Collaborative Paradigms of Generative AI and Human Intelligence for Equitable Learning Futures

Faizan Ahmad
Cardiff Metropolitan University, UK

Jay Kumar Pandey
https://orcid.org/0000-0003-4086-5730
Shri Ramswaroop Memorial University, Barabanki, India

Momina Shaheen
https://orcid.org/0000-0001-9424-9787
University of Roehampton, London, UK

IGI Global
Scientific Publishing
Publishing Tomorrow's Research Today

Vice President of Editorial Melissa Wagner
Director of Acquisitions Mikaela Felty
Director of Book Development Jocelynn Hessler
Production Manager Mike Brehm
Cover Design Jose Rosado

Published in the United States of America by
IGI Global Scientific Publishing
701 East Chocolate Avenue
Hershey, PA, 17033, USA
Tel: 717-533-8845 | Fax: 717-533-7115
Website: https://www.igi-global.com E-mail: cust@igi-global.com

Library of Congress Cataloging-in-Publication Data

Names: Ahmad, Faizan, 1988- editor | Pandey, Jay Kumar, 1987- editor | Shaheen, Momina, 1993- editor
Title: Collaborative paradigms of generative AI and human intelligence for equitable learning futures / edited by: Faizan Ahmad, Jay Kumar Pandey, Momina Shaheen.
Description: Hershey, PA : IGI Global Scientific Publishing, [2026] | Includes bibliographical references and index. | Summary: "This book is a timely and authoritative resource that contributes significantly to the evolving discourse on generative AI in education. By focusing on the synergistic collaboration between humans and GenAI, it provides critical insights and practical guidance for fostering educational futures that are not only technologically advanced but also deeply inclusive and equitable"-- Provided by publisher.
Identifiers: LCCN 2025036583 (print) | LCCN 2025036584 (ebook) | ISBN 9798337360638 hardcover | ISBN 9798337360645 paperback | ISBN 9798337360652 ebook
Subjects: LCSH: Artificial intelligence--Educational applications | Generative artificial intelligence in higher education
Classification: LCC LB2395.72 .C65 2026 (print) | LCC LB2395.72 (ebook)
LC record available at https://lccn.loc.gov/2025036583
LC ebook record available at https://lccn.loc.gov/2025036584

British Cataloguing in Publication Data
A Cataloguing in Publication record for this book is available from the British Library.

Table of Contents

Detailed Table of Contents

to action for institutions, policymakers, and communities to co-design educational ecosystems that are ethical, visionary, and collaborative.

This chapter introduces the Gamified LLM Lifecycle, a seven-stage conceptual framework that reimagines large language model (LLM) development as an inclusive and participatory ecosystem. Although LLMs support education and productivity, their design and governance remain centralized and opaque. The proposed framework transforms the traditional pipeline—data collection, annotation, fine-tuning, alignment, evaluation, prompting, and deployment—into gamified stages that integrate learning theory, motivational design, and human–AI collaboration. Grounded in Self-Regulated Learning, the Octalysis Framework, and human–AI symbiosis, each stage embeds quests, peer review, ethical duels, and community-based evaluation to foster engagement and skill development. By turning technical contributions into meaningful learning experiences, the model aims to democratize AI creation and amplify underrepresented voices. The chapter positions AI development as a transparent process in which users act not merely as consumers, but as contributors, evaluators, and ethical stewards of intelligent systems.

The goal of inclusive education is to provide all students with the same opportunities to learn. However, language barriers, disabilities, and lack of access to technology can make it difficult for everyone to participate fully. This chapter discusses how Generative AI (GenAI) can make classrooms more welcoming and open to everyone, especially for students who feel left out or not represented. Teachers can utilize ChatGPT (language generation), Whisper and Indic Whisper (speech-to-text), mT5 and NLLB (multilingual translation), and TTS engines (text-to-speech) to make learning more flexible, apply multiple approaches, and fit the needs of each student. We recommend a three-part framework comprising Input, Processing, and Output. With this technology, people who speak different languages can communicate with each other, modify content in real-time, and share it in various ways. In this chapter, we will learn how GenAI can help children with disabilities, children who do not speak much English, and children who do not have much money.

This chapter explores how Generative AI (GenAI) is transforming assessment and feedback in education through Intelligent Tutoring Systems (ITS). As learning shifts toward more personalized, inclusive, and data-driven approaches, GenAI enables real-time adaptive feedback, conversational learning, and dynamic assessment tailored to individual needs. It examines the integration of GenAI technologies—like natural language processing—into ITS architectures to create personalized, context-aware evaluations. Ethical concerns such as bias, transparency, and inclusion are addressed, emphasizing the need for human-AI collaboration. Case studies from K–12, higher education, and vocational training highlight practical applications. The chapter also discusses how GenAI, supported by learning analytics and formative assessment, can move evaluation beyond summative tests toward continuous, learner-centered progress tracking. Ultimately, GenAI is presented as a powerful tool for deeper learning and meaningful feedback—provided it is developed responsibly and with strong educator engagement.

This chapter critically examines the role of generative artificial intelligence (AI) in history education through the lenses of collective memory, historical consciousness, and human-centred pedagogy. It conceptualises generative AI not as a neutral instructional tool but as a dialogic and provisional partner whose educational value depends on sustained human mediation. Drawing on interdisciplinary literature from history education, memory studies, digital pedagogy, and AI ethics, the chapter analyses how AI-generated historical representations may either reproduce dominant narratives or open spaces for multiperspectivity and ethical reflection. It highlights key epistemic risks, including narrative closure, bias reproduction, and the erosion of evidentiary reasoning, and proposes a memory-sensitive pedagogical

This chapter focuses on the artificial intelligence (AI) applications in education from a Culturally Responsive Teaching (CRT) perspective. Following a review of the theoretical background of multicultural education and CRT, the chapter critically examines how AI technologies may both support and challenge efforts to foster cultural and linguistic inclusivity. It identifies key potentials and challenges, such as personalization, translanguaging support, digital equity, algorithmic bias, and linguistic hierarchies. Existing frameworks for ethical and culturally responsive AI are explained, with attention to an identified gap in current models. In response, the chapter introduces a Culturally Responsive Artificial Intelligence Evaluation Framework (CRAI-EF) designed to assist educators, researchers, and policymakers in making informed decisions regarding the responsible deployment of AI tools. The chapter concludes by outlining pedagogical implications, with an emphasis on teacher responsibility, AI literacy for students and the principles of culturally responsive design.

The deployment of Artificial Intelligence (AI) in learning is rapidly changing teaching, learning, and governance, establishing what can be termed human–AI learning ecosystems AI presents a chance for individualized education, coincidence, and effectiveness; however, it introduces the dangers of prejudice, injustice, and loss of trust among people. Issues of justice, such as fairness, accountability, transparency, and privacy, as well as social pressures, such as the digital divide, transformations in teacher-student relationships, and reaching a more inclusive society, are also important. Participatory AI is an alternative to embedding democratic values in AI systems. Institutions such as global policy and ethics boards are considered systems of governance that enable responsible adoption . Among these technological innovations, explainable AI (XAI), reinforcement learning based on human feedback (RLHF), multimodal interaction, and federated learning have been noted when discussing increased transparency and participation.

As generative AI tools, such as GitHub Copilot and ChatGPT, become embedded in programming education, they are reshaping how students learn and write code. While these tools increase access, speed, and engagement, they also raise concerns related to insecure code, plagiarism, and reduced understanding of core concepts. This chapter examines how educators can strike a balance between the benefits of AI-assisted coding and the technical and ethical responsibilities associated with secure software development. Drawing on classroom cases and student insights, it presents a framework that integrates AI literacy, secure-by-design principles, and ethical reflection. Key topics include common vulnerabilities in AI-generated code, strategies for pairing AI output with human review, and approaches for assessing human-AI collaboration. The chapter offers practical recommendations for curriculum redesign and educator training to help students develop safe, responsible, and ethical coding practices in an AI-rich learning environment.

This chapter reviews how artificial intelligence is reshaping education by moving traditional teacher-centered systems toward more personalized, creative, and inquiry-driven learning. It outlines the historical shift from conventional instruction to AI-supported models that use adaptive pathways, competency-based structures, collaborative learning, and continuous assessment. The discussion explains how teacher responsibilities are expanding toward roles as learning designers, AI supervisors, and ethical stewards, while students gain greater autonomy, agency, and metacognitive skills. Key ethical and policy concerns, including privacy, bias, accessibility, and governance, are addressed to guide responsible adoption. Global cases show varied approaches and offer lessons for effective integration. The chapter closes with a view of emerging AI-native ecosystems featuring hybrid learning spaces, lifelong AI assistance, and analytics-driven credentialing aimed at building a more equitable and human-centered educational future.

This chapter explores the paradigm shift in education from rigid traditional models to dynamic human-AI collaborative learning systems. Based on criticism of standard curricula and unfair assessment practices, this chapter advocates for the integration of artificial intelligence not as a replacement for educators, but as a cognitive partner that enriches human learning. Drawing on AI theories centred on social construction and human-centred approaches, this chapter proposes an inclusive and adaptive framework designed to support diverse learners through personalised feedback, real-time analysis, and collaborative problem-solving. Using case studies and practical models, this chapter highlights how human-AI collaboration can address existing systemic inequalities and foster a more equitable, learner-centred learning environment. It offers conceptual and empirical insights for reimagining education as a partnership between human intelligence and machine learning—with the goal of creating an ethical, inclusive, and sustainable future of learning.

In an era increasingly defined by artificial intelligence (AI), automation, and rapid technological advancement, AI on work, education, and everyday life. The traditional model of acquiring a fixed set of skills early in life and relying on them throughout one's career is no longer viable. AI systems are evolving at an unprecedented pace, leading to the automation of routine and even some complex tasks, while simultaneously creating new roles and industries that demand new competencies. As such, individuals must constantly reskill and upskill to remain relevant in the job market, adapt to shifting career landscapes, and leverage the benefits of AI tools effectively and ethically.The necessity for lifelong learning is underscored by the disruptive impact of AI on the workforce.Automation technologies are projected to displace millions of jobs globally, especially those involving repetitive manual labor or routine cognitive tasks. However, while AI renders some jobs obsolete, it also generates new opportunities in fields like data science, machine learning, cybersecurity.

Preface

INTRODUCTION

As editors of *Collaborative Paradigms of Generative AI and Human Intelligence for Equitable Learning Futures*, we are pleased to present a volume that engages deeply with one of the most consequential transformations in contemporary education: the integration of Generative Artificial Intelligence with human and collective intelligence.

This book emerges at a pivotal moment when education systems across the globe are grappling with questions of access, equity, and relevance in an increasingly digital and interconnected world. The chapters assembled here collectively argue that the future of learning lies not in the replacement of human educators by intelligent systems, but in the thoughtful collaboration between them. By bringing together Generative AI (GenAI), Human Intelligence (HI), and Collective Intelligence (CI), the contributors articulate a paradigm in which technology amplifies, rather than diminishes, the human dimensions of teaching and learning.

Central to this volume is the vision of learner-centric, inclusive, and future-ready education. The integration of AI enables scalable personalization—adapting content, pace, and pathways to individual learners—while human educators provide the empathy, ethical judgment, creativity, and contextual understanding that remain irreplaceable. This synergy creates opportunities to address long-standing disparities in educational access and quality, particularly for underserved and marginalized communities.

The book also reimagines the evolving role of educators. Rather than serving solely as transmitters of knowledge, teachers are positioned as orchestrators of dynamic, hybrid learning ecosystems. In such environments, learners engage in dialogic inquiry supported by AI tools, while educators guide critical thinking, nurture emotional development, and cultivate collaborative knowledge-building. This shift underscores the importance of preparing educators not only to use technology, but to shape its pedagogical and ethical applications.

We are equally mindful that technological advancement must be accompanied by ethical responsibility. Accordingly, this volume addresses critical concerns such as algorithmic bias, data privacy, transparency, and equitable access to AI-driven tools. The contributors emphasize that the promise of GenAI in education can only be realized if its deployment is guided by principles of fairness, inclusivity, and accountability.

Through a combination of conceptual frameworks, empirical studies, and practical applications, this book offers both vision and guidance. It is our intention that this work serves as a meaningful resource for a wide and diverse audience: academics and researchers exploring the frontiers of AI in education; educators and practitioners seeking to integrate these tools into their teaching; policymakers and institutional leaders shaping educational futures; technology developers designing learning systems; and students engaging with the intersection of computing and pedagogy.

We believe that this volume contributes substantively to the ongoing discourse on Generative AI in education. More importantly, we hope it inspires collaborative, thoughtful, and ethical innovation. By embracing the complementary strengths of human and artificial intelligence, we can move toward learning ecosystems that are not only technologically advanced, but also profoundly equitable and inclusive.

ORGANIZATION OF THE BOOK

Chapter 1 examines the evolution of Generative AI from rule-based systems to sophisticated, data-driven models powered by deep learning and transformer architectures. The discussion highlights the expanding range of educational applications—from personalized tutoring to creative, multimodal learning tools—while also critically engaging with ethical, pedagogical, and equity considerations. The chapter emphasizes the need for responsible, human-centered integration of these technologies.

In **Chapter 2**, the editors present the conceptual core of the book, articulating collaborative paradigms that place human values at the center of AI integration. Moving beyond purely technocentric approaches, the chapter offers frameworks that emphasize co-agency between humans and machines, supported by case studies and policy recommendations. It calls for educational ecosystems that advance social justice, cultural diversity, and inclusive participation.

Chapter 3 introduces an innovative perspective on AI development through the Gamified LLM Lifecycle framework. By reimagining the creation and governance of large language models as participatory and gamified processes, the chapter highlights how learners and communities can actively contribute to AI systems. This approach democratizes AI development, fostering transparency, engagement, and ethical stewardship.

In **Chapter 4**, the focus shifts to inclusive pedagogy, demonstrating how Generative AI can help overcome barriers related to language, disability, and access. The chapter proposes a practical framework for designing inclusive learning experiences, showcasing how multimodal AI tools can support diverse learners. It underscores the potential of AI to create more equitable classrooms by adapting to varied needs and contexts.

Chapter 5 explores the transformation of assessment and feedback through AI-powered Intelligent Tutoring Systems. The contributors illustrate how Generative AI enables real-time, adaptive, and personalized evaluation, moving beyond traditional testing toward continuous, learner-centered assessment. At the same time, the chapter highlights the importance of addressing ethical concerns and maintaining strong human oversight.

In **Chapter 6**, the discussion turns to history education, where Generative AI is examined through the lenses of collective memory and historical consciousness. The chapter presents AI as a dialogic partner rather than a neutral tool, emphasizing the need for human mediation to ensure critical inquiry and ethical interpretation. It warns against risks such as bias and narrative simplification while proposing a memory-sensitive pedagogical framework.

Chapter 7 examines the evolving role of teachers in AI-augmented classrooms. Educators are repositioned as designers, curators, and facilitators who guide personalized and ethically grounded learning experiences. The chapter highlights both the opportunities and risks of AI integration, arguing that teacher agency and professional development are essential for meaningful and equitable implementation.

In **Chapter 8**, attention shifts to policy and governance, identifying these as central challenges in AI-driven educational transformation. The chapter analyzes gaps in regulatory frameworks and their implications for equity and access. It offers a governance-first approach, advocating for ethical standards, data protection, and coordinated global efforts to ensure responsible AI adoption.

In **Chapter 9**, the focus is on culturally responsive AI in global education contexts. The chapter examines how AI can both support and challenge efforts toward cultural and linguistic inclusivity. By introducing a dedicated evaluation framework, it provides practical guidance for ensuring that AI systems align with the principles of culturally responsive teaching and equitable design.

Chapter 10 emphasizes the importance of community and stakeholder engagement in shaping human–AI learning ecosystems. It highlights participatory approaches that embed democratic values into AI development and deployment. The chapter also explores emerging technologies that enhance transparency and trust, advocating for inclusive governance structures and collaborative decision-making.

In **Chapter 11**, the discussion centers on programming education, where Generative AI tools are transforming how students learn to code. The chapter addresses both the opportunities and risks associated with AI-assisted coding, including concerns about security and academic integrity. It proposes a framework that integrates technical competence with ethical awareness, preparing students for responsible practice.

Chapter 12 examines the broader shift from traditional education models to AI-supported, collaborative learning environments. It outlines how personalization, continuous assessment, and learner agency are redefining educational practices. Drawing on global examples, the chapter provides insights into effective integration strategies and highlights emerging AI-native learning ecosystems.

Chapter 13 further develops this theme by framing human–AI collaboration as a paradigm shift in education. The chapter critiques rigid curricula and inequitable assessment systems, proposing adaptive and inclusive frameworks that leverage AI as a cognitive partner. Through case studies and conceptual analysis, it envisions a more equitable and learner-centered educational landscape.

Finally, **Chapter 14** addresses the critical importance of lifelong learning in the age of AI. As technological change accelerates, the chapter underscores the need for continuous reskilling and upskilling. It highlights both the disruptive and generative impacts of AI on the workforce, advocating for learning systems that enable individuals to adapt, thrive, and engage ethically with emerging technologies.

Collectively, these chapters offer a comprehensive and forward-looking exploration of how Generative AI, when aligned with human values and collaborative principles, can reshape education into a more inclusive, adaptive, and equitable enterprise.

CONCLUSION

As we bring this volume to a close, we are reminded that the conversation surrounding Generative Artificial Intelligence in education is neither finite nor settled—it is evolving, dynamic, and deeply -centric in its implications. The chapters in this book collectively affirm that the future of education will not be defined by technology alone, but by the ways in which human intelligence, values, and collaboration shape and guide its use.

Across diverse contexts and perspectives, this volume has emphasized a unifying principle: that meaningful educational transformation arises from synergy rather than substitution. Generative AI, when thoughtfully integrated, has the capacity to expand access, personalize learning, and enhance creativity. Yet, it is human insight—ethical judgment, cultural awareness, empathy, and critical reasoning—that ensures these technological capabilities are directed toward equitable and inclusive ends.

We have seen how educators are re-envisioned as designers of learning experiences, facilitators of inquiry, and stewards of ethical practice. We have explored how learners, too, become active participants in co-creating knowledge alongside intelligent systems. At the same time, the discussions on governance, policy, and cultural responsiveness underscore that the success of AI in education depends on collective responsibility, institutional foresight, and sustained engagement with issues of justice and inclusion.

Importantly, this book highlights that the challenges before us—ranging from bias and inequity to questions of access and accountability—are not merely technical problems, but societal ones. Addressing them requires interdisciplinary collaboration, participatory design, and a commitment to aligning innovation with shared human values. The frameworks, case studies, and critical reflections presented herein offer not only insights but also pathways for action.

As editors, we hope this volume serves as both a reference and a catalyst: a resource that informs, a guide that supports, and an invitation to continue reimagining education in ways that are bold, ethical, and inclusive. The promise of Generative AI lies not in its novelty, but in its potential to help us build learning ecosystems that honor diversity, foster agency, and empower all learners to thrive.

The future of education, as envisioned in these pages, is collaborative, adaptive, and just. It is a future that calls upon all of us—educators, researchers, policymakers, technologists, and learners—to engage thoughtfully and act responsibly. In this shared endeavor, we find not only the challenges of transformation, but also its greatest possibilities.

Chapter 1
Overview of Generative AI:
Its Evolution, Core Technologies, and Its Potential Impact on Education

Nayla Fadiya
http://orcid.org/0009-0007-8389-911X
Universitas Esa Unggul, Indonesia

Azizaturridha Fitria Wibowo
http://orcid.org/0009-0008-1927-3101
Universitas Esa Unggul, Indonesia

Binastya Anggara Sekti
http://orcid.org/0000-0001-5489-4888
Universitas Esa Unggul, Indonesia

ABSTRACT

The evolution of Generative Artificial Intelligence (Generative AI) marks a transformative shift in intelligent system development, moving from rule-based algorithms to data driven models capable of generating human-like content. Enabled by deep learning, particularly transformer-based architectures, this shift has opened new frontiers in education. Generative models like GPT-3 and DALL·E now empower various educational applications ranging from personalized tutoring and curriculum generation to multimodal tools that enhance creativity and inclusion. This chapter explores the historical development and foundational technologies of Generative AI, highlighting its growing role in reshaping teaching and learning processes. It critically assesses ethical, pedagogical, and equity-related implications, and out-

DOI: 10.4018/979-8-3373-6063-8.ch001

lines strategic directions for integrating AI responsibly in education. The aim is to foster collaborative, human-centered educational futures that align innovation with social and pedagogical values.

INTRODUCTION

The educational landscape is undergoing a profound transformation with the rapid emergence and adoption of Generative Artificial Intelligence (Generative AI). This shift marks a departure from traditional, static methods of content delivery toward a dynamic, interactive, and intelligent learning environment. Generative AI refers to AI systems capable of creating new content, whether textual, visual, auditory, or multimodal, that mimics human creativity. This capability has significant implications for how knowledge is accessed, internalized, and applied by learners across the globe. Generative Artificial Intelligence is quickly transforming music education with the ability to create new creative experiences, opportunities of cultural interaction, and tailored learning (Kaushik et al., 2025).

Unlike previous technologies that focused on automating repetitive tasks or enhancing administrative processes, Generative AI reshapes the very fabric of teaching and learning. It can simulate human-like interactions, provide personalized tutoring, adapt content to individual learning styles, and even engage in Socratic questioning. Students no longer depend solely on teachers or textbooks; they can now learn through conversations with intelligent agents that provide explanations, clarify doubts, and offer encouragement. This personalization fosters deeper engagement, intrinsic motivation, and improved retention. The advancement of digital illustration has led to a revolution stage whereby it entails the application of generative artificial intelligence which integrates the human creativity and the computational creativity (Riyat et al., 2025).

Generative AI is also democratizing knowledge creation. Learners from diverse backgrounds can generate essays, solve complex problems, visualize historical events, or create original music and art using AI tools. These affordances enhance inclusivity and empower voices that were previously underrepresented in academic discourse. Moreover, Generative AI supports teachers by automating routine tasks such as grading, feedback generation, and curriculum design, allowing them to focus more on mentoring and relationship-building.

However, the integration of Generative AI into education is not without challenges. There are valid concerns regarding the authenticity of student work, data privacy, algorithmic bias, and the potential deskilling of educators. Ethical questions arise around the authorship of AI-generated content, the reproduction of stereotypes, and the accountability for misinformation. Institutions must balance innovation with responsibility, ensuring that the deployment of AI aligns with educational values and human dignity. Generative artificial intelligence (AI) has taken the world by storm, with notable tension transpiring in the field of education (Taulli & Deshmukh, 2025).

In terms of infrastructure, the successful adoption of Generative AI requires robust digital ecosystems. These include reliable internet access, adequate hardware, secure platforms, and teacher training programs. Without such infrastructure, the benefits of AI risk being concentrated in affluent regions, exacerbating existing educational inequalities. To mitigate this, policy frameworks must promote equitable access, culturally relevant content, and local language support. AI refers to the broader concept of machines or systems simulating human intelligence, enabling decision- making, problem- solving, and task automation (Sekti, 2025c).

Furthermore, Generative AI brings about a pedagogical shift from content delivery to inquiry-based, project-based, and competency-based learning. Teachers evolve into facilitators of knowledge construction, guiding students to critically engage with AI outputs, verify information, and apply insights to real-world problems. This co-intelligent learning environment enhances 21st-century skills such as critical thinking, digital literacy, collaboration, and creativity.

To fully realize the potential of Generative AI, stakeholders must collaborate across disciplines and sectors. Governments, academia, industry, and civil society need to co-develop standards, ethics, and accountability mechanisms. Interdisciplinary research is essential to understand the cognitive, emotional, and social impacts of learning with AI. Moreover, international cooperation is necessary to ensure that AI in education serves as a global public good, rather than a tool for commercial exploitation or surveillance. Generative artificial intelligence (AI) has emerged as a powerful technology with numerous applications in various domains (Bandi, Adapa, & Kuchi, 2023).

This chapter aims to offer a comprehensive overview of Generative AI in education by addressing four core themes: (1) the technological foundations and evolution of generative models, (2) current applications and innovations in various educational settings, (3) ethical, pedagogical, and societal implications, and (4) future directions and recommendations for responsible integration. Drawing on current research, case studies, and expert perspectives, this chapter provides a critical and constructive lens through which educators, policymakers, technologists, and learners can navigate the complex landscape of AI-enhanced education.

In doing so, the chapter not only highlights the transformative potential of Generative AI but also emphasizes the importance of human agency, empathy, and inclusivity in shaping educational futures. As we stand at the intersection of machine intelligence and human aspiration, it becomes imperative to ensure that technology amplifies our collective capacity to learn, grow, and contribute to a more just and enlightened society. Generative artificial intelligence (AI) has taken the world by storm, with notable tension transpiring in the field of education (Lim, Gunasekara, Pallant, Pallant, & Pechenkina, 2023).

While much of the existing discourse on generative AI in education emphasizes its technical capabilities and efficiency gains, fewer studies critically examine how these systems reshape the epistemological and pedagogical foundations of learning itself. In particular, there remains limited consensus on whether generative AI should be understood primarily as an automation tool, a cognitive aid, or a collaborative partner in human learning processes. This ambiguity has contributed to fragmented debates, where enthusiasm for innovation often coexists with concerns about dehumanization, dependency, and inequity.

This chapter addresses this gap by situating generative AI within a collaborative intelligence paradigm, in which human judgment, creativity, and ethical agency remain central. Rather than treating generative AI as a standalone solution, the chapter examines how its educational impact depends on institutional design, pedagogical intent, and governance structures. By integrating technological foundations with educational theory and ethical considerations, the chapter advances a more analytical understanding of how generative AI can support equitable and human-centered learning futures.

THE EVOLUTION OF GENERATIVE AI: FROM RULES TO INTELLIGENCE

Artificial Intelligence (AI) began with symbolic, rule-based systems, such as expert systems that relied on explicit programming to simulate decision-making. These systems, while useful in limited domains, lacked flexibility and adaptability. The evolution to machine learning, and later deep learning, marked a turning point. The introduction of neural networks, particularly deep neural networks, allowed machines to identify patterns and make decisions based on data rather than pre-defined rules. Artificial intelligence (AI) is being increasingly integrated into scientific discovery to augment and accelerate research, helping scientists to generate hypotheses, design experiments, collect and interpret large datasets, and gain insights that might not have been possible using traditional scientific methods alone (H. Wang et al., 2023).

The rise of Generative AI stems from advances in deep learning, notably through Generative Adversarial Networks (GANs), Variational Autoencoders (VAEs), and Transformer-based models such as GPT (Generative Pre-trained Transformer). The introduction of OpenAI's GPT-2 and GPT-3 highlighted the extraordinary capabilities of large language models (LLMs) trained on vast corpora of text. These models demonstrated the ability to generate coherent, context-aware text and answer complex queries with increasing fluency. The advent of generative artificial intelligence (AI) offers transformative potential in the field of education (Cooper, 2023).

Transformer-based architectures, especially those employing self-attention mechanisms, have become the cornerstone of generative models. Tools such as ChatGPT, Bard, Claude, and DALL·E are powered by these architectures and have become increasingly integrated into educational tools and platforms. Generative Artificial Intelligence (AI) tools, including DALL-E (GPT-powered), Midjourney, Gatekeep (GPT-powered) and Globe Explorer, can be used to generate images, videos as well as search, and group resources in science education (Liao, Han, & Xu, 2025). As generative models continue to scale in terms of parameters and training data, their capacity to mimic human-like reasoning, engage in contextual dialogue, and generate domain-specific content will further strengthen their relevance in educational settings. ChatGPT is revolutionizing the field of higher education by leveraging deep learning models to generate human-like content (Michel-Villarreal, Vilalta-Perdomo, Salinas-Navarro, Thierry-Aguilera, & Gerardou, 2023).

In parallel, the open-source movement has also empowered educational institutions to experiment with lightweight generative models tailored to local languages and curricula. From research prototypes in AI labs to open datasets and training toolkits, the democratization of generative AI is paving the way for global educational inclusion.

Figure 1. Application of generative AI

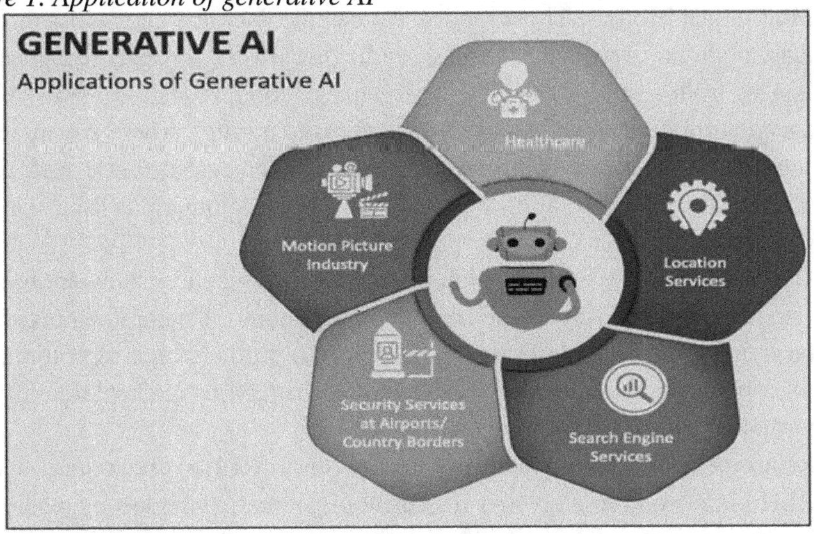

CORE TECHNOLOGIES BEHIND GENERATIVE AI

Generative AI technologies are grounded in several core innovations:

- Neural Networks and Deep Learning: At the heart of Generative AI are artificial neural networks, particularly deep learning architectures that consist of multiple layers enabling complex pattern recognition. These models mimic the structure of the human brain to process input data through multiple hidden layers, extracting features and mapping complex relationships. Convolutional Neural Networks (CNNs) have been central to the Deep Learning revolution and played a key role in initiating the new age of Artificial Intelligence (R. Wang & Demszky, 2023).
- Transformers: The Transformer architecture revolutionized natural language processing. It allows models to attend to different parts of a sequence simultaneously, enabling better context understanding. The attention mechanism helps AI understand long-range dependencies and nuanced relationships between words and phrases, making it ideal for dialogue and content generation.
- Self-Supervised Learning: Instead of relying on labeled datasets, many generative models use self-supervised methods, predicting parts of the input based on other parts. This is crucial for scaling up training on massive unstructured datasets such as web text, allowing models to learn patterns and associations without human annotation.
- Multimodal Models: These models can handle and generate across different data modalities (e.g., text, images, audio). DALL·E, for instance, generates images from text prompts. The emergence of models such as GPT-4-Vision and Gemini multimodal architectures points to a future where AI can understand and respond to complex, cross-modal educational tasks, such as describing images, annotating videos, or generating simulations from scientific descriptions.
- Diffusion Models: Used for high-fidelity image and audio generation, diffusion models iteratively transform random noise into structured outputs based on training data distributions. Their ability to produce high-resolution, lifelike visuals and audio makes them ideal for visual arts, medical training, and virtual laboratory environments in education.
- Reinforcement Learning with Human Feedback (RLHF): Techniques such as RLHF improve the safety and alignment of generative models by incorporating human preferences and ethical constraints into the training loop, making AI more useful and trustworthy in classroom environments.

These technologies provide the computational and algorithmic foundation for building applications that interact with learners in human-like ways, offering responsive and empathetic support that enhances traditional teaching methods. The evolution from rule-based systems to large-scale generative models is not merely a technical progression but represents a qualitative shift in how machines participate in knowledge production. In educational contexts, this shift blurs traditional boundaries between content delivery, tutoring, and assessment. Unlike earlier educational technologies that supported predefined instructional pathways, generative models actively shape learning trajectories through dialogue, adaptation, and synthesis. This raises fundamental questions about authority, expertise, and the role of human educators in AI-mediated learning environments.

CURRENT APPLICATIONS IN EDUCATION

The application of Generative AI in education is expanding rapidly, revolutionizing how knowledge is accessed, created, and delivered. From personalized tutoring to curriculum development, its influence spans every layer of the educational ecosystem. Effective implementation of GenAI tools, can ultimately enhancing teaching and learning experiences in higher education (Chan & Hu, 2023). The following areas highlight key current applications and their broader implications:

- Personalized Learning Assistants: Tools like ChatGPT, Claude, Gemini, and others have evolved into on-demand intelligent tutors capable of interacting naturally with students. These AI agents provide real-time responses to academic queries, generate summaries of complex readings, simulate quizzes, and adapt their responses based on learner behavior. With access to students' learning history, these assistants tailor explanations, examples, and challenges to suit diverse proficiency levels, learning styles, and emotional states. They can mimic scaffolding strategies used by human tutors and promote metacognitive skills by prompting self-reflection and strategy selection. Transformative artificially intelligent tools, such as ChatGPT, designed to generate sophisticated text indistinguishable from that produced by a human, are applicable across a wide range of contexts (Dwivedi et al., 2023).
- Automated Content Creation: One of the most impactful uses of Generative AI lies in its ability to support teachers in generating pedagogical materials. Instructors can prompt AI to produce quizzes, test banks, rubrics, reading guides, writing prompts, learning objectives, course syllabi, and even full lesson sequences. These tools significantly reduce teacher workload while allowing for rapid customization based on course level, subject, and cultural

context. Advanced platforms also allow instructors to fine-tune AI on their own course material, enhancing alignment and coherence. Generative AI is able to create text, images, music, animation, video and even build software code from simple, user-generated text prompts will simplify business processes in a multitude of ways (Pearson, 2024).

- Language Learning and Translation: Generative AI supports language acquisition by offering tools that simulate conversation practice, provide instant grammar correction, recommend vocabulary, and deliver context-aware explanations. Learners can engage in interactive dialogues in multiple languages, practice pronunciation using text-to-speech models, and receive real-time translation of foreign language content. These capabilities extend beyond mainstream languages to low-resource languages, potentially preserving endangered dialects and enhancing cultural inclusion.
- Accessibility and Universal Design for Learning (UDL): Students with disabilities benefit significantly from AI-powered personalization and content transformation. For example, visually impaired students can use AI to generate audio versions of written texts, while students with cognitive disabilities can request simplified summaries. Generative AI can dynamically convert diagrams into verbal descriptions, create interactive braille-compatible outputs, or provide sign-language avatars. These advancements bring education closer to the goals of UDL by accommodating learner variability at scale.
- STEM, Programming, and Technical Skill Development: Students in science, technology, engineering, and mathematics (STEM) fields increasingly rely on AI tools for computational support. GitHub Copilot and ChatGPT can explain algorithms, generate code snippets, simulate engineering systems, and visualize abstract mathematical concepts. In laboratory-based disciplines, generative models create virtual experiments that mirror real-world outcomes. In vocational education, AI simulations replicate industrial environments, allowing students to train in safety protocols, machinery operation, or chemical analysis.
- Creative and Interdisciplinary Exploration: Creative subjects like art, literature, and music benefit from AI tools that can co-create content with learners. Students can generate short stories, poems, paintings, or music compositions with real-time AI collaboration. This nurtures imagination and encourages experimentation across disciplines. In design and architecture, AI can generate concept sketches, assist in modeling, and simulate environmental factors. Such co-creation supports inquiry-based learning and fosters innovation by removing entry barriers to creative expression.
- Administrative and Institutional Support: Beyond classroom instruction, Generative AI streamlines educational management. AI-driven systems au-

tomate email responses, monitor academic progress, predict student attrition, and recommend interventions. In admissions and student services, chatbots support application processes, scholarship searches, and course registration. For faculty, AI offers assistance with research summarization, academic writing, and peer review preparation.

- MOOCs, Microlearning, and Continuous Professional Development: Generative AI transforms online education by enabling dynamic, conversational experiences at scale. Learners in Massive Open Online Courses (MOOCs) interact with AI tutors embedded in videos or text-based modules. These tutors pause content to explain concepts, test understanding, or suggest related readings. In microlearning contexts, short, AI-generated modules are created on-demand for just-in-time training. Professionals in medicine, law, or engineering can use AI to stay current with regulations, case studies, and best practices.
- Data-Driven Instruction and Formative Assessment: Generative AI can create diagnostic quizzes, simulations, and reflective prompts based on student performance data. These assessments are tailored in difficulty and format, offering learners instant feedback and tracking progress over time. Teachers receive dashboards that visualize learning trajectories, identify misconceptions, and suggest differentiated strategies. Through continuous formative assessment, students are guided toward mastery in an adaptive and responsive system.
- Collaborative AI-Learner Projects: Students and teachers are increasingly engaging in projects where AI is not just a tool but a collaborator. For example, students co-write articles or design experiments with AI input. In some classrooms, students fine-tune open-source models on custom datasets, learning about machine learning in a hands-on manner (Sekti, 2025c). This encourages deeper engagement with both subject matter and the principles behind AI technology itself.
- Emotionally Responsive Learning Systems: Emerging research in affective computing enables AI to detect learners' emotional states through text cues, facial expressions, or voice. Generative systems can then adjust tone, provide encouragement, or suggest breaks. These emotionally intelligent systems support mental well-being and create a more humanized digital learning space.
- Gamified and Immersive Learning Environments: AI is being used to generate storylines, quests, and adaptive challenges in educational games. It can respond to player choices and skill levels, ensuring an engaging, personalized, and pedagogically sound game-based learning experience. Combined with

AR/VR technologies, Generative AI populates virtual environments with intelligent agents and real-time adaptive content.

Together, these applications signal a paradigm shift toward a learner-centric model where AI serves not only as a content generator, but also as a mentor, facilitator, and co-creator. As these tools mature and are increasingly integrated into digital ecosystems, they redefine boundaries between subjects, roles, and learning modalities. Ultimately, the synergy between human educators and Generative AI can foster more inclusive, creative, and transformative learning experiences than ever before.

Across these diverse applications, a common pattern emerges: generative AI shifts education from standardized content delivery toward adaptive, dialogic, and learner-centered environments. However, the pedagogical value of these applications depends less on technological sophistication than on how they are embedded within instructional design. When aligned with principles of scaffolding, formative feedback, and reflective learning, generative AI can enhance understanding and agency. When deployed without pedagogical intent, it risks promoting surface learning, overreliance, and diminished critical engagement.

ETHICAL, PEDAGOGICAL, AND EQUITY-RELATED CHALLENGES

The ethical, pedagogical, and equity-related challenges associated with the integration of Generative Artificial Intelligence in education are both complex and urgent. As institutions and stakeholders rapidly incorporate AI-powered technologies into classrooms and learning systems, they must simultaneously confront the moral, instructional, and access-related questions that arise from such accelerated technological advancement. Addressing these challenges requires a multidimensional exploration that is grounded not only in technology ethics but also in educational theory, public policy, and principles of social justice. Artificial Intelligence (AI) has become an influential force shaping modern society, raising urgent ethical questions about responsibility, fairness, transparency, and human dignity (Sekti, 2025b).

From an ethical standpoint, one of the most pressing concerns relates to authorship and academic integrity. Generative AI systems are capable of producing essays, solving mathematical problems, generating computer code, and simulating complex dialogues, all of which may be submitted as student work. This capability fundamentally alters traditional conceptions of originality, authorship, and academic misconduct. Conventional plagiarism detection tools are often ineffective in identifying AI-generated content, necessitating a critical re-evaluation of assessment practices, collaborative learning models, and trust-based educational frameworks.

Moreover, excessive reliance on AI tools may unintentionally undermine the development of critical thinking, reflective judgment, and problem-solving skills, which are central to meaningful learning. Rather than prohibiting AI use entirely, educators are increasingly exploring pedagogical strategies that integrate AI as a learning companion while safeguarding academic integrity.

Ethical challenges also extend to data governance and privacy. Generative AI systems require vast volumes of data for training, frequently collected from publicly available sources without explicit user consent. When deployed in educational environments, these systems may capture sensitive student data, including learning behaviors, performance metrics, and personal identifiers, often without transparent disclosure or informed consent. If improperly managed, such data can be vulnerable to misuse, commercial exploitation, or surveillance. In educational contexts that already face significant concerns regarding digital safety, the implementation of opaque and proprietary AI technologies intensifies risks related to data privacy and child protection. Although regulatory frameworks such as the General Data Protection Regulation in the European Union provide important safeguards, their application and enforcement within educational institutions remain uneven and insufficient, highlighting the need for stronger governance and accountability mechanisms.

Bias and discrimination embedded in AI models present another ethical quandary. Since most AI systems are trained on data from dominant cultural, linguistic, and ideological perspectives, they often fail to represent the diversity of learners across different geographies. This leads to content that may be subtly exclusionary or overtly prejudiced, reinforcing stereotypes and marginalizing minority voices. For example, an AI that associates scientific achievements primarily with Western figures may inadvertently neglect contributions from non-Western civilizations, thus distorting historical and cultural narratives. Such algorithmic bias undermines the promise of inclusive education and can perpetuate systemic inequities unless intentionally countered with diverse training datasets, localized content, and community-informed design.

From a pedagogical perspective, the integration of Generative AI challenges long-established models of instruction, cognition, and student engagement. Traditional pedagogical approaches emphasize human interaction, inquiry-based learning, and the co-construction of knowledge between teachers and students. The introduction of AI systems, particularly those capable of responding faster and with apparent greater accuracy than humans, raises critical questions regarding the evolving role of educators. Will teachers primarily become facilitators of AI-generated content? Will students increasingly depend on machine tutors rather than human mentors? These questions underscore the need for careful pedagogical reflection and thoughtful instructional design. Generative AI technologies have the potential to drastically change teaching and learning approaches and necessitate new ways of thinking (Matthew, Bakare, Ebong, Ndukwu, & Nwanakwaugwu, 2023).

In fact, one major concern is the depersonalization of learning. AI systems may provide standardized feedback and adaptive learning pathways, but they often lack the contextual understanding, emotional intelligence, and relational depth that human educators bring to the classroom. Students who interact more with machines than with peers or teachers may experience a diminished sense of belonging, motivation, and socio-emotional development. This is particularly problematic for younger learners, who rely heavily on social cues and emotional resonance for cognitive and emotional growth.

To safeguard pedagogical integrity, educators must be equipped to critically integrate AI into their teaching strategies, not as a replacement for human instruction, but as an enhancement of it. This requires systematic reskilling initiatives, continuous professional development, and collaborative curriculum design that effectively blends human creativity with machine efficiency. New pedagogical models, such as AI-augmented inquiry, flipped learning supported by AI, and co-intelligent collaboration, can emerge only when teachers are empowered and actively engaged in shaping how AI is implemented in classroom practices.

The equity-related implications of Generative AI in education are perhaps the most concerning. Education systems across the globe are already marked by disparities in access to quality resources, infrastructure, and opportunities. The introduction of AI, if not carefully managed, risks deepening these divides. Students in high-income regions may have access to sophisticated AI tools, high-speed internet, and tech-savvy educators, while those in low-income or rural settings may be left behind. Without proactive intervention, AI could become yet another privilege of the elite, rather than a tool for universal learning.

Digital literacy represents another significant axis of inequality. Even when AI tools are accessible, not all students or educators possess the knowledge, skills, or confidence required to use them effectively. This digital competence gap can intensify existing educational disparities, as learners who receive stronger technological support and guidance are more likely to benefit disproportionately. Furthermore, many AI systems are not designed with accessibility as a primary consideration. For learners with disabilities, including visual, auditory, cognitive, and physical impairments, mainstream AI tools may create additional barriers rather than meaningful solutions unless they are intentionally developed to support inclusive and universal design principles.

Governments and international bodies must intervene with policies that mandate equitable access, promote open-source AI tools, and fund infrastructure in underserved areas. AI systems should be localized in terms of language, culture, and curriculum relevance. Global collaborations between AI developers, educators, and community leaders can help design tools that are inclusive, context-sensitive, and aligned with the needs of diverse learners. Table 1 shows the complex interplay of the challenge area.

Table 1. Complex interplay of the challenge area

Challenge Area	Ethical Implications	Pedagogical Implications	Equity Implications
Authorship & Plagiarism	Blurs lines between original and generated content	Undermines authentic assessment and learning	Disproportionately benefits students with access to tools
Data Privacy	Risk of surveillance and data misuse	Discourages open engagement in digital learning spaces	Marginalized students more vulnerable to exploitation
Bias in AI Models	Reinforces stereotypes, cultural erasure	Promotes skewed or incomplete learning	Disadvantages underrepresented groups
Teacher Role	Questions about responsibility and agency	Shifts educators toward AI facilitation roles	Requires training that may not be equitably distributed
Student Dependency	Overreliance reduces critical thinking	Reduces resilience and problem-solving skills	Students without guidance may misuse tools or underperform
Accessibility	Fails to address needs of students with disabilities	Limits inclusive learning design	AI tools may be unusable for learners with special needs
Infrastructure	High cost of tech deployment and maintenance	Limits pedagogical innovation in underfunded schools	Widening of global and local digital divides

The integration of Generative AI in education presents a transformative opportunity, but only when guided by ethical foresight, pedagogical integrity, and a firm commitment to equity. Educational institutions must move beyond mere adoption to critically examine the values embedded within AI systems, the assumptions they encode, and the power structures they may reinforce or challenge. Education should remain a fundamentally human-centered endeavor, even in an era increasingly shaped by intelligent technologies. This work emphasizes the importance of building inclusive educational ecosystems in which technology supports pedagogy rather than dictating it. Only through intentional, reflective, and collective effort can Generative AI realize its potential as a democratizing force in global education.

These ethical and equity-related challenges indicate that generative AI in education is not a neutral technological intervention but a normative choice that reflects underlying values about knowledge, authority, and inclusion. Decisions about data governance, model design, and access determine whose knowledge is amplified and whose is marginalized. As such, ethical integration of generative AI requires moving beyond compliance-based regulation toward value-sensitive design and participatory governance involving educators, learners, and communities.

Artificial Intelligence's Impact on Various Industries

To survive, grow, and remain competitive in increasingly dynamic markets, companies must strategically adopt advanced technologies. This imperative is particularly pronounced in developed economies, where rapid innovation and intense competition continuously reshape business landscapes. Among emerging technologies, artificial intelligence (AI) stands out as a critical source of competitive advantage, enabling organizations to enhance efficiency, effectiveness, productivity, and creativity. Unlike human labor, AI systems can rapidly process and analyze massive datasets, automate routine tasks, optimize operations, streamline business processes, reduce labor costs, and conduct large-scale market analysis. These capabilities allow managerial teams to reallocate time, energy, and resources toward higher-value strategic activities. In a short span of time since its introduction, generative artificial intelligence (AI) has garnered much interest at both personal and organizational levels (Ooi et al., 2025).

Generative AI (GenAI) further amplifies these benefits by fundamentally transforming organizational strategies, operational models, and customer interactions across diverse industries. As highlighted by Bill Gates, "2024 is the year of GenAI," underscoring its accelerating adoption and impact. Empirical evidence supports this trend. According to Statista, the global AI market is projected to surpass USD 1.8 trillion by 2030, reflecting unprecedented growth. For comparison, the United Kingdom's gross domestic product in 2021 amounted to approximately USD 3.1 trillion. Similarly, forecasts indicate that the market for Generative AI alone is expected to reach USD 1.3 trillion by 2032, signaling its central role in shaping the future of global economic and technological development. The dawn of AI agents is upon us. Tech visionaries like Bill Gates, Andrew Ng, and Vinod Khosla have highlighted the monumental potential of this powerful technology (Taulli & Deshmukh, 2025). The distribution of AI investments by individual industries is shown in the following Figure:

Figure 2. Worldwide spending on AI, by industries

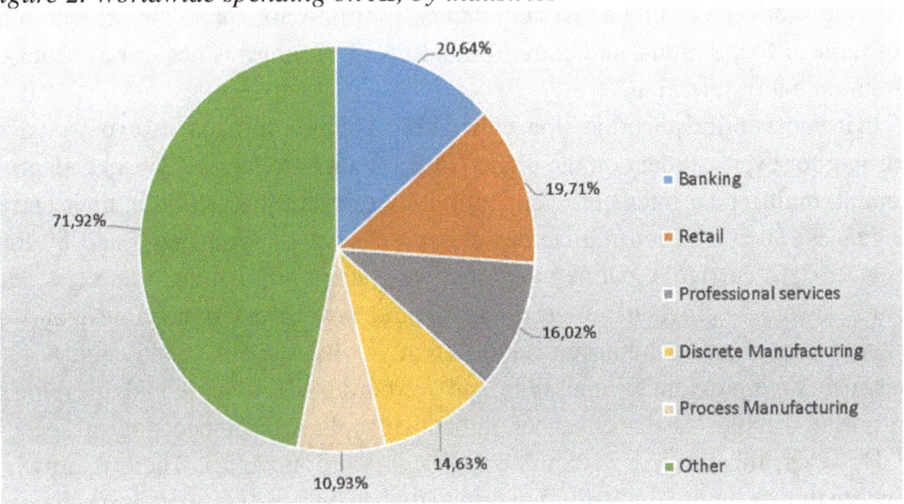

FUTURE OUTLOOK AND DIRECTIONS

The contribution of this chapter lies in advancing an integrative perspective on generative AI in education that connects technological evolution with pedagogical theory, ethical governance, and equity considerations. By framing generative AI as a component of collaborative human–AI intelligence rather than a replacement for human cognition, the chapter offers a conceptual lens that moves beyond descriptive accounts. This perspective supports educators and policymakers in critically evaluating not only what generative AI can do, but how it should be designed and governed to support equitable learning futures.

As the integration of Generative Artificial Intelligence (Generative AI) in education gains momentum, it is imperative to consider not only the current applications and challenges but also the long-term trajectory of its evolution. The future of education, when viewed through the lens of Generative AI, reveals an expansive terrain of possibilities—some inspirational, others cautionary. These possibilities span across technological, pedagogical, sociocultural, psychological, and geopolitical domains. The horizon is not merely shaped by technical capabilities but also by human choices, values, and governance structures that determine how these technologies are built, deployed, and institutionalized.

The direction in which Generative AI will evolve in education is not predetermined. Rather, it is a terrain shaped by critical negotiation—among educators, policymakers, technologists, students, communities, and global institutions. Whether

Generative AI reinforces existing inequalities or fosters a democratized, inclusive, and empowering learning ecosystem depends on how we shape the present policies, ethical foundations, and cultural mindsets. The future is not just a matter of invention but of intention.

In its most optimistic projection, Generative AI holds the capacity to personalize learning for every student on the planet, offering them tailored feedback, adaptive content, multimodal interaction, and culturally relevant instruction in their native languages. Such a vision reimagines classrooms not as spaces confined by four walls or rigid curricula, but as intelligent ecosystems—dynamic, borderless, and context-aware. Learners in remote villages could have access to the same quality of instruction as those in urban centers; differently-abled students could interact with content in ways previously impossible; and overburdened teachers could find relief in AI-powered assistance that enhances, rather than replaces, their pedagogical agency.

However, this utopian vision coexists with valid anxieties. There is growing concern that Generative AI, if left unchecked, may become yet another mechanism through which educational institutions are commodified, surveillance is normalized, and knowledge is standardized into machine-readable formats. The future, therefore, must be critically envisioned—not as a passive outcome of innovation but as an active construction involving multiple stakeholders.

To understand where we might be headed, it is essential to examine emerging trajectories in AI research and practice, and how these might interface with the evolving needs and complexities of education systems globally. Among the most prominent developments that will shape the future landscape of Generative AI in education are the maturation of explainable AI (XAI), the emergence of federated and on-device learning, the integration of co-intelligent systems between humans and machines, the evolution of multimodal learning environments including extended reality (XR), and the institutionalization of global governance frameworks for AI ethics and policy in education.

Let us begin with the first: explainable AI. Current Generative AI systems, including large language models, often operate as "black boxes." While they generate impressive outputs, the mechanisms underlying these outputs remain largely inaccessible to end users, educators, and even developers. This lack of interpretability can undermine trust, especially in high-stakes educational settings. In the future, we anticipate a strong shift towards explainability—AI systems that can not only generate answers but also explain their reasoning, cite their sources, and offer alternative perspectives. Explainable AI will empower educators to better evaluate AI-generated feedback, and will equip learners with metacognitive tools to interrogate, reflect upon, and contextualize machine output. In teacher training, such systems can also facilitate a deeper understanding of how AI processes knowledge, how it frames biases, and how it may be guided through prompts and constraints.

Federated learning represents another paradigm shift that will profoundly impact education's digital infrastructure. Unlike traditional machine learning models, which centralize data collection for training, federated learning enables models to learn directly on user devices. This approach has significant implications for privacy, data sovereignty, and personalization. Students will be able to engage with AI tutors that adapt to their learning styles and progress, without having their data sent to central servers. Such architectures could enable education systems to comply with stricter data regulations and to serve populations that are particularly sensitive to surveillance, such as children, refugees, and indigenous communities. Furthermore, on-device AI may allow real-time adaptation in low-bandwidth or offline environments, thus closing the connectivity gap that persists across many parts of the Global South. As industrial systems increasingly integrate machine learning (ML) for cybersecurity, they face a growing threat from adversarial machine learning (AML) attacks (Sekti, 2025a).

Beyond infrastructure, the pedagogical future of Generative AI is likely to revolve around co-intelligent systems, namely environments in which human intelligence and machine intelligence collaborate symbiotically. This extends beyond current assistant-like roles toward more participatory and dialogic learning models. Such platforms enable students to co-create knowledge with AI agents, critically challenge machine-generated responses, and construct iterative learning narratives that evolve over time. In parallel, teachers are expected to transition into co-designers of intelligent curricula by orchestrating AI-driven simulations, customizing instructional pathways, and facilitating epistemic dialogues informed by both human and machine reasoning. Within this landscape, AI is not positioned as a replacement but as a co-learner, an adaptive entity that evolves through interaction to better support human understanding and creativity.

Multimodal Environments Dan Extended Reality (XR)

The evolution of multimodal learning environments, enhanced by the integration of Extended Reality (XR), marks another transformative direction for the future of education. Multimodal systems are those that engage learners through various sensory and communicative channels—text, audio, video, images, simulations, haptic feedback, and increasingly, real-time gesture and emotion recognition. While traditional e-learning platforms have attempted to simulate multimodal experiences through multimedia, the integration of AI into these systems dramatically expands the possibilities. Generative AI, with its ability to synthesize realistic voices, generate animations, build interactive simulations, and respond to emotional cues, allows for the creation of learning spaces that are not only multimodal but also deeply interactive and adaptive. Advances in artificial intelligence and human-computer interaction will likely lead to extended reality (XR) becoming pervasive (Bozkir et al., 2024).

Imagine a biology student donning an augmented reality headset to enter a fully-rendered, AI-generated simulation of the human circulatory system, where she can manipulate virtual organs, listen to AI narrators explain physiological processes, and receive instant, personalized feedback. Or consider a history class where students "walk" through an ancient city reconstructed in virtual reality, guided by AI avatars capable of engaging in Socratic dialogue, offering differing historical interpretations based on primary sources. These are not distant dreams, but imminent possibilities. Already, several universities and ed-tech firms are piloting immersive XR courses that combine Generative AI with spatial computing to create fully personalized learning adventures.

What distinguishes this new wave of XR education from earlier models is the integration of real-time generative responsiveness. Rather than relying on pre-scripted pathways, AI agents embedded in these environments can adapt narrative flow, difficulty levels, and interaction styles based on learner engagement and progress. This adaptability enables what may be described as living curricula, namely educational experiences that evolve dynamically rather than remaining static. The potential impact of such systems on student engagement, knowledge retention, and cross-disciplinary exploration is substantial. For learners with disabilities, multimodal and XR-based systems also provide more inclusive interfaces by enabling gesture-based navigation for individuals with mobility impairments and voice-activated tutoring for visually impaired learners.

As these technologies mature, the need for comprehensive global policy frameworks becomes increasingly urgent. The educational application of Generative AI, particularly in immersive and data-intensive environments, raises critical concerns related to cognitive manipulation, surveillance, and equity. Fundamental questions emerge regarding data ownership, the prevention of behavioral advertising and ideological influence, and the protection of learners from misinformation, especially when AI systems are capable of producing highly realistic simulations of historical events or scientific phenomena.

In response to these challenges, international organizations such as UNESCO, the OECD, and the World Economic Forum have initiated multi-stakeholder dialogues aimed at developing governance frameworks specifically tailored to educational AI. These initiatives seek to balance innovation with regulatory oversight, ensuring that AI systems used in education are transparent, explainable, accountable, equitable, and aligned with human rights principles. They promote algorithmic transparency, meaningful human oversight, participatory design involving educators and learners, and continuous ethical auditing of classroom technologies. Furthermore, these global efforts emphasize cultural pluralism in AI development, advocating for localized approaches that reflect linguistic diversity, epistemic traditions, and socio-political contexts.

Looking ahead, a critical priority is the systematic integration of AI literacy into teacher education, curriculum design, and public education policy. Assuming that educators will naturally acquire the competencies required to effectively integrate AI tools is both unrealistic and inequitable. Teachers require comprehensive professional development that extends beyond technical training to include philosophical inquiry and ethical reflection. They must be equipped to critically examine how AI systems frame knowledge, embed assumptions about learning and cognition, and amplify or marginalize particular perspectives within educational contexts.

AI literacy must go beyond functional usage. It must cultivate in educators and students a critical awareness of how AI systems work, what data they are trained on, what biases they might harbor, and what limitations they face. This kind of literacy is foundational for any future in which humans and AI collaborate meaningfully. Without it, there is a risk that educational systems will become over-reliant on AI outputs without interrogating their epistemological implications. In such a scenario, education could devolve into the passive consumption of machine-generated knowledge, rather than remaining a site of human inquiry, reflection, and creativity.

Another significant direction is the development of co-intelligent governance systems, namely organizational and institutional frameworks in which human decision-makers work in tandem with AI systems to craft educational policy, monitor learning outcomes, and allocate resources. These systems do not replace human leadership but rather augment it by using AI-driven insights to identify areas of inequality, forecast future workforce needs, and simulate the potential impact of new curricula. For instance, AI models trained on economic, demographic, and environmental data can support ministries of education in designing more adaptive, resilient, and responsive policies. However, for such governance models to be trustworthy, the underlying algorithms must be auditable, transparent, and subject to democratic oversight. Table 2 shows the Comparative Scenarios for the Future of Generative AI in Education.

Table 2. Comparative scenarios for the future of generative AI in education

Scenario Name	Core Vision	Role of AI	Educator Agency	Equity Implications	Risks/ Warnings
Equitable Co-Intelligence	Human-AI partnerships for inclusive, personalized learning	Assistive, explainable, and adaptive	Empowered as co-designers and facilitators	High equity; locally adaptable; accessible	Requires strong policy, infrastructure, and ethical regulation
Corporate EduTech Dominance	Centralized platforms dominate global education delivery	Proprietary, opaque, profit-driven	Reduced to content managers	Widened gaps; data exploitation; algorithmic bias	Monopolization, cultural loss, surveillance capitalism
AI-Driven Standardization	Optimization of learning through metrics, automation, and testing	Autonomous evaluator and content generator	Minimal role; supervised automation	One-size-fits-all; exclusion of diverse learning models	Pedagogical reductionism, creativity loss, learner disempowerment
Community-Led AI Learning	Grassroots development and deployment of open, ethical AI tools in schools	Transparent, participatory, open-source	Highly engaged; AI tailored to community	Local empowerment, linguistic diversity, resilient learning systems	Requires funding, capacity-building, and open infrastructure

These scenarios are not exhaustive nor mutually exclusive. Elements of each may emerge simultaneously across different regions and systems, depending on local contexts and decisions. For instance, affluent private schools may experience "Equitable Co-Intelligence," while underfunded public schools are trapped in "AI-Driven Standardization." Meanwhile, indigenous or marginalized communities may resist both, opting for "Community-Led AI Learning" grounded in their cultural epistemologies.

Navigating this complexity requires global coordination and ethical leadership. Institutions such as UNESCO have already laid the groundwork for AI ethics in education, emphasizing human rights, sustainability, and transparency. Yet, implementation varies widely across countries. Some governments have embraced AI without sufficient safeguards, while others have banned its use entirely due to concerns over misinformation, bias, or dependency.

What becomes clear is that there is no neutral AI in education. Every system reflects the assumptions, values, and priorities embedded within its design. Therefore, one of the most important future directions is the development of AI design literacy among educators, curriculum developers, and community stakeholders. Rather than treating AI as a fixed product, educational systems must approach it as a negotiable and evolving process that remains open to critical scrutiny, iterative refinement, and local adaptation.

Such a participatory approach also implies the establishment of AI research centers within teacher education institutions, where educators can experiment with emerging tools, co-design pedagogical applications, and conduct classroom-based research on learning effectiveness, equity, and social impact. These centers could function as hubs of innovation and democratic oversight, ensuring that Generative AI advances pedagogical goals rather than serving purely commercial or political interests.

Moreover, a critical frontier in AI development is epistemic pluralism, which refers to the capacity of AI systems to represent and generate knowledge across diverse cultural, philosophical, and disciplinary traditions. Current models predominantly reflect Western and Anglophone data corpora. For future AI systems to serve global educational communities equitably, they must support indigenous languages, accommodate non-linear learning pathways, and promote pluralistic epistemologies that transcend dominant paradigms.

This vision aligns with the broader project of decolonizing education through AI, wherein machine intelligence is not just a tool for efficiency but a platform for reimagining knowledge, voice, and agency in more equitable and pluralistic ways.

Epistemological Transformation in Education with Generative AI

Much of the current discourse surrounding Generative AI in education has focused on its roles in content delivery, assessment automation, and personalized learning. However, the most profound impact of this technology may not lie in what is taught, but in how knowledge itself is understood, constructed, and validated. Generative AI has the potential to fundamentally transform the epistemology of education, namely the ways in which knowledge is defined, acquired, and meaningfully engaged. Instances of complete generation were recorded in 16% of cases, indicative of hyperdelegation and the erosion of intentionality, and revealed epistemological polarization regarding the AI perception (Horban, Stadnyk, Vintoniv-Bakharieva, Panasiuk, & Yatyshchuk, 2025).

In traditional educational paradigms, knowledge is often structured as linear and hierarchical, flowing from authoritative sources such as teachers, textbooks, or institutions to students. Learning is frequently conceptualized as the transmission and internalization of established facts or procedures. Success is measured primarily by the ability to recall, reproduce, or apply this knowledge within standardized formats.

Generative AI challenges this paradigm. When students can ask a large language model like ChatGPT virtually any question and receive complex, synthesized, and often dialectical responses, the notion of the "singular source of truth" begins to unravel. Moreover, when AI systems can generate new hypotheses, alternative perspectives, or novel connections between ideas, they shift from being passive repositories to active participants in knowledge creation.

This opens up the possibility of human–AI dialogic learning environments in which learners and machines co-construct knowledge through iterative questioning, reflection, and feedback. In such settings, students do not merely learn from AI; they learn with it. They may challenge AI-generated claims, explore divergent viewpoints, or even retrain local models using culturally relevant data. This co-intelligent exchange represents a shift from knowledge transmission toward knowledge emergence.

Consequently, curricula may need to be redesigned around processes of inquiry, creativity, and synthesis rather than rigid content standards. The goals of learning may shift from knowing what to knowing how and knowing why, emphasizing metacognition, epistemic humility, and critical thinking. Assessment practices would also need to evolve. If AI systems can generate essays or solve problems instantly, the educational value of such tasks must be reconsidered. Alternative assessment approaches may include collaborative inquiry, reflective learning journals, and dialogical reasoning activities.

Another future direction is epistemic pluralism, which refers to the capacity of AI systems to represent and generate knowledge derived from diverse cultural, linguistic, and philosophical traditions. Current AI models are predominantly trained on Western and English-language data corpora. A more equitable educational future requires sustained investment in datasets and algorithms that respect Indigenous knowledge systems, oral traditions, community practices, and non-linear epistemologies. In this way, AI should function not as a mechanism of epistemological domination, but as a platform for epistemic justice.

Educational researchers, anthropologists, technologists, and philosophers must work together to develop AI systems that not only perform tasks but understand and respect how different cultures conceptualize truth, learning, and evidence. This collaborative endeavor will define whether AI becomes an agent of homogenization or a catalyst for cognitive diversity.

Likewise, learners should be educated in the limitations and assumptions of AI systems. AI literacy must include understanding how AI models process information, what they omit, how they can be biased, and how to challenge their outputs. Without this awareness, there is a risk that learners will outsource their cognitive agency to machines, mistaking fluency for truth.

AI as a Creative Partner in Curriculum Innovation and Experiential Learning Simulations

As education shifts from content delivery to dynamic engagement, the role of AI is also evolving—from a tool for automation to a co-creative partner in the design and delivery of meaningful learning experiences. This transformation opens up new frontiers in curriculum innovation, instructional design, and experiential learning.

Reimagining Curriculum Design with Generative AI

Traditionally, curriculum development has been a slow, labor-intensive process, often constrained by bureaucratic structures, static textbooks, and rigid assessment frameworks. Generative AI can radically accelerate and personalize this process by co-designing learning pathways that are modular, adaptive, and aligned with learner needs and contexts.

Imagine a curriculum designer collaborating with an AI system that can instantly analyze:

- National competency standards
- Local community needs
- Learner profiles and prior knowledge
- Multimodal content repositories

Based on this input, the AI can generate customized learning modules, propose interdisciplinary connections, or even recommend culturally relevant materials in multiple languages. Rather than replacing human educators, this approach empowers them to make better, faster, and more inclusive design decisions.

More importantly, Generative AI can facilitate responsive curriculum cycles—where content is not "fixed" for years but updated in real time based on learner performance data, global developments, or newly available resources. This is especially valuable in fields like environmental science, data ethics, or digital literacy, where knowledge is constantly evolving.

For example:

- In climate education, AI can generate local simulations of carbon emissions based on real data.
- In history, AI can synthesize primary sources and present contrasting narratives for analysis.
- In literature, AI can create parallel versions of a story from different cultural perspectives, prompting comparative discussions.

Simulated Learning Environments and AI-Generated Scenarios

Generative AI is also reshaping experiential learning, a pedagogical model in which students learn through direct experience, reflection, and practical application. Through tools such as AI-generated simulations, virtual role-play scenarios, and narrative branching environments, learners can explore complex real-world systems in safe, adaptive, and cost-effective ways. Generative AI could become a cost-effective complement to expert feedback by serving as an automated teacher coach (R. Wang & Demszky, 2023).

Consider the following examples:

- A student in a global studies class enters an AI-generated diplomatic simulation, playing the role of a UN delegate navigating a climate treaty negotiation. The AI dynamically generates responses based on the student's choices and presents plausible outcomes.
- In a healthcare course, learners participate in an AI-powered emergency scenario, where they must make decisions under pressure and receive feedback in real time, complete with virtual patient responses.
- In ethics education, learners engage with AI-generated moral dilemmas and explore competing ethical frameworks before articulating their personal reasoning.

Such simulations develop critical thinking, empathy, decision-making, and systems thinking, which are difficult to cultivate through lectures or standard assessments. Moreover, these environments can be personalized to learner readiness, escalating in complexity as the student grows, and integrating reflection points along the way.

AI's creative capacity also makes it possible to design entirely new genres of educational media:

- Immersive storyworlds based on curriculum themes
- Dynamic escape rooms using subject-specific puzzles
- Procedural poetry generators for language learning
- Historical "what if" engines for speculative historiography

These formats not only support learning objectives but also increase engagement, motivation, and learner autonomy—especially for students who struggle in traditional academic environments.

Ensuring Pedagogical Alignment

While the possibilities are exciting, they must be grounded in sound pedagogical principles. AI-generated experiences must align with learning goals, cognitive load considerations, developmental stages, and assessment frameworks. Randomly generated content can easily become overwhelming, misleading, or irrelevant if not curated carefully.

Therefore, the future of creative AI in education depends not on automation alone but on the formation of AI–educator partnerships. Educators should be trained not just as users of AI, but as co-designers and curators—able to shape and adapt what the AI creates to ensure rigor, accessibility, and meaning.

To make this process transparent and manageable, AI systems should provide explainability features, such as:

- Learning objective tagging for generated content
- Source traceability and cultural contextualization
- Options for human feedback and content iteration

This allows teachers to trust the output, correct biases, and align materials with their learners' unique profiles.

CONCLUSION

Generative AI holds transformative potential for education by enabling more personalized, inclusive, and creative learning experiences. From intelligent tutoring systems and adaptive content generation to multimodal accessibility and cross-cultural knowledge creation, these technologies offer unprecedented opportunities to enhance teaching and learning. However, such potential can only be realized through deliberate, ethical, and collaborative implementation. Beyond technical sophistication, generative AI must be guided by purposeful design that centers human values, pedagogical integrity, and social responsibility. Achieving this requires human-centered design principles, inclusive learning frameworks, robust governance structures, and a strong commitment to equity and justice.

As educational systems increasingly integrate AI tools into everyday practice, there is a growing need to reconsider foundational assumptions about teaching, learning, and knowledge construction. This transformation extends beyond technological adoption and calls for a broader philosophical and epistemological reorientation. Education must actively shape the design and deployment of AI rather than passively adapt to technological change. Meaningful collaboration among educators, technologists, learners, policymakers, and communities is essential to ensure that AI enhances human connection, learner autonomy, and critical reflection, rather than diminishing them.

The integration of generative AI into learning environments should not be driven solely by efficiency or innovation, but by a commitment to building systems that are transparent, responsive, culturally sensitive, and resilient. Ethical safeguards and accountability mechanisms must be embedded throughout the AI lifecycle to mitigate risks related to bias, privacy, and unintended consequences. Equally important is the empowerment of educators, who should remain central agents in pedagogical innovation, supported by AI as a reflective partner rather than replaced by automated systems. Furthermore, equitable access to infrastructure and digital resources must be prioritized to ensure that AI-enhanced education benefits all learners, particularly those from historically marginalized and underserved communities.

Ultimately, the future of education in the age of generative AI is not merely a technological challenge but a profoundly human one. It requires sustained cross-disciplinary collaboration among educators, engineers, social scientists, ethicists, and learners to shape learning ecosystems grounded in empathy, ethics, and inclusivity. The central question is not whether AI can teach, but how educational systems can preserve human agency, critical judgment, and cultural plurality while embracing intelligent technologies. By aligning innovation with human values, generative AI and human intelligence can work together to foster a more just, humane, and meaningful educational future.

REFERENCES

Bandi, A., Adapa, P. V. S. R., & Kuchi, Y. E. V. P. K. (2023). The Power of Generative AI: A Review of Requirements, Models, Input–Output Formats, Evaluation Metrics, and Challenges. *Future Internet, 15*(8), 260. Advance online publication. DOI: 10.3390/fi15080260

Bozkir, E., Özdel, S., Lau, K. H. C., Wang, M., Gao, H., & Kasneci, E. (2024). Embedding Large Language Models into Extended Reality: Opportunities and Challenges for Inclusion, Engagement, and Privacy. In *Proceedings of the 6th Conference on ACM Conversational User Interfaces, CUI 2024*. DOI: 10.1145/3640794.3665563

Chan, C. K. Y., & Hu, W. (2023). Students' voices on generative AI: Perceptions, benefits, and challenges in higher education. *International Journal of Educational Technology in Higher Education, 20*(1), 43. Advance online publication. DOI: 10.1186/s41239-023-00411-8

Cooper, G. (2023). Examining Science Education in ChatGPT: An Exploratory Study of Generative Artificial Intelligence. *Journal of Science Education and Technology, 32*(3), 444–452. DOI: 10.1007/s10956-023-10039-y

Dwivedi, Y. K., Kshetri, N., Hughes, L., Slade, E. L., Jeyaraj, A., Kar, A. K., Baabdullah, A. M., Koohang, A., Raghavan, V., Ahuja, M., Albanna, H., Albashrawi, M. A., Al-Busaidi, A. S., Balakrishnan, J., Barlette, Y., Basu, S., Bose, I., Brooks, L., Buhalis, D., & Wright, R. (2023). Opinion Paper: "So what if ChatGPT wrote it?" Multidisciplinary perspectives on opportunities, challenges and implications of generative conversational AI for research, practice and policy. *International Journal of Information Management, 71*, 102642. 10.1016/j.ijinfomgt.2023.102642. DOI: 10.1016/j.ijinfomgt.2023.102642

Horban, O., Stadnyk, M., Vintoniv-Bakharieva, S., Panasiuk, L., & Yatyshchuk, O. (2025). Artificial Intelligence as an Integral Component of the Digital Culture within Contemporary Higher Education. *Journal of Educational Technology and Learning Creativity, 3*(2), 451–467. DOI: 10.37251/jetlc.v3i2.2333

Kaushik, V., Narayana, A., Satha, D. S., Grace, J., Elankavi, R., & Chavan, G. (2025). Generative Ai For Multicultural Music Education. *ShodhKosh: Journal of Visual and Performing Arts, 6*(5s), 547–557. DOI: 10.29121/shodhkosh.v6.i5s.2025.6910

Liao, S. J., Han, P., & Xu, Y. (2025). Capability and Potential of Generative Artificial Intelligence (AI) Tools in Science Education: An Exploratory Study of ChatGPT-Powered Tools (DALL-E and Globe Explore), Midjourney and Gatekeep in Multimodal Science Education. *Journal of College Science Teaching*, *54*(6), 477–493. DOI: 10.1080/0047231X.2025.2480575

Lim, W. M., Gunasekara, A., Pallant, J. L., Pallant, J. I., & Pechenkina, E. (2023). Generative AI and the future of education: Ragnarök or reformation? A paradoxical perspective from management educators. *International Journal of Management Education*, *21*(2), 100790. Advance online publication. DOI: 10.1016/j.ijme.2023.100790

Matthew, U. O., Bakare, K. M., Ebong, G. N., Ndukwu, C. C., & Nwanakwaugwu, A. C. (2023). Generative Artificial Intelligence (AI) Educational Pedagogy Development: Conversational AI with User-Centric ChatGPT4. *Journal of Trends in Computer Science and Smart Technology*, *5*(4), 401–418. DOI: 10.36548/jtcsst.2023.4.003

Michel-Villarreal, R., Vilalta-Perdomo, E., Salinas-Navarro, D. E., Thierry-Aguilera, R., & Gerardou, F. S. (2023). Challenges and Opportunities of Generative AI for Higher Education as Explained by ChatGPT. *Education Sciences*, *13*(9), 856. Advance online publication. DOI: 10.3390/educsci13090856

Ooi, K.-B., Tan, G. W.-H., Al-Emran, M., Al-Sharafi, M. A., Capatina, A., Chakraborty, A., Dwivedi, Y. K., Huang, T.-L., Kar, A. K., Lee, V.-H., Loh, X.-M., Micu, A., Mikalef, P., Mogaji, E., Pandey, N., Raman, R., Rana, N. P., Sarker, P., Sharma, A., & Wong, L.-W. (2025). The Potential of Generative Artificial Intelligence Across Disciplines: Perspectives and Future Directions. *Journal of Computer Information Systems*, *65*(1), 76–107. DOI: 10.1080/08874417.2023.2261010

Pearson, A. (2024). Creativity: Firing on all generative AI cylinders. *Journal of Digital and Social Media Marketing*, *12*(1), 52–64. DOI: 10.69554/VSKL5622

Riyat, S., Gandhi, J., Kumar, A., Das, K., Panigra, A., Jennifer, D., & Manav, O. M. (2025). Reinventing Digital Illustration With Generative Ai Tools. *ShodhKosh: Journal of Visual and Performing Arts*, *6*(5s), 1–11. DOI: 10.29121/shodhkosh.v6.i5s.2025.6876

Sekti, B. A. (2025a). Adversarial Machine Learning in Industrial Cybersecurity: Challenges and Solutions. In *AI-Enhanced Cybersecurity for Industrial Automation* (pp. 363–386). IGI Global Scientific Publishing. DOI: 10.4018/979-8-3373-3241-3.ch018

Sekti, B. A. (2025b). Foundations of Artificial Intelligence Ethics. In *Navigating Social Trust in the AI Era* (pp. 23–47). DOI: 10.4018/979-8-3373-7011-8.ch002

Sekti, B. A. (2025c). Machine Learning vs. AI: Key Concepts. In *Implementing Enterprise Cybersecurity With AI* (pp. 1–27). DOI: 10.4018/979-8-3373-2252-0.ch001

Taulli, T., & Deshmukh, G. (2025). *Building Generative AI Agents: Using LangGraph, AutoGen, and CrewAI. Building Generative AI Agents: Using LangGraph.* AutoGen, and CrewAI., DOI: 10.1007/979-8-8688-1134-0

Wang, H., Fu, T., Du, Y., Gao, W., Huang, K., Liu, Z., Chandak, P., Liu, S., Van Katwyk, P., Deac, A., Anandkumar, A., Bergen, K., Gomes, C. P., Ho, S., Kohli, P., Lasenby, J., Leskovec, J., Liu, T.-Y., Manrai, A., & Zitnik, M. (2023). Scientific discovery in the age of artificial intelligence. *Nature*, *620*(7972), 47–60. DOI: 10.1038/s41586-023-06221-2 PMID: 37532811

Wang, R., & Demszky, D. (2023). Is ChatGPT a Good Teacher Coach? Measuring Zero-Shot Performance For Scoring and Providing Actionable Insights on Classroom Instruction. In *Proceedings of the Annual Meeting of the Association for Computational Linguistics* (pp. 626–667). Retrieved from https://www.scopus.com/inward/record.uri?eid=2-s2.0-85172178508&partnerID=40&md5=c3131386676854c615e0acae66264a4b

Chapter 2
Collaborative Paradigms of Generative AI and Human Intelligence for Equitable Learning Futures

Rafael Luberto Sinaga
http://orcid.org/0009-0004-0433-7054
Universitas Esa Unggul, Indonesia

Binastya Anggara Sekti
http://orcid.org/0000-0001-5489-4888
Universitas Esa Unggul, Indonesia

ABSTRACT

This book explores collaborative paradigms between generative artificial intelligence (Generative AI) and human intelligence in shaping a fair, inclusive, and sustainable future of learning. Moving beyond technocentric approaches, it offers both conceptual and practical frameworks for integrating AI in education that centers human values. Emphasizing ethics, social justice, participation, and cultural diversity, each chapter provides a roadmap for learning systems that foster co-agency between humans and machines. Case studies, adaptive frameworks, and multi-level policy recommendations are presented to ensure that AI in education does not widen existing inequalities but instead expands access and strengthens human dignity. This book is a global call to action for institutions, policymakers, and communities to co-design educational ecosystems that are ethical, visionary, and collaborative.

DOI: 10.4018/979-8-3373-6063-8.ch002

1. INTRODUCTION

Artificial intelligence (AI) is now in a new phase in its role in transforming various aspects of life, including the social, cultural, global economy, and education systems. Over the past two decades, AI has been a catalyst in a wide range of learning innovations, from smart tutors, automated grading systems, to data-driven adaptive learning. While these advancements bring significant benefits such as efficiency and personalization, the dominant approach is still firmly rooted in a technocentric paradigm: making AI the center of control over the learning process. This paradigm often ignores critical dimensions in education such as empathy, participation, cultural context, and social justice. As a result, AI in education risks not only magnifying the already existing digital divide, but also reinforcing systemic exclusion and bias structures.

To answer the various challenges that arise from the application of AI in education, an approach known as *Human-Centric Artificial Intelligence* (HCAI) comes as a promising alternative. This approach emphasizes the importance of placing humans in a central position in the entire technological process, both as users who interact directly with the system, as learners who receive the impact of its implementation, and as designers and decision-makers who determine the direction of its development. Thus, HCAI aims to ensure that artificial intelligence not only supports the learning process technically, but is also aligned with human values such as empathy, active participation, and diversity of social contexts. HCAI does not simply emphasize user convenience, but rather champions human values such as autonomy, participation, transparency, and fairness in every stage of AI design and implementation. In the context of education, this means that AI is not only a teaching tool, but also a collaborative medium that respects the diversity of learning experiences and encourages a more equitable pedagogical transformation.

Recent literature trends show that although the term HCAI has received widespread attention, its application in the context of education is still very limited. A systematic study conducted by (Horvatić & Lipic, 2021) identifies that most research on AI in education focuses on technological innovation, but has not adequately touched on participatory design aspects or real engagement of learners and educators. They highlight the gap between the rhetoric of inclusivity and the reality of implementation, particularly in different cultural and social contexts. This is reinforced by the study (Le Dinh et al., 2025) which found that very few educational AI systems were actually built with ethical design principles from the very beginning. Most still adopt an approach that positions the user as a passive object, rather than as a subject who actively contributes to the system design and development process.

Furthermore, the *human-centered learning analytics* approach shows that important elements such as transparency, accountability, and system reliability are still underpaid in the development of educational AI systems. They also noted that AI literacy among teachers and students is still very low, leading to a power imbalance and understanding between system makers and end-users. This condition raises ethical concerns, especially when it comes to how data is collected, analyzed, and used to make educational decisions that directly impact students.

In the framework of global development, education is not only a matter of transferring knowledge, but also a tool to achieve social justice and equality between generations. In this context, the application of AI must be in line with sustainable development values, in particular the fourth goal of *the Sustainable Development Goals* (SDG 4): ensuring inclusive and quality education for all. Unfortunately, as systematic studies reveal (Rivas & Zhao, 2023), most educational AI systems are still being developed by institutions in northern global countries with the assumption of universality that often does not match the needs and realities of the global south. This can lead to algorithmic colonization, where learning and evaluation models from one cultural context are exported and applied uncritically to another, very different context.

A more recent literature review of (Moustaghfir & Brigui, 2024) also highlights how the dominance of logic of efficiency and performativity in AI education systems tends to ignore the principles of inclusion and fairness. In this study, it is explained that there are still few systems that explicitly include a digital accessibility component for people with disabilities, students from indigenous communities, or those in remote areas. As a result, AI, which should be an empowerment tool, actually strengthens the existing gap.

In crafting a vision for the future of AI in education, it is important to not only talk about efficiency, but also about participation, transparency, and diversity of values. Education is a domain that is inherently human and contextual. Therefore, the AI applied in it must also be able to understand and interact with this socio-cultural complexity. Good AI in education is not one that replaces teachers or dictates students, but rather one that strengthens human connections in the learning ecosystem. In other words, AI must be a co-actor in shaping meaningful learning experiences, not just content providers or automated decision-makerss.

The shift to a humanist AI paradigm also has far-reaching policy implications. A governance framework is needed that ensures the involvement of all stakeholders, such as students, teachers, parents, and policymakers, in the process of developing and overseeing AI systems. This governance must include the principles of data protection, algorithmic justice, ethical audits, as well as public accountability mechanisms. This is not only the responsibility of educational institutions, but also technology companies, government agencies, and international organizations involved in the development of educational technology.

As part of this transformation process, AI literacy must become a basic competency in today's education system. Students and educators need to understand how AI systems work, how they are developed, and what impact they have on their rights and lives. AI literacy is not only about technical skills, but also about critical awareness, digital ethics, and empowerment in the face of increasingly complex systems. Without literacy and equitable participation, AI risks becoming an elitist technology, which can only be understood by a small percentage of individuals while the majority of other users tend to accept it passively.

In conclusion, to realize a just and sustainable future of education, AI must be positioned as a tool that supports human dignity, not as a substitute or controller. The human-centric approach in educational AI development offers a path to a more inclusive, ethical, and collaborative learning system. However, this vision will not be realized without a profound paradigm shift, which includes the fields of research, technology design, public policy, and also pedagogical practices in daily life. This chapter will present a conceptual and practical roadmap to guide the next step towards a learning ecosystem that makes AI an equal partner in achieving global education goals.

2. REINTERPRETING AI IN EDUCATION FROM AUTOMATION TO HUMANITY

Table 1. The evolution of AI in the education system

Period	AI Technology Focus	Implementation Examples	Excess	Limitations
1980–2000	Intelligent Tutoring Systems (ITS)	Carnegie Learning, AutoTutor	Individual learning	High cost, less scalable
2000–2015	Learning Analytics	Learning Record Stores (LRS), OpenLearnerModel	Processing performance data	Quantitative focus, potential bias
2015–sekarang	Predictive AI Systems	Early warning systems, adaptive LMS	Early intervention, efficiency	Labeling risk, minimal human agency

The development of artificial intelligence (AI) in the world of education has undergone a significant transition in the last decade. Initially, AI was implemented through systems such as *Intelligent Tutoring Systems* (ITS) which function to provide direct feedback and limited personalization to learners. However, as educational data has increased and advances in algorithmic modeling have evolved, these systems have evolved into more complex predictive systems. The system not only responds to user learning behavior, but is also capable of estimating learning outcomes, identifying academic risks, and automatically recommending interventions (Nuranti et al., 2022)

While these technological advancements provide benefits in operational efficiency and scale of implementation, criticism is beginning to emerge against the technocratic approach that dominates the design and development of AI in education. This approach often puts technology at the center of the decision-making process, assuming that efficiency and optimization are the primary goals. In practice, this results in a system that takes less into account human values such as justice, empathy, and participation. As noted by (Holmes et al., 2022), This technocratic paradigm creates a gap between system developers and end-users, where educators and learners are rarely actively involved in the process of designing the technology they will use.

In response to this criticism, an alternative approach known as *Human-Centric Artificial Intelligence* (HCAI) has emerged. Paraphase this sentence so that the em dash disappears. (Guesmi et al., 2022) emphasizes that HCAI in education aims to create a collaborative, transparent, and accountable learning environment, where educators retain control and agency over the use of AI systems in learning.

The HCAI approach has four main pillars, namely autonomy, empathy, diversity, and justice. The autonomy pillar emphasizes the importance of giving users, especially educators, control to determine when and how AI is used in teaching and learning activities. The empathy pillar refers to the system's ability to understand the user's emotional and social context, as well as respond in a way that supports psychological well-being. The diversity pillar ensures that the system is designed to reflect and respect different cultural backgrounds, languages, and individual needs. Meanwhile, the justice pillar focuses on efforts to eliminate algorithmic bias and prevent discrimination in the decision-making process carried out by the system (Schiff, 2022) .

The implementation of HCAI principles in education demands fundamental changes in the way technology is developed. One promising approach is *socio-technical co-design*, which is a collaborative design process that involves stakeholders from various social and technical backgrounds in every stage of system development. In the context of education, this means involving teachers, students, administrators, technology developers, and local communities in designing technology solutions that are relevant to their needs and values. This approach is believed to be able to increase social relevance, cultural acceptance, and the effectiveness of AI implementation in diverse learning contexts (Ahrweiler et al., 2025).

Although the concept of co-design has been widely discussed in the literature, its application in the field of *Artificial Intelligence in Education* (AIED) is still relatively limited. A systematic study conducted by (Samuli Laato, 2022) It shows that only a small part of the learning analytics system actually engages the end user in the design process. Even when that engagement exists, it often occurs at the final evaluation stage, rather than at the initial conceptualization phase. This poses a risk that the developed system will not meet the real needs of users or may even exacerbate existing inequalities.

More than just user engagement, co-design within the HCAI framework also includes efforts to understand and integrate local values in the technology development process. In a diverse global context, educational AI must be able to adapt to different social norms, languages, and value systems. Otherwise, AI systems have the potential to reproduce the cultural hegemony of technology-developing countries and ignore the local educational context. Therefore, co-design is not only about technical participation, but also about the recognition of cultural rights and alternative epistemology in education.

The transformation from a technocratic paradigm to a humanistic paradigm in educational AI is not an easy task. It requires collective and interdisciplinary efforts involving the fields of technology, pedagogy, psychology, philosophy, and public policy. However, this direction is the only way to ensure that developing educational technologies are not only technically sophisticated, but also socially meaningful. Truly human-centric AI is AI that is capable of supporting learning as a complex human process, not just an algorithmically automated activity.

This chapter emphasizes that reinterpreting AI in education is not just a matter of replacing old technology with newer ones. It's about reimagining the relationship between humans and machines, as well as ensuring that the technology we build reflects the values we want to instill in the educational process. In the next chapter, the discussion will focus on the core principles of equitable AI integration, as the basis for the development of more inclusive technology-based education policies and practices.

3. CORE PRINCIPLES FOR EQUITABLE AI INTEGRATION

3.1 Ethics-by-Design and Participatory Engagement

The concept *of ethics-by-design* is a proactive approach in the development of artificial intelligence (AI) systems that places ethical values as a core element from the conceptualization stage to implementation. In the context of education, this approach emphasizes the importance of ensuring that any technical decision is aligned with the principles of justice, participation, inclusion, and digital rights. Instead of treating ethics as a final evaluation or corrective step, ethics-by-design makes ethics the systemic cornerstone of the technology architecture itself (Lampou R., 2023).

To realize ethics-by-design effectively, participatory involvement is an indispensable requirement. This means that students, teachers, parents, and other stakeholders must be actively involved in the design and decision-making process. This participation not only enriches the context of the system, but also strengthens the sense of belonging and social legitimacy towards the use of AI in education (Oliveira et al., 2021). Participatory design practices encourage policymakers and system developers to accommodate the diversity of end-user needs and experiences.

Figure 1. Ethics by design

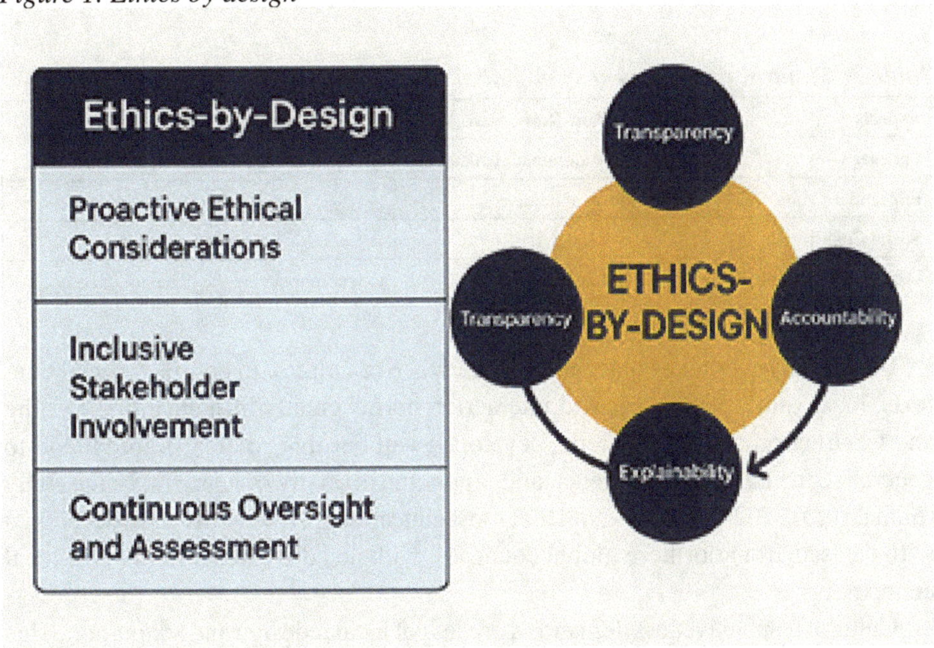

3.2 Transparency, Accountability, and Explainability in Educational Algorithms

In the AI-based education ecosystem, algorithmic systems are often used to recommend materials, monitor student performance, or conduct automated assessments. Therefore, transparency and accountability are fundamental principles so that users can understand, review, and even reject decisions that are considered inappropriate. Otherwise, then AI systems will actually strengthen *the information asymmetry* between developers and users, and magnifying the potential for algorithm-based discrimination (Guesmi et al., 2022).

Explainability or the ability to explain AI decisions to users is also a major concern. Studies have shown that educators tend to be reluctant to rely on AI systems if they don't understand how recommendations are given (Eguchi et al.,

2021). Without an adequate explanatory mechanism, the system risks losing trust from its users and failing to integrate into daily learning practices. Therefore, the design of the system must include *user-facing explanations* that can be understood by different groups of users.

3.3 Cultural Responsiveness and Global Context

Table 2. Cultural responsiveness in global

Aspects	Cultural Non-Responsive AI	Culturally Responsive AI
Language	Only supports dominant languages	Supports multilingual and local dialects
Educational Value	Uniform and universal	Adjusted to local values
Social Context	Ignored	Integrated in design
Data Representation	Global dominance bias	Accommodating the diversity of contexts

Education never takes place in a sterile space of culture. In contrast, social contexts, local values, language, and interaction norms greatly influence the learning and teaching process. AI systems developed without this context in mind tend to generalize the learning experience and ignore the diversity of learners. In the study (Samala et al., 2024), It was found that most educational AI systems were developed with datasets from northern global countries, with no adjustments for diverse local contexts.

Cultural responsiveness demands a process of local redesign and adaptation. This includes the use of representative local data, translation of interfaces into regional languages, as well as community involvement in system testing. This responsiveness is not only about language inclusion, but also the recognition of *alternative epistemology* and the uniqueness of pedagogy in a particular community.

3.4 Digital Rights and Data Protection

One of the most obvious implications of the use of AI in education is the increasing collection and processing of large amounts of student data. This data includes learning preferences, academic track record, digital activities, and highly sensitive personal information. Without adequate data protection, the digital learning ecosystem can become a field of commercial or even political exploitation (Akbari & Fithry, 2024).

The principles *ofdata sovereignty* and *informed consent* must be part of the digital education framework. This means that students and guardians should have the right to know how data is collected, used, stored, and given the choice to access or delete that data. Regulations such as GDPR in Europe have become a global reference, but their implementation in the context of education still faces challenges, especially in developing countries.

3.5 Global Policy Studies and Ethical Frameworks

The application of ethical principles in educational AI does not only depend on technology and local actors, but also requires policy support from the national to global levels. A number of international initiatives such as *(Chan, 2023)* and guidance from the OECD has tried to frame universal principles to ensure fairness, inclusion, and sustainability in the use of AI.

However, as criticized by (Chan, 2023), many of these global frameworks are still declarative and lack binding implementation mechanisms. Concrete national policies and ethical oversight tools are needed to ensure the implementation of these principles on a local scale. In addition, cross-border collaboration and exchange of best practices are important strategies in building responsible and equitable governance of educational AI globally.

4. A VISIONARY FRAMEWORK FOR BUILDING A SUSTAINABLE EDUCATION AI ECOSYSTEM

4.1 Ecosystem Approaches: The Role of Students, Educators, Institutions, and Communities

Figure 2. Ecosystem approach

In building sustainable artificial intelligence (AI) systems in education, ecosystem-based approaches have become highly relevant. Instead of viewing technology as a stand-alone entity, this approach emphasizes that AI must function within a complex social network, where students, educators, institutions, and communities are dynamically connected and contributing. This approach also recognizes that the success of a technology is not solely determined by the sophistication of the algorithm, but also by the social and cultural context in which it is applied (Casal-Otero et al., 2023a).

Students in this ecosystem are not just passive users, but active actors who have a voice in how AI impacts their learning experience. AI literacy, understanding digital rights, and awareness of algorithmic bias need to be part of the learning curriculum so that students can become empowered digital citizens (Bobby L. Asirit & H. Hua, 2023a). On the other hand, educators need to be positioned not only as system implementers, but also as pedagogical designers who are able to direct the use of AI according to local educational values and student learning needs.

Educational institutions, including schools and colleges, act as a link between technological innovation and pedagogical practice. They have the responsibility to provide digital infrastructure, formulate policies on the use of AI, and ensure teacher training in integrating technology ethically. Communities that include parents, civil society organizations, and the industrial world also have an important role to play as partners in the co-creation and evaluation of AI-based learning systems.

4.2 AI Governance Model in Human Rights and Social Justice-Based Education

The application of AI in education cannot be separated from the principles of human rights (HAM) and social justice. AI governance in sustainable education must guarantee the protection of the fundamental rights of every individual, including the right to education, the right to privacy, and the right not to be discriminated against by algorithmic decisions (Papagiannidis et al., 2023a). This framework demands the development of systems that are not only technically efficient, but also ethically and legally legitimate.

An effective governance model must prioritize the principles of *transparency*, *accountability*, and *participation*. Transparency means that decision-making processes involving AI must be explainable and accessible to all parties. Accountability ensures that there is an accountability mechanism when the system fails or results in adverse decisions. Participation refers to the involvement of various stakeholders in each stage of system design and evaluation (Birkstedt et al., 2023a).

Various countries have begun to develop policies and regulations to regulate the use of AI in the education sector. However, as stated by (Agbese et al., 2023), This policy is still very varied and has not fully reached the deeper ethical aspects. Therefore, an adaptive governance model is needed that can adapt to social dynamics and technological advances, as well as be able to maintain a balance between innovation and protection of rights.

4.3 Case Study: Best Practices of Human–AI Collaborative Learning Systems

To understand how the educational AI ecosystem can be implemented in a sustainable manner, a number of case studies from various countries can be used as references. One prominent example is the *CoLearn* program in Finland, which combines an adaptive learning system with hands-on teacher intervention. The system not only provides data-driven learning material recommendations, but also provides interpretive reports that allow teachers to tailor their teaching strategies. This model succeeds in increasing student engagement without reducing the central role of teachers as the main facilitators (Yang, 2022a).

Another study in China developed an AI-based learning platform that integrates individual learning preferences with students' socio-cultural contexts. The system not only measures academic performance, but also takes into account social-emotional well-being indicators. This approach demonstrates the potential of AI as a holistic and contextual learning tool (Samuel et al., 2023a).

Meanwhile, the *EdTech Justice Lab project* in Kenya developed a community-based recommendation system designed in conjunction with local teachers and students. The technology used is open-source and can be modified by schools according to local needs. Preliminary results show an increased sense of ownership of technology and the growth of a digital literacy culture based on community ethics.

The three case studies show that best practices in AI integration are always rooted in local participation, sensitivity to context, and appreciation of human roles. The most successful systems are not the most technically advanced, but the ones that are most capable of bridging technology and educational values.

4.4 Adaptive Systems Framework: From Policy to Implementation Design

For the educational AI ecosystem to run sustainably, an adaptive systems framework is needed that brings together the dimensions of policy, technology design, and pedagogical practices. This framework must be modular and flexible, so that it can be adapted to local needs, institutional capacity, and the latest technological developments.

This framework includes four main components: (1) *strategic policy alignment*, i.e. the adjustment of education policies with the ethical principles of AI; (2) *technological infrastructure*, in the form of a system that can be customized and audited openly; (3) *capacity building*, which is continuous training for teachers and education staff in understanding and managing AI; and (4) *participatory monitoring*, a participation-based evaluation mechanism involving students, teachers, and the community.

(Mandeville et al., 2023) suggests that this adaptive system be supported by *learning analytics* that is not only used to predict academic outcomes, but also to evaluate the social and ethical impacts of the use of AI in learning. With this approach, decision-making is not only data-driven, but also value-based.

5. COLLABORATIVE INTELLIGENCE CREATES CO-AGENCY BETWEEN AI, TEACHERS, AND STUDENTS

5.1 Definition and Concept of Collaborative Intelligence in Education

Collaborative intelligence refers to the synergistic integration between human and machine intelligence in completing tasks or achieving common goals. In the context of education, this concept positions AI not as a substitute for teachers or students, but as a cooperative partner that strengthens the learning and teaching process. This collaboration occurs when humans and AI complement each other: AI provides fast, data-driven analysis, while humans interpret, align, and direct those results according to social and social values pedagogis (Ren & Wang, 2025)

In a learning system that adopts this approach, learning decisions are made not by AI independently, but rather as a result of continuous interaction between humans and intelligent systems. Collaborative intelligence rests on the principle of co-agency, which is the ability of teachers and students to actively shape and modify systems based on local needs and contexts With this principle, AI is not just a technical tool, but develops into a reflective partner that plays a role in educational decision-making. Therefore, human-AI collaboration in education requires the design of systems that allow for the negotiation of meaning, user participation, and openness to local and cultural values.

5.2 The Role of Educators in Shaping AI-Based Curriculum

AI-based education transformation will not succeed without the active role of educators as the main architects in the curriculum. Teachers have a strategic role in contextualizing data and recommendations from AI systems into meaningful learning practices. The human-in-the-loop approach provides room for teachers to assess, filter, or adjust input from the system to keep it in line with the student's specific social-emotional conditions and classroom dynamics (Albosaif et al., 2025)

More than that, teachers need to be professionally empowered so that they do not become passive users of technology, but become designers and key decision-makers in AI integration. Teacher training and capacity building programs related to technology need to focus on a critical understanding of how AI systems work, not just its operational aspects. As highlighted, The curriculum of future teacher education should include dimensions of digital ethics, explainability principles, and AI-based co-design skills.

The role of teachers is increasingly complex in the AI era because they must be mediators between the technical results provided by AI and the need for holistic education. Teachers must be able to assess whether AI recommendations are in line with the pedagogical values they want to develop, and how to ensure that the resulting learning approach remains humane, relevant, and inclusive.

5.3 Co-Design of AI-Driven Learning Experiences

Co-design is a collaborative process that involves students, teachers, and technology developers in designing AI-powered learning experiences. This approach allows for the emergence of systems that are more responsive to the real needs of users, more culturally representative, and more socially accountable. Through co-design, students not only become objects of the system, but also contribute to shaping technology-education interactions (Abraham & Dev, 2026)

A real-world example of co-design is an AI platform that allows students to provide immediate feedback on learning recommendations, allowing the system to learn and adapt its approach. On the other hand, teachers can propose parameters of local values or contextual pedagogy so that AI systems do not run with generic standards that are universalistic. Co-design encourages a personalization approach based on ethics and fairness, not just efficiency-based.

In addition, the co-design approach strengthens students' and teachers' sense of ownership of the technology they use, increases trust in the system, and opens up space for local innovation based on user experience. In the context of multicultural education, co-design can bridge the cultural gap between system developers who may come from different backgrounds and users in the field.

5.4 Improving AI Literacy for All Stakeholders

AI literacy is a fundamental requirement for successful collaboration between humans and machines. This literacy includes not only technical knowledge of how AI systems work, but also a critical understanding of algorithmic bias, the social impact of technology, and the digital rights of users. AI literacy has diverse dimensions, covering technological, ethical, pedagogical, and even political aspects, and needs to be developed at all levels of education and education management levels (Cordeiro et al., 2026)

Students need to be equipped with a basic understanding of how adaptive learning systems work, how their data is used, and how to critique the results that AI provides. Teachers, as managers of the learning process, need to have a deeper understanding of the limitations and potential of AI systems, as well as the skills to facilitate critical discussions in the classroom about the impact of technology. Educational institutions, including principals and policy managers, must be able to formulate guidelines for the use of AI that are ethical and in accordance with the vision of inclusive and humanistic education

Furthermore, AI literacy also involves the ability to actively participate in public discussions regarding the use of AI in the education sector and in policy decision-making. This literacy strengthens the position of all stakeholders to not only become consumers of technology, but also critical and responsible digital citizens.

5.5 Practical Challenges and Solutions: Resistance, Competency Gaps, and Algorithmic Bias

Although the concept of co-agency and collaborative intelligence offers a more adaptive and inclusive future of education, its implementation on the ground still faces real challenges. One of the main challenges is the resistance of teachers and institutions to technological change. Some educators feel they lose autonomy when technology is too dominant, while others are not competently ready to integrate AI into their pedagogy (Weng et al., 2026).

On the other hand, algorithmic bias is a serious challenge in AI systems used for learning or assessment. If the system is trained with data that is not representative or without considering a particular cultural context, then the resulting recommendations may be discriminatory or irrelevant. Therefore, the development of AI systems needs to be accompanied by algorithmic auditing and ethical evaluation processes that directly involve affected communities.

The solution to these challenges lies in strengthening the capacity of all stakeholders through ongoing training, inclusion-based policy support, and the adoption of collaborative and adaptive design approaches. It is also necessary to build a monitoring and evaluation mechanism that involves the community to ensure system accountability. Only in this way, AI can truly be a partner in realizing equitable, meaningful, and sustainable education.

6. THE SUSTAINABLE FUTURE OF AI, EDUCATION, AND INTERGENERATIONAL JUSTICE

6.1 Linking Educational AI to the Sustainable Development Goals (SDGs)

The integration of artificial intelligence (AI) in the education sector needs to be carried out strategically and value-aware to support the achievement of the Sustainable Development Goals (SDGs), especially SDG 4 which emphasizes access to quality, inclusive, and equal education for all. AI in education can help answer various structural challenges, such as teacher shortages, limited quality teaching materials in remote areas, and the need for personalization in learning. AI-based learning systems have great potential to reach learners in areas previously isolated from adequate educational infrastructure, as well as deliver content tailored to individual needs in real-time(Ocrospoma et al., 2023).

Sustainability in the context of education should not be limited to environmental aspects alone. Instead, this concept includes social and pedagogical sustainability that involves building human capacity, respect for local wisdom, and the sustainability of democratic values in the learning process. AI must not only be technically effective, but it must also be socially fair and ethically accountable. AI-powered education should develop students' critical thinking skills towards technology, as well as instill awareness of how technology affects their future and society at large(Ocrospoma et al., 2023).

6.2 Reducing Digital Exclusion and the Impact of Work Disruption

The adoption of AI in education risks deepening digital exclusion if it is not accompanied by serious efforts to bridge the gap in access and competence. Digital exclusion does not only concern the absence of devices or internet networks, but also includes inequities in digital skills, low technological literacy, and limited critical understanding of how AI systems work. This situation is most evident in communities in remote areas, schools with minimal budgets, and social groups that have been structurally marginalized (Alexander Sotiriou & X. Bogner, 2023)

AI also has a major impact on the transformation of the labor market. AI-driven automation threatens repetitive job positions, including some administrative jobs in the education sector. In order for students to be prepared for the future affected by this disruption, the curriculum must be focused on developing non-routine skills based on creativity, empathy, communication skills, and critical thinking. These are qualities that are still difficult to replace by machines and will be an important capital in a knowledge-based and innovation-based economy(Ahuja & Bala, 2021).

6.3 Future-Proofing Strategy: Resilient to Uncertainty and Automation

Future-proofing is an important concept in building a resilient and flexible education system in the face of global uncertainty. In the rapidly changing era of AI, education is not enough just to teach current skills, but it must also prepare individuals for unpredictable changes. This includes technological change, environmental crises, global pandemics, and social shifts that occur rapidly and complexly(Oyebola Olusola Ayeni et al., 2024a).

Future-proofing strategies in AI-based education can start with designing a curriculum that is flexible and open to updates. Additionally, it is important to facilitate lifelong learning that allows individuals to continue learning and adapt as times change. AI ethical literacy must be part of the curriculum so that students and teachers understand the limits and responsibilities in the use of technology. Education must provide the ability to navigate a world filled with advanced technology, while maintaining the principles of justice and humanity(Bulathwela et al., 2024a).

The implementation of AI technology in education must also pay attention to the adaptive capabilities of the system itself. A good adaptive learning system not only measures academic performance, but also considers the social, emotional, and cultural context of students. AI must be able to read the needs of students in different situations and respond with appropriate approaches. This is important to create an education that is truly responsive to the realities of students' daily lives(Alfredo et al., 2024).

Finally, the success of future-proofing is inseparable from the capacity building of educational institutions. Schools and universities need to have organizational structures that are responsive to change, a robust risk management system, and adequate technological support and resources. Future-proof education not only answers today's challenges, but also prepares individuals and institutions for an ever-changing future.

6.4 Ethnographic and Intergenerational Approaches in AI Policy Design

AI policy design in education requires an approach rooted in social realities, not just technocratic models. The ethnographic approach provides space for an in-depth understanding of how AI is used and interpreted by various groups of people. Ethnography not only reveals what happened, but also why it happened, as well as how local values, cultures, and experiences shaped perceptions of technology. In this context, the policies built will be more contextual, relevant, and accepted by the end user(Chine et al., 2022).

The use of ethnographic approaches also strengthens the principle of community participation in the decision-making process. In the education system, teachers and students are not only recipients of technology, but also have a voice in designing, implementing, and evaluating the AI systems used. Policies that ignore the local context risk failing in implementation because they are not in line with the needs and values of the community. Therefore, ethnography is an important tool to ensure social accountability in the development of educational AI systems (Martinez-Maldonado, 2023).

Combining ethnographic and intergenerational approaches provides a robust and holistic framework for the development of equitable, inclusive, and sustainable AI policies. Policies like this are not only relevant at the national level, but can also be implemented at the local scale by involving community actors. Thus, AI in education is not only about technological sophistication, but about how technology can serve human needs meaningfully across time and across cultures(Vinella et al., 2022).

7. A ROADMAP TO INCLUSIVE AND ETHICAL LEARNING WITH AI

7.1 Long-Term Vision: Equitable, Collaborative, and Empowered Learning Systems

The vision of artificial intelligence-based education must be transformative and put social justice as its main goal. Education is not solely the transmission of information, but the process of building a society that is aware, critical, and active in advancing civilization. In this long-term vision, AI is positioned as a catalyst to drive a more adaptive and inclusive education system, not as a substitute for educators or students. This technology must be a means to strengthen the relationship between people and knowledge, between teachers and students, as well as between communities and the wider learning ecosystem(Reyes-Galindo et al., 2023).

The application of AI in education should not end up with administrative efficiency or optimization of academic outcomes alone. It must be able to present a learning approach that values each individual's unique experiences, including cultural backgrounds, languages, and learning styles. This requires AI systems that are able to learn from local contexts and not rely solely on universalistic models that often ignore diversity. Thus, personalization does not mean atomization, but rather an appreciation of the complexity of student identity (Yang, 2022b).

7.2 Policy Recommendations and Multi-Level Implementation

The implementation of an ethical AI-based learning system requires a comprehensive and coordinated policy approach. Each level of school, regional, national, and international education governance has a strategic role in creating a fair and inclusive learning environment. Policies at the micro level should provide space for teachers and students to innovate and voice their experiences with technology. This is important to ensure that AI integration runs in a contextual, participatory manner, and does not create a dominance effect by external actors(Birkstedt et al., 2023b).

Furthermore, policy evaluation must be carried out collaboratively and continuously. It is not enough to just create regulations and initial training, but also to build a feedback system that allows policy adjustments based on real-world experience on the ground. The involvement of the education community, including teachers, students, parents, and NGOs, in the policy evaluation process is essential to avoid the exclusionary effect. This is what is meant by a holistic multi-level approach that is responsive to the changing times(Wood et al., 2021).

7.3 Strategic Steps: Education, Regulation, and Social Innovation

Transformation towards an inclusive AI-based education system cannot be achieved without a planned and layered strategy. Education is the main foundation of this transformation, not only in the traditional sense like formal teaching, but also as a process of collective awareness of the meaning, risks, and potential of AI in everyday life. AI literacy needs to be part of the basic curriculum at all levels of education. It includes not only a technical understanding of how algorithms work, but also an understanding of social impacts, algorithmic biases, and their ethical implications (Papagiannidis et al., 2023b).

Regulation is an important instrument to ensure that the development and use of AI in education does not get out of control. Without adequate regulation, AI systems risk creating new inequalities, reinforcing discrimination, or eroding the autonomy of teachers and schools. Effective regulation must be based on public values such as fairness, transparency, accountability, and partiality for vulnerable groups. More importantly, regulations should not be reactive alone, but should be adaptive and proactive in anticipating rapid technological changes(Casal-Otero et al., 2023b).

These strategic steps must be carried out simultaneously and mutually reinforcing. Education enhances critical understanding, regulation maintains ethical and legal corridors, while social innovation opens up space for community participation and ownership. These three are the foundations of building an AI learning ecosystem that not only adopts technology, but also reshapes educational values in a more humanistic, democratic, and equitable direction (Brown & Klein, 2020).

7.4 Success Indicators of Human-Centered AI Integration

To ensure that the integration of AI in education is truly human-oriented, we need to use broader indicators of success than test scores or system efficiency. This indicator must be able to capture the humanitarian dimension such as increased student agency, teacher involvement in the technology design process, and the perception of fairness in the use of AI. For example, if students feel that an AI system gives them control over learning, that's a success that can't be measured with conventional academic metrics alone (Bobby L. Asirit & H. Hua, 2023b).

Success can also be measured through AI's ability to respond to the needs of students from diverse backgrounds, including those who have disabilities, come from minority communities, or live in remote areas. Inclusive AI will be able to offer contextual differentiation of learning, rather than a one-size-fits-all standard. Therefore, success indicators must also include aspects of diversity, social inclusion, and accessibility (Agesilaou & Kyza, 2022).

7.5 The Role of Future Technologies: Generative AI, Multimodal Models, and Beyond GPT

AI technology continues to evolve beyond what we previously imagined. Generative AI, as seen in GPT-4 and similar models, allows for the automatic creation of content in various forms: text, images, audio, and video. This multimodal model combines different types of inputs and outputs to create a much richer and more contextual learning experience. In the world of education, this technology can be used to create virtual tutors, scenario-based simulations, or learning environments that can adapt in real-time to students' learning styles (Zerilli et al., 2022).

However, this progress also brings serious challenges. When AI can create historical narratives, cultural visuals, or academic recommendations, the potential to generate bias or distortion of information becomes greater. There is a risk that the resulting digital representation does not reflect local values or true cultural diversity. As such, future technologies require stronger governance, including explainability principles, user engagement, and rigorous ethical testing before large-scale implementation(Han, 2021).

8. REVIEW AI

8.1 Reflections from Previous Chapters

The journey that has been taken in the previous chapters shows that artificial intelligence in education is not just a neutral technology that works automatically without social implications. AI brings with it a set of values, assumptions, and perspectives that reflect the interests of developers, institutional policies, and the culture in which it is implemented. In the context of education, this means that AI cannot be separated from ethical, fair, and sustainability considerations. AI should be understood not only as a technical tool, but as an integral part of a vibrant and dynamic educational ecosystem(Gerdes, 2022).

Through an exploration of concepts such as co-agency, collaborative intelligence, co-design, future-proofing, and intergenerational sustainability, the book has emphasized the importance of putting humans at the center of every educational AI design, implementation, and evaluation process. Value-based and contextual approaches are key principles for AI to function as a catalyst for meaningful learning, not just a data collection engine or a student rating tool. Any technological innovation must be balanced with a critical understanding of its impact on identity, autonomy, and relationships between humans in the learning process(Sellar & Gulson, 2021).

8.2 Collaborative Invitations to Global Institutions, Governments, and Communities

AI-based education transformation will never succeed if it is done in a sectoral and fragmented manner. Therefore, this chapter underscores the importance of building active collaboration between educational institutions, governments, and the global community. Educational institutions are at the forefront of this process. They are not only responsible for adopting technology pedagogically, but also for creating a democratic and ethical learning environment. Teachers, principals, and curriculum managers should be involved as key decision-makers, not just outside-determined technology users(Zytko et al., 2022).

The government, on the other hand, plays a strategic role in creating a regulatory framework that supports digital justice. Regulations must go beyond the aspects of data security and privacy protection, and include algorithm audit mechanisms, educational technology licenses, and developer transparency obligations. The government is also obliged to allocate resources to ensure equal access to technology for all regions, as well as to provide incentives for local community- and cultural-based innovation. Without fair and progressive policy intervention, AI integration risks deepening structural inequalities(Vallée & Hsu, 2023).

innovations, such as community learning spaces, ethics-based hackathons, and open-source movements, are becoming important channels in voicing a more humane form of education of the future. The co-evolution of AI and humanity is only possible if all parties work together critically, collaboratively, and responsibly(Korir et al., 2023).

8.3 Collective Responsibility Framework

To address the challenges of AI in education, a framework is needed that goes beyond a technocratic approach. The collective responsibility framework is an approach that brings all stakeholders together in a collaborative ecosystem, where each party has roles, responsibilities, and decision-making space. The framework emphasizes the importance of cross-sectoral and cross-generational dialogue to ensure that the benefits of AI are not only felt by a handful of elites, but are equally and fairly for all walks of life, including those most vulnerable(Huang, 2023).

The application of collective responsibility can be realized through a multi-stakeholder forum with deliberative authority, an independent algorithmic oversight body, and a mechanism for public participation in system oversight. For example, schools can form a technology ethics committee made up of teachers, students, and parents to review the use of AI in learning environments. At the national level, governments can establish AI ethics boards that represent different levels of society, including indigenous communities and disability groups, to make policies more inclusive(Oyebola Olusola Ayeni et al., 2024b).

8.4 Conclusion: AI Is Not a Substitute for Humans, but a Reinforcer of Humanity's Potential

This chapter closes with an important affirmation that AI is not a threat to human existence in education, but rather a potential companion that expands human capacity. The role of humans as teachers, mentors, and facilitators of learning will not be replaced by machines, because true education is not solely related to information, but also to values, relationships, and self-transformation. Therefore, the ideal AI in education is not a system that replaces, but one that strengthens and deepens the humanized educational process(Bulathwela et al., 2024b).

8.5 Inspirational Quotes and Emphasis on Universal Values in Future Education

In closing the course of thought regarding the co-evolution between artificial intelligence and humanity in education, it is important to return to the fundamental principles that are at the heart of every learning system: universal values. Education is not just an effort to educate individuals, but a process of humanizing humans. Values such as justice, empathy, solidarity, inclusion, and human dignity should be the primary compass in any AI-based education design, policy, and practice. In this context, the quote from Nelson Mandela "Education is the most powerful weapon which you can use to change the world" is not just an inspirational slogan, but a philosophical foundation in designing a just education future(Samuel et al., 2023b).

These values are very important in the midst of a global trend that is increasingly technocratic and transactional in looking at education. When learning is reduced to algorithm scores, quantitative performance, and system efficiency, the risk that arises is the marginalization of relational, contextual, and cultural aspects that are the essence of education. In this case, AI should be designed to serve those values, not replace them. Technology is not a substitute for teachers, nor is it a shortcut to the future. It will only be useful if it strengthens the human capacity to think critically, create collaboratively, and live meaningfully in diversity(Pawan et al., 2023).

REFERENCES

Abraham, M. M., & Dev, S. (2026). AI-driven surveillance in India: Reconciling privacy, national security and legal oversight. *Journal of Data Protection and Privacy, 8*(2), 183–207. DOI: 10.69554/BZBZ5748

Agbese, M., Alanen, H.-K., Antikainen, J., Erika, H., Isomaki, H., Jantunen, M., Kemell, K.-K., Rousi, R., Vainio-Pekka, H., & Vakkur, V. (2023). Governance in Ethical, Trustworthy AI Systems: Extension of the ECCOLA Method for AI Ethics Governance Using GARP. *E-Informatica Software Engineering Journal, 17*(1), 230101. DOI: 10.37190/e-Inf230101

Agesilaou, A., & Kyza, E. A. (2022). Whose data are they? Elementary school students' conceptualization of data ownership and privacy of personal digital data. *International Journal of Child-Computer Interaction, 33*, 100462. DOI: 10.1016/j.ijcci.2022.100462

Ahrweiler, P., Späth, E., Siqueiros García, J. M., Capellas, B. L., & Wurster, D. (2025). *Inclusive Technology Co-design for Participatory AI.*, DOI: 10.1007/978-3-031-71678-2_2

Ahuja, K., & Bala, I. (2021). Role of Artificial Intelligence and IoT in Next Generation Education System. In *Intelligence of Things: AI-IoT Based Critical-Applications and Innovations* (pp. 189–208). Springer International Publishing. DOI: 10.1007/978-3-030-82800-4_8

Akbari, R. N., & Fithry, A. (2024). MENGANALISIS PENGARUH HAK CIPTA DALAM GANGGUAN AI PADA SEKTOR MEDIA. *Prosiding SNAPP : Sosial Humaniora, Pertanian. Kesehatan Dan Teknologi, 2*(1), 377–383. DOI: 10.24929/snapp.v2i1.3159

Albosaif, W. K., Aljughaiman, A. M., & Alsayed, A. K. (2025). The role of diversity in enrichment programs in shaping the career paths of gifted individuals: An analysis of influential factors and emerging trends. *International Journal of Advanced and Applied Sciences, 12*(11), 82–92. DOI: 10.21833/ijaas.2025.11.009

Alexander Sotiriou, S., & Bogner, X. F. (2023). Discovery Space: A Technology-Enhanced Classroom for Deeper Learning in STEM. In *Reimagining Education - The Role of E-Learning, Creativity, and Technology in the Post-Pandemic Era.* IntechOpen. DOI: 10.5772/intechopen.1002649

Alfredo, R., Echeverria, V., Jin, Y., Yan, L., Swiecki, Z., Gašević, D., & Martinez-Maldonado, R. (2024). Human-centred learning analytics and AI in education: A systematic literature review. *Computers and Education: Artificial Intelligence*, *6*, 100215. DOI: 10.1016/j.caeai.2024.100215

Ayeni, O. O., Al Hamad, N. M., Chisom, O. N., Osawaru, B., & Adewusi, O. E. (2024a). AI in education: A review of personalized learning and educational technology. *GSC Advanced Research and Reviews*, *18*(2), 261–271. DOI: 10.30574/gscarr.2024.18.2.0062

Ayeni, O. O., Al Hamad, N. M., Chisom, O. N., Osawaru, B., & Adewusi, O. E. (2024b). AI in education: A review of personalized learning and educational technology. *GSC Advanced Research and Reviews*, *18*(2), 261–271. DOI: 10.30574/gscarr.2024.18.2.0062

Birkstedt, T., Minkkinen, M., Tandon, A., & Mäntymäki, M. (2023a). AI governance: Themes, knowledge gaps and future agendas. *Internet Research*, *33*(7), 133–167. DOI: 10.1108/INTR-01-2022-0042

Birkstedt, T., Minkkinen, M., Tandon, A., & Mäntymäki, M. (2023b). AI governance: Themes, knowledge gaps and future agendas. *Internet Research*, *33*(7), 133–167. DOI: 10.1108/INTR-01-2022-0042

Bobby, L. Asirit, L., & H. Hua, J. (. (2023a). Converging perspectives: Assessing AI readiness and utilization in Philippine higher education. *Polaris Global Journal of Scholarly Research and Trends*, *2*(3), 1–50. DOI: 10.58429/pgjsrt.v2n3a152

Bobby, L. Asirit, L., & H. Hua, J. (. (2023b). Converging perspectives: Assessing AI readiness and utilization in Philippine higher education. *Polaris Global Journal of Scholarly Research and Trends*, *2*(3), 1–50. DOI: 10.58429/pgjsrt.v2n3a152

Brown, M., & Klein, C. (2020). Whose Data? Which Rights? Whose Power? A Policy Discourse Analysis of Student Privacy Policy Documents. *The Journal of Higher Education*, *91*(7), 1149–1178. DOI: 10.1080/00221546.2020.1770045

Bulathwela, S., Pérez-Ortiz, M., Holloway, C., Cukurova, M., & Shawe-Taylor, J. (2024a). Artificial Intelligence Alone Will Not Democratise Education: On Educational Inequality, Techno-Solutionism and Inclusive Tools. *Sustainability (Basel)*, *16*(2), 781. DOI: 10.3390/su16020781

Casal-Otero, L., Catala, A., Fernández-Morante, C., Taboada, M., Cebreiro, B., & Barro, S. (2023a). AI literacy in K-12: A systematic literature review. *International Journal of STEM Education*, *10*(1), 29. DOI: 10.1186/s40594-023-00418-7

Chan, C. K. Y. (2023). A comprehensive AI policy education framework for university teaching and learning. *International Journal of Educational Technology in Higher Education, 20*(1), 38. DOI: 10.1186/s41239-023-00408-3

Chine, D. R., Brentley, C., Thomas-Browne, C., Richey, J. E., Gul, A., Carvalho, P. F., Branstetter, L., & Koedinger, K. R. (2022). *Educational Equity Through Combined Human-AI Personalization: A Propensity Matching Evaluation.*, DOI: 10.1007/978-3-031-11644-5_30

Cordeiro, C. M., Adomaitis, L., & Huang, L. (2026). The AI-policy-governance nexus: How regulation and AI shift corporate governance toward stakeholders. *Technology in Society, 84*, 103117. Advance online publication. DOI: 10.1016/j.techsoc.2025.103117

Eguchi, A., Okada, H., & Muto, Y. (2021). Contextualizing AI Education for K-12 Students to Enhance Their Learning of AI Literacy Through Culturally Responsive Approaches. *KI - Künstliche Intelligenz, 35*(2), 153–161. DOI: 10.1007/s13218-021-00737-3

Gerdes, A. (2022). A participatory data-centric approach to AI Ethics by Design. *Applied Artificial Intelligence, 36*(1), 2009222. Advance online publication. DOI: 10.1080/08839514.2021.2009222

Guesmi, M., Chatti, M. A., Tayyar, A., Ain, Q. U., & Joarder, S. (2022). Interactive Visualizations of Transparent User Models for Self-Actualization: A Human-Centered Design Approach. *Multimodal Technologies and Interaction, 6*(6), 42. DOI: 10.3390/mti6060042

Han, I. (2021). Immersive virtual field trips and elementary students' perceptions. *British Journal of Educational Technology, 52*(1), 179–195. DOI: 10.1111/bjet.12946

Holmes, W., Porayska-Pomsta, K., Holstein, K., Sutherland, E., Baker, T., Shum, S. B., Santos, O. C., Rodrigo, M. T., Cukurova, M., Bittencourt, I. I., & Koedinger, K. R. (2022). Ethics of AI in Education: Towards a Community-Wide Framework. *International Journal of Artificial Intelligence in Education, 32*(3), 504–526. DOI: 10.1007/s40593-021-00239-1

Horvatić, D., & Lipic, T. (2021). Human-Centric AI: The Symbiosis of Human and Artificial Intelligence. *Entropy (Basel, Switzerland), 23*(3), 332. DOI: 10.3390/e23030332 PMID: 33799841

Huang, L. (2023). Ethics of Artificial Intelligence in Education: Student Privacy and Data Protection. *Science Insights Education Frontiers, 16*(2), 2577–2587. DOI: 10.15354/sief.23.re202

Korir, M., Slade, S., Holmes, W., Héliot, Y., & Rienties, B. (2023). Investigating the dimensions of students' privacy concern in the collection, use and sharing of data for learning analytics. *Computers in Human Behavior Reports, 9*, 100262. DOI: 10.1016/j.chbr.2022.100262

Samuli Laato. (2022). *How to explain AI systems to end users: a systematic literature review and research agenda.*

Lampou R. (2023). *The Integration of Artificial Intelligence in Education: Opportunities and Challenges.*

Le Dinh, T., Le, T. D., Uwizeyemungu, S., & Pelletier, C. (2025). Human-Centered Artificial Intelligence in Higher Education: A Framework for Systematic Literature Reviews. *Information (Basel), 16*(3), 240. DOI: 10.3390/info16030240

Mandeville, C. P., Nilsen, E. B., Herfindal, I., & Finstad, A. G. (2023). Participatory monitoring drives biodiversity knowledge in global protected areas. *Communications Earth & Environment, 4*(1), 240. DOI: 10.1038/s43247-023-00906-2

Martinez-Maldonado, R. (2023). Human-centred learning analytics: Four challenges in realising the potential. *Journal of Learning Letters.* DOI: 10.59453/FIZJ7007

Moustaghfir, S., & Brigui, H. (2024). Navigating Critical Thinking in the Digital Era: An Informative Exploration. *International Journal of Linguistics. Literature and Translation, 7*(1), 137–143. DOI: 10.32996/ijllt.2024.7.1.11x

Nuranti, E. Q., Yulianti, E., & Husin, H. S. (2022). Predicting the Category and the Length of Punishment in Indonesian Courts Based on Previous Court Decision Documents. *Computers, 11*(6), 88. DOI: 10.3390/computers11060088

Ocrospoma, G., Fuster-Guillén, D., Ocaña-Fernández, Y., & Villalba-Condori, K. O. (2023). Enseñanza recíproca influenciado por los niveles de alfabetización informacional en estudiantes de Ciencias de la Comunicación. *PUBLICACIONES, 53*(2), 125–155. DOI: 10.30827/publicaciones.v53i2.26819

Oliveira, G., Grenha Teixeira, J., Torres, A., & Morais, C. (2021). An exploratory study on the emergency remote education experience of higher education students and teachers during the COVID-19 pandemic. *British Journal of Educational Technology, 52*(4), 1357–1376. DOI: 10.1111/bjet.13112 PMID: 34219758

Papagiannidis, E., Enholm, I. M., Dremel, C., Mikalef, P., & Krogstie, J. (2023a). Toward AI Governance: Identifying Best Practices and Potential Barriers and Outcomes. *Information Systems Frontiers, 25*(1), 123–141. DOI: 10.1007/s10796-022-10251-y PMID: 35464171

Pawan, F., Li, S., Nijiati, S., Dopwell, M., Harris, A., & Iruoje, T. (2023). Culturally- and Linguistically-Responsive Online Teacher Learning Professional Development. *Online Learning : the Official Journal of the Online Learning Consortium, 27*(4). Advance online publication. DOI: 10.24059/olj.v27i4.4003

Ren, X., & Wang, R. (2025). Integrating human–AI collaboration into translation education: A comprehensive protocol for assessment, diagnosis, and strategy development. *PLOS ONE, 20*(12 December). DOI: 10.1371/journal.pone.0338089

Reyes-Galindo, V., Jaramillo-Correa, J. P., Carrasco Nava, K., De-la-Rosa-González, A. E., Flores Flores, D., Martínez, M., Monroy-De-la-Rosa, L. A., Morelos Zamora, M. Á., Ramírez Morales, B. E., Ramírez Morales, O. T., Rodríguez, M., Salazar Zamora, M., Zamora Callejas, C., Zamora Callejas, R., Zamora, C., Zamora, T., González-Camacho, V. A., Rebollo, E., Torres-Jardón, R., & Mastretta-Yanes, A. (2023). Evaluating pollution-related damage and restoration success in urban forests with participatory monitoring and digital tools. *Conservation Biology, 37*(5), e14112. Advance online publication. DOI: 10.1111/cobi.14112 PMID: 37204008

Rivas, P., & Zhao, L. (2023). Marketing with ChatGPT: Navigating the Ethical Terrain of GPT-Based Chatbot Technology. *AI, 4*(2), 375–384. DOI: 10.3390/ai4020019

Samala, A. D., Zhai, X., Aoki, K., Bojic, L., & Zikic, S. (2024). An In-Depth Review of ChatGPT's Pros and Cons for Learning and Teaching in Education. [IJIM]. *International Journal of Interactive Mobile Technologies, 18*(02), 96–117. DOI: 10.3991/ijim.v18i02.46509

Samuel, Y., Brennan-Tonetta, M., Samuel, J., Kashyap, R., Kumar, V., Krishna Kaashyap, S., Chidipothu, N., Anand, I., & Jain, P. (2023a). Cultivation of human centered artificial intelligence: Culturally adaptive thinking in education (CATE) for AI. *Frontiers in Artificial Intelligence, 6*, 1198180. Advance online publication. DOI: 10.3389/frai.2023.1198180 PMID: 38106981

Schiff, D. (2022). Education for AI, not AI for Education: The Role of Education and Ethics in National AI Policy Strategies. *International Journal of Artificial Intelligence in Education, 32*(3), 527–563. DOI: 10.1007/s40593-021-00270-2

Sellar, S., & Gulson, K. N. (2021). Becoming information centric: The emergence of new cognitive infrastructures in education policy. *Journal of Education Policy, 36*(3), 309–326. DOI: 10.1080/02680939.2019.1678766

Vallée, E., & Hsu, Y.-C. (2023). Protecting Students: Data Privacy in the African Union. *TechTrends, 67*(2), 203–206. DOI: 10.1007/s11528-023-00834-0

Vinella, F. L., Koppelaar, S., & Masthoff, J. (2022). Forming Teams of Learners Online in a User as Wizard Study with Openness, Conscientiousness, and cognitive Ability. *Adjunct Proceedings of the 30th ACM Conference on User Modeling, Adaptation and Personalization*, 283–292. DOI: 10.1145/3511047.3537660

Weng, K., Jia, M., Nguyen, T. T., Hu, X., Zhang, G., & Zeng, Q. (2026). Coupled data-driven and experience-informed neural networks for prediction of pile base resistance with consideration of data limitation. *Engineering Applications of Artificial Intelligence*, *165*, 113384. Advance online publication. DOI: 10.1016/j.engappai.2025.113384

Wood, E. A., Ange, B. L., & Miller, D. D. (2021). Are We Ready to Integrate Artificial Intelligence Literacy into Medical School Curriculum: Students and Faculty Survey. *Journal of Medical Education and Curricular Development*, *8*, 23821205211024078. Advance online publication. DOI: 10.1177/23821205211024078 PMID: 34250242

Yang, W. (2022a). Artificial Intelligence education for young children: Why, what, and how in curriculum design and implementation. *Computers and Education: Artificial Intelligence*, *3*, 100061. DOI: 10.1016/j.caeai.2022.100061

Zerilli, J., Bhatt, U., & Weller, A. (2022). How transparency modulates trust in artificial intelligence. *Patterns (New York, N.Y.)*, *3*(4), 100455. DOI: 10.1016/j.patter.2022.100455 PMID: 35465233

Zytko, D. J., Wisniewski, P., Guha, S. P. S., Baumer, E., & Lee, M. K. (2022). Participatory Design of AI Systems: Opportunities and Challenges Across Diverse Users, Relationships, and Application Domains. *CHI Conference on Human Factors in Computing Systems Extended Abstracts*, 1–4. DOI: 10.1145/3491101.3516506

Chapter 3
Gamification for Inclusive Large Language Models

Leila Samimi-Dehkordi
http://orcid.org/0000-0002-2842-0256
Shahrekord University, Iran

Shekoufeh Kolahdouz Rahimi
University of Roehampton, UK

Shabih Fatima
University of Roehampton, UK

ABSTRACT

This chapter introduces the Gamified LLM Lifecycle, a seven-stage conceptual framework that reimagines large language model (LLM) development as an inclusive and participatory ecosystem. Although LLMs support education and productivity, their design and governance remain centralized and opaque. The proposed framework transforms the traditional pipeline—data collection, annotation, fine-tuning, alignment, evaluation, prompting, and deployment—into gamified stages that integrate learning theory, motivational design, and human–AI collaboration. Grounded in Self-Regulated Learning, the Octalysis Framework, and human–AI symbiosis, each stage embeds quests, peer review, ethical duels, and community-based evaluation to foster engagement and skill development. By turning technical contributions into meaningful learning experiences, the model aims to democratize AI creation and amplify underrepresented voices. The chapter positions AI development as a transparent process in which users act not merely as consumers, but as contributors, evaluators, and ethical stewards of intelligent systems.

DOI: 10.4018/979-8-3373-6063-8.ch003

INTRODUCTION

Large Language Models (LLMs) have rapidly evolved from research prototypes into widely used socio-technical systems that influence learning, communication, and productivity (Zhang & Dong, 2024; Torkamaan et al., 2024). Contemporary models such as GPT-4o, Llama 3, Claude 3.5, and Mistral function as tutors, collaborators, translators, and reasoning assistants across formal and informal educational contexts (García-Méndez et al., 2025; Sharma et al., 2025). By adapting to individual learning paths, they expand opportunities for self-directed and personalized learning (Yankouskaya et al., 2025).

Despite this promise, LLM development remains centralized and opaque. Data resources, computational infrastructure, and human oversight are concentrated in a small number of organizations and regions. As a result, many communities particularly in the Global South, rural areas, Indigenous contexts, and low-resource language environments—remain passive users rather than active contributors (Hernández et al., 2025). This imbalance affects not only access to AI benefits but also whose knowledge, values, and cultural norms are embedded in these systems (Bender et al., 2021; Birhane et al., 2022). For instance, some LLMs provide psychological advice designed for Western countries, which may not be appropriate in Eastern countries with different cultural norms.

To realize the full educational potential of LLMs, their development must become more inclusive and participatory. This chapter argues that gamification (Seaborn & Fels, 2015) can help transform LLM development into an engaging ecosystem that broadens community involvement, supports learning, and ensures more diverse representation in AI systems.

The LLM Revolution and Its Hidden Cost

The rapid expansion of LLMs has created new possibilities for autonomous and lifelong learning, but it has also exposed structural inequities in AI development (Zhang & Dong, 2024; Torkamaan et al., 2024). Most widely used models are trained primarily on English-dominated datasets, which can marginalize multilingual, indigenous, and dialect-rich communities (Bender et al., 2021).

Alignment processes such as Reinforcement Learning from Human Feedback (RLHF) often rely on a limited pool of annotators, frequently reflecting Western cultural norms and dominant political perspectives (Chaudhari et al., 2025; Tao et al., 2024). These constraints can introduce systematic bias into model behavior. In addition, effective use of LLMs frequently depends on advanced prompt engineering skills, which remain inaccessible to many learners (Federiakin et al., 2024).

Consequently, those who benefit most from LLM technologies are typically individuals with high digital literacy, linguistic privilege, and access to computational resources. This creates a paradox: systems promoted as tools for democratizing knowledge are developed through processes that exclude much of the global population. The challenge is therefore not only technical (Vidal et al., 2025), but also educational and participatory. A key question emerges: how can the LLM development pipeline be redesigned so that learners worldwide can actively contribute to, and grow alongside, AI systems?

Gamification as the Missing Link

Gamification applies game elements such as quests, rewards, progression systems, and social recognition to non-game contexts. Research in motivation and gamified learning shows that such structures enhance engagement, persistence, and skill development (Hydari et al., 2023).

This approach is particularly relevant for LLM development, where tasks like data curation, annotation, ethical alignment, and evaluation require scale, diversity, and sustained participation. Platforms such as Mozilla Common Voice[1] demonstrate how game-inspired structures can mobilize global communities around complex tasks. Yet, systematic gamification has not been applied across the full LLM lifecycle. Reframing this lifecycle as a structured learning journey could broaden participation while increasing transparency and educational value.

Research Questions

This chapter introduces the Gamified LLM Lifecycle, a seven-stage framework that reimagines the traditional LLM pipeline as an open and participatory learning environment. The central claim is that gamification can democratize AI creation by integrating structured learning, meaningful incentives, and human–AI collaboration throughout model development. Instead of relying exclusively on engineers and annotators, future LLMs could be shaped by global learners who contribute data, annotations, ethical judgments, prompts, and evaluations through structured missions.

The framework is built on three principles:

1. **Every technical step becomes a learning quest.** Tasks such as data validation, prompt construction, and preference ranking are reframed as structured challenges with clear goals and feedback.
2. **Every human contribution earns progression and agency.** Participants receive recognition, skill-based advancement, and expanded responsibilities.

3. **Every AI agent evolves through playful collaboration.** AI systems function as companions and co-learners within continuous feedback loops.

Based on these principles, the chapter addresses three research questions:

1. **Participation:** How can gamification broaden participation across the LLM pipeline, especially for marginalized and low-resource communities?
2. **Mechanics and Design:** Which game mechanics best support inclusive, ethical, and scalable AI development?
3. **Learning Outcomes:** How does co-creating AI through gamified processes enhance autonomy, metacognition, digital citizenship, and critical thinking?

This work presents a conceptual and normative framework rather than a technical implementation plan. The Gamified LLM Lifecycle serves as a theoretical blueprint intended to stimulate scholarly discussion and guide future research toward more inclusive, transparent, and learner-centered AI ecosystems.

Structure of the Chapter

The chapter follows the seven stages of the Gamified LLM Lifecycle, each corresponding to a phase of model development and its gamified structure. It begins with theoretical foundations drawn from self-regulated learning, motivational design, and human–AI symbiosis. The stages include:

- Open-World Data Quest (inclusive data collection),
- Data Detective (data cleaning and annotation),
- World Builder (fine-tuning and collaborative evaluation),
- Ethics Duel Arena (ethical alignment),
- Prompt Dojo (structured prompt mastery),
- AI Lab (evaluation through testing and simulation), and
- Living with AI (deployment as continuous engagement).

The chapter concludes by reflecting on the conceptual implications of the Gamified LLM Lifecycle and outlining directions for future scholarly inquiry. It frames the seven stages as a theoretical lens for rethinking how LLM development can become more inclusive, participatory, and learner-centered. Together, these stages conceptualize the LLM pipeline as a transparent and globally collaborative learning ecosystem. Figure 1 illustrates the overall structure of the seven-stage framework and the flow of participation across stages.

Figure 1. Overall structure of the seven-stage gamified LLM lifecycle

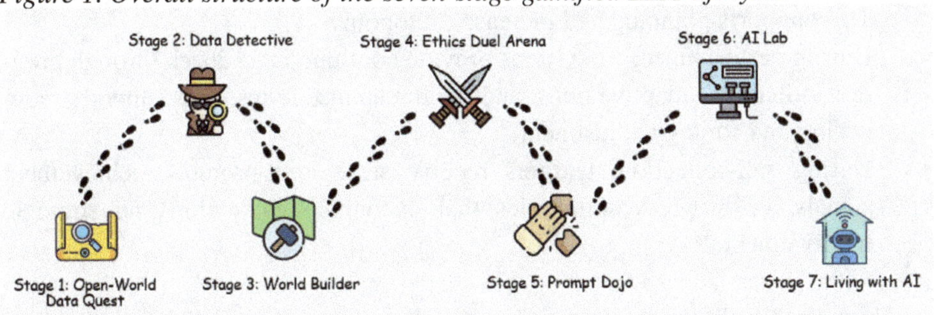

THEORETICAL FOUNDATIONS

The Gamified LLM Lifecycle is grounded in three complementary theoretical foundations:

1. Self-Regulated Learning (SRL)
2. Octalysis Framework of motivation
3. Human–AI symbiosis

Together, these perspectives explain how gamification can structure learning, sustain motivation, and enable meaningful collaboration between humans and AI systems. Gamification is therefore not an additional feature, but a structural design approach for participatory AI development.

Self-Regulated Learning (SRL) and AI Agents

Self-Regulated Learning (SRL), as defined by Zimmerman (2013), describes how learners actively guide their own learning through three cyclical phases: forethought, performance, and self-reflection. Effective learners set goals, monitor their progress, and evaluate their outcomes. However, many learners struggle with these metacognitive processes without structured support.

Gamified AI agents can scaffold the SRL cycle. Instead of treating self-regulation as a purely internal skill, it can be supported through external structures and feedback. This aligns with Self-Determination Theory, which emphasizes autonomy, competence, and relatedness as key motivational needs (Johnson et al., 2016).

In a gamified LLM environment:

- During forethought, learners select structured quests aligned with clear goals. This supports planning and increases autonomy.
- During performance, AI systems provide continuous feedback through progress indicators, adaptive hints, and rapid response loops. This supports monitoring and strategy adjustment.
- During self-reflection, learners receive structured prompts, achievement signals, or progress summaries that encourage evaluation and strategic improvement.

Through this alignment, metacognitive processes become visible, guided, and socially supported. Gamified AI agents therefore provide a scalable way to cultivate self-regulated learning skills within human–AI interaction.

Octalysis Framework for Motivation

While SRL explains how learning is regulated, the Octalysis Framework explains why individuals choose to participate and persist. According to Chou (2015), motivation in gamified systems can be understood through eight core drives that balance intrinsic and extrinsic incentives.

Applied to LLM development, these drives can support sustained participation in tasks such as data contribution, prompt design, evaluation, and ethical review. Several core drives are especially relevant:

- **Meaning:** Contributions are framed as benefiting one's community or language group.
- **Accomplishment:** Progress systems such as experience points or levels reinforce mastery.
- **Empowerment:** Creative tasks, such as prompt experimentation, encourage exploration.
- **Social Influence:** Collaborative missions and community recognition broaden participation.

Other drives (e.g., ownership, unpredictability, scarcity) can be integrated carefully, but they must remain aligned with educational and ethical goals.

Human–AI Symbiosis

The third pillar is human–AI symbiosis. In this model, humans and AI systems act as complementary partners (Seeber et al., 2020).

Humans contribute ethical judgment, empathy, contextual understanding, and creativity in novel situations. AI contributes large-scale data processing, rapid pattern recognition, instant feedback, and optimization.

Gamification supports this partnership by structuring collaboration as shared missions rather than top-down control processes. AI systems can detect patterns or generate alternatives, while humans evaluate meaning, fairness, and cultural relevance.

This view aligns with constructionist learning theory, which emphasizes active knowledge building in meaningful contexts (Papert, 1996). When development tasks are framed as collaborative quests, participation becomes more balanced and engaging.

Gamification also strengthens ethical governance. For example, participants can be rewarded for identifying harmful outputs or contributing to community-based review processes. This increases transparency and distributes responsibility more broadly, addressing concerns about centralization in current LLM practices.

Integrated Perspective

Together, these three foundations form a coherent conceptual base:

- SRL explains the cognitive structure of learning through planning, action, and reflection (Zimmerman, 2013).
- Octalysis explains sustained motivation through structured incentive design (Chou, 2015).
- Human–AI symbiosis explains how collaboration between humans and AI can be complementary and balanced (Seeber et al., 2020).

Their integration frames LLM development and refinement as a structured learning journey rather than a purely technical process. Figure 2 illustrates this conceptual integration within the Gamified LLM Lifecycle framework.

Figure 2. Theoretical integration of the gamified LLM lifecycle

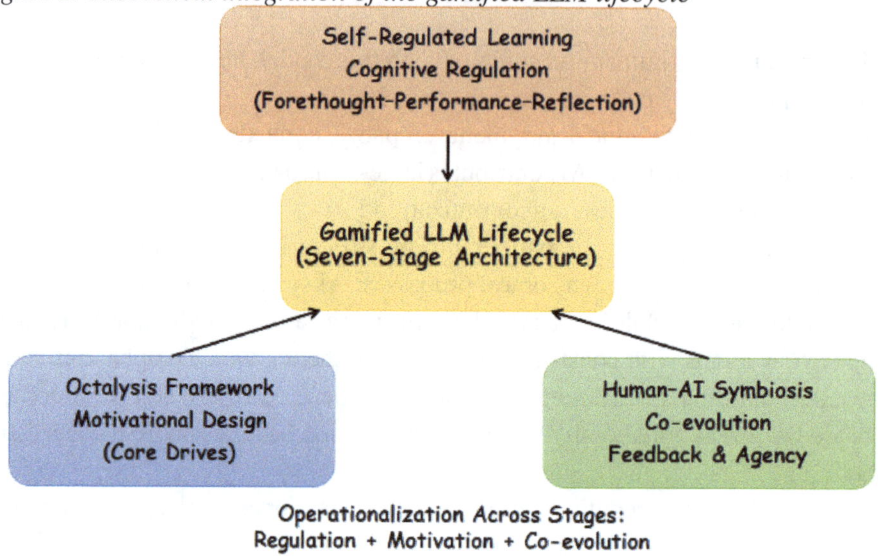

RELATED WORK

Research on LLMs, lifecycle governance, and gamification has expanded rapidly, yet these strands remain largely disconnected. Existing studies contribute structural foundations, operational practices, or engagement models, but none integrates them into a unified lifecycle-aligned architecture. This section situates the proposed Gamified LLM Lifecycle at the intersection of these streams.

Lifecycle, Governance, and Gamified Systems

Several works formalize LLM lifecycles in domain or production settings. Lee et al. (2024) propose an education-focused lifecycle covering data, fine-tuning, deployment, and classroom use, while identifying bias injection points across stages. From an operational perspective, LLMOps extends MLOps by emphasizing continuous fine-tuning, deployment, monitoring, governance, security, and scalability (Pahune and Akhtar, 2025). Related studies expand lifecycle awareness into software engineering and knowledge-graph–integrated pipelines (Xing et al., 2025; Pan et al.,

2024). These approaches provide structural and governance foundations but treat development primarily as a technical production process.

A parallel stream embeds LLMs within gamified or adaptive environments. Huber et al. (2024), Ge et al. (2025), and Goslen et al. (2025) demonstrate how LLMs support iterative prompting, adaptive planning, and self-regulated learning cycles. Gallotta et al. (2024) and Leslie et al. (2025) position LLMs in dynamic narrative-driven game systems. Other studies explore adaptive gameplay and behavioral modeling (Hassan & Aboulhassan, 2024; Lorè & Heydari, 2024; Yang et al., 2025). These works show that LLMs function effectively within gamified systems, but mainly at the interaction or deployment level rather than across full development lifecycles.

Recent research also formalizes engagement dynamics. Costa (2025) models task adaptation and reward optimization mathematically, while Gianni et al. (2025) design adaptive feedback mechanisms in XR learning contexts. In parallel, participatory modeling research demonstrates how gamification can scaffold collaborative data contribution and ethical reflection (Bakhanova et al., 2020, 2023). The P2Si framework embeds iterative co-design cycles resembling user-in-the-loop processes (Heras et al., 2021), and Narayanan and Kumaravel (2024) integrate gamification with machine learning in adaptive tutoring systems. These studies confirm that gamification can structure collaboration and refinement, yet they do not extend this logic to foundation-model operational lifecycles.

Synthesis and Research Gap

The literature provides complementary but separate components:

- Lifecycle and bias governance structures (Lee et al., 2024; Pahune & Akhtar, 2025)
- Gamified and adaptive LLM-enabled interaction models (Huber et al., 2024; Leslie et al., 2025)
- Mathematical engagement modeling (Costa, 2025; Gianni et al., 2025)
- Participatory data-generation frameworks (Bakhanova et al., 2023)

What remains absent is an explicit architectural integration that:

1. Aligns game mechanics with each stage of an established LLM lifecycle
2. Treats gamified interaction as a structured data and evaluation pipeline
3. Embeds governance, monitoring, and bias-aware refinement within a participatory framework

The proposed Gamified LLM Lifecycle addresses this gap by structurally embedding motivational and participatory dynamics into a seven-stage lifecycle architecture spanning data, alignment, evaluation, governance, and lived deployment contexts.

Critical Structural Comparison

This section positions the proposed framework conceptually. Table 1 compares representative approaches across five structural criteria:

- Full lifecycle coverage
- Governance and monitoring integration
- Gamification as a structural element
- Participatory data contribution
- End-to-end architectural integration

Table 1. Structural comparison of conceptual frameworks relevant to a gamified LLM lifecycle

Framework	Full Lifecycle Coverage	Governance & Monitoring	Gamification as Structural Element	Participatory Data Contribution	End-to-End Integration
Lee et al. (2024)	Education-focused lifecycle; domain-specific	Strong bias analysis	Not central	Not emphasized	No
Pahune & Akhtar (2025)	Production pipeline stages	Strong operational governance	Not included	Not included	No
Huber et al. (2024); Goslen et al. (2025); Ge et al. (2025)	Interaction loops at learner level	Limited	Central at application layer	Indirect	No
Costa (2025); Costa et al. (2025); Gianni et al. (2025)	Dynamic interaction modeling	Not lifecycle-governed	Central in engagement modeling	Not primary focus	No

continued on following page

Table 1. Continued

Framework	Full Lifecycle Coverage	Governance & Monitoring	Gamification as Structural Element	Participatory Data Contribution	End-to-End Integration
Bakhanova et al. (2020; 2023); Heras et al. (2021)	Early-stage participatory modeling	Ethical participation focus	Used to scaffold collaboration	Strong	No
Proposed Gamified LLM Lifecycle	Seven gamified stages aligned with the LLM lifecycle (Open-World Data Quest → Living with AI)	Integrated within Ethics Duel Arena, AI Lab, and Living with AI	Embedded structurally in all seven stages	Formalized in early and iterative stages	Yes

The comparison shows that existing approaches provide partial components—lifecycle structure without gamification, gamified interaction without lifecycle governance, or participatory modeling without foundation-model integration. None formalizes gamification as a structural layer across the full LLM lifecycle while simultaneously integrating governance and participatory data pipelines. The proposed framework synthesizes these dimensions within a unified architecture.

STAGE 1: OPEN-WORLD DATA QUEST

Stage 1 redesigns data collection as an open and voluntary learning process. Instead of treating training data as something silently extracted from the web, this stage invites users and communities to actively co-create it. The goal is to transform data gathering from a hidden technical operation into a transparent, participatory activity where contribution, learning, and consent are central. Figure 3 illustrates this shift. Data collection is reframed as a gamified, community-driven ecosystem in which learners complete structured quests, contribute diverse and consent-based data, and participate in shared quality control.

Figure 3. Stage 1 – open-world data quest. Gamified data collection

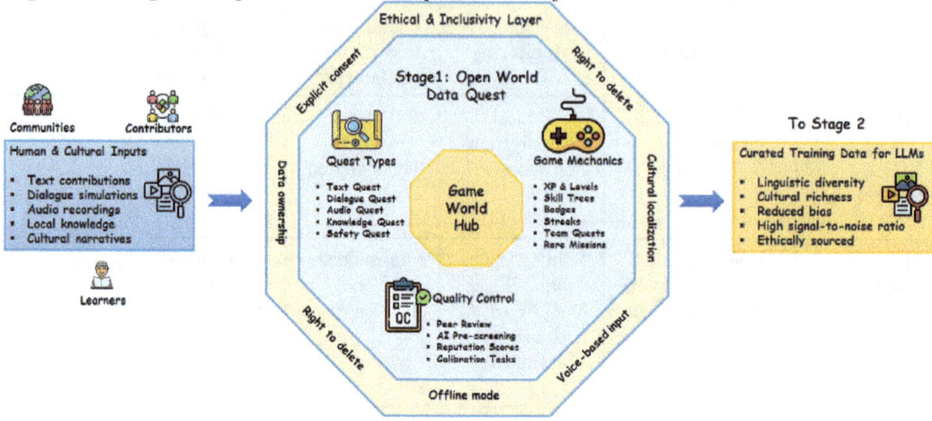

Current large language models depend heavily on large-scale web scraping (Brown et al., 2020; Dodge et al., 2021). This approach has created several problems, including repetition, declining data quality, toxic or machine-generated content, and strong language imbalance. English dominates most datasets, while many languages and cultural contexts remain underrepresented. As a result, models often perform unevenly across regions and communities. Stage 1 shifts from passive data collection to active data co-creation, inviting users to contribute content that reflects their language and experiences, with the goal of improving diversity, contextual relevance, and consent-based governance.

Contribution is organized as an open-world quest system (Morschheuser et al., 2017; Hinterreiter et al., 2024). Tasks are short and clearly defined. Participants may write narratives, simulate conversations, record speech, or review biased outputs. Simple game elements structure this process: contributors earn experience points for validated submissions, follow visible progress paths, and receive feedback through peer review and reputation signals. Light leaderboard features or community milestones encourage collective effort within language groups.

Quality control is embedded in the quest structure. Submissions are reviewed by peers, and reputation mechanisms reward careful evaluation. AI-based prechecks can detect duplication or formatting issues before human validation. In this way, validation becomes part of participation rather than a separate technical step. Mozilla Common Voice illustrates this approach by collecting over 200,000 hours of speech data in more than 100 languages through community participation and gamified engagement. It supports speech technologies for low-resource languages such as Swahili and Quechua, demonstrating that inclusive, community-driven data collection can scale effectively.

Beyond data production, Stage 1 has a strong educational function. When participants create or review data, they directly observe how training datasets shape model behavior. They learn that quality, balance, and representation influence outcomes. This builds practical data literacy rather than abstract awareness (Long & Magerko, 2020; Ng et al., 2021; Vuorikari, 2022). Through structured contribution and peer feedback, participants also develop critical thinking and ethical sensitivity toward AI systems (Gholiagha et al., 2025).

Ethically, this stage embeds consent and transparency from the beginning. Participation is voluntary, data usage is explained, and contributors can request removal of their submissions (Guillen-Aguinaga et al., 2025). Community-based review and moderation increase shared responsibility, while inclusive design features help reduce barriers to participation (Ahrweiler et al., 2025).

In relation to the research questions, Stage 1 shows how the LLM lifecycle can begin as a participatory process, how simple gamified structures can support engagement and quality, and how early involvement in data creation strengthens AI literacy and inclusive governance.

STAGE 2: DATA DETECTIVE

Stage 2 focuses on improving the quality, fairness, and reliability of the data collected in Stage 1. Even when data is voluntarily contributed, it may still contain noise, duplication, labeling errors, bias, or culturally sensitive issues. The goal of this stage is to clean and annotate data in a careful, human-centered way so that model training is based on trustworthy and inclusive datasets.

Figure 4 presents this stage as a gamified human–AI collaboration process. Raw data from Stage 1 is examined through detective-style quests, where participants work alongside AI partners to identify duplicates, bias, toxicity, and inconsistencies under shared governance.

Figure 4. Stage 2 – Data detective. Gamified human–AI collaboration for data cleaning

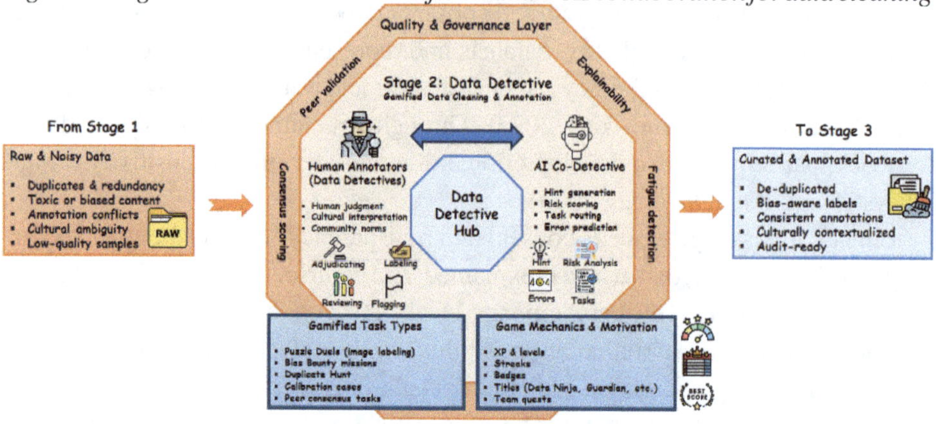

In traditional machine learning pipelines, data annotation is often performed by large distributed teams under repetitive and rigid workflows. These processes can be slow, expensive, and cognitively exhausting. They also tend to privilege dominant languages and overlook cultural nuances (Snow et al., 2008; Kittur et al., 2008). If errors or biases remain in the dataset, they directly affect model behavior and may reinforce unfair outcomes.

Stage 2 reframes data cleaning as a structured and meaningful activity. Annotation tasks are organized as short "Data Detective" missions (Krohmann et al., 2025). Participants examine pieces of data as individual "cases," such as identifying biased language, checking factual consistency, correcting labels, or flagging culturally inappropriate content. A light narrative frames contributors as investigators who solve problems and improve the integrity of the dataset (Warsinsky et al., 2022). Gamified elements such as points, levels, reputation signals, and team challenges encourage contributors to produce accurate annotations and collaboratively resolve complex cases.

AI agents function as co-detectives rather than replacements. They can suggest possible issues, highlight uncertain cases, provide brief explanations, and adapt task difficulty based on participant performance (Khakpour & Colomo-Palacios, 2021). This human–AI collaboration reduces fatigue, improves consistency, and keeps final judgment in human hands. By combining automated pre-checks with peer validation, the system balances scalability with contextual sensitivity.

A practical example of structured annotation at scale is *Scale AI*[2]. The platform demonstrates how clear workflows, performance feedback, and fair compensation can improve annotation quality and retention. While not fully gamified, its structured task design shows that organized and incentive-based annotation systems can achieve lower error rates. The addition of lightweight gamification, as proposed here, could further strengthen motivation and collaboration.

Stage 2 also has a strong educational dimension. Through detective-style tasks and AI-supported feedback, participants learn how small labeling decisions influence model outputs. They practice spotting bias, evaluating context, and reflecting on fairness. This supports key elements of AI literacy, including understanding how data shapes AI behavior and recognizing ethical implications in data processing (Chiu et al., 2024; Miao & Shiohira, 2024).

Ethically, this stage promotes shared responsibility in data governance. Cultural knowledge and diverse perspectives are valued during review, helping prevent the dominance of a single viewpoint. Explainable AI support reduces cognitive overload and increases transparency in the annotation process (Pham et al., 2025; Warsinsky et al., 2022). By embedding review, reflection, and accountability into a structured yet accessible system, Stage 2 contributes to cleaner, more representative datasets and strengthens trust in the overall LLM lifecycle. Stage 2 demonstrates how gamified human–AI collaboration can enhance data quality, maintain participant engagement, and foster awareness of bias, fairness, and responsible AI development.

STAGE 3: WORLD BUILDER

Stage 3, illustrated in Figure 5, enables continuous, community-driven model evolution, where users contribute to refinement, alignment, and specialization through structured participation, creating, evaluating, and merging variants under shared governance. Large-scale pre-training usually takes place inside centralized organizations with significant computational resources. However, later phases such as refinement and parameter-efficient fine-tuning are more accessible, especially with techniques like LoRA and other lightweight adaptation methods (Hu et al., 2022; Tan et al., 2024). Stage 3 builds on this shift by inviting community members to help improve model behavior. Participants may review outputs, identify weaknesses, suggest better alignment choices, or contribute domain-specific examples. In this way, users move from passive consumers to active co-creators of model development (Vaughan, 2018).

Gamification structures this participation without making it overly technical. Improvement tasks are framed as small quests. Contributors earn experience points and visible progression based on the quality of their evaluations and suggestions. AI agents act as guides, recommending tasks that match a participant's expertise and the system's current needs (Krohmann et al., 2025).

Model variants are presented as accessible "builds" with distinct strengths, such as a domain-adapted medical model or a debate-focused reasoning model, and are compared through structured evaluation tasks. A "Model Merge Arena" enables blind comparisons where community members assess outputs for clarity, reasoning, safety, or bias, with votes weighted by prior review accuracy. High-performing variants advance and may be merged into the main system using techniques such as LoRA fusion or preference optimization (Radeta et al., 2024).

Figure 5. Stage 3 – World builder: Gamified model evolution

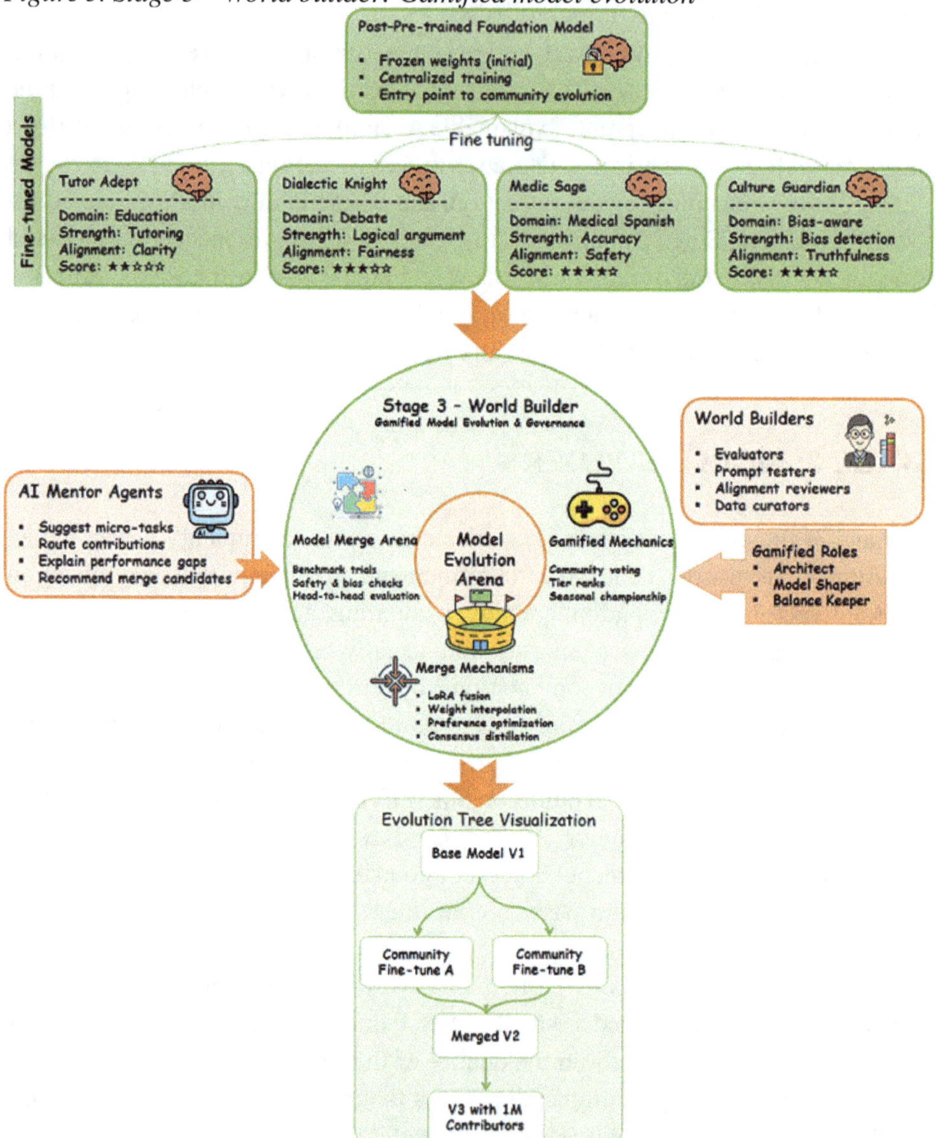

An evolution tree visualization makes this process transparent. Each branch shows the goal of a variant, the data sources used, evaluation results, alignment decisions, and key contributors. This makes model development traceable rather than opaque.

A real-world example of community-driven AI improvement is *AWS AI League*[3]. The initiative builds on the earlier AWS DeepRacer and engages developers worldwide in hands-on AI challenges using services such as Amazon SageMaker[4] and Bedrock[5]. Through ranked challenges, structured evaluation, and performance-based feedback, participants iteratively improve models and gain practical experience. While not identical to the framework proposed here, it demonstrates how structured competition and community incentives can support large-scale model refinement.

Stage 3 also has clear educational value. Participants observe how small changes in data, alignment criteria, or evaluation metrics affect model behavior (Kong et al., 2021). By comparing variants and reviewing outputs, they learn how reasoning quality, bias mitigation, and domain specialization are shaped. This supports core dimensions of AI literacy emphasized in international frameworks, including understanding model evaluation, alignment, and responsible design (Chiu et al., 2024; Miao & Shiohira, 2024).

From an ethical perspective, this stage promotes transparency and shared governance. Each model variant has a visible lineage, showing contributors, adaptation goals, and evaluation results. Community review reduces the concentration of decision-making power and allows diverse perspectives to influence alignment choices (Washington, 2024; Gilman, 2023). By turning post–pre-training development into a traceable and participatory process, Stage 3 strengthens accountability while maintaining technical rigor.

In relation to the research questions, Stage 3 demonstrates how the later phases of the LLM lifecycle can become participatory rather than centralized, how structured and gamified evaluation can sustain engagement in complex improvement tasks, and how transparent model evolution contributes to AI literacy and responsible governance.

STAGE 4: ETHICS DUEL ARENA

Stage 4, illustrated in Figure 6, focuses on aligning large language models with human values such as fairness, honesty, safety and empathy through transparent, participatory evaluation. Users compare model behaviors, justify ethical choices and contribute structured preference data in a gamified, community-driven process under shared governance.

Traditional alignment methods, such as reinforcement learning from human feedback (RLHF), preference optimization, or constitutional approaches, are often conducted within relatively closed settings (Christiano et al., 2017). While effective, these processes can be difficult for the public to inspect. Ethical decisions may appear abstract, and the reasoning behind them may not be visible. Stage 4 addresses this limitation by turning alignment into an interactive and educational process.

Alignment tasks are organized as short "duels." In each duel, participants compare two anonymous model responses to the same prompt. A clear ethical focus is defined, such as avoiding stereotype bias, providing safe advice, remaining truthful, or demonstrating empathy (Bai et al., 2022). Users select the response they consider better aligned with the stated value and briefly explain their reasoning. In this way, alignment becomes an act of reflective judgment rather than simple labeling.

Figure 6. Stage 4 – Ethics duel arena. Gamified AI alignment

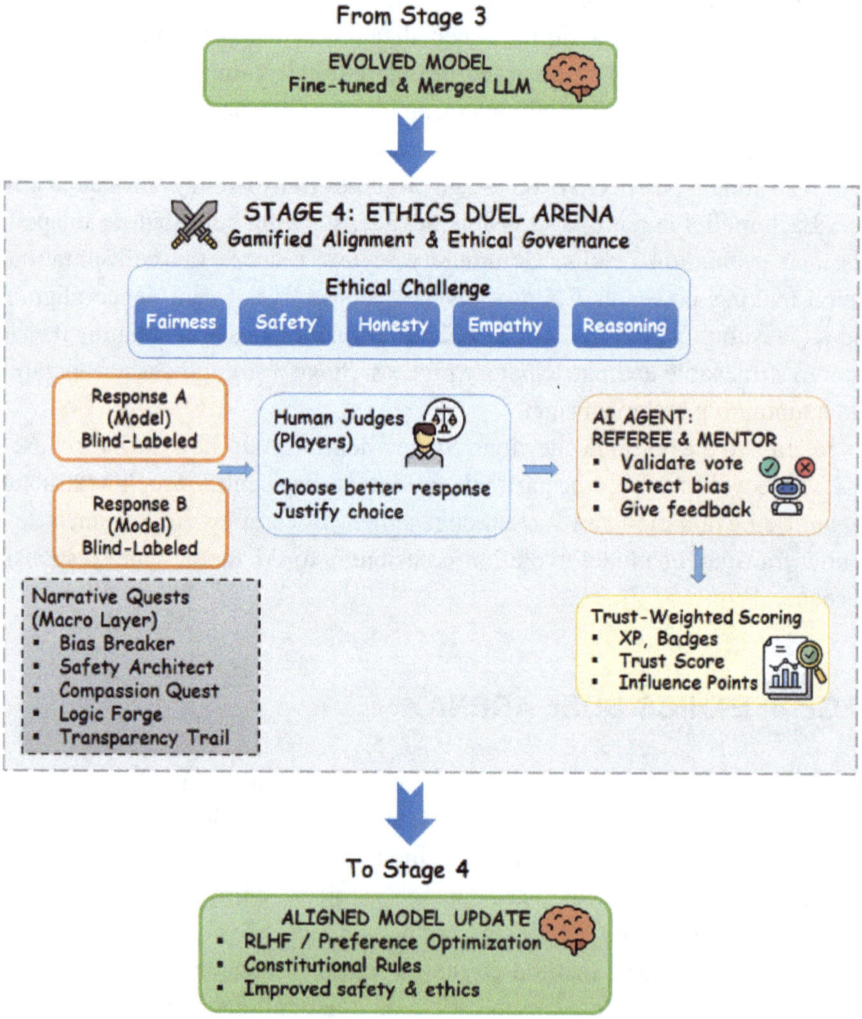

Different types of duels emphasize different ethical dimensions. Some focus on fairness and bias, others on hallucination and factual accuracy, safety in sensitive domains, emotional support, or logical consistency. More complex or high-impact tasks may carry higher rewards, encouraging participants to engage with challenging alignment issues.

Gamification structures the experience without trivializing it. Contributors earn experience points for consistent and well-justified evaluations. A trust score reflects the reliability of past judgments and determines the weight of future votes. Beginners can participate in lower-risk comparisons, while high-trust participants have greater influence in updating preference data. AI agents act as referees: they check for inconsistent judgments, provide brief feedback, and highlight strong reasoning patterns (Kamar, 2016). This combination of human judgment and AI support helps maintain quality while keeping the system open.

Scenario-based quests add depth to the process (Xenos & Velli, 2018). For example, participants may encounter a biased chatbot response or an unsafe medical suggestion and work step by step to identify the ethical issue and improve the output. Community voting can help select the most appropriate revisions. Recognition mechanisms, such as badges for sustained engagement in bias detection or safety review, support long-term participation.

A related real-world example is *Anthropic and its Constitutional AI approach* (Bai et al., 2022). In this method, written principles guide model self-critique and improvement. Public input can inform the formulation of such principles, increasing legitimacy and diversity. A gamified extension, as proposed in this stage, would allow users to compare alternative principles, vote on refinements, and contribute to an evolving and inspectable ethical framework.

Stage 4 has strong educational value. By repeatedly comparing responses and explaining their choices, participants practice ethical reasoning in concrete situations. They learn to detect bias, assess honesty, evaluate safety risks, and consider the social impact of language (Friedman et al., 2011; Bai et al., 2022). This supports key dimensions of AI literacy, including value alignment, ethical reflection, and critical evaluation of AI systems (Chiu et al., 2024; Miao & Shiohira, 2024).

From a governance perspective, Stage 4 broadens ethical oversight by incorporating diverse cultural perspectives, reducing the influence of a single group on shared norms. Trust scores, peer review, and AI-supported feedback help prevent misuse while maintaining openness. Making alignment visible and participatory enhances transparency, accountability, and public trust in model behavior.

In relation to the research questions, Stage 4 shows how alignment can become a civic and educational process rather than a closed technical procedure, how structured gamified comparisons can sustain engagement in complex ethical evaluation, and how participatory value formation contributes to more inclusive and trustworthy AI systems.

STAGE 5: PROMPT DOJO

Stage 5 focuses on developing users' skills in communicating effectively with AI systems. While earlier stages address data, annotation, alignment, and model refinement, this stage centers on human capability. The goal is to transform prompt design from an expert-only technique into an accessible, structured, and learnable skill.

Figure 7 illustrates this stage as a level-based learning environment in which users practice prompt writing through guided quests, receive AI-supported feedback, and contribute high-quality prompts to a shared community space.

Figure 7. Stage 5 – Prompt Dojo. Gamified prompt mastery environment

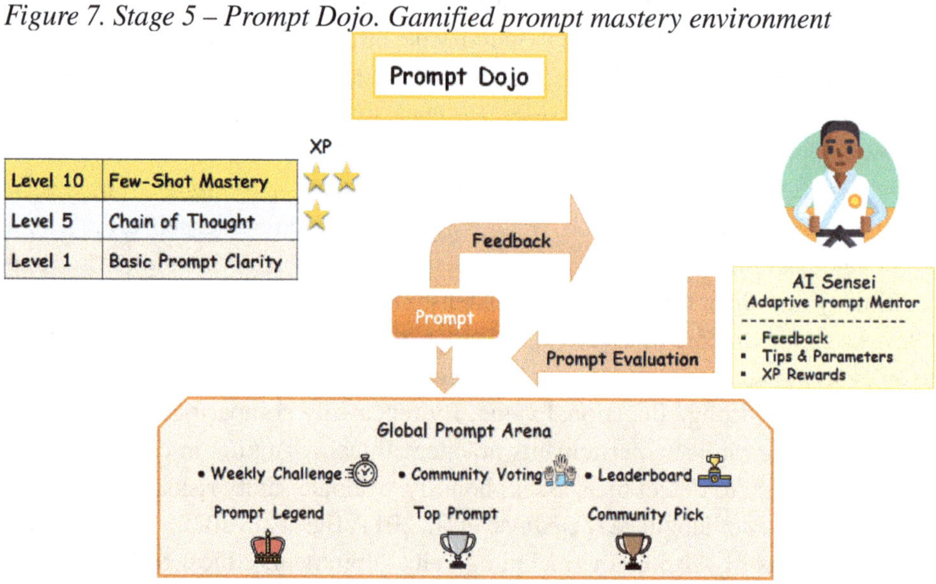

Prompt engineering has become a critical skill for guiding large language models toward accurate, safe, and useful outputs (Liu et al., 2023). However, it is often treated as informal experimentation or insider expertise. Stage 5 reframes it as deliberate practice. Prompting is broken down into small, progressive steps so that users can move from basic clarity to more advanced reasoning techniques (Zamfirescu-Pereira et al., 2023).

Gamification structures this learning journey. Participants progress through levels that reflect increasing mastery (Deterding et al., 2011; Wei et al., 2022). Early quests focus on writing clear and specific instructions. Users learn to define scope, specify output formats, and avoid ambiguity. Immediate feedback highlights vague phrasing or missing constraints.

Intermediate challenges develop structured reasoning by having participants prompt the model to explain steps, check logic, and reduce hallucinations. By rewriting prompts and comparing outputs, they learn how structure affects quality. Advanced levels introduce few-shot prompting, template design, and multi-part task orchestration, with progress tracked through experience points, titles, and unlocked challenges to maintain engagement.

A collaborative dimension complements individual progression. Community challenges invite users to submit prompts for shared themes, such as lesson design, tutoring scenarios, or problem-solving tasks (Kittur et al., 2013). First, AI agents evaluate submissions for clarity and usefulness. Then, community voting highlights the most effective prompts. High-quality contributions enter a shared prompt library, creating a collective resource while rewarding contributors.

A related real-world example is *The Prompt Dojo*[6], an online platform that offers structured prompt-engineering challenges with progressive difficulty. Through daily exercises, instant feedback, and ranking systems, it demonstrates how systematic practice can improve prompting skills and sustain engagement. While independent from the full lifecycle proposed here, it shows that gamified, tiered learning can effectively support prompt mastery.

Stage 5 has clear educational value. Participants learn that small changes in wording, structure, or constraints can significantly alter model behavior (Wei et al., 2022). AI agents act as mentors by offering short, adaptive suggestions such as clarifying objectives or separating complex tasks (Fortuna et al., 2025). This supports deliberate practice and reduces frustration. Over time, users develop confidence in controlling AI outputs rather than relying on trial and error.

From an AI literacy perspective, this stage strengthens practical competence in human–AI interaction. It supports responsible use by teaching users how to reduce bias, avoid unsafe instructions, and anticipate potential misinterpretations (Long & Magerko, 2020; Ukwandu et al., 2025). Prompt design becomes not only a technical skill but also an ethical practice.

Governance in this stage is community-based. Shared prompt libraries, peer review, and voting mechanisms help surface high-quality and responsible examples. AI mentors provide safeguards by flagging potentially harmful or misleading instructions (Amershi et al., 2019). By embedding structured progression, feedback, and collaboration into prompt learning, Stage 5 improves interaction quality while reinforcing transparency and accountability.

In relation to the research questions, Stage 5 demonstrates how gamified progression can transform prompt design into an inclusive and learnable skill, how structured feedback sustains engagement in skill development, and how improved human–AI communication strengthens responsible and effective AI use.

STAGE 6: AI LAB

Stage 6, referred to as the AI Lab, focuses on evaluating and testing language models under real-world and diverse conditions. While traditional evaluation often relies on fixed benchmarks and expert-designed metrics, this stage opens assessment to a broader community. Users participate as testers, bug hunters, and co-investigators, working alongside AI agents to identify failures, contextual limitations, and areas for improvement. Figure 8 illustrates this stage as a community-driven evaluation environment in which structured activities contribute to a shared and continuously updated Model Report Card.

Figure 8. Stage 6 – AI Lab (Model Report Card). Transparent, community-informed model evaluation dashboard visualizing performance metrics, trends, and updates

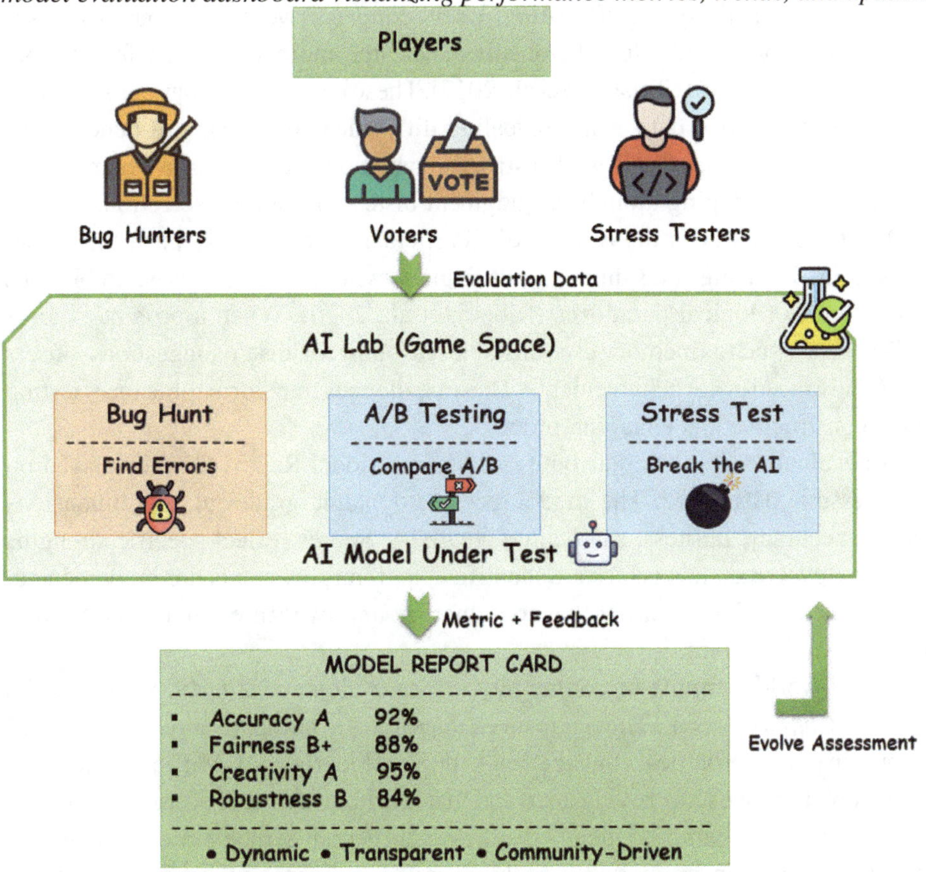

Model evaluation is traditionally conducted by experts using predefined datasets and technical metrics, which can miss practical failures, cultural variation, and unexpected behavior (Raji et al., 2020). The AI Lab transforms evaluation into an open, participatory process, where users examine strengths, weaknesses, and contextual behavior of the model (Kittur et al., 2013). This collective scrutiny enhances reliability and robustness.

Gamification structures this evaluation through three main types of activities.

The first is the Bug Hunt. Participants carefully inspect model outputs to detect hallucinations, logical inconsistencies, factual errors, or misleading claims (Huang et al., 2025). When a confirmed issue is reported with clear reasoning, contributors earn experience points and recognition titles that reflect analytical skill, such as achievements for detecting complex reasoning flaws. Error detection becomes an investigative challenge rather than a passive complaint mechanism.

The second activity is A/B testing. Users compare two anonymous responses to the same prompt and select the one that is clearer, more accurate, safer, or more culturally appropriate (Christiano et al., 2017). These pairwise comparisons generate structured preference data while revealing differences that standard benchmarks may ignore. Consistent and well-justified evaluations strengthen a contributor's reputation, encouraging thoughtful judgment instead of random selection.

The third activity is the Stress Test. Participants deliberately push the model to its limits by using long inputs, multilingual switching, edge cases, ambiguous instructions, or logical paradoxes (Ribeiro et al., 2020). When a prompt exposes weaknesses—such as memory loss, unstable reasoning, or unsafe suggestions—users unlock advanced tester achievements. These challenges transform robustness testing into a constructive and engaging process.

All evaluation results contribute to a shared Model Report Card displayed on an accessible dashboard. The model receives dynamic grades across dimensions such as accuracy, fairness, safety, and creativity. Scores reflect specific strengths and gaps, evolve as new issues are identified, and improvements are implemented, treating the model as a learner that continuously improves through feedback rather than as a static system.

A real-world example of community-driven evaluation is *LMSYS Org* and its platform *Chatbot Arena*[7]. The platform enables users to compare anonymous model outputs in pairwise battles, contributing to public leaderboards. Millions of interactions from diverse users provide open and real-world assessment of frontier models. Although not fully gamified in the sense proposed here, it demonstrates the power of crowdsourced comparison, public ranking, and transparent benchmarking. Adding structured achievements, recognition titles, and a visible report card system could further strengthen engagement and educational value.

Stage 6 has strong educational benefits. By participating in bug hunts, comparative evaluations, and stress challenges, users learn how models are tested and why benchmark scores alone are insufficient (Huang et al., 2025). They practice critical observation, logical analysis, and bias detection. They also recognize that model quality is multi-dimensional and context-dependent (Long & Magerko, 2020; Southworth et al., 2023).

From an AI literacy perspective, this stage makes evaluation visible and understandable. Users learn to question outputs, assess reliability across situations, and interpret performance claims critically. Evaluation becomes a shared civic practice rather than an opaque technical procedure.

Ethically, the AI Lab promotes transparency and collective oversight. Open reporting of strengths and weaknesses reduces blind trust in AI systems. Community-based testing reveals cultural blind spots that centralized benchmarks may miss (Raji et al., 2020). Reputation systems and AI guidance encourage responsible participation while limiting noise. By embedding structured investigation, public reporting, and shared accountability into the lifecycle, Stage 6 strengthens trust, robustness, and inclusive governance.

In relation to the research questions, Stage 6 demonstrates how evaluation can become participatory and educational, how gamified investigative tasks sustain engagement in quality assurance, and how transparent reporting supports responsible and trustworthy AI development.

STAGE 7: LIVING WITH AI

Stage 7, Living with AI, extends the framework from development and evaluation to long-term human–AI coexistence. While earlier stages focus on design, testing, and improvement, this stage addresses what happens after deployment. AI systems become embedded in daily routines, and their value unfolds gradually through sustained interaction. Rather than treating deployment as a technical endpoint, this stage frames it as the beginning of an evolving partnership in which both users and AI systems adapt over time (Amershi et al., 2019).

The goal of this stage is to make everyday AI use intentional, reflective, and developmentally meaningful. Language models evolve through updates and contextual exposure, while users refine their goals, expectations, and habits. Living with AI is seen as continuous cohabitation, where AI supports learning, creativity, productivity, and communication, and users shape its behavior through feedback, boundary-setting, and repeated engagement (Jiang et al., 2024). The focus shifts from performance alone to sustainable, responsible integration into daily life.

Gamification in this stage is lightweight and longitudinal. Daily Quests turn routine interactions into small, purposeful missions, while a Personal Agent adapts to user goals and preferences, reinforcing co-adaptation and agency (Kocielnik et al., 2019). The XP Passport tracks achievements, creative outputs, and ethical reflections, supporting visible long-term engagement. Together, these mechanics create a sustained, user-centered journey aligned with core gamification principles (Deterding et al., 2011).

A practical example is Duolingo's streak system, where short daily interactions, adaptive difficulty, and personalization improve retention and learning continuity (Loewen et al., 2019). Stage 7 applies this approach to general-purpose large language model use, showing how structured daily engagement can support long-term growth at scale.

Figure 9. Stage 7 – Living with AI. Deployment as a continuous, gamified human–AI partnership supporting lifelong learning, creativity, and ethical engagement

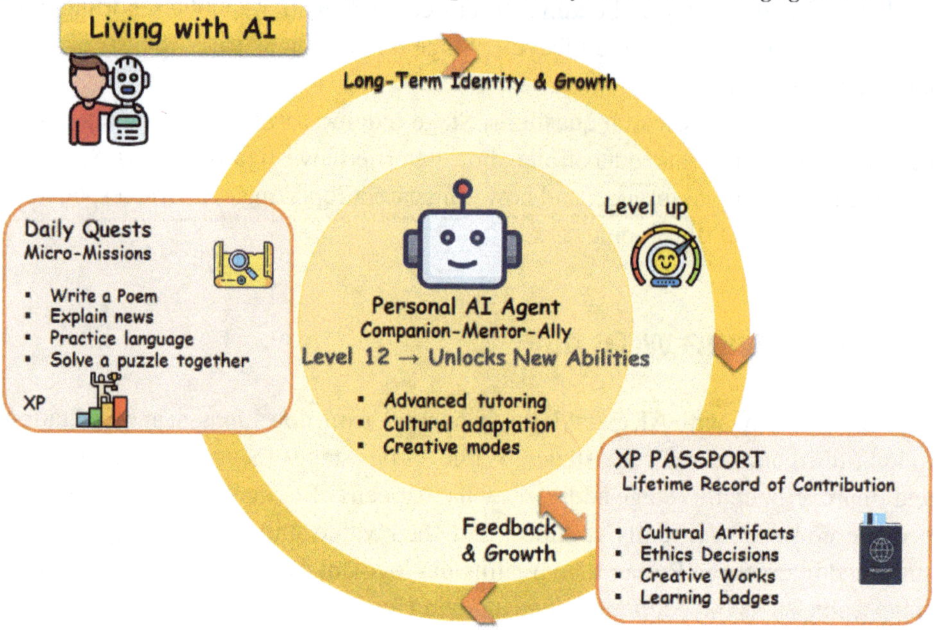

Educationally, this stage strengthens AI literacy through sustained practice. Users develop habits of goal setting, critical reflection, and adaptive communication, while learning to recognize evolving limitations and risks over time. AI quality is understood not as a static metric but as a dynamic balance between usefulness, safety, fairness, and autonomy (Southworth et al., 2023; Floridi & Cowls, 2022).

Ethically, Stage 7 emphasizes user agency and transparency. Users control what the Personal Agent remembers, its behavior, and the interactions they engage in. Clear memory boundaries, privacy settings, and visible progress records maintain accountability, while transparent logs, feedback loops, and shared norms support responsible governance. This frames AI use as a balanced, evolving partnership that promotes lifelong learning, autonomy, and cultural respect.

DISCUSSION

The Gamified LLM Lifecycle presents a transformative, participatory vision for human–AI co-evolution, embedding learning, ethics, and governance into a persistent, bidirectional cycle (Kulynych et al., 2020). Unlike linear AI pipelines, it treats users as active co-creators whose contributions (intentions, judgments, and creativity) directly shape model evolution through feedback loops. The framework's modularity enables cross-disciplinary application across education and ethics, while its conceptual design avoids technical constraints, ensuring adaptability to diverse cultural and infrastructural contexts.

Figure 10 depicts the high-level flow of participation, mission-based interaction, model adaptation, and renewed engagement. Arrows indicate conceptual influence and feedback loops rather than technical data flows.

At the heart of the cycle lies a co-evolutionary dynamic:

- Users gain skills, metacognitive awareness, and agency through sustained participation.
- The model improves through diverse, community-sourced signals of preference, judgment, and creativity.

This mutual adaptation persists indefinitely, extending well beyond initial deployment.

Figure 10. Conceptual architecture of the gamified LLM lifecycle

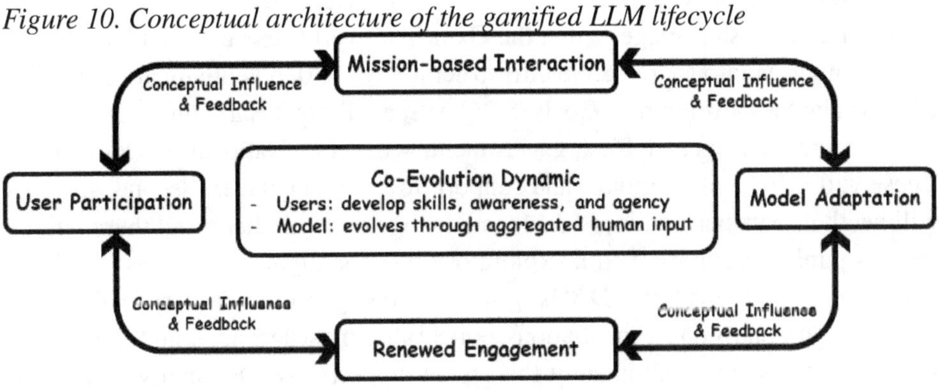

Key innovations include structured roles: users as learners and ethical stewards, AI agents as adaptive companions, and missions as dual-purpose units for engagement and data generation. Progress signals (XP, badges) foster agency and responsibility, while governance mechanisms ensure transparency and inclusivity.

However, challenges persist. The first challendge is gaming the system, in which users might exploit the system for quick XP by submitting copied content, low-effort repeats, or bot help (Petter et al., 2020). It is mitigated via AI pre-filtering and peer duels. The second challenge is digital divide; it means the people in low-connectivity areas, with basic phones, high data costs, or limited digital skills may be left out exactly the groups already underrepresented in AI data (Deursen and

Van Dijk, 2019). It is addressed through offline mode and SMS quests. The third one is burnout, which means heavy use of streaks, daily quests, and leaderboards can create pressure and guilt (Hammedi et al., 2021). It is countered by wellness streaks and sabbatical badges. Final challenge is bias in rewards where a small group often collects most XP and visibility, discouraging newcomers and reinforcing real-world inequalities (Tadimalla and Kunkeler, 2024). The last challenge is reduced via progressive XP taxation and collaboration incentives.

This LLM development framework promotes a decentralized, shared vision. However, it recognizes that current power structures are controlled by big tech companies that own the infrastructure and data. These companies will likely centralize key decisions on architecture and deployment. This limits real decentralization, as platform governance research suggests (Khan, 2017; Srnicek, 2017). Also, mechanisms like DAOs provide transparency, but they face legal uncertainty. They can cause power to gather among a few token holders, which may create digital oligarchies (Hassan & De Filippi, 2021). Similarly, voting based on reputation can make existing inequalities worse. Therefore, fair AI governance needs more than just gamification. It requires regulatory oversight, clear audits, and protections against power concentration to support the design goal (O'Neil, 2017).

The Future Vision suggests that the Gamified LLM Lifecycle is a blueprint for transforming AI into shared civic infrastructure by 2030, potentially aligning with UN Sustainable Development Goals (SDGs) (Spanellis and Harviainen, 2021). Key changes will be happened. First, governments will set up National AI Quest Hubs. These will help local AI groups and support different languages. Second, students will get their own personalized LLMs, made together with them, and these will be seen as public resources. Third, exploratory models might involve Decentralized Autonomous Organizations (DAOs) governing AI agents, where earned XP could serve as high-quality data contributions, ethical alignment decisions, and community mentoring and support. Ultimately, this vision supports SDG 4 (Quality Education) through personalized learning, SDG 10 (Reduced Inequalities) via inclusive participation mechanisms like progressive XP taxation, and SDG 17 (Partnerships) by creating a collaborative platform for global, ethical AI progress, positioning AI as an equitable force.

CONCLUSION

The Gamified LLM Lifecycle is more than a technical architecture or a design strategy—it represents a new philosophy of education, participation, and human–AI coevolution. Across its seven stages, the Lifecycle reframes AI development not as an opaque process reserved for a small cadre of experts, but as a dynamic, game-based learning ecosystem in which every user becomes a contributor, evaluator, and co-designer.

By transforming data creation into quests, alignment into ethical duels, evaluation into playful testing, and deployment into daily adventure, the Lifecycle establishes a developmental loop in which AI improves because people learn and people learn because AI improves. This reciprocal growth is the foundation of a more democratic and pedagogically grounded AI future.

At its core, the Lifecycle operationalizes three commitments:

1. **Democratization of AI Creation:** The traditional boundaries between developers and users collapse. Through micro-contributions, SMS quests, community duels, and decentralized governance, individuals across the globe gain agency in shaping the behavior, values, and linguistic diversity of the models that increasingly structure public life.
2. **Education through Contribution:** Each interaction doubles as a learning opportunity. As users annotate, evaluate, reason, and create alongside AI agents, they develop metacognition, critical literacy, ethical sensitivity, and collaborative problem-solving. Learning becomes embedded in civic participation rather than confined to formal institutions.
3. **Empowerment of Learners as Co-Creators:** The Lifecycle positions humans not as passive consumers of AI outputs, but as active co-evolutionary partners. Personal Agents that level up, XP Passports that track long-term growth, and DAO-governed ecosystems that reward meaningful participation signal a future in which users exercise real influence over AI's trajectory.

Together, these commitments articulate a vision of AI that is not merely more inclusive, but fundamentally more educational, participatory, and socially embedded.

DISCLOSURE STATEMENT

The authors confirm that ChatGPT was used during the manuscript preparation process solely for language editing and minor stylistic improvements.

REFERENCES

Ahrweiler, P., Späth, E., Siqueiros García, J. M., Capellas, B. L., & Wurster, D. (2025). Inclusive technology co-design for participatory AI. *Participatory Artificial Intelligence in Public Social Services: From Bias to Fairness in Assessing Beneficiaries*, 35-62.

Amershi, S., Weld, D., Vorvoreanu, M., Fourney, A., Nushi, B., Collisson, P., & Horvitz, E. (2019, May). Guidelines for human-AI interaction. In *Proceedings of the 2019 chi conference on human factors in computing systems* (pp. 1-13).

Bai, Y., Kadavath, S., Kundu, S., Askell, A., Kernion, J., Jones, A., . . . Kaplan, J. (2022). Constitutional AI: Harmlessness from AI Feedback. *arXiv preprint arXiv:2212.08073.*

Bakhanova, E., Garcia, J. A., Raffe, W. L., & Voinov, A. (2020). Targeting social learning and engagement: What serious games and gamification can offer to participatory modeling. *Environmental Modelling & Software, 134*, 104846. DOI: 10.1016/j.envsoft.2020.104846

Bakhanova, E., Garcia, J. A., Raffe, W. L., & Voinov, A. (2023). Gamification framework for participatory modeling: A proposal. *Group Decision and Negotiation, 32*(5), 1167–1182. DOI: 10.1007/s10726-023-09838-w

Bender, E. M., Gebru, T., McMillan-Major, A., & Shmitchell, S. (2021, March). On the dangers of stochastic parrots: Can language models be too big? In *Proceedings of the 2021 ACM conference on fairness, accountability, and transparency* (pp. 610-623). DOI: 10.1145/3442188.3445922

Birhane, A., Isaac, W., Prabhakaran, V., Diaz, M., Elish, M. C., Gabriel, I., & Mohamed, S. (2022, October). Power to the people? Opportunities and challenges for participatory AI. In *Proceedings of the 2nd ACM Conference on Equity and Access in Algorithms, Mechanisms, and Optimization* (pp. 1-8). DOI: 10.1145/3551624.3555290

Brown, T., Mann, B., Ryder, N., Subbiah, M., Kaplan, J. D., Dhariwal, P., & Amodei, D. (2020). Language models are few-shot learners. *Advances in Neural Information Processing Systems, 33*, 1877–1901.

Chaudhari, S., Aggarwal, P., Murahari, V., Rajpurohit, T., Kalyan, A., Narasimhan, K., Deshpande, A., & Castro da Silva, B. (2025). RLHF deciphered: A critical analysis of reinforcement learning from human feedback for LLMs. *ACM Computing Surveys*, *58*(2), 1–37. DOI: 10.1145/3743127

Chiu, T. K., Ahmad, Z., Ismailov, M., & Sanusi, I. T. (2024). What are artificial intelligence literacy and competency? A comprehensive framework to support them. *Computers and Education Open*, *6*, 100171. DOI: 10.1016/j.caeo.2024.100171

Christiano, P. F., Leike, J., Brown, T., Martic, M., Legg, S., & Amodei, D. (2017). Deep reinforcement learning from human preferences. *Advances in Neural Information Processing Systems*, •••, 30.

Costa, C. J. (2025). Integrating LLM usage in gamified systems. *WSEAS Transactions on Mathematics*, *24*, 258–267. DOI: 10.37394/23206.2025.24.25

Costa, C. J., Aparicio, M., & Aparicio, J. T. (2025, May). Gamifying Human-AI Interaction: Using Large Language Models for Enhanced Engagement and Learning. In *2025 IEEE 5th International Conference on Human-Machine Systems (ICHMS)* (pp. 325-331). IEEE.

Deterding, S., Dixon, D., Khaled, R., & Nacke, L. (2011, September). From game design elements to gamefulness: defining" gamification". In *Proceedings of the 15th international academic MindTrek conference: Envisioning future media environments* (pp. 9-15). DOI: 10.1145/2181037.2181040

Dodge, J., Sap, M., Marasović, A., Agnew, W., Ilharco, G., Groeneveld, D., & Gardner, M. (2021). Documenting Large Webtext Corpora: A Case Study on the Colossal Clean Crawled Corpus. In *Proceedings of the 2021 Conference on Empirical Methods in Natural Language Processing*. Association for Computational Linguistics. DOI: 10.18653/v1/2021.emnlp-main.98

Federiakin, D., Molerov, D., Zlatkin-Troitschanskaia, O., & Maur, A. (2024, November). Prompt engineering as a new 21st century skill. [). Frontiers Media SA.]. *Frontiers in Education*, *9*, 1366434. DOI: 10.3389/feduc.2024.1366434

Floridi, L., & Cowls, J. (2022). A unified framework of five principles for AI in society. *Machine learning and the city: Applications in architecture and urban design*, 535-545.

Fortuna, A., Prasetya, F., Samala, A. D., Rawas, S., Criollo-C, S., Kaya, D., Raihan, M., Andriani, W., Safitri, D., & Nabawi, R. A. (2025). Artificial intelligence in personalized learning: A global systematic review of current advancements and shaping future opportunities. *Social Sciences & Humanities Open*, *12*, 102114. DOI: 10.1016/j.ssaho.2025.102114

Friedman, B., Hendry, D. G., & Borning, A. *A survey of value sensitive design methods, foundations and trends® in human–computer interaction 11 (2)(2011) 63–125.*

Gallotta, R., Todd, G., Zammit, M., Earle, S., Liapis, A., Togelius, J., & Yannakakis, G. N. (2024). Large language models and games: A survey and roadmap. *IEEE Transactions on Games*, 1–18. DOI: 10.1109/TG.2024.3461510

García-Méndez, S., de Arriba-Pérez, F., & Somoza-López, M. D. C. (2025). A review on the use of large language models as virtual tutors. *Science & Education*, *34*(2), 877–892. DOI: 10.1007/s11191-024-00530-2

Ge, W., Sun, Y., Wang, Z., Zheng, H., He, W., Wang, P., . . . Wang, B. (2025). SRLAgent: Enhancing Self-Regulated Learning Skills through Gamification and LLM Assistance. *arXiv preprint arXiv:2506.09968*.

Gholiagha, S., Neyer, J., Sienknecht, M., Wolska, M. A., Kiesel, D., Riehmann, P., Voigt, J., Wiegmann, M., López García, I., Girgensohn, K., Stein, B., & Fröhlich, B. (2025). From annotation to reflection: How participatory AI training enhances critical thinking. *AI & Society*, •••, 1–14. DOI: 10.1007/s00146-025-02539-9

Gianni, A. M., Nikolakis, N., & Antoniadis, N. (2025). An LLM based learning framework for adaptive feedback mechanisms in gamified XR. *Computers & Education: X Reality, 7*, 100116.

Gilman, M. E. (2023). *Democratizing AI: Principles for meaningful public participation*. Data & Society.

Goslen, A., Kim, Y. J., Rowe, J., & Lester, J. (2025). LLM-based student plan generation for adaptive scaffolding in game-based learning environments. *International Journal of Artificial Intelligence in Education, 35*(2), 533–558. DOI: 10.1007/s40593-024-00421-1

Guillen-Aguinaga, M., Aguinaga-Ontoso, E., Guillen-Aguinaga, L., Guillen-Grima, F., & Aguinaga-Ontoso, I. (2025). Data quality in the age of AI: A review of governance, ethics, and the FAIR principles. *Data, 10*(12), 201. DOI: 10.3390/data10120201

Hammedi, W., Leclercq, T., Poncin, I., & Alkire, L. (2021). Uncovering the dark side of gamification at work: Impacts on engagement and well-being. *Journal of Business Research, 122*, 256–269. DOI: 10.1016/j.jbusres.2020.08.032

Hassan, S., & De Filippi, P. (2021). Decentralized autonomous organization. *Internet Policy Review, 10*(2). Advance online publication. DOI: 10.14763/2021.2.1556

Hassan, Y. M., & Aboulhassan, A. (2024, November). A framework for adaptive game play and adversary creation based on gamer behavioral analysis and large language (llm) models. In *2024 International Mobile, Intelligent, and Ubiquitous Computing Conference (MIUCC)* (pp. 413-417). IEEE.

Heras, S. C., Gargalo, C. L., Weitze, C. L., Mansouri, S. S., Gernaey, K. V., & Krühne, U. (2021). A framework for the development of Pedagogical Process Simulators (P2Si) using explanatory models and gamification. *Computers & Chemical Engineering, 151*, 107350. DOI: 10.1016/j.compchemeng.2021.107350

Hernández, A. D., Mosquera, D., & Gallegos, F. (2025). Lessons from the margins: Contextualizing, reimagining, and hacking generative AI in the Global South. *Harvard Data Science Review*.

Hinterreiter, S., Spinde, T., Oberdörfer, S., Echizen, I., & Latoschik, M. E. (2024). News Ninja: Gamified annotation of linguistic bias in online news. *Proceedings of the ACM on Human-Computer Interaction, 8*(CHI PLAY), 1-29. DOI: 10.1145/3677092

Hu, E. J., Shen, Y., Wallis, P., Allen-Zhu, Z., Li, Y., Wang, L., & Chen, W. (2022). LoRA: Low-rank adaptation of large language models. *International Conference on Learning Representations (ICLR)*.

Huang, L., Yu, W., Ma, W., Zhong, W., Feng, Z., Wang, H., Chen, Q., Peng, W., Feng, X., Qin, B., & Liu, T. (2025). A survey on hallucination in large language models: Principles, taxonomy, challenges, and open questions. *ACM Transactions on Information Systems, 43*(2), 1–55. DOI: 10.1145/3703155

Huber, S. E., Kiili, K., Nebel, S., Ryan, R. M., Sailer, M., & Ninaus, M. (2024). Leveraging the potential of large language models in education through playful and game-based learning. *Educational Psychology Review, 36*(1), 25. DOI: 10.1007/s10648-024-09868-z

Hydari, M. Z., Adjerid, I., & Striegel, A. D. (2023). Health wearables, gamification, and healthful activity. *Management Science, 69*(7), 3920–3938. DOI: 10.1287/mnsc.2022.4581 PMID: 37547027

Jiang, T., Sun, Z., Fu, S., & Lv, Y. (2024). Human-AI interaction research agenda: A user-centered perspective. *Data and Information Management*, *8*(4), 100078. DOI: 10.1016/j.dim.2024.100078

Johnson, D., Deterding, S., Kuhn, K. A., Staneva, A., Stoyanov, S., & Hides, L. (2016). Gamification for health and wellbeing: A systematic review of the literature. *Internet Interventions : the Application of Information Technology in Mental and Behavioural Health*, *6*, 89–106. DOI: 10.1016/j.invent.2016.10.002 PMID: 30135818

Kamar, E. (2016, July). Directions in Hybrid Intelligence: Complementing AI Systems with Human Intelligence. In *IJCAI* (pp. 4070-4073).

Khakpour, A., & Colomo-Palacios, R. (2021). Convergence of gamification and machine learning: A systematic literature review. *Technology. Knowledge and Learning*, *26*(3), 597–636. DOI: 10.1007/s10758-020-09456-4

Khan, L. M. (2017). Amazon's antitrust paradox. *The Yale Law Journal*, *126*(3), 710–805.

Kittur, A., Chi, E. H., & Suh, B. (2008, April). Crowdsourcing user studies with Mechanical Turk. In *Proceedings of the SIGCHI conference on human factors in computing systems* (pp. 453-456). DOI: 10.1145/1357054.1357127

Kittur, A., Nickerson, J. V., Bernstein, M., Gerber, E., Shaw, A., Zimmerman, J., & Horton, J. (2013, February). The future of crowd work. In *Proceedings of the 2013 conference on Computer supported cooperative work* (pp. 1301-1318). DOI: 10.1145/2441776.2441923

Kocielnik, R., Amershi, S., & Bennett, P. N. (2019, May). Will you accept an imperfect ai? Exploring designs for adjusting end-user expectations of ai systems. In *Proceedings of the 2019 CHI conference on human factors in computing systems* (pp. 1-14).

Kong, S. C., Cheung, W. M. Y., & Zhang, G. (2021). Evaluation of an artificial intelligence literacy course for university students with diverse study backgrounds. *Computers and Education: Artificial Intelligence*, *2*, 100026. DOI: 10.1016/j.caeai.2021.100026

Krohmann, S., Rank, S., Schmidt-Kraepelin, M., Thiebes, S., & Sunyaev, A. (2025). Quest for quality: A review of design knowledge on gamified AI training data annotation systems. *Behaviour & Information Technology*, •••, 1–26. DOI: 10.1080/0144929X.2025.2568932

Kulynych, B., Madras, D., Milli, S., Raji, I. D., Zhou, A., & Zemel, R. (2020, July). Participatory approaches to machine learning. In *International Conference on Machine Learning Workshop* (Vol. 7).

Lee, J., Hicke, Y., Yu, R., Brooks, C., & Kizilcec, R. F. (2024). The life cycle of large language models in education: A framework for understanding sources of bias. *British Journal of Educational Technology*, *55*(5), 1982–2002. DOI: 10.1111/bjet.13505

Leslie, L. G., Jali, N., Yahia, S. B., Shiang, C. W., & Junaini, S. N. (2025, August). Exploring Large Language Models in Gamified Environments: A Systematic Literature Review. In *2025 14th International Conference on Information Technology in Asia (CITA)* (pp. 119-124). IEEE. DOI: 10.1109/CITA66455.2025.11198821

Liu, P., Yuan, W., Fu, J., Jiang, Z., Hayashi, H., & Neubig, G. (2023). Pre-train, prompt, and predict: A systematic survey of prompting methods in natural language processing. *ACM Computing Surveys*, *55*(9), 1–35. DOI: 10.1145/3560815

Loewen, S., Crowther, D., Isbell, D. R., Kim, K. M., Maloney, J., Miller, Z. F., & Rawal, H. (2019). Mobile-assisted language learning: A Duolingo case study. *ReCALL*, *31*(3), 293–311. DOI: 10.1017/S0958344019000065

Long, D., & Magerko, B. (2020, April). What is AI literacy? Competencies and design considerations. In *Proceedings of the 2020 CHI conference on human factors in computing systems* (pp. 1-16). DOI: 10.1145/3313831.3376727

Lorè, N., & Heydari, B. (2024). Strategic behavior of large language models and the role of game structure versus contextual framing. *Scientific Reports*, *14*(1), 18490. DOI: 10.1038/s41598-024-69032-z PMID: 39122801

Miao, F., & Shiohira, K. (2024). *AI competency framework for students*. UNESCO Publishing.

Morschheuser, B., Hamari, J., Koivisto, J., & Maedche, A. (2017). Gamified crowdsourcing: Conceptualization, literature review, and future agenda. *International Journal of Human-Computer Studies*, *106*, 26–43. DOI: 10.1016/j.ijhcs.2017.04.005

Narayanan, K. S., & Kumaravel, A. (2024). Hybrid gamification and AI tutoring framework using machine learning and adaptive Neuro-fuzzy inference system. *Journal of Advanced Research in Applied Sciences and Engineering Technology*, *42*(2), 221–233. DOI: 10.37934/araset.42.2.221233

Ng, D. T. K., Leung, J. K. L., Chu, S. K. W., & Qiao, M. S. (2021). Conceptualizing AI literacy: An exploratory review. *Computers and Education: Artificial Intelligence*, *2*, 100041.

O'neil, C. (2017). *Weapons of math destruction: How big data increases inequality and threatens democracy*. Crown.

Pahune, S., & Akhtar, Z. (2025). Transitioning from MLOps to LLMOps: Navigating the unique challenges of large language models. *Information (Basel)*, *16*(2), 87. DOI: 10.3390/info16020087

Pan, S., Luo, L., Wang, Y., Chen, C., Wang, J., & Wu, X. (2024). Unifying large language models and knowledge graphs: A roadmap. *IEEE Transactions on Knowledge and Data Engineering*, *36*(7), 3580–3599. DOI: 10.1109/TKDE.2024.3352100

Papert, S. (1996). *The Connected Family: Bridging the digital generation gap*. Longstreet Press.

Petter, S., Barber, C. S., & Barber, D. (2020). Gaming the system: The effects of social capital as a resource for virtual team members. *Information & Management*, *57*(6), 103239. DOI: 10.1016/j.im.2019.103239

Pham, N., Ngoc, H. P., & Nguyen-Duc, A. (2025). Fairness for machine learning software in education: A systematic mapping study. *Journal of Systems and Software*, *219*, 112244. DOI: 10.1016/j.jss.2024.112244

Radeta, M., Freitas, R., Rodrigues, C., Zuniga, A., Nguyen, N. T., Flores, H., & Nurmi, P. (2024). Man and the machine: Effects of AI-assisted human labeling on interactive annotation of real-time video streams. *ACM Transactions on Interactive Intelligent Systems*, *14*(2), 1–22. DOI: 10.1145/3649457

Raji, I. D., Smart, A., White, R. N., Mitchell, M., Gebru, T., Hutchinson, B., & Barnes, P. (2020, January). Closing the AI accountability gap: Defining an end-to-end framework for internal algorithmic auditing. In *Proceedings of the 2020 conference on fairness, accountability, and transparency* (pp. 33-44). DOI: 10.1145/3351095.3372873

Ribeiro, M. T., Wu, T., Guestrin, C., & Singh, S. (2020). Beyond accuracy: Behavioral testing of NLP models with CheckList. *arXiv preprint arXiv:2005.04118*. DOI: 10.18653/v1/2020.acl-main.442

Seaborn, K., & Fels, D. I. (2015). Gamification in theory and action: A survey. *International Journal of Human-Computer Studies*, *74*, 14–31. DOI: 10.1016/j.ijhcs.2014.09.006

Sharma, S., Mittal, P., Kumar, M., & Bhardwaj, V. (2025). The role of large language models in personalized learning: A systematic review of educational impact. *Discover Sustainability*, *6*(1), 1–24. DOI: 10.1007/s43621-025-01094-z

Snow, R., O'connor, B., Jurafsky, D., & Ng, A. Y. (2008, October). Cheap and fast–but is it good? Evaluating non-expert annotations for natural language tasks. In *Proceedings of the 2008 conference on empirical methods in natural language processing* (pp. 254-263).

Southworth, J., Migliaccio, K., Glover, J., Glover, J. N., Reed, D., McCarty, C., Brendemuhl, J., & Thomas, A. (2023). Developing a model for AI Across the curriculum: Transforming the higher education landscape via innovation in AI literacy. *Computers and Education: Artificial Intelligence, 4*, 100127. DOI: 10.1016/j.caeai.2023.100127

Spanellis, A., & Harviainen, J. T. (2021). *Transforming society and organizations through gamification*. Springer International Publishing. DOI: 10.1007/978-3-030-68207-1

Srnicek, N. (2017). *Platform Capitalism*. Polity Press.

Tadimalla, S. Y., & Kunkeler, T. (2024, October). Exploring Capital and Privilege in Computing and Engineering Education Through Gamification. In *2024 IEEE Frontiers in Education Conference (FIE)* (pp. 1-9). IEEE. DOI: 10.1109/FIE61694.2024.10893030

Tan, Z., Zeng, Q., Tian, Y., Liu, Z., Yin, B., & Jiang, M. (2024, November). Democratizing Large Language Models via Personalized Parameter-Efficient Fine-tuning. In *Proceedings of the 2024 Conference on Empirical Methods in Natural Language Processing* (pp. 6476-6491). DOI: 10.18653/v1/2024.emnlp-main.372

Tao, Y., Viberg, O., Baker, R. S., & Kizilcec, R. F. (2024). Cultural bias and cultural alignment of large language models. *PNAS Nexus, 3*(9), pgae346. DOI: 10.1093/pnasnexus/pgae346 PMID: 39290441

Torkamaan, H., Steinert, S., Pera, M. S., Kudina, O., Freire, S. K., Verma, H., Kelly, S., Sekwenz, M.-T., Yang, J., van Nunen, K., Warnier, M., Brazier, F., & Oviedo-Trespalacios, O. (2024). Challenges and future directions for integration of large language models into socio-technical systems. *Behaviour & Information Technology*, •••, 1–20. DOI: 10.1080/0144929X.2024.2431068

Ukwandu, E., Omisade, O., Jones, K., Thorne, S., & Castle, M. (2025). The future of teaching and learning in the context of emerging artificial intelligence technologies. *Futures, 171*, 103616. DOI: 10.1016/j.futures.2025.103616

Van Deursen, A. J., & Van Dijk, J. A. (2019). The first-level digital divide shifts from inequalities in physical access to inequalities in material access. *New Media & Society, 21*(2), 354–375. DOI: 10.1177/1461444818797082 PMID: 30886536

Vaughan, J. W. (2018). Making better use of the crowd: How crowdsourcing can advance machine learning research. *Journal of Machine Learning Research, 18*(193), 1–46.

Vidal, J., Estoquia, C., & Concepcion, M. (2025). Quasi-Development: Access alone to Artificial Intelligence like ChatGPT Is Not Enough.

Vuorikari, R. (2022, June). DigComp helping shape the education ecosystem in Europe. In *Annual Conference of European Distance and E-Learning Network* (pp. 137-143). Cham: Springer International Publishing. DOI: 10.1007/978-3-031-20518-7_11

Warsinsky, S., Schmidt-Kraepelin, M., Thiebes, S., Wagner, M., & Sunyaev, A. (2022, May). Gamified expert annotation systems: meta-requirements and tentative design. In *International Conference on Design Science Research in Information Systems and Technology* (pp. 154-166). Cham: Springer International Publishing. DOI: 10.1007/978-3-031-06516-3_12

Washington, P. (2024). A perspective on crowdsourcing and human-in-the-loop workflows in precision health. *Journal of Medical Internet Research, 26*, e51138. DOI: 10.2196/51138 PMID: 38602750

Wei, J., Wang, X., Schuurmans, D., Bosma, M., Xia, F., Chi, E., & Zhou, D. (2022). Chain-of-thought prompting elicits reasoning in large language models. *Advances in Neural Information Processing Systems, 35*, 24824–24837.

Xenos, M., & Velli, V. (2018, September). A serious game for introducing software engineering ethics to university students. In *International Conference on Interactive Collaborative Learning* (pp. 579-588). Cham: Springer International Publishing.

Xing, X., Wang, W., Ma, L., Yang, W., & Zheng, J. (2025). Lifecycle-Aware code generation: Leveraging Software Engineering Phases in LLMs. *arXiv preprint arXiv:2510.24019.*

Yang, F., Liu, J., & Li, K. (2025). LLM-Guided Reinforcement Learning for Interactive Environments. *Mathematics, 13*(12), 1932. DOI: 10.3390/math13121932

Yankouskaya, A., Babiker, A., Rizvi, S., Alshakhsi, S., Liebherr, M., & Ali, R. (2025). LLM-D12: A Dual-Dimensional Scale of Instrumental and Relational Dependencies on Large Language Models. *ACM Transactions on the Web.*

Zamfirescu-Pereira, J. D., Wong, R. Y., Hartmann, B., & Yang, Q. (2023, April). Why Johnny can't prompt: how non-AI experts try (and fail) to design LLM prompts. In *Proceedings of the 2023 CHI conference on human factors in computing systems* (pp. 1-21). DOI: 10.1145/3544548.3581388

Zhang, Y., & Dong, C. (2024). Exploring the digital transformation of generative ai-assisted foreign language education: A socio-technical systems perspective based on mixed-methods. *Systems*, *12*(11), 462. DOI: 10.3390/systems12110462

Zimmerman, B. J. (2013). Theories of self-regulated learning and academic achievement: An overview and analysis. *Self-regulated learning and academic achievement*, 1-36.

KEY TERMS AND DEFINITIONS

AI Lab: A gamified evaluation environment where users conduct bug hunts, A/B testing, and stress tests to assess robustness, fairness, and reliability of language models.

Data Detective: A human–AI collaborative annotation model in which participants identify bias, errors, and inconsistencies in datasets through investigative, game-inspired tasks.

Ethics Duel Arena: A structured alignment mechanism in which users compare model outputs, justify ethical judgments, and contribute preference data to shape value-sensitive AI behavior.

Gamified LLM Lifecycle: A seven-stage conceptual framework that restructures large language model development as a participatory, game-based ecosystem in which users contribute to data creation, alignment, evaluation, and long-term AI governance.

Human–AI Symbiosis: A collaborative model of interaction in which humans provide contextual judgment and ethical reasoning while AI systems contribute scale, feedback, and pattern recognition.

Open-World Data Quest: A gamified approach to data collection where individuals voluntarily contribute culturally grounded and consent-based data through structured micro-tasks designed as quests.

Prompt Dojo: A progressive learning environment that develops prompt engineering skills through level-based challenges, guided feedback, and community evaluation.

World Builder: A participatory fine-tuning stage where community members iteratively refine, evaluate, and merge model variants, treating model evolution as a transparent and collective process.

XP Passport: A longitudinal record of user contributions, skills, and governance participation that reflects earned influence and sustained engagement within the ecosystem.

ENDNOTES

1 https://commonvoice.mozilla.org/

2 https://scale.com/

3 https://aws.amazon.com/ai/aileague

4 https://docs.aws.amazon.com/sagemaker/

5 https://docs.aws.amazon.com/bedrock/

6 https://thepromptdojo.com/

7 https://arena.ai

Chapter 4
Designing Inclusive Learning Experiences With Generative AI

S. Sriharshaa
SASTRA University, India

Akshay Bhuvaneswari Ramakrishnan
http://orcid.org/0009-0000-1578-0984
Johns Hopkins University, USA

S. Srijanani
http://orcid.org/0009-0008-4233-2958
SASTRA University, India

R. Manikandan
http://orcid.org/0000-0001-6116-2132
SASTRA University, India

S. Magesh
http://orcid.org/0000-0003-2876-7337
Dr. M.G.R. Educational and Research Institute, India

ABSTRACT

The goal of inclusive education is to provide all students with the same opportunities to learn. However, language barriers, disabilities, and lack of access to technology can make it difficult for everyone to participate fully. This chapter discusses how Generative AI (GenAI) can make classrooms more welcoming and open to everyone, especially for students who feel left out or not represented. Teachers can utilize ChatGPT (language generation), Whisper and Indic Whisper (speech-to-text), mT5

DOI: 10.4018/979-8-3373-6063-8.ch004

and NLLB (multilingual translation), and TTS engines (text-to-speech) to make learning more flexible, apply multiple approaches, and fit the needs of each student. We recommend a three-part framework comprising Input, Processing, and Output. With this technology, people who speak different languages can communicate with each other, modify content in real-time, and share it in various ways. In this chapter, we will learn how GenAI can help children with disabilities, children who do not speak much English, and children who do not have much money.

1. INTRODUCTION

Education plays a central role in promoting social mobility, economic participation, and cultural continuity, yet equitable access to quality learning opportunities remains uneven across populations. Becoming a developed nation involves studying, learning, and embracing the contemporary economic environment and business culture. As a result, processes that would drive development need to be in place, foremost among which is the creation of a strong educational system. Education caters to humanity's need for improvement and opens doors to self-employment, culture and civilization. However, the scenario of educating disadvantaged groups remains poor. Many Indigenous communities have remained marginalized, facing social and economic challenges due to their limited access to quality education (UNESCO, 2021; United Nations, 2022). Active participation in cultural preservation and transformation likewise requires an improved level of education, as the mechanization of cultural activities is strongly correlated with higher educational attainment (World Bank 2020).

Therefore, education for all must include Indigenous and disadvantaged learners as well. These issues underscore the importance of designing inclusive education that strives for equality, accessibility, and adaptability for learners at every stage (Holmes et al., 2022; Luckin et al., 2016). The purpose is not to impose a one-size-fits-all system but to create flexible systems that adapt to diverse learning methods (Bulger 2016; Kumar et al. 2021).

With the rapid development of generative AI technologies, new opportunities have emerged to address these gaps in the literature. Tools such as Whisper for speech-to-text (Narayanan et al., 2023; AI4Bharat, 2023), mT5 and NLLB for multilingual translation (Xue et al., 2021; Meta AI, 2022), and ChatGPT/GPT-4 for language comprehension and response generation (Radford et al., 2023; Brown et al., 2020) demonstrate how AI can meaningfully personalize instruction, provide bilingual instructional support, transcribe speech to text (and vice versa), and make complex concepts more accessible in classroom settings (Banerjee & Dey, 2022; Rose & Dalton, 2009). This matter becomes even more urgent as AI becomes central to educational design and delivery. As recent scholarship emphasizes, GenAI tools hold potential to enhance equity, improve access, and tailor learning to the needs of diverse learners worldwide (Holmes, Bialik, & Fadel, 2019; Singh & Gupta, 2025; Melo-López et al., 2025).

This chapter explores the potential of Generative AI (GenAI) to help create inclusive learning environments for marginalized, multilingual, and low-resource learner populations. This chapter discusses some of the main barriers faced by these learners within education, provides details about the available capabilities of GenAI technologies, and presents a layered approach to inclusive learning design. Finally, this chapter presents some of the ethical implications and future directions for this area of research and practice.

2. THE RISE OF GENERATIVE AI IN EDUCATION

Generative AI (GenAI) has rapidly emerged as a transformative force in education, altering the dynamics of content creation, transmission, and adaptation. Unlike ordinary AI applications that rely on rule-based logic or predictions from structured data, GenAI models can generate text in a human-like manner, respond to voice commands, translate languages, summarize content and formulate questions (Raffel et al., 2020; Vaswani et al., 2017; Devlin et al., 2019). These capabilities make them particularly suitable for personalized and accessible learning experiences (Holmes, Bialik, & Fadel, 2019; Kumar et al., 2021). Large Language Models (LLMs), such as ChatGPT, Claude, and Gemini, have already been incorporated into classrooms to answer students' questions, rewrite information at different levels of complexity, and clarify explanations in simplified language (Brown et al., 2023; Brown et al., 2020; Singh & Gupta, 2025). For instance, a high school student struggling with chemistry might pose a challenging question to ChatGPT and receive a response tailored to their learning level, thereby bridging knowledge gaps in real time.

A further powerful tool is Whisper, an open-source speech-to-text system by OpenAI, which enables students to vocalize questions and responses in their native language, providing significant benefits to learners with reading or typing difficulties (Banerjee & Dey, 2023; Banerjee & Dey, 2022). Similarly, Google's mT5 and Meta's NLLB (No Language Left Behind) extend multilingual support by translating curriculum-based content across hundreds of languages, thereby enabling instruction in a learner's first language (Xue et al., 2021; Meta AI, 2022).

These advancements are not merely theoretical in nature. In India, initiatives such as Bhashini and AI4Bharat are developing AI-driven language tools for rural students using regional voice inputs (Muralidhar et al., 2023; AI4Bharat, 2023). Meanwhile, schools in the UK and US have piloted Gen AI-based tutoring systems that provide real-time assistance during self-paced learning (Holmes et al., 2022; Melo-López et al., 2025).

As these technologies become increasingly open-source and widely available, their role in classrooms is expanding. Their real value lies not merely in automation but in enabling human-like interaction, multilingual communication, and adaptive personalization, all of which are crucial for inclusive education (Gupta & Kaul, 2024; Choudhury & Deshmukh, 2022). By enabling real-time adaptation to learner needs, generative AI systems can reduce the linguistic, cognitive, and accessibility barriers that persist in conventional digital learning environments. GenAI serves as a foundational technology for designing equitable, learner-centered educational systems. Table 1 describes how key Gen AI tools support learning through Q&A, speech-to-text conversion and multilingual translation.

Table 1. Technology-enabled learning support tools

Tool	Function	Relevance in Learning
ChatGPT	Natural language Q&A, explanation	Simplifies complex topics
Whisper	Speech-to-text	Helps with voice input and accessibility
mt5	Multilingual text generation	Supports translation for regional learners
NLLB	Language translation (200+ langs	Enables access for minority language users

3. EDUCATIONAL BARRIERS IN DIVERSE LEARNER POPULATIONS

Despite improvements in digital education, many students continue to face significant challenges that hinder their ability to learn effectively. Socioeconomic limitations, language barriers, disabilities, and lack of access to technology and adaptive learning materials often cause these challenges. Designing inclusive learning systems requires an understanding of the unique challenges faced by different learner groups (UNESCO, 2021; United Nations, 2022; Gupta-Kaul, 2024).

3.1 Language Barriers

Individuals who are novices in mainstream languages typically struggle with experiences that are almost exclusively relevant to Hindi and English. For example, a Tamil-language student in a rural school may have trouble engaging with national-level learning platforms that do not provide Tamil content. Even when translated content is available, it often situates the course content too literally and lacks cultural nuance. Consequently, it frequently fails to provide sufficient cultural context for complete understanding (Choudhury & Deshmukh, 2022; Xue et al., 2021; Meta AI, 2022; Muralidhar et al., 2023).

3.2 Disabilities

Students with difficulties in seeing, hearing, or thinking often cannot use regular learning tools effectively. Without assistive technologies such as screen readers, voice interfaces, or simplified text, these learners fall behind their peers. For instance, a student with dyslexia might find text-to-speech content helpful, but most platforms lack this feature by default (Banerjee and Dey, 2022; Kasinathan et al., 2023; Sharma and Kalra, 2020).

3.3 Digital Divide and Connectivity

Students who live in rural areas or areas with low incomes often lack access to smartphones, reliable Internet connections, or the latest digital devices. Due to this digital divide, they are unable to benefit from basic online learning tools. While urban students may have access to a wide range of learning apps, rural students often rely solely on textbooks and community classes (World Bank, 2020; United Nations, 2022; Bardia and Agrawal, 2025).

3.4 Lack of Personalisation in Learning Systems

Although learners progress at different speeds, have varying prior knowledge, and prefer different modes of learning, many current systems provide identical materials to all. This lack of personalization excludes both fast and slow learners, who require more adaptive pathways to learn effectively. Scholars emphasize that AI-powered personalization can better meet the diverse needs of learners, but its widespread implementation remains limited (Bulger et al., 2021; Bulger, 2016; Holmes et al., 2019). These barriers highlight the multidimensional nature of educational exclusion, indicating the need for integrated and inclusive technological approaches rather than isolated interventions.

4. GENAI CAPABILITIES FOR EQUITY IN LEARNING

GenAI, or generative AI, is an effective means of closing educational gaps through tailored content, eliminating language barriers, and allowing people to connect more flexibly (Zawacki-Richter et al., 2019; Dwivedi et al., 2023). They should work better than e-learning systems because they are multimodal, evolve, and are designed for each user (Kasneci et al. 2023). This is invaluable to students who are low-income or have other conditions preventing them from having a strong educational background (Holmes et al. 2019).

Generative AI models have abilities that implementations with rule sets do not have, such as reasoning, translating across many languages, summarizing long portions, or working according to voice or text commands (Bommasani et al., 2021; Dwivedi et al., 2023). This is how they can help make education fair, where students customize their studies rather than having them customized for them (Kasneci et al., 2023):

Speech-to-text models, such as Whisper, can assist learners with reading, typing, and other challenges (Radford et al., 2022). Learners can also utilize multilingual models such as mT5 or NLLB to receive learning materials in their original language (Xue et al. 2021; Costa-jussà et al. 2022). ChatGPT and other large language models can help individuals comprehend ideas or concepts and provide them with various explanations based on their current understanding of the topic (OpenAI, 2023; Dwivedi et al., 2023).To better understand these capabilities, Table 2 maps key Gen AI tools to the challenges they address in terms of inclusion.

Table 2. GenAI tools and their roles in inclusive learning

Tool	Function	Use case Example	Inclusion Benefit
ChatGPT	Text-based Q&A, explanation generator	Explaining science concepts in simpler language	Supports learners with different reading levels or prior knowledge
Whisper	Speech-to-text (automatic speech recognition)	Converting spoken Tamil questions into text input	Helps students with dyslexia, visual impairment, and low literacy
mT5	Multilingual text generation	Translating English learning materials into Tamil or Hindi	Enables access for regional and minority language speakers
NLLB (Meta)	Translation across 200+ languages	Making quizzes available in tribal languages	Supports linguistic minorities and preserves language equity
TTS (Text-to-Speech)	Converts text into spoken audio	Reading out Instructions for visually impaired learners	Improves access for blind or low-vision users
Gemini / Claude	Conversational tutoring with contextual memory	Providing real-time feedback in student writing tasks	Encourages deeper learning and engagement

continued on following page

Table 2. Continued

Tool	Function	Use case Example	Inclusion Benefit
Bark / Tortoise TTS	Advanced voice synthesis (text-to-speech with natural tone)	Reading out storybooks in a child-friendly voice	Enhances engagement for early readers learners
Indic Whisper (AI4Bharat)	Speech recognition for Indian languages	Transcribing Hindi or Tamil speech into accurate text	Localized support for Indian students with limited typing skills

5. FRAMEWORK: DESIGNING ADAPTIVE AND INCLUSIVE LEARNING SYSTEMS

Generative AI can help schools become more equitable and accessible to all the stakeholders. To maximize the benefits of this opportunity, a structured system that acknowledges the diverse needs of learners throughout the experience and utilizes AI to adapt the experience as needed is required. This section describes a three-level system, known as Input, Processing, and Output, which enables GenAI to assist learners and potentially provide a more flexible and accessible learning experience.

5.1 Input Layer: Understanding User Needs

Layer one of the framework collects learner input in various forms.

- Text input, in which learners type in either natural language or local languages,
- Spoken input, where automatic speech recognition (ASR) tools like OpenAI's Whisper and AI4Bharat's Indic Whisper are used,
- Learner contextual data, which captures preferred language, reading level, and some aspects of disability (i.e., vision impaired, speech impaired)
- This layer collects multilingual and multimodal input, thus catering to learners with different language and technology backgrounds.

5.2 Processing Layer: Processing and Adaptation

At the very center of the framework, the processing layer harnesses Gen AI tools to review, generate, and customize the learning content. In particular, the elements of the processing layer are as follows:

- Large Language Models (LLMs) (e.g., ChatGPT, Claude) interpret learners' input as they engage with the learning content, generating descriptions or explanations of the learner input.
- Multilingual models (e.g., mT5 or Meta's NLLB) convert content into the learner's language or, in some instances, simplify the content if the learner's language is not included in the model.
- Personalization algorithms adjust the level of difficulty and visual presentation of information, drawing on the associated learner profile data and the learning engagement history.

Overall, the processing layer facilitates learning by providing content tailored to the learner's language, cognitive level, and needs on demand.

5.3 Output Layer: Delivering Accessible Learning

The final layer produces the generated outputs in various formats.

- Text (simple or in event language)
- Audio using text-to-speech (TTS) engines such as Google TTS, Bark, or Tortoise;
- Visual representations, including breakdowns or diagrams, wherever possible

This layer enables output flexibility for different learners; for example, a student with dyslexia may require audio output, or a multilingual learner may need an explanation in their native language.

5.4 Illustrative Example

A Tamil-speaking student with no knowledge of reading and writing requests knowledge and experience questions about photosynthesis by speaking into their phone. Whisper converts audio inputs into text (Radford et al., 2023). mT5 converts text to basic English to comprehend questions (Xue et al., 2021). ChatGPT uses this information to create shorter explanations (OpenAI, 2023). The output was spoken in Tamil using TTS, making it completely accessible. This scaffolded process demonstrates how Gen AI tools can be applied in inclusive education systems, and this approach can be scaled to a significant extent (Holmes et al., 2022). This pipeline illustrates how various AI models can collaborate to overcome barriers related to language, literacy, and disability (Khalil & Er, 2023). This demonstrates how Gen AI can transform classrooms into inclusive learning spaces where every learner can succeed (Luckin, 2023). Figure 1 depicts the framework for learning using Generative AI.

5.5 Operationalizing the Framework: Turn-Key Checklists

Although the proposed frameworks intend to provide guidelines on how to leverage the potential of Generative AI to facilitate inclusive learning paradigms, it is imperative to provide operational considerations to ensure its practical application and adoption. To this effect, three checklists are proposed to ensure the practical application and adoption of the proposed frameworks by educational institutions and individuals involved in the education process. Tables 3 and 4 provide checklists for various features of Gen AI deployment.

Table 3. Classroom readiness checklist for inclusive GenAI deployment

Component	Checklist Item	Description / Minimum Requirement
Devices	Learner devices	Availability of smartphones, tablets, or computers suitable for text and voice interaction
Audio hardware	Microphone/headset	Built-in or external microphones to support speech-to-text input
Connectivity	Internet bandwidth	Low to medium bandwidth support (2G/3G/4G/Wi-Fi), adaptive to local conditions
Offline support	Offline content cache	Ability to cache lessons, audio explanations, or transcripts for offline access
Platform access	Browser/app compatibility	Compatibility with low-end Android devices and standard web browsers
Power	Charging availability	Access to charging points or shared charging facilities in classrooms

Table 4. Accessibility, governance, and audit checklist for inclusive GenAI systems

Category	Checklist Item	Purpose
Accessibility	Multimodal access (text, audio, captions)	Supports learners with visual, hearing, and reading difficulties
Accessibility	Text-to-Speech (TTS) support	Enables access for low-literacy and visually impaired learners
Accessibility	Language toggle	Allows switching between English and regional or minority languages
Accessibility	Simplified content mode	Adapt learning materials for varied cognitive and reading levels.

continued on following page

Table 4. Continued

Category	Checklist Item	Purpose
Governance	Bias evaluation across groups	Monitors fairness across language, gender, and socioeconomic slices
Governance	Human oversight and override	Enables teachers to correct or moderate AI-generated outputs
Governance	Appeal and feedback mechanism	Allows reporting of incorrect or inappropriate system responses
Governance	Periodic audit and review	Ensures accountability, transparency, and responsible AI use

5.6 Alignment with Educational and Accessibility Standards

In addition, to facilitate adoption by institutions, the proposed framework must adhere to universally adopted pedagogical, accessibility, and learning technology standards. In terms of pedagogical alignment, it adheres to the Universal Design of Learning standards, as it provides multiple channels of engagement, representation, and expression, such as voice and text, in terms of content delivery. From an accessibility point of view, it ensures that the input and output interfaces are compatible with various accessibility standards, including screen readers, keyboards, alternative text, captioning, and text-to-speech functionality, as per WCAG, WAI ARIA, etc. In terms of system alignment, it can be easily integrated into various Learning Management Systems already in use through standard integration frameworks, such as Learning Tools Interoperability and Experience API, so that various learning system usages can also be recorded without having to change existing Learning Management System architectures.

5.7 Low-Resource Deployment Pathways

To be used in low-resource learning environments, the proposed framework contains multiple different ways for it to be rolled out in low-resource scenarios. The tiered-device guidance enables the framework to be used with simple on-device speech recognition and text-to-speech for fundamental interactions, and the cloud-based option can be activated when the user is in an area with reliable Internet service. For users who may not have access to the Internet regularly or have spotty Internet access, the framework provides a way for users to access cached instructional content, send asynchronous voice queries, and communicate using text as alternatives to online connectivity. In addition, users could exploit various available operational funding and access mechanisms - for example, community learning centers available in the community - and develop appropriate shared-device pool models or school-based lending models to lessen the financial and access burden on individual students while promoting equitable access for all students.

Figure 1. Inclusive learning framework using generative AI

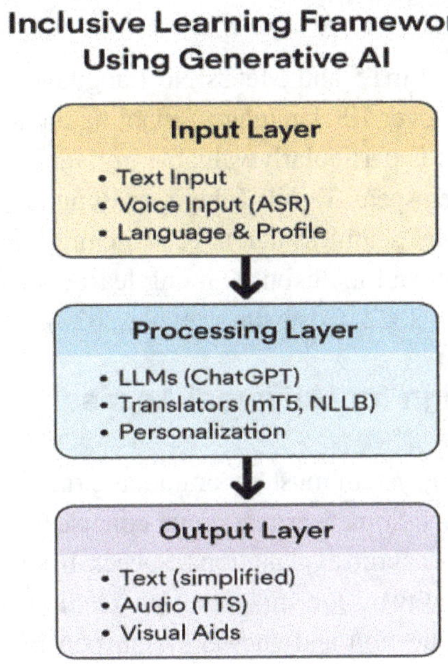

6. VOICE, LANGUAGE, AND MULTIMODAL INTERACTION FOR ACCESSIBILITY

Multimodal interaction, which combines voice, text, images, and gestures, has emerged as a key enabler of educational inclusivity. When integrated with Generative AI (GenAI), these interactions enable students with linguistic, physical, or cognitive challenges to access and engage with learning materials more effectively.

6.1 The Role of Voice Interfaces

Voice-based systems reduce reliance on continuous reading and provide accessibility for students with visual impairments. Natural language processing (NLP) enables students to communicate and consume content via speech. For example, text-to-speech (TTS) systems, such as Google TTS or Bark, can convert learning materials into spoken form, helping learners with visual disabilities or reading problems. Voice interfaces remove barriers to participation in traditional screen-based learning environments (Kumar et al., 2023).

6.2 Multilingual Accessibility

GenAI models, such as mT5 and Meta's No Language Left Behind (NLLB), support translation across over 100 languages, enabling the real-time translation of classroom materials. This is particularly valuable in multilingual contexts such as India, where students often speak Tamil, Telugu, or Bengali as their first language. Multilingual GenAI enables seamless language switching in bilingual classrooms, promoting comprehension and inclusivity among learners from diverse linguistic backgrounds (Goyal et al., 2022; Costa-Jussà et al., 2022).

6.3 Multimodal Design for Universal Access

An inclusive education system must accommodate the diverse learning preferences and needs of students. Some learners prefer concise text summaries, whereas others benefit from visual or audio explanations. Speech-based explanations provide an alternative learning pathway for students with reading or vision difficulties. Furthermore, interactive question-and-answer systems enable learners to engage in their preferred learning modality, fostering a deeper understanding of the material. GenAI-powered multimodal systems can thus personalize learning by offering flexible combinations of text, visuals, and audio to ensure universal access. Figure.2 Illustrates the multimodal interaction cycle enabled by Generative AI.

Figure 2. Multimodal interaction cycle in generative AI

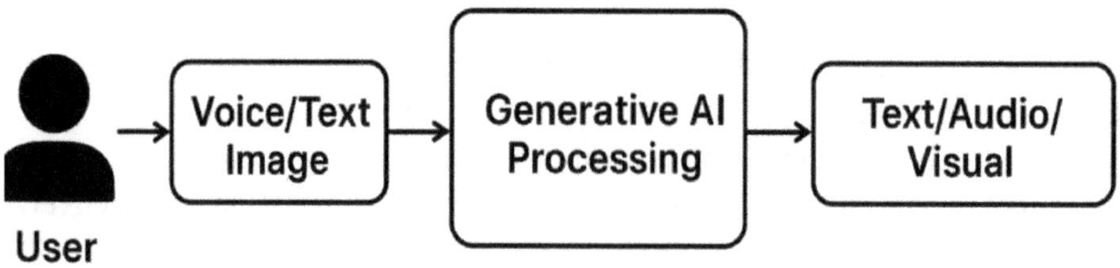

6.4 Measuring the Impact of Inclusive GenAI Systems

Although an assessment of Generative AI technology-enhanced Inclusive Learning Systems is made using subjective criteria, it is important to note that effectiveness must also be measured quantitatively. Accordingly, to facilitate learning centers/ institutions/teachers/educators, a metrics starter pack along with an example of a mini-case is presented. Even though the proposed frameworks intend to provide guidelines on how to leverage the potential of Generative AI to facilitate inclusive learning paradigms, it is imperative to provide operational considerations to ensure its practical application and adoption. To this effect, three checklists are proposed to ensure the practical application and adoption of the proposed frameworks by educational institutions and individuals involved in the education process.

Table 5. Metrics starter pack for evaluating inclusive GenAI systems

Metric	Purpose
Word Error Rate (WER)	Measures speech-to-text accuracy
Coverage	Indicates percentage of learners supported
Latency	Reflects system response time
Usage frequency	Shows learner adoption and engagement
Equity delta	Captures learning gains for marginalized learners

6.5 Role of Educators in Moderating Multimodal GenAI Interactions

Generative AI tools are multimodal and allow flexible access to learning through voice, text, and language. Generative AI can be used in classrooms; however, teacher input is necessary for its use with Generative AI tools. In this capacity, teachers are human-in-the-loop moderators who approve the output produced by the AI to verify that the information is accurate, age-appropriate, and culturally and curriculum aligned. With multilingual and voice-based interactions, teachers can identify errors made by the system during speech recognition by translating them into other languages and literally and contextually clarifying AI-generated responses as needed. If an AI-generated response is inaccurate, unclear, or pedagogically invalid, the teacher may modify or update it to maintain instructional integrity. In addition, teachers can create consistent and responsible behaviors for generative AI tools by using structured and consistent prompt templates to guide their interactions with AI. By using these types of teacher-moderated methods with generative AI, both accessibility and inclusion can be improved while allowing the teacher to maintain pedagogical control.

7. GENAI FOR LOW-RESOURCE AND LINGUISTIC MINORITY STUDENTS

Students in many rural or low socioeconomic status (SES) settings face a multitude of issues, including inadequate Internet access, a lack of digital devices, and insufficiently trained teachers to use them. GenAI tools can help address some of these issues as on-demand learning resources that are always available (Banerjee & Dey, 2022; Rose & Dalton, 2009; United Nations, 2022). For example, educational apps operating on mobile devices with small LLMs or speech models could potentially provide instant explanations, even with limited Internet access or bandwidth (Raffel et al., 2020; Xue et al., 2021; Brown et al., 2020). Speech recognition tools (e.g., Whisper and Indic Whisper) are invaluable in these instances because they allow students to speak instead of typing on a QWERTY keyboard or using any text input (Narayanan et al., 2023; AI4Bharat, 2023; Sharma & Kalra, 2020). Reducing reliance on infrastructure and reaching students who would never or cannot learn digitally at any other time is important (Holmes et al., 2022; World Bank, 2020).

7.1 Enhancing Access for Linguistic Minority Students

The use of multiple languages poses a considerable challenge to inclusive education in the following ways. Students who communicate in endangered languages or those limited to specific regions find it challenging to understand courses conducted primarily in English or Hindi (Choudhury & Deshmukh, 2022; Sahu, 2025). Multilingual GenAI models, such as mT5, NLLB from Meta, and Bhashini, which is based in India, help address this gap by enabling people to translate and create content in multiple Indian and global languages (Xue et al., 2021; Meta AI, 2022; Muralidhar et al., 2023). These tools enable learners to access information in their own language, pose questions, and have responses remain in their native language, thereby expanding their understanding of concepts in their own language. GenAI can also support bilingual or multilingual classrooms by presenting content in multiple languages (Kasinathan et al., 2023; Gupta & Kaul, 2024).

7.2 Built-in Personalisation for Equity

Even in groups with few resources or people who speak a minority language, learners have very different levels of prior knowledge, learning speeds, and ways of accessing information (Banerjee & Dey, 2016; Banerjee & Dey, 2022). GenAI models can dynamically adjust their output by altering the level of detail in their explanations, choosing between text and audio, and simplifying complex definitions (Holmes, Bialik, & Fadel, 2019; Kumar et al., 2021; Bardia & Agrawal, 2025). This ability allows each student to receive information in their preferred format. Personalization is particularly significant in areas where teachers cannot or do not provide individual support, making Gen AI a strong tool for equitable education (Singh & Gupta, 2025; Melo-López et al., 2025).

8. ETHICAL, SOCIAL AND TECHNICAL LIMITATIONS

Generative AI (GenAI) can transform learning into a more inclusive experience; however, its implementation also presents significant ethical, social, and technical challenges. These issues must be addressed meticulously to ensure that AI-enhanced education is equitable, accountable, and sustainable.

8.1 Ethical Concerns-Bias and Fairness

Generative AI models learn from large amounts of data gathered from the Internet, which often contain historical and societal biases. Consequently, these systems risk unintentionally amplifying existing stereotypes related to race, gender, caste, and language. Generative AI models, such as AI-powered tutors, may use biased restatements towards one gender, package examples that reflect the most common language rules, or discriminate against groups that are already underrepresented. To ensure that content generation is free of bias, a large amount of representative training data and strong tools for bias detection are required.

8.2 Social Concerns: Over-Reliance and Cultural Sensitivity

The fear of dependence on automated tools is a growing concern for both learners and educators in AI-enhanced educational settings. Learners and educators may treat AI-generated content as independent learning without questioning its accuracy, which can potentially lead to misinformation and misunderstandings (Bender & Friedman, 2018; Zou & Schiebinger, 2018; Suresh & Guttag, 2019). AI tools that lack cultural awareness cannot adequately interpret idioms or regional variations in meaning, particularly in multilingual contexts (Choudhury & Deshmukh, 2022; Kasinathan et al., 2023). Translation models may produce overly literal translations that omit cultural nuances, confusing and reducing learners' engagement (Meta AI, 2022; Xue et al., 2021; Muralidhar et al., 2023).

8.3 Technical Limitations: Accessibility and Infrastructure Gaps

Although GenAI tools are highly scalable, they face significant usability challenges in low-resource settings such as healthcare. Many of these tools require reliable Internet connectivity, substantial processing power, and ongoing updates, which may be unavailable in rural or underdeveloped areas (Banerjee & Dey, 2022; United Nations, 2022; Rose & Dalton, 2009). Additionally, speech models may perform poorly when confronted with accents, dialects or environmental noise (Narayanan et al., 2023; AI4Bharat, 2023; Sharma & Kalra, 2020). Most models currently support only major languages, leaving hundreds of tribal or regional languages spoken by millions of learners underrepresented or inadequately modeled (Xue et al., 2021; Meta AI, 2022; Muralidhar et al., 2023).

9. DIRECTIONS FOR SCALABLE, INCLUSIVE AI TOOLS IN EDUCATION

To leverage the use of Generative AI in schools, new tools must be intentionally designed for extensibility, inclusivity, and longevity (Holmes, Bialik, & Fadel, 2019; Luckin et al., 2016; Banerjee & Dey, 2022). A key goal is to develop AI models that are compact, multilingual, and functional in low-resource contexts, particularly in situations with limited Internet access or where mobile devices are the primary option (Xue et al. 2021; Muralidhar et al. 2023; Sahu 2025). This ensures that students in remote or under-resourced areas are not disadvantaged. Another important focus is the creation of open-source educational datasets and models tailored to regional languages and curricula, allowing local communities to develop culturally relevant solutions (Choudhury & Deshmukh, 2022; Kasinathan et al., 2023). Future tools should include adaptive learning paths that continuously adjust to each student's learning needs, capacities, and interests (Kumar et al., 2021; Bardia & Agrawal, 2025). For students with disabilities, systems must be controllable via voice, touch, and vision while maintaining performance comparable to the standard interaction design (Sharma & Kalra, 2020; Banerjee & Dey, 2022). Governments, edtech companies, teachers, and AI researchers must collaborate to create classrooms in which Gen AI is used ethically and effectively. If designed and deployed fairly, scalable AI tools can provide a truly personalized and universal educational experience (Singh & Gupta, 2025; Melo-López et al., 2025).

10. CONCLUSION

Generative AI has the potential to improve education by democratizing, personalizing, and enhancing accessibility for individual learners (Banerjee & Fadel, 2019; Luckin et al., 2016; Banerjee & Dey, 2022). This chapter highlights several AI tools that can help reduce barriers for students facing language, cognitive, physical, or socioeconomic challenges. Examples include multilingual large language models, speech-based interaction interfaces, and multimodal content delivery systems that support learners left behind by traditional educational pathways (Xue et al. 2021; Narayanan et al. 2023; Sahu 2025). It is essential to design these tools ethically to ensure cultural relevance and fairness for all students (Choudhury and Deshmukh, 2022; Kasinathan et al., 2023). Pedagogical platforms can support learners from diverse backgrounds if AI development follows protocols grounded in universal design, equity and diversity recognition (Singh & Gupta, 2025; Melo-López et al., 2025). To responsibly create such innovative educational platforms, collaboration among educators, governments, technology developers, and communities is crucial (Holmes et al., 2022; Bardia and Agrawal, 2025). Generative AI can help illuminate pathways towards an educational landscape in which equity is the fundamental principle of every learning experience.

Through the study of educational barriers, assessment of the capabilities of Generative AI, and development of an adaptive and inclusive learning framework, this chapter emphasizes the potential of GenAI to be designed in a way that is beneficial to marginalized and multilingual learners. When integrated with ethical guidelines, these systems provide scalable solutions for more inclusive learning environments.

REFERENCES

Banerjee, A., & Dey, D. (2022). Speech-to-text and text-to-speech systems for inclusive education in India. *IEEE Access : Practical Innovations, Open Solutions, 10*, 121456–121468. DOI: 10.1109/ACCESS.2022.3222563

Bardia, A., & Agrawal, A. (2025). MindCraft: Revolutionizing education through AI-powered personalized learning and mentorship in rural India. *arXiv preprint arXiv:2502.05826*. https://doi.org//arXiv.2502.05826DOI: 10.48550

Bender, E. M., & Friedman, B. (2018). Data statements for NLP: Toward mitigating system bias and enabling better science. *Transactions of the Association for Computational Linguistics, 6*, 587–604. DOI: 10.1162/tacl_a_00041

Brown, T. B., Mann, B., Ryder, N., Subbiah, M., Kaplan, J., Dhariwal, P., & Amodei, D. (2020). Language models are few-shot learning models. *Advances in Neural Information Processing Systems, 33*, 1877–1901. DOI: 10.48550/arXiv.2005.14165

Bulger, M. (2016). *Personalized learning: The conversations we are not having*. Data & Society Research Institute. DOI: 10.69985/OBUE9001

Choudhury, M., & Deshmukh, A. (2022). Designing linguistic diversity in AI systems. *Proceedings of CHI 2022 Workshops*. DOI: 10.48550/arXiv.2203.12632

Devlin, J., Chang, M.-W., Lee, K., & Toutanova, K. (2019). BERT: Pre-training of deep bidirectional transformers for language understanding. In *Proceedings of NAACL-HLT 2019* (pp. 4171–4186). Association for Computational Linguistics. DOI: 10.48550/arXiv.1810.04805

Gupta, M., & Kaul, S. (2024). AI in inclusive education: A systematic review of opportunities and challenges in the Indian context. *MIER Journal of Educational Studies Trends & Practices, 14*(2), 429–461. DOI: 10.52634/mier/2024/v14/i2/2702

Holmes, W., Bialik, M., & Fadel, C. (2019). *Artificial intelligence in education: Promises and implications for teaching and learning*. Center for Curriculum Redesign.

Holmes, W., Persson, J., Choi, J., & Maeda, Y. (2022). *Artificial intelligence and the future of teaching and learning: Insights and recommendations*. US Department of Education.

Kasinathan, G.. (2023). Inclusive AI: Bridging language, disability, and digital divides in Indian classrooms. *International Journal of Inclusive Education*. Advance online publication. DOI: 10.1080/13603116.2023.2184212

Kumar, V., Singh, V., Pandey, A., & Tiwari, P. (2021). AI-powered personalized learning systems: A review. *International Journal of Educational Technology in Higher Education, 18*(1), 1–23. DOI: 10.1186/s41239-021-00292-2 PMID: 34926790

Luckin, R., Holmes, W., Griffiths, M., & Forcier, L. B. (2016). *Intelligence unleashed: An argument for AI in education*. Pearson Education.

. Melo-López, V.-A., Basantes-Andrade, A., Gudiño-Mejía, C.-B., & Hernández-Martínez, E. (2025). The impact of artificial intelligence on inclusive education: A systematic review. *Education Sciences, 15*(5), Towardsttps://DOI: 10.3390/educsci15050539

Meta, A. I. (2022). No language left behind (NLLB): Scaling human-centered machine translation. *arXiv preprint arXiv:2207.04672*. https://doi.org//arXiv.2207.04672DOI: 10.48550

Muralidhar, S., Srinivasan, A., Jha, A., & Kumar, P. (2023). Bhashini: Enabling inclusive AI in the Indian language. *arXiv preprint arXiv:2305.15207*. https://doi.org//arXiv.2305.15207DOI: 10.48550

Open, A. I. (2023). GPT-4 technical report. *arXiv preprint arXiv:2303.08774*. https://doi.org//arXiv.2303.08774DOI: 10.48550

Radford, A., Kim, J. W., Xu, T., Brockman, G., McLeavey, C., & Sutskever, I. (2023). Robust speech recognition via large-scale weak supervision (Whisper). *arXiv preprint arXiv:2212.04356*. https://doi.org//arXiv.2212.04356DOI: 10.48550

Raffel, C., Shazeer, N., Roberts, A., Lee, K., Narang, S., Matena, M., & Liu, P. J. (2020). Exploring the limits of transfer learning with a unified text-to-text transformer. *Journal of Machine Learning Research, 21*(140), 1–67. DOI: 10.5555/3455716.3455856

Rose, D. H., & Dalton, B. (2009). Learning to read in the digital age. *Mind, Brain and Education : the Official Journal of the International Mind, Brain, and Education Society, 3*(2), 74–83. DOI: 10.1111/j.1751-228X.2009.01057.x

Sahu, P. (2025). AI and digital tools supporting multilingual primary education in India. *International Journal of Multidisciplinary Educational Research, 14*(5[2]). Advance online publication. DOI: 10.5281/zenodo.10982345

Sharma, G., & Kalra, A. (2020). Designing accessible voice user interfaces for low-literacy users. In *Proceedings of IDC 2020* (pp. 77–88). ACM. DOI: 10.1145/3392063.3394431

Singh, A., & Gupta, P. (2025). Perspective of generative AI for UNESCO inclusive education. *SSRN*. DOI: 10.2139/ssrn.5181859

Suresh, H., & Guttag, J. V. (2019). A framework for understanding the unintended consequences of machine learning. *Communications of the ACM, 63*(11), 62–71. DOI: 10.1145/3376897

UNESCO. (2021). *Reimagining our futures together: A new social contract for education*. UNESCO Publishing.

. United Nations. (2022). *Digital inclusion for all: Bridging the digital divide.*

Vaswani, A., Shazeer, N., Parmar, N., Uszkoreit, J., Jones, L., Gomez, A. N., & Polosukhin, I. (2017). Attention is all you need. *Advances in Neural Information Processing Systems, 30*. Advance online publication. DOI: 10.48550/arXiv.1706.03762

. World Bank. (2020). *The COVID-19 pandemic: Shocks to education and policy responses.*

Xue, L., Constant, N., Roberts, A., Kale, M., Al-Rfou, R., Siddhant, A., & Raffel, C. (2021). mT5: A massively multilingual pre-trained text-to-text transformer. In *Proceedings of NAACL 2021*. DOI: 10.18653/v1/2021.naacl-main.41

Zou, J. Y., & Schiebinger, L. (2018). AI can be sexist and racist; it is time to make it fair. *Nature, 559*(7714), 324–326. DOI: 10.1038/d41586-018-05707-8 PMID: 30018439

Chapter 5
Assessment and Feedback Through Generative AI Intelligent Tutoring Systems

Rupam Hazra
http://orcid.org/0009-0003-0332-2128
Global Institute of Management and Technology, Krishnanagar, India

Parag Chatterjee
http://orcid.org/0000-0003-1243-9582
Global Institute of Management and Technology, Krishnanagar, India

Soumen Ghosh
http://orcid.org/0009-0008-3778-6090
Global Institute of Management and Technology, Krishnanagar, India

ABSTRACT

This chapter explores how Generative AI (GenAI) is transforming assessment and feedback in education through Intelligent Tutoring Systems (ITS). As learning shifts toward more personalized, inclusive, and data-driven approaches, GenAI enables real-time adaptive feedback, conversational learning, and dynamic assessment tailored to individual needs. It examines the integration of GenAI technologies—like natural language processing—into ITS architectures to create personalized, context-aware evaluations. Ethical concerns such as bias, transparency, and inclusion are addressed, emphasizing the need for human-AI collaboration. Case studies from K–12, higher education, and vocational training highlight practical applications. The chapter also discusses how GenAI, supported by learning analytics and forma-

DOI: 10.4018/979-8-3373-6063-8.ch005

tive assessment, can move evaluation beyond summative tests toward continuous, learner-centered progress tracking. Ultimately, GenAI is presented as a powerful tool for deeper learning and meaningful feedback—provided it is developed responsibly and with strong educator engagement.

1. INTRODUCTION

The landscape of education is undergoing a profound transformation, driven by advances in artificial intelligence—particularly the emergence of Generative AI (GenAI). As traditional modes of assessment struggle to keep pace with the complexities of personalized and competency-based learning, GenAI offers a compelling opportunity to reimagine how we evaluate and support learners. Intelligent Tutoring Systems (ITS), once confined to rigid rule-based interactions, are now being revitalized through the integration of generative models capable of producing real-time, context-aware feedback and dialogue. These developments mark a shift from one-size-fits-all testing to dynamic, adaptive, and inclusive learning ecosystems. This chapter introduces the foundational ideas underpinning GenAI's role in transforming assessment and feedback. It explores how GenAI enhances the personalization, scalability, and equity of ITS by enabling natural language interactions, real-time learner modeling, and content generation tailored to individual progress. The chapter also frames the challenges ahead, including algorithmic bias, data ethics, and the need for transparent, explainable AI systems in education. Most importantly, it highlights the critical importance of human-AI collaboration—ensuring that GenAI supports, rather than supplants, the pedagogical insight, empathy, and judgment of educators. By contextualizing these emerging technologies within broader educational goals, this chapter sets the stage for a deeper examination of how GenAI can meaningfully enhance learning outcomes, empower educators, and create more equitable and responsive assessment environments in the digital age.

2. FOUNDATIONS OF INTELLIGENT TUTORING SYSTEMS (ITS)

Intelligent Tutoring Systems (ITS) represent a significant milestone in the evolution of educational technologies, designed to simulate the one-on-one guidance of a human tutor by adapting instruction to the needs of individual learners. Rooted in cognitive science, artificial intelligence, and learning theory, ITS aim to personalize the learning experience by dynamically analyzing learner responses, identifying knowledge gaps, and delivering targeted instructional support. Traditionally, these systems are composed of four key components: the domain model (which defines the subject knowledge), the learner model (which tracks the student's evolving understanding), the pedagogical model (which determines the teaching strategy), and the user interface (which facilitates interaction). Over time, ITS have evolved from rule-based systems to more flexible architectures that integrate machine learning, natural language processing, and data-driven analytics to support more nuanced forms of assessment and feedback.

Artificial intelligence in education matures in systems referred to as "intelligent tutors," advancing beyond conventional computer-assisted instruction. Computer-assisted instruction advances to intelligent tutoring systems (ITSs) by meeting three criteria of intelligence (Polson & Richardson, 2013). As education shifts toward more personalized, competency-based models, the foundational structure of ITS provides a critical framework for integrating generative AI, enabling more dynamic, conversational, and responsive learning environments that reflect the complex needs of diverse learners.

A. Evolution and Architecture of ITS

Initially, ITS followed fixed scripts and decision trees, offering limited adaptability to individual learners. With advances in artificial intelligence, especially in machine learning and natural language processing, modern ITS can now personalize learning pathways, adapt to student responses in real time, and provide more natural, conversational interactions. The genetic architecture refers to the configuration of genetic factors that contribute to the development and regulation of a particular phenotypic trait, as well as its associated variability characteristics(Hansen,2006). The architecture of ITS has also become more modular, typically including four main components: the domain model (what is being taught), the student model (what the learner knows), the tutor model (how to teach), and the user interface (how the system communicates). GenAI further enhances this architecture by enabling dynamic feedback generation, nuanced learner modeling, and greater flexibility in instructional dialogue.

a) AI-Enhanced Personalization

Generative AI empowers ITS to deliver truly personalized learning by analyzing a student's performance, behavior, and preferences in real time. Unlike traditional systems, which provide the same feedback to all users, GenAI can tailor explanations, hints, and practice problems to suit individual learning styles and levels of understanding. It can simulate human-like dialogue, allowing students to ask questions and receive contextually relevant responses, creating a more engaging learning experience. This level of personalization helps identify learning gaps early and adapt instruction accordingly, leading to improved outcomes. Over time, the system becomes more refined as it gathers data, continuously enhancing its ability to support each learner uniquely.

b) Modular System Design

The architecture of modern ITS is based on interconnected modules—each with a specific function—that work together to deliver effective instruction. The domain model holds the subject matter content, while the student model tracks a learner's current knowledge and misconceptions. The tutor model uses this information to decide what and how to teach next, and the user interface presents this content in an accessible, often interactive, format. GenAI enhances this modularity by improving the accuracy of learner modeling and enabling the generation of personalized, context-aware feedback within the tutor model. This modular, flexible design also makes it easier to update or expand individual components as educational needs evolve or new AI capabilities become available.

B. Traditional vs. AI-Driven Tutoring Models

Traditional tutoring models—whether in-person or digital—often follow linear, one-size-fits-all instructional pathways with limited adaptability to individual learners' needs. These systems typically rely on pre-programmed rules or static content sequences, which can lead to disengagement or unmet learning goals when students struggle or advance at different paces. In contrast, AI-driven tutoring models powered by GenAI can dynamically adjust instruction, content delivery, and feedback based on real-time analysis of learner behavior, performance, and preferences. In contrast to conventional educational frameworks, ITS promotes a learner-focused method, allowing students to advance at their own speed while obtaining personalized support(Ali,2024). These systems simulate human-like adaptability by diagnosing misconceptions, offering personalized hints, and modifying difficulty levels to support ongoing growth. As a result, AI-driven tutoring not only increases instructional efficiency but also promotes a more equitable and personalized learning experience for diverse learners.

a) Static vs. Dynamic Instruction

Traditional systems deliver static instruction, meaning all students receive the same sequence of lessons, regardless of their prior knowledge or learning speed. This often results in boredom for advanced learners and frustration for those who need more support. AI-driven models, however, enable dynamic instruction that adjusts content difficulty, pacing, and feedback in real time. By continuously analyzing a learner's input and progress, the system selects the most appropriate next step to keep the learner challenged but supported. This responsiveness fosters more effective learning and better retention.

b) Limited Feedback vs. Adaptive Support

In traditional tutoring, feedback is often limited to right-or-wrong answers, lacking depth or personalization. Students may not understand why they made a mistake or how to improve. AI-driven tutoring systems overcome this by offering rich, adaptive feedback tailored to the specific error or misconception. GenAI can provide detailed explanations, generate targeted practice problems, or rephrase content in simpler terms based on the learner's needs. This type of feedback helps learners reflect, self-correct, and build confidence over time.

C. Core Components: Learner Modeling, Instructional Planning, and Feedback Delivery

At the heart of Intelligent Tutoring Systems (ITS) are three core components that drive effective personalization: learner modeling, instructional planning, and feedback delivery. Learner modeling involves continuously analyzing and updating a profile of the student's knowledge, skills, misconceptions, and learning preferences. Instructional planning uses this profile to determine the most appropriate content, strategies, and sequencing of instruction. A challenge for educators is creating educational systems that equip students to succeed in a constantly evolving world (Tucci & Hursh, 1991). Feedback delivery, in turn, provides timely and targeted guidance that supports learning and fosters metacognition. Together, these components enable ITS—especially when enhanced by GenAI—to create highly responsive, adaptive learning environments that evolve in real time with each learner's needs.

a) Learner Modeling

Learner modeling is the process of creating a dynamic, data-driven representation of a student's current understanding, progress, and learning behaviours. Traditional systems often rely on static assessments, but AI-enhanced ITS continuously gather input from student interactions to refine this model in real time. GenAI allows for more nuanced modeling by capturing subtle cues such as hesitation, error patterns, or natural language input. This enables a deeper understanding of the learner's cognitive state, misconceptions, and affective needs. As the model evolves, it informs every subsequent instructional and feedback decision made by the system.

b) Instructional Planning

Instructional planning refers to how the ITS determines what to teach, when to teach it, and how to present it most effectively. Using data from the learner model, GenAI helps select optimal learning paths and adjust instructional strategies to align with individual student goals and abilities. It can identify prerequisite gaps, prioritize learning objectives, and sequence content accordingly. GenAI can even simulate instructional decision-making similar to a human tutor, customizing support based on both short-term needs and long-term learning goals. This level of planning ensures instruction remains targeted, flexible, and learner-centered.

c) Feedback Delivery

Feedback delivery is a critical component that directly influences learner engagement and understanding. While traditional systems often provide basic right-or-wrong responses, GenAI enables rich, context-sensitive feedback that explains *why* an answer is correct or incorrect. It can also suggest alternate strategies, clarify misunderstandings, or generate examples tailored to the learner's level and style. Feedback is delivered in a timely, conversational manner, increasing its impact on student learning. By aligning feedback with the learner model and instructional plan, GenAI ensures that every response contributes meaningfully to growth and retention.

3. GENERATIVE AI AND ITS INTEGRATION INTO ITS

Generative AI (GenAI) introduces transformative capabilities to Intelligent Tutoring Systems (ITS) by enabling more natural, adaptive, and scalable interactions between learners and machines. Unlike traditional ITS, which rely heavily on predefined rules and static feedback, GenAI models—such as large language models—can generate real-time, context-sensitive responses that simulate human-like tutoring. This advancement significantly enhances the system's ability to engage learners through personalized dialogue, Socratic questioning, and tailored content creation. GenAI also strengthens the learner model by interpreting open-ended inputs, identifying patterns in language use, and dynamically adjusting instructional strategies based on learner progress. For example, a GenAI-powered ITS can provide scaffolding for complex problem-solving, summarize student responses, or reframe explanations based on prior misconceptions—all in natural language. Integration with multimodal capabilities further expands these systems to include visual and auditory feedback, making them more inclusive and accessible. Additionally, generative AI can occasionally generate results that exceed normal human abilities

(Zhong, 2024). However, successful integration of GenAI into ITS also requires careful attention to transparency, explainability, and alignment with pedagogical goals. As such, GenAI-enhanced ITS are not only a leap forward in technological sophistication but also a reimagining of how digital systems can support human-centered, responsive, and equitable learning.

A. Capabilities of GenAI: Language, Reasoning, and Adaptivity

Generative AI brings powerful capabilities that significantly enhance Intelligent Tutoring Systems (ITS) through advanced language understanding, sophisticated reasoning, and adaptive learning processes. Its natural language processing (NLP) allows systems to interpret, generate, and engage in human-like conversations, making interactions more intuitive and accessible for learners. Beyond language, GenAI demonstrates complex reasoning abilities that enable it to analyze problems, infer student misconceptions, and devise effective instructional strategies. Generative AI (GenAI) is essential in enhancing personalized education by dynamically customizing learning resources to meet students' individual needs and skills (Huynh & McNamara, 2025). Adaptivity is a key strength, as GenAI continuously adjusts content, feedback, and pacing based on ongoing learner data and contextual factors. Together, these capabilities enable ITS to deliver personalized, responsive, and scalable education tailored to diverse learner needs.

a) Advanced Language Understanding

GenAI's proficiency in natural language processing allows ITS to understand student queries, explanations, and even emotional cues expressed through text. This enables conversational interfaces where learners can ask questions in their own words and receive meaningful, context-aware responses. It also supports the generation of explanations, examples, and feedback in clear, natural language tailored to individual comprehension levels. Such language flexibility makes learning more engaging and reduces barriers caused by rigid or overly technical system prompts.

b) Sophisticated Reasoning

GenAI models can perform complex reasoning tasks, such as diagnosing errors, predicting misconceptions, and selecting the most effective instructional interventions. By simulating human-like cognitive processes, the system can analyze multiple factors simultaneously, including learner history, task difficulty, and learning objectives. This reasoning capability allows ITS to provide targeted hints, scaffold difficult concepts, and adapt challenges to optimize learning outcomes. As a result,

GenAI-powered ITS function more like expert human tutors, offering deeper support beyond rote instruction.

c) Continuous Adaptivity

One of GenAI's most impactful features is its ability to adapt continuously to learner behavior and context in real time. This means adjusting content difficulty, feedback style, and pacing dynamically based on immediate performance data and evolving learner needs. Unlike static or scheduled interventions, this adaptivity fosters more responsive and personalized learning experiences that can accommodate diverse learning speeds and styles. Over time, as the system gathers more data, it refines its adaptive strategies to become even more precise and effective.

B. Natural Language Processing for Conversational Learning

Natural Language Processing (NLP) is a cornerstone capability of Generative AI that enables Intelligent Tutoring Systems (ITS) to support conversational learning. Through NLP, ITS can understand and interpret learner inputs expressed in everyday language, making interactions more natural and intuitive. This allows students to ask questions, explain their thinking, and receive personalized, context-aware responses in real time. In the era of digital communication, straightforward and dependable human-machine interaction has emerged as a vital issue. Natural Language Processing has been crucial in advancing the field of conversational artificial intelligence (Bataineh et al., 2023). Conversational learning facilitated by NLP promotes active engagement, helps learners articulate their understanding, and encourages deeper reflection. Additionally, NLP supports multilingual and inclusive learning environments by adapting communication styles and content to diverse linguistic and cultural backgrounds.

a) Understanding Learner Input

NLP enables ITS to process diverse student inputs, including questions, explanations, and even errors, by interpreting the meaning behind natural language expressions. This helps the system identify specific misconceptions or knowledge gaps rather than just assessing right-or-wrong answers. By recognizing nuances in learner language, ITS can tailor responses that directly address the student's current thought process and needs. This level of understanding fosters more meaningful, individualized dialogue and reduces learner frustration. It also supports a more flexible, learner-driven interaction style, empowering students to guide their own learning.

b) Generating Personalized Responses

Using advanced language generation, NLP allows ITS to craft responses that are clear, relevant, and tailored to each learner's context. The system can explain concepts in simpler terms, offer examples, or rephrase questions based on the learner's proficiency and prior interactions. This personalization makes feedback more accessible and effective, supporting comprehension and retention. Moreover, the conversational tone encourages learners to stay engaged and motivated, simulating the experience of interacting with a skilled human tutor. By adapting communication dynamically, NLP-driven ITS create a supportive, dialogic learning environment.

C. Creating Dialogue Agents for Developmental Feedback and Socratic Inquiry

Dialogue agents powered by Generative AI play a crucial role in providing formative feedback and facilitating Socratic questioning within Intelligent Tutoring Systems (ITS). These agents engage learners in meaningful, guided conversations that promote critical thinking and self-reflection rather than simply delivering answers. By asking open-ended, thought-provoking questions, dialogue agents encourage students to explore underlying concepts and articulate their reasoning. Formative feedback is delivered in a timely, personalized manner, helping learners identify misconceptions and deepen understanding. The Socratic method, valued for its ability to enhance critical thinking and promote profound understanding, has acquired new importance in the age of AI (Chukhlomin,2024). This conversational approach supports metacognition and active learning, fostering deeper engagement and long-term knowledge retention.

a) Facilitating Socratic Questioning

Dialogue agents use Socratic questioning techniques to stimulate learners' thinking and guide them toward discovering answers independently. Instead of providing direct solutions, the agent poses carefully designed questions that challenge assumptions, highlight contradictions, and encourage explanation. This method helps students develop problem-solving skills and promotes a deeper grasp of subject matter. By adapting questions based on learner responses, the agent creates a personalized learning dialogue that respects each student's pace and cognitive level. This reflective process builds critical thinking and self-directed learning abilities.

b) Delivering Formative Feedback

Formative feedback through dialogue agents is interactive, context-aware, and responsive to learner input in real time. Unlike static feedback, it targets specific errors or gaps, offering hints, explanations, or additional resources tailored to the individual's needs. This ongoing support helps learners adjust strategies and correct misunderstandings before moving forward. The conversational format makes feedback feel supportive rather than evaluative, reducing anxiety and encouraging persistence. Overall, dialogue agents enhance the feedback process by making it continuous, personalized, and integral to the learning journey.

4. PERSONALIZED ASSESSMENT STRATEGIES THROUGH GENAI

Generative AI revolutionizes personalized assessment by enabling real-time, adaptive strategies that respond to the unique needs, abilities, and learning trajectories of individual students. Unlike traditional assessments that offer standardized tasks and fixed feedback, GenAI-powered systems can dynamically generate questions, problems, and tasks tailored to a learner's current level of understanding, engagement style, and even emotional tone. By analyzing learner inputs—whether written responses, speech, or behavioural patterns—GenAI can infer cognitive strengths and gaps, adjust difficulty levels, and provide instant, formative feedback that supports deeper understanding. These systems can also simulate authentic learning environments, offering scenario-based assessments that reflect real-world application of knowledge and skills. Importantly, GenAI supports multimodal personalization, allowing for diverse learning preferences by delivering assessments in text, audio, or visual formats. With personalized learning at the forefront of digital education, the emergence of GenAI—particularly large language models (LLMs)—provides fresh avenues for creating content tailored to individual learners (Hu & Shao, 2025). Additionally, the conversational nature of GenAI allows for reflective questioning and iterative clarification, encouraging metacognitive awareness in students. This continuous, embedded form of assessment shifts the focus from grading to growth, aligning with inclusive and learner-centered pedagogies. By facilitating nuanced, equitable, and responsive evaluation, GenAI makes personalized assessment a practical and scalable reality in modern education.

A. Adaptive Testing Based on Real-Time Learner Input

Adaptive testing powered by Generative AI transforms traditional assessments by dynamically adjusting to a learner's performance in real time. Unlike fixed tests, adaptive assessments modify question difficulty, format, and sequencing based on immediate learner responses. This personalized approach helps accurately gauge a student's knowledge, skills, and progress without unnecessary repetition or frustration. Real-time data analysis allows the system to identify strengths and weaknesses promptly, providing insights that guide both learners and educators. By tailoring the testing experience to individual needs, adaptive testing fosters more precise, efficient, and meaningful evaluation. Most importantly, the advancement in learning improved notably, increasing from 65% to 78%. These findings emphasize the capacity of our DL-powered method to adaptively modify the learning process according to real-time feedback, resulting in enhanced student comprehension, involvement, and general growth (Ahamed & Hanirex, 2024).

a) Dynamic Question Selection

Adaptive testing systems use learner responses to select subsequent questions that are neither too easy nor too difficult. This dynamic selection keeps learners appropriately challenged, maintaining engagement while preventing discouragement. The system continually refines its understanding of the learner's ability level, ensuring that each question provides maximum diagnostic value. As a result, assessments become more efficient, requiring fewer questions to accurately measure proficiency. This responsiveness enhances both the learner experience and the reliability of test outcomes.

b) Real-Time Performance Analysis

Real-time analysis during adaptive testing enables immediate insight into learner performance patterns, including common errors or misconceptions. This data supports timely interventions, such as hints or tailored feedback, to help learners overcome difficulties. For educators, real-time reports provide actionable information for personalized instruction and progress monitoring. Continuous updating of learner profiles throughout the assessment allows for ongoing refinement of both testing and instructional strategies. Ultimately, this integration of testing and learning supports a more formative and learner-centered evaluation process.

B. Context-Aware Formative Feedback Generation

Context-aware formative feedback uses Generative AI to deliver personalized, timely, and relevant guidance that responds directly to a learner's unique situation and actions. Unlike generic feedback, this approach considers the learner's current knowledge state, recent responses, and even emotional cues to craft responses that truly support growth. By integrating contextual data, feedback becomes more precise—addressing specific misconceptions, reinforcing strengths, and suggesting targeted next steps. The initial step is to identify a corresponding relationship among functions in the students' submissions (Song et al., 2021). This dynamic interaction helps learners understand not just *what* is wrong but *why*, fostering deeper conceptual clarity. Such tailored feedback enhances motivation and engagement by making learners feel seen and supported throughout their educational journey.

a) Personalization Based on Learner Data

Formative feedback is personalized using real-time data about the learner's progress, errors, and interaction patterns. GenAI analyses this data to identify precise areas of difficulty and adapts feedback accordingly. For example, it might simplify explanations for struggling students or challenge advanced learners with deeper questions. This personalization ensures that feedback meets learners where they are, promoting effective scaffolding and growth. It also enables a more learner-centered approach, shifting the focus from rote correctness to meaningful understanding.

b) Integration of Emotional and Contextual Cues

Advanced systems can detect emotional or contextual signals, such as frustration or hesitation, through language cues or interaction patterns. Incorporating this information allows the feedback to be more empathetic and encouraging, helping reduce learner anxiety. Context-aware feedback might adjust tone, offer motivational support, or provide additional resources depending on the learner's current state. This holistic approach creates a supportive learning environment that recognizes the learner as a whole person, not just a knowledge repository. By addressing both cognitive and emotional needs, the system enhances engagement and resilience.

C. Differentiation for Diverse Learning Styles and Needs

Generative AI enables Intelligent Tutoring Systems to differentiate instruction by tailoring content and feedback to accommodate diverse learning styles, preferences, and abilities. Recognizing that learners vary in how they process information—whether visually, auditorily, kinaesthetically, or through reading/writing—GenAI adapts its teaching strategies to match these modalities. The idea of learning styles is highly attractive both logically and intuitively, making educators' interest in emphasizing them easy to comprehend (Landrum & McDuffie, 2010). It can also address special educational needs by adjusting pace, complexity, or presentation format, ensuring accessibility and inclusion. This personalized differentiation fosters a more engaging and effective learning experience for all students. By embracing diversity, ITS powered by GenAI promote equity and help every learner reach their full potential.

a) Multi-Modal Content Delivery

To support various learning preferences, GenAI can present material in multiple formats—such as text, images, audio, or interactive simulations. For example, visual learners might receive diagrams and videos, while auditory learners benefit from narrated explanations. This flexibility helps ensure concepts are accessible and understandable to a broader range of students. Offering multiple ways to engage with content also encourages deeper comprehension and retention. By personalizing delivery modes, ITS make learning more adaptable and inclusive.

b) Accessibility and Support for Special Needs

GenAI-driven ITS can detect and respond to learners with special needs by modifying instructional approaches accordingly. This might include simplifying language for learners with reading difficulties, providing additional scaffolding, or offering alternative interaction modes for those with physical or sensory impairments. The system's ability to continuously monitor learner progress allows it to adjust support dynamically, ensuring that barriers to learning are minimized. Such differentiation ensures that all students, regardless of ability, receive equitable opportunities to succeed.

5. EQUITY, INCLUSION, AND BIAS IN AI-DRIVEN ASSESSMENT

While Generative AI offers powerful tools for personalization and scalability in assessment, it also raises critical concerns around equity, inclusion, and algorithmic bias. AI systems are trained on large datasets that may reflect historical inequalities, cultural stereotypes, or linguistic imbalances—factors that can inadvertently disadvantage certain learner groups, particularly those from marginalized, multilingual, or neurodiverse backgrounds. In AI-driven assessments, biased data can result in inappropriate question generation, misinterpretation of learner responses, or unequal feedback quality, undermining fairness and trust. Moreover, lack of transparency in how these systems make decisions can prevent students and educators from understanding or challenging biased outcomes. To address these issues, it is essential to design GenAI systems with inclusive pedagogical frameworks, incorporating diverse linguistic, cultural, and cognitive representations. AI-powered learner models can assist in tackling issues encountered by existing K-12 evaluations (Sato et al., 2024). Regular audits, fairness metrics, and stakeholder engagement—especially from underrepresented communities—should guide development and deployment. Ethical AI assessment also requires explainability, allowing learners and educators to see how conclusions are drawn, and offering opportunities for correction or human override. When designed responsibly, GenAI can actually promote equity by identifying underserved learning needs, offering differentiated supports, and reducing one-size-fits-all educational barriers. Thus, equity and inclusion must be built into the foundation—not treated as optional features—of AI-driven assessment systems.

A. Risks of Algorithmic Bias in Feedback and Evaluation

Algorithmic bias poses significant risks in AI-driven feedback and evaluation systems, potentially reinforcing existing inequalities and unfair treatment of learners. Biases can emerge from training data that reflect historical prejudices, unrepresentative samples, or flawed assumptions embedded in algorithms. If unchecked, these biases may lead to inaccurate assessments, unfair feedback, or marginalization of certain groups based on factors such as race, gender, language, or socioeconomic status. Moreover, biased feedback can undermine learner confidence and perpetuate educational disparities. Addressing these risks requires careful design, diverse data sets, and ongoing monitoring to ensure that AI systems promote fairness and equity in learning environments. The issue of bias in educational assessments has been recorded since the 1960s and foreshadowed numerous elements of contemporary discussions on algorithmic bias and equity (Baker & Hawn, 2022).

a) Sources of Bias in AI Systems

Bias can originate from various sources, including biased training data that overrepresent certain demographics or perspectives. Additionally, the design choices made by developers—such as feature selection or model objectives—can unintentionally embed biases. Feedback algorithms that rely heavily on standardized data may fail to capture the diversity of learner backgrounds and abilities. Without deliberate intervention, these systemic biases can distort learner evaluations and feedback quality. Recognizing and mitigating these sources is essential to create trustworthy and inclusive ITS.

b) Consequences for Learners and Education

Algorithmic bias can negatively impact learners by delivering inaccurate feedback or unfair assessments that affect motivation and learning outcomes. Marginalized groups may be disproportionately affected, experiencing lower-quality support or being misjudged based on biased criteria. This can widen achievement gaps and reduce trust in AI-driven educational tools. Educators may also struggle to identify when bias affects system recommendations, complicating intervention efforts. Thus, addressing bias is not only a technical challenge but a critical ethical imperative to uphold educational justice.

B. Ensuring Fairness Across Linguistic, Cultural, and Cognitive Dimensions

Ensuring fairness in AI-driven tutoring requires addressing the diverse linguistic, cultural, and cognitive backgrounds of learners. Language differences, including dialects and proficiency levels, can affect how learners interact with Intelligent Tutoring Systems (ITS) and the quality of feedback they receive. Cultural contexts influence learning styles, communication preferences, and content relevance, which AI systems must recognize to avoid misunderstandings or bias. Cognitive diversity, including variations in prior knowledge and learning needs, demands flexible adaptation to support all learners equitably. Designing ITS with inclusivity in mind fosters respectful, relevant, and effective learning experiences that honour each student's unique identity. The idea of fairness is intricate in the literature since it is understood through multiple perspectives (Falavarjani & Mousavi, 2024).

a) Linguistic Fairness

AI systems must accommodate different languages, dialects, and proficiency levels to ensure learners fully understand and benefit from feedback. This includes supporting multilingual interactions and adapting language complexity appropriately. Failure to do so can lead to confusion, misinterpretation, or exclusion, disadvantaging non-native speakers. Implementing robust natural language processing models that reflect linguistic diversity is essential for equitable communication.

b) Cultural and Cognitive Inclusivity

Cultural fairness involves recognizing and respecting learners' backgrounds, values, and norms, which shape their educational experiences. ITS should avoid cultural bias in examples, analogies, and content presentation. Cognitive inclusivity means adapting to varied learning styles, prior knowledge, and abilities to meet individual needs effectively. Together, these considerations help create a more equitable learning environment that validates diverse learner identities and supports success for all.

C. Designing GenAI Systems for Accessibility and Ethical Responsiveness

Creating Generative AI systems for education requires intentional design focused on accessibility and ethical responsiveness to ensure all learners benefit fairly. Accessibility involves making systems usable by individuals with diverse abilities, including those with visual, auditory, motor, or cognitive impairments. Ethical responsiveness demands transparency in data use, respect for learner privacy, and mechanisms to prevent harm, such as mitigating bias and avoiding over-reliance on AI at the expense of human judgment. By embedding inclusive design principles and ongoing ethical evaluation, GenAI systems can support equitable learning environments that uphold learner dignity and promote trust. Additionally, this study highlights the essential importance of regulatory structures, AI education initiatives, and faculty development in promoting the responsible application of GenAI in educational environments (Hirpara et al., 2024).

a) Accessibility by Design

Ensuring accessibility means integrating features such as screen reader compatibility, adjustable text sizes, alternative input methods, and multimodal content delivery. These accommodations help remove barriers for learners with disabilities, allowing equal participation and engagement. Designing for accessibility from the outset, rather than as an afterthought, leads to more effective and universally usable ITS. Continuous testing with diverse users ensures that accessibility needs are met across contexts.

b) Ethical Safeguards and Transparency

Ethical design requires clear communication about how learner data is collected, stored, and used, fostering informed consent and trust. Systems must include safeguards to detect and mitigate biases or errors that could disadvantage learners. Importantly, GenAI should complement—not replace—educator expertise, preserving human oversight in critical instructional decisions. Regular audits, accountability measures, and stakeholder involvement are key to maintaining ethical standards and responsiveness over time.

6. HUMAN-AI COLLABORATION IN THE FEEDBACK LOOP

Human-AI collaboration in the feedback loop represents a hybrid model where educators and generative AI systems work together to enhance the quality, timeliness, and personalization of learner feedback. Rather than replacing teachers, AI acts as a co-tutor—analyzing student inputs, generating formative feedback, and identifying patterns or misconceptions that might otherwise go unnoticed. Teachers can then review, contextualize, or supplement this feedback with their pedagogical judgment, emotional intelligence, and knowledge of individual learner needs. This collaborative model empowers educators to focus on higher-order guidance—such as motivation, critical thinking, and socio-emotional support—while AI handles scalable and repetitive feedback tasks. For learners, this dual approach fosters a deeper sense of trust and clarity. GenAI can provide immediate, adaptive, and low-stakes responses, while human educators reinforce or refine those insights to ensure alignment with curricular goals and cultural contexts. Overall, these findings suggest that human bias is greatly heightened in interactions between humans and AI, more so than in human-to-human interactions (Glickman & Sharot, 2025). Explainable AI systems further support collaboration by making machine-generated feedback interpretable and editable by humans. Moreover, collaborative feedback loops allow for continuous improvement: educators can fine-tune AI models through feedback on accuracy and tone, while students benefit from more consistent, timely, and pedagogically sound support. Ultimately, this human-AI synergy strengthens feedback as a dialogic, learner-centered process rather than a one-way evaluation.

A. Teachers as Co-Designers and Interpreters of AI Feedback

Teachers play a vital role in the effective integration of AI-driven feedback within Intelligent Tutoring Systems (ITS). As co-designers, educators collaborate in developing AI tools that align with pedagogical goals, ensuring feedback is relevant, actionable, and supportive of diverse learners. The education of Artificial Intelligence (AI) is becoming an increasingly popular subject for K-12 educators (Lin & Van Brummelen, 2021). Their expertise guides the refinement of algorithms and content, helping to create systems that complement classroom instruction. Teachers also serve as interpreters of AI feedback, contextualizing automated suggestions to meet individual student needs and address nuances that AI might miss. This partnership between human educators and AI promotes more meaningful, ethical, and effective learning experiences.

a) Collaborative Development with Educators

Involving teachers in the design process ensures that AI feedback tools reflect real classroom challenges and pedagogical priorities. Educators contribute insights on learner behaviours, instructional strategies, and assessment goals, shaping AI functionalities that are practical and classroom-friendly. This collaboration helps prevent misalignment between AI outputs and teaching objectives, enhancing system usability and effectiveness.

b) Contextualizing AI Feedback

Teachers interpret and adapt AI-generated feedback to suit each student's context, considering factors such as motivation, emotional state, and learning history. They provide the human judgment needed to address ambiguous or sensitive situations that AI might not fully grasp. By bridging the gap between automated insights and personalized instruction, teachers ensure that feedback supports holistic learner development.

B. Empowering Learners Through Explainable AI

Explainable AI (XAI) enhances learner autonomy by making AI-driven feedback and decisions transparent and understandable. When students can see *why* a particular suggestion or assessment was made, they gain insights into their learning processes and develop metacognitive skills. This transparency fosters trust in AI systems and encourage learners to take ownership of their progress. XAI also helps demystify complex algorithms, reducing anxiety or scepticism toward AI-driven instruction. By empowering learners with clear explanations, ITS promote deeper engagement and more informed self-regulated learning. They finish by promoting wider conversation about explainable AI in education, enhanced research and implementation of these models, and engagement of various stakeholders in creating tools and systems (Gašević et al., 2023).

a) Transparency in Feedback

Explainable AI provides learners with clear reasons behind feedback, helping them understand their mistakes and how to improve. This clarity supports reflection and encourages a growth mindset by showing that errors are part of the learning journey. Transparent feedback also makes AI decisions more predictable, reducing frustration and building confidence.

b) Supporting Metacognition and Self-Regulation

By revealing the logic behind AI assessments, XAI helps learners monitor their own understanding and adjust strategies proactively. This supports the development of skills like goal setting, self-assessment, and strategic learning. When learners grasp how AI systems evaluate their work, they become more active participants in their education rather than passive recipients of feedback.

C. Hybrid Feedback Models: Blending Human Insight With Machine Scalability

Hybrid feedback models combine the strengths of human educators with the efficiency and scalability of AI-driven systems to create richer, more effective learning experiences. While Generative AI can quickly analyze vast amounts of learner data and provide immediate, personalized feedback, human teachers bring empathy, contextual understanding, and pedagogical judgment that machines cannot replicate. This partnership ensures feedback is both timely and nuanced, addressing cognitive and emotional learner needs. The progression of Artificial Intelligence from conventional inference-driven systems to advanced generative models has diminished the distinctions between machine and human abilities, leading to the emergence of Hybrid Intelligence (Mestre, 2024). By blending automated insights with educator interpretation, hybrid models balance consistency with flexibility and foster deeper engagement. Ultimately, such collaboration maximizes the potential of ITS to support diverse learners at scale while maintaining high-quality, human-centered instruction.

a) Leveraging AI for Efficiency

AI systems handle routine feedback tasks at scale, delivering personalized hints, explanations, and progress tracking without delay. This frees educators to focus on complex, creative, or sensitive teaching moments that require human insight. The speed and breadth of AI enable continuous learner support beyond the constraints of traditional classrooms.

b) Integrating Educator Expertise

Teachers contextualize and refine AI-generated feedback, ensuring it aligns with learner emotions, motivations, and individual circumstances. Their expertise helps interpret ambiguous cases and tailor interventions to maximize impact.

7. CASE STUDIES AND IMPLEMENTATION EXAMPLES

Real-world case studies and implementation examples offer critical insights into how Generative AI is transforming assessment and feedback within Intelligent Tutoring Systems (ITS) across diverse educational contexts. In K–12 education, platforms like Scribe Sense and Grade scope have integrated AI-driven feedback to streamline grading and provide immediate, formative responses, especially in STEM and language subjects. These tools have demonstrated improved student engagement and teacher workload reduction, particularly in large classrooms. In higher education, institutions have piloted GenAI-based writing assistants and virtual tutors that offer real-time critiques on student essays, enabling iterative improvement and deeper reflection. For example, one university implemented a GPT-powered writing lab that guided students through argumentative structure, grammar correction, and source evaluation—while still allowing human tutors to review final drafts. In vocational and lifelong learning settings, AI-driven simulations have enabled real-time scenario-based assessments, such as diagnosing machinery faults or responding to workplace dilemmas, with adaptive feedback based on learner choices. Meanwhile, global initiatives have focused on inclusivity by deploying multilingual GenAI tutoring systems in underserved regions, demonstrating potential for equitable access. These implementation cases reveal that while challenges like bias, infrastructure, and teacher training remain, the thoughtful integration of GenAI into ITS can create scalable, context-aware, and responsive learning environments. Collectively, these examples underscore the transformative potential of GenAI—when guided by ethical design and pedagogical alignment—to personalize learning at scale.

A. Deployment of GenAI Tutoring in K–12 and Higher Education

In K–12, GenAI supports differentiated instruction by adapting to varied student skill levels and providing interactive, engaging feedback that fosters foundational skill development. Higher education leverages GenAI to facilitate complex problem-solving, critical thinking, and research skills through advanced, adaptive dialogue and real-time assessment. Both contexts benefit from scalable, data-driven insights that inform instruction and monitor learner progress continuously. Despite varying educational goals and learner maturity, GenAI tutors enable more responsive, inclusive, and learner-centered environments across educational levels.

a) Enhancing Foundational Skills in K–12

In K–12 education, GenAI tutoring systems tailor content to meet diverse learner needs, providing scaffolded support in core subjects like math and literacy.

Interactive features, such as conversational agents, encourage curiosity and active engagement, helping younger learners build confidence and mastery. The technology also assists teachers by offering real-time analytics that inform differentiated instruction strategies.

b) Supporting Advanced Learning in Higher Education

Higher education applications of GenAI focus on fostering higher-order thinking and personalized mentorship. Adaptive tutoring assists with complex tasks such as writing, data analysis, and conceptual synthesis, allowing students to explore ideas deeply and at their own pace. GenAI's ability to provide timely, formative feedback complements traditional teaching methods, promoting autonomous and reflective learning.

B. Success Stories and Challenges From Global Pilot Programs

Global pilot programs deploying GenAI tutoring reveal promising successes alongside notable challenges. Many initiatives report improved learner engagement, personalized support, and higher achievement, particularly in underserved or remote areas where traditional resources are limited. For example, adaptive tutoring has helped students master difficult concepts faster and increased motivation through real-time, context-aware feedback. However, challenges include addressing infrastructure disparities, ensuring cultural relevance, and mitigating algorithmic bias. Additionally, teacher training and acceptance vary, impacting effective integration. These pilots highlight the importance of ongoing refinement, inclusive design, and strong educator involvement for sustainable, equitable deployment.

a) Positive Outcomes in Diverse Contexts

Pilot programs demonstrate that GenAI tutoring can bridge educational gaps by offering tailored support that adapts to learners' unique needs across regions. Increased engagement and personalized learning pathways have led to measurable improvements in student outcomes. These successes underline GenAI's potential to democratize quality education globally.

b) Challenges in Implementation and Equity

Despite benefits, pilot programs face hurdles such as unequal access to technology, varying teacher readiness, and the need to localize content culturally and linguistically. Addressing these challenges requires investment in infrastructure, professional development, and ethical oversight to ensure fairness. Balancing innovation with sensitivity to local contexts remains critical.

C. Lessons from Cross-Disciplinary Applications (e.g., STEM, Language Learning)

The deployment of Generative AI tutoring across various disciplines such as STEM and language learning has revealed important lessons about the adaptability and design considerations necessary for effective Intelligent Tutoring Systems (ITS). In STEM education, the complexity of subject matter demands that GenAI not only provide correct answers but also guide students through multi-step problem-solving processes, conceptual visualizations, and critical thinking exercises. The system's ability to break down abstract or challenging concepts into manageable parts through adaptive hints and scaffolding proves essential for learner comprehension and confidence. Additionally, the integration of interactive simulations and dynamic visual aids enhances engagement and helps translate theoretical knowledge into practical understanding.

a) STEM-Specific Adaptations

GenAI systems tailored for STEM education focus on guiding learners through complex, multi-step problem-solving tasks. They provide adaptive scaffolding by offering hints that gradually reduce in detail, helping students build independent reasoning skills without overwhelming them. Visualizations, such as interactive graphs or simulations, play a crucial role in making abstract concepts tangible and fostering conceptual understanding. Furthermore, real-time feedback on errors allows students to correct misconceptions promptly, supporting continuous learning. This approach encourages persistence, critical thinking, and application of knowledge in real-world scenarios.

b) Language Learning Innovations

In language learning, GenAI-powered conversational agents create authentic practice opportunities by simulating dialogues and providing instant, personalized feedback. This interactive environment helps learners develop speaking, listening, reading, and writing skills in an integrated manner. The system can adapt feedback complexity based on proficiency, offering simplified explanations or advanced linguistic nuances as needed. Pronunciation coaching and contextualized grammar corrections enable learners to refine their skills iteratively. Additionally, incorporating cultural context within language exercises ensures that learners appreciate the social and pragmatic aspects of communication, fostering more holistic language competence.

8. MEASURING LEARNING OUTCOMES IN GENAI-ENHANCED ENVIRONMENTS

Measuring learning outcomes in GenAI-enhanced environments requires rethinking traditional assessment metrics to align with the dynamic, interactive, and personalized nature of AI-driven education. Unlike standardized tests that capture static snapshots of performance, GenAI-enabled systems offer continuous, real-time monitoring of learner progress across cognitive, behavioural, and even affective domains. These systems can analyze a wide array of learner data—including response accuracy, time-on-task, self-corrections, engagement patterns, and dialogue quality—to build rich, multidimensional profiles of learning. Importantly, GenAI allows for the evaluation of process over product, meaning it can track how students arrive at solutions, how they revise thinking after feedback, and how their metacognitive skills develop over time. These insights enable educators to assess not only mastery of content but also critical thinking, persistence, and learning strategies. Dashboards and visual analytics can present this information in interpretable ways for teachers, learners, and guardians. However, the use of such data must be governed by ethical and transparent practices, ensuring privacy, consent, and non-discrimination.

A. Redefining Assessment Metrics Beyond Grades

Generative AI offers transformative potential to move assessment beyond traditional grading systems toward more holistic and meaningful measures of learner progress. Standard grades often reduce learning to a single number or letter, which may fail to capture the depth of understanding, skills development, or critical thinking abilities. GenAI enables continuous, formative assessment that tracks a variety of learner behaviours—such as problem-solving approaches, creativity, persistence, and collaboration—providing a richer picture of student growth. By analyzing patterns over time, AI-driven systems can identify strengths and challenges more precisely, allowing educators and learners to focus on mastery rather than merely performance. This shift supports more personalized learning trajectories and fosters a growth mindset, encouraging learners to view assessment as an ongoing process rather than a final judgment.

a) Moving from Summative to Formative Assessment

Traditional summative assessments typically occur at the end of a learning period and offer limited opportunities for feedback or adjustment. GenAI enables continuous, real-time formative assessment by analyzing student interactions, responses, and learning behaviours. This approach supports timely interventions, helping learners address difficulties as they arise and adapt instruction to their evolving needs. Formative metrics emphasize progress and understanding over time, encouraging reflection and self-regulation.

b) Expanding the Scope of Assessment

Beyond right or wrong answers, GenAI systems can evaluate complex competencies such as critical thinking, creativity, problem-solving strategies, and collaboration skills. This broader scope recognizes multiple dimensions of learning essential for real-world success. AI can analyze student writing for coherence and argument quality, track collaboration patterns in group work, and assess persistence in challenging tasks, providing a multi-faceted view of learner achievement.

B. Behavioural and Engagement Analytics

Generative AI-powered systems collect and analyze rich behavioural and engagement data to deepen understanding of how learners interact with content and tools. Beyond just measuring correctness, these analytics examine patterns such as time spent on tasks, frequency of attempts, navigation paths, and response times. By interpreting this data, AI can infer learner motivation, persistence, and frustration levels, which are critical for tailoring support. Engagement metrics help identify when students are disengaged or overwhelmed, enabling timely intervention to re-engage or scaffold learning. This nuanced insight into learner behavior promotes more responsive and adaptive instruction that supports sustained motivation and improved outcomes.

a) Tracking Learning Behaviours

AI systems monitor detailed behaviours like how learners approach problems, their strategies, and adjustments made after feedback. For example, repeated attempts or hesitation can indicate areas of struggle, while efficient problem-solving suggests mastery. Understanding these behaviours allows ITS to personalize feedback and adjust challenge levels dynamically.

b) Detecting Engagement Patterns

Engagement analytics assess indicators such as interaction frequency, session duration, and participation in collaborative tasks. Drops in engagement may signal boredom, confusion, or external distractions. By identifying these patterns early, AI tutors can modify content delivery or prompt reflective activities to re-energize learners, fostering sustained involvement.

C. Using Learning Data Ethically and Effectively

The collection and use of learner data through Generative AI systems offer powerful opportunities to enhance education but also raise significant ethical considerations. Ensuring data privacy, security, and transparency is essential to maintain trust among students, educators, and institutions. Ethical data use involves obtaining informed consent, clearly communicating how data will be stored and used, and allowing learners control over their information. Moreover, careful analysis is needed to avoid reinforcing biases or misinterpreting data, which can lead to unfair or inaccurate evaluations. Responsible use of learning data promotes not only personalized and effective instruction but also respects learner dignity and fosters an inclusive, equitable educational environment.

a) Protecting Privacy and Security

AI systems need to establish strong protections to safeguard sensitive learner data from unauthorized access or breaches. Encryption, anonymization, and safe storage methods are essential elements. Moreover, clear policies must educate learners regarding what data is gathered and the manner in which it will be utilized.

b) Preventing Bias and Misuse

Data analysis should be approached critically to detect and mitigate biases related to race, gender, language, or disability. Algorithms need continual auditing and refinement to ensure fairness and accuracy. Ethical use also means avoiding over-reliance on AI judgments and maintaining human oversight in decision-making processes.

9. CONCLUSION

This chapter has explored how Generative AI, when integrated thoughtfully into Intelligent Tutoring Systems (ITS), redefines assessment and feedback as more responsive, inclusive, and learner-centered processes. By moving beyond static evaluation models, GenAI enables adaptive, real-time feedback loops that support continuous learning, differentiated instruction, and deeper engagement. Through natural language processing and contextual awareness, these systems can offer nuanced, personalized support that mirrors the pedagogical strategies of skilled human tutors—while also scaling to meet the demands of diverse and global classrooms. Importantly, the chapter emphasizes that the power of GenAI lies not merely in automation or efficiency, but in its potential to enhance human relationships in education. Effective implementation depends on collaborative design, where educators, learners, and AI systems work in concert to promote equity, inclusion, and trust. Ethical considerations—particularly around bias, data privacy, and transparency—must remain at the forefront to ensure these technologies serve all learners fairly and responsibly. As education systems evolve, the role of GenAI in assessment and feedback will only grow in significance. This chapter calls for a future where technology does not replace the human touch, but rather extends it—amplifying the reach, responsiveness, and relevance of education in an increasingly complex world.

REFERENCES

Ahamed, H. R., & Hanirex, D. K. (2024, August). A deep learning-enabled approach for real-time monitoring of learner activities in adaptive e-learning environments. In *2024 7th International Conference on Circuit Power and Computing Technologies (ICCPCT)* (Vol. 1, pp. 846-851). IEEE. DOI: 10.1109/ICCPCT61902.2024.10673041

Ali, M. (2024). AI and Intelligent Tutoring Systems: A New Paradigm for Student-Centered Learning. *Journal of AI Integration in Education, 1*(2), 1–11.

Baker, R. S., & Hawn, A. (2022). Algorithmic bias in education. *International Journal of Artificial Intelligence in Education, 32*(4), 1052–1092. DOI: 10.1007/s40593-021-00285-9

Bataineh, A. Q., Abu-AlSondos, I. A., Almazaydeh, L., El Mokdad, S. S., & Allahham, M. (2023, December). Enhancing natural language processing with machine learning for conversational AI. In *IET Conference Proceedings CP870* (Vol. 2023, No. 39, pp. 229-237). Stevenage, UK: The Institution of Engineering and Technology.

Chukhlomin, V. (2024). Socratic Prompts: Engineered Dialogue as a Tool for AI-Enhanced Educational Inquiry. *Latin American Business and Sustainability Review, 1*(1), 1–13. DOI: 10.70469/labsreview.v1i1.10

Falavarjani, M., & Mousavi, A. (2024). Rethinking fairness in classroom assessment: The influence of cultural dimensions. *American Journal of STEM Education, 2*, 22–49.

. Gašević, D., Siemens, G., & Sadiq, S. (2023). Empowering learners for the age of artificial intelligence. *Computers and education: artificial intelligence, 4*, 100130.

Glickman, M., & Sharot, T. (2025). How human–AI feedback loops alter human perceptual, emotional and social judgements. *Nature Human Behaviour, 9*(2), 345–359. DOI: 10.1038/s41562-024-02077-2 PMID: 39695250

Hansen, T. F. (2006). The evolution of genetic architecture. *Annual Review of Ecology, Evolution, and Systematics, 37*(1), 123–157. DOI: 10.1146/annurev.ecolsys.37.091305.110224 PMID: 17017054

Hirpara, N., Weber, M., Szakonyi, A., Cardona, T., & Singh, D. (2024, November). Exploring the Role of GenAI in Shaping Education. In *International Conference on Intelligent Human Computer Interaction* (pp. 121-134). Cham: Springer Nature Switzerland.

Hu, W., & Shao, Z. (2025). Design and Evaluation of a GenAI-Based personalized Educational Content System Tailored to Personality Traits and Emotional Responses for Adaptive Learning. *Computers in Human Behavior Reports*, *19*, 100735. DOI: 10.1016/j.chbr.2025.100735

Huynh, L., & McNamara, D. S. (2025). GenAI-Powered Text Personalization: Natural Language Processing Validation of Adaptation Capabilities. *Applied Sciences (Basel, Switzerland)*, *15*(12), 6791. DOI: 10.3390/app15126791

Landrum, T. J., & McDuffie, K. A. (2010). Learning styles in the age of differentiated instruction. *Exceptionality*, *18*(1), 6–17. DOI: 10.1080/09362830903462441

Lin, P., & Van Brummelen, J. (2021, May). Engaging teachers to co-design integrated AI curriculum for K-12 classrooms. In *Proceedings of the 2021 CHI conference on human factors in computing systems* (pp. 1-12). DOI: 10.1145/3411764.3445377

Mestre, A. (2024, May). Towards a Hybrid Intelligence Paradigm: Systematic Integration of Human and Artificial Capabilities. In *International Conference on Research Challenges in Information Science* (pp. 149-156). Cham: Springer Nature Switzerland. DOI: 10.1007/978-3-031-59468-7_17

Polson, M. C., & Richardson, J. J. (2013). *Foundations of intelligent tutoring systems*. Psychology Press. DOI: 10.4324/9780203761557

Sato, E., Shyyan, V., Chauhan, S., & Christensen, L. (2024). Putting ai in fair: A framework for equity in ai-driven learner models and inclusive assessments. *Egitimde ve Psikolojide Ölçme ve Degerlendirme Dergisi*, *15*(Special Issue), 263–281. DOI: 10.21031/epod.1526527

Song, D., Lee, W., & Oh, H. (2021, August). Context-aware and data-driven feedback generation for programming assignments. In *Proceedings of the 29th ACM Joint Meeting on European Software Engineering Conference and Symposium on the Foundations of Software Engineering* (pp. 328-340). DOI: 10.1145/3468264.3468598

Tucci, V., & Hursh, D. (1991). Competent Learner Model: Instructional programming for teachers and learners. *Education & Treatment of Children*, •••, 349–360.

Zhong, H. (2024). Optimal Integration: Human, Machine, and Generative AI. *Machine, and Generative AI (July 18, 2024)*.

Chapter 6
Bridging Memory and Machine:
Generative AI and the Human-Centred Transformation of History Education

Tolgahan Ayantaş
http://orcid.org/0000-0003-4348-0975
Ankara University, Turkey

ABSTRACT

This chapter critically examines the role of generative artificial intelligence (AI) in history education through the lenses of collective memory, historical consciousness, and human-centred pedagogy. It conceptualises generative AI not as a neutral instructional tool but as a dialogic and provisional partner whose educational value depends on sustained human mediation. Drawing on interdisciplinary literature from history education, memory studies, digital pedagogy, and AI ethics, the chapter analyses how AI-generated historical representations may either reproduce dominant narratives or open spaces for multiperspectivity and ethical reflection. It highlights key epistemic risks, including narrative closure, bias reproduction, and the erosion of evidentiary reasoning, and proposes a memory-sensitive pedagogical framework to guide responsible AI use. The chapter argues that generative AI can enrich historical inquiry only when human judgment, ethical accountability, and student authorship remain epistemically primary.

DOI: 10.4018/979-8-3373-6063-8.ch006

INTRODUCTION

While artificial intelligence offers potential for personalisation, automated feedback, and adaptive learning, its educational value is highly context-dependent. Rule-based systems and machine learning are effective in procedural domains with stable knowledge and measurable outcomes, and in large-scale assessment based on consistent data (Güven, 2025). However, from a history education perspective, these strengths reveal limits: historical learning relies on interpretation, contextualisation, evidentiary reasoning, and ethical judgment rather than rule-based mastery. Uncritical transfer of AI models from structured disciplines may therefore narrow historical understanding. Meaningful integration requires human-centred pedagogy in which teachers critically mediate AI outputs; without this grounding, AI may increase efficiency but not support the complex aims of history education.

History education extends beyond transmitting facts; it organises collective memory, legitimises identities, and shapes civic orientation. Textbooks and curricula function as "psychological tools" that construct belonging and marginalisation through selective narratives (Sakki, 2025), reproducing social hierarchies and power relations (Oksuzoglu, 2024). Classrooms thus institutionalise memory and normalise particular historical meanings.

National history courses play a central role in nation building and identity formation, especially in multicultural or polarised contexts. Comparative research shows they often promote cohesion and continuity under conditions of contested pasts (Ishak & Ahmad, 2025; Kirs, 2023; Sandhu et al., 2023), yet they may also privilege dominant narratives and exclude alternative experiences (Muis et al., 2024). This dual function highlights the tension between AI's technical capacities and the epistemic nature of historical knowledge: because history shapes memory and identity, technological interventions require careful mediation to avoid reinforcing dominant narratives.

Scholarship further frames history education as cultivating historical consciousness—the ability to connect past, present, and future and to recognise narratives as constructed and value-laden (Burgos-Videla et al., 2025; Edling et al., 2020a; Fesenko et al., 2025; Ishak & Ahmad, 2025). Such awareness supports critical thinking and civic judgment by enabling students to interrogate dominant accounts (Burgos-Videla et al., 2025; Mollès & Parada-Ulloa, 2025; Muis et al., 2024). History education therefore shapes not only understandings of the past but also visions of the future.

Collective memory narratives operate as moral frameworks that classify historical actors and structure intergroup relations (Barreiro & Pérez-Manjarrez, 2025; Oksuzoglu, 2024; Silfver & Myyry, 2022). While they may reinforce binary identities, multiperspectival approaches foregrounding moral ambiguity can foster ethical reflection and historical empathy (Muis et al., 2024; Silfver & Myyry, 2022; Harnes, 2025). Yet such approaches require careful scaffolding; without guidance, empathy may lead to presentism or simplified moral judgments.

Historical empathy involves both cognitive contextualisation and affective engagement (Bartelds et al., 2020; Burgos-Videla et al., 2025; Harnes, 2025) and is cultivated through explicit instruction and diverse sources (Burgos-Videla et al., 2025; Bartelds et al., 2020). Engagement with traumatic pasts, however, carries ethical risks, potentially reinforcing exclusion or hostility if instrumentalised (Oksuzoglu, 2024; Stoddard, 2021). Trauma-informed pedagogies therefore emphasise emotional safety, critical distance, and ethical responsibility (Stoddard, 2021; Harnes, 2025).

Research increasingly challenges linear national narratives and promotes inquiry-based, socio-critical approaches that treat history as a site of deliberation rather than reproduction (Burgos-Videla et al., 2025; Ishak & Ahmad, 2025; Alvén, 2024; Mollès & Parada-Ulloa, 2025). Such approaches support plural identities and inclusive belonging by recognising diverse historical experiences (Vakulik et al., 2024; Sandhu et al., 2023), positioning curriculum design as an ethical and political act shaping both memory and membership.

Transnational initiatives—including collaborative textbooks and cross-border exchanges—seek to move beyond methodological nationalism by emphasising interconnected histories and global responsibility (Alvén, 2024; Koyama, 2023). However, significant empirical gaps remain regarding assessment, teacher preparation, and long-term effects on civic outcomes (Barreiro & Pérez-Manjarrez, 2025; Burgos-Videla et al., 2025; Harnes, 2025). While the theoretical case for critical and inclusive history education is strong, translating these ideals into sustainable classroom practice continues to pose a major challenge.

CHALLENGES IN HISTORY EDUCATION

A growing body of international research shows that history education remains marked by structural and pedagogical tensions. Across contexts, curricula are often overloaded, textbook-centred, and exam-driven, while learners' identities and digital habits rapidly evolve (Grever & Vlies, 2017; Miller & Spohnholz, 2023; Delaben et al., 2025). Many classrooms prioritise content coverage and memorisation over inquiry and interpretation.

From a history educator's perspective, transnational initiatives are promising but reveal a weak link between normative aims and classroom practice. Limited clarity on assessment, teacher preparation, and sustainability risks leaving global approaches symbolic, while exam-driven systems reward recall rather than critical reflection.

A persistent problem is excessive content load and assessment regimes that privilege recall. History courses are often organised as dense survey narratives or "content dumps" (Miller & Spohnholz, 2023), leaving little space for source analysis, causal reasoning, or ethical reflection. Students frequently experience history as overwhelming and disconnected from contemporary life (Delaben et al., 2025; Amoakwa et al., 2025), reinforcing simplified narratives that obscure historiographical debate and the constructed nature of knowledge (Grever & Vlies, 2017).

Equally significant is the dominance of national narratives and marginalisation of alternative voices. Textbooks often reproduce national myths and state-centred perspectives while limiting the visibility of minoritised histories (Stoddard, 2021; Sakki, 2025). Although calls for inclusive curricula highlight the underrepresentation of racialised, Indigenous, and other marginalised groups (Bekturganov & Nurpeissova, 2025; Gunter, 2025; Miles, 2018), these reforms require careful teacher preparation. Without disciplinary expertise and pedagogical support, introducing sensitive topics may reinforce simplistic moral interpretations, particularly in polarised contexts shaped by nationalism and conflict.

A related challenge concerns temporal abstraction and controversial knowledge. Many students struggle to connect past and present, especially when history is taught as a linear narrative of progress (Alvén, 2024; Delaben et al., 2025). Teachers often feel unprepared to address traumatic or contested pasts, leading to avoidance strategies that flatten complexity and depoliticise moral issues (Stoddard, 2021; Miles, 2018; Alvén, 2024).

These issues are intensified by a mismatch between traditional teaching and digital learning environments. Students engage with interactive and visual media, making text-heavy instruction appear disengaging (Firmansyah & Atmaja, 2025; Malysheva et al., 2022; Evurulobi et al., 2024). Although social media increases exposure to historical content, it may discourage critical inquiry and contextual reasoning (Grata & Llaneta, 2024). At the same time, formal education shows uneven digital integration due to infrastructural inequalities and limited teacher preparation (Nkolika, 2025; Aminullah et al., 2025; Anggiani et al., 2025), widening the gap between classroom practice and students' media experiences (Malysheva et al., 2022; Firmansyah & Atmaja, 2025).

Social media further complicates historical understanding by allowing experts and non-experts to circulate interpretations with equal visibility. While seemingly democratic, such environments often spread decontextualised or inaccurate content and encourage presentism and sensationalism, weakening evidentiary reasoning. Without pedagogical guidance, these dynamics risk reinforcing misconceptions rather than developing critical historical literacy.

Overall, the literature reveals a troubling pattern: history education remains shaped by curricular overload, narrow national narratives, limited engagement with difficult pasts, and pedagogies misaligned with students' realities. Addressing these challenges requires not incremental reform but a fundamental rethinking of history education to support critical citizenship, moral reflection, and inclusive belonging in a digital world.

TECHNOLOGY-ENHANCED HISTORY EDUCATION

Over the past two decades, research on technology-enhanced history education has consistently demonstrated that digital archives, interactive maps, simulations, virtual and augmented reality environments, educational games, and online platforms can significantly enrich students' engagement with the past. By visualising historical time and space, enabling direct interaction with primary sources, and supporting inquiry-oriented learning, these tools have been shown to increase motivation, participation, and epistemic agency in history classrooms (Firmansyah & Atmaja, 2025; Banerjee, 2024; Corrales et al., 2024; Lee, 2023; Umar, 2024). Digital history, in this sense, promised not merely efficiency but a pedagogical reorientation—from transmission to exploration, from memorisation to interpretation.

Yet empirical studies repeatedly reveal that this promise has only been partially realised. In many educational contexts, technology remains layered onto traditional pedagogies rather than fundamentally reshaping them. Classrooms continue to rely heavily on lecture-based instruction and textbook-centred content, with digital tools often used to deliver the same narratives more quickly or attractively rather than to challenge epistemic assumptions or foster historical inquiry (Malysheva et al., 2022; Corrales et al., 2024; Toktamysov et al., 2022; Villena-Taranilla & Diago, 2025). As a result, the transformative potential of digital history is frequently reduced to instrumental efficiency, reinforcing rather than disrupting established curricular logics.

The literature identifies several interrelated barriers to meaningful digital integration. These include uneven infrastructure and access, persistent digital divides, limited teacher digital literacy, and institutional cultures that prioritise the accumulation of digital resources over critical pedagogical use (Firmansyah & Atmaja, 2025; Malysheva et al., 2022; Umar, 2024; Hetharion et al., 2025; Toktamysov et al., 2022; Villena-Taranilla & Diago, 2025). Importantly, researchers warn that an abundance of digital materials does not automatically translate into deeper historical understanding; without explicit scaffolding, students may engage superficially with sources, confuse information access with interpretation, or reproduce unexamined narratives in digital form (Banerjee, 2024).

GENERATIVE AI IN HISTORY EDUCATION

Generative artificial intelligence is increasingly reshaping the educational landscape, emerging not merely as a digital tool but as a qualitatively different actor capable of generating texts, images, and narratives in real time. Research suggests AI can support personalised learning, historical source analysis, and reflection on causality and narrative construction when accompanied by AI literacy and critical evaluation of outputs (Moskalyuk & Len, 2025; Hetharion et al., 2025; Bhagat et al., 2025; Yan et al., 2025). In online history education, AI environments may expand access but also risk superficial engagement if pedagogical guidance is weak or inequalities persist (Banerjee, 2024; Umar, 2024; Toktamysov et al., 2022; Villena-Taranilla & Diago, 2025).

Recent scholarship rejects replacement models, instead advocating dialogic, human-centred integration in which AI expands learning dialogue rather than replacing human cognition (Ruiz-Rojas et al., 2024; Tang et al., 2024). When embedded in inquiry-based tasks, AI can support collaboration, metacognition, and critical questioning, though studies also warn of over-reliance and uncritical trust, especially without guidance on the probabilistic and biased nature of AI systems (Ruiz-Rojas et al., 2024; Bhagat et al., 2025; Yan et al., 2025).

History-specific research similarly frames AI as a partner in inquiry rather than an authoritative source. For example, simulations of the French Revolution show AI generating scenarios that learners critique and verify within a TPACK framework (Kindenberg, 2025). Scholars also emphasise validating AI outputs, preventing misuse, and ensuring traditional source analysis precedes AI use (Fareed et al., 2024; Pope, 2024; Kindenberg, 2025). Across studies, AI's value lies in provoking questioning about plausibility, perspective, and omission.

Overall, the literature suggests that generative AI's educational potential emerges when it functions as a dialogic, co-interpretive partner within human-led historical inquiry. Such integration requires strong teacher agency, attention to bias and authorship, and pedagogies centred on source criticism, multiperspectivity, and ethical reflection (Moskalyuk & Len, 2025; Hetharion et al., 2025; Ruiz-Rojas et al., 2024; Tang et al., 2024; Bhagat et al., 2025; Kindenberg, 2025; Yan et al., 2025).

POSITIONING GENERATIVE AI IN HUMAN-CENTRED HISTORY EDUCATION

AI-supported history education can slow historical thinking by revealing how memory is constructed through selection and interpretation, yet this depends on pedagogical intent rather than technological sophistication. Only critically supervised, equity-oriented, pedagogy-first uses of generative AI can support reflective, inclusive, and socially responsible historical understanding.

This chapter reconceptualises generative AI in history education by situating it within broader structural, pedagogical, and ethical debates. Rather than treating AI as a neutral tool, it positions it as a human-centred partner in shaping historical meaning. The study examines how AI may reshape historical consciousness, collective memory, and moral reasoning while addressing its epistemic and ethical risks. It aims to analyse AI's role in reproducing or challenging dominant narratives, clarify the limits of AI-generated historical representations, and propose human–AI collaborative models that preserve teacher agency and student authorship. Rather than delegating memory to machines, it proposes a framework in which memory and responsibility are negotiated between humans and AI to support more reflective and pluralistic history education.

THEORETICAL FRAMEWORK: MEMORY, ETHICS, AND HUMAN–AI CO-CREATION IN HISTORY EDUCATION

Generative AI can support historical understanding, but its value is neither automatic nor neutral. Its impact depends on framing AI use through memory theory, moral reasoning, and human–AI collaboration that preserves human interpretive authority. Without such framing, AI may reinforce dominant narratives. The key issue is therefore not whether AI produces historical representations, but how they shape collective memory and classroom practice.

Research on collective memory shows that historical narratives actively shape power, identity, and moral judgment rather than simply reflecting the past (Barreiro & Pérez-Manjarrez, 2025; Webb et al., 2019; Stoddard, 2021). What societies remember or forget defines belonging and responsibility, positioning history education at the intersection of knowledge and ethics, where historical consciousness and moral reasoning are cultivated (Barreiro & Pérez-Manjarrez, 2025; Edling et al., 2020b; Stoddard, 2021).

Hybrid-intelligence models challenge techno-solutionist views by treating learning as a collaboration between human and machine capacities (Cohn et al., 2024; Ifenthaler & Schumacher, 2023; Nguyen et al., 2024). Humans provide ethical judgment and contextual sensitivity, while AI offers speed and pattern recognition. Yet large language models lack truth-tracking and moral accountability, reinforcing the need for human epistemic authority in history education (Tirado-Olivares et al., 2023; Kansteiner, 2022).

Overall, research highlights three points: AI should function as a co-creator requiring human evaluation (Cohn et al., 2024; Ifenthaler & Schumacher, 2023; Kansteiner,

2022; Tirado-Olivares et al., 2023; Nguyen et al., 2024); it can enhance empathy and inclusion in heritage practices (Poce et al., 2025; He et al., 2024; Capistrán et al., 2025); and its benefits depend on pedagogies that emphasise ethical and epistemic guidance, treating AI outputs as situated interpretations rather than authoritative histories (Barreiro & Pérez-Manjarrez, 2025; Webb et al., 2019; Kansteiner, 2022).

GENERATIVE AI, CULTURAL MEMORY, AND HERITAGE PRACTICES

Generative AI increasingly shapes museum and heritage education through AI-enhanced Object-Based Learning environments that expand access to cultural heritage, especially for learners with disabilities or limited museum access (Poce et al., 2025; Pataranutaporn et al., 2021; Ly et al., 2025). Using adaptive content, multimodal artefacts, and AI-mediated dialogue, these tools support inquiry, personalisation, and emotional engagement with historical objects.

However, AI-supported heritage initiatives also raise epistemic and ethical tensions. Generative models can visualise local or marginalised histories and amplify excluded voices (He et al., 2024; Capistrán et al., 2025; Poce et al., 2025), yet they risk algorithmic bias, misrepresentation, and symbolic appropriation when shaped by dominant data or weak community input (Sánchez-Martín et al., 2025; Kansteiner, 2022). Effective use therefore requires careful curation, ethical framing, and clear negotiation of authorship and authority.

Beyond formal education, AI is also used to reconstruct fragmented archives for communities affected by displacement or violence, supporting emotional repair and challenging dominant memory regimes (Capistrán et al., 2025; VanGorder, 2025). Yet such projects raise unresolved concerns about data sovereignty, consent, and the commodification of trauma, showing that AI-driven inclusion remains politically and ethically contested (He et al., 2024; Sánchez-Martín et al., 2025).

GENERATIVE AI AS A DIALOGIC PARTNER IN HISTORICAL INQUIRY

Empirical comparisons of AI-generated historical texts and student writing reveal AI's ambivalent role. Systems such as ChatGPT can produce formally coherent arguments aligned with historical-thinking criteria, yet often lack emotional depth, ethical positioning, and sensitivity to moral complexity (Tirado-Olivares et al., 2023;

Kindenberg, 2024). This highlights AI's value for modelling structure and offering feedback, while exposing its limits as a moral or interpretive agent.

Research on human–AI co-writing shows stronger learning outcomes when interaction is iterative and critical. Students who revise and re-prompt AI outputs engage more deeply with causality and narrative construction (Cohn et al., 2024; Nguyen et al., 2024). In history education, such practices support co-created timelines and counterfactual inquiry, similar to historical fiction approaches that foster empathy—provided speculation remains grounded in evidence (Savenije & De Bruijn, 2017; Stoddard, 2021; VanGorder, 2025; Kindenberg, 2024).

In classrooms, AI-generated texts and images increasingly function as "co-authors" that provoke source analysis rather than provide closure. By revealing how prompts and data shape representations, these tools encourage reflection on memory politics and moral judgment (Webb et al., 2019; Kansteiner, 2022; VanGorder, 2025), aligning with concerns about whose histories are represented (Barreiro & Pérez-Manjarrez, 2025; Stoddard, 2021).

However, significant gaps remain. The long-term effects of AI-generated history on students' memory, identity, and moral judgment are unclear, and methods for assessing whether AI-supported scenarios genuinely enhance historical thinking are still developing (Barreiro & Pérez-Manjarrez, 2025; Stoddard, 2021; Capistrán et al., 2025; Tirado-Olivares et al., 2023; Savenije & De Bruijn, 2017; Kindenberg, 2024; Kansteiner, 2022).

EPISTEMIC RISKS AND PEDAGOGICAL PRECONDITIONS FOR AI IN HISTORY EDUCATION

Existing research suggests that generative AI should be understood as a collaborative, memory-sensitive partner in history education rather than an autonomous narrator. When embedded in human-led inquiry, it can support inclusive and multimodal engagement with the past, yet this potential requires strong ethical grounding—centred on human judgment, source criticism, and attention to power, representation, and memory.

From a history education perspective, claims that AI deepens historical understanding warrant caution. Its rapid and uneven adoption means many users treat AI outputs as equivalent to historical knowledge. Where critical reading and source evaluation skills are weak, AI-generated narratives—often simplified or decontextualised—may mislead learners, reinforcing epistemic passivity rather than critical thinking. This highlights a structural issue: historical analysis is not innate but cultivated through comparison, multiperspectivity, and engagement with diverse evidence.

Although AI is ideally a dialogic partner that provokes questioning and revision, in practice it often reinforces existing views through confirmation-seeking use. Such patterns risk narrowing interpretation and weakening contextual judgment, increasing the likelihood of presentism and ethical simplification. Uneven teacher expertise, curricular pressures, and classroom constraints further encourage one-directional use of AI for convenience rather than sustained inquiry.

Ultimately, the key challenge is not AI's technical capacity but whether history education systems are prepared to integrate it responsibly. Without prioritising analytical depth, epistemic vigilance, and moral reasoning, AI may amplify existing weaknesses. Transformative use therefore requires shifting pedagogical priorities from content coverage toward comparative evidence analysis, dialogic interpretation, and critical examination of historical narratives, enabling AI to sharpen—rather than replace—human historical judgment.

PEDAGOGICAL DESIGN PATTERNS IN AI-SUPPORTED HISTORY EDUCATION

Research on AI-assisted history and heritage education consistently shows that learning improves only when students retain epistemic control over historical interpretation. AI tools are most effective when treated as provisional co-authors, while responsibility for interpretation and justification remains with learners (VanGorder, 2025; Moldovan et al., 2025). When AI outputs are accepted as authoritative, learning shifts to epistemic outsourcing, weakening historical reasoning.

Studies on virtual exhibitions and AI-augmented heritage learning stress design principles that prioritise student authorship. Learners must curate sources, construct narratives, and justify interpretations, using AI outputs as material to critique and contextualise rather than final accounts (VanGorder, 2025; Yu & Hu, 2025; Fareed et al., 2024; Moldovan et al., 2025). Similarly, chatbot interactions with historical figures may increase engagement but often reveal weak source validation and contextual analysis, showing that immersion alone does not ensure understanding (Luprichová, 2025; Tirado-Olivares et al., 2023; Oger et al., 2025).

Research on interactive agents and AI-mediated dialogues further highlights risks of over-trust and "narrative seduction," where emotional realism reduces critical judgment (Kouzelis & Spantidi, 2024; Oger et al., 2025; Moldovan et al., 2025). Effective practice therefore requires strong teacher mediation, transparent signalling of speculative elements, and systematic comparison with historical sources.

Prompt engineering has also emerged as a key pedagogical practice. Designing and refining prompts helps students see how framing shapes historical representation and reveals interpretive contingencies in AI systems (VanGorder, 2025; Walter,

2024; Cain, 2023; Lazovsky et al., 2024). Such iterative use fosters meta-historical awareness of narrative construction and representation (Kouzelis & Spantidi, 2024; Moldovan et al., 2025).

Although AI outputs often contain inaccuracies or biases, these limitations can support learning by enabling source criticism and evidentiary evaluation (VanGorder, 2025; Yu & Hu, 2025; Tirado-Olivares et al., 2023; Foka, 2024; Fareed et al., 2024; Moldovan et al., 2025). When critically examined, AI becomes a tool for analysing historical narration; when accepted uncritically, it encourages superficial understanding.

Overall, the literature emphasises that students must act as curators, critics, and validators of knowledge. AI-supported history learning is effective only within human-centred pedagogy that requires evidence verification, critical reflection, and awareness of bias (VanGorder, 2025; Yu & Hu, 2025; Luprichová, 2025; Tirado-Olivares et al., 2023; Oger et al., 2025; Moldovan et al., 2025). Without such guidance, AI produces plausible narratives rather than genuine historical understanding.

COLONIALITY, EPISTEMIC INJUSTICE, AND THE RISKS OF GENERATIVE AI IN HISTORY EDUCATION

Critical scholarship increasingly shows that generative AI in history education is not neutral but embedded in colonial power relations and epistemic hierarchies. Large language and image models are largely trained on Western datasets and infrastructures, reproducing Western perspectives as universal while reinforcing existing asymmetries (Mohamed et al., 2020; Mollema, 2024; Muldoon & Wu, 2023). Without critical framing, their use in classrooms risks normalising these imbalances.

Scholars identify several mechanisms behind this dynamic. First, AI development reflects forms of digital colonialism, where Western epistemologies and curricular models are globalised while data and resources are extracted from the Global South (Mohamed et al., 2020; Maimela & Mbonde, 2025; Mollema, 2024; Muldoon & Wu, 2023), leading to the standardisation of Western historical frameworks. Second, cognitive imperialism marginalises Indigenous and non-Western knowledge, producing epistemicide by erasing alternative perspectives (Ofosu-Asare, 2024; Maimela & Mbonde, 2025; Mollema, 2024; Muzanenhamo & Power, 2024; Khurana, 2025). Third, AI may reinforce epistemic injustice by privileging dominant voices while rendering marginalised testimonies and interpretive frameworks less credible (Ajmani et al., 2024; Miragoli, 2024; Muzanenhamo & Power, 2024).

These risks are especially visible in cultural heritage contexts, where biased archives and datasets privilege Eurocentric perspectives while misrepresenting or omitting non-Western histories (Błoch et al., 2025; De Andrade & Gobbi, 2025;

Foka & Griffin, 2024). Similarly, AI-generated educational content often defaults to Western norms, reinforcing digital neocolonialism and narrowing curricular diversity (Nyaaba et al., 2024; Zembylas, 2021; Maimela & Mbonde, 2025). Such dynamics contribute to "machine memory," where algorithmic systems shape which pasts become visible and legitimate (Kansteiner, 2022; Miragoli, 2024; Mollema, 2024; Muldoon & Wu, 2023; De Andrade & Gobbi, 2025).

To address these challenges, scholars advocate decolonial and critically digital pedagogies that treat AI as an object of ethical and historical inquiry (Mohamed et al., 2020; Zembylas, 2021; Maimela & Mbonde, 2025; VanGorder, 2025). This involves teaching students to analyse how AI systems are designed, whose data they use, and whose interests they serve (Ofosu-Asare, 2024; Mohamed et al., 2020; Muldoon & Wu, 2023), while developing critical digital and historical literacies that interrogate bias, representation, and archival power (Foka & Griffin, 2024; Kansteiner, 2022; Miragoli, 2024; De Andrade & Gobbi, 2025; VanGorder, 2025).

Decolonial AI pedagogy also emphasises integrating Indigenous and local knowledge, community archives, and marginalised perspectives, using AI to expose rather than reproduce exclusion (Błoch et al., 2025; Ofosu-Asare, 2024; Moldovan et al., 2025; Maimela & Mbonde, 2025; Muzanenhamo & Power, 2024; Khurana, 2025). Human-centred prompt design can further reveal bias and support plural interpretations (Nyaaba et al., 2024; VanGorder, 2025; Zembylas, 2021).

Overall, research suggests that uncritical use of generative AI may reinforce Western-centric "machine memory" and digital colonialism. Ethical use in history education therefore requires decolonial approaches that prioritise critical literacy, local knowledge, and scrutiny of whose histories AI represents, enabling AI to support historical justice rather than epistemic domination.

PEDAGOGICAL IMPLICATIONS AND FUTURE DIRECTIONS

Teacher education is the key site where the promises and risks of generative AI in history education are either critically addressed or unreflectively reproduced. Preparing future teachers requires more than technical training; it demands technological–pedagogical–ethical competence to evaluate, mediate, and challenge AI-generated knowledge. Extensions of the TPACK model, such as Intelligent-TPACK, emphasise that teachers need not only technological knowledge but also pedagogical judgment and ethical awareness to assess reliability and design historically responsible learning tasks (Celik, 2022). Without this competence, AI risks being used merely as an efficiency tool rather than a contested epistemic actor.

Research on pre-service history teachers reveals gaps in pedagogical readiness and ethical awareness. Although many express openness toward AI, they often lack experience designing inquiry-based tasks or addressing bias, authorship, and accountability (Antin & Dzulkifli, 2025). This highlights the need for experiential AI training in teacher education that integrates design practice, critical reflection, and institutional support. More broadly, scholars argue that AI should function as a human-centred, dialogic medium that strengthens rather than replaces empathy, moral responsibility, and critical reflection (Karaoulas, 2025; Ren, 2025; Siddiqui et al., 2025). In history education, teachers remain responsible for ethical interpretation and historical meaning.

The literature identifies key design principles for AI-supported history pedagogy. First, inquiry and student agency must remain central, with AI used to support questioning and evidentiary reasoning rather than content reproduction (Burgos-Videla et al., 2025; Sleeter et al., 2020; Conn, 2024). Second, plurality and inclusivity require deliberate attention to diverse sources and safeguards against bias (Burgos-Videla et al., 2025; Chatzichristofis, 2025; Ni & Shin, 2025; Pansoni et al., 2023; Jaillant & Rees, 2022). Third, transparency and accountability demand clear labelling of AI outputs and discussion of data and roles within learning environments (Airaj, 2024; Karaoulas, 2025; Balasubramanian et al., 2023; Siddiqui et al., 2025; Jaillant & Rees, 2022). Fourth, critical digital and historical literacy must enable teachers to analyse AI bias and the conditions of knowledge production (Burgos-Videla et al., 2025; Airaj, 2024; Ren, 2025; Ni & Shin, 2025; Chamo et al., 2025; Atchley et al., 2024). Finally, human-centred collaboration should guide integration, preserving teacher agency and contextual judgment (Celik, 2022; Kim, 2023; Ren, 2025; Atchley et al., 2024; Siddiqui et al., 2025).

Overall, research emphasises embedding AI-supported history pedagogy within structured frameworks such as Intelligent-TPACK or AI-TEACH that foreground inquiry, plurality, transparency, and teacher responsibility. Without such preparation, AI may reinforce inequities and epistemic shortcuts; when carefully integrated, it can support critical and inclusive history education. From a history educator's perspective, the key issue is not AI's capacity to generate persuasive content, but whether education systems can prevent it from gaining epistemic authority. Premature inclusion of sensitive topics without adequate preparation may also reproduce simplified interpretations. Accordingly, Table 1 outlines conditions under which AI use becomes pedagogically productive or epistemically risky, challenging assumptions that greater representation or technological sophistication automatically deepens historical understanding.

Table 1. A memory-sensitive pedagogical risk framework

Dimension	Productive / Defensible Use (Conditions to Meet)	Fragile / High-Risk Use (Where Caution is Warranted)
Epistemic status of AI	AI is treated as a *provisional* generator of hypotheses, alternatives, or representations to be scrutinised.	AI is treated as a *neutral narrator* or "answer engine," quietly inheriting epistemic authority.
Teacher role and preparedness	Teacher acts as an epistemic mediator: designs tasks, sets boundaries, models critique, and monitors ethical/affective dynamics (supported by Intelligent-TPACK/AI-TEACH type training).	Teacher is positioned as a tool user or content distributor; limited preparation leads to "plug-in" adoption and reliance on AI outputs.
Student agency and authorship	Students remain authors and critics: prompting is iterative; outputs are revised, justified, and documented; responsibility for meaning-making stays with learners.	Students become consumers; AI replaces drafting, interpretation, or argumentation, producing epistemic outsourcing and passive acceptance.
Evidence and source discipline	Outputs must be corroborated with primary/ secondary sources; AI is used to *surface* gaps, bias, and alternative framings, not to settle claims.	Outputs are used without verification; plausibility substitutes for evidence; "access" is conflated with "validity."
Narrative openness vs. closure	Tasks are designed to slow down thinking: competing interpretations, uncertainty, and contingency are made explicit; narrative construction is discussed.	AI is used to speed up coverage; streamlined narratives and closure are rewarded; complexity is reduced to neat storylines.
Bias, representation, and inclusion	Plurality is *designed*: diverse archives and standpoints are intentionally curated; students are trained to detect omission, silencing, and dataset-driven bias.	"More voices" is assumed to be automatically democratic; AI reproduces dominant statistical narratives, colonial frames, or single-story accounts.
Sensitive/traumatic and identity-laden histories	Inclusion of difficult knowledge is scaffolded: trauma-informed mediation, ethical distance, and classroom safety protocols are in place; teacher education is explicit.	Sensitive topics are inserted prematurely without preparation; classroom discussion risks moralising, presentism, polarisation, or identity conflict.
Visual representations (images, reenactments, XR)	Images are labelled as reconstructed/ speculative where relevant; anachronism and aesthetic distortion are used as prompts for source criticism and historiographical debate.	Visual realism seduces judgment; anachronistic or biased imagery is consumed as evidence, reinforcing presentism and "narrative seduction."

continued on following page

Table 1. Continued

Dimension	Productive / Defensible Use (Conditions to Meet)	Fragile / High-Risk Use (Where Caution is Warranted)
Assessment and accountability	Assessment rewards reasoning: sourcing, contextualisation, corroboration, ethical justification, and reflection on AI limitations; provenance is documented.	Assessment rewards output quality/speed; provenance is opaque; students' reasoning disappears behind polished AI artefacts.
Institutional alignment and equity	Policies, infrastructure, and support reduce uneven adoption; time and guidance enable dialogic use rather than convenience-driven shortcuts.	Digital divides persist; AI becomes an efficiency patch for overloaded curricula, amplifying inequities and "shortcut" cultures.

While Table 1 summarises key design principles and normative conditions for ethical AI use in history education, such principles remain abstract unless their epistemic consequences are made visible. To address this gap, Figure 1 conceptualises AI-supported history pedagogy as a dynamic epistemic space, illustrating how shifts in pedagogical intent and human interpretive authority produce qualitatively different educational outcomes (see Figure 1).

Figure 1. Epistemic–pedagogical boundary framework for generative AI in history education

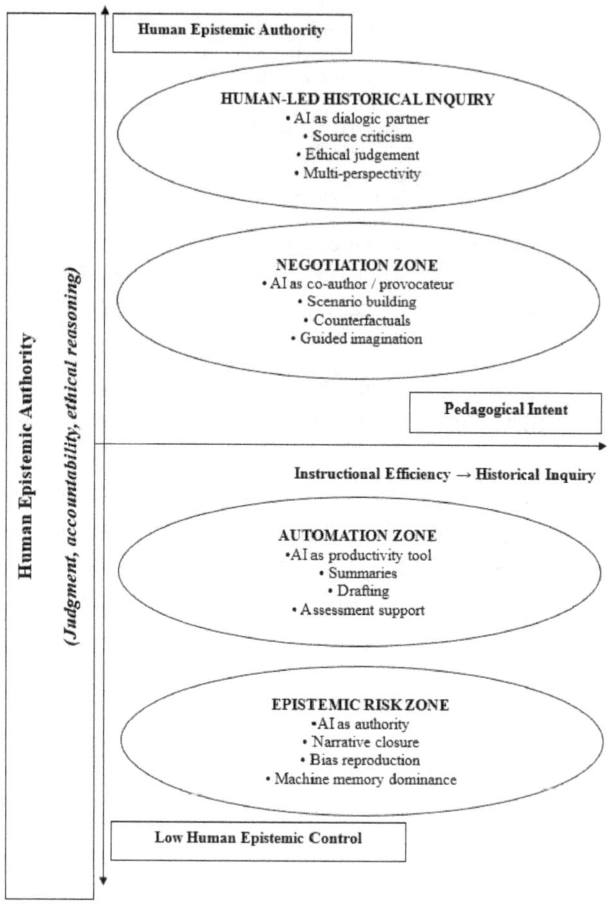

Building on the epistemic boundaries articulated in Figure 1, Figure 2 synthesises the dispersed findings of the reviewed literature into an integrated pedagogical framework. Rather than proposing another prescriptive model, Figure 2 visualises the conditions under which generative AI shifts from epistemic risk to pedagogical resource in history education. By mapping zones of automation, co-interpretation, and human-led inquiry, the framework foregrounds the central claim of this chapter: that the educational value of generative AI lies not in efficiency or substitution, but in its capacity to operate as a critically mediated, human-centred partner within historically grounded learning (See Figure 2).

Figure 2. An integrated epistemic–pedagogical boundary framework for generative AI in history education

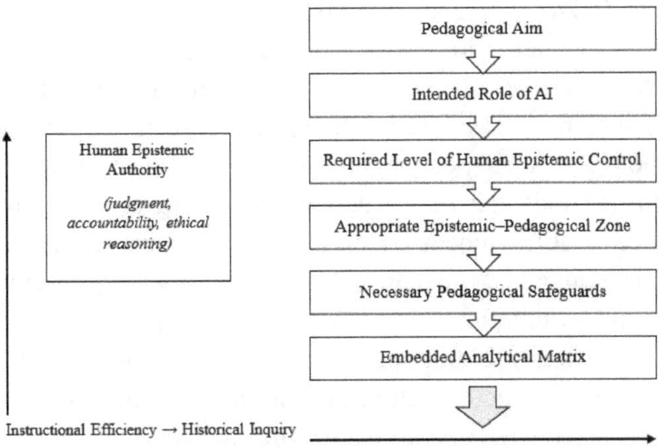

Embedded Analytical Matrix

Zone	Pedagogical Aim	AI Role	Epistemic Control Level	Teacher Preconditions
Zone 1: Human-led Inquiry	Historical inquiry, source interpretation, causal reasoning; counterfactual thinking, historical imagination, empathy	Dialogic partner / co-interpreter; provocateur / co-author	Very High / High	Mandatory source comparison; AI outputs explicitly labelled; teacher-mediated discussion; ethical reflection
Zone 2: Co-interpretive Use	Summarisation, drafting support, organisational help	Productivity tool	Moderate	Explicit separation of evidence vs speculation; revision and critique of AI outputs
Zone 3: Instrumental Use	Summarisation, drafting support, organisational help	Productivity tool	Moderate	No substitution for analysis; outputs not assessed as historical interpretation
Zone 4: Epistemic Risk	Knowledge delivery, narrative explanation	Authoritative narrator	Low (problematic)	Use discouraged; requires explicit deconstruction if used

Pedagogical Intent: Instructional Efficiency → Historical Inquiry

CONCLUSION

The growing presence of generative AI in history education has renewed debates on authorship, authority, and the ethics of historical knowledge. Research shows AI can broaden how students engage with the past, but only when human judgment remains central. Treated as a neutral narrator, AI risks oversimplifying complexity and reinforcing dominant narratives; embedded in human-centred, ethical pedagogy, however, it can support deeper inquiry rather than replace historical thinking.

Studies in history and architectural history education demonstrate that generative AI can stimulate curiosity, affective engagement, and interpretive exploration through practices such as AI-generated images, reconstructed environments, or conversational interactions with simulated historical figures (VanGorder, 2025; Kong & Yang, 2024; Mierwald, 2024). These encounters often create a sense of immediacy and personal connection that traditional textual sources struggle to achieve, particularly for learners who experience the past as abstract or distant. Importantly, the educational value of such practices does not lie in their realism, but in their capacity to provoke questions about perspective, representation, and absence.

Research further indicates that structured prompting grounded in primary and secondary sources enables students to surface narrative gaps, test alternative explanations, and practise contextual reasoning while simultaneously observing how training data, framing, and assumptions shape AI outputs (VanGorder, 2025; Kansteiner, 2022; Fareed et al., 2024). In this way, generative AI becomes a reflective surface through which the constructed nature of historical narratives—and of "machine memory" itself—is rendered visible. Rather than delivering answers, AI-supported activities can destabilise certainty and invite comparative, evidence-based analysis.

Beyond history-specific contexts, the broader educational literature frames generative AI as a potential knowledge producer capable of supporting personalised learning pathways, self-regulation, and sustained engagement—provided that teachers retain orchestration and evaluative authority (Wang & Guo, 2023; Kong & Yang, 2024; Mittal et al., 2024). Human-centred frameworks consistently stress that AI should augment attentiveness, dialogue, and reflection, not replace human judgment or ethical responsibility (Airaj, 2024; Karaoulas, 2025; Fowlin et al., 2025). In history education, this distinction is especially consequential, as the discipline's core questions are inseparable from moral interpretation, responsibility, and contested memory.

Across this literature, a convergent set of ethical and pedagogical principles emerges that defines when and how generative AI can meaningfully enrich history education.

First, transparency and accountability are foundational. Scholars emphasise the importance of explicitly labelling AI-generated content, discussing data provenance and model limitations, and confronting the "black box" character of generative systems (Airaj, 2024; Bearman & Ajjawi, 2023; Pope, 2024). Such practices prevent the silent transfer of epistemic authority from historians and educators to algorithms and reinforce students' awareness of AI as a situated, fallible system rather than an objective arbiter of the past.

Second, plurality and inclusion must be actively designed rather than assumed. Research highlights the potential of AI to surface overlooked narratives and supplement dominant accounts, but also warns that this potential is realised only when educators intentionally foreground marginalised voices, diverse archives, and non-canonical perspectives (VanGorder, 2025; Atenas et al., 2025; Kong & Yang,

2024; Mierwald, 2024; Yusuf et al., 2024). Without such intentionality, AI tends to reproduce the statistical dominance of already-privileged histories.

Third, critical engagement is non-negotiable. Multiple studies stress that AI responses should be framed as provisional hypotheses to be tested against historical evidence, rather than as authoritative explanations. Teaching students to evaluate AI outputs for bias, error, anachronism, and omission strengthens evaluative judgment and aligns AI use with the disciplinary practices of history (VanGorder, 2025; Kansteiner, 2022; Choi, 2025; Siddiqui et al., 2025; Bearman & Ajjawi, 2023; Mierwald, 2024).

Finally, student agency is central to ethical AI integration. When students are positioned as designers of prompts, constructors of scenarios, and critics of AI-generated artefacts, they engage with AI as historical actors rather than passive consumers of algorithmic narratives (VanGorder, 2025; Kong & Yang, 2024; Lim et al., 2023; Fowlin et al., 2025; Williams et al., 2022). This shift reinforces authorship, responsibility, and reflexivity—key dimensions of historical consciousness.

Current research suggests that the key issue in history education is not whether generative AI is used, but how it is pedagogically framed. Within human-centred and ethically grounded approaches, AI can deepen historical understanding and inclusive engagement; treated as an autonomous knower, however, it risks narrowing interpretation and obscuring the moral dimension of historical inquiry. The task is therefore not to delegate memory to machines, but to use them to make the work of memory more visible and critically examined.

AI USE STATEMENT

As English is not the author's first language, limited use of AI-based language tools (e.g., ChatGPT) was made solely for linguistic editing and clarity. All academic content, arguments, interpretations, and scholarly responsibility remain entirely with the author.

REFERENCES

Airaj, M. (2024). Ethical artificial intelligence for teaching-learning in higher education. *Education and Information Technologies*, *29*(13), 17145–17167. DOI: 10.1007/s10639-024-12545-x

Ajmani, L., Foriest, J., Taylor, J., Pittman, K., Gilbert, S., & Devito, M. (2024). Whose Knowledge is Valued? Epistemic Injustice in CSCW Applications. *Proceedings of the ACM on Human-Computer Interaction*, *8*(CSCW2), 1–28. DOI: 10.1145/3687062

Alvén, F. (2024). Controversial issues in history teaching. *Journal of Curriculum Studies*, *56*(5), 537–553. DOI: 10.1080/00220272.2024.2322502

Aminullah, M., Susanto, H., Nadilla, D. F., & Mardiani, F. (2025). Challenges And Strategies Of History Teachers In Utilizing Digital Learning Media: A Case Study At SMKN 1 Banjarmasin. *Jurnal Pendidikan Ips*, *15*(3), 751–758. DOI: 10.37630/jpi.v15i3.3257

Amoakwa, A., Asante, G., & Gyimah, E. (2025). Implementing History Curriculum in Basic Schools: Techniques and Challenges. *East African Journal of Education Studies.*, *8*(3), 306–317. DOI: 10.37284/eajes.8.3.3524

Anggiani, A., Dewi, O., Simanjuntak, C., Barus, A., & Sari, I. (2025). Challenges and Opportunities for High School History Teachers in Using TikTok and Other Social Media for Learning. *Riwayat: Educational Journal of History and Humanities.*, *8*(3), 2623–2631. DOI: 10.24815/jr.v8i3.47375

Atchley, P., Pannell, H., Wofford, K., Hopkins, M., & Atchley, R. A. (2024). Human and AI collaboration in the higher education environment: Opportunities and concerns. *Cognitive Research: Principles and Implications*, *9*(1), 20. DOI: 10.1186/s41235-024-00547-9

Atenas, J., Havemann, L., & Nerantzi, C. (2025). Critical and creative pedagogies for artificial intelligence and data literacy: An epistemic data justice approach for academic practice. *Research in Learning Technology*, *32*, 3296. DOI: 10.25304/rlt.v32.3296

Balasubramanian, S., Devarajan, H. R., Raparthi, M., Dodda, S. B., Maruthi, S., & Adnyana, I. M. D. M. (2023). Ethical considerations in ai-assisted decision-making for end-of-life care in healthcare. *Power System Technology*, *47*(4), 167–182. DOI: 10.52783/pst.168

Banerjee, D. (2024). The Impact of Digital Tools on the Teaching of History: A Comparative Study of Traditional and Technology-Integrated Teaching Methods. *International Journal For Multidisciplinary Research*, *3*(3), 22919. DOI: 10.36948/ijfmr.2024.v06i03.22919

Bañuelos Capistrán, J., Zavala Scherer, D., & Lugo Rodríguez, N. (2025). Art, community and AI: Images for an affective memory. *Frontiers in Communication*, *10*, 1567694. DOI: 10.3389/fcomm.2025.1567694

Barreiro, A., & Pérez-Manjarrez, E. (2025). Collective memory, moral judgements, and history education. *Current Opinion in Psychology*, *66*, 102113. DOI: 10.1016/j.copsyc.2025.102113

Bartelds, H., Savenije, G., & Van Boxtel, C. (2020). Students' and teachers' beliefs about historical empathy in secondary history education. *Theory and Research in Social Education*, *48*(4), 529–551. DOI: 10.1080/00933104.2020.1808131

Bearman, M., & Ajjawi, R. (2023). Learning to work with the black box: Pedagogy for a world with artificial intelligence. *British Journal of Educational Technology*, *54*(5), 1160–1173. DOI: 10.1111/bjet.13337

Bekturganov, K., & Nurpeissova, E. (2025). Digital History: Students' Opportunities to Eradicate National Nihilism Using Smart Products. *3i intellect idea innovation - интеллект идея инновация*. *1*(1), 308-314. DOI: 10.52269/22266070_2025_1_308

bin Antin, A. & Dzulkifli, D.N. (2025). A concept paper on readiness in artificial intelligence (AI) mastery and its impact on 21st century pedagogy among pre-service history teachers. *International Journal of Research and Innovation in Social Science (IJRISS)*, *9*(7), 1630–1636. DOI: 10.47772/IJRISS.2025.907000135

Bhagat, S., Meenakshi, Bakshi, P., & Aman. (. (2025). Integrating technology in history education: Digital pathways and transformative practices aligned with nep 2020. *International Journal on Science and Technology.*, *16*(2), 1–12. DOI: 10.71097/IJSAT.v16.i2.4531

Błoch, A., Oms, G., & Santana, C. (2025). Decolonizing Archival Narratives: Exploring Digital Bias in the Catalogs of Portuguese-Colonized African Territories. *Journal of African History*, *66*, e19. DOI: 10.1017/S0021853725100601

Burgos-Videla, C., Parada-Ulloa, M., & Martínez-Díaz, J. (2025). Critical thinking in the classroom: The historical method and historical discourse as tools for teaching social studies. *Frontiers in Sociology*, *10*, 1526437. DOI: 10.3389/fsoc.2025.1526437

Cain, W. (2023). Prompting Change: Exploring Prompt Engineering in Large Language Model AI and Its Potential to Transform Education. *TechTrends*, *68*(1), 47–57. DOI: 10.1007/s11528-023-00896-0

Celik, I. (2022). Towards Intelligent-TPACK: An empirical study on teachers' professional knowledge to ethically integrate artificial intelligence (AI)-based tools into education. *Computers in Human Behavior*, *138*, 107468. DOI: 10.1016/j.chb.2022.107468

Chamo, N., Biberman-Shalev, L., Bar-Tal, S., & Broza, O. (2025). Heutagogy Meets Generative AI in Teacher Education: Examining an Evolving Synergy. *Journal of Posthumanism.*, *5*(7), 1189–1208. DOI: 10.63332/joph.v5i7.2906

Chatzichristofis, S. (2025). Reframing AI in Education: A Pedagogical Opportunity, Not a Technocratic Threat. *Journal of Research in Science Teaching*, *63*(1), 97–103. DOI: 10.1002/tea.70024

Choi, B. (2025). Identifying Issues and Seeking Improvements in History Education Through the Use of Generative AI. *Education Research International*, *45*(1), 283–300. DOI: 10.34245/jed.45.1.283

Cohn, C., Snyder, C., & Fonteles, J., T. s., A., Montenegro, J., & Biswas, G. (. (2024). A multimodal approach to support teacher, researcher and AI collaboration in STEM+C learning environments. *British Journal of Educational Technology*, *56*, 595–620. DOI: 10.1111/bjet.13518

Conn, Z. (2024). A HOUSE WITH EXPOSED BEAMS: INQUIRY-BASED LEARNING AND HISTORIANS' ETHICAL RESPONSIBILITIES AS SCHOLAR-TEACHERS. *History and Theory*, *63*(4), 106–127. DOI: 10.1111/hith.12366

Corrales, M., Rodríguez, F., Merchán, M., Merchán, P., & Pérez, E. (2024). Comparative Analysis between Virtual Visits and Pedagogical Outings to Heritage Sites: An Application in the Teaching of History. *Heritage.*, *7*(1), 366–379. DOI: 10.3390/heritage7010018

De Andrade, T., & Gobbi, M. (2025). O algoritmo como arquivista: Curadoria algorítmica, apagamentos estruturais e a luta pela memória coletiva no século XXI. *Revista Memorare., 12*(1), e27026–e27026. DOI: 10.59306/memorare.v12e12025e27026

Delaben, R., Bual, J., & Madrigal, D. (2025). Student's Achievement of Learning Competencies and Challenges in Learning World History in Public High Schools. *Technium Social Sciences Journal., 72*, 312–331. DOI: 10.47577/tssj.v72i1.12903

Edling, S., Sharp, H., Löfström, J., & Ammert, N. (2020a). The good citizen: Revisiting moral motivations for introducing historical consciousness in history education drawing on the writings of Gadamer. *Citizenship. Social and Economics Education, 19*(2), 133–150. DOI: 10.1177/2047173420936622

Edling, S., Sharp, H., Löfström, J., & Ammert, N. (2020b). Why is ethics important in history education? A dialogue between the various ways of understanding the relationship between ethics and historical consciousness. *Ethics and Education, 15*(3), 336–354. DOI: 10.1080/17449642.2020.1780899

Evurulobi, C., Dagunduro, A., & Ajuwon, O.Chinasa Iroabughichi EvurulobiAdebukola Olufunke DagunduroOlanike Abiola Ajuwon. (2024). Digital narratives and historical representation: A review - analyzing how digital mediums are revolutionizing the way history is taught and perceived. *World Journal of Advanced Research and Reviews., 24*(1), 2083–2096. DOI: 10.30574/wjarr.2024.24.1.2852

Fareed, M., Nassif, A., & Nofal, E. (2024). Exploring the Potentials of Artificial Intelligence Image Generators for Educating the History of Architecture. *Heritage., 7*(3), 1727–1753. DOI: 10.3390/heritage7030081

Fesenko, A., Gurevych, R., Yarova, A., Gotsuliak, V., Dovhalets, O., & Perekhodko, N. (2025). Neuroethics and the Politics of Historical Memory: Rethinking Polish-Ukrainian Relations Through Education. *BRAIN. Broad Research in Artificial Intelligence and Neuroscience, 16*(2), 169–177. DOI: 10.70594/brain/16.2/13

Firmansyah, H., & Atmaja, T. (2025). Transformation of history learning methods in the digital era: Challenges and opportunities in schools. [IJED]. *Indonesian Journal of Educational Development, 6*(1), 264–277. DOI: 10.59672/ijed.v6i1.4791

Foka, A. (2024). A Framework for Critical Evaluation of Text-to-Image Models: Integrating Art Historical Analysis, Artistic Exploration, and Critical Prompt Engineering. *ArXiv*, abs/2412.12774. https://doi.org//arxiv.2412.12774DOI: 10.48550

Foka, A., & Griffin, G. (2024). AI, Cultural Heritage, and Bias: Some Key Queries That Arise from the Use of GenAI. *Heritage., 7*(11), 6125–6136. DOI: 10.3390/heritage7110287

Fowlin, J., Coleman, D., Ryan, S., Gallo, C., Soares, E., & Hazelton, N. (2025). Empowering Educators: Operationalizing Age-Old Learning Principles Using AI. *Education Sciences*, *15*(3), 393. DOI: 10.3390/educsci15030393

Grata, A., & Llaneta, R. (2024). *Understanding Philippine History Education in the Age of Disinformation: A Phenomenological Exploration*. International Journal of Education and Humanities., DOI: 10.58557/(ijeh).v4i4.262

Grever, M., & Vlies, T. (2017). Why national narratives are perpetuated: A literature review on new insights from history textbook research. *London Review of Education*, *15*(2), 286–301. DOI: 10.18546/LRE.15.2.11

Gunter, D. (2025). Integrating Marginalized Voices into History Education. *Journal of Educational Impact.*, *2*(1), 56–64. DOI: 10.70617/eduimpact.2025.12

Güven, İ. (2025). Yapay zekâya (YZ) ilişkin teorik çerçeve ve eğitimsel temeller. [Theoretical framework and educational foundations of artificial intelligence (AI)] In Güven, İ., & Ayantaş, T. (Eds.), *Sosyal bilgiler eğitiminde yapay zekâ (YZ)* [*Artificial intelligence (AI) in social studies education*]. Pegem Akademi.

Harnes, H. (2025). What can empirical research tell us about how to develop students' historical empathy? A scoping review. *History Education Research Journal.*, *22*(1), 1–18. DOI: 10.14324/HERJ.22.1.18

He, Z., Su, J., Chen, L., Wang, T., & Lc, R. (2024). 'I Recall the Past': Exploring How People Collaborate with Generative AI to Create Cultural Heritage Narratives. *Proceedings of the ACM on Human-Computer Interaction*, *9*(2), 1–30. DOI: 10.1145/3711006

Hetharion, B., Yafie, E., Bakri, T., Ilyas, S., Nirmala, B., & Setyaningsih, D. (2025). Using Emerging Digital Technologies Adoption for History Teaching: A Teacher-Centric Unified Theory of Acceptance and Use of Technology Analysis of Motivational and Environmental Influences. *European Journal of Educational Research.*, *14*(3), 999–1014. DOI: 10.12973/eu-jer.14.3.999

Ifenthaler, D., & Schumacher, C. (2023). Reciprocal issues of artificial and human intelligence in education. *Journal of Research on Technology in Education*, *55*(1), 1–6. DOI: 10.1080/15391523.2022.2154511

Ishak, N., & Ahmad, A. (2025). History Education and Students' Historical Consciousness in Malaysian Primary Schools. *International Journal of Academic Research in Progressive Education and Development.*, *14*(2). Advance online publication. DOI: 10.6007/IJARPED/v14-i2/25307

Jaillant, L., & Rees, A. (2022). Applying AI to digital archives: Trust, collaboration and shared professional ethics. *Digit. Scholarsh. Humanit.*, *38*(2), 571–585. DOI: 10.1093/llc/fqac073

Kansteiner, W. (2022). Digital Doping for Historians: Can History, Memory, And Historical Theory Be Rendered Artificially Intelligent? *History and Theory*, *61*(4), 119–133. DOI: 10.1111/hith.12282

Karaoulas, A. (2025). Supervision and Teaching in Education: Historical Development and Contemporary Transformation in The Digital Age. *International Journal of Research in Education Humanities and Commerce.*, *6*(3), 73–91. DOI: 10.37602/IJREHC.2025.6306

Khurana, S. (2025). Decolonizing Artificial Intelligence: Indigenous Knowledge Systems, Epistemic Pluralism, and the Ethics of Technology. *Journal of Computer Allied Intelligence.*, *3*(3), 1–10. DOI: 10.69996/jcai.2025013

Kim, J. (2023). Leading teachers' perspective on teacher-AI collaboration in education. *Education and Information Technologies*, *29*(7), 8693–8724. DOI: 10.1007/s10639-023-12109-5

Kindenberg, B. (2024). ChatGPT-Generated and Student-Written Historical Narratives: A Comparative Analysis. *Education Sciences*, *14*(5), 330. DOI: 10.3390/educsci14050530

Kindenberg, B. (2025). The Role of AI in Historical Simulation Design: A TPACK Perspective on a French Revolution Simulation Design Experience. *Education Sciences*, *15*(2), 192. DOI: 10.3390/educsci15020192

Kirs, E. (2023). Historical reflection as a source of inspiration for youth resistance in illiberal regimes – a qualitative study of the FreeSZFE movement in Hungary. *Journal of Youth Studies*, *28*(1), 213–235. DOI: 10.1080/13676261.2023.2261861

Kong, S., & Yang, Y. (2024). A Human-Centered Learning and Teaching Framework Using Generative Artificial Intelligence for Self-Regulated Learning Development Through Domain Knowledge Learning in K–12 Settings. *IEEE Transactions on Learning Technologies*, *17*, 1588–1599. DOI: 10.1109/TLT.2024.3392830

Kouzelis, L., & Spantidi, O. (2024). Enhancing Historical Extended Reality Experiences: Prompt Engineering Strategies for AI-Generated Dialogue. *Applied Sciences (Basel, Switzerland)*, *14*(15), 6405. DOI: 10.3390/app14156405

Koyama, S. (2023). The potential of transnational history education: Attempts at university teaching practice in East Asia. *Memory Studies*, *16*(6), 1663–1670. DOI: 10.1177/17506980231204203

Lazovsky, G., Raz, T., & Kenett, Y. (2024). The Art of Creative Inquiry—From Question Asking to Prompt Engineering. *The Journal of Creative Behavior*, *59*(1), e671. DOI: 10.1002/jocb.671

Lee, B. (2023). Digital Tools & Inquiry-Based Learning in History Education. *Muallim Journal of Social Science and Humanities.*, *7*(4), 78–88. DOI: 10.33306/mjssh/255

Lim, W., Gunasekara, A., Pallant, J., Pallant, J., & Pechenkina, E. (2023). Generative AI and the future of education: Ragnarök or reformation? A paradoxical perspective from management educators. *International Journal of Management Education*, *21*(2), 100790. DOI: 10.1016/j.ijme.2023.100790

Luprichová, J. (2025). Enhancing Historical Understanding, Gender Perspectives, and Critical Thinking. *Resource*, *12*, 188–197. DOI: 10.53349/re-source.2025.is1.a1391

Ly, C., Peng, E., Liu, K., Qin, A., Howe, G., Cheng, A., & Cuadra, A. (2025). Museum in the Classroom: Engaging Students with Augmented Reality Museum Artifacts and Generative AI. *Proceedings of the Extended Abstracts of the CHI Conference on Human Factors in Computing Systems*. 1-8. DOI: 10.1145/3706599.3719787

Maimela, C., & Mbonde, P. (2025). Artificial intelligence in South African universities: Curriculum transformation and decolonisation—aid or obstacle? *Frontiers in Sociology*, *10*, 1543471. DOI: 10.3389/fsoc.2025.1543471

Malysheva, O., Tokareva, E., Orchakova, L., & Smirnova, Y. (2022). The effect of online learning in modern history education. *Heliyon*, *8*(7), e09965. Advance online publication. DOI: 10.1016/j.heliyon.2022.e09965

Mierwald, M. (2024). Chatting about the Past with Artificial Intelligence. *Journal of Educational Media. Memoria y Sociedad : Revista del Departamento de Historia y Geografia*, *16*(2), 143–173. DOI: 10.3167/jemms.2024.160206

Miles, J. (2018). Teaching history for truth and reconciliation: The challenges and opportunities of narrativity, temporality, and identity. *McGill Journal of Education*, *53*(2). Advance online publication. DOI: 10.7202/1058399ar

Miller, B., & Spohnholz, J. (2023). Collaboratively Reforming General Education History Teaching and Learning: A Roadmap for the Twenty-First Century. *Proceedings of the H-Net Teaching Conference*. Vol 1. 77-87. DOI: 10.33823/phtc.v1i1.203

Miragoli, M. (2024). Conformism, Ignorance & Injustice: AI as a Tool of Epistemic Oppression. *Episteme (Edinburgh)*, *22*(2), 522–540. DOI: 10.1017/epi.2024.11

Mittal, U., Sai, S., Chamola, V., & Sangwan, D. (2024). A Comprehensive Review on Generative AI for Education. *IEEE Access : Practical Innovations, Open Solutions*, *12*, 142733–142759. DOI: 10.1109/ACCESS.2024.3468368

Mohamed, S., Png, M., & Isaac, W. (2020). Decolonial AI: Decolonial Theory as Sociotechnical Foresight in Artificial Intelligence. *Philosophy & Technology*, *33*(4), 659–684. DOI: 10.1007/s13347-020-00405-8

Moldovan, S., Moldovan, I., & Rice, T. (2025). Speculative Memory and Machine Augmentation: A Polyvocal Rendering of Brutalist Architecture Through AI and Photogrammetry. *Heritage.*, *8*(10), 401. DOI: 10.3390/heritage8100401

Mollema, W. J. T. (2024). Decolonial AI as Disenclosure. *Open Journal of Social Sciences*, *12*(2), 574–603. DOI: 10.4236/jss.2024.122032

Mollès, D., & Parada-Ulloa, M. (2025). The classroom as a space of resistance. Cooperation, gratitude and collective memory between neuroscience and social science. *Frontiers in Sociology*, *10*, 1567675. Advance online publication. DOI: 10.3389/fsoc.2025.1567675

Moskalyuk, M., & Len, A. (2025). Digital Technologies and Their Role in Studying History. *Open Educational E-Environment of Modern University*, (18), 92–102. DOI: 10.28925/2414-0325.2025.188

Muis, A., Lukin, S., Sharif, S., Rashid, N., & Hamid, Z. (2024). Nation-Building through History Education: Mutual Goals in Shaping Student Character. *International Journal of Academic Research in Progressive Education and Development.*, *13*(3), 2391–2397. DOI: 10.6007/IJARPED/v13-i3/22157

Muldoon, J., & Wu, B. (2023). Artificial Intelligence in the Colonial Matrix of Power. *Philosophy & Technology*, *36*(4), 1–24. DOI: 10.1007/s13347-023-00687-8

Muzanenhamo, P., & Power, S. (2024). ChatGPT and accounting in African contexts: Amplifying epistemic injustice. *Critical Perspectives on Accounting*, *99*, 102735. DOI: 10.1016/j.cpa.2024.102735

Nguyen, A., Hong, Y., Dang, B., & Huang, X. (2024). Human-AI collaboration patterns in AI-assisted academic writing. *Studies in Higher Education*, *49*(5), 847–864. DOI: 10.1080/03075079.2024.2323593

Ni, L., & Shin, C. (2025). Humanism Enhancing Student Motivation in History Learning Through AI-Driven e-Cooperative and e-Collaborative Methods in Rural Education. *Randwick International of Education and Linguistics Science Journal.*, *6*(1), 99–108. DOI: 10.47175/rielsj.v6i1.1132

Nkolika, C. (2025). Pedagogical Challenges Encountered by Teachers in Some Content Areas of the Reintroduced History Curriculum in Junior Secondary Schools in Awka Education Zone. *Indonesian Journal of Innovative Teaching and Learning.*, *2*(1), 72–80. DOI: 10.64420/ijitl.v2i1.176

Nyaaba, M., Wright, A., & Choi, G. L. (2024). Generative AI and digital neocolonialism in global education: Towards an equitable framework. *arXiv preprint arXiv:2406.02966.*

Ofosu-Asare, Y. (2024). Cognitive imperialism in artificial intelligence: Counteracting bias with indigenous epistemologies. *AI & Society*, *40*(4), 3045–3061. DOI: 10.1007/s00146-024-02065-0

Oger, A., Gorisse, G., Fleury, S., & Christmann, O. (2025). MemorIA, an Architecture for Creating Interactive AI Historical Agents in Educational Contexts. *Computer Animation and Virtual Worlds*, *36*(3), e70032. DOI: 10.1002/cav.70032

Oksuzoglu, G. (2024). Construction of collective memory through official history education in North Cyprus (1971-2003). *Turkish History Education Journal.*, *13*(1), 142–169. DOI: 10.17497/tuhed.1423137

Pansoni, S., Tiribelli, S., Paolanti, M., Frontoni, E., & Giovanola, B. (2023). Design of an Ethical Framework for Artificial Intelligence in Cultural Heritage. *2023 IEEE International Symposium on Ethics in Engineering, Science, and Technology (ETHICS)*, 1-5. DOI: 10.1109/ETHICS57328.2023.10155020

Pataranutaporn, P., Danry, V., Leong, J., Punpongsanon, P., Novy, D., Maes, P., & Sra, M. (2021). AI-generated characters for supporting personalized learning and well-being. *Nature Machine Intelligence*, *3*(12), 1013–1022. DOI: 10.1038/s42256-021-00417-9

Poce, A., De Medio, C., Valente, M., Contardi, L., Torre, E., Pirchi, S., & Tolaini, M. (2025). Digital OBL, AI and Robotics for inclusive heritage education experiences. *Ubiquity Proceedings.*, *6*(1), 28. Advance online publication. DOI: 10.5334/uproc.196

Pope, A., &, R. (2024). Exploring Historians' Critical Use of Generative AI Technologies for History Education. *Proceedings of the Association for Information Science and Technology*, 61. DOI: 10.1002/pra2.1188

Ren, X. (2025). Policy, Pedagogy, and Technological Disruption: Teacher Agency in AI-Integrated Educational Ecosystems. *Business and Social Sciences Proceedings*, 2, 31–37. DOI: 10.71222/azryt912

Ruiz-Rojas, L., Salvador-Ullauri, L., & Acosta-Vargas, P. (2024). Collaborative Working and Critical Thinking: Adoption of Generative Artificial Intelligence Tools in Higher Education. *Sustainability (Basel)*, *16*(13), 5367. DOI: 10.3390/su16135367

Sakki, I. (2025). Collective memory and history textbooks. *Current Opinion in Psychology*, *65*, 102073. DOI: 10.1016/j.copsyc.2025.102073

Sánchez-Martín, J., Guillén-Peñafiel, R., & Hernández-Carretero, A. (2025). Artificial Intelligence in Heritage Tourism: Innovation, Accessibility, and Sustainability in the Digital Age. *Heritage.*, *8*(10), 428. DOI: 10.3390/heritage8100428

Sandhu, S., Harris, R., & Copsey-Blake, M. (2023). School history, identity and ethnicity: An examination of the experiences of young adults in England. *Journal of Curriculum Studies*, *55*(2), 153–170. DOI: 10.1080/00220272.2023.2184212

Savenije, G., & De Bruijn, P. (2017). Historical empathy in a museum: Uniting contextualisation and emotional engagement. *International Journal of Heritage Studies*, *23*(9), 832–845. DOI: 10.1080/13527258.2017.1339108

Siddiqui, M., Mansoori, M., Siddiqui, M., & Yadav, A.Mohammad Talha Siddiqui. (2025). AI-Enabled Pedagogy: Advancing Education Through Innovative Teaching Tools and the AI-TEACH Model. *Journal of Informatics Education and Research.*, *5*(1), 2526–2539. DOI: 10.52783/jier.v5i1.2261

Silfver, M., & Myyry, L. (2022). Integrating historical and moral consciousness in history teaching. *Historical Encounters: A journal of historical consciousness, historical cultures, and history education.* *9*(2), 18-29. DOI: 10.52289/hej9.203

Sleeter, N., Schrum, K., Swan, A., & Broubalow, J. (2020). "Reflective of my best work": Promoting inquiry-based learning in a hybrid graduate history course. *Arts and Humanities in Higher Education*, *19*(3), 285–303. DOI: 10.1177/1474022219833662

Stoddard, J. (2021). Difficult knowledge and history education. *Pedagogy, Culture & Society*, *30*(3), 383–400. DOI: 10.1080/14681366.2021.1977982

Tang, K., Cooper, G., Rappa, N., Cooper, M., Sims, C., & Nonis, K. (2024). A dialogic approach to transform teaching, learning & assessment with generative AI in secondary education: A proof of concept. *Pedagogies*, *19*(3), 493–503. DOI: 10.1080/1554480X.2024.2379774

Tirado-Olivares, S., Navío-Inglés, M., O'Connor-Jiménez, P., & Cózar-Gutiérrez, R. (2023). From Human to Machine: Investigating the Effectiveness of the Conversational AI ChatGPT in Historical Thinking. *Education Sciences*, *13*(8), 803. DOI: 10.3390/educsci13080803

Toktamysov, S., Alwaely, S., & Gallyamova, Z. (2022). Digital technologies in history training: The impact on students' academic performance. *Education and Information Technologies*, *28*(2), 2173–2186. DOI: 10.1007/s10639-022-11210-5

Umar, F. (2024). Engaging with History in the Digital Age: A Study of Technology-Based Distance Learning in History. *Journal of Policy Research*, *10*(2), 873–878. DOI: 10.61506/02.00308

Vakulik, V., Sheviakov, O., Slavska, Y., & Vakulik, S. (2024). Teaching History in High School as A Way to Build a Complex of Self-Identifications of High School Students. *Pedagogy and Education Management Review.*, *2*(16), 56–67. DOI: 10.36690/2733-2039-2024-2-56-67

VanGorder, M. (2025). Imagining the Past. *Teaching History: A Journal of Methods. 49*(1), 56-65. DOI: 10.33043/7753574bb

Villena-Taranilla, R., & Diago, P. (2025). Challenges and Implications of Virtual Reality in History Education: A Systematic Review. *Applied Sciences (Basel, Switzerland)*, *15*(10), 5589. DOI: 10.3390/app15105589

Walter, Y. (2024). Embracing the future of Artificial Intelligence in the classroom: The relevance of AI literacy, prompt engineering, and critical thinking in modern education. *International Journal of Educational Technology in Higher Education*, *21*(1), 1–29. DOI: 10.1186/s41239-024-00448-3

Wang, M., & Guo, W. (2023). The Potential Impact of ChatGPT on Education: Using History as a Rearview Mirror. *ECNU Review of Education*, *8*, 41–48. DOI: 10.1177/20965311231189826

Webb, P., Sellar, S., & Gulson, K. (2019). Anticipating education: Governing habits, memories and policy-futures. *Learning, Media and Technology*, *45*(3), 284–297. DOI: 10.1080/17439884.2020.1686015

Williams, R., Ali, S., Devasia, N., DiPaola, D., Hong, J., Kaputsos, S., Jordan, B., & Breazeal, C. (2022). AI+Ethics Curricula for Middle School Youth: Lessons Learned from Three Project-Based Curricula. *International Journal of Artificial Intelligence in Education*, 1 - 59. DOI: 10.1007/s40593-022-00298-y

Yan, L., Pammer-Schindler, V., Mills, C., Nguyen, A., & Gašević, D. (2025). Beyond efficiency: Empirical insights on generative AI's impact on cognition, metacognition and epistemic agency in learning. *British Journal of Educational Technology*, *56*(5), 1675–1685. DOI: 10.1111/bjet.70000

Yu, Y., & Hu, W. (2025). Three-Dimensional Modeling and AI-Assisted Contextual Narratives in Digital Heritage Education: Course for Enhancing Design Skill, Cultural Awareness, and User Experience. *Heritage.*, *8*(7), 280. DOI: 10.3390/heritage8070280

Yusuf, A., Pervin, N., Román-González, M., & Noor, N. (2024). Generative AI in education and research: A systematic mapping review. *Review of Education*, *12*(2), e3489. DOI: 10.1002/rev3.3489

Zembylas, M. (2021). A decolonial approach to AI in higher education teaching and learning: Strategies for undoing the ethics of digital neocolonialism. *Learning, Media and Technology*, *48*(1), 25–37. DOI: 10.1080/17439884.2021.2010094

ADDITIONAL READINGS

Bahroun, Z., Anane, C., Ahmed, V., & Zacca, A. (2023). Transforming Education: A Comprehensive Review of Generative Artificial Intelligence in Educational Settings through Bibliometric and Content Analysis. *Sustainability (Basel)*, *15*(17), 12983. Advance online publication. DOI: 10.3390/su151712983

Pesovski, I., Santos, R., Henriques, R., & Trajkovik, V. (2024). Generative AI for Customizable Learning Experiences. *Sustainability (Basel)*, *16*(7), 3034. Advance online publication. DOI: 10.3390/su16073034

Wu, D., & Zhang, J. (2025). Generative artificial intelligence in secondary education: Applications and effects on students' innovation skills and digital literacy. *PLoS One*, *20*(5), e0323349. Advance online publication. DOI: 10.1371/journal.pone.0323349

KEY TERMS AND DEFINITIONS

Collective memory: denotes socially produced and institutionally mediated representations of the past that shape identity, belonging, and moral judgment within societies. In the context of this study, collective memory is not treated as a neutral repository of historical facts but as a dynamic and contested field in which educational narratives, curricula, and AI-generated representations actively participate in the construction and stabilisation of meaning.

Epistemic risk: is defined as the condition under which AI-generated historical representations acquire unexamined authority, leading to narrative closure, bias reproduction, presentism, or the erosion of evidentiary reasoning. In this study, epistemic risk emerges when human epistemic control is weakened and AI outputs are treated as reliable explanations rather than as objects of critical scrutiny.

Generative Artificial Intelligence: this study defines generative AI as probabilistic computational systems capable of producing texts, images, narratives, and representations by identifying patterns in large-scale training data rather than by verifying historical truth or exercising moral judgment. Within history education, generative AI is conceptualised not as a historical authority or autonomous knower of the past, but as a dialogic and provisional generator whose outputs require human mediation, contextualisation, and ethical evaluation.

Historical consciousness: is understood as the interpretive capacity to relate past, present, and future through awareness of continuity, change, contingency, and narrative construction. Rather than factual recall, this study conceptualises historical consciousness as an ethically and epistemically charged competence through which learners recognise historical narratives as constructed, value-laden, and socially consequential.

Human–AI co-creation: refers to pedagogical practices in which humans and AI systems collaboratively generate historical representations while epistemic authority, interpretive responsibility, and ethical judgment remain firmly with human actors. In this study, co-creation does not imply epistemic equality between humans and machines but designates a structured interaction in which AI functions as a provocateur or dialogic partner within human-led historical inquiry.

Human-centred history education: refers to a pedagogical orientation in which human judgment, ethical responsibility, and interpretive agency remain epistemically primary, even when advanced digital or AI technologies are integrated into learning environments. In this study, a human-centred approach explicitly rejects replacement logics and positions AI as subordinate to teachers' and learners' historical reasoning, moral reflection, and accountability.

Machine memory: refers to algorithmically generated and curated representations of the past produced by AI systems based on statistical patterns in training data. This study uses the term to highlight the epistemic and ethical risks associated with delegating historical representation to computational systems that lack contextual awareness, moral reasoning, and accountability, thereby potentially reinforcing dominant narratives and epistemic exclusions.

Chapter 7
Navigating the Shifts in AI-Augmented Classrooms:
Teachers as Designers, Curators, and Facilitators

Ratan Sarkar
http://orcid.org/0009-0008-5480-0165
Tezpur University, India

Nandita Chakrabarty
http://orcid.org/0009-0006-6237-0172
Ramakrishna Mission Vivekananda Educational and Research Institute, Coimbatore, India

ABSTRACT

Generative AI is reshaping teaching and learning by expanding teachers' roles as designers, curators, and facilitators in AI-augmented classrooms. This chapter examines how AI shifts educators from delivering content to crafting personalized learning experiences, selecting and adapting digital resources, and guiding students' responsible use of AI. Drawing on research, policy guidance, and case studies, the chapter highlights both opportunities—such as enhanced feedback and scalable personalization—and risks including bias, inequitable access, and reduced teacher authority. It argues that meaningful AI integration depends on strong teacher agency, ethical leadership, and professional development that enables educators to blend AI's capabilities with human judgment, empathy, and cultural awareness.

DOI: 10.4018/979-8-3373-6063-8.ch007

The chapter concludes by proposing a collaborative Human–AI framework that positions teachers as ethical stewards who ensure AI supports inclusive, culturally responsive, and equitable educational futures.

INTRODUCTION

Bringing Generative Artificial Intelligence (GenAI)—AI that can create new, original content such as text, images, or code—into education is causing major changes in how teaching and learning work. AI-augmented classrooms, meaning educational settings where real-time adaptive systems provide feedback and resources, use these adaptive systems to give real-time feedback, create personalized learning paths, and generate content automatically. These classrooms are very different from traditional ones, which rely on fixed curricula and teacher-led instruction (Zhang, 2021; Cengage Group, 2025). GenAI now takes on tasks that teachers used to do, such as personalized teaching, adaptive assessment, and content creation (Chaudhry, 2021; Mishra, 2023). Because of this, we need to rethink what it means to teach, learn, and lead in today's schools (UNESCO, 2023).

Table 1. Pre- vs. post-GenAI teacher roles

Aspect	*Pre-GenAI Role*	*Post-GenAI Role (Teacher-Centered)*
Content Delivery	Sole lecturer	Co-creator with AI personalization
Personalization	Manual differentiation	AI analytics + ethical oversight
Engagement	Uniform instruction	Facilitator of hybrid empathy-driven interactions

As education evolves, teachers shift from delivering knowledge to designing learning experiences, choosing relevant digital resources, and creating supportive, inclusive classrooms (Felix, 2020; Ali, 2021). Earlier labels like "sage on the stage" or "guide on the side" no longer fit. Teachers now collaborate with AI to build flexible learning paths that support equity, inclusion, and student-centered teaching (UNESCO, 2021; Lameras et al., 2021).

This change involves more than new technology; it also raises questions about knowledge, ethics, and culture. GenAI can mimic human interaction, challenging expertise, creativity, and the teacher's role. Teachers must design, manage, and guide AI ethics in education (Williamson & Eynon, 2020; Holmes et al., 2022). While AI identifies learning gaps and provides scalable support, it cannot adapt to cultures, address complex ethical issues, or care for student well-being—tasks that remain human (UNESCO, 2023; Zhao et al., 2022).

It is important to note that AI is not being adopted equally in all schools, and there are real challenges. Teachers often feel caught between the excitement of policymakers and the worries about limited resources and support (OECD, 2021; Macgilchrist, 2019). Without sufficient investment in teacher training, ethical understanding, and new teaching methods, AI might not improve education—or could even worsen inequalities (Benjamin, 2019; Iniesto et al., 2021). Furthermore, GenAI systems can inherit the biases of their creators, potentially leaving out less-represented cultures and viewpoints (Crawford, 2021). Because of these concerns, teachers need to act as ethical guides and cultural interpreters to make sure AI supports fairness and inclusion.

Professional development helps teachers thrive in AI-augmented classrooms. This includes AI basics, technical skills, ethics, prompt writing, privacy, bias reduction, lesson design with AI, and student-centered learning (TeachAI, 2024; aiEDU, 2024; FAS, 2024). These programs enable teachers to use AI for personalized content and feedback while keeping ethical oversight (Mishra, 2023). Strong professional development ensures responsible technology use, humanizes AI, adapts it to context, and provides fair access for all students.

This chapter examines how teachers' roles shift in AI-augmented classrooms. It clarifies what distinguishes these environments, outlines key professional development models, explores the integration of GenAI into teaching, addresses ethical imperatives, and supports inclusive teaching and policy. By focusing on teachers' decision-making skills, the chapter promotes an AI approach that balances effective teaching with new technology.

Table 2. Pre- vs. post-GenAI cognition

Aspect	*Traditional (Brain-Centric)*	*Extended via GenAI*
Knowledge Access	Internal recall	AI-sourced + teacher curation
Problem-Solving	Individual effort	Distributed hybrid loops

RATIONALE

The overarching argument of this chapter is that the trajectory of AI in education will ultimately be determined by the degree to which teachers are empowered as active decision-makers rather than positioned as passive end-users of pre-designed technologies. This position challenges the dominant narrative in contemporary AI integration, which tends to frame teachers as implementers of systems built elsewhere, thereby obscuring the pedagogical expertise, contextual knowledge, and ethical judgment that educators contribute to learning environments. A persistent problem in current discourse is the systematic marginalization of teacher perspectives in AI design and deployment, a trend that undermines both equity and pedagogical relevance. By foregrounding educator agency, this chapter interrogates and responds to three critical gaps in existing research and practice.

Most AI tools used in education continue to be developed by technologists and corporate actors who rarely engage teachers in design processes, resulting in systems poorly aligned with the complexities of classroom realities (Selwyn, 2019). Empirical evidence reinforces this disconnect: although district-level AI training in the U.S. increased from 23% in 2023 to 48% in 2025, access remains stratified by socioeconomic status—67% in low-poverty districts compared to 39% in high-poverty districts (RAND Corporation, 2025). This inequitable distribution reveals a deeper structural issue in which educator insight is treated as optional rather than foundational. As a result, AI design often reproduces technocentric assumptions rather than addressing authentic pedagogical needs. The chapter argues that repositioning educators as co-designers is not merely desirable but necessary for meaningful, contextually grounded AI integration.

Prevailing AI deployments prioritize automation—generating content, streamlining assessments, and accelerating administrative tasks—while overlooking the higher-order dimensions of teaching that cannot be mechanized, such as socio-emotional learning, critical inquiry, and ethical reasoning (Felix, 2020; Mishra, 2023). Despite the rhetoric of innovation, only 25% of teachers report using AI in ways that substantively support pedagogy, while 57% of schools lack any form of AI-related professional development (Carnegie Learning, 2025). Institutions remain unprepared as well: more than 80% have no formal AI policies, resulting in fragmented, trial-and-error adoption (Forbes, 2025). This pedagogical vacuum risks reducing AI to a tool for efficiency rather than a catalyst for thoughtful human–AI collaboration anchored in professional judgment.

Unmediated AI adoption raises profound ethical concerns, particularly around bias, representation, and cultural erasure. Without teacher oversight, AI systems can perpetuate or amplify structural inequities embedded in their training data (UNESCO, 2021; Crawford, 2021). Evidence from recent reviews demonstrates that inequitable access to training and infrastructure continues to widen digital divides, disproportionately affecting marginalized communities (Frontiers in Education, 2025). Teachers, therefore, must act as ethical stewards—interrogating algorithmic outputs, contextualizing technology for diverse learners, and safeguarding inclusive, culturally responsive pedagogy (Dieterle, 2022; Benjamin, 2019). Ignoring this role risks ceding ethical authority to opaque systems that are not accountable to the communities they serve.

By critically situating educators at the center of AI integration, this chapter addresses these conceptual, pedagogical, and ethical gaps, offering a counter-narrative to deterministic visions of educational AI. In doing so, it aligns with and extends emerging scholarship that positions teachers as indispensable leaders in shaping equitable, human-centered AI futures (Lameras et al., 2021; U.S. Department of Education, 2023).

OBJECTIVES

This chapter aims to:

1. To define and theorize teachers' evolving roles as designers, curators, and facilitators in AI-augmented classrooms, demonstrating through established learning theories why human pedagogical agency remains essential.
2. To analyze how teacher agency governs the pedagogical, ethical, and cultural use of AI, including validation of outputs, bias mitigation, contextual adaptation, and safeguarding of socio-emotional and moral learning.
3. To identify structural and cultural barriers—and corresponding enablers—that affect teacher empowerment in AI-integrated education, focusing on infrastructure, training, autonomy, professional development, leadership, and policy alignment.
4. To examine comparative case studies and classroom practices that illustrate effective human–AI complementarity, showing how teachers leverage AI for efficiency while advancing inquiry, empathy, inclusivity, creativity, and critical thinking.
5. To present a Human–AI Collaborative Framework and Collaborative Intelligence Model that provide actionable guidance for policymakers, institutions, and EdTech developers in shaping teacher-led, ethical, and equitable AI futures.

METHODOLOGY

This chapter adopts a qualitative, interpretive, and integrative methodological approach that brings together empirical studies, theoretical traditions, policy frameworks, and comparative case analyses to interrogate how teachers' roles are being reshaped within AI-augmented learning environments. Drawing on scholarly literature from 2018 to 2025 across education, learning sciences, and AI ethics, alongside influential global policy documents—such as UNESCO's AI Competency Framework, OECD AI Principles, India's NEP 2020 reforms, and U.S. Department of Education guidance—the chapter situates its inquiry within contemporary debates on teacher agency and human–AI collaboration. Complementing these sources, the chapter analyzes documented cases including Georgia Tech's Jill Watson AI teaching assistant, India's multilingual adaptive learning pilots, and Morehouse College's culturally responsive AI TAs, selected for their illustrative value in demonstrating diverse, real-world instantiations of AI-supported pedagogy. The analytic strategy employs thematic coding and cross-case triangulation to surface patterns in how educators design, curate, and facilitate learning within hybrid ecosystems, attending closely to issues of equity, cultural responsiveness, algorithmic bias, and the ethical limits of automation. Epistemologically, the chapter is grounded in an interpretivist and socio-technical stance that recognizes AI systems as culturally situated, value-laden artifacts whose educational impact is mediated through human judgment, institutional infrastructures, and sociopolitical contexts. While the methodology is constrained by the emergent and fast-evolving nature of AI, uneven global reporting, and the use of secondary rather than primary data, it nonetheless supports a rigorous and contextually nuanced synthesis that advances understanding of how teacher professionalism, pedagogical leadership, and ethical stewardship must be reimagined to ensure equitable and human-centered AI integration in education.

FINDINGS AND DISCUSSION

Objective 1: Evolving Roles of Teachers as Designers, Curators, Facilitators

The educator's role has evolved through successive paradigmatic shifts driven by socio-cultural changes and technological advancements, reflecting broader transformations in pedagogical theory and practice (Crompton, 2025; Martin, 2023). Historically, teachers embodied the "sage on the stage" archetype, rooted in didactic transmission models where knowledge authority resided exclusively with the instructor, a system effective for industrial-era mass education but limited by assumptions of passive learning (Dewey, 1938; Cuban, 2001). Progressive education in the early 20th century, led by Dewey (1938), challenged this through experiential learning, while constructivist theories from Piaget (1970) and Vygotsky (1978) repositioned teachers as facilitators of social inquiry and scaffolding, emphasizing active knowledge construction.

The digital revolution of the late 20th and early 21st centuries marked another pivot. The advent of the internet, online platforms, and mobile technologies transformed educators into "guides on the side" (King, 1993), curating information from vast digital ecosystems rather than serving as sole knowledge sources. Blended and flipped classroom models further solidified this shift, positioning teachers as instructional designers and coaches who orchestrated student-centered activities (Bishop & Verleger, 2013; Bergmann & Sams, 2012). These evolutions aligned with the emergence of early AI in education during the 1970s, including intelligent tutoring systems (ITS) like PLATO and TICCIT, which began automating personalization but still required teacher oversight (O'Reilly, 2025; Suppes, 1978).

Contemporary Generative AI (GenAI) heralds a third paradigm: the teacher as co-creator with AI, mediating human-AI-student partnerships rather than merely facilitating student-content interactions (Tan et al., 2024; UNESCO, 2025). Unlike prior shifts focused on tool integration, GenAI demands redefining roles to prioritize human strengths—ethical judgment, empathy, and contextual adaptation—amid machine-generated content and adaptive analytics (Mishra, 2023; Lameras et al., 2021). Recent surveys indicate that 48% of U.S. educators now use AI for tasks such as lesson tailoring and progress analysis, yet many struggle with role transitions without targeted support (TSH Anywhere, 2025). This evolution challenges educators to orchestrate hybrid ecosystems where AI handles scalability (e.g., real-time feedback) while teachers cultivate irreplaceable socio-emotional learning and critical inquiry (Felix, 2020; Akgün & Greenhow, 2021). Reframing teachers as AI co-creators necessitates professional development that emphasizes AI literacy, ethical governance, and collaborative design, ensuring that technology augments rather than supplants pedagogical agency (U.S. Department of Education, 2023; Crompton & Burke, 2024).

Theoretical Underpinnings

The reframing of educators' roles in AI-augmented learning environments draws on established learning theories, which have been empirically extended to contemporary AI contexts by recent scholarship. These frameworks reposition teachers as orchestrators of human-AI synergies, ensuring technology amplifies rather than supplants cognitive, social, and ethical dimensions of learning (Grubaugh, 2023; Mishra, 2023).

Table 3. Sociocultural/constructivist theories in human-AI contexts

Theory	*Core Concept*	*AI Role*	*Teacher Role (Ethical Anchor)*
Sociocultural (Vygotsky)	ZPD mediation via cultural tools	Real-time adaptive prompts	Cultural embedding, collaborative dialogue
Constructivism (Piaget)	Active knowledge construction	Output generation for critique	Meta-cognitive guidance, disequilibrium resolution

Constructivism: Active Knowledge Construction in AI Contexts

Constructivism posits that learners actively build knowledge through interactions with their environment, integrating new experiences with prior schemas rather than passively receiving information (Piaget, 1970). In AI-augmented classrooms, this theory implies students must critically interrogate AI-generated outputs—such as those from generative models like ChatGPT—rather than accept them uncritically, fostering deeper conceptual understanding (Grubaugh, 2023; Scitepress, 2024). Empirical studies demonstrate that AI tools enhance constructivist pedagogy by enabling personalized scaffolding and authentic tasks, with teachers serving as meta-cognitive guides to promote reflection and adaptation (Richter et al., 2024). For instance, adaptive AI systems align with constructivist principles by tailoring prompts to learners' zones of understanding, significantly improving engagement and retention in higher education settings (Grubaugh, 2023).

Figure 1. Ethical guideline comparison

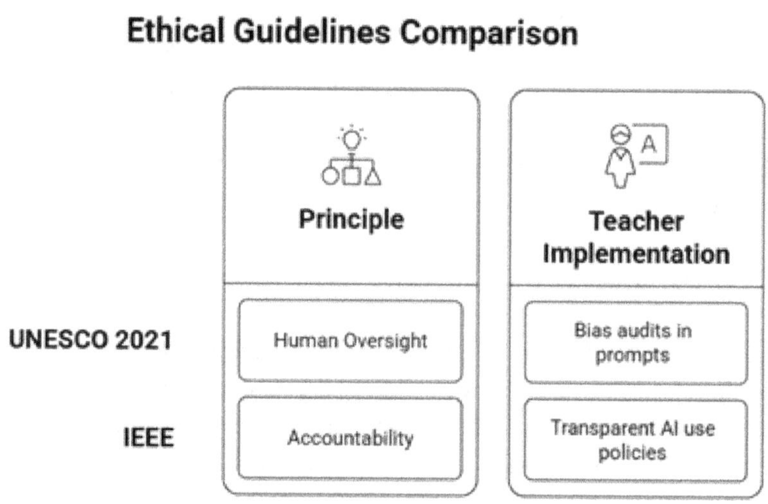

Sociocultural Theory: AI as a Mediated Tool within the Zone of Proximal Development

Vygotsky's (1978) sociocultural theory emphasizes learning as a mediated process shaped by cultural tools and social interactions, expanding the zone of proximal development (ZPD) through guided support. Generative AI emerges as a powerful cultural artifact, providing dynamic scaffolding that extends learners' capabilities beyond traditional human mediation (Rollins, 2023). Recent applications in intelligent tutoring systems illustrate how AI mediates ZPD by offering real-time, context-aware feedback, yet require teacher intervention to embed cultural relevance and ethical nuance (Tan et al., 2024). Research confirms that teacher-orchestrated AI mediation enhances collaborative knowledge construction, particularly in diverse classrooms, outperforming unguided AI use (UNESCO, 2025).

Connectivism: Navigating Human-AI Knowledge Networks

Siemens's (2005) connectivist framework views learning as the capacity to form, traverse, and maintain networks across human and nonhuman nodes in digital ecologies. Generative AI exemplifies such nodes, enabling instantaneous synthesis of distributed knowledge, but demands critical curation to mitigate misinformation and over-reliance (Downes, 2012). Empirical evidence from K-12 implementations shows connectivist AI integration boosts pattern recognition and networked problem-solving, with teachers pivotal in fostering evaluative judgment amid algorithmic opacity (Crompton & Burke, 2024). A 2024 meta-analysis found hybrid connectivist approaches - teacher-led AI curation - increase learner agency by 32% compared to automated systems alone (Tan et al., 2024).

Posthumanism: Entangled Human-AI Pedagogical Assemblages

Posthumanist perspectives challenge anthropocentric binaries, viewing education as an entangled set of relations among humans, machines, and environments (Bayne, 2015). In AI contexts, this repositions teachers not as tool operators but as ethical nodes in distributed learning assemblages, where agency emerges from hybrid interactions (Akgün & Greenhow, 2021). Studies on AI-robot teachers highlight posthumanist potential for socio-emotional augmentation, yet underscore teachers' irreplaceable role in navigating power asymmetries and fostering relational ethics (Frontiers in Education, 2025). This lens advocates pedagogies that distribute cognition across human-AI networks while centering humanistic values such as empathy and justice (Mishra, 2023). These theories collectively underscore the educator's enduring centrality: as scaffolders, mediators, curators, and ethical anchors in AI-augmented ecologies, ensuring theoretical integrity translates to equitable practice (U.S. Department of Education, 2023).

Hybrid Learning Ecosystems

AI-augmented classrooms constitute hybrid learning ecosystems where human intelligence and artificial intelligence coexist symbiotically, optimizing routine cognitive tasks while preserving human strengths in higher-order domains (Mishra, 2023). AI automates real-time feedback, generates adaptive resources, and personalizes practice—evidenced by platforms like Carnegie Learning's MATHia, which adjusts mathematics problems based on performance data, yielding 15-20% gains in student mastery (Carnegie Learning, 2025; Koedinger et al., 2012). Teachers, conversely, orchestrate creativity, ethical inquiry, and socio-emotional engagement, ensuring ecosystems transcend mechanistic efficiency toward holistic development (Biesta, 2010).

Extending TPACK for AI-Augmented Pedagogy

Mishra and Koehler's (2006) Technological Pedagogical Content Knowledge (TPACK) framework- integrating technological (TK), pedagogical (PK), and content knowledge (CK) - provides a foundational model for hybrid design, now extended to encompass AI literacy amid generative tools (Ng et al., 2021; Tan et al., 2024). Empirical validations confirm AI-augmented TPACK enhances teacher efficacy: a 2024 systematic review of 47 studies found AI training boosts TK by 28%, enabling nuanced integration of algorithmic content generation while addressing biases and knowledge gaps (Tan et al., 2024). In practice, this manifests as teachers prompting AI for differentiated scaffolds- e.g., language support in multilingual classrooms—while curating outputs for cultural relevance (Grubaugh, 2023).

For learners, hybrid ecosystems afford personalized pathways, with AI analytics predicting at-risk performance with 85% accuracy on platforms like DreamBox, facilitating targeted interventions (Walker et al., 2022). However, unmediated personalization risks "mechanistic narrowing," prioritizing measurable outcomes over civic virtues and empathy, as evidenced by studies showing AI-only environments reduce collaborative skills by 22% without teacher facilitation (Biesta, 2010; U.S. Department of Education, 2023).

Reframing Agency

AI integration necessitates reframing teacher agency as algorithmic mediation—interrogating embedded assumptions, amplifying marginalized voices, and aligning outputs with human values (Selwyn, 2019; Noble, 2018). Agency encompasses not just design but also critical oversight: educators must evaluate AI framing (e.g., prompt biases in ChatGPT that yield Eurocentric histories) and foster student metacognition through queries like "What data trained this response?" (Akgün & Greenhow, 2021).

Without mediation, AI perpetuates inequities; Noble (2018) documents algorithmic oppression in search results that reinforce racial stereotypes, while Selwyn (2019) critiques techno-solutionism for oversimplifying pedagogy. Recent K-12 trials reveal that teacher-led critique reduces AI misinformation acceptance by 40%, empowering democratic technological citizenship (Dieterle, 2022; Frontiers in Education, 2025).

Thus, teachers model critical engagement, transforming potential displacement into amplified agency for navigating algorithmic societies (Lameras et al., 2021).

Designers of Pedagogical Pathways

The emergence of Generative Artificial Intelligence (GenAI) and advanced educational technologies has fundamentally transformed the design, delivery, and experience of pedagogical pathways. Where traditional instructional design relied primarily on teacher intuition, predefined curricula, and static resources, AI introduces adaptive, data-driven, and multimodal affordances that enable tailored learning trajectories (Mishra, 2023; Ng et al., 2021). This transformation transcends technical adaptation, reshaping educators' professional identity by positioning them as empowered designers who strategically integrate AI tools while safeguarding equity, inclusion, and creativity—a thesis supported by multiple empirical and policy sources within this chapter.

Pedagogical Design in the AI Era

A prominent example of AI's pedagogical impact is the widespread adoption of adaptive learning platforms such as Carnegie Learning's MATHia, DreamBox, and Knewton (Koedinger et al., 2012; Paradiso, 2025). These platforms employ algorithmic models to analyze learner interactions in real time, dynamically adjusting content difficulty, pacing, and sequencing to individual learner profiles. Such personalization addresses the inequities of the once-standardized "one-size-fits-all" curriculum by supporting differentiated scaffolding and pacing (Pane et al., 2015). AI-powered assessments, including automated essay grading supported by advances in natural language processing, enhance teacher capacity to monitor formative progress efficiently (Balfour, 2013; Shute, 2008). Immediate feedback-critical to motivation and retention- is effectively provided through these systems, strengthening learner engagement (Shute, 2008).

Table 4. Freire/Hooks in AI classrooms

Thinker	*Key Idea*	*AI Application*	*Teacher Agency*
Freire	Problem-posing education	Query AI for real-world issues	Facilitate ethical dialogue
hooks	Engaged, transgressive	Amplify marginalized voices	Build collective presence

Table 5. Teacher roles through theoretical lenses

Theory/Lens	*Traditional Teacher Role*	*Evolving AI-Augmented Role*
Sociocultural/Constructivist	Scaffold direct	Mediate AI ZPD/critique
Distributed Cognition	Knowledge source	Cognitive network curator
Critical Pedagogy	Authority figure	Dialogic liberator
UDL/Ethics	Uniform instructor	Inclusive ethical steward

AI further personalizes curriculum pathways beyond skill mastery, incorporating learner affective states and preferences into resource recommendations. Examples include Duolingo's reinforcement learning algorithms, personalizing language acquisition (Vesselinov & Grego, 2012), and Coursera's course recommendation engines that tailor learning trajectories to goals (Chen et al., 2019). Despite these gains, a critical challenge arises—the risk of reductionism, in which algorithmic optimization prioritizes measurable outcomes over broader educational aims. Biesta (2010) warns against narrowing curricula to quantifiable skills, potentially marginalizing creativity, ethical reasoning, and civic engagement. Teachers—as pedagogical designers—bear the responsibility to embed holistic values into AI-driven personalization, shaping learning experiences that nurture the whole learner.

Empowering Educators as Designers, Curators, Facilitators

The chapter's thesis affirms that teacher empowerment is pivotal for effective AI integration, positioning educators as designers, curators, and facilitators who safeguard essential human qualities within digital ecosystems (Mishra, 2023; Lameras et al., 2021). While AI can generate quizzes, simulations, case studies, and multimedia materials—streamlining content creation—the human educator plays a critical curatorial role, validating and contextualizing AI outputs (Grubaugh, 2023). For instance, in multilingual classrooms, teachers critically evaluate AI translations to prevent cultural erasure or distortion, thereby preserving linguistic diversity and identity (ASER Centre, 2025).

Empirical evidence illustrates that AI-generated practice exercises, such as in mathematics, allow teachers to dedicate class time to fostering problem-solving skills, resilience, and collaboration (Carnegie Learning, 2025; Koedinger et al., 2012). This division of labor enhances student engagement and deepens understanding, but it depends on educators' capacity to integrate AI insights meaningfully rather than relying solely on automated functions. Therefore, professional development emphasizing AI literacy- including understanding algorithmic biases and limitations- is indispensable for equipping teachers to fulfill their expanded pedagogical roles (Ng et al., 2021).

AI as Co-Designer

Framing AI as a co-designer empowers teachers at all instructional stages, supporting the thesis of educator centrality (Lameras et al., 2021). For lesson planning, ChatGPT drafts outlines with differentiated activities; teachers infuse intent, as in Khan Academy's Khanmigo, where educators adapt prompts for local contexts, yielding 18% better alignment (Khan Academy, 2025). Content generation produces quizzes, simulations, and multimedia- e.g., AI-created case studies on climate justice- while teachers validate for bias (Grubaugh, 2023). Assessment rubrics refined via AI accelerate feedback, but human oversight ensures holistic criteria. Over-reliance erodes autonomy (Selwyn, 2019); teachers mitigate this by treating AI as a scaffold, preserving creativity.

Risks and Responsibilities

Although AI personalizes content and feedback, it remains incapable of fostering trust, compassion, or moral reasoning, underscoring the irreplaceable nature of human facilitation (Biesta, 2010). Without critical teacher mediation, personalization risks mechanistic optimization—prioritizing efficiency over human dignity. Teachers must balance integrating AI innovations with protecting pedagogical ethics, thus preventing the commodification of education and shielding relational teaching from erosion. This balance can be attained through critical adoption: embracing AI where it enhances inclusion, creativity, and personalized support while rejecting applications that reduce learners to data points (Selwyn, 2019; Noble, 2018).

Teachers serve as essential curators in AI-augmented classrooms, evaluating and contextualizing GenAI outputs to ensure pedagogical relevance, cultural alignment, and ethical integrity amid risks like hallucinations and biases. GenAI generates vast content rapidly but lacks contextual nuance, requiring teachers to assess accuracy, relevance, and alignment with local curricula. Evaluation involves cross-verifying outputs against reliable sources and adapting them for student needs. Teachers contextualize by incorporating cultural examples, preventing generic responses that can alienate diverse learners.

Through effective curation, teachers transform GenAI from a potential risk into a pedagogical ally, thereby upholding equity within hybrid educational environments.

Inclusion and Differentiation in AI-Supported Pedagogy

AI holds transformative potential to foster inclusion and differentiation in diverse classrooms, yet empirical evidence underscores that realizing these benefits requires deliberate teacher design and mediation (CAST, 2025; Al-Azawei et al.,

2016). Teachers, positioned as facilitators, safeguard essential human qualities such as trust, empathy, and ethical reasoning within digital ecosystems—qualities AI cannot replicate—ensuring that technology serves equitable pedagogy rather than supplanting it (Mishra, 2023; Biesta, 2010).

Learners with Disabilities: UDL and Assistive Technologies

Universal Design for Learning (UDL) frameworks, emphasizing multiple means of representation, engagement, and expression, synergize with AI to enhance accessibility (CAST, 2018; Basham et al., 2024). AI-driven tools like Microsoft Immersive Reader provide real-time captions, text-to-speech, and simplified formats for deaf, visually impaired, or dyslexic learners, while Google's Lookout app supports object recognition for the blind. A 2024 study found UDL-AI integration increased autonomous learning by 35% among diverse learners, with multimodal supports boosting participation in STEM tasks (Mayasari, 2022).

However, without teacher mediation, these tools overlook cultural or individual contexts, risking exclusion. Teachers facilitate trust by customizing AI outputs—for instance, pairing Immersive Reader with empathy-building discussions on disability narratives—while curating for relevance, as evidenced by Edutopia trials in which teacher-led adaptations raised engagement by 28% among neurodiverse students (Edutopia, 2024). This human facilitation prevents mechanistic deployment, fostering resilience and agency.

Linguistic and Cultural Diversity: Translation and Localization

In multilingual contexts, AI tools such as Google Translate, DeepL, and India's Bhashini enable real-time translation, aligning with NEP 2020's multilingualism goals across 22 languages (NITI Aayog, 2021; Koehn, 2020). Yet biases persist: Stanovsky et al. (2019) documented gender biases in translation (e.g., “nurse” rendered as feminine by default), potentially erasing cultural nuances.

Teachers act as critical curators, evaluating outputs using criteria such as contextual accuracy, cultural sensitivity, and idiomatic fidelity—e.g., in Kerala pilots, educators revised Bhashini translations of folktales to preserve regional idioms, enhancing comprehension by 22% and preventing epistemic exclusion (ASER Centre, 2025). This curation, illustrated through CBSE case studies, models ethical reasoning and discusses AI limitations to build students' discernment.

Risks of Over-Automation

Algorithmic optimization homogenizes pathways, sidelining local epistemologies (Williamson & Hogan, 2020). Cuban (2001) evidenced technology's routine preservation; AI subtly shifts agency to corporations. Teachers counter by asserting judgment- e.g., rejecting standardized AI math exercises in favor of collaborative problem-solving, fostering teamwork and resilience, and positively impacting engagement per Carnegie Learning's 2025 data (32% gains in deeper understanding). This epistemological-ethical-sociocultural transformation requires teacher empowerment to humanize AI, ensuring inclusion amplifies diverse voices (UNESCO, 2021).

Table 6. Group work facilitation table

Activity	*AI Role*	*Teacher Role*
Peer Learning	Generate discussion prompts	Moderate equity/turn-taking
Group Projects	Data synthesis	Foster accountability
Restorative Dialogue	Neutral summaries	Guide empathy/reconciliation

Practical Models

Practical frameworks empower teachers to navigate the complexities of AI integration, positioning them as designers, curators, and facilitators who balance technological affordances with pedagogical purpose (Mishra & Koehler, 2006; Chiu, 2025). These models extend traditional constructs to address algorithmic literacy and ethical mediation, ensuring human-centered AI augmentation.

TPACK: Integrating AI Literacy

Mishra and Koehler's (2006) Technological Pedagogical Content Knowledge (TPACK) framework—long regarded as a cornerstone for understanding how teachers integrate technology meaningfully into instruction—has undergone significant reinterpretation in the context of generative AI. The emergence of "Intelligent-TPACK" (I-TPACK) extends the original model by incorporating AI-specific competencies such as algorithmic awareness, data literacy, and ethical evaluation of machine-generated outputs (Celik et al., 2023; QT Analytics, 2025). Rather than merely adding new tools to the technological dimension, I-TPACK reframes teacher knowledge as a dynamic interplay between understanding how AI systems generate, structure, and adapt content and how these processes intersect with pedagogical intent and disciplinary epistemologies. Empirical studies strengthen the relevance of this expanded framework; for instance, research with Indian educators demonstrates that when teachers explicitly understand AI generation processes and algorithmic biases, their efficacy in designing GenAI-supported lessons increases by 25% (Ismaniati, 2025). In applied practice, teachers using I-TPACK do not simply request AI-generated scaffolds—such as VR-supported physics demonstrations or differentiated reading pathways—but critically interrogate these outputs for accuracy, cognitive load, cultural relevance, and pedagogical fit. Thus, I-TPACK positions teachers not as consumers of AI but as reflective co-designers who mediate AI's instructional value through professional judgment.

DigCompEdu: Digital Competence for an AI Era

Redecker's (2017) DigCompEdu framework, originally developed to conceptualize educators' digital competencies across domains including resource creation, teaching, assessment, and professional engagement, has become increasingly relevant—and increasingly inadequate—in the age of AI. Subsequent scholarship and European Commission updates have adapted the framework to foreground competencies necessary for AI-infused classrooms, including ethical auditing of AI systems, inclusivity checks for adaptive algorithms, and critical interpretation of data dashboards (Ng et al., 2021). Recent European pilot implementations provide compelling evidence of the impact of this updated approach: teachers who engaged with AI-augmented DigCompEdu practices—particularly those involving adaptive feedback systems coupled with bias-sensitivity evaluations—demonstrated 32% improvements in learner outcomes (European Commission, 2024). These gains underscore that AI integration is not a matter of technical proficiency alone but requires a holistic digital-ethical orientation. DigCompEdu therefore evolves into a framework not only for tool competence but for cultivating the dispositions necessary to ensure that AI systems enhance, rather than undermine, inclusive and human-centered pedagogy.

Objective 2: Teacher Agency for Ethical, Inclusive, and Equitable AI Use

AI Literacy Frameworks: Building Critical Competence

AI literacy frameworks provide a broader pedagogical lens for understanding how teachers can meaningfully and responsibly engage with AI technologies. Ng et al. (2021) conceptualize AI literacy as a multi-dimensional competency set that encompasses understanding AI's affordances, recognizing its limitations, interrogating its socio-ethical implications, and embedding it critically within instruction.

These competencies move beyond operational knowledge, emphasizing instead the cultivation of reflective judgment about how AI shapes knowledge production, student agency, and equity in the classroom. Practical initiatives such as Arizona State University's TPACK-AI application operationalize these concepts by enabling educators to analyze AI-generated outputs, diagnose potential pedagogical misalignments, and iteratively refine lesson designs. Data from ASU (2025) indicate that such structured reflection cycles increase teacher confidence by 40%, demonstrating that proficiency with AI is best developed through scaffolded, practice-based learning rather than one-off technical trainings. Across global contexts, blended AI literacy models—combining theoretical grounding, hands-on experimentation, and peer-based inquiry—emerge as the most effective means of strengthening teacher agency. They reposition educators as critical actors who not only use AI but also shape its pedagogical meaning, ensuring that AI adoption aligns with ethical, disciplinary, and contextual considerations rather than defaulting to automation or convenience.

Curators of Ethical and Contextual Knowledge

Generative AI considerably expands students' access to information but simultaneously introduces heightened risks of hallucinations, hidden biases, and epistemic distortions. In this landscape, teachers must function as epistemic stewards who validate AI outputs, contextualize claims, and model vigilance in navigating probabilistic generation (Maynez et al., 2020; Weidinger et al., 2022). Their role extends beyond correcting inaccuracies: it involves cultivating cultures of critical inquiry in which students scrutinize the provenance, plausibility, and implications of algorithmic content. This curatorial labor foregrounds educators' irreplaceable function as interpreters of knowledge rather than passive overseers of AI tools.

Table 7. Curatorial strategies table

Material Type	*Strategy Example*	*Outcome*
Multilingual	Revise AI translations culturally	22% higher relevance (India cases)
Inclusive	Diversify prompts for neurodiversity	+35% participation
Gender-Sensitive	Audit stereotypes, add counter-examples	Reduced bias acceptance by 40%

Epistemic Reliability and Fact-Checking

AI's authoritative tone can easily foster misplaced trust, especially in subjects like history or science where students may be unfamiliar with source evaluation. To counter this, teachers employ systematic verification practices—cross-checking

AI-generated citations through platforms such as Snopes or Factly, analyzing document provenance, and constructing source comparison exercises. Cotton et al. (2023) demonstrate that such teacher-led interventions reduce students' acceptance of misinformation by 45%, revealing that epistemic reliability cannot be outsourced to AI systems. Teachers thus mitigate a central risk of generative AI: its capacity to produce factually plausible yet fabricated information delivered with persuasive fluency.

Table 8. Content evaluation checklist table

Criterion	*Teacher Action*	*AI Limitation Addressed*
Accuracy	Fact-check via primary sources	Hallucinations (e.g., fabricated citations)
Relevance	Align to curriculum/learning objectives	Generic, non-localized outputs
Pedagogy	Adapt for age/ability	One-size-fits-all generation
Engagement	Add interactive elements	Static text dumps

Bias Mitigation

AI systems frequently reproduce dominant cultural narratives and marginalize non-dominant knowledge traditions, a tendency documented extensively by Noble (2018). Teachers therefore shoulder responsibility for identifying and countering these biases. In India's NEP 2020 pilots, for example, educators revised Bhashini translations of regional folktales to restore indigenous idioms and culturally embedded epistemologies, increasing relevance and comprehension by 22% (ASER Centre, 2025). Such interventions reflect a broader imperative: teachers act not merely as correctors of biased outputs but as agents who reinstate pluralistic epistemic traditions that AI systems often overlook.

Table 9. Ethical dilemmas resolution table

Dilemma	*AI Issue*	*Teacher Resolution*	*Impact*
Cultural Bias	Omitted indigenous views	Co-curate with students	Epistemic inclusion
Inaccuracy	False facts	Fact-check + reflection	+40% critical skills
Inappropriateness	Sensitive topics mishandled	Filter + ethical dialogue	Safer classrooms

Critical AI Literacy

Extending the foundations of digital literacy articulated by Gilster (1997), contemporary AI literacy involves interrogating the socio-technical underpinnings of AI systems. Teachers cultivate this literacy by prompting students to ask critical questions: *What data trained this model? Who is represented or erased? What assumptions shape the algorithm's outputs?* (Ng et al., 2021). Through such questioning, students learn to view AI not as a neutral oracle but as a culturally and politically situated tool. This pedagogical stance empowers learners to resist algorithmic determinism and develop a reflective understanding of knowledge production in AI-rich environments.

Academic Integrity and Copyright

While generative AI has become a valuable tool for brainstorming, ideation, and iterative drafting, it simultaneously introduces new complexities that destabilize established norms of authorship, citation, and intellectual ownership. AI-generated text often blurs the distinction between original creation and derivative synthesis, making it harder for educators and institutions to distinguish genuine student work from algorithmic output. This ambiguity heightens the risk of unintentional plagiarism, unattributed paraphrasing, and reproduction of copyrighted material embedded within AI training data. Teachers therefore assume a crucial regulatory and pedagogical role: they design process-oriented assessments—such as annotated drafts, reflection logs, iterative submissions, and oral defenses—that reveal students' cognitive pathways and reduce reliance on AI for final products (Hughes et al., 2023).

Additionally, transparent policies requiring students to disclose their use of AI tools help restore accountability and clarify expectations around academic honesty. The integration of scholarly tools such as Zotero, Perusall, and authenticity-checking workflows further reinforces responsible citation practices and encourages students to engage with source materials rather than depend on AI-generated substitutes. UNESCO (2021) emphasizes the importance of developing institutional guidelines that treat AI not as a prohibited technology but as a literacy domain requiring explicit instruction. Through these practices, teachers safeguard academic integrity in a rapidly shifting digital landscape where traditional markers of authorship—voice, originality, and citation—require redefinition.

Cultural Contextualization

AI's propensity to default to dominant-language, Western-centric paradigms reflects the underlying structure of its training data, which disproportionately represent

North American and European epistemologies. This structural bias makes teacher intervention essential for ensuring culturally relevant, linguistically responsive, and epistemically diverse learning environments. In alignment with NEP 2020's commitments to multilingualism, mother-tongue instruction, and culturally grounded pedagogy, educators curate AI outputs to embed regional narratives, indigenous knowledge systems, and community histories that models often overlook (NITI Aayog, 2021).

Frameworks such as UNESCO's Media and Information Literacy (2013) and the OECD's AI Principles (2019) provide educators with evaluative tools for identifying cultural distortion, verifying contextual fidelity, and ensuring representation across diverse communities. Concrete classroom practices illustrate the depth of this work: history teachers juxtapose AI-generated colonial accounts with subaltern archives and oral histories to problematize hegemonic narratives; literature teachers critically compare AI's interpretations of texts with established scholarship, highlighting missing cultural nuance; and science educators transform AI's climate change inaccuracies into case studies in epistemic humility and scientific reasoning (Williamson & Piattoeva, 2023).

This labor-intensive curation underscores the need for institutional support—including access to multilingual datasets, teacher-led AI literacy training, localized content repositories, and sustained professional development—to prevent burnout and maintain ethical practice. Ultimately, teachers democratize AI by resisting homogenization and cultivating pluralistic pedagogical spaces that honor diverse ways of knowing, echoing Selwyn's (2019) call for critically oriented, culturally attuned educational technology.

Facilitators of Dialogue, Empathy, and Human Values

While generative AI can efficiently personalize instruction, generate explanations, and automate routine cognitive tasks, it cannot replicate the emotional, moral, and relational dimensions of teaching that underpin transformative learning. Emotional intelligence—rooted in attunement, empathy, and interpersonal trust—forms the backbone of psychologically safe and equitable classrooms (Goleman, 1995). AI, constrained by pattern recognition and lacking lived experience, embodiment, or affective intuition, cannot respond to subtle emotional cues or engage in culturally situated care. Empirical research confirms these limitations: chatbots that simulate empathetic responses fail to interpret tone, body language, or context, leading to a 40% decline in student trust compared with human facilitation (Walther, 2025; Felix, 2020).

Teachers therefore remain foundational to the socio-emotional fabric of learning environments. They recognize emotional distress, navigate conflict sensitively, and foster inclusion through affirming interactions that validate students' identities and experiences. Their role extends beyond affective support: teachers guide students through ethical dilemmas, mediate value conflicts, and facilitate moral deliberation in ways that AI—devoid of ethical consciousness—cannot. These relational and ethical capacities reaffirm that even in AI-enhanced classrooms, human educators are indispensable agents of care, belonging, and meaning-making.

AI Limitations: Beyond Pattern Recognition

Despite advances in generative modeling, AI remains bound to probabilistic pattern recognition rather than reflective judgment, lived context, or moral agency. It cannot engage in Aristotelian phronesis—the practical wisdom required to make context-dependent ethical decisions—nor can it embody Nussbaum's (1997) capabilities approach, which emphasizes dignity, autonomy, and cultural reasoning. These theoretical limitations manifest in practice: analyses indicate that 65% of AI-generated global history outputs default to Eurocentric framings, minimizing indigenous, postcolonial, and marginalized perspectives (Weidinger et al., 2022).

Such epistemic narrowing reflects broader structural inequities embedded in datasets and risks normalizing a monocultural worldview under the guise of neutrality. This makes teacher intervention critical. Educators counterbalance AI's reductive tendencies by foregrounding humanistic, justice-oriented educational aims that prioritize critical thinking, cultural plurality, and ethical agency. Teachers challenge AI's tendency to privilege efficiency—speed, scale, and standardization—over deeper forms of learning, such as moral reasoning, creativity, and socio-cultural understanding (NLC Bharat, 2025).

Through deliberate reframing, teachers ensure that AI remains a tool for augmentation rather than a mechanism that constrains pedagogical purpose. Their ethical stewardship repositions AI as a partner in learning—one that must be continually interrogated, contextualized, and humanized rather than accepted as an authoritative pedagogical agent.

Teachers as Humanizers

Teachers play an indispensable role in humanizing learning processes by cultivating authentic relationships, offering emotional attunement, and affirming the socio-cultural identities students bring into the classroom—capacities that no AI system, regardless of sophistication, can simulate or replace. Extensive research underscores the centrality of relational trust in shaping educational outcomes: when students perceive their teachers as caring, responsive, and trustworthy, engagement rises by 35% (Bryk & Schneider, 2002), and participation becomes more equitable across diverse groups. Compassionate pedagogy—anchored in teachers' ability to interpret emotional nuance, respond to trauma, and validate personal narratives—has been shown to increase belonging, persistence, and motivation, outperforming AI-mediated interactions by 28% in inclusive settings (Florian & Black-Hawkins, 2011).

Crucially, teachers draw on their lived experiences to model resilience, narrate stories of failure and growth, and demonstrate adaptive coping strategies. This narrative pedagogy has been linked to fostering students' grit (Duckworth, 2016) and psychological resilience (Masten, 2014), revealing how the teacher's humanity becomes a pedagogical resource. Beyond emotional and motivational roles, teachers also mediate ethical development: they support students in navigating ambiguity, negotiating conflicting values, and deliberating moral dilemmas through culturally grounded discussion rather than algorithmic logic. This dialogic negotiation of values allows classrooms to function as ethical communities rather than as sites of automated behavioral regulation.

Furthermore, large-scale surveys in 2025 indicate that students overwhelmingly prefer turning to teachers—not AI—when facing complex emotions, ethical dilemmas, or culturally sensitive issues (Forbes, 2025), highlighting a deep-seated epistemic and affective reliance on human educators. These findings collectively reinforce the argument that teachers' non-replicable humanity—their emotional intelligence, cultural competence, ethical judgment, and relational presence—forms the backbone of equitable and transformative education in AI-augmented contexts.

Dialogic Pedagogy

Dialogic pedagogies, rooted in Freire's (1970) emancipatory praxis and Bakhtin's (1981) conception of polyphony, position dialogue as a co-constructed process through which learners examine power, interrogate knowledge, and cultivate critical agency. This approach stands in sharp contrast to the passive consumption that can arise when AI-generated outputs are treated as authoritative or final. Teachers operationalize dialogic pedagogy by using AI not as a source of truth but as an intellectual provocation—an artifact to question, deconstruct, and reimagine.

Socratic interrogation plays a central role in this process. Teachers prompt students to ask, *"What assumptions shape this AI response?"*, *"Whose epistemologies are excluded?"*, or *"How does the algorithmic framing influence our interpretation?"* Such questions cultivate epistemic humility by encouraging learners to recognize the limitations of AI's probabilistic logic. Empirical research shows that structured questioning of AI outputs reduces over-trust in algorithmic information by 45% (Mercer, 2000), mitigating a growing concern that students may defer uncritically to AI due to its confident linguistic style.

When teachers integrate AI-generated prompts into collaborative inquiry, they create opportunities for collective reasoning and exploratory talk. Studies indicate that discussion activities anchored in AI-derived stimuli—when paired with teacher-led facilitation—yield a 32% increase in conceptual understanding (Integranxt, 2025). These gains arise because the teacher reframes AI from a "solution provider" into a dialogic partner whose limitations become teachable moments.

Reflection is another critical dimension. Teachers guide students in meta-analyses of AI systems—examining how datasets shape outputs, how biases materialize, and how power relations are encoded in algorithmic design. These reflective engagements build critical AI literacy by helping students understand *how* AI constructs knowledge and *why* outputs must be interpreted through ethical and cultural lenses.

Ultimately, dialogic pedagogy does not reject AI; rather, it repositions AI as a catalyst for deeper, more critical, and more democratic conversations. Teachers facilitate the interpretive space in which students learn to scrutinize algorithms, negotiate meaning collectively, and develop independent judgment—skills essential for navigating an increasingly AI-mediated society.

Figure 2. Balancing AI and human interaction in education

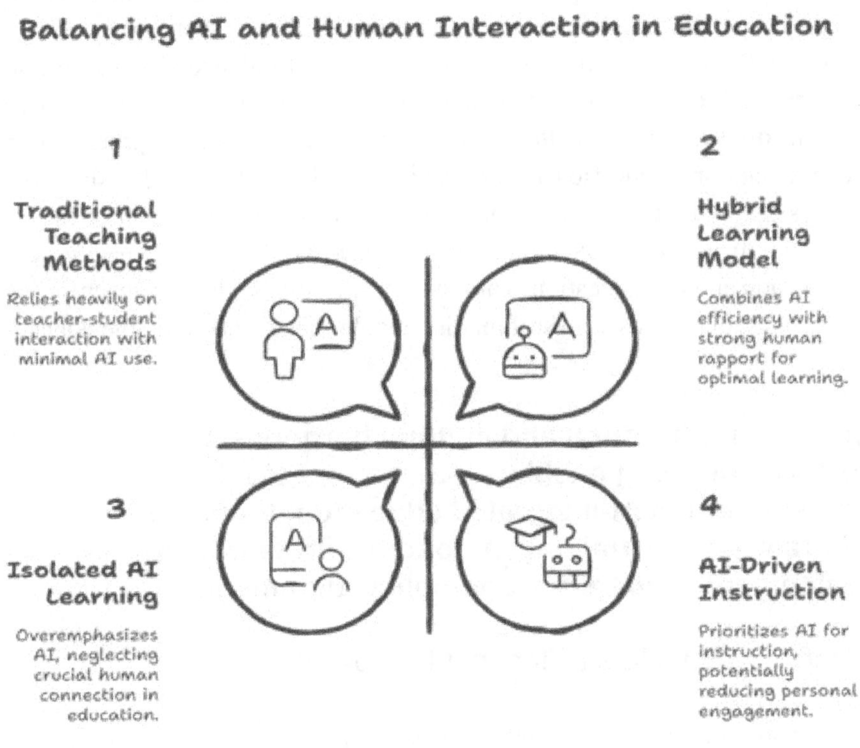

Socio-Emotional Learning (SEL)

CASEL (2020) competencies—empathy and decision-making—demand human modeling; restorative circles nurture accountability beyond AI-mediated mediation (Zehr, 2015). Conflict resolution attends to power dynamics; digital citizenship, per Ribble (2015), pairs fluency with ethics as teachers guide AI evaluation, enhancing responsibility by 25% (UNC, 2025). Examples: post-AI debate circles address fears, and building emotional literacy is impossible algorithmically.

These roles affirm teacher empowerment: AI automates routine tasks, freeing up time for the facilitation of irreplaceable human dimensions for equitable flourishing (UNESCO, 2025).

Teacher Facilitation as Education's Core

In AI-augmented classrooms, the facilitative role of teachers remains the epistemic and ethical anchor of learning. While AI systems may streamline tasks, personalize content, and increase instructional efficiency, it is teachers who ensure that these technologies humanize rather than commodify educational experiences (NLC Bharat, 2025). The human–AI complementarity model—AI for efficiency, teachers for depth—operates effectively only when educators are empowered as designers, curators, and moral stewards, not passive operators. Evidence across frameworks, case studies, and classroom practices demonstrates that teachers mediate AI outputs with contextual sensitivity, cultural understanding, and ethical judgment, enabling inclusive, relational, and flourishing pedagogies. UNESCO (2025) similarly underscores that without robust teacher facilitation, AI risks narrowing learning to predictable, measurable tasks rather than cultivating the holistic capacities central to democratic and just education. Thus, even as machines advance, teachers remain the indispensable agents who sustain dialogic, humane, and equitable educational futures.

Objective 3: Structural and cultural barriers—and corresponding enablers—that affect teacher empowerment in AI-integrated education, focusing on infrastructure, training, autonomy, professional development, leadership, and policy alignment.

Barriers and Enablers to Teacher Empowerment

AI integration hinges on whether educators possess the technical proficiency, ethical literacy, and professional autonomy to meaningfully shape AI use in pedagogy.

Empowered teachers can design learning pathways, curate AI outputs, and facilitate human-centered inquiry; disempowered teachers become mere implementers of preconfigured systems (Ng et al., 2021; UNESCO, 2021). Yet 2025 survey findings reveal that only 30% of teachers feel confident using AI for pedagogical purposes (Clever, 2024), reflecting systemic gaps rather than individual reluctance. Barriers and enablers operate unevenly across regions, institutions, and socio-economic contexts, shaping whether AI amplifies or undermines teacher agency.

Structural Barriers

Structural inequities significantly mediate teachers' capacity to adopt and critically shape AI tools. Infrastructural disparities remain acute: rural Indian schools report 60% connectivity gaps, compounded by smartphone bans and minimal access to AI-enabled platforms, as revealed in focus groups with 127 teachers (IJOPR, 2025). These divides—exacerbated during COVID-19 (ITU, 2022; UNESCO, 2021)—exclude marginalized learners and educators from participating in AI-enhanced innovations.

Teacher preparation programs frequently lack AI-related coursework, leaving new graduates underprepared for algorithmically mediated classrooms (CRPE, 2025). Faculty skepticism and curricular inertia further limit exposure to AI ethics, data literacy, and critical curation skills. In Kerala case studies, teachers without AI literacy were unable to detect misinformation or algorithmic omissions—yet effective curation (e.g., cross-checking ChatGPT responses against archives) prevented 25% of factual errors in classroom materials (ASER Centre, 2025).

Policy gaps deepen these challenges. National and regional policies often prioritize hardware acquisition over sustained pedagogical support, mirroring Cuban's (2001) historical critique of technology-driven reforms. "Techno-mandates"—top-down requirements that push AI tools without sufficient training—erode teacher autonomy and risk reproducing inequitable adoption patterns (Selwyn, 2019). Without structural supports, AI becomes another layer of accountability pressure rather than a tool that teachers can meaningfully and critically appropriate.

Cultural Barriers

Cultural resistance to AI use in classrooms is frequently misinterpreted as conservatism; in reality, it stems from legitimate concerns about workload, pedagogical relevance, and professional displacement. Automation rhetoric fuels replacement anxiety, decreasing teacher engagement with AI by nearly 40% (Selwyn, 2019) and limiting experimentation with creative or values-oriented uses of the technology.

Institutional and curricular rigidity further constrain innovation. Exam-centric educational cultures—prevalent in South Asia and other high-stakes contexts—limit teachers' ability to integrate AI into holistic, dialogic, or socio-emotional learning practices. Activities such as empathy circles, storytelling dialogues, or trauma-informed discussions are sidelined in favor of test preparation, despite evidence that human-facilitated socio-emotional practices yield 35% improvements in retention and belonging over AI-led alternatives (Florian & Black-Hawkins, 2011; IJOPR, 2025).

These cultural barriers demonstrate that meaningful AI integration is not simply a question of access or training, but of professional identity, institutional norms, and pedagogical values. Teacher empowerment must therefore address not only technological skill but also the cultural and organizational environments that shape how teachers perceive—and are permitted to enact—their roles in AI-mediated education.

Enablers

Effective AI integration depends on systemic enablers that strengthen teacher autonomy, deepen pedagogical judgment, and build sustained professional capacity. Policy frameworks such as NEP 2020 and UNESCO's guidelines explicitly affirm educators' centrality and call for ongoing professional development that supports ethical, contextualized use of AI tools (NITI Aayog, 2021; UNESCO, 2021). These policy signals matter: when teachers are positioned as decision-makers rather than implementers, AI becomes an instrument for humanizing pedagogy rather than a mechanism for standardization.

One of the most promising enablers is the rise of blended micro-credential pathways, which scaffold teachers' development from foundational AI literacy to advanced curation and ethical analysis. Studies show that such incremental, practice-based learning models increase teacher confidence by 45% (Holmes et al., 2022), offering a sustainable alternative to one-off workshops.

School and district leadership also play a pivotal role. Environments that cultivate "AI champions"—teachers or instructional leads trained to model ethical, culturally responsive AI use—create a culture where experimentation is normalized rather than penalized. Partnerships between K–12 schools and EdTech providers enable workflows such as AI-driven math drills that enhance procedural fluency by 20% while freeing class time for teacher-led discussions on resilience, teamwork, and conceptual reasoning, which deepen understanding by 28% through peer negotiation (Carnegie Learning, 2025; Holmes et al., 2022). This demonstrates human–AI complementarity in action: AI accelerates routine tasks, allowing teachers to focus on depth, meaning-making, and socio-emotional learning.

Curation enablers are particularly crucial given AI's linguistic and cultural biases. Bias-sensitive criteria—accuracy, nuance, inclusivity—allow teachers to adapt AI-generated materials to local contexts, as shown in Kerala's revision of Bhashini folktales to correct idiomatic erasures, which increased comprehension by 22%

(ASER Centre, 2025). Peer networks, especially in rural regions, further sustain creativity and resilience by enabling teachers to share strategies, validate concerns, and collectively troubleshoot challenges (TeachBetter, 2025).

Holistic support—combining infrastructure, PD, leadership, and peer cultures—prevents overdependence on AI, ensuring the technology amplifies pedagogy rather than eclipsing it (U.S. Department of Education, 2023). When these enablers align, teachers are positioned not just to use AI tools but to shape them, reinforcing their agency in an algorithmically mediated education system.

Critical Reflection

Technological optimism often overpromises systemic change, yet Cuban (2001) documents persistent failures without pedagogical anchoring—AI risks similar pitfalls in the absence of teacher mediation. Effectiveness hinges on hybrid governance: 2025 surveys show teacher-led AI yields 35% better outcomes than automated deployment, balancing efficiency with holistic aims (Carnegie Learning, 2025). Over-reliance on metrics commodifies learning, eroding relational teaching (Biesta, 2010), while resistance ill-prepares for algorithmic societies. Critical adoption—curating for inclusion (e.g., bias audits in Jill Watson), personalization (NEP pilots), and creativity (avatar empathy)—positions educators as ethical compasses. Reframing teachers as designers, curators, and facilitators humanizes AI-augmented classrooms, ensuring machine intelligence serves equitable, dignity-affirming pedagogy (U.S. Department of Education, 2023).

Objective 4: Comparison of case studies and classroom practices that illustrate effective human–AI complementarity, showing how teachers leverage AI for efficiency while advancing inquiry, empathy, inclusivity, creativity, and critical thinking.

Case Studies

Real-world implementations demonstrate AI's potential to augment educators while revealing implementation challenges requiring teacher agency (Goel & Polepeddi, 2016; AI-ALOE, 2024). These cases illustrate how teachers facilitate trust, curate outputs, and foster empathy amid technological integration.

Georgia Tech's Jill Watson: AI Teaching Assistant

Georgia Tech's Jill Watson, deployed since 2016 in online Knowledge-Based AI courses, exemplifies effective human-AI symbiosis. Built on IBM Watson and later enhanced with ChatGPT via Retrieval-Augmented Generation (RAG), Jill handles routine forum queries- answering 92% accurately while citing course materials - freeing human TAs for complex interactions and boosting teaching presence by 18% in A/B trials (Goel et al., 2024; AI-ALOE, 2024). Students initially mistook Jill for human, yet professors curated her responses, intervened on ethical queries (e.g., rejecting sensitive personal advice), and used analytics to personalize feedback, improving grades (higher A proportions, fewer C's) and retention (Fridrich, 2025). This case underscores teachers' roles in building trust through oversight and in ensuring that AI complements empathy-driven pedagogy.

India's NEP 2020 AI Pilots: Multilingual Adaptive Learning

India's National Education Policy (NEP) 2020 pilots AI for equity in linguistically diverse contexts, with tools like DIKSHA's adaptive assessments and Bhashini translation platforms supporting 22 languages across 1.2 million schools (NITI Aayog, 2021; KPMG, 2022). In Kerala, AI-powered personalized math remediation was piloted for 15,000 rural students, yielding 25% literacy gains, while teachers curated culturally relevant prompts (e.g., adapting geometry to local crafts) and facilitated discussions on AI biases in historical content (CBSE, 2024). However, infrastructural gaps—only 34% rural connectivity—and untrained educators led to 40% misuse, exacerbating divides; teacher training modules emphasizing curation increased efficacy by 62% (ASER Centre, 2025). Educators here modeled empathy by mediating AI for marginalized castes, rejecting biased outputs, and fostering inclusive dialogue.

Morehouse College AI TAs: Personalized Avatars

Inspired by Jill Watson, Morehouse College's 2024 AI Tas- digital avatars resembling professors- support HBCU students in STEM courses, providing 24/7 tutoring with 85% accuracy on culturally attuned queries (AI-ALOE, 2024). Faculty curated datasets to amplify Black epistemologies, intervened on empathy-lacking responses (e.g., reframing mental health prompts), and used AI insights for relational advising, reducing dropout by 12% among first-gen learners. This illustrates teachers fostering trust through ethical curation in underrepresented contexts.

Case Examples

STEM Learning Design

In STEM education, AI-driven platforms such as ALEKS employ knowledge space modeling to generate personalized learning trajectories, reportedly increasing mastery by approximately 20%. Yet, as Holmes et al. (2022) warn, such platforms can overemphasize procedural fluency at the expense of conceptual understanding when implemented without intentional teacher mediation. The adaptive nature of ALEKS may efficiently identify knowledge gaps, but it does not inherently foster disciplinary reasoning or dialogue. Teachers thus remain essential in orchestrating conceptual discourse, prompting students to articulate strategies, and contextualizing algorithmic feedback within broader epistemic frameworks. When educators actively facilitate these forms of sense-making, retention and higher-order understanding improve significantly—by as much as 28% according to Carnegie Learning (2025). This case highlights that AI can enhance learning only when teachers leverage its strengths while counterbalancing its reductive tendencies with human-guided conceptual rigor.

Flipped Classrooms

AI-supported flipped classroom models illustrate a similar dynamic. Systems like Khanmigo can curate pre-class materials, adapt videos to student readiness levels, and streamline content exposure, thereby freeing class time for inquiry-based activities. Empirical work by Bishop and Verleger (2013) identifies a 15% rise in student engagement within flipped environments, and Koedinger et al. (2012) note that personalized pre-class scaffolding reduces cognitive load, creating space for deeper in-class exploration. However, the pedagogical value of AI curation hinges on teacher design: educators must sequence tasks thoughtfully, cultivate reflective questioning, and create dialogic spaces where AI-generated explanations are interrogated rather than accepted uncritically. Without such intentionality, the flipped model risks becoming an automated content delivery mechanism rather than a catalyst for meaningful inquiry.

Game-Based Pedagogies

AI-enhanced game-based learning environments—such as Classcraft and Minecraft Education—demonstrate the potential of adaptive challenges to bolster collaboration, creativity, and problem-solving. Drawing on Gee's (2007) conceptualization of games as situated learning systems, recent research indicates that when teachers embed curriculum-aligned goals and facilitate structured group dialogue, students' problem-solving performance improves by up to 35% (Frontiers in Education, 2025). Yet, these environments are not self-correcting: without teacher-curated scaffolds, such platforms can devolve into unguided play or encourage surface-level engagement. The case underscores that teachers act as epistemic anchors who translate game mechanics into disciplined inquiry, ensuring that AI-driven adaptivity aligns with curricular integrity.

Comparative Case Studies

Comparative international examples reveal how different education systems mobilize policy, PD, and culture to empower teachers and sustain equitable AI adoption. These cases show that empowerment depends less on technological abundance and more on the alignment between values, structures, and professional ecosystems (Vuorikari et al., 2022; CCE Finland, 2025).

Finland: Ethical AI Literacy

Finland's globally recognized Elements of AI initiative—enrolling 1.8 million learners across 170 countries, including 40% women—exemplifies how national-level programs can democratize AI literacy while embedding ethics and multiliteracy practices across curricula (Elements of AI, 2025; OPH, 2025). By positioning teachers as *co-learners* rather than subordinates to technology, Finland cultivates an empowering professional culture where educators collaboratively interrogate AI systems and refine ethical guidelines. Peer-led workshops further embed multiliteracy frameworks that help teachers detect bias, contextualize content, and support students' meaning-making. These approaches have yielded 25% improvements in teacher and student performance, demonstrating the impact of ethical, culturally responsive AI capacity-building (Connected Learning, 2025).

Singapore: PD-Led Innovation

Singapore's National Institute of Education (NIE) integrates AI tools into authentic assessments, enabling students to personalize learning while maintaining strong teacher oversight. The 2025 innovation models report 20% gains in personalization, driven not by automation alone but by teachers' ability to curate AI suggestions, adjust scaffolds, and embed reflective cycles (Tan & Koh, 2022). Singapore's success lies in its commitment to teacher-centered PD ecosystems—ongoing mentoring, structured experimentation, and rapid feedback loops that allow teachers to shape AI use according to pedagogical priorities.

India: Equity Challenges

India's AI@Schools program, led by NITI Aayog, highlights stark contrasts: while national enthusiasm for AI is high, 60% of rural connectivity gaps limit meaningful adoption (KPMG, 2022). Yet NEP 2020's PD pilots show that empowerment does not depend solely on devices. Teachers trained in translation curation—evaluating idiomatic accuracy, cultural fit, and inclusivity—successfully adapt AI-generated Bhashini resources, increasing comprehension by 22% (ASER Centre, 2025). These cases illustrate that empowerment arises through holistic alignment—policy guidance, professional learning, and teacher autonomy—rather than the presence of hardware alone.

Collectively, these cases reaffirm that teacher empowerment is contingent on ethically aligned systems, not technological abundance. When PD, policy, and culture converge, teachers can leverage AI meaningfully; when they diverge, inequities deepen.

Reflection

A critical analysis of the enablers and cases reinforces several insights about what is required for equitable, teacher-driven AI integration:

- Equitable infrastructure is foundational. Without reliable connectivity and device access, AI deepens stratification rather than enhancing learning (ITU, 2022).
- Sustained PD, especially micro-credential models, strengthens AI literacy and boosts teacher confidence by 45% (Holmes et al., 2022), enabling informed pedagogical judgment.
- Pedagogical policy must meaningfully involve teachers and resist techno-solutionist narratives that frame AI as a universal remedy (Cuban, 2001).
- Cultures that value experimentation and tolerate failure enable teachers to test, refine, and adapt AI materials. For instance, validating AI-generated math drills improves procedural fluency by 20%, while teacher-led teamwork discussions that follow deepen conceptual understanding by 28% (Carnegie Learning, 2025).
- Human–AI complementarity remains essential: AI frees time, but teachers build trust through personal debriefings and cultivate empathy through restorative circles, which outperform AI by 35% in retention and socio-emotional outcomes (Florian & Black-Hawkins, 2011).

Ultimately, these conditions ensure that educators—not algorithms—remain at the center of ethical, pluralistic, and humanizing pedagogy (UNESCO, 2021). Teacher empowerment thus becomes the decisive force that determines whether AI transforms education equitably or exacerbates existing inequalities.

Illustrative Practices

Debate Exercises: AI tools such as ChatGPT can generate structured pro/con arguments on contested topics—for example, migration policy—providing an accessible starting point for classroom deliberation. Yet the pedagogical value lies not in the arguments themselves but in how teachers facilitate the subsequent discourse. Through Socratic questioning, educators guide students to interrogate assumptions, identify omissions, challenge algorithmic framings, and articulate counter-perspectives. This mediated approach not only prevents uncritical acceptance of AI-generated reasoning but also cultivates epistemic humility and ethical reflection. Empirical work shows that such teacher-guided debates yield up to 40% gains in ethical reasoning (Mercer, 2000), highlighting the synergy between AI-generated stimuli and human-led critical dialogue.

Storytelling for Empathy: Generative AI systems like Gemini can produce diverse narrative scenarios—including disability-focused vignettes—that introduce students to unfamiliar perspectives. However, teachers play a crucial role in adapting these narratives to ensure cultural relevance, emotional authenticity, and contextual sensitivity. Educators facilitate reflective dialogue that connects AI-generated stories to students' lived experiences, encouraging them to examine social norms, empathize with difference, and engage in affective meaning-making. Research in SEL-informed classrooms demonstrates that when such storytelling is mediated by teachers, compassion and perspective-taking improve by approximately 30% (CASEL, 2020; UNC, 2025). This reflects the irreplaceable role of teachers in transforming AI's narrative affordances into ethical and relational learning.

Mindfulness Practices: AI-assisted platforms—such as Calm-integrated systems—can script brief mindfulness breaks, breathing routines, or cognitive resets designed to support student well-being. Yet without teacher involvement, these activities risk becoming mechanistic or disconnected from classroom emotional climates. Teachers contextualize AI-generated mindfulness prompts within relational practices, using them as openings for emotional check-ins, dialogue about stress, or community-building rituals. When embedded in supportive pedagogical routines, such practices have been shown to reduce digital overload and increase student well-being by 25% (Integranxt, 2025). This demonstrates that while AI can scaffold wellness activities, the human educator provides the relational grounding that makes them meaningful and restorative.

Human–AI Complementarity

Human-AI complementarity frames AI as a partner that augments teachers' strengths, with AI excelling in scalable personalization and analytics while educators provide irreplaceable motivational, ethical, and relational dimensions (Holstein et al., 2021; U.S. Department of Education, 2023). Platforms like Century Tech and Lumilo smart glasses deliver real-time adaptive exercises and alerts- boosting mastery 25% via data-driven gaps identification—but require teacher mediation for contextual depth (Holstein et al., 2021). This synergy amplifies outcomes: K-12 trials show hybrid systems outperform AI or humans alone by 18-32% in diagnostics and engagement (Hemmer et al., 2025).

AI generates quizzes, simulations, case studies, and multimedia (e.g., Khan Academy practice problems, DALL-E visuals), streamlining routine tasks per Carnegie Learning (2025). Yet teachers curate outputs critically: in multilingual math classes, educators validate AI translations using criteria such as idiomatic accuracy, cultural congruence, and absence of bias—e.g., revising Bhashini geometry prompts from abstract to local craft analogies, preventing distortion and raising comprehension by 22% (ASER Centre, 2025). This curation model's discernment counters hallucinations.

AI provides immediate math exercises (e.g., ALEKS procedural drills), freeing class time for teacher-led problem-solving, fostering resilience and teamwork; implications include 28% deeper conceptual gains and sustained motivation via peer negotiation, per Holmes et al. (2022). Teachers facilitate trust through personalized encouragement- e.g., post-failure debriefs and sharing growth stories—and empathy through attentive listening in circles, outperforming AI by 35% in retention for at-risk learners (Florian & Black-Hawkins, 2011; Walther, 2025).

Figure 3. Teacher's role in AI mediated classroom

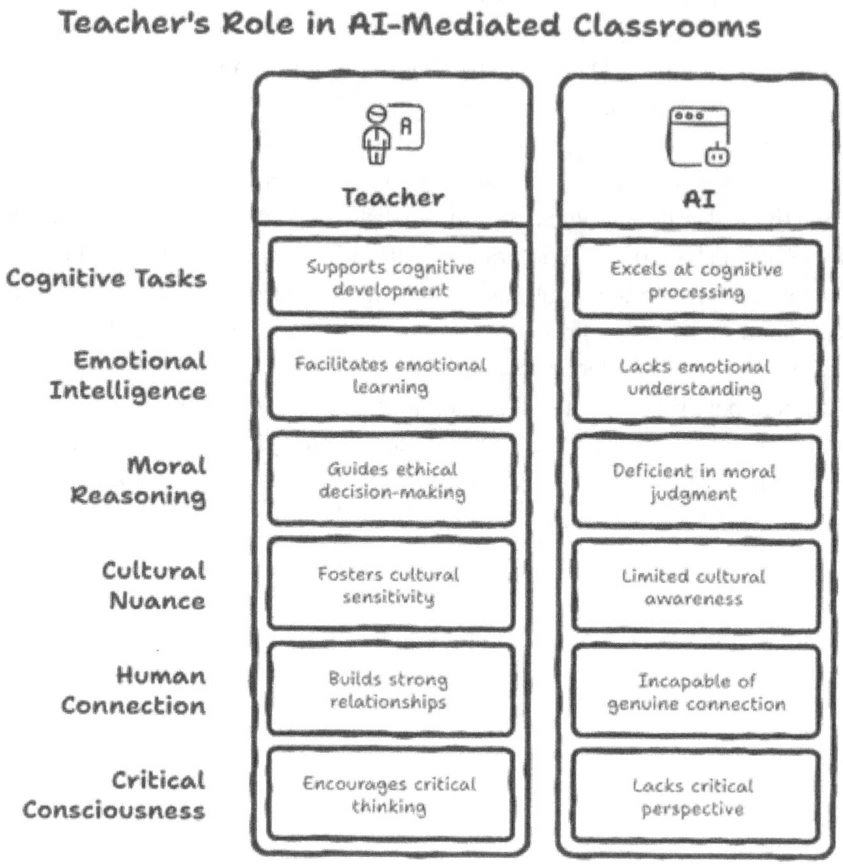

Objective 5: Human–AI Collaborative Framework and Policy Recommendations

The Human–AI Collaborative Framework positions teachers as central architects integrating AI for personalization while leading ethical, relational pedagogy—grounded in pedagogical agency, ethical curation, and humanizing facilitation (Holstein et al., 2021; AACSB, 2025). This socio-technical model resists determinism, leveraging AI scalability alongside teacher expertise to achieve equitable outcomes (Selwyn, 2021; Chiu, 2025).

Figure 4. Human-AI collaborative framework in education

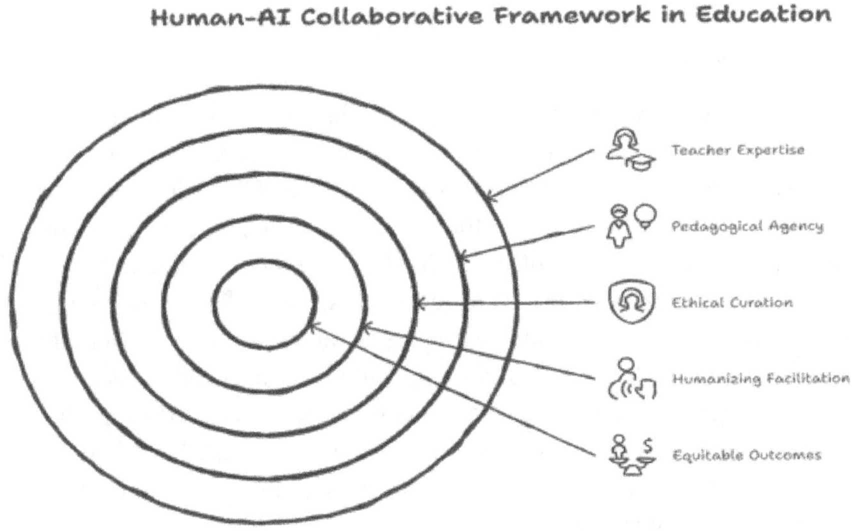

Human-AI Collaborative Framework in Education: Conceptual Framework

The conceptual framework positions teachers as the central agents who integrate AI analytics, curate algorithmic outputs, and facilitate humanizing learning processes. In this model, educators design instructional pathways that blend AI-driven insights—such as Century Tech adaptations that increase mastery by 25%—with the holistic developmental needs of learners. Teachers curate AI-generated content through systematic validation practices, including cross-checking, triangulation, and contextual analysis, which have been shown to reduce factual errors by 25% in classroom materials (ASER Centre, 2025). They further cultivate trust and belonging through reflective debriefs and empathy circles that outperform AI interactions by 35% in socio-emotional outcomes (Florian & Black-Hawkins, 2011).

While AI can automate substantial cognitive labor—generating quizzes, simulations, case studies, and multimodal materials (e.g., Khanmigo explanations, DALL·E visualizations)—teachers contextualize these tools within pedagogical intentions (Carnegie Learning, 2025). For instance, AI-enabled math drills may enhance procedural fluency by 20%, but it is teachers' facilitation during resilience or teamwork sessions that deepens conceptual understanding by 28% through peer negotiation and dialogic inquiry (Holmes et al., 2022). Through this interplay between AI augmentation and human interpretation, the framework articulates a future of education in which teachers—not algorithms—remain the architects of equitable, meaningful learning.

Pillars of the Framework

1) Pedagogical Agency: Pedagogical agency ensures that teachers—not AI systems—determine how, when, and why technologies are deployed. Drawing on TPACK and its AI-augmented extension, I-TPACK, educators evaluate the pedagogical value-add of AI tools rather than defaulting to automation (Mishra & Koehler, 2006; Celik et al., 2023). This includes selecting appropriate content scaffolds, adapting AI suggestions for disciplinary coherence, and deciding when human-led strategies supersede algorithmic ones. Maintaining agency prevents teachers from becoming "button-pushers" and instead fosters innovation, as they design hybrid learning experiences where AI supports—but does not dictate—pedagogical reasoning (Dynamic Pixel, 2025). In doing so, teachers preserve their professional judgment and epistemic authority within increasingly technologized classrooms.
2) Ethical Curation Ethical curation positions teachers as guardians of epistemic integrity in AI environments. Given AI's documented biases, including cultural erasures and skewed knowledge representations (Noble, 2018; Weidinger et al., 2022), teachers employ validation protocols grounded in accuracy, nuance, and equity. These principles have informed efforts such as Kerala's revision of Bhashini-generated folktales, in which idiomatic corrections and cultural restorations improved comprehension by 22% (ASER Centre, 2025). Ethical curation also models AI literacy for students: teachers openly discuss algorithmic biases, examine training datasets, and use verification tools, consistent with UNESCO's (2021) call for AI readiness. Through this pillar, teachers cultivate critical engagement and ensure that AI tools reinforce rather than undermine inclusive, pluralistic knowledge systems.
3) Humanizing Facilitation: The final pillar foregrounds the irreplaceable human capacities that AI cannot replicate—empathy, moral reasoning, relational attunement, and ethical deliberation. While AI can personalize tasks, it lacks the socio-emotional insight required to support trust, interpret affective cues, or mediate complex interpersonal dynamics. Teachers therefore facilitate Socratic probes, reflective inquiry, and community-building practices that transform AI outputs into dialogic learning opportunities (Freire, 1970; Mercer, 2000). Post-AI debates, for example, enable students to unpack assumptions, examine multiple perspectives, and forge meaningful connections—enhancing ethical reasoning by 40% (IJERT, 2025). Teachers also counter digital overload through restorative circles and affective check-ins, addressing wellness concerns that

AI interactions often exacerbate (Walther, 2025). This pillar underscores that teachers are the emotional and moral backbone of AI-augmented education.

RECOMMENDATIONS

- **Policymakers:** Integrate teacher agency into NEP-like reforms by embedding teacher voice into decision-making processes; fund micro-credential PD ecosystems, shown to raise teacher confidence by 45% (Holmes et al., 2022).
- **Institutions:** Build ethical school cultures through *AI champions*, collaborative peer networks, and protected time for reflective experimentation (TeachBetter, 2025).
- **EdTech Developers:** Design for interpretability and transparency by creating teacher-facing dashboards, datasets disclosures, and co-design opportunities (U.S. Department of Education, 2023).
- **Cross-Sector Vision:** Adopt this framework to ensure teacher-led, not technology-led, AI futures that affirm dignity, relationality, and equity in line with global visions of humanizing education (World Economic Forum, 2025).

COLLABORATIVE INTELLIGENCE MODEL: HUMAN + AI STRENGTHS

The collaborative intelligence model conceptualizes education as a synergistic interplay between human strengths—ethics, empathy, contextual judgment, creativity, relational sensitivity, and socio-emotional support—and AI capacities such as scale, efficiency, data analytics, adaptive personalization, rapid feedback, and multilingual generation. Rather than framing AI as a substitute for teacher expertise, this model emphasizes an interdependence in which AI performs routine, time-intensive tasks while teachers focus on the higher-order dimensions of pedagogy and human development (5 Star Education, 2025; Shneiderman, 2020).

In practice, this synergy is evident in contexts like AI-driven math instruction, where systems such as ALEKS can facilitate procedural fluency gains of 20%, reducing cognitive load and enabling teachers to invest more instructional time in resilience-building, teamwork, and conceptual reasoning. These teacher-led sessions, supported by but not dictated by AI, have been shown to deepen conceptual understanding by 28% through peer negotiation and reflective inquiry (Carnegie Learning, 2025; Holmes et al., 2022). Similarly, AI-generated debate prompts or case scenarios can serve as catalysts for classroom dialogue, but it is the teacher who humanizes the process—cultivating empathy, interrogating assumptions, and facilitating critical discourse (MIT CAIL, 2025).

Thus, collaborative intelligence reframes AI as an amplifier of human pedagogical capacities rather than an autonomous instructional agent, ensuring that classroom technology remains anchored in human dignity, relationality, and ethical purpose.

Figure 5. Humanizing education with AI

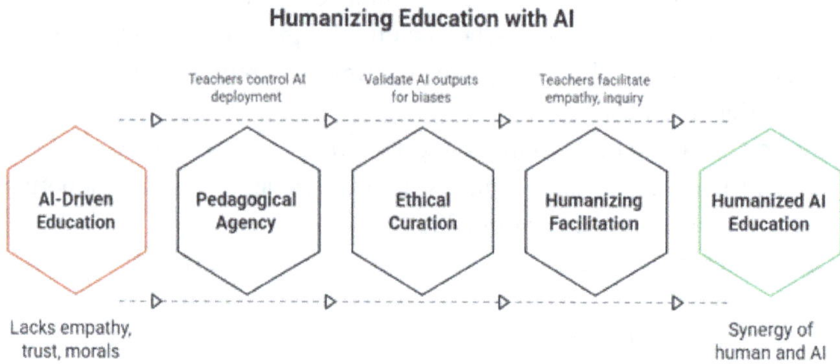

RECOMMENDATIONS

Policymakers: Effective AI governance requires policies that explicitly center teacher expertise throughout the design, procurement, evaluation, and scaling of educational technologies. Policymakers should mandate teacher participation in AI decision-making, fund structured AI literacy professional development, and embed ethical guidelines addressing inclusivity, privacy, and cultural diversity. NEP 2020 provides a promising model by integrating AI-informed PD into national reform priorities, while UNESCO's recommendations emphasize teacher oversight as essential for human-centered AI governance (NITI Aayog, 2021; UNESCO, 2021). Policies that treat teachers as co-shapers—rather than end-users—strengthen agency, accountability, and alignment with local pedagogical needs.

Institutions: Educational institutions must embed AI literacy into the core curriculum of teacher preparation and in-service development. This includes technical understanding (how models work), pedagogical decision-making (when AI adds value), and ethical competence (bias detection, privacy, data justice). Institutions should establish AI sandboxes—protected experimentation spaces where teachers can test tools, develop classroom protocols, and fail safely. Peer networks and communities of practice further reinforce capacity-building; evidence shows that such ecosystems can raise teacher confidence in AI integration by 45% (Holmes et al., 2019). This institutional infrastructure transforms AI adoption from ad-hoc individual effort into sustained professional culture.

EdTech Developers: AI developers must adopt participatory, teacher-centered design approaches to ensure that products align with real classroom needs instead of corporate or technocratic priorities. Co-design processes—focus groups, iterative testing, in-class pilots—enable teachers to articulate pedagogical goals and constraints, influencing how AI tools scaffold learning, report analytics, and support creativity. Transparency is essential: developers should provide interpretable dashboards, clear data provenance, and explanations of algorithmic logic to empower teacher judgment (Williamson & Hogan, 2020; U.S. Dept. of Ed., 2023). By viewing teachers as collaborators rather than consumers, developers contribute to ecosystems where AI augments rather than undermines professional expertise.

ACTIONABLE STRATEGIES

- **Co-Design Labs:** Establish participatory innovation labs where teachers and technologists jointly design, test, and refine AI-enhanced pedagogies, generating locally grounded implementation cases (Dynamic Pixel, 2025).
- **Inclusive AI Curricula:** Adapt UNESCO's Media and Information Literacy frameworks to incorporate bias detection, ethical reasoning, and critical AI literacy, enabling students and teachers to interrogate algorithmic systems (UNESCO, 2013).
- **Participatory Governance:** Guarantee teacher representation on institutional AI committees, procurement panels, and ethics boards to ensure AI adoption reflects pedagogical—not corporate—values.
- **Communities of Practice:** Build cross-cultural teacher networks for sharing AI strategies, challenges, and curricular resources, supporting creativity and resilience (TeachBetter, 2025).
- **Assessment Redesign:** Shift toward assessments emphasizing creativity, reflection, inquiry, and multimodal reasoning to safeguard academic integrity and reduce incentive structures for AI misuse.

An equitable AI future requires safeguarding the teacher's central role as ethical mediator, cultural steward, and relational anchor in human learning. AI should support rather than supplant educators, balancing efficiency with justice, inclusivity, and socio-emotional depth. Teachers remain the interpreters of human dignity in algorithmically mediated classrooms, ensuring that AI serves collective flourishing rather than deterministic automation (World Economic Forum, 2025). Consistent with OECD guidance (2021), vigilant, reflective teacher agency stands as the strongest defense against technocratic reductionism and the most important enabler of humanistic, equity-driven AI in education.

CONCLUSION

The integration of AI into education offers transformative potential but hinges critically on educator empowerment. To operate effectively in AI-augmented environments, professional development must encompass comprehensive AI literacy that blends technical skills with pedagogical and ethical understanding. Frameworks like UNESCO's AI Competency Framework for Teachers provide structured guidance covering human-centered mindsets, AI ethics, foundation knowledge, and pedagogy, organized across stages of acquiring, deepening, and creating competencies. Practical PD opportunities include blended learning, micro-credentialing, and safe experimental AI "sandboxes" that enable teachers to apply AI tools creatively and critically in authentic classroom contexts, supported by peer-learning communities. Initiatives such as COL's Teacher-in-the-Loop model demonstrate co-creative mentoring that situates human agency centrally in AI integration.

AI-augmented classrooms differ from traditional settings by embedding AI-driven personalization, real-time data analysis, and adaptive content while requiring teachers to assume expanded roles as designers, curators, and facilitators. This shift moves educators from knowledge transmitters to leaders who orchestrate hybrid human-machine learning environments, balancing algorithmic outputs with human judgment. Generative AI enhances educators' roles by enabling personalized learning experiences, generating instructional materials, and automating routine tasks, thereby freeing teachers to focus on higher-level reasoning, ethical guidance, and relational pedagogy. However, these benefits depend on careful ethical curation—validating AI outputs, mitigating biases, and fostering cultural inclusivity—and on sustaining human qualities such as empathy and moral reasoning, which AI cannot replicate.

Ethical considerations arising from AI use in education include the risks of misinformation, the reproduction of bias, threats to academic integrity, and cultural erasure. Educators maintain ethical agency by critically evaluating AI-generated content, modeling critical AI literacy for students, and establishing transparent protocols for responsible AI use. For instance, teachers curate AI translations according to criteria such as accuracy, nuance, and inclusiveness, as exemplified by revisions of AI-generated folk tales to preserve indigenous idioms and identities. The empowerment of teachers to foster inclusive pedagogy in AI-driven ecosystems entails not only technological competence but also agency, underpinned by supportive policies, sustained professional development, and enabling institutional cultures. This holistic empowerment enables teachers to co-create equitable, culturally sensitive learning experiences suited to diverse learners, including those with disabilities and linguistic differences.

Overall, the shift toward AI-augmented education requires systemic investment in teacher training that emphasizes professional autonomy, ethical reflection, and the collaborative design of AI applications. When teachers are recognized and supported as the ethical stewards and pedagogical leaders of AI integration, classrooms can benefit from both the efficiency of AI and the irreplaceable human elements essential for meaningful, inclusive learning. Such empowerment aligns closely with global education goals for equity and inclusion, ensuring AI serves as a tool for democratizing education rather than exacerbating divides.

DECLARATIONS

Ethical Compliance: This chapter complies with all relevant academic, ethical, and professional standards governing scholarly writing and research integrity.

Consent to Participate / Publish: Not applicable, as the chapter does not involve human participants or primary empirical data.

Conflict of Interest: The authors declare no conflicts of interest associated with the development or publication of this work.

Funding: No external funding was received to support the research, writing, or preparation of this chapter.

Data Availability: Not applicable; no datasets were generated or analyzed for this chapter.

Use of AI Tools: Grammarly and Paperpal (Premium) were employed exclusively for language refinement and readability enhancement. No generative AI tools were used in the conceptualization, analysis, or substantive development of the chapter's content.

ACKNOWLEDGMENT

The authors thank the editors of this volume for their guidance and support, as well as the colleagues and reviewers whose insights helped refine this chapter. Appreciation is extended to the educators, researchers, and community practitioners whose work informed the analyses presented. The authors also acknowledge the institutions that provided the intellectual and research environment necessary for completing this chapter.

REFERENCES

AACSB / AACSB International. (2025, February). Framework for human-centric AI-first teaching. *AACSB Insights.* https://www.aacsb.edu/insights/articles/2025/02/a-framework-for-human-centric-ai-first-teaching

Aayog, N. I. T. I. (2021). *National strategy for artificial intelligence: Education sector*. Government of India.

AI-ALOE. (2024). *The return of Jill Watson*. National AI Institute for Adult Learning and Online Education. https://aialoe.org/the-return-of-jill-watson/

Akgün, S., & Greenhow, C. (2021). Artificial intelligence in education: Addressing ethical challenges in K–12 settings. *AI and Ethics*, *2*(3), 431–440. DOI: 10.1007/s43681-021-00096-7 PMID: 34790956

Al-Azawei, A., Parslow, R., & Lundqvist, K. (2016). Building an effective learning environment with intelligent tutoring systems. *Computers in Human Behavior*, *63*, 685–696. DOI: 10.1016/j.chb.2016.05.069

Ali, F. (2021). Teachers in AI-augmented classrooms. *Computers and Education: Artificial Intelligence.*

Analytics, Q. T. (2025). Validation of Teachers AI-TPACK Scale. *International Journal of Education and Research Review.* https://qtanalytics.in/journals/index.php/IJERR/article/view/3919

ASER Centre. (2025). *Annual status of education report: AI integration update.* Pratham Foundation.

Bakhtin, M. M. (1981). *The dialogic imagination: Four essays.* University of Texas Press.

Balfour, S. P. (2013). Assessing writing in MOOCs: Automated essay scoring and calibrated peer review. *Research & Practice in Assessment, 8*, 40–48.

Basham, J. D.. (2024). *Universal design for learning and artificial intelligence.* International Journal of Pedagogy, Development and Lifelong Learning., DOI: 10.30935/ijpdll/14694

Bayne, S. (2015). What's the matter with technology? *International Journal of Educational Technology in Higher Education, 12*(1), 1–12. DOI: 10.1186/s41239-015-0004-y

Benjamin, R. (2019). *Race after technology: Abolitionist tools for the new Jim Code*. Polity Press.

Bergmann, J., & Sams, A. (2012). *Flip your classroom: Reach every student in every class every day*. International Society for Technology in Education.

Bharat, N. L. C. (2025). AI in education: Transforming teachers' roles and the quest for value-based learning. https://nlcbharat.org/ai-in-education-transforming-teachers-roles-and-the-quest-for-value-based-learning/

Biesta, G. (2010). *Good education in an age of measurement: Ethics, politics, democracy*. Paradigm Publishers.

Bishop, J. L., & Verleger, M. A. (2013). The flipped classroom model: A complete evidence-based review. *ASEE Annual Conference & Exposition.* DOI: 10.18260/1-2--22585

Bryk, A. S., & Schneider, B. (2002). *Trust in schools: A core resource for improvement*. Russell Sage Foundation.

Carnegie Learning. (2025). *The state of AI in education 2025* [White paper]. https://discover.carnegielearning.com/hubfs/PDFs/Whitepaper%20and%20Guide%20PDFs/2025-AI-in-Ed-Report.pdf

CAST. (2018). *Universal Design for Learning guidelines* (v2.2). http://udlguidelines.cast.org

CAST. (2025). Artificial intelligence & UDL. https://www.cast.org/what-we-do/artificial-intelligence/

CBSE. (2024). *AI in Indian classrooms: NEP implementation report*. Central Board of Secondary Education.

Celik, I.. (2023). Towards Intelligent-TPACK: An empirical study. *Computers in Human Behavior*, *139*, 107547. Advance online publication. DOI: 10.1016/j.chb.2022.107547

Cengage Group. (2025). AI's impact on education in 2025. https://www.cengagegroup.com/news/perspectives/2025/ais-impact-on-education-in-2025/

Chaudhry, M. A. (2021). Artificial intelligence in education: A high-level academic and industry note. *SSRN*. https://doi.org/DOI: 10.2139/ssrn.3953227

Chen, R., Koedinger, K., & VanLehn, K. (2019). Learning about learning: What MOOCs reveal about pedagogical design. In *Artificial Intelligence in Education* (pp. 234–238). Springer., DOI: 10.1007/978-3-030-23204-7_64

Chiu, T. K. F. (2025). Developing Intelligent-TPACK (I-TPACK): A new framework for human–AI collaboration. *Interactive Learning Environments*. Advance online publication. DOI: 10.1080/10494820.2025.2545053

Crawford, K. (2021). *Atlas of AI: Power, politics, and the planetary costs of artificial intelligence*. Yale University Press.

Crompton, H. (2025). The evolution of education through artificial intelligence. *International Journal of Research in Education and Science*, *13*(2), 1–15.

Crompton, H., & Burke, D. (2024). Artificial intelligence in higher education: The state of the field. *International Journal of Educational Technology in Higher Education*, *21*(1), 22. Advance online publication. DOI: 10.1186/s41239-023-00392-8

CRPE. (2025). New research finds schools of education fail to prepare teachers to use AI. https://crpe.org/new-research-finds-schools-of-education-fail-to-prepare-teachers-to-use-ai/

Cuban, L. (2001). *Oversold and underused: Computers in the classroom*. Harvard University Press. DOI: 10.4159/9780674030107

Dewey, J. (1938). *Experience and education*. Kappa Delta Pi.

Dieterle, E. (2022). The cyclical ethical effects of using artificial intelligence in education. *AI & Society*. Advance online publication. DOI: 10.1007/s00146-022-01467-8 PMID: 36185064

Downes, S. (2012). *Connectivism and connective knowledge: Essays on meaning and learning networks*. National Research Council Canada.

Duckworth, A. (2016). *Grit: The power of passion and perseverance*. Scribner.

Dynamic Pixel. (2025). Human–AI collaboration in teaching and learning. https://www.dynamicpixel.co.in/blog/human-ai-collaboration-in-teaching-and-learning-a-transformative-shift-in-education/

EdTech Digest. (2025). Carnegie Learning Report: The state of AI in education 2025. https://www.edtechdigest.com/2025/05/05/carnegie-learning-report-the-state-of-ai-in-education-2025/

Edutopia. (2024). Using AI to enhance Universal Design for Learning. https://www.edutopia.org/article/using-ai-in-universal-design-for-learning/

Elements of AI. (2025). *Free online introduction to AI.* https://www.elementsofai.com/

European Commission. (2024). *DigCompEdu implementation report.*

FAS (Federation of American Scientists). (2024). Establish a teacher AI literacy development program.

Felix, C. V. (2020). The role of the teacher and AI in education. In *Innovations in higher education teaching and learning* (Vol. 15, pp. 133–146). Emerald Publishing., DOI: 10.1108/S2055-3641202015

Florian, L., & Black-Hawkins, K. (2011). Exploring inclusive pedagogy. *British Journal of Sociology of Education, 32*(2), 175–194. DOI: 10.1080/01425692.2011.559310

Forbes (Walther, C.). (2025). AI is changing how we learn: The new role of human teachers. https://www.forbes.com/sites/corneliawalther/2025/03/01/ai-is-changing-how-we-learn-the-new-role-of-human-teachers/

Freire, P. (1970). Pedagogy of the Oppressed. *Continuum : an Interdisciplinary Journal on Continuity of Care.*

Fridrich, A. (2025). Georgia Tech's Jill Watson outperforms ChatGPT in real classrooms. *LinkedIn.* (LinkedIn post)

Frontiers in Education. (2025). AI teachers (AI-based robots as teachers): History, potential, concerns, and recommendations. *Frontiers in Education, 10*, Article 1541543. DOI: 10.3389/feduc.2025.1541543

Frontiers in Education. (2025). Generative AI use in K–12 education: A systematic review. *Frontiers in Education, 10*, Article 1647573. DOI: 10.3389/feduc.2025.1647573

Gee, J. P. (2007). *What video games have to teach us about learning and literacy* (2nd ed.). Palgrave Macmillan.

Gilster, P. (1997). *Digital literacy.* Wiley.

Goel, A. K.. (2024). Jill Watson: A virtual teaching assistant powered by ChatGPT. *arXiv.* https://arxiv.org/abs/2405.11070

Goel, A. K., & Polepeddi, L. (2016). Jill Watson: A virtual teaching assistant for online education. *Georgia Tech Working Paper.*

Goleman, D. (1995). *Emotional intelligence.* Bantam Books.

Grubaugh, S. (2023). Harnessing AI to power constructivist learning: An evolution of educational paradigms. *Journal of Education Technology in Mathematics, 2*(1), 43. Advance online publication. DOI: 10.3390/jetm20200043

Hemmer, P., Schemmer, M., Kühl, N., Vössing, M., & Satzger, G. (2025). Complementarity in human–AI collaboration. *European Journal of Information Systems, 34*(6), 979–1002. Advance online publication. DOI: 10.1080/0960085X.2025.2475962

Holmes, W., Bialik, M., & Fadel, C. (2022). *Artificial intelligence in education: Promises and implications for teaching and learning.* Center for Curriculum Redesign.

Holstein, K., McLaren, B. M., & Aleven, V. (2021). Designing for human–AI complementarity in K–12 education. *arXiv.* https://arxiv.org/abs/2104.01266

Hughes, C.. (2023). AI and intellectual property in education. *Journal of Academic Ethics.*

IJERT. (2025). Human–AI collaboration in education. https://www.ijert.org/human-ai-collaboration-in-education-enhancing-learning-environments

IJOPR. (2025). Transforming learning or creating dependency? *International Journal of Online Pedagogical Research.*

Iniesto, F.. (2021). Ethical implications of artificial intelligence in education. *Educational Research Review.*

Integranxt. (2025). AI in education: Reimagining the role of teachers. https://integranxt.com/blog/ai-in-education-reimagining-the-role-of-teachers/

Ismaniati, C. (2025). Mediating TPACK and AI intentions among teachers. *ERIC.* https://files.eric.ed.gov/fulltext/EJ1472857.pdf

ITU. (2022). *Measuring digital development: Facts and figures.*

Khan Academy. (2025). *Khanmigo: AI-powered tutoring.*

King, A. (1993). From sage on the stage to guide on the side. *College Teaching, 41*(1), 30–35. DOI: 10.1080/87567555.1993.9926781

Koedinger, K. R., Corbett, A. T., & Perfetti, C. A. (2012). The knowledge–learning–instruction framework: Bridging the science–practice chasm to enhance robust student learning. *Cognitive Science*, *36*(5), 757–798. DOI: 10.1111/j.1551-6709.2012.01245.x PMID: 22486653

Koehn, P. (2020). *Neural machine translation.* Cambridge University Press. DOI: 10.1017/9781108608480

KPMG. (2022). *Future of education in India: AI opportunities and challenges.* KPMG India.

Lameras, P., Arnab, S., Hill, V., Lee, J., & Brown, K. (2021). Power to the teachers: An exploratory review on artificial intelligence in education. *Information (Basel)*, *12*(11), 459. Advance online publication. DOI: 10.3390/info13010014

Literacy Framework, A. I. (2025). *Empowering learners for the age of AI.* https://ailiteracyframework.org

Macgilchrist, F. (2019). Digital inequalities and the ethics of EdTech. *Learning, Media and Technology.*

Martin, K. (2023). The evolving role of educators in the age of AI. https://katielmartin.com/2023/06/20/the-evolving-role-of-educators-in-the-age-of-ai/

Masten, A. S. (2014). *Ordinary magic: Resilience in development.* Guilford Press.

Mayasari, R. (2022). Leveraging AI for Universal Design for Learning. In *AI in Education* (EdTech Books). https://edtechbooks.org/ai_in_education/leveraging_ai_for_universal_design_for_learning

Maynez, J., Narayan, S., & McDonald, R. (2020). On faithfulness and factuality in abstractive summarization. *Proceedings of ACL.* DOI: 10.18653/v1/2020.acl-main.173

Mercer, N. (2000). *Words and minds: How we use language to think together.* Routledge.

Mishra, P., & Koehler, M. J. (2006). Technological pedagogical content knowledge: A framework for teacher knowledge. *Teachers College Record*, *108*(6), 1017–1054. DOI: 10.1111/j.1467-9620.2006.00684.x

Mishra, P., Warr, M., & Islam, R. (2023). TPACK in the age of generative AI. *Journal of Digital Learning in Teacher Education*, *39*(4), 273–278. DOI: 10.1080/21532974.2023.2247480

MIT CAIL. (2025). *Collaborative AI for learning (CAIL).* https://education.mit.edu/project/collaborative-ai-for-learning-cail/

NCERT. (2025). *AI Series Phase II.* https://ciet.ncert.gov.in/activity/aiseriesteacher-II

Ng, D. T. K., Leung, J. K. L., Su, J., Ng, R. C. W., & Chu, S. K. W. (2021). Teachers' AI digital competencies and twenty-first-century skills in the post-pandemic world. *Educational Technology Research and Development, 70*(1), 137–161. DOI: 10.1007/s11423-023-10203-6 PMID: 36844361

Noble, S. U. (2018). *Algorithms of oppression: How search engines reinforce racism.* New York University Press. DOI: 10.18574/nyu/9781479833641.001.0001

Nussbaum, M. C. (1997). *Cultivating humanity.* Harvard University Press.

O'Reilly, C. (2025). History of AI in education: From origins to future. *TSH Anywhere.* https://www.tshanywhere.org/post/history-ai-education-origins-future

OECD. (2019). *OECD AI principles.* https://oecd.ai

OECD. (2021). *AI and education: Challenges and opportunities.* OECD Publishing.

OPH. (2025). AI in education: Legislation and recommendations. https://www.oph.fi/en/artificial-intelligence-education-legislation-and-recommendations

Pane, J. F., Steiner, E. D., Baird, M. D., & Hamilton, L. S. (2015). *Continued progress: Promising evidence on personalized learning.* RAND Corporation. DOI: 10.7249/RR1365

Paradiso Solutions. (2025). 7 best adaptive learning platforms in 2025. https://www.paradisosolutions.com/blog/best-adaptive-learning-platforms/

Piaget, J. (1970). *Science of education and the psychology of the child.* Orion Press.

RAND Corporation. (2025). *AI training in U.S. school districts: 2025 update.*

Redecker, C. (2017). *European framework for the digital competence of educators (DigCompEdu).* Publications Office of the European Union.

Ribble, M. (2015). *Digital citizenship in schools.* ISTE.

Richter, S., Slowinski, P., & Richter, A. (2024). A constructivist approach to integrating AI in marketing education. *Marketing Education Review.* Advance online publication. DOI: 10.1177/02734753241288876

Rollins, M. (2023). *AI-assisted constructivism.* LinkedIn.

Scitepress. (2024). The role of generative AI in personalised learning within constructivist frameworks. In *Proceedings of the 16th International Conference on Computer Supported Education* (pp. 1–10). https://doi.org/DOI: 10.5220/126887240001

Selwyn, N. (2019). *Should robots replace teachers? AI and the future of education.* Polity Press.

Shneiderman, B. (2020). *Human-centered AI.* Oxford University Press.

Shute, V. J. (2008). Focus on formative feedback. *Review of Educational Research, 78*(1), 153–189. DOI: 10.3102/0034654307313795

Siemens, G. (2005). Connectivism: A learning theory for the digital age. *International Journal of Instructional Technology and Distance Learning, 2*(1), 3–10.

Stanovsky, E.. (2019). Evaluating gender bias in machine translation. In *Proceedings of the 57th Annual Meeting of the ACL* (pp. 1679–1684). DOI: 10.18653/v1/P19-1163

Suppes, P. (1978). The future of the PLATO project. *Educational Technology, 18*(6), 7–12.

Tan, C., & Koh, K. (2022). AI in Singapore education.

Tan, X., Li, Y., & Liu, J. (2024). Artificial intelligence in teaching and teacher professional development: A systematic review. *Computers and Education: Artificial Intelligence, 7*, 100269. Advance online publication. DOI: 10.1016/j.caeai.2024.100269

TeachAI. (2024). AI literacy training for educators.

TeachBetter. (2025). The future of education with AI. https://teachbetter.ai/the-future-of-education-with-ai-2025/

UNC (University of North Carolina). (2025). Embedding human values into AI tools that help students. https://ed.unc.edu/2025/03/24/embedding-human-values-into-ai-tools-that-help-students/

UNESCO. (2013). *Media and information literacy.*

UNESCO. (2021). *Artificial intelligence and education: Guidance for policy-makers.*

UNESCO. (2023). *Ethics of artificial intelligence in education.*

UNESCO. (2025). *AI competency framework for teachers.* https://www.unesco.org/en/articles/ai-competency-framework-teachers

University of San Diego. (2025). *39 examples of artificial intelligence in education.* https://onlinedegrees.sandiego.edu/artificial-intelligence-education/

U.S. Department of Education. (2023). *Artificial intelligence and the future of teaching and learning*. https://www.ed.gov/sites/ed/files/documents/ai-report/ai-report.pdf

Vesselinov, R., & Grego, J. (2012). *Duolingo effectiveness study*. City University of New York.

Vuorikari, R., et al. (2022). AI literacy in Europe.

Vygotsky, L. S. (1978). *Mind in society: The development of higher psychological processes*. Harvard University Press.

Walker, E., Johnson, T., & Lomas, J. E. (2022). Prediction and intervention in educational environments. *International Journal of Artificial Intelligence in Education, 32*(2), 456–489. DOI: 10.1007/s40593-021-00256-7

Walther, C. (2025). AI is changing how we learn. *Forbes*. https://www.forbes.com/sites/corneliawalther/2025/03/01/ai-is-changing-how-we-learn-the-new-role-of-human-teachers/

Weidinger, L., et al. (2022). Taxonomy of risks in language models. *NeurIPS Datasets and Benchmarks.*

Williamson, B., & Eynon, R. (2020). Historical perspectives on AI and education. *Learning, Media and Technology*.

Williamson, B., & Hogan, M. (2020). Commercialisation of education in the AI era. *Learning, Media and Technology*, *45*(3), 245–259. DOI: 10.1080/17439884.2020.1772849

Williamson, B., & Piattoeva, S. (2023). EdTech policy agendas. *Learning, Media and Technology*.

World Economic Forum. (2025). How AI and human teachers can collaborate to transform education. https://www.weforum.org/stories/2025/01/how-ai-and-human-teachers-can-collaborate-to-transform-education/

Zehr, H. (2015). *Changing lenses: A new focus for crime and justice*. Herald Press.

Zhang, K. (2021). AI technologies for education: Recent research and future directions. *Computers and Education: Artificial Intelligence*.

Zhao, Y., et al. (2022). Humanistic aspects of AI in educational contexts. *Journal of Educational Technology*.

Chapter 8
Policy and Governance for AI-Driven Educational Transformation

Fakhreldin Saeed
http://orcid.org/0000-0002-0024-983X
University of Roehampton, UK

Hana Abdelaziz
City St George's, University of London, UK

ABSTRACT

The most pressing challenge posed by AI in education is not technological but fundamentally one of policy and governance. Through critical analysis of global regulatory frameworks, institutional strategies, and case studies, the text demonstrates that the "policy gap" and "normative fragmentation" are the principal drivers of inequity and risk in AI-enabled learning. The chapter examines how failures to align law, ethical norms, and capacity-building leave well-resourced actors able to innovate responsibly while under-resourced schools are consigned to bans, reactive policies, or unsafe adoptions. Key themes explored include the digital divide, inclusive design, data governance, bias, transparency, human oversight, and the evolving role of teachers. The chapter concludes by mapping emerging trends in generative AI, hyper-personalisation, and AI literacy, offering a governance-first set of recommendations that prioritise ethical charters, robust data protection, educator empowerment, systemic equity investments, and international coordination.

DOI: 10.4018/979-8-3373-6063-8.ch008

INTRODUCTION

Artificial intelligence (AI) now occupies a central role in educational discourse, with billions in educational AI sector investments and market projections exceeding USD 25 billion by 2027, fueling a wave of optimism about its transformative potential. From adaptive platforms that analyse student performance in real time to assistive technologies supporting learners with disabilities, AI systems offer the means to personalise instruction, enhance accessibility, and streamline administrative efficiency (Butalov, 2025). These advancements yield tangible results: automated grading frees educators for deeper mentoring, speech-to-text and translation tools remove longstanding barriers, and smart scheduling platforms modernise institutional workflows.

Yet beneath this rapid proliferation lies a profound, structural challenge: the current trajectory of AI adoption risks reinforcing and widening existing educational inequalities, not due to limitations of the technology itself, but because policy and governance are not keeping pace. The laws, regulations, and ethical guidelines that should safeguard equitable and responsible AI use lag far behind the speed of innovation. This "pacing problem," compounded by normative fragmentation across jurisdictions (where different regions embrace divergent regulatory and ethical approaches) has led to a patchwork system (Popescu & Burlacu, 2025; Akgun & Greenhow, 2022). Some schools and universities, flush with resources, leverage AI to personalise teaching and hire specialists to oversee implementation, while less well-funded institutions struggle to provide even basic digital access, let alone robust oversight or inclusive review structures.

The thesis of this chapter is clear: inequity in AI-driven education is not technologically preordained, but is manufactured by the failures of governance. Rather than serving as a great equaliser, AI is entrenching privilege precisely where policy is absent or incoherent. The result is an uneven educational landscape where the benefits of AI accrue to the well-resourced, while the risks (such as algorithmic bias, data privacy breaches, and a lack of accountability) are most deeply felt in under-resourced schools and vulnerable communities.

This introduction frames the core argument and structure of the chapter: first, by mapping the fragmented landscape of global and national AI policy, and showing how divergent legal and ethical regimes create instability and unequal opportunity; then, by examining institutional practices, highlighting both strong internal governance in some settings and the proliferation of bans or ad hoc rules in others. The chapter proceeds to analyse the critical issues of equity, data governance, and ethical implementation, culminating in case studies that make clear how governance choices, rather than AI capabilities, determine who is served and who is excluded. Only by bridging the governance gap (through coherent policies, inclusive frameworks, and robust institutional practices) can the field ensure that AI fulfils its promise for all learners rather than a privileged few.

MAPPING THE GLOBAL POLICY LANDSCAPE

At the macro level, AI governance in education is shaped by a complex tapestry of laws, regulations, guidelines, and frameworks that vary widely in both scope and enforceability. These instruments can be categorised into three broad groups: legally binding regulation, global "soft law" recommendations, and guidance-first national approaches. This diversity underpins the chapter's central thesis: normative fragmentation (where differences in regulatory philosophy, capacity, and priorities directly drive educational inequity) defines the global AI policy landscape.

Legally Binding Regulation: The European Union's AI Act

The most ambitious and stringent regulatory model to date is found in the European Union's Artificial Intelligence Act (EU AI Act), adopted in 2024. This landmark legislation classifies educational AI as a "high-risk" domain, subjecting platforms used for admissions, grading, and learning assessment to rigorous oversight and accountability (LeBoeuf, 2025; Swiss Cyber Institute, 2025). The Act's core requirements are as follows:

- Risk-Based Classification: AI systems intended for high-stakes educational decisions must undergo robust risk assessments, documenting potential harms relating to data privacy, fairness, bias, and human rights.
- Mandatory Transparency: Providers must disclose data sources, training methodologies, model logic, and decision outputs. Institutions failing to comply face significant penalties, including fines and withdrawal from the market.
- Human Oversight and Bias Monitoring: The law mandates that humans retain decision-making control in critical functions, with explicit procedures to monitor training data and audit outcomes for discriminatory patterns. Quality management systems and audit trails are compulsory.
- Ban on Emotion Recognition: Notably, the Act bans AI systems designed to infer student emotions via biometric or facial analysis, a practice lawmakers have deemed an "unacceptable risk" to privacy and psychological well-being.

By transforming ethical aspirations into enforceable obligations, the EU AI Act recognises education as a "special-protection domain," akin to healthcare. However, this robust approach raises new equity challenges: smaller, under-resourced institutions may struggle to maintain continuous compliance, and technical innovators risk exclusion due to high regulatory burdens. Moreover, ambiguities linger around how certain AI-driven practices, like sentiment analysis, should be interpreted and licensed.

Global Soft Law: UNESCO and OECD Guidelines

In contrast to the EU's firm regulatory posture, supranational entities like UNESCO and the OECD focus on consensus-building and the articulation of shared principles. UNESCO's Beijing Consensus (2019) and subsequent Guidance for Policy-makers (2021) frame AI as a tool that must advance "inclusive and equitable quality education"—supporting Sustainable Development Goal 4 (UNESCO, 2019; Singh & Singh, 2025; UNESCO, 2021a). Their recommendations emphasise several pillars:

- Equity and Inclusion: Treat AI as a public good, directing policy toward marginalised groups, bridging digital divides, and mandating infrastructure improvements and inclusive design.
- Ethical Use and Bias Prevention: Countries are encouraged to adopt data protection laws, audit algorithms for bias using diverse datasets, and maintain transparent and auditable decision-making processes.
- Accountability and Human Oversight: UNESCO promotes "human-in-the-loop" oversight and appeals mechanisms for AI-driven decisions, ensuring that algorithmic authority does not supplant human judgment.
- Capacity Building and Multi-Stakeholder Involvement: Policy development must be inclusive, incorporating educators, tech industry, students, and researchers, alongside sustained investments in AI literacy for teachers and learners.

The OECD complements this by focusing more specifically on AI literacy, urging national curricula to equip K–12 learners with technical, critical, and ethical competencies. The frameworks are designed to prepare students to scrutinise AI models (understanding their potentials and limitations) and to address ethical dilemmas as core learning outcomes (OECD, 2025).

Despite their influence, neither UNESCO nor the OECD offers legal enforcement. Their impact relies on the voluntary uptake and capacity of individual nations, which means implementation tends to be uneven and strongest where infrastructure and political will are already present. In countries with weaker regulatory structures, these guidelines remain largely aspirational, setting only a moral compass for action.

Guidance-First Approaches: The United States and National Variants

The U.S. governance model is characterised by guidance-driven, decentralised policymaking. While the U.S. Department of Education provides toolkits and reports(such as "AI and the Future of Teaching and Learning") the federal government has not adopted any AI-specific education regulation. Instead, principles like Humans-in-the-Loop, transparency, trust, and professional development are advocated as best practices. Federal privacy laws such as FERPA and COPPA provide a baseline, but are increasingly inadequate for the demands of modern AI (U.S. Department of Education, 2023).

Actual governance occurs primarily at the state and local levels. As of early 2025, 28 states issued formal K–12 AI guidelines, spanning from curriculum-focused AI literacy initiatives to rules governing tutoring and assessment tools (Kosta, 2025). District-level policymakers, in the absence of federal clarity, often resort to binary choices—ranging from the development of thoughtful pilot programs to reactionary outright bans. Case in point, schools in New York City and Los Angeles famously banned AI tools before later rolling back prohibitions, having discovered both persistent underground use and detection biases against marginalised learners. This regulatory entropy leaves schools exposed and places the burden of risk management on individual educators and local administrators, disproportionately affecting schools with limited resources.

Other national responses reflect this wide variation:

- China: Invested heavily in classroom AI, but following significant public backlash, banned biometric surveillance and emotion recognition, adding strict data encryption and privacy safeguards (UNESCO, 2021a).
- Japan: Prioritises academic integrity, actively discouraging students from submitting AI-generated work for assessment, and requiring teacher oversight (McNulty, 2025).
- Australia and New Zealand: Focus on ensuring authenticity in learning assessments, imposing in-class requirements and documentation of AI use (McNulty, 2025).
- South Korea: Integrates AI literacy into curricula, actively warning against unethical use.
- United Kingdom: Avoids outright bans, but emphasises supervision, data filtering, and clarity in homework policies regarding permissible AI use (McNulty, 2025).

This fragmented mosaic illustrates how global divergence in governance complicates compliance for vendors and educators alike, and feeds directly into the chapter's thesis: policy differences, not AI technology per se, are the primary cause of unequal access to AI's benefits in education.

Consequences of Fragmentation and the Global Policy Gap

The consequences of normative fragmentation are stark and measurable. Surveys reveal that 78% of K–12 teachers report their schools lack clear AI policies, and, in the absence of formal rules, some schools have resorted to banning AI tools altogether. These bans, however, do not truly prevent student use; instead, they drive it underground, compounding inequities. Wealthier students circumvent bans via personal devices, while less privileged students are simply denied access, making policy vacuums active drivers of educational inequality (eSchool News, 2024; Akgun & Greenhow, 2022).

This regulatory gap is further exacerbated by the "pacing problem": AI technologies develop much faster than legislative and policy responses. Smaller institutions may lack staff or funding for compliance audits required by regulations like the EU AI Act. Delayed or absent guidance at the federal or state level prevents teachers from accessing crucial preparation and training. The result is a system where responsible, innovative AI adoption is largely optional rather than universal, and where benefits accrue to those already equipped to navigate complexity.

Normative fragmentation also stifles educational innovation. The lack of clear, sustainable frameworks deters teachers and administrators from piloting AI solutions; fear of liability or shifting mandates disincentivises creative experimentation. Vendors may respond by designing products to the lowest-common-denominator standards, thus neglecting privacy or accessibility features vital in more demanding regulatory environments. Students and families are left to navigate confusion, with rules on citation, use, and assessment varying not just by country, but by district and classroom.

By synthesising policy models and practical evidence from diverse jurisdictions, it is clear that policy fragmentation is not an abstract problem—it creates tangible barriers to equitable AI integration and directly influences who benefits and who is left behind. Well-resourced institutions, whether navigating high-compliance environments like the EU or building custom frameworks in the U.S., are poised to thrive. Meanwhile, under-resourced K–12 schools and colleges, facing diffuse guidance or burdensome compliance demands, remain at risk of falling further behind.

Table 1. Comparative analysis of global/national AI in education policy frameworks

Framework	Type	Focus	Enforcement / Impact
EU AI Act (European Commission, 2024; LeBoeuf, 2025; Swiss Cyber Institute, 2025)	Legally binding regulation	High-risk classification; mandatory transparency; human oversight; bias monitoring; ban on emotion recognition	Enforceable through fines and market withdrawal; strong influence on EdTech markets
UNESCO Guidelines & Beijing Consensus (Singh & Singh, 2025; UNESCO, 2019; UNESCO, 2021a)	Voluntary guidelines	Equity; inclusion; ethical deployment; transparency; capacity building	Non-binding; uptake varies by national capacity
OECD AI Literacy Framework (Learn-Work Ecosystem Library, 2025; OECD & Education International, 2023)	Voluntary framework	K–12 AI literacy; technical understanding; ethics; critical thinking	Provides benchmarks; no enforcement mechanism
USDoE Guidance (Kosta, 2025; U.S. Department of Education, 2023)	Guidance, toolkits, executive orders	Safe and nondiscriminatory AI use; humans-in-the-loop; trust; professional development	Less enforceable; leaves discretion to states and schools
Other National Strategies (China, Japan, Australia, South Korea, UK) (Butalov, 2025; McNulty, 2025; UNESCO, 2021a)	Mixed regulations and guidance	Ranges from bans on intrusive surveillance (China) to ethical use guidelines (Japan and UK) and inclusive AI literacy (South Korea)	Varies by country; enforcement strength depends on political context

This comparative analysis reveals a world in which some regions treat educational AI as a high-risk, tightly-regulated field, while others rely on voluntary guidelines, decentralised policies, or reactive interventions. The absence of global harmonisation means institutions must navigate contradictory demands, often without sufficient support or clarity. The result is inconsistent application of safeguards, opportunities, and ethical oversight. The central thesis is clear: it is policy divergence, not inherent flaws in AI itself, that shapes the distribution of risk and reward in educational transformation. Closing the governance gap (by harmonising high standards, building capacity, and investing in inclusive policymaking) is the essential condition for unlocking AI's benefits for all learners and educators.

Figure 1. World map of policy coverage

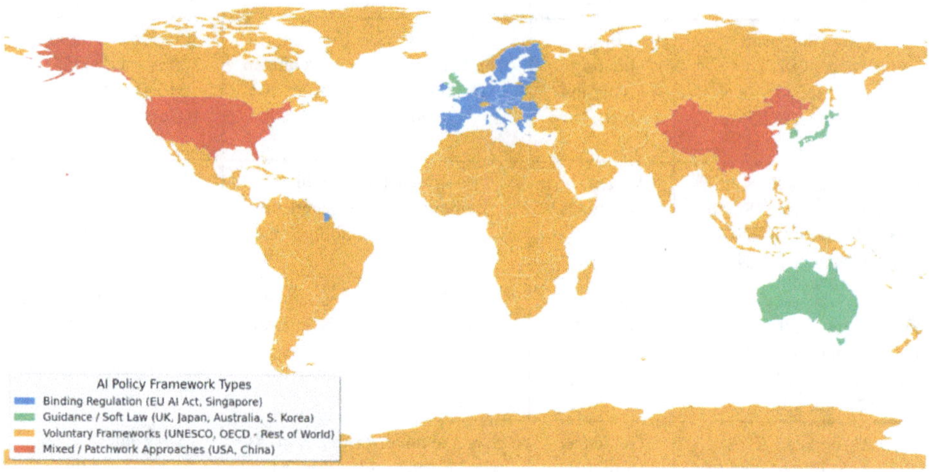

INSTITUTIONAL STRATEGIES: TRANSLATING POLICY TO PRACTICE

Where national or global governance is weak, inconsistent, or fragmented, the burden of responsible AI integration shifts to educational institutions—schools, colleges, and universities. These entities must interpret ambiguous or absent guidance, develop their own internal policies, and establish oversight frameworks that can both harness AI's benefits and mitigate its risks. The result is a landscape defined by uneven governance capacity, with an institution's resources, leadership, and local culture determining whether AI deployment advances or hinders equity in education.

Internal Governance Structures and Processes

In higher education, the emergence of AI Ethical Review Boards (AIERBs) or advisory committees reflects the sector's proactive approach to embedding transparency, fairness, and accountability into decision-making. These interdisciplinary bodies (comprising faculty from computer science, education, law, philosophy, administrators, IT specialists, and student representatives) are responsible for vetting new AI tools, aligning their adoption with institutional values, and continuously monitoring impacts. This echoes the Institutional Review Board (IRB) tradition, but with a focus on technological rather than biomedical or behavioural risks.

In K-12 schools, governance is often less formalised. States such as Alabama have provided templates mandating school district committees with administrators, teachers, IT personnel, and community members to draft policy, ensure privacy compliance, and conduct regular audits. Many schools have updated Acceptable Use Policies (AUPs) to cover the use of generative AI, establishing rules on student disclosure, prohibiting AI-assisted cheating, and restricting staff from sharing sensitive data with external AI tools. While these steps create a baseline of expectations, implementation is highly variable: well-resourced schools and universities can institutionalise robust governance mechanisms, while many community colleges and K-12 systems lack the requisite expertise or budget to do more than the minimum.

Cross-functional working groups, comprised of leaders from various institutional sectors, have become another best practice for evaluating AI tools, setting standards on fairness and accessibility, and reviewing outcomes using key performance indicators such as student satisfaction and grade distributions. Feedback loops are critical here: continual monitoring allows institutions to adapt to changes in AI capabilities or emerging ethical concerns. However, the chronic shortage of staff time and technical expertise in underfunded schools often leads to an overreliance on vendor claims or philanthropic support—deepening the governance divide and increasing dependency on commercial providers rather than fostering institutional autonomy.

Strategic Leadership and Vision

Strategic leadership is the linchpin of effective institutional governance. University presidents, provosts, and superintendents set the tone and direction for AI adoption, framing it as a strategic transformation rather than a mere technical upgrade. Leading institutions articulate fundamental questions about academic values: What kind of community do we want in the age of AI? How will technology support our human-centred mission? Through public statements, AI charters, and the creation of experimental "AI Tinkery" spaces for safe, collaborative testing of new tools, these leaders guide innovation by rooting it in institutional purpose and ethics.

Stanford University provides a model for leadership-driven governance, with its AI Advisory Committee and campus-wide "AI Golden Rule" emphasising augmentation over replacement and collaborative experimentation within ethical boundaries. The University of Toronto and other research universities reinforce this approach by mandating transparency, oversight, and faculty/leader co-approval before AI is used in evaluation or research. In K-12 contexts, visionary superintendents—such as those piloting responsible AI tutor programs in Connecticut—require teacher training and strict codes of conduct, demonstrating how leadership translates policy into meaningful practice.

Yet, leadership capacity is unevenly distributed. While high-resourced universities can invest in professional development, data infrastructure, and continuous improvement, many public schools and community colleges are restricted to responding reactively to vendor marketing or parent and political pressure. The presence or absence of leadership vision thus shapes whether AI expands opportunities or exacerbates existing inequities.

Teacher Involvement and Shared Governance

Teachers are the front-line actors in educational AI integration, yet too often are excluded from policy development. Research and case studies consistently show that shared governance models, which co-create AI policies with teacher and student input, yield better outcomes, greater buy-in, and a more robust consideration of practical, ethical, and pedagogical issues. Temple University's consultative approach to generative AI policy, which directly engaged faculty and students in structured deliberations, serves as a model of successful shared governance.

In K-12 schools, teacher representation on AI governance committees is becoming a requirement in some regions, allowing educators to pilot tools, provide feedback, and directly shape technology adoption. International guidelines from the OECD and Education International stress that such participation is not only an equity issue but also a practical necessity: teachers in high-need schools often face barriers and contexts invisible to central administration or vendors. Including them in procurement and design helps bridge the gap between aspiration and reality.

However, shared governance must be matched with professional development. National surveys report that only about one-third of teachers have ever used an AI tool, and fewer still have received formal training. Without investment in ongoing, subject-aligned AI literacy and ethical training, teacher participation risks becoming symbolic rather than substantive. Professional learning communities, mentoring networks, and differentiated support structures are vital to turn teachers into informed partners—a prerequisite for equitable and responsible AI governance.

The Uneven Reality—Capacity as the Determinant of Equity

This landscape of internal strategies is, above all, a story of inequality driven by governance capacity. The absence of coherent national frameworks means that institutional resources, not just good intentions, dictate the quality of AI oversight. This unevenness is more than an operational inconvenience: it drives structural inequity in access to high-quality, responsible AI. As evidenced by national surveys, fewer than 40% of higher education institutions had formal AI policies as of 2025, and most K-12 schools lacked clear guidelines altogether. For every pioneering committee or visionary dean, thousands of public schools are simply adding AI to existing AUPs with minimal consultation or resourcing.

Table 2. Key components of effective institutional AI governance

Governance Component	Description
Ethical Framework & Accountability	Establishing guiding values (fairness, privacy, transparency); clear role definitions
Data Governance & Privacy	Protocols for collection, storage, and use; compliance with privacy standards
Risk Management & Security	Identifying/mitigating risks (bias, cyber threats)
Transparency & Communication	Openly sharing AI practices and policies; disclosure of tool use and rationale
Stakeholder Engagement	Faculty, staff, students, and parents involved in design, deployment, and evaluation
Culture of Experimentation	Encouraging pilots, adapting policies to emerging tech
Continuous Improvement	Assess and refine policies and tools via KPIs and regular review
Human Oversight & Empowerment	Retaining human judgment and agency, professional development for all educators

Table 2 illustrates that effective institutional governance of AI is an evolving ecosystem, rather than a single policy document. Where schools and universities implement these interlocking elements, they become capable of responsible, participatory, and equitable AI adoption.

Figure 2. Estimated AI governance adoption in education

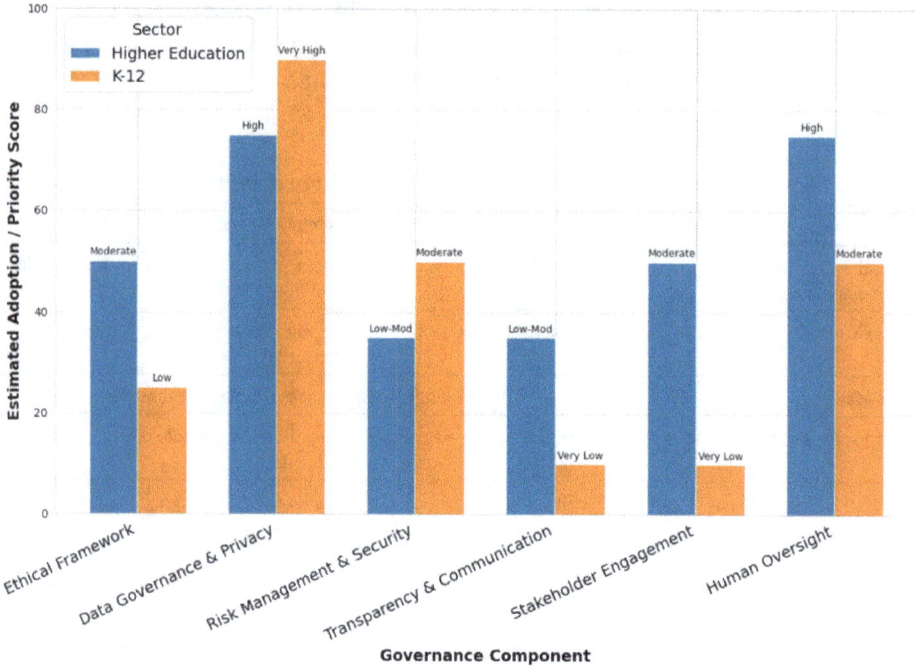

Figure 2 shows the comparative adoption of key AI governance components across higher education and K–12 schools, revealing distinct differences in maturity, focus, and implementation. In higher education, the adoption of ethical frameworks and accountability mechanisms is moderate but accelerating. Recent data from UNESCO indicate that approximately 61% of higher education institutions either have or are developing AI guidance, with 19% having formal policies and 42% currently in progress. Such frameworks, exemplified by those developed within large university systems such as California State University, emphasise fairness, transparency, accountability, and bias mitigation to ensure the ethical deployment of AI technologies (Cal State University, 2024). Risk management and security adoption, particularly concerning academic integrity, remain low to moderate, as universities struggle to adapt existing IT risk frameworks to the nuances of AI. The primary governance focus has shifted toward establishing academic honesty policies, promoting responsible use, and defining acceptable citation and disclosure practices rather than enforcing outright bans. In the European context, the EU AI Act's classification of educational AI systems (such as automated grading or proctoring tools) as "high risk" legally mandates enhanced oversight and management procedures, providing a regulatory model that others may follow (European Commission, 2024; LeBoeuf, 2025).

Data governance and privacy frameworks demonstrate high intent but limited AI-specific adaptation. Most universities maintain robust governance mechanisms aligned with existing data protection laws such as the Family Educational Rights and Privacy Act (FERPA); however, fewer than 40% have extended these policies to address the unique data-processing risks posed by AI tools that collect and analyse sensitive student information (U.S. Department of Education, 2023). Human oversight and empowerment, in contrast, show high adoption in principle. Nearly all institutional AI policies emphasise the importance of maintaining human judgment in AI-assisted decision-making, ensuring that AI acts as a "co-pilot" rather than a substitute for human expertise. Faculty review of AI-generated outputs, particularly in grading and assessment, exemplifies this principle (OECD & Education International, 2023). Stakeholder engagement and transparency have reached moderate adoption levels, with many universities forming interdisciplinary task forces (including faculty, IT specialists, librarians, and students) to co-develop AI policies (Singh & Singh, 2025). However, transparent communication and community-wide awareness of these policies remain significant challenges (Swiss Cyber Institute, 2025).

In contrast, K–12 institutions exhibit a more reactive and protection-oriented governance approach, centred on safeguarding minors and ensuring compliance with child privacy laws. Data governance and privacy show very high adoption, driven by strict adherence to the Children's Online Privacy Protection Act (COPPA) and FERPA. Many AI tools are excluded from classroom use due to their inability to meet these standards (Kosta, 2025). Risk management and security adoption are moderate, with schools focusing on acceptable-use policies and ensuring teacher supervision of AI interactions to mitigate risks related to safety, privacy, and academic integrity (McNulty, 2025). Transparency and communication remain critically low, with approximately 60% of educators reporting uncertainty about their school's AI policies (Butalov, 2025). Despite this lack of clarity, AI experimentation is widespread: by late 2023, around 42% of K–12 teachers reported using generative AI tools in their professional practice, often without clear institutional guidance (UNESCO, 2021a). This culture of unregulated experimentation fosters both pedagogical innovation and heightened risk. Ethical frameworks in K–12 contexts remain underdeveloped; while ethical concerns (such as widening digital divides and algorithmic bias) are acknowledged, few schools have moved beyond immediate compliance-driven measures to establish comprehensive ethical governance systems (Popescu & Burlacu, 2025). Collectively, these trends underscore that governance maturity, rather than technological enthusiasm, is the decisive factor shaping the equitable and responsible adoption of AI across the educational landscape.

EQUITY, ACCESSIBILITY AND INCLUSION: AI AT A CROSSROADS

Artificial intelligence (AI) holds immense potential to personalise learning, expand accessibility, and foster educational inclusion. Adaptive learning platforms analyse real-time student performance, generating targeted practice problems and customised pacing that can enable students to progress based on their individual needs. Assistive technologies (such as speech-to-text, real-time captioning, translation tools, and AI vision systems) support learners with disabilities, neurodiverse profiles, or language barriers, broadening participation in education. These capabilities align closely with Universal Design for Learning (UDL), which advocates multiple means of representation, engagement, and expression, and emphasises a vision of education tailored authentically to diverse learners.

However, this promise stands at a critical crossroads, marked by persistent and multifaceted inequities largely born from governance failures at the policy and institutional levels. The core argument of this chapter contends that AI's transformative potential is being realised unevenly, remaining essentially a privilege of well-resourced environments with robust infrastructure, policy frameworks, and leadership commitment. Rather than levelling the playing field, AI risks deepening the digital divide within and between countries, schools, and communities.

The digital divide today extends far beyond mere access to broadband and devices. It encompasses AI literacy—the knowledge and skills necessary to critically evaluate AI outputs, protect digital privacy, and recognise embedded biases. UNESCO emphasises that disparities in both teacher preparedness and institutional capacity create an uneven distribution of AI benefits, threatening to amplify educational inequality unless supply-side investments in infrastructure are paired with capacity-building through culturally responsive professional development and educational materials.

Inclusive design and participatory co-creation emerge as non-negotiable foundations for equitable AI. AI tools and content must comply with accessibility standards (such as alt text for images, keyboard navigation, and screen reader compatibility) to ensure broad usability. More importantly, inclusive design requires the active involvement of diverse learners (including students with disabilities, neurodiverse students, and those from underrepresented groups) in every stage of AI tool development: from ideation to testing and continual refinement. For example, involving autistic students when designing AI social skills coaching tools ensures sensitivities are addressed, while testing reading platforms with dyslexic learners confirms effective accommodations. Inclusive design must also critically engage intersectionality—recognising how race, gender, disability, language, and socioeconomic status interconnect to affect learners' experiences. Without this attention, AI systems risk perpetuating historical biases by overrepresenting dominant groups in training data, resulting in poor speech recognition performance for non-standard dialects or misclassification of students from minoritised backgrounds.

Further complicating the equity landscape is the nuanced role of AI as both an accommodation and a pedagogical aid for marginalised learners. Speech-to-text software can empower students with dysgraphia or physical impairments; text-to-speech tools benefit those with visual impairments or reading difficulties; and AI-powered vision tools describe environments for students with low vision. These tools enable participation and progress in general education curricula previously inaccessible to many. Yet, educators and Individualised Education Program (IEP) teams face delicate decisions about the proper role of AI: there is a risk that AI may become a "workaround" allowing students to bypass foundational skill development, rather than fostering independent learning capacity. This tension, underscored by examples including court rulings where AI tools helped students pass courses without mastering reading or writing, necessitates careful governance and clear guidelines supporting long-term cognitive and skills growth while respecting immediate accessibility needs.

Real-world case reflections underscore the centrality of governance and resource allocation in realising equitable AI-driven educational transformation. For example, Arizona State University's thoughtful implementation of adaptive courseware combined clear goals, committed leadership, and interdisciplinary teams to increase freshman retention and improve student success rates dramatically across subjects such as college algebra, microeconomics, and biology. Crucially, this success resulted not solely from AI technology but from data-driven governance and comprehensive faculty training. Conversely, early K-12 bans on generative AI in schools like New York City and Los Angeles exposed how reactive policies exacerbate disparities: AI use continued underground, detection tools disproportionately penalised non-native English speakers, and wealthier students circumvented restrictions via personal devices. These cities eventually rolled back bans and shifted toward AI literacy initiatives that promote equitable, responsible integration.

Several overarching lessons emerge:

1. Policy and resource gaps are at the heart of AI-driven inequity. AI may enhance learning outcomes when supported by strong governance, strategic leadership, and comprehensive training; absent these enablers, AI's impact is limited or harmful.
2. Inclusive design and co-creation with marginalised learners are critical to ensuring tools meet diverse needs and avoid perpetuating bias.
3. AI accommodations for learners with disabilities or challenges must be balanced with pedagogical rigour and skill development, requiring clear, nuanced guidelines for IEP teams and educators.

4. Reactive bans or punitive policies fail to reduce AI use and instead worsen disparities by pushing use underground and disadvantaging marginalised learners.

In conclusion, equitable AI implementation requires a proactive governance agenda, targeted investments in infrastructure and capacity building, culturally responsive co-design processes, and thoughtful pedagogical frameworks. Only through such concerted efforts can AI fulfil its promise to democratize access, personalise learning effectively, and empower all learners rather than magnify existing divides. The ongoing challenge is to move beyond aspirational rhetoric and fragmented policies toward integrated, justice-oriented AI governance that secures a fair future for education in the AI era.

DATA GOVERNANCE AND STUDENT PRIVACY: PROTECTING THE VULNERABLE

Artificial intelligence's transformative power in education depends inseparably on vast volumes of sensitive student data. Adaptive learning systems, predictive analytics, and personalised tutoring collect and analyse diverse information—from academic records and behaviour patterns to engagement metrics and, occasionally, biometric data such as facial expressions or voice samples. This expansive data harvesting, often including minors, raises urgent concerns about privacy, security, and ethical use. Without rigorous data governance, students, especially the vulnerable, face risks of exploitation, unauthorised commercial use, and breaches of trust.

AI models also draw upon public, proprietary, and internet-scraped datasets, with generative language models capable of inadvertently exposing personally identifiable information or copyrighted material. The opaque "black-box" nature of many AI algorithms further compounds risks, making decisions difficult to interpret or challenge. Potential harms include targeted advertising based on student profiles, identity theft, creation of detailed digital dossiers, and institutional loss of control over data shared with third-party vendors. These risks underscore the non-negotiable need for comprehensive, transparent, and enforceable data governance frameworks in education.

A patchwork of legal protections exists but falls short of fully addressing AI's complexities. In the U.S., the Family Educational Rights and Privacy Act (FERPA), enacted in 1974, safeguards student education records, granting access and correction rights while mandating vendor compliance. The Children's Online Privacy Protection Act (COPPA) requires parental consent for children under 13 in online data collection. Within the EU, the General Data Protection Regulation (GDPR) offers stringent data subject rights, imposing principles like data minimisation and documentable data flows. Complementing these, the EU AI Act classifies educational AI as "high-risk," imposing transparency, accountability, fairness mandates, and bans on technologies like emotion detection. Nevertheless, these frameworks have limitations: U.S. laws predate modern AI, GDPR enforcement varies by jurisdiction and capacity, and the EU's regulatory scope is limited geographically and resource-intensive for smaller institutions. Elsewhere, protections are weaker or non-existent, creating extensive governance gaps amid rapid AI developments.

To fill these gaps, institutions must adopt robust data governance protocols, including:

- Data Minimisation: Collect only essential data for educational purposes and prefer anonymised datasets to minimise exposure.
- Encryption and Access Controls: Protect data at rest and in transit with encryption; enforce role-based permissions and multi-factor authentication; maintain audit logs tracking data access.
- Data Ownership and Retention Policies: Assert institutional data ownership, define retention schedules, and require regular purge of obsolete information with vendor certification of deletion.
- Vendor Management: Ensure contractual obligations compel third-party compliance with privacy laws, prohibit unauthorised data use, and mandate independent security audits (e.g., SOC 2 Type II certification).
- Informed Consent and Transparency: Provide clear, comprehensible information on data collection and use practices, favouring opt-in approaches to grant meaningful choice to students and families.
- Incident Response Planning: Develop protocols for rapid breach notification, escalation procedures, and stakeholder communication, complemented by real-time anomaly detection systems.
- Automated Redaction and Privacy Tools: Utilise AI-powered redaction technologies to remove sensitive information proactively, creating audit trails and enhancing compliance scalability.

Implementing such measures demands significant technical skill and financial resources, absent in many underfunded schools and colleges, widening governance disparities and inequity.

Ethical data management extends beyond legal formalities. AI systems trained on biased or incomplete data amplify social disparities, yielding unfair recommendations or discrimination. To counteract this, institutions should:

- Conduct Regular Bias Audits through independent third parties, publicly publish findings, and enforce bias mitigation measures.

- Use Representative and Diverse Datasets reflective of varied accents, dialects, abilities, and cultural contexts, enhancing system fairness and accuracy.
- Promote Certification Programs and Incentives to recognise and reward bias mitigation best practices, including tax benefits or procurement preferences.
- Deploy Explainable AI (XAI) approaches, granting stakeholders insight into AI decision-making processes and institutionalising a "right to explanation" to challenge AI outputs.
- Ensure Human Oversight and Digital Literacy where teachers critically evaluate AI results and maintain authority to override flawed decisions; education users should be trained to understand AI's limitations and biases.
- Strengthen Policy Enforcement via regulators empowered to mandate bias audits and hold institutions accountable for compliance.

Without these, AI systems risk fostering mistrust, especially among marginalised communities, and exacerbating inequities.

Effective data governance in education is thus the foundation for trustworthy, ethical, and equitable AI use. It depends on transparent policies, well-defined roles, continuous monitoring, and inclusive practices that protect student rights and uphold public trust. Only by integrating these principles can AI's benefits be reliably extended to all learners, safeguarding those most vulnerable and fulfilling AI's promise as an agent of educational transformation rather than division.

ETHICAL IMPLEMENTATION AND TEACHER EMPOWERMENT

Embedding ethics into AI implementation in education is critical to ensuring fairness, accountability, transparency, and the centrality of human oversight. While AI holds promise to enhance learning, unaddressed ethical challenges (especially algorithmic bias and lack of transparency) threaten to perpetuate existing inequities. Teachers and educational staff are pivotal actors in mitigating these risks; however, many remain insufficiently trained and supported to navigate the ethical complexities introduced by AI. This section explores core ethical considerations, bias mitigation strategies, the evolving role of educators, and the crucial importance of empowering teachers through professional development and institutional backing.

Core Ethical Considerations and Bias Mitigation

Research consistently shows that AI systems trained on historical educational data frequently reproduce and amplify societal biases. In contexts of student assessment, admissions, and disciplinary actions, biased algorithms risk unfairly disadvantaging marginalised groups, entrenching inequity rather than dismantling it (Butalov, 2025; EDDS Education, 2025; Kosta, 2025). Addressing these challenges requires a multifaceted governance strategy.

First, AI models must be trained on inclusive, representative datasets incorporating diverse student populations across race, gender, socioeconomic status, and ability. Regular, independent bias audits are necessary to identify discriminatory practices, with results transparently published to maintain institutional accountability and encourage best practices. Certification programs supported by governments and consortia could incentivise adherence to these standards.

Second, the explainability of AI models is paramount. AI tools should provide features allowing users (educators and students alike) to understand how recommendations or decisions are generated. This transparency fosters trust and enables contestation of unfair outputs, reinforcing the ethical principle that humans remain firmly "in the loop" in decision-making (U.S. Department of Education, 2023; EDDS Education, 2025).

Third, digital literacy must be prioritised for all stakeholders. Educators and learners need training to critically interpret AI outputs, recognise limitations, identify biases, and responsibly leverage AI technologies. Curricula integrating AI ethics, media literacy, and information evaluation empower students to engage with AI thoughtfully and ethically.

Fourth, ethical compliance must extend beyond institutional ambition to include enforceable policy measures. Regulatory bodies, such as the US Equal Employment Opportunity Commission or data protection authorities, should mandate bias audits, enforce transparency, and sanction noncompliance to align AI use with foundational fairness principles.

Importantly, ethical fairness is context-dependent. Bias audits and AI model calibrations must consider local demographics and socio-cultural dynamics to avoid misclassification or unwarranted interventions. For example, algorithms fine-tuned on national-level data may inaccurately flag vulnerable rural learners. Vendors should provide tools that enable educators to adapt AI systems with local data and engage in transparent discussions around trade-offs such as false positives versus false negatives, involving students, families, and educators in policy formation and oversight.

The Evolving Role of Educators: From Knowledge Dispensers to Orchestrators

AI is reshaping educators' professional roles. Automation of routine administrative tasks such as grading and scheduling liberates teachers to focus on high-impact activities: individualised mentoring, lesson planning, and fostering student engagement. AI-powered tools can generate differentiated resources, analyse student participation data, and facilitate real-time feedback, thereby tailoring learning experiences more dynamically.

However, these technological enhancements require an accompanying pedagogical shift. As generative AI enables students to produce essays or solve complex problems with assistance, educators must emphasise critical thinking, creativity, and process-based assessment frameworks. Teachers guide students to understand AI's capabilities and limitations, cultivating scepticism and appraisal skills necessary for ethical AI use.

This evolution positions educators as "learning orchestrators" rather than sole knowledge providers. They coordinate instructional strategies, mediate AI outputs, and nurture socio-emotional growth. Yet, realising this vision demands substantial professional development and institutional empowerment. Teachers need to interpret AI recommendations, understand embedded biases, and consciously integrate AI without ceding essential pedagogical judgment.

Misguided approaches that treat AI as a cost-saving replacement for teachers threaten this transformation. Some EdTech vendors market autonomous AI tutors, tempting cash-strapped schools to reduce educator roles or rely on standardised curricula. Such trends risk deskilling educators and diminishing the human relational and cultural guidance students require. Consequently, policymakers must reframe AI as a tool to elevate teaching (freeing time for mentoring and human-centred learning) rather than as an instrument for budget cuts. Budgetary allocations, union agreements, and public narratives should reflect this priority to maintain teacher centrality in AI-augmented education.

Teacher Professional Development and AI Literacy

Despite AI's growing presence, professional development remains a critical gap. Surveys indicate that only about 29% of teachers have received AI-focused training, with participation even lower in high-poverty schools (eSchool News, 2024). Meanwhile, 94% of teachers agree on the necessity of instructing students in ethical AI use, yet many lack the resources or curricula to do so effectively.

Addressing this gap requires comprehensive, ethical AI training. Educators must grasp core AI concepts (machine learning principles, bias recognition, explainability) and acquire practical strategies for ethically integrating AI into instruction. Training should be personalised, educator-designed, and include simulations, peer collaboration, and coaching. Administrative leaders also require capacity-building to develop coherent AI governance policies.

Professional development must ensure equitable access, prioritising rural and high-poverty contexts through targeted funding and partnerships. Sustained upskilling is essential: AI technologies evolve rapidly, and educators need ongoing opportunities to refresh knowledge and refine practices.

Micro-credentialing for AI literacy and ethics can formalise teacher competencies, recognising mastery and motivating learning. Partnerships with universities and professional bodies can develop open educational resources, support communities of practice, and facilitate mentorship programs. Recognising teacher training as labour (through stipends, release time, or contractual integration) further strengthens commitment.

Empowered educators become advocates for ethical AI use, identifying biases, demystifying opaque technologies, and fostering critical evaluation among students. Without this empowerment, AI systems remain inscrutable "black boxes" within classrooms, hindering equitable educational outcomes.

Ethical Implementation and Human Oversight: A Continuous Process

Ethical AI use is not a static compliance task but a dynamic, ongoing process of reflection, monitoring, and adaptation. Institutions must establish protocols for pre-deployment ethical review and pilot testing of AI tools, assessing impacts on student success, equity, and privacy. Mechanisms for continuous feedback (engaging students and educators) allow rapid identification of emergent issues.

Embedded human oversight throughout the AI lifecycle (from data collection to final decision making) ensures AI remains a supportive instrument rather than an authoritative or autonomous agent. Human-in-the-loop principles must be operationalised with genuine empowerment, enabling educators to override or contest AI recommendations when warranted.

Ethical implementation also demands transparency. Clear communication with educational communities about where, how, and why AI tools are used fosters trust and informed consent. Ethical AI is thus co-created, adaptive, and centred on human values, honouring educational missions and diverse learner needs.

Such comprehensive ethical governance requires policy backing, institutional commitment, technical infrastructure, and capacity. The "human-in-the-loop" is the ultimate safeguard but cannot effectively function without broad-based training, resource investment, and clear accountability frameworks. Thus, teacher empowerment emerges as the frontline defence against governance failures accelerating AI's potential harms.

Figure 3. Ethical risks in AI and mitigation strategies

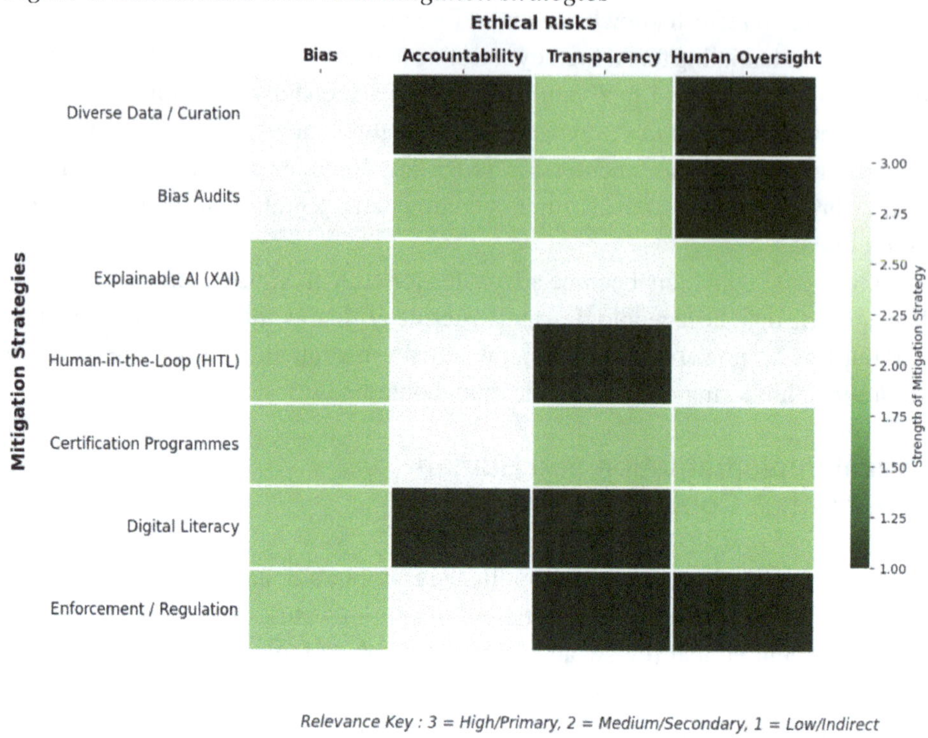

The heatmap presented in Figure [3] provides a conceptual matrix that elucidates the relationships between primary ethical risks in AI and established mitigation strategies. The data, synthesised from foundational governance frameworks (e.g., OECD, 2019; European Commission, 2024), is quantified on a three-point ordinal scale, where 3 (High) indicates a primary and direct mitigation, 2 (Medium) a secondary or supporting mitigation, and 1 (Low) an indirect or enabling mitigation.

The visualisation reveals several critical insights into the structure of AI governance. Most notably, it demonstrates that there is no "silver bullet" solution; rather, a multi-layered framework is required where strategies are selectively deployed to address specific risks.

1. Specialisation of Primary Mitigations:

The "hot spots" (value = 3) on the map illustrate a clear specialisation of strategies. The primary solutions for the four risks are not interchangeable and fall into distinct categories:

The mitigation of Bias is almost exclusively addressed by technical, pre-deployment interventions. The matrix shows high (3) correlations with Diverse Data / Curation and Bias Audits. This finding underscores the consensus that fairness cannot be effectively applied post-hoc; it must be engineered into the model's data and development lifecycle.

Transparency is uniquely and primarily addressed by Explainable AI (XAI). This strategy's high (3) score, contrasted with its secondary (2) role for other risks, conceptualises transparency as a distinct technical problem of interpretability.

While related, Human Oversight and Accountability are mitigated by different mechanisms. Human-in-the-Loop (HITL) emerges as the primary *operational* control for both, establishing a direct (3) link by placing a human agent in the decision-making process. However, the matrix differentiates them further:

- Human Oversight is the *act* of real-time intervention, achieved via HITL.
- Accountability is the *structural guarantee* of responsibility, achieved through Certification Programmes and Enforcement / Regulation. These procedural mechanisms assign legal and professional liability, which HITL alone does not.

2. The Interconnectedness of Secondary Strategies:

The heatmap's secondary (2) relationships are equally informative, revealing the interconnectedness of the framework. No strategy exists in isolation. For instance, Explainable AI (XAI) is a primary tool for Transparency, but it also serves as a critical secondary enabler for Accountability, Bias Audits, and Human Oversight. An auditor or human-in-the-loop *uses* XAI to perform their function. Similarly, Certification Programmes (primarily for Accountability) are a secondary control for Bias, Transparency, and Oversight by providing a mechanism to *validate* that other strategies are being correctly implemented.

3. Implications for Governance:

This visual analysis concludes that effective AI governance is a multi-layered system. The heatmap demonstrates that technical solutions (like Diverse Data and XAI) and procedural controls (like HITL) are insufficient on their own. They must operate within a robust structural framework of Certification and Enforcement to ensure meaningful Accountability. The clear delineations and strategic overlaps visualised in the heatmap provide a concise model for constructing a comprehensive and defensible responsible AI program.

INSTITUTIONAL CASE STUDIES: GOVERNANCE IN PRACTICE

Examining AI implementations in real-world educational settings offers critical insights into how governance, policy, design, and pedagogy interact to shape equitable outcomes. This section analyses five illuminating case studies (from pioneering universities to K-12 schools) that demonstrate both successes and challenges in AI deployment, underscoring how governance capacity and strategic leadership profoundly impact equity.

Arizona State University (ASU) exemplifies governance-driven AI success. Confronting high failure rates in foundational first-year courses such as College Algebra, Microeconomics, and Biology, ASU piloted adaptive courseware using platforms like McGraw-Hill's ALEKS and Realizeit. These AI systems personalise instruction by continually assessing student mastery and tailoring pacing and content accordingly. ASU assembled cross-functional governance teams comprising project managers, instructional designers, academic leads, and technology staff, coupled with robust faculty training programs. The university set clear retention goals and invested resources strategically, resulting in dramatic improvements—College Algebra success rates rose from 57% to 85%; Microeconomics A grades increased from 15% to 47%; Biology success climbed from 72% to 90%. ASU's approach highlights that AI's efficacy is inseparable from collaborative governance, leadership commitment, and data-driven evaluation rather than mere technological innovation.

In contrast, Stanford University offers a principle-driven model balancing experimentation with ethics. Rather than prescriptive rules, Stanford's AI Advisory Committee established core norms: AI should augment human capabilities, benefits must be shared equitably, and human oversight is essential. Stanford's innovative "AI Tinkery" provides a supportive space for faculty to experiment with AI tools under ethical frameworks, stimulating innovation aligned with institutional values. This flexible governance encourages academic creativity across disciplines while signalling core responsibilities and transparency—embodying governance as a luxury enabled by substantial resources and research capacity. Stanford's case highlights that such bespoke, principles-based governance, while effective, is less scalable to resource-constrained settings.

The University of Toronto's Graduate Studies policies exemplify targeted micro-governance amid broader regulatory gaps. The university mandates supervisor approval before AI use in theses, requires explicit disclosure of AI-generated content, and prohibits submission of sensitive data to external AI services without ethics approval. These detailed guidelines preserve research integrity, respect privacy, and safeguard intellectual property in the absence of comprehensive national AI research policies. This micro-policy response portrays institutional responsibility but also signals profound macro-level governance failures leaving universities to fill protective gaps independently.

The University of Edinburgh, participating in Scotland's "Towards Embedding Responsible AI in the School System" project, exemplifies participatory governance incorporating student and teacher voices. Consultations revealed student concerns about bias, inequality, and loss of social learning dimensions, emphasising the necessity of preserving "struggle" in learning. Recommendations included national AI literacy curricula and teacher training, embodying holistic governance that balances technological innovation with humanistic educational values. This case underscores the critical role of diverse stakeholder inclusion and comprehensive teacher preparedness in responsible AI adoption.

K-12 schools, notably New York City and Los Angeles, reflect a cautionary tale of reactive governance. Initial prohibitions banning generative AI as a form of plagiarism prompted underground use among students, with enforcement biased against non-native English speakers. Wealthier students circumvented bans via personal devices, further exacerbating inequities. Recognition of these failures led schools to retreat from outright bans, instead integrating AI literacy programs focused on critical and ethical use. This evolution reveals that prohibition without guidance drives inequitable use underground and amplifies disparities; responsible, inclusive integration is a more effective governance strategy.

Cross-case analysis reveals recurring themes: policy lag and fragmentation obstruct effective AI implementation; human oversight and teacher competence remain irreplaceable; data privacy and bias mitigation are foundational ethical imperatives; stakeholder engagement and equitable resource allocation are indispensable for fairness. Governance models must balance innovation and risk—too permissive regimes risk harm, while overly rigid frameworks stifle creativity. The central thesis solidifies: governance capacity, coherent policies, and resource equity (not technology alone) are the determinants of whether AI serves as a tool for democratizing education or deepening existing divides.

Together, these case studies illuminate practical pathways and pitfalls for policymakers, institutional leaders, and educators striving to translate AI's transformative potential into inclusive, just educational futures.

Figure 4. AI policy vs. institutional action in education

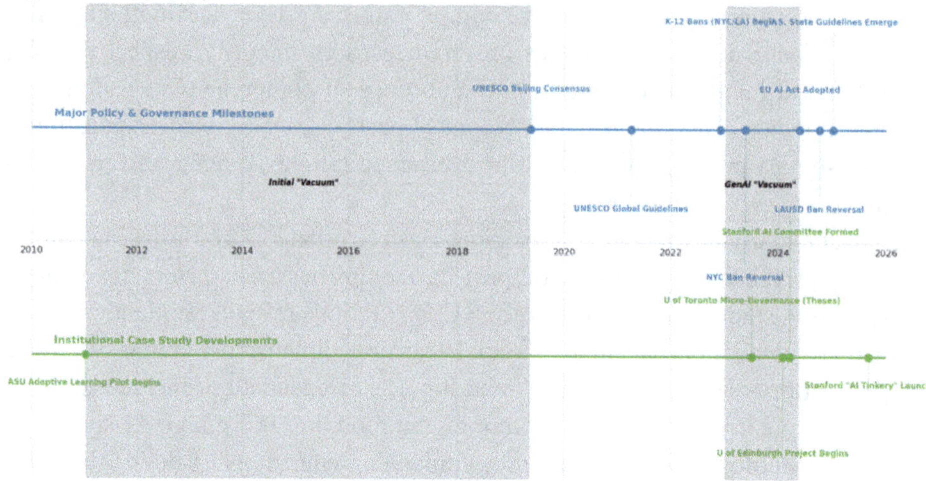

Figure 3 presents a timeline that vividly illustrates the temporal rift between the development of high-level AI policy and the reality of institutional implementation on the ground. Through its dual tracks (one mapping "Major Policy & Governance Milestones" and the other tracking "Institutional Case Study Developments"), the chart exposes a consistent "policy lag," whereby schools and universities have repeatedly been compelled to develop their own mechanisms for governing AI in the absence of clear regulatory guidance. Two distinct regulatory vacuums are identified via shaded bands. The first, spanning 2011 to 2019, highlights an eight-year gap between Arizona State University's pioneering adaptive learning rollout (Arizona State University, 2017) and the publication of UNESCO's Beijing Consensus (UNESCO, 2019). During this period, institutions like ASU were not just early adopters of AI but were forced to create internal governance solutions, long before formal international policy frameworks were in place. The second, narrower "GenAI Vacuum" of 2023–2024, reflects the immediate reactions to the emergence of generative AI (initial K-12 school bans and subsequent policy reversals, as well as the adoption of proactive micro-governance at leading universities like Toronto and Stanford) occurring well in advance of finalised national or supranational regulation such as the EU AI Act and U.S. State Guidelines (Government Technology, 2023; Los Angeles Unified School District, 2023; Flores, 2023; European Commission, 2024). The overall message of the timeline is clear: institutional governance is frequently a matter of necessity in the face of policy inertia. The appearance of formal regulatory milestones consistently lags behind institutional action, establishing strong internal capacity for ethical and agile governance as the decisive factor in whether AI adoption is responsible, equitable, and aligned with educational values, or whether it devolves into new forms of risk and inequity.

EMERGING TRENDS AND POLICY RECOMMENDATIONS: SHAPING THE FUTURE OF AI IN EDUCATION

The future of AI in education is poised to be shaped by continual technological advances, evolving ethical norms, and dynamic regulatory frameworks. As AI technologies (especially generative tools such as Large Language Models (LLMs)) grow increasingly sophisticated and pervasive, they promise transformative impacts on content creation, personalised tutoring, and administrative efficiency. However, these advancements bring complex challenges including concerns about academic integrity, authorship, and embedded biases.

One major trend is hyper-personalisation through adaptive learning platforms that utilise diverse data sources (demographic, behavioural, and affective) to predict student performance and recommend individualised interventions. This capability holds great promise for tailoring education, but also escalates privacy and consent issues, making robust ethical frameworks around data governance and minimisation ever more critical. Simultaneously, AI continues to automate routine administrative tasks such as grading, scheduling, and resource allocation, prompting institutions to carefully consider accountability for automated decisions and effects on employment structures.

As AI becomes foundational in education, AI literacy is emerging as a core competency, anticipated to be as essential as reading or numeracy. Curricula will increasingly encompass AI fundamentals along with ethical usage and critical evaluation skills, preparing learners to navigate an AI-enhanced societal landscape. Inclusive education benefits from advancements in assistive technologies, enhancing accessibility for students with disabilities; nonetheless, debates about balancing accommodations with skill development remain unresolved.

Policy landscapes globally exhibit both convergence and divergence. While some regions embrace stringent regulations akin to the EU AI Act, others adopt softer guidance-based approaches. This normative fragmentation necessitates international cooperation and harmonised standards to manage cross-border educational technologies and mitigate inequities.

Institutions have begun scrutinising vendors more rigorously, favouring those committed to fairness, privacy, safety, and transparency. The rise of responsible AI platforms embedding governance features is signalling an evolving market preference. Additionally, new professional roles (AI ethicists, data stewards, and AI-enhanced instructional designers) are poised to emerge, with educators collaborating closely with technologists in co-creating adaptive curricula and assessments.

The integration of generative AI into ubiquitous productivity tools blurs lines between human and machine contributions, sparking critical discourse on academic integrity, authorship, and intellectual property. Policymakers will grapple with disclosure requirements for AI-assisted work, recognition of AI contributions, and defining what constitutes original student effort. Environmental sustainability is also climbing the agenda, as training large AI models consumes significant energy. Emerging governance frameworks may begin incorporating sustainability metrics to align AI usage with climate goals.

Building on these trends and lessons, this chapter advocates for a "governance-first" approach, presenting strategic recommendations:

1. Develop Comprehensive and Adaptable AI Governance Frameworks: Institutions should implement enforceable ethical charters emphasising fairness, transparency, and human oversight. Cross-functional governance bodies involving academic, technical, legal, and student stakeholders must institutionalise iterative policy evaluation to adapt governance in step with technological evolution.
2. Prioritise Data Governance and Student Privacy: Robust data protections require minimising data collection, encryption, controlled access, and clear retention policies. Rigorous vendor vetting to ensure compliance with legal and ethical standards including FERPA and GDPR is essential, alongside demands for algorithmic transparency and a formal right to explanation.
3. Address Equity and Accessibility Systemically: Policymakers must invest strategically in infrastructure for underserved communities while mandating inclusion and Universal Design for Learning (UDL) principles in AI tools. Financial support should enable all students and institutions to access the requisite technologies for meaningful participation.
4. Empower Educators and Foster AI Literacy: Ongoing, practical educator training on AI concepts, ethical use, and bias detection is critical. AI literacy should be embedded across curricula, with policy reinforcing human-in-the-loop approaches placing educators at the centre of AI integration.
5. Foster Collaboration and Knowledge Exchange: Cross-sector partnerships spanning universities, K-12 schools, policymakers, and industry should promote the sharing of best practices and joint research on ethical AI. Engagement of students, families, and communities ensures that governance reflects diverse needs and values.
6. Enable Continuous Adaptation and Collaborative Governance: Governance systems should be agile, centred on human rights and environmental sustain-

ability, and shaped through co-creation involving policymakers, educators, technologists, students, and parents.

7. Create Mechanisms for International Coordination: To reduce normative fragmentation, governments should establish forums or consortia to harmonise AI standards, recognise certifications, and share bias mitigation research. This cooperation is necessary to prevent a regulatory "race to the bottom" amid global EdTech market dynamics.

Collectively, these recommendations emphasise governance evolution as parallel and indispensable to technological progress. Only by embedding comprehensive, just, and adaptive governance can AI realise its potential as an enabler of inclusion, rather than an amplifier of existing educational inequities.

Ultimately, the chapter reaffirms the central thesis that the defining challenge is not AI as technology, but systemic governance failures. The urgency to bridge the governance gap is critical; without it, increasing AI sophistication and integration will compound risks and deepen disparities. Policymakers, institutional leaders, and educators must act decisively to build frameworks grounded in ethics, equity, and human-centred values, securing a future where AI advances educational justice for all learners.

REFERENCES

Akgun, S., & Greenhow, C. (2022). Artificial intelligence in education: Addressing ethical challenges in K-12 settings. *AI and Ethics*, *2*(3), 431–440. DOI: 10.1007/s43681-021-00096-7 PMID: 34790956

Butalov, D. (2025, February 26). *Navigating the AI-Driven Transformation in Education*. EdTech Digest. Retrieved from https://www.edtechdigest.com/2025/02/26/navigating-the-ai-driven-transformation-in-education/

EDDS Education. (2025, June 5). *Ensuring Fairness in AI for Education: A Framework for Trustworthy Systems*. Retrieved from https://www.edds-education.org/post/ensuring-fairness-in-ai-for-education-a-framework-for-trustworthy-systems

eSchool News. (2024, November 13). *Equitable access to AI in classrooms is a problem–the solution is*. Retrieved from https://www.eschoolnews.com/digital-learning/2024/11/13/equitable-access-ai-professional-development/

European Commission. (2024). *Regulation of the European Parliament and of the Council laying down harmonized rules on Artificial Intelligence (AI Act)*. European Union.

Kosta, D. (2025, January 13). *State AI guidance for K-12 schools (updated July 2025)*. AI for Education Initiative. Retrieved from https://aiforeducation.org/state-guidance-2025

Learn-Work Ecosystem Library. (2025, July 8). *AI Literacy Framework for Primary & Secondary Education—OECD-EC*. Retrieved from https://learnworkecosystemlibrary.com/initiatives/ai-literacy-framework-for-primary-secondary-education-oecd-ec/

LeBoeuf, R. (2025, February 12). *From regulation to innovation: What the EU AI Act means for EdTech*. FeedbackFruits Blog. Retrieved from https://feedbackfruits.com/blog/2025-eu-ai-act-edtech

McNulty, N. (2025, March 21). *Comparative analysis of generative AI policies in education: Australia, Japan, New Zealand, Korea, United Kingdom*. Retrieved from https://niallmcnulty.com/ai-policies-international-overview

OECD. (2025, January 23). *Trends Shaping Education 2025*. Retrieved from https://www.oecd.org/en/publications/trends-shaping-education-2025_ee6587fd-en/full-report/global-trends-and-the-future-of-education-in-2025_7358e77a.html

OECD & Education International. (2023). Opportunities, guidelines and guardrails for effective and equitable use of AI in education. In *OECD Digital Education Outlook 2023*. OECD Publishing.

Popescu, A. I., & Burlacu, M. (2025). Knowledge Governance and AI Awareness in Higher Education. *MDPI, 15*(6), 144. Retrieved from https://www.mdpi.com/2075-4698/15/6/144

Singh, R., & Singh, A. (2025). *Integrating AI in Education: Navigating UNESCO Global Guidelines, Emerging Trends, and Its Intersection with Sustainable Development Goals*. ResearchGate. Retrieved from https://www.researchgate.net/publication/389936132_Integrating_AI_in_Education_Navigating_UNESCO_Global_Guidelines_Emerging_Trends_and_Its_Intersection_with_Sustainable_Development_Goals

Stanford University. (2025a, January 9). *Report outlines Stanford principles for use of AI*. Retrieved from https://news.stanford.edu/stories/2025/01/report-outlines-stanford-principles-for-use-of-ai

Stanford University. (2025b, January 9). *Report of the AI at Stanford Advisory Committee*. Retrieved from https://provost.stanford.edu/2025/01/09/report-of-the-ai-at-stanford-advisory-committee/

Swiss Cyber Institute. (2025, July 4). *The EU AI Act: Implications for Ethical AI in Education*. Retrieved from https://swisscyberinstitute.com/blog/eu-ai-act-implications-ethical-ai-education/

UNESCO. (2019). *Beijing consensus on artificial intelligence and education*. Paris: UNESCO. https://unesdoc.unesco.org/ark:/48223/pf0000370307

UNESCO. (2021a). *AI and education: Guidance for policy-makers* (Miao, F., Holmes, W., Huang, R., & Zhang, H.). Paris: UNESCO. https://unesdoc.unesco.org/ark:/48223/pf0000376709

University of Toronto. (2025, March 31). *Guidance on the Use of Generative Artificial Intelligence*. Retrieved from https://www.sgs.utoronto.ca/about/guidance-on-the-use-of-generative-artificial-intelligence/

U.S. Department of Education, Office of Educational Technology. (2023). *Artificial intelligence and the future of teaching and learning: Insights and recommendations*. Washington, DC: USDOE. https://tech.ed.gov/files/2023/05/AI-Teaching-Learning-Report-2023.pdf

Chapter 9
Culturally Responsive Artificial Intelligence in Global Education

Kübra Okumuş Dağdeler
http://orcid.org/0000-0002-3781-3182
Sivas Cumhuriyet University, Turkey

ABSTRACT

This chapter focuses on the artificial intelligence (AI) applications in education from a Culturally Responsive Teaching (CRT) perspective. Following a review of the theoretical background of multicultural education and CRT, the chapter critically examines how AI technologies may both support and challenge efforts to foster cultural and linguistic inclusivity. It identifies key potentials and challenges, such as personalization, translanguaging support, digital equity, algorithmic bias, and linguistic hierarchies. Existing frameworks for ethical and culturally responsive AI are explained, with attention to an identified gap in current models. In response, the chapter introduces a Culturally Responsive Artificial Intelligence Evaluation Framework (CRAI-EF) designed to assist educators, researchers, and policymakers in making informed decisions regarding the responsible deployment of AI tools. The chapter concludes by outlining pedagogical implications, with an emphasis on teacher responsibility, AI literacy for students and the principles of culturally responsive design.

1. INTRODUCTION

In the contemporary digital era, the expanding integration of Artificial Intelligence (AI) into educational systems is fundamentally transforming teaching,

DOI: 10.4018/979-8-3373-6063-8.ch009

learning, and assessment across the globe. Technologies such as adaptive learning platforms, intelligent tutoring systems, predictive analytics, and automated feedback mechanisms present considerable opportunities for enhancing personalization and scalability in education. However, these advances, especially when examined from the perspectives of equality, cultural diversity, and inclusivity, also bring complex challenges. Therefore, the question of whether artificial intelligence can truly function in a culturally sensitive manner is of critical importance, particularly in diverse educational settings. Since education involves students from diverse backgrounds and societies, this diversity poses potential risks if not consciously addressed. Therefore, the implementation of artificial intelligence in schools and learning environments should be guided by a commitment to ensure that its use does not inadvertently disadvantage or harm students, educators, or other education stakeholders.

Despite its risks, AI also has considerable potential to contribute to more personalized, inclusive, and equitable educational experiences. It provides resources that a wide range of users can benefit. However, AI presents a paradox: it can both widen and reduce the digital divide. Moreover, there are three key dilemmas—creativity versus standardization, inclusion versus fixity, and meaning versus form—that educators are likely to encounter when integrating AI into their classrooms (Jeon et al, 2025). Whether AI becomes a tool that worsens inequalities in the classroom or one that minimizes them depends largely on how it is developed, trained, and implemented. This means that creating culturally sensitive AI applications is not simply a technical process; it requires a holistic and interdisciplinary approach that focuses on social justice, equality, and inclusivity in education. Within this context, the relationship between AI and cultural responsiveness emerges as a multidimensional field of both research and practice. Accordingly, the purpose of this chapter is to critically examine AI in education through the lens of culturally responsive teaching and to propose a new framework for evaluating culturally responsive AI. It focuses on culturally responsive AI by first outlining the theoretical foundation—specifically, Culturally Responsive Teaching (CRT). It then examines issues of digital equity, exploring both the potential and challenges of AI in promoting cultural inclusion and fairness. Next, it reviews existing culturally responsive AI frameworks proposed for educational settings, and finally, it introduces a new framework designed to evaluate culturally responsive AI applications.

2. MULTICULTURAL EDUCATION AND CRT

Multicultural education emerged as a response to increasing cultural, ethnic, and linguistic diversity in schools, as well as the persistent inequities experienced by marginalized student groups. By taking the principles from social justice, democratic participation, and equal opportunity, its primary aim is to reform educational structures, curricula, and pedagogical practices so that all learners with diverse backgrounds experience both academic success and cultural affirmation. Rather than viewing diversity as an obstacle, multicultural education emphasizes respect for multiple perspectives, encourages critical reflection on cultural assumptions, and prepares students to participate meaningfully in pluralistic societies. As Gay (2015) explains, multicultural education is a broad ideological and curricular movement involving educational philosophy, policy, content selection, assessment, and instructional practices.

Culturally Responsive Teaching (CRT) was developed as a focused, classroom-level extension of multicultural education (Gay, 2015). Geneva Gay (2000, 2010) introduced the concept to describe an instructional approach centred on "*using the cultural knowledge, prior experiences, frames of reference, and performance styles of ethnically diverse students to make learning encounters more relevant to and effective for them.*" (Gay, 2000; p.31). At the centre of Gay's framework is the notion of *cultural congruence*, which requires aligning instructional materials, teaching strategies, and classroom interactions with students' cultural backgrounds and lived realities. This approach assumes that when academic content is situated within familiar cultural frames, learning becomes more meaningful, engaging, and durable. Consequently, CRT reframes cultural diversity not as a problem to be managed, but as a resource that enriches the teaching–learning process. As Gay (2010) emphasizes, culturally responsive instruction calls for educators to intentionally integrate students' cultural and linguistic identities into academic content so that learners perceive school knowledge as relevant, valuable, and connected to their own lives—thus enhancing motivation, comprehension, and retention.

Vavrus (2008) characterizes CRT as an educational reform movement designed to improve the engagement, achievement, and sense of belonging of students of colour who have historically faced academic underperformance and social marginalization in public schools. Effective CRT implementation, therefore, requires educators to adopt inclusive curricula and culturally relevant materials, cultivate cultural competence, and build positive and respectful teacher–student relationships (Abdalla & Moussa, 2024). Building on this foundation, Aceves and Orosco (2014) conceptualize CRT as an innovative framework for addressing the needs of culturally and linguistically diverse (CLD) learners. They identify six essential components: (1) instructional engagement, (2) culture, language, and racial identity, (3) multicultural awareness, (4) high expectations, (5) critical thinking, and (6) social justice. Each dimension encourages educators to view students' cultural and linguistic repertoires as assets to be intentionally incorporated into curriculum and pedagogy.

A growing body of research highlights pedagogical strategies associated with CRT that enhance academic achievement, inclusivity, and student engagement.

These include student-centred approaches, involving learners in curriculum design, adapting instruction to diverse learning needs and styles, embedding cultural references in teaching materials, and offering ongoing professional development for educators. However, implementing CRT often faces practical barriers, such as limited funding, insufficient institutional support, and resistance from educators accustomed to traditional methods. To ensure the effective integration of CRT into teacher education and schooling, institutional and policy-level backing is essential (Liu et al., 2025). Importantly, CRT extends beyond the pursuit of equality to advocate for *equity*—a principle aligned with social justice. While equality provides the same resources and opportunities to all students, equity recognizes that learners' diverse experiences, needs, and abilities require differentiated support to achieve fair outcomes (Bronfenbrenner, 1973). CRT therefore seeks to transform educational systems, so they empower all students to succeed, especially those from historically underserved communities.

Beyond CRT, related pedagogical movements such as Culturally Relevant Pedagogy (CRP) and Culturally Sustaining Pedagogy (CSP) have also contributed to the field. According to Ladson-Billings (1995), culturally relevant pedagogy rests on three elements: academic achievement, cultural competence, and sociopolitical or critical consciousness. Any pedagogical approach that does not embody all three elements cannot be considered culturally relevant pedagogy. Paris (2012), building on Ladson-Billings's (1995) foundational work on CRP, introduced the concept of CSP, questioning whether the terms "relevant" and "responsive" fully capture the depth required to value, maintain, and sustain the cultural and linguistic practices of communities marginalized by systemic inequalities. CSP emphasizes the active maintenance and celebration of multilingual and multicultural practices in schools.

Although there are minor differences in the conceptualization and terminology of these approaches, they all focus on educational practices in which cultural differences are respected and meaningfully integrated into teaching and learning. CRT has become particularly influential as a theoretically grounded and practical model that translates the principles of multicultural education into instructional practice. Ultimately, CRT represents a paradigm shift in education—from standardized, one-size-fits-all models to dynamic, personalized, and equity-oriented approaches that intentionally value and support students' cultural backgrounds as foundations for rigorous learning, identity development, and inclusive educational environments.

3. DIGITAL DIVIDE AND EQUITY

Although technology offers substantial advantages for teaching and learning, it simultaneously introduces concerns related to digital equity and the digital divide.

The benefits of technological integration can only be fully realized when all learners have equitable access to the tools, infrastructure, and support required to use them effectively. Learners with limited access to technology frequently remain restricted to conventional learning experience (Gruber & Köse, 2025). In reality, disparities in connectivity, device availability, digital skills, and institutional support continue to limit the transformative potential of educational technologies. Moreover, despite rapid advancements in AI, scholars emphasize that AI-driven solutions alone cannot address systemic educational inequalities without concurrent investments in robust infrastructure and comprehensive digital literacy initiatives (Waghid & Waghid, 2021). Thus, addressing the digital divide remains a foundational prerequisite for ensuring that technology meaningfully contributes to equitable and inclusive education.

Digital divide refers to disparities in accessing to digital technologies such as the internet, computing devices, and AI-powered educational tools (Ahmed, 2024). The Organization for Economic Co-operation and Development (OECD) (2001) defines the digital divide as "*the gap between individuals, households, businesses, and geographic areas at different socioeconomic levels with regard both to their opportunities to access information and communication technologies and to their use of the Internet for a wide variety of activities*" (p. 5). The digital divide persists globally as a result of multiple interconnected factors, including unequal access to hardware and internet connectivity, limited autonomy in technology use, gaps in digital and literacy skills, insufficient technical and social support, and inequitable access to educators proficient in information and communication technologies (ICTs) (Resta & Laferrière, 2015). Similarly, DiMaggio and Hargittai (2001) suggest five dimensions along which inequalities may exist: 1) inequality in technical apparatus; 2) inequality in autonomy of use; 3) inequality in skill; 4) inequality in the availability of social support; and 5) variation in the purposes for which people use the technology.

Digital divide is countered by the concepts of digital justice and equality. The concepts of digital divide, digital equity, and digital equality are closely interconnected yet represent distinct dimensions of technology access in education. While digital equality seeks to provide all learners with the same technological tools, this approach often falls short because it does not account for variations in learners' socioeconomic backgrounds, linguistic needs, or levels of digital literacy. In contrast, digital equity emphasizes fairness by ensuring that each learner receives the specific resources, support, and culturally relevant content necessary to engage meaningfully with digital technologies. In this sense, digital equity functions as a targeted response to the digital divide, recognizing that closing access gaps requires more than equal distribution—it requires meeting learners' diverse needs to achieve true inclusion. Thus, digital equity is a multifaceted issue that goes beyond access to hardware, software, and Internet connectivity to include the availability of meaningful, high-quality, and culturally relevant content in local languages, as well as the capacity to create, share, and exchange knowledge. According to United States-based organisation the National Digital Inclusion Alliance (2019), digital equity is defined as:

> *"a condition in which all individuals and communities have the information technology capacity needed for full participation in our society, democracy and economy. Digital Equity is necessary for civic and cultural participation, employment, lifelong learning, and access to essential services."*

To provide digital equity, Jackson et al. (2024) suggest a framework which contains five main domains including a) leadership for digital transformation, b) coherent systems, resources, and policies, c) consistent access to devices and connectivity, d) digital competency, and e) powerful learning propelled by technology (see Figure 1). *Leadership for Digital Transformation* refers to the strategic, collaborative, and future-oriented leadership provided by district, school, and community stakeholders to articulate and implement a clear vision for meaningful technology integration throughout the education system. *Coherent Systems, Resources, and Policies* involves ensuring that organizational structures, resources, and policy frameworks are intentionally aligned with a strategic and ongoing improvement plan designed to support sustained and effective technology integration. *Consistent Access to Devices and Connectivity* focuses on guaranteeing that every learner has reliable, continuous access to high-speed internet, digital devices, emerging technologies, and essential learning tools, both within the school environment and beyond. *Digital Competency* refers to the deliberate development of the digital skills, mindsets, dispositions, and behaviours required for all individuals to use technology confidently and responsibly, enabling full participation in a digitally mediated world. *Powerful Learning Propelled by Technology* emphasizes implementing learner-centred instructional approaches in which digital resources and emerging technologies are seamlessly embedded into research-based teaching practices, fostering high engagement and deep, meaningful learning.

Figure 1. Digital equity framework (Jackson et al. 2024, p. 18)

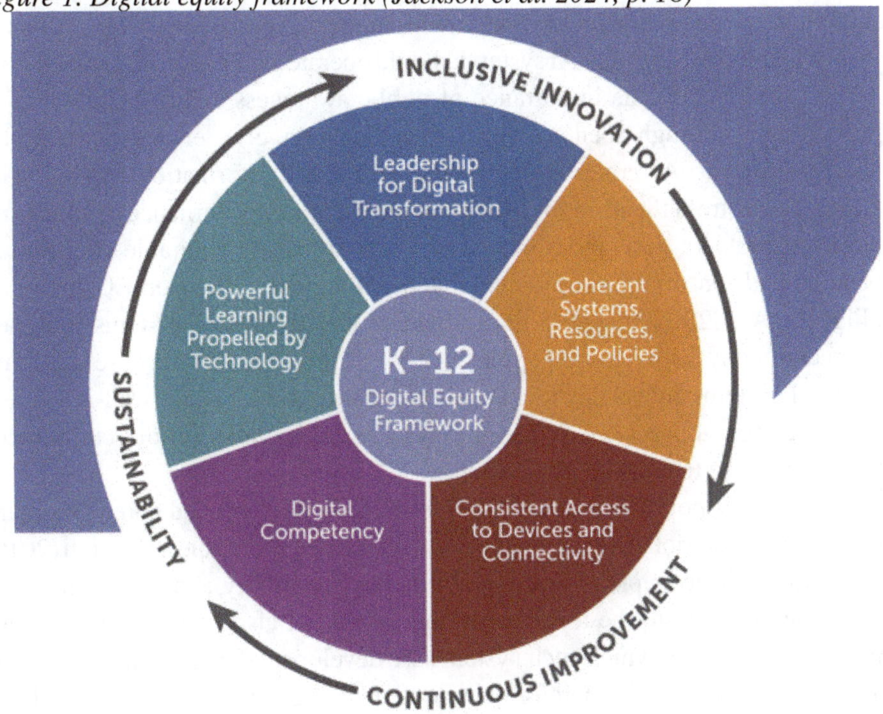

4. RESPONSIBLE AI

AI systems are inherently socio-technical, embedded within complex social environments shaped by diverse stakeholders, institutions, norms, and cultural contexts (Dignum, 2021). Since their development and use directly influence people and society, ensuring their responsible operation is essential. As AI adoption accelerates, a range of ethical challenges—such as fairness, privacy, transparency, and accountability—become increasingly prominent, making clear the need for robust guidelines to govern their use. Among the leading global efforts, UNESCO's Recommendation on the Ethics of Artificial Intelligence (2022) outlines ten foundational principles for the responsible development and deployment of AI, offering a comprehensive framework for promoting ethical and trustworthy practices. The principles include proportionality and do no harm, fairness and non-discrimination, safety and security, sustainability, the right to privacy and data protection, human oversight and determination, transparency and explainability, responsibility and accountability, awareness and literacy, and multi-stakeholder and adaptive governance.

UNESCO emphasizes that AI systems should operate in fair, safe, and responsible ways, and underscores the importance of public awareness and understanding of AI technologies through open and accessible education, civic engagement, digital skills development, AI ethics training, and media and information literacy. The guidelines also stress the need for inclusive, participatory governance by engaging diverse stakeholders throughout the AI lifecycle to ensure equitable distribution of benefits and contributions to sustainable development. Moreover, EU Artificial Intelligence Act (2024) suggests that providers ensure that AI systems designed to interact directly with natural people clearly inform users that they are engaging with an AI system, unless this fact is self-evident to a reasonably well-informed, observant, and circumspect individual, taking into account the specific circumstances and context of use to enhance transparency.

Beyond global policy-level guidelines, scholars have proposed complementary frameworks to operationalize responsible AI in practice. For instance, Dignum (2019) proposes the ART principles—Accountability, Responsibility, and Transparency—which apply not only to the technical design of AI but also to the broader socio-technical ecosystem in which such systems are developed, deployed, and used (see Figure 2). Ensuring ART therefore requires an integrated approach that aligns software design with governance structures, regulatory mechanisms, and ethical oversight. *Accountability* involves ensuring that AI decisions can be explained, justified, and traced back to the mechanisms and values that shaped them. *Responsibility* emphasizes the essential role of human actors throughout the AI lifecycle. It requires clear attribution of how decisions arise—from input data to algorithmic outputs—and highlights that responsibility lies not only in regulating AI systems but also in how individuals and institutions use and interpret them. *Transparency* requires the ability to describe, inspect, and reproduce the processes by which AI systems make decisions and learn from data.

Figure 2. ART principles (Dignum, 2019)

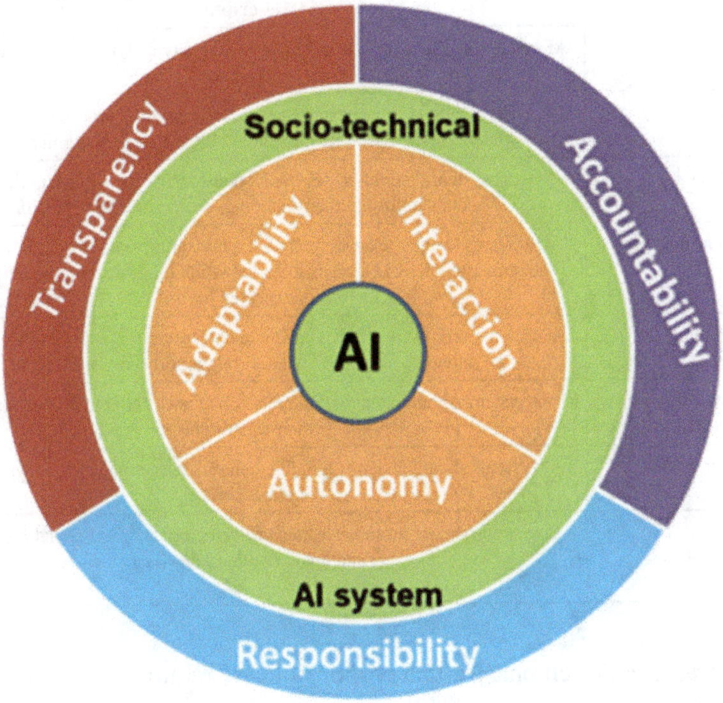

Across global discussions on responsible AI, there is broad agreement that these principles ensure the ethical, accountable, and trustworthy use of AI in alignment with user expectations, organizational values, and societal norms (Accenture, 2021). In line with this consensus, responsible AI is viewed as a set of requirements that must be upheld throughout the entire system lifecycle (European Commission, 2019). Building on the European Commission's indicators of trustworthy AI, Mikalef et al. (2022) present a comprehensive framework outlining the key components and definitions of responsible AI (See Table 1).

Table 1. Responsible AI dimensions (Mikalef et al., 2022)

Dimension	Description
Fairness	AI systems should enable inclusion and diversity and not lead to discriminatory outcomes.
Transparency	AI systems should be open and transparent regarding processes and outcomes and facilitate traceability, explainability, and user communication.
Accountability	AI systems should be developed considering the responsibility and accountability of their outcomes with ethics and principles.
Robustness and safety	AI systems should be developed with a preventative approach to risks and in a manner that they behave as intended while minimising unintentional and unexpected harm.
Data governance	AI systems should ensure that adequate data governance covers the quality and integrity of the data used throughout the entire lifecycle.
Laws and regulations	AI systems should adhere to the respective laws and regulations that dictate their functioning.
Human Oversight	AI systems should generate tangible benefits for people and always stay under human control.
Societal and Environmental well-being	AI systems should promote sustainability, ecological, and social responsibility and not cause them any harm.

These frameworks emphasise that responsible AI requires a holistic, ongoing commitment that spans the entire lifecycle of AI systems, rather than being a single principle or technical fix. UNESCO's ethical guidelines, Dignum's (2019) ART principles, the European Commission's (2019) trustworthy AI indicators, EU Artificial Intelligence Act (2024) and Mikalef et al.'s (2022) multidimensional framework collectively highlight the need for fairness, accountability, transparency, human oversight and societal well-being as core pillars of trustworthy AI. These approaches affirm that AI must ultimately serve human values and social good by integrating ethical design, robust governance, and active stakeholder participation. Therefore, ensuring responsible AI requires continuous reflection, regulation and collaboration to ensure that technological innovation advances in an inclusive and equitable manner that is aligned with the broader public interest.

5. POTENTIAL OF AI FOR CRT

The growing integration of artificial intelligence into educational environments has created new opportunities for supporting CRT, particularly through personalization, linguistic support, and enhanced accessibility. Increasingly, scholars argue that AI can serve as a powerful tool for addressing the diverse needs of learners by offering differentiated, adaptable, and inclusive learning experiences. In this sense,

AI has the potential not only to supplement existing pedagogical practices but also to expand the possibilities of culturally sustaining and equitable education.

One of the most frequently cited potentials of AI is its ability to enhance personalized learning and academic support. Technological advances in Generative Artificial Intelligence (GenAI) have led to sophisticated multimodal and multilingual models that hold significant potential for advancing a long-standing educational goal which is promoting equity and expanding access for linguistically diverse learners (Jeon et al., 2025). AI-powered virtual tutors can provide individualized assistance and instruction, making high-quality learning experiences more accessible to students who may not have direct access to human educators. In addition, AI-based translation and speech recognition tools have significantly improved access to educational content for non-native speakers by lowering linguistic barriers and expanding participation (Ahmed, 2024). Building on this, Roshanaei (2024) emphasizes that AI holds considerable promise for democratizing education by offering adaptive learning pathways that respond to learners' diverse needs, thereby enabling each student to reach their full potential. GenAI extends this potential by promoting the inclusion of learners with varied cultural, linguistic, and cognitive profiles. As Szabó and Szoke (2024) note, GenAI can effectively enhance inclusivity by accommodating individual learning differences. This includes supporting translanguaging practices, which allow learners to draw upon multiple linguistic resources; fostering neurodiverse inclusion through universal design for learning principles that generate accessible instructional materials (Paiz et al., 2025); and providing specialized tools such as dictation services for learners with disabilities, reading supports for students with dyslexia, and real-time conversational learning via chatbots (Szabó & Szoke, 2024). These capacities illustrate how AI can help broaden educational participation by recognizing and responding to the varied ways in which students learn and engage.

Another potential is AI's ability to raise awareness of linguistic diversity and challenge monolithic language ideologies. For example, a study with Korean preservice English teachers showed that interacting with virtual agents using diverse English varieties reduced participants' native-speaker bias, strengthened their sense of ownership of the language, and provided affective support (Lee et al., 2025). Such findings highlight the value of AI tools in promoting linguistic pluralism, validating diverse language practices, and encouraging more inclusive attitudes toward Global Englishes—principles that strongly align with CRT.

AI tools can also contribute to CRT by supporting personalization and contextualization across culturally diverse classrooms. Real-time translation systems, adaptive learning platforms, and natural language processing (NLP) applications can help narrow linguistic and cultural gaps, making learning more meaningful and accessible. Akdemir and Ulaş (2024) highlight that these technologies assist learners from varied linguistic and cultural backgrounds by responding to their individual learning requirements and reducing cultural mismatches. When designed with cultural sensitivity, such tools can provide students from marginalized or underrepresented groups with more relevant, affirming, and empowering learning experiences that reflect their identities and socio-cultural realities.

However, research also indicates that the presence of AI alone is insufficient to ensure culturally responsive outcomes. For instance, Li and Yu (2025) found that although AI tools could help teachers create learning materials aligned with students' cultural backgrounds and interests, pre- and post-survey results showed no statistically significant improvement in CRT skills based on AI usage. This implies that the effective integration of AI into CRT requires intentional strategies, pedagogical guidance, and critical awareness—rather than a reliance on technology itself.

The literature shows that AI's potential is shaped by design choices and implementation contexts. Akdemir and Ulaş (2024) argue that AI-supported educational applications can contribute to inclusivity and equality by acknowledging students' cultural backgrounds, though this potential is contingent upon culturally sensitive technology design. In a similar vein, Grab's qualitative research at the higher education level emphasizes that while AI tools can promote inclusivity through personalization, they may also overlook students' cultural experiences and exhibit socio-cultural blind spots (Grab, 2025). Thus, the benefits of AI for CRT depend strongly on the extent to which technologies are developed and deployed with explicit attention to cultural diversity and equity.

Grab (2025) synthesizes the potential of AI for CRT into four key advantages. First, *Culturally Stipulated Learning* illustrates how AI-powered systems can analyse learners' backgrounds and recommend culturally relevant materials to enhance engagement. Second, *Minimizing Implicit Bias* highlights AI's capacity to reduce subjective grading and support equitable assessment practices, particularly for historically underserved populations. Third, *Broadening Access to Educational Resources from an Array of Sources* shows that AI can offer global perspectives by providing diverse content and materials in learners' native languages or dialects. Finally, *Enhancing the Effectiveness of the Teacher* demonstrates how AI-driven analytics can inform real-time instructional decisions, enabling educators to better support culturally diverse learners. These dimensions outline the significant potential of AI to enrich CRT practices and promote inclusive, equitable learning environments. Overall, these findings suggest that AI has considerable capacity to strengthen culturally responsive teaching by supporting personalization, linguistic diversity, socio-cultural relevance, and equitable access.

6. CHALLENGES

While artificial intelligence has a great potential for expanding access to high-quality instruction and addressing educational inequalities, its integration into CRT presents several critical challenges that require sustained scrutiny. Although AI-driven tools—such as intelligent tutoring systems, open-source learning platforms, and automated assessment systems—have been hailed for their potential to bridge educational gaps for underserved communities (Warschauer & Matuchniak, 2010) scholars caution that these advantages are accompanied by serious concerns regarding cultural representation, linguistic diversity, and algorithmic fairness (Oyetada et al., 2025).

One of the most important challenges is algorithmic bias, which can reproduce and reinforce disparities across educational settings. Empirical studies identify the presence of implicit biases in AI systems along dimensions such as race, ethnicity, and gender, disproportionately affecting underrepresented groups (Roshanaei, 2024). These biases may originate from developers' assumptions, skewed training data, or the technological ecosystems in which AI systems are created (Baker & Hawn, 2022). The problem is especially acute in language-related technologies; NLP tools have been shown to amplify gendered associations, and automated speech recognition (ASR) systems exhibit measurable racial bias (Mengesha et al., 2021). The cumulative effect of these biases manifests in discriminatory outputs, opaque decision-making processes, and potentially inequitable learning opportunities (Mikalef et al., 2022). Within assessment contexts, AI-based scoring tools risk perpetuating existing inequalities or producing biased outcomes, thereby undermining the principles of fairness and educational justice (Rane et al., 2024).

Another problem is training datasets that GenAI applications use for creating content. The data foundations of many LLMs are disproportionately derived from materials associated with white, Western, industrialized, and highly educated cultural contexts, often described as the WEIRD paradigm (Atari et al., 2023). This imbalance results in AI systems that reflect epistemologies and worldviews rooted in whiteness (Jones, 2025), thereby narrowing the cultural lens through which knowledge is interpreted, produced, and disseminated. Even when AI tools expand access through open-source platforms, underlying cultural assumptions in algorithmic logic can constrain their inclusivity and authenticity, particularly for communities historically marginalized in digital knowledge production (Warschauer & Matuchniak, 2010).

Linguistic issues represent one of the most challenging aspects of AI use, as many systems are primarily developed and optimized in English, resulting in noticeably higher-quality outputs in that language. As AI systems predominantly operate within English-centric datasets and models, they frequently struggle to accurately interpret and respond to the linguistic variations, accents, and dialects of non-native English speakers (Park, 2024). As a result, these users often encounter systemic biases that create disparities in access to AI-powered services, such as voice recognition technologies, language translation tools, and automated decision-making systems (Park, 2024).

Beyond what the literature shows about AI's linguistic bias, users can also notice this bias themselves when they interact with these systems. As a GenAI user, I personally have observed some differences in response quality between English and Turkish (my first language), particularly when the topic is universally discussed. Although this discrepancy is understandable given that much of the data used to train AI models is in English—the current lingua franca—the long-standing dominance of English in digital technologies has contributed to this imbalance. Despite promises of multilingual support, many AI tools continue to exhibit inherent linguistic and cultural biases due to the predominance of English in training datasets, the underrepresentation of minority languages and dialects, and the cultural assumptions embedded within algorithmic systems.

The dominance of these technologies poses challenges for non-native English speakers, as it not only restricts their access to information but also risks fostering a monocultural AI ecosystem that is primarily proficient in English while neglecting other languages and cultural contexts (Park, 2024). Large language models (LLMs) are typically trained on standardized varieties of first language (L1) English (Dai et al., 2025), which leads to the privileging of normative language forms and the marginalization of diverse linguistic identities. These limitations can result in unequal access to high-quality educational experiences and may inadvertently reinforce stereotypes or perpetuate cultural marginalization. As Capraro et al. (2024) put forward use of GenAI in education has some challenges such as perpetuation of biases and discriminatory patterns as in the example they present:

> *"An example is the translation bias observed in tools like Google Translate, where gender stereotypes are inadvertently perpetuated in language translations. Translating the phrase "she/he is a nurse" from Turkish (which is "genderless") to English (which is "gendered") yielded the feminine form (i.e. "she is a nurse"), while the phrase "she/he is a doctor" yielded the masculine form (i.e. "he is a doctor" (Johnson, 2021)). Failing to account for these biases could amplify inequalities and injustices, specifically towards historically marginalized groups." (p. 7).*

Such bias stands in contrast to the principles of CRT, which emphasize linguistic diversity, cultural hybridity, and the recognition of students' linguistic repertoires as valuable assets for learning. Within educational contexts, multilingual education and translanguaging have become central areas of focus. Multilingual education enables use of two or more languages in schooling with the explicit aim of fostering multilingualism and multiliteracy (Cenoz & Gorter, 2015). As an essential dimension of multilingual education, translanguaging is "*a process by which students and teachers engage in complex discursive practices that include ALL the language practices of ALL students in a class in order to develop new language practices and sustain old ones, communicate and appropriate knowledge, and give voice to new sociopolitical realities by interrogating linguistic inequality.*" (García & Kano, 2014; p. 261). From this standpoint, AI tools should actively support translanguaging by offering multiple language and dialect options and by enabling learners to draw from their full linguistic repertoires rather than restricting them to standardized or dominant-language practices. Otherwise, monolingual policies and practices that prevent speakers of diverse languages from using their full linguistic resources can exacerbate social injustice by contributing to unequal learning environments (Piller, 2016).

Beyond representational concerns, the personalization capabilities of AI raise pedagogical challenges. Although personalization is frequently celebrated as a key advantage of AI-enhanced learning environments, it may inadvertently compromise cultural relevance. AI-generated instructional content can be aligned with learners' cognitive profiles or academic needs while remaining disconnected from their socio-cultural realities. Such mismatches risk diminishing learner engagement, fostering alienation, and reproducing the very forms of cultural invisibility that CRT seeks to counteract. These tensions emphasize urgent questions surrounding ethical design, transparency, and the cultural situatedness of AI-generated materials.

Barnes and Hutson (2024) highlight 7 potential negative impacts of bias in higher education including perpetuation of inequality, misguided decision-making, erosion of trust, legal and ethical repercussions, reduction in diversity, hindrance to personalized learning, damage to institutional reputation. Similarly, Li and Yu (2025) identify four risks of integration of AI in lesson planning such as accuracy concerns, over-reliance on AI, limited cultural specificity. Addressing these challenges necessitates systemic, culturally grounded frameworks for AI development and implementation. Ożegalska-Łukasik and Łukasik (2023) emphasize the need for AI enculturation—an approach that enables AI systems to adapt responsively to the demands of multicultural societies—and advocate for regulatory mechanisms that promote ethical, culturally sensitive design. While AI holds considerable potential for supporting educational innovation and expanding opportunities for learners worldwide, its integration into CRT is fraught with substantial challenges related to bias, linguistic exclusion, cultural misrepresentation, and ethical ambiguity. These limitations reveal that technological sophistication alone is insufficient to ensure equity in AI-mediated learning. Instead, culturally responsive AI requires deliberate efforts to diversify training data, incorporate multicultural perspectives, ensure transparency, and design systems that honour learners' lived experiences. Without such intentionality, AI risks perpetuating rather than dismantling the inequities that

CRT seeks to address. AI actors must promote social justice and uphold fairness and non-discrimination in accordance with international law, which requires an inclusive approach to ensuring that the benefits of AI technologies are both available and accessible to all individuals, taking into account the specific needs of different age groups, cultural and linguistic communities, persons with disabilities, girls and women, and those who are disadvantaged, marginalized, or in vulnerable situations (UNESCO, 2022).

7. A BRIEF SUMMARY OF THEORETICAL FOUNDATIONS

The theoretical perspectives reviewed in this chapter—CRT, translanguaging and linguistic justice, digital equity, and responsible AI—share a common commitment to recognizing diversity and respecting human differences in educational contexts. CRT emphasizes on cultural congruence, identity affirmation, and the use of learners' lived experiences as assets for learning (Gay, 2010), and related approaches such as culturally relevant and culturally sustaining pedagogy also highlight academic success, cultural competence, and critical consciousness (Ladson-Billings, 1995; Paris & Alim, 2017). Translanguaging theory and linguistic justice frameworks challenge monolingual and deficit-oriented language ideologies by recognizing learners' full linguistic repertoires as legitimate resources for meaning-making (García & Wei, 2014; Baker-Bell, 2020).

Scholarship on digital equity and responsible AI highlights that technological innovation alone does not guarantee inclusive or fair educational outcomes. Digital equity research emphasizes the importance of contextual access, differentiated support, and meaningful participation, while AI ethics frameworks emphasize fairness, transparency, accountability, and human oversight throughout the AI lifecycle (Dignum, 2019; UNESCO, 2022; EU Artificial Intelligence Act, 2024). Collectively, these perspectives stress that AI systems are socio-technical tools whose value depends on how they are designed, evaluated, and mediated by human actors within specific cultural and institutional contexts.

Although these theoretical foundations offer substantial contributions to both educational theory and practice, they have not yet been integrated into a unified framework for evaluating AI through a culturally responsive lens. In response to this gap, the present chapter proposes a Culturally Responsive AI Evaluation Framework (CRAI-EF) grounded in these foundations, following a review of related approaches in the literature in the next section.

8. FRAMEWORKS FOR CULTURALLY RESPONSIVE IN EDUCATION

As artificial intelligence becomes increasingly embedded in educational systems, a number of frameworks have been introduced to guide ethical, culturally responsive, and pedagogically sound AI design and use. These frameworks collectively highlight the need to address issues of fairness, cultural diversity, human oversight, and contextual relevance in AI-enhanced learning environments. Although diverse in their scope and methodologies, they converge on a shared goal: ensuring that AI technologies support equitable and culturally grounded educational practices.

In addition to global ethical standards, recent scholarship has introduced models specifically aimed at operationalizing cultural responsiveness in AI-supported education. To begin with, Nyaaba and Zhai (2025) propose the Culturally Responsive Lesson Planner (CRLP), a custom GPT tool designed to assist teachers in developing lesson plans that reflect local cultural and contextual realities. Unlike generic, Western-oriented outputs, CRLP integrates local languages, traditions, knowledge systems, and community practices into instructional design. Their study demonstrates that CRLP produces lesson plans with stronger cultural representation—such as incorporating Asante Twi examples in Ghana—while maintaining higher factual accuracy and closer curriculum alignment. Importantly, CRLP preserves teacher agency by allowing educators to review, adjust, and refine AI-generated content. It also enhances AI literacy by enabling teachers to learn how to guide generative AI more effectively while strengthening culturally responsive pedagogy.

Similarly, Naidoo and Chadhaa (2025) introduce the Culturally Responsive Artificial Intelligence (Chatbot) Framework (CRAIF-C), a modular structure for developing AI chatbots capable of understanding and respecting cultural diversity across contexts. CRAIF-C is distinctive in its effort to operationalize cultural responsiveness across the entire AI lifecycle. It brings together domain-specific technical methods, validated measurement tools, and multi-context empirical testing across four core domains: enculturation, adaptive interaction, explainability and transparency, and governance and accountability. Together, these domains ensure that chatbots adapt to cultural norms, offer transparent interaction mechanisms, and adhere to ethical, accountable AI governance.

Louie et al. (2022) proposed the Culturally Localized User Experience (CLUE) Framework for designing social robots and evaluated its principles through a series of case studies. The first principle, *Gather Stakeholder Beliefs and Expectations*, emphasizes the importance of understanding the cultural views and anticipations of the communities who will interact with the robot. The second principle, *Utilize Non-Verbal Co-Design Methods*, involves engaging students through non-verbal design activities to ensure that English proficiency is not a barrier to participating in robotic education. This approach made the project accessible to learners regardless of language ability, while also fostering a desire to verbalize ideas in both English and home languages, as well as encouraging peer-supported translation among multilingual learners during debriefings. As cultural informants, students offered suggestions for revising and improving the robot's interactions. The third principle, *Provide an Experiential Robot Interaction*, highlights the need to offer multilingual learners a direct and embodied interaction with the robot. Such experiential engagement is essential because learners rely on immediate and concrete context to provide meaningful feedback about their preferences and experiences.

Extending the focus to AI education, Samuel et al. (2023) propose the Culturally Adaptive Thinking in Education for AI (CATE-AI) framework, which addresses the need for AI instruction that is responsive to culturally diverse learners. The model is built upon five principles: (1) grounding AI education in theoretical and philosophical foundations that consider human behaviour, technological capacities, and human-centred AI; (2) adapting AI education to sociocultural contexts and equipping learners to recognize and counter AI biases; (3) fostering richer and more engaging learning experiences through culturally adaptive thinking; (4) ensuring that AI education remains dynamic and responsive to evolving interactions between AI technologies and human behaviour; and (5) using philosophical foundations of human–AI interaction to guide ethical, values-based, human-centred AI development and education. CATE-AI thus frames culturally adaptive AI literacy as both an educational and ethical imperative.

A complementary perspective is offered by He et al. (2025), who propose a Framework for Teachers' Co-Creation of Culturally Responsive Educational Materials with AI. Their framework identifies the essential components of effective teacher–AI collaboration by emphasizing three critical areas of teacher expertise: cultural understanding, pedagogical knowledge, and AI literacy. According to this model, teachers draw on these areas to guide the co-creative process when using generative AI for ideation or material production. The same knowledge domains also inform how teachers interpret, evaluate, and refine AI-generated content to ensure that it aligns with culturally responsive educational goals. This framework highlights the importance of teacher agency and professional judgment in AI-mediated content creation.

The existing frameworks demonstrate increasing recognition of the need for AI systems that are culturally informed, ethically governed, and pedagogically meaningful. However, despite these important contributions, no existing framework—based on current knowledge—specifically evaluates AI systems through a comprehensive Culturally Responsive Teaching (CRT) lens. The absence of such a model represents a significant gap, particularly given the growing reliance on AI in multilingual and multicultural classrooms. To address this need, the following section introduces a new framework designed to evaluate AI systems explicitly within the context of CRT, offering a holistic and systematic approach that integrates cultural, linguistic, ethical, and pedagogical considerations.

9. A PROPOSAL FOR EVALUATING AI THROUGH A CRT LENS

Drawing on the existing theoretical foundations, an AI evaluation framework within the context of CRT has been proposed, as no such model—based on current knowledge—appears in the literature (see Figure 3). Given its significance for both educators and researchers, this framework has been developed to address a critical gap in the field. Collectively, its domains constitute a holistic and systematic model for evaluating AI through a CRT lens.

In addition to its evaluative function, the framework contributes to the conceptual clarification of *culturally responsive AI*, a construct that, to the best of our knowledge, has not yet been explicitly defined in the literature. While responsible AI has been extensively conceptualized and operationalized (see the section on Responsible AI), cultural responsiveness in relation to AI systems remains largely implicit and under-theorized. To address this gap, culturally responsive AI is defined in this chapter as AI systems that recognize, respect, and respond to cultural and linguistic differences while promoting inclusivity for diverse user groups across different contexts. The CRAI-EF is developed in alignment with this definition and is grounded in established theoretical traditions, which are outlined in the following paragraph. These foundations inform the framework's domains and guide its focus on cultural relevance, linguistic justice, equity, and pedagogical alignment.

The development of this evaluation framework is grounded in several theoretical foundations. The core structure draws on CRT, particularly Gay's (2010) principles of cultural congruence, validation of students' cultural knowledge, and the creation of inclusive learning environments. The emphasis on multilingualism and linguistic equity is based on translanguaging theory (García & Wei, 2014) and research on linguistic justice (Baker-Bell, 2020). The domains relating to access, fairness, and bias are aligned with the literature on algorithmic justice, AI bias (Buolamwini & Gebru, 2018) and AI ethics frameworks emerging from UNESCO (2021) and OECD (2022). Finally, alignment with CRT pedagogy reflects the shift toward culturally sustaining pedagogy (Paris & Alim, 2017), which highlights that technologies must not only reflect culture but actively sustain diverse cultural and linguistic practices. Collectively, these foundations form the theoretical justification for each component of the framework.

Figure 3. Culturally responsive AI evaluation framework (CRAI-EF)

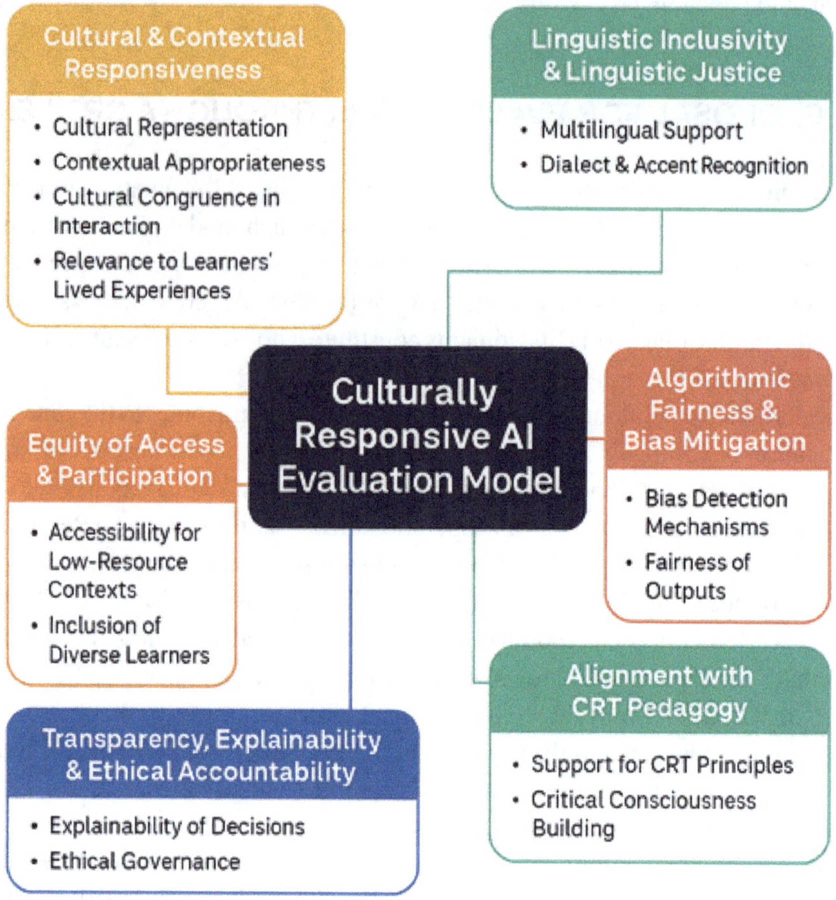

9.1. Defining the Domains of the Culturally Responsive AI Evaluation Framework

The Culturally Responsive AI Evaluation Framework (CRAI-EF) consists of six domains that together capture the cultural, linguistic, ethical, and pedagogical dimensions necessary for evaluating AI tools in global education. Each domain includes specific subdomains that articulate the principles of culturally responsive teaching (Ladson-Billings, 1995; Gay, 2010), linguistic justice (Baker-Bell, 2020), and responsible AI governance (UNESCO, 2022; Baeza-Yates, 2023). These domains collectively ensure that AI does not simply improve efficiency but actively supports culturally sustaining and equitable learning environments.

Cultural and Contextual Responsiveness: This domain evaluates whether the AI system recognises, respects and accurately represents the cultural identities, histories and sociocultural realities of learners. Since culture and context are interwoven, they have been taken together in this framework. This domain involves four sub-dimensions. Firstly, *Cultural Representation* examines whether the AI system incorporates diverse cultural perspectives, avoids stereotypes, and reflects the lived realities of marginalised and underrepresented communities. Secondly, *Contextual Appropriateness* assesses whether AI-generated examples, explanations and scenarios are situated within learners' cultural, historical and community contexts, rather than relying on generic, decontextualised content. Thirdly, *Cultural Congruence in Interaction* evaluates whether the AI system aligns with culturally specific communication norms (e.g. politeness strategies, narrative styles and discourse patterns). Finally, *Relevance to Learners Lived Experiences* determines whether AI outputs help students to connect learning to their personal, cultural and community-based experiences, thereby supporting identity affirmation.

Linguistic Inclusivity & Linguistic Justice: This domain assesses whether AI tools promote, rather than undermine, linguistic diversity. It is grounded in translanguaging theory (García & Wei, 2014) and linguistic justice frameworks (Baker-Bell, 2020). It examines how AI responds to the multilingual realities of global education. The *Multilingual Support* section of this dimension assesses the breadth, quality and accessibility of multilingual features, such as translation, multilingual interfaces and bilingual outputs. On the other hand, The *Dialect and Accent Recognition* tool evaluates the accuracy with which AI processes non-dominant dialects, accented speech and linguistic varieties that are often excluded from training data.

Equity of Access & Participation: This domain focuses on material and structural access, recognizing that AI can unintentionally widen inequalities if it assumes high-income settings or standardized digital infrastructure. *Accessibility for Low-Resource Contexts* assesses whether AI works effectively in low-bandwidth environments, offline modes, or on basic devices while *Inclusion ofDiverse Learners* evaluates whether the AI accommodates disabilities, neurodiversity, varied learning preferences, and diverse linguistic repertoires.

Algorithmic Fairness & Bias Mitigation: Based on research into AI bias (Buolamwini & Gebru, 2018), this domain examines whether AI systems can identify, mitigate and reduce discriminatory patterns. The *Bias Detection Mechanisms* sub-domain assesses whether AI systems include processes, documentation, or audits for checking for bias. *Fairness of Outputs* sub-domain evaluates whether the system's responses are free from stereotyping, discrimination, or uneven treatment across demographic, cultural, and linguistic groups.

Transparency, Explainability & Ethical Accountability: This domain addresses whether AI behaviour is transparent, interpretable, and guided by ethical standards aligned with global policymaking bodies such as UNESCO, OECD and EU. It consists of two-subdomains which are explainability of decisions and ethical governance. *Explainability of Decisions* evaluates whether the AI provides understandable explanations for outputs, recommendations, or automated classifications. *Ethical Governance* assesses whether the AI adheres to responsible data practices, privacy standards, accountability protocols, and ethical guidelines.

Alignment with CRT Pedagogy: Based on the Culturally Responsive Teaching (Gay, 2000, 2010, 2015), Culturally Relevant Pedagogy (Ladson-Billings, 1995), and Culturally Sustaining Pedagogy (Paris & Alim, 2017), this domain evaluates whether AI strengthens pedagogical practices that affirm students' identities, promote critical thinking, and support culturally grounded learning. *Support for CRT Principles* examines whether AI-generated materials, guidance, and tasks align with core CRT principles. *Critical Consciousness Building* assesses whether the AI promotes opportunities for sociopolitical awareness, cultural reflection, and discussions of identity, equity, and justice.

9.2. OPERATIONALIZING THE CRAI-EF: AN ILLUSTRATIVE CLASSROOM SCENARIO AND EVALUATION

To demonstrate how the Culturally Responsive AI Evaluation Framework (CRAI-EF) can be applied in educational practice, this section presents an illustrative classroom scenario. This scenario is not intended as a prescriptive lesson plan, but rather as a conceptual demonstration of how educators and researchers may use the framework to critically examine AI-generated learning materials in culturally and linguistically diverse contexts.

Scenario: AI-Generated Reading Comprehension Texts in Teacher Education

Context: The scenario is situated within an English Language Teacher Education program, specifically in a course focusing on the teaching of the four main language skills—reading, writing, listening, and speaking—in multicultural and multilingual classrooms.

Task Description: Pre-service teachers use an AI tool to generate reading comprehension texts that represent both local and global cultural contexts. They prompt the AI to produce three reading texts aligned with a specified proficiency level and topic determined by the pre-service teachers. These texts are intended to simulate materials that might later be used in K–12 EFL classrooms.

Use of the CRAI-EF: Rather than adopting the AI-generated texts directly, pre-service teachers critically examine the outputs using the CRAI-EF guiding questions presented in the following table (see Table 2), which consists of questions regarding how to evaluate AI outputs in terms of cultural responsiveness, linguistic justice and inclusivity, transparency, algorithmic bias, ethics, equity of access, and alignment with CRT. The sample CRAI-EF evaluation questions help teachers and learners to measure to what extent the AI systems and outputs align with CRT and AI ethics.

In this scenario, the CRAI-EF supports pre-service teachers in deciding whether the texts are culturally appropriate, linguistically inclusive, and pedagogically suitable for their target learners. The same framework is subsequently applied to other AI-assisted materials prepared for listening, speaking, and writing activities, highlighting the flexibility of the CRAI-EF across different language skills.

This scenario illustrates how the CRAI-EF can function as a reflective and pedagogically grounded tool, enabling educators to move beyond surface-level efficiency and engage critically with AI-generated materials before integrating them into classroom practice.

Table 2. Sample CRAI-EF evaluation questions

Domain	Sub-Domain	Questions
Cultural & Contextual Responsiveness	Cultural Representation	Do the AI outputs reflect diverse cultural perspectives without relying on stereotypes or dominant (e.g., Western-centric) narratives?
	Contextual Appropriateness	Are the AI outputs situated within learners' local, historical, or community contexts rather than generic settings?
	Cultural Congruence in Interaction	Does the AI's interaction style align with culturally appropriate communication norms?
	Relevance to Learners' Lived Experiences	Do the AI outputs help learners connect academic content to their personal, cultural, or community-based experiences?
Linguistic Inclusivity & Linguistic Justice	Multilingual Support	Does the AI provide accurate, accessible, and pedagogically meaningful support across multiple languages used by learners?
	Dialect & Accent Recognition	How effectively does the AI recognise and respond to non-dominant dialects, accents, or localized language varieties?
Equity of Access & Participation	Accessibility for Low-Resource Contexts	Can the AI tool function effectively under constraints such as low bandwidth, limited devices, or unstable connectivity?
	Inclusion of Diverse Learners	Does the AI tool accommodate learners with disabilities and/or diverse learners?

continued on following page

Table 2. Continued

Domain	Sub-Domain	Questions
Algorithmic Fairness & Bias Mitigation	Bias Detection Mechanisms	Does the AI system provide mechanisms and documentation regarding how potential cultural, linguistic, or demographic biases are identified and mitigated?
	Fairness of Outputs	Are the AI outputs consistent and equitable across users from different cultural, linguistic, or socioeconomic backgrounds?
Transparency, Explainability & Ethical Accountability	Explainability of Decisions	Does the AI provide understandable explanations for its recommendations, feedback, or automated decisions to educators and learners?
	Ethical Governance	Are data use, privacy protection, accountability structures, and ethical standards clearly articulated and aligned with international AI ethics guidelines?
Alignment with CRT Pedagogy	Support for CRT Principles	Do the AI outputs affirm learners' identities, value cultural knowledge, and support relationship-centred pedagogy?
	Critical Consciousness Building	Does the AI tool create opportunities for reflection on issues of culture, power, equity, language, and social justice within learning activities?

Although the scenario is presented in a generalized form, it is intended to illustrate how the CRAI-EF may be applied across diverse global educational contexts rather than to represent practices in any single region. Moreover, instructional materials may be generated by AI systems; however, their pedagogical use requires careful evaluation and revision by educators. Even in contexts where inclusivity appears relatively high—such as when English is used as the primary language of prompting—human judgment remains essential, as AI systems are not fully sensitive to cultural differences, local norms, or contextual nuances. Accordingly, teachers may align AI-generated texts with culturally preferred discourse patterns, classroom norms, and sociocultural expectations prior to classroom use. Across such contexts, culturally inclusive outcomes are therefore not assumed to emerge from AI systems alone, but from the collaborative interplay between AI-generated resources and human pedagogical judgment.

This emphasis on human–AI collaboration is supported by emerging empirical work. For example, Ewart (2025) demonstrates that AI-driven prompting approaches can foster inclusive, equitable, and culturally sustaining learning environments when educators actively guide the alignment of instructional materials with learners' cultural identities, linguistic backgrounds, and learning needs. Drawing on a mixed-methods study involving 292 educators across two Canadian provinces, Ewart shows that AI-enhanced CRT practices can promote equity, affirm cultural identity, and expand inclusive access to knowledge when grounded in educators' contextual expertise. Thus, these considerations underscore that culturally responsive AI in education is not a property of technology itself, but an outcome of intentional human–AI collaboration guided by culturally responsive pedagogical principles.

9.3. Validation Considerations

The Culturally Responsive AI Evaluation Framework (CRAI-EF) presented in this chapter is grounded in well-established theoretical traditions, including CRT (Gay, 2000; 2010; 2015), Culturally Relevant Pedagogy (Ladson-Billings, 1995), Culturally Sustaining Pedagogy (Paris & Alim, 2017), Translanguaging (García & Wei, 2014), Multilingual Pedagogy (García & Wei, 2014), Linguistic Justice (Baker-Bell, 2020) and International AI Ethics Guidelines (UNESCO, 2022). As this chapter which proposes a preliminary framework adopts a narrative review approach which *"allows researchers to describe what is known on a topic while conducting a subjective examination and critique of an entire body of literature"* (Sukhera, 2022; p. 414), future empirical work is needed to examine its reliability and validity further. To establish content validity, experts in CRT, AI in education and multilingual learning can review the framework using the Content Validity Index (Polit & Beck, 2006). Pilot testing with educators could assess face validity and practical applicability, and inter-rater reliability could be evaluated if the framework were operationalised as a checklist or rubric. Construct and criterion validity could be investigated by mapping the framework onto existing ethical AI standards, or by comparing results with those from established evaluation tools. These methodological steps will ensure that the framework is both theoretically robust and empirically sound, enabling its use in diverse educational and cultural contexts.

10. PEDAGOGICAL IMPLICATIONS

The rapid proliferation of artificial intelligence tools such as ChatGPT, Gemini, and DeepSeek has reshaped learning environments, despite the fact that these technologies are not originally designed for educational purposes. While teachers and students are not responsible for developing AI applications—because doing so requires advanced technical expertise—they are nevertheless central users whose pedagogical decisions determine how AI ultimately influences learning. Thus, culturally responsive AI in education necessarily involves both stakeholders within the education system (e.g., teachers, school leaders, students) and actors outside the system (e.g., AI developers, policymakers, technology companies). This aligns closely with UNESCO's (2022) AI ethics guidelines, which address both member states and AI actors, emphasizing collaborative responsibility for ensuring that AI technologies operate in fair, equitable, and culturally respectful ways.

Emerging research suggests that GenAI can significantly contribute to the development of key 21st-century competencies. Studies by Michalon and Camacho-Zúñiga (2023) and McCallum (2024) demonstrate that tools such as ChatGPT can foster critical thinking, intercultural competence, and communication skills. Similarly, Rospigliosi (2023) reports that the integration of ChatGPT supports learner-centred pedagogies by stimulating creative thinking and enhancing problem-solving strategies in language tasks. These findings indicate that AI, when thoughtfully integrated, can enrich learning processes and expand opportunities for personalized and culturally responsive instruction. On the other hand, it has important limitations such as the lack of human interaction, constrained contextual understanding, bias in training datasets, limited creativity, excessive dependence on input data, privacy concerns, and restricted capacity for meaningful personalization (Baidoo-Anu & Ansah, 2023).

To benefit from AI in a pedagogically meaningful and culturally sustaining way, both teachers and students must develop robust AI literacy. As defined by Druga et al. (2019), AI literacy encompasses the competencies needed to critically evaluate, communicate, and collaborate effectively with AI systems. This includes understanding how AI works, recognizing its limitations, and being able to detect potential biases embedded in AI outputs. AI education extends beyond technological knowledge; it also involves cultivating critical reflection on how trustworthy, ethical, and socially responsible AI should be developed, as well as the consequences of failing to do so.

As Tikız-Ertürk and Taşpınar (2023) argue, one of the fundamental challenges of AI integration is sustaining human-centred learning environments, as education is inherently a collaborative process involving teachers, students, families, and communities. Teachers therefore remain essential not only as facilitators of learning but also as cultural mediators and critical decision-makers who guide when, how, and why AI should be used. Because teachers are not AI designers, their primary responsibility lies in selecting appropriate AI tools and integrating them in pedagogically sound ways. The CRAI-EF proposed in this chapter can support teachers in making informed choices by helping them assess whether a given AI application aligns with CRT principles, respects digital equity, and meets the cultural and linguistic needs of their students. Of course, teachers must also consider more traditional pedagogical concerns—such as curricular goals, subject-matter alignment, and instructional approaches—but the framework offers a structured pathway for ensuring that culturally responsive considerations are not overlooked.

As students increasingly use AI tools independently—often outside the supervision of teachers—they must also develop the competencies needed to select AI tools wisely and use them responsibly. AI literacy is therefore essential not only for educators but equally for learners. Empowering students with critical understanding of how AI systems function, what their limitations are, and how to detect cultural or linguistic biases enables them to become responsible, reflective, and culturally aware users of technology.

These pedagogical implications highlight the need for a holistic approach to AI integration in education—one that places cultural responsiveness, equity, and human-centred design at the centre. By ensuring that teachers and students are equipped with the necessary AI literacy skills, maintaining teacher agency, and promoting collaborative governance across educational and technological stakeholders, education systems can move toward an AI ecosystem that supports—not undermines—multiculturalism, linguistic diversity, and culturally sustaining pedagogies. The CRAI-EF provides a practical tool to support these goals, offering educators a structured way to evaluate AI applications through the lens of CRT and digital equity.

REFERENCES

Abdalla, H., & Moussa, A. (2024). Culturally responsive teaching: Navigating models and implementing effective strategies. *Acta Pedagogia Asiana*, *3*(2), 91–100. DOI: 10.53623/apga.v3i2.432

Accenture. (2021). Artificial intelligence services. https://www.accenture.com/us-en/services/data-ai

Aceves, T. C., & Orosco, M. J. (2014). *Culturally responsive teaching* (Document No. IC-2). University of Florida, Collaboration for Effective Educator, Development, Accountability, and Reform Centre. http://ceedar.education.ufl.edu/tools/innovation-configurations/

Ahmed, F. (2024). The digital divide and AI in education: Addressing equity and accessibility. *AI Edify Journal*, *1*(2), 12–22.

Akdemir, A. S., & Ulaş, A. H. (2024). Culturally responsive teaching in the age of artificial intelligence. In Akdemir, A. S. (Ed.), *Emerging Trends, Multilingualism, and AI Integration in Language Studies* (pp. 42–53). Shanlax Publications.

Artificial Intelligence Act, E. U. (2024). Available on https://artificialintelligenceact.eu/article/50/

Atari, M., Xue, M. J., Park, P. S., Blasi, D. E., & Henrich, J. (2023, September 22). Which humans? DOI: 10.31234/osf.io/5b26t

Baeza-Yates, R. (2023). An introduction to responsible AI. *European Review (Chichester, England)*, *31*(4), 406–421. DOI: 10.1017/S1062798723000145

Baidoo-Anu, D., & Owusu Ansah, L. (2023). Education in the era of generative Artificial Intelligence (AI): Understanding the potential benefits of ChatGPT in promoting teaching and learning. *Journal of AI.*, *7*(1), 52–62. DOI: 10.61969/jai.1337500

Baker, R. S., & Hawn, A. (2022). Algorithmic Bias in Education. *International Journal of Artificial Intelligence in Education*, *32*(4), 1052–1092. DOI: 10.1007/s40593-021-00285-9

Baker-Bell, A. (2020). *Linguistic justice: Black language, literacy, identity, and pedagogy*. Routledge. DOI: 10.4324/9781315147383

Barnes, E., & Hutson, J. (2024). Navigating the ethical terrain of AI in higher education: Strategies for mitigating bias and promoting fairness. *Forum for Education Studies*, *2*(2), 1229. DOI: 10.59400/fes.v2i2.1229

Bronfenbrenner, M. (1973). Equality and equity. *The ANNALS of the American Academy of Political and Social Science, 409*(1), 9-23. (Original work published 1973)DOI: 10.1177/000271627340900103

Buolamwini, J., & Gebru, T. (2018). Gender shades: Intersectional accuracy disparities in commercial gender classification. In *Proceedings of the 1st Conference on Fairness, Accountability and Transparency* (pp. 77–91). PMLR.

Capraro, V., Lentsch, A., Acemoglu, D., Akgun, S., Akhmedova, A., Bilancini, E., Bonnefon, J.-F., Brañas-Garza, P., Butera, L., Douglas, K. M., Everett, J. A. C., Gigerenzer, G., Greenhow, C., Hashimoto, D. A., Holt-Lunstad, J., Jetten, J., Johnson, S., Kunz, W. H., Longoni, C., & Viale, R. (2024). The impact of generative artificial intelligence on socioeconomic inequalities and policy making. *PNAS Nexus*, *3*(6), 1–18. DOI: 10.1093/pnasnexus/pgae191 PMID: 38864006

Cenoz, J., & Gorter, D. (2015). *Multilingual education: Between language learning and translanguaging*. Cambridge University Press. DOI: 10.1017/9781009024655

Dai, D., Suzuki, S., & Chen, G. (2025). Generative AI for professional communication training in intercultural contexts: Where are we now and where are we heading? *Applied Linguistics Review*, *16*(2), 763–774. DOI: 10.1515/applirev-2024-0184

Dignum, V. (2019). *Responsible artificial intelligence: How to develop and use AI in a responsible way*. Springer. DOI: 10.1007/978-3-030-30371-6

Dignum, V. (2021). The role and challenges of education for responsible AI. *London Review of Education, 19* (1), 1, 1–11. DOI: 10.14324/LRE.19.1.01

DiMaggio, P., & Hargittai, E. (2001). From the 'digital divide' to 'digital inequality': Studying Internet use as penetration increases. Working Papers 47, Princeton University, School of Public and International Affairs, Center for Arts and Cultural Policy Studies. Accessed on https://ideas.repec.org/p/pri/cpanda/15.html

Druga, S., Vu, S. T., Likhith, E., & Qiu, T. (2019). Inclusive AI literacy for kids around the world. [Association for Computing Machinery.]. *Proceedings of FabLearn, 2019*, 104–111. DOI: 10.1145/3311890.3311904

Ewart, K. (2025). Leveraging Generative AI for Culturally Responsive Teaching: A Shift in Educator Planning and Practice. In R. Jake Cohen (Ed.), *Proceedings of Society for Information Technology & Teacher Education International Conference* (pp. 2030-2035). Orlando, FL, USA: Association for the Advancement of Computing in Education (AACE). Available on https://www.learntechlib.org/p/225764

García, O., & Kano, N. (2014). Translanguaging as process and pedagogy: Developing the English writing of Japanese students in the US. In Conteh, J., & Meier, G. (Eds.), *The multilingual turn in languages education: Opportunities and challenges* (pp. 258–277). Multilingual Matters. DOI: 10.21832/9781783092246-018

García, O., & Wei, L. (2014). Translanguaging, bilingualism, and bilingual education. In Wright, W., Boun, S., & García, O. (Eds.), *The handbook of bilingual and multilingual education* (pp. 223–240). Wiley-Blackwell.

Gay, G. (2000). *Culturally responsive teaching: Theory, research, and practice.* Teachers College Press.

Gay, G. (2010). *Culturally responsive teaching: Theory, research, and practice* (2nd ed.). Teachers College Press.

Gay, G. (2015). The what, why, and how of culturally responsive teaching: International mandates, challenges, and opportunities. *Multicultural Education Review, 7*(3), 123–139. DOI: 10.1080/2005615X.2015.1072079

Grab, M. O. (2025). Teaching for equity: An exploration of AI's role in culturally responsive teaching in higher education settings. *Innovative Higher Education.* Advance online publication. DOI: 10.1007/s10755-025-09801-4

Gruber, A., & Köse, N. (2025). Language education amid digital disruption: In-service and pre-service teacher perspectives on AI language bias and curriculum integration. *Language Awareness*, 1–19. Advance online publication. DOI: 10.1080/09658416.2025.2590680

He, K., Liu, X., Xu, Y., Bustamante, A. S., & Warschauer, M. (2025). "Carlitos the Curious Caterpillar": Exploring teacher–AI co-creation of culturally responsive educational materials. In *Interaction Design and Children (IDC '25)* (pp. 1–19). ACM. DOI: 10.1145/3713043.3727056

Jackson, J., Starr, J., and Weaver, D. (2024, August). *A Framework for Digital Equity. Digital Promise.* DOI: 10.51388/20.500.12265/223

Jeon, J., Wei, L., Tai, K. W. H., & Lee, S. (2025). ç Generative AI and its dilemmas: Exploring AI from a translanguaging perspective. *Applied Linguistics, 46*(4), 709–717. DOI: 10.1093/applin/amaf049

Johnson, M. (2021). Scalable approach to reducing gender bias in Google translate. Accesed on https://ai.googleblog.com/2020/04/a-scalable-approach-to-reducing-gender.html

Jones, R. (2025). Culture machines. *Applied Linguistics Review*, *16*(2), 753–762. DOI: 10.1515/applirev-2024-0188

Ladson-Billings, G. (1995). Toward a theory of culturally relevant pedagogy. *American Educational Research Journal*, *32*(3), 465–491. DOI: 10.3102/00028312032003465

Lee, S., Jeon, J., & Choe, H. (2025). Enhancing pre-service teachers' global Englishes awareness with technology: A focus on AI chatbots in 3D metaverse environments. *TESOL Quarterly*, *59*(1), 49–74. DOI: 10.1002/tesq.3300

Li, X., & Yu, S. (2025). Culturally responsive AI module in early childhood teacher education: An action research. *Journal of Early Childhood Teacher Education*, 1–17. Advance online publication. DOI: 10.1080/10901027.2025.2552973

Liu, W., Jamaludin, K. A., & Hamzah, M. I. (2025). Systematic review of culturally responsive teaching and implications for technical communication education. *Multidisciplinary Reviews*, *8*(4), 2025117. DOI: 10.31893/multirev.2025117

Louie, B., Björling, E. A., Kuo, A. C., & Alves-Oliveira, P. (2022). Designing for culturally responsive social robots: An application of a participatory framework. *Frontiers in Robotics and AI*, *9*, 983408. Advance online publication. DOI: 10.3389/frobt.2022.983408 PMID: 36340576

McCallum, L. (2024). New takes on developing intercultural communicative competence: Using AI tools in telecollaboration task design and task completion. *Journal for Multicultural Education*, *18*(1/2), 153–172. DOI: 10.1108/JME-06-2023-0043

Mengesha, Z., Heldreth, C., Lahav, M., Sublewski, J., & Tuennerman, E. (2021). "I don't think these devices are very culturally sensitive."—Impact of automated speech recognition errors on African Americans. *Frontiers in Artificial Intelligence*, *4*(725911), 725911. Advance online publication. DOI: 10.3389/frai.2021.725911 PMID: 34901836

Michalon, B. & Camacho- Zúñiga, C. (2023). ChatGPT, a brand-new tool to strengthen timeless competencies. *Frontiers in Education, 8 (*1251163), DOI: 10.3389/feduc.2023.1251163

Mikalef, P., Conboy, K., Lundström, J. E., & Popovič, A. (2022). Thinking responsibly about responsible AI and 'the dark side' of AI. *European Journal of Information Systems*, *31*(3), 257–268. DOI: 10.1080/0960085X.2022.2026621

Naidoo, V., & Chadhaa, K. K. (2025). Culturally responsive AI chatbots: From framework to field evidence. *Computers in Human Behavior: Artificial Humans*, *6*, 100224. Advance online publication. DOI: 10.1016/j.chbah.2025.100224

National Digital Inclusion Alliance. (2019). Definitions. Retrieved from https://www.digitalinclusion.org/definitions/

Nyaaba, M., & Zhai, X. (2025). Developing a theory-grounded AI tool for generating culturally responsive lesson plans. *Computers and Education: Artificial Intelligence*. DOI: 10.1016/j.caeai.2025.100474

Ożegalska-Łukasik, N. & Łukasik, S. (2023). Culturally responsive artificial intelligence – problems, challenges and solutions. *Intercultural Relations, 7*(2(14), 106-119. DOI: 10.12797/RM.02.2023.14.07

Paiz, J. M., Toncelli, R., & Kostka, I. (2025). *Artificial intelligence, real teaching: A guide to AI in ELT*. University of Michigan Press. DOI: 10.3998/mpub.14329762

Paris, D. (2012). Culturally sustaining pedagogy: A needed change in stance, terminology, and practice. *Educational Researcher, 41*(3), 93–97. DOI: 10.3102/0013189X12441244

Paris, D., & Alim, H. S. (2017). *Culturally sustaining pedagogies*. Teachers College Press.

Park, S. (2024). AI chatbots and linguistic injustice. *Journal of Universal Language, 25*(1), 99–119. DOI: 10.22425/jul.2024.25.1.99

Piller, I. (2016). *Linguistic diversity and social justice*. Oxford University Press. DOI: 10.1093/acprof:oso/9780199937240.001.0001

Polit, D. F., & Beck, C. T. (2006). The content validity index: A critical review. *Research in Nursing & Health, 29*, 489–497. DOI: 10.1002/nur.20147 PMID: 16977646

Rane, N. L., Choudhary, S. P., & Rane, J. (2024). Education 4.0 and 5.0: Integrating Artificial Intelligence (AI) for personalized and adaptive learning. *Journal of Artificial Intelligence and Robotics, 1*(1), 29–43. DOI: 10.61577/jaiar.2024.100006

Resta, P., & Laferrière, T. (2015). Digital equity and intercultural education. *Education and Information Technologies, 20*(4), 743–756. DOI: 10.1007/s10639-015-9419-z

Roshanaei, M. (2024). Towards best practices for mitigating artificial intelligence implicit bias in shaping diversity, inclusion and equity in higher education. *Education and Information Technologies, 29*(14), 18959–18984. DOI: 10.1007/s10639-024-12605-2

Rospigliosi, P. (2023). Artificial intelligence in teaching and learning: What questions should we ask of Chat GPT? *Interactive Learning Environments, 31*(1), 1–3. DOI: 10.1080/10494820.2023.2180191

Samuel, Y., Brennan-Tonetta, M., Samuel, J., Kashyap, R., Kumar, V., Krishna Kaashyap, S., Chidipothu, N., Anand, I., & Jain, P. (2023). Cultivation of human centred artificial intelligence: Culturally adaptive thinking in education (CATE) for AI. *Frontiers in Artificial Intelligence*, *6*(1198180), 1198180. Advance online publication. DOI: 10.3389/frai.2023.1198180 PMID: 38106981

Sukhera, J. (2022). Narrative reviews: Flexible, rigorous, and practical. *Journal of Graduate Medical Education*, *14*(4), 414–417. DOI: 10.4300/JGME-D-22-00480.1 PMID: 35991099

Szabó, F., & Szoke, J. (2024). How does generative AI promote autonomy and inclusivity in language teaching? *ELT Journal*, *78*(4), 478–488. DOI: 10.1093/elt/ccae052

The Organization for Economic Co-operation and Development (OECD). (2001). *Understanding the digital divide*. OECD Publications.

Tıkız-Ertürk, G., & Taşpınar, H. K. (2023). Applications of artificial intelligence (AI) in EFL classrooms. In S. Uçar (Ed.), *Digital pedagogy in the 21st century: Emerging technologies in foreign language classrooms* (ss. 27–44). Efe Akademi Publishing.

United Nations Educational, Scientific and Cultural Organization (UNESCO). (2022). *Recommendation on the ethics of artificial intelligence*. https://unesdoc.unesco.org/ark:/48223/pf0000381137

Vavrus, M. (2008). Culturally responsive teaching. In T. L. Good (Ed.), *21st century education: A reference handbook* (Vol. 2, pp. 49–57). SAGE. https://www.scribd.com/document/636505197/VavrusCulturallyResponsiveTeaching

Waghid, Y., & Waghid, Z. (2021). *Artificial intelligence and education: Philosophical perspectives on innovation and equity*. Springer.

Warschauer, M., & Matuchniak, T. (2010). New technology and digital learning: Addressing educational inequity. *Harvard Educational Review*, *80*(4), 698–730.

ADDITIONAL READING

Aler Tubella, A., Mora-Cantallops, M., & Nieves, J. C. (2024). How to teach responsible AI in Higher Education: Challenges and opportunities. *Ethics and Information Technology*, *26*(3), 3. Advance online publication. DOI: 10.1007/s10676-023-09733-7

Banks, J. A. (2004). Multicultural education: Historical development, dimensions, and practice. In Banks, J. A., & Banks, C. A. M. (Eds.), *Handbook of research on multicultural education* (2nd ed., pp. 3–29). Jossey-Bass.

Chomsky, N., Roberts, I., & Watumull, J. (2023). The false promise of ChatGPT, *The New York Times*. https://www.nytimes.com/2023/03/08/opinion/noam-chomsky-chatgpt-ai.html

Curtis, C. (1998). Creating culturally responsive curriculum: Making race matter. *The Clearing House: A Journal of Educational Strategies, Issues and Ideas*, *71*(3), 135–139. DOI: 10.1080/00098659809599344

EUR-Lex. (2024). Regulation (EU) 2024/1689 of the European Parliament and of the Council of 13 June 2024 laying down harmonised rules on artificial intelligence and amending Regulations (EC) No 300/2008, (EU) No 167/2013, (EU) No 168/2013, (EU) 2018/ 858, (EU) 2018/1139 and (EU) 2019/2144 and Directives 2014/90/EU, (EU) 2016/ 797 and (EU) 2020/1828 (Artificial Intelligence Act) (Text with EEA relevance)PE/24/ 2024/REV/1. https://data.europa.eu/eli/reg/2024/1689/oj

European Commission. (2023). Proposal for a regulation of the European Parliament and of the Council laying down harmonised rules on artificial intelligence (Artificial Intelligence Act) and amending certain Union legislative acts. Accessed on https://eur-lex.europa.eu/legal content/EN/TXT/?uri=CELEX:52021PC0206

Gay, G. (2013). Teaching to and through cultural diversity. *Curriculum Inquiry*, *43*(1), 48–70. DOI: 10.1111/curi.12002

Jayasinghe, S., Arm, K., & Gamage, K. A. A. (2025). Designing culturally inclusive case studies with Generative AI: Strategies and considerations. *Education Sciences*, *15*(6), 645. DOI: 10.3390/educsci15060645

Ladson-Billings, G. (2006). "Yes, but how do we do it?" Practicing culturally relevant pedagogy. In J. Landsman & C. W. Lewis (Eds.), *White teachers/diverse classrooms: A guide to building inclusive schools, promoting high expectations, and eliminating racism*. Sterling, VA: Stylus.

Smith, G., & Rustagi, I. (2020). Mitigating bias in artificial intelligence: An equity fluent leadership playbook. *Berkeley Haas Centre for Equity, Gender, and Leadership*. https://haas.berkeley.edu/wp-content/uploads/UCB_Playbook_R10_V2_spreads2.pdf

KEY TERMS AND DEFINITIONS

AI Bias: Refers to systematic preferences or unfair outcomes in AI systems that arise when algorithms rely too heavily on narrow or unbalanced datasets, such as those dominated by particular genders, races, or ethnic groups. These patterns can lead to unequal or inaccurate results for other groups.

Culturally Responsive AI: Refers to AI applications that recognize, respect, and respond to cultural differences. Such systems aim to function in ways that reflect the values, communication styles, and lived experiences of diverse user groups rather than assuming one cultural norm.

Culturally Responsive Teaching: Refers to a teaching approach that actively incorporates learners' cultural backgrounds—such as race, ethnicity, language, and community experiences—into instruction. It aims to make learning more relevant, supportive, and engaging for diverse students.

Digital Divide: Refers to disparities among individuals or communities regarding access to digital technologies, internet connectivity, and the skills needed to use them. It highlights structural inequalities that prevent some groups from fully participating in digital environments.

Digital Equity: Refers to ensuring fair access to technology, digital resources, and opportunities so that all users—regardless of background or circumstance—can meaningfully participate in digital life. It goes beyond equal treatment by focusing on providing what people need to engage fully and successfully.

Inclusivity: Refers to practices that intentionally involve people with diverse abilities, needs, languages, and cultural backgrounds. It emphasizes creating environments where everyone feels valued, represented, and able to participate.

Linguistic Justice: Refers to fairness in the treatment of languages and language varieties. It stresses equal respect for different linguistic backgrounds and seeks to eliminate discrimination based on how people speak or use language.

Chapter 10
Community and Stakeholder Engagement in Human–AI Learning Ecosystems

S. Magesh
http://orcid.org/0000-0003-2876-7337
Dr. M.G.R. Educational and Research Institute, India

S. Vijayalakshmi
SRM Institute of Science and Technology, India

V. Nivedha
SRM Institute of Science and Technology, India

P. S. Rajakumar
Dr. M.G.R. Educational and Research Institute, India

R. Manikandan
http://orcid.org/0000-0001-6116-2132
SASTRA University, India

ABSTRACT

The deployment of Artificial Intelligence (AI) in learning is rapidly changing teaching, learning, and governance, establishing what can be termed human–AI learning ecosystems AI presents a chance for individualized education, coincidence, and effectiveness; however, it introduces the dangers of prejudice, injustice, and loss of trust among people. Issues of justice, such as fairness, accountability, transparency, and privacy, as well as social pressures, such as the digital divide, transformations

DOI: 10.4018/979-8-3373-6063-8.ch010

in teacher-student relationships, and reaching a more inclusive society, are also important. Participatory AI is an alternative to embedding democratic values in AI systems. Institutions such as global policy and ethics boards are considered systems of governance that enable responsible adoption . Among these technological innovations, explainable AI (XAI), reinforcement learning based on human feedback (RLHF), multimodal interaction, and federated learning have been noted when discussing increased transparency and participation.

1. INTRODUCTION

Artificial intelligence (AI) can be discussed as a revolutionary tendency that has changed the landscape of different spheres, such as the industrial production sector, healthcare, and education, among others. When it comes to education, AI has evolved past elementary mortifying projects or one-time innovations and is now being implemented on general platforms and in the actual classroom, as well as in institutional approaches. AI technologies, including adaptive tutoring systems, generative AI tools, predictive analytics, and learning management systems, are slowly transforming how students engage with content, teachers deliver instruction, and administrators develop curricula. However, this transformation is associated with several issues. The introduction of AI into classrooms cannot be considered a technical breakthrough. Instead, it must be viewed as the evolution of what researchers have come to call human-AI learning ecosystems: interconnected networks in which human actors (students, teachers, policymakers, developers, communities) and AI systems learn together in the broader contexts of culture, institutions, and ethics.

1.1 The Participatory Turn in AI and Education

These ecosystems are based on participatory designs. The need to integrate AI differs in that it cannot be implemented top-down, unlike conventional educational reforms. Members, students, and other stakeholders cannot sit and wait to become recipients of AI-driven innovations. They must assume the role of co-creators and purposefully direct technologies towards harmony with human values, learning goals, and social justice mandates. Such a participatory turn can be considered an acknowledgement of the fact that AI can replicate disparities unless created in a participatory and inclusive manner; on the contrary, it can bring a lot more inclusivity when guided by governance through a partnership and unobservable decision-making (Delgado et al., 2023; van den Broek et al., 2024).

1.2 The Need for AI Literacy

The next aspect that is also much needed is AI literacy. As artificial intelligence becomes increasingly integrated into everyday life, learning systems require students, teachers, and communities to possess the knowledge and expertise necessary for a critical approach to AI tools. AI literacies encompass not only technical literacy but also the ability to challenge bias, understand the ethical risks associated with their use, analyse algorithm transparency, and employ effective decision-making strategies (Almatrafi et al., 2024; Chiu and Sanusi, 2024). The application of AI literacy as a tool to empower learners must be widely adopted, as it is crucial to prevent the emergence of dependency risks associated with opaque systems.

1.3 Ethical and Responsible AI

The issue of responsible and ethical AI is also important in this context. Human -AI learning ecosystems are not neutral; instead, they have embedded assumptions and values, governance styles, and cultural beliefs. Existing social, economic, and racial disparities, as well as gender divisions, predispose the use of AI, since biases in the training data, the intransparency of algorithms, and unequal access to AI systems can cause a further widening of the gap. Consequently, educational AI must also be evaluated in terms of pedagogical performance and fairness, accountability, transparency, and ethics (Kashyap et al., 2023; Kashyap et al., 2024).

1.4 Generative AI in Education

As the use of generative AI in learning expands, exciting possibilities and complications arise. Such systems, as large language models, can increase creativity, provide instant feedback, and facilitate collaborative learning. Nevertheless, they also raise concerns such as academic integrity, overreliance on automated products, and erosion of critical thinking abilities. Such difficulties underscore the need for balanced integration approaches that utilise generative AI entities as augmentation tools rather than reduction tools in the context of replacing human judgment and knowledge (Khosravi et al., 2025).

1.5 Institutional and Policy Dimensions

Human institutions and policies also affect AI learning systems because of their backgrounds. Members of states, universities, and global organisations are becoming increasingly interested in formulating principles for the implementation of AI in the educational process. Policy frameworks address data privacy, principles of moral conduct, access to infrastructure, and R&D financing. In this manner, educational AI will present not only a technological challenge but also a policy and governance challenge because it will require balancing technical potential and social priorities (Ahrweiler et al., 2025; Al-Zahrani & Alasmari, 2024).

1.6 Conceptual Framework

The conceptual scope of the same dynamic is depicted in the figure below, reflecting the main layers of stakeholder engagement that characterise human learning ecosystems involving AI.

Figure 1. Stakeholder engagement in human–AI learning ecosystems

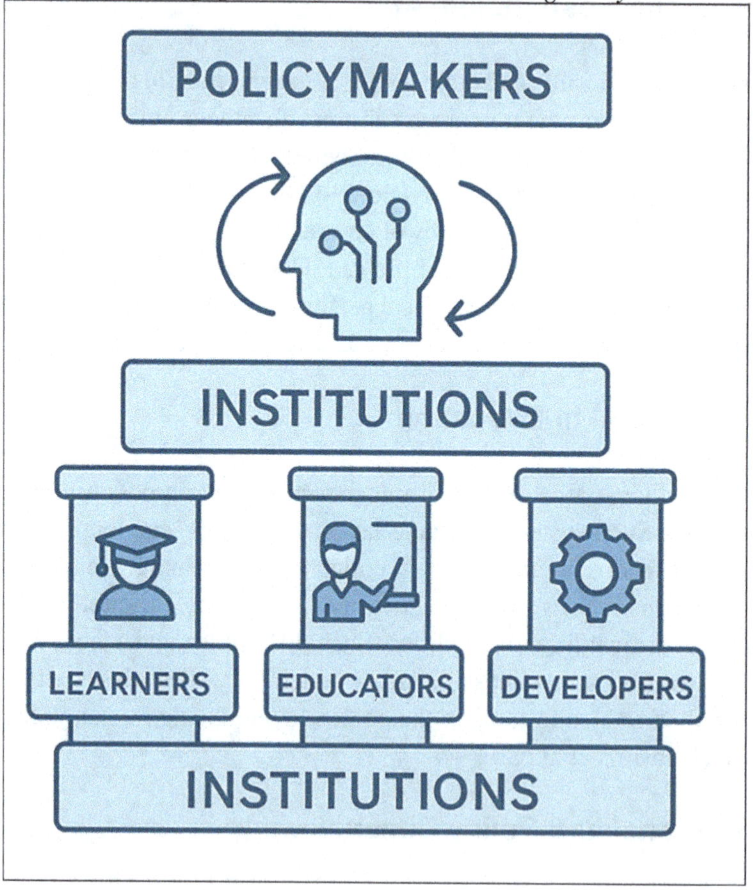

The pillar structure of stakeholder involvement in human–AI learning ecosystems is shown in Figure 1. The most fundamental are learners and educators, including institutions, policymakers, and developers. The arrows symbolise co-creation, accountability, and mutual influence at various levels.

1.7 Chapter Overview

This chapter begins by contextualising AI within the broader background of participatory education and critically evaluating the current literature on AI literacy, participatory design, and ethical governance. It examines existing patterns within generative AI and provides examples of participatory co-design and multi-stakeholder approaches to adopting responsible AI. The chapter concludes with suggestions for an inclusive, transparent, and sustainable human-AI learning ecosystem. The way the notion of AI is theoretically nuanced and practically put into practice in this chapter helps move away from thinking of it as a toolset to a paradigm-shifting sociotechnical system, which, when judiciously crafted, governed, and incorporated into education, can become a source of empowerment and improve equity of the education provision process in a way that an equally improperly done AI can further broaden the inequality gap.

2. BACKGROUND AND LITERATURE REVIEW

2.1 Historical Evolution of AI in Education

Over the past five decades, artificial intelligence (AI) has increasingly transformed the field of education. The the 1970s and the 1980s saw the introduction of Intelligent Tutoring Systems (ITS) that demonstrated the possibility of human-like tutoring conducted with the help of a computational model. Learning Management Systems (LMS) and original analytics began to provide educators with previously unseen information about student performance on a broad but small scale in the 1990s and the 2000s. The 2010s saw a paradigm shift, marked by the development of new tools such as adaptive testing, advanced analytics, and recommender systems, which created personalised learning paths. By the 2020s, the combination of technologies such as generative AI, multimodal learning environments, and AI-driven assessment marked an important step towards intelligent adaptive environments, moving beyond the classroom to lifelong learning.

Figure 2. Timeline of AI in education

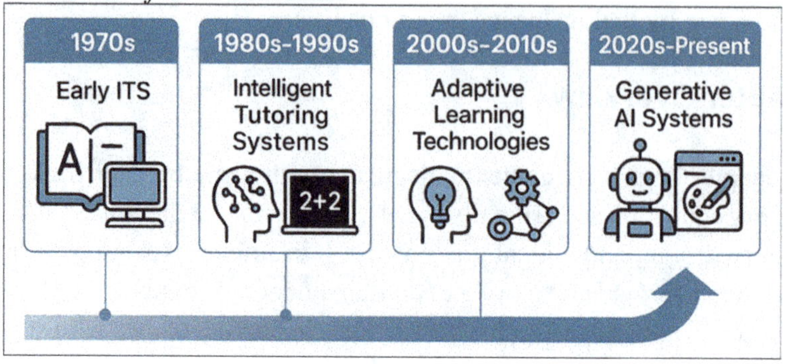

Figure 2 presents a chronicle of AI development in education since the emergence of the first ITS and the creation of generative AI systems. The scope and level of complications are increasing in each period. The history of innovations can be traced, which are made up of innovations that create human-AI learning ecosystems.

2.2 Defining Human-AI Learning Ecosystems

Learning ecosystems built between humans and AI involve more than just the introduction of AI tools to learning. They consist of interconnected systems of students, teachers, policymakers, developers, and communities who live in the learning space collectively. Such ecosystems are based on participatory design methodologies that enhance inclusive perspectives, equity, and flexibility. Delgado et al. (2023) state that ecosystems emphasize participatory evolution in designing AI, the central aspect of which is the engagement of the stakeholders in collaborative processes. The inclusive frame highlights the importance of equitable education and a comprehensive understanding of how AI systems interact with social, cultural and institutional forces.

2.3 Theoretical Underpinnings of Stakeholder Engagement

A wide range of theoretical models have been used for stakeholder engagement in AI-enabled learning systems. Participatory design theory emphasises participatory design processes, during which end users are considerably involved in shaping the tools and policies leading to the process of co-creation. Social constructivism theory is concerned with the construction of knowledge through collaboration, whereas sociotechnical systems theory focuses on the mutual influence between technology and human behaviour. These are theoretical ways of looking at the development of educational innovations, where a balance between technological advances and human demands is achieved. Similarly, van Leeuwen et al. (2023) presented how participatory dashboards, which could be successfully applied in teacher training, capitalised on professional vision, and thus the implementation domain of theoretical models that were converted into practical capacity-building techniques.

Figure 3. Theoretical foundations of stakeholder engagement in AI-enabled education

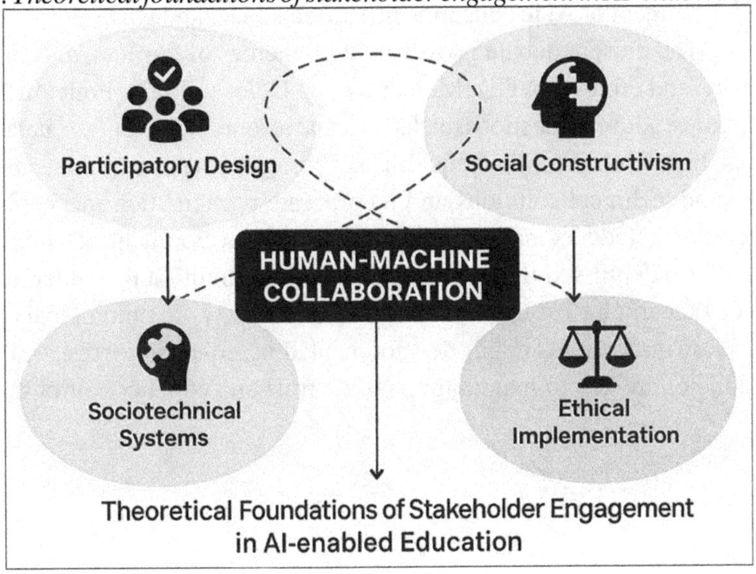

The significant theories that affect stakeholder engagement are depicted in the map in Figure 3, which includes participatory design, social constructivism and sociotechnical systems. This underscores the fact that the two theories intersect in advancing the human-machine collaboration. This framework provides information on sustainable and ethical implementations.

2.4 AI Literacy: A Foundational Competency

The sustainability of human-AI ecosystems of learning is facilitated by AI literacy, including the aptitude to comprehend, criticise, and co-create AI technologies. According to Chiu and Sanusi (2024), the authors underlined that both students and teachers should possess clear structures of AI literacy, which comprise technical expertise, critical reasoning, and awareness of ethics. In terms of teacher education, AI literacy sharpens the professional perspective such that educators are more capable of critically analysing the decisions made by algorithmic systems and effectively incorporating them into their instructions without putting too much responsibility on them (Sperling et al., 2024). Among students, AI literacy would be connected to the sphere of project-based learning, which, in addition to the development of technical skills, would bring about reflective abilities related to ethical questions regarding bias, transparency, and accountability.

2.5 Ethical and Governance Considerations

The advancement of AI in education has raised ethical and governance dilemmas for teachers. The present debate is overrun with themes of fairness, accountability, transparency, and ethics (FATE) (Memarian and Doleck, 2023). Policymakers and institutions must address questions related to equal resource distribution, data privacy, algorithmic bias, and systemic inequalities. Thus, governance mechanisms should extend beyond technical solutions and incorporate participation mechanisms that involve teachers, students, and communities in the development of policies. Karran et al. (2025) expressed the view in support of the multi-stakeholder models of governance that emphasize innovation and responsibility. Technological evolution usually leads to institutional policy development; thus, constant correspondence and flexible policies are key to maintaining public trust and equal conditions.

Figure 4. Ethical and governance framework for human-AI learning ecosystems

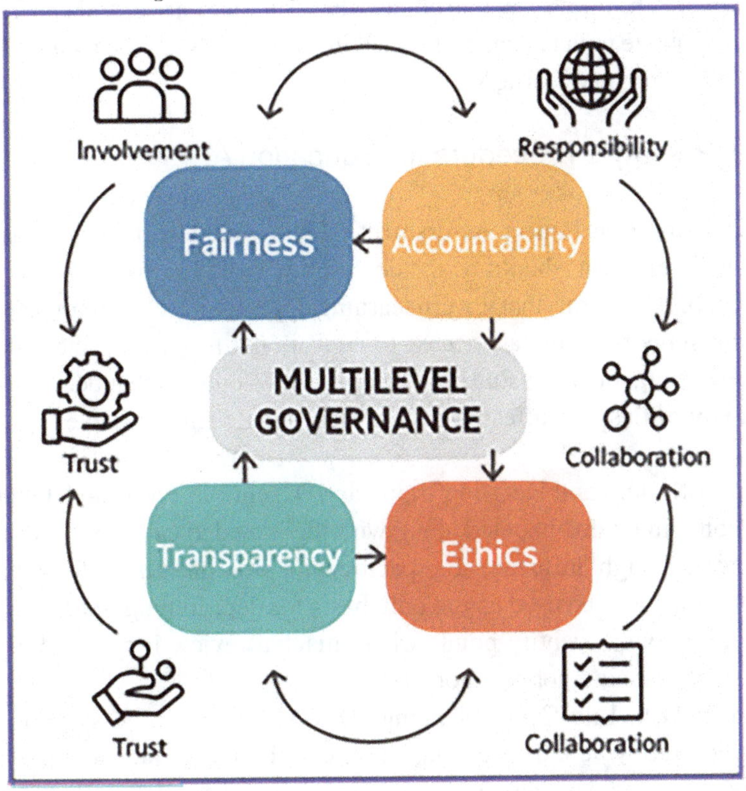

As shown in Figure 4, various aspects of fairness, accountability, transparency, and ethics are interlinked. It emphasises involvement and multilevel governance. This framework emphasises the issue of collective responsibility in AI use.

In principle, and especially in the context of the education sector, discussions about "ethical AI" are mostly theoretical and abstract. In this case, and given the scope of the chapter, fairness and other philosophical questions surrounding the governance of AI will not be dealt with. This chapter provides a conceptual working model for responsible engagement with human–AI learning systems by outlining the attributes of decision rights, documentation, and procedural safeguards to ensure that deployment is auditable and contestable.

Within the educational domain, governance is a balancing act of protective legal and technical oversight while addressing the unique stakes involved: a lack of agency on the part of the students, some degree of developmental fragility, and the potential for automated outputs to assume the role of policy in a matter of seconds. The procedural safeguards that would implement the ethical intent comprise information governance practices that identify points of potential harm and the associated legal, technical, and policy margins that prevent misuse, ensure some degree of oversight in cases where contestable outcomes arise, and ensure that the system is adaptable to the changes that will inevitably arise in the parameters of the model, curriculum, and learners.

2.5.1 A DPIA-Style Procedure for Education AI

A Data Protection Impact Assessment (DPIA) framework, or alternatively, a DPIA-style assessment, should be the default threshold for institutions in the pre-deployment of AI systems that govern learning opportunities, assessment practices, and student support, or dictate access to educational resources. The following is designed to be practical in nature and offers a set of outputs that decision-makers, oversight authorities, and affected stakeholders should find valuable.

Step 1: System and Decision Boundary Definition. Each model and vendor version will be documented along with the intended users and decisions that the system might influence. Be specific with prohibited uses (for instance, the system may not be used as the only basis for determining grades, discipline, or admissions). Identify points where manual review is required and where the system should not be automated.

Step 2: Data Life Cycle Mapping (DLCM). Discuss the system data that is processed, where data are gathered, how long data are stored, who could view processed data, and where the processing of the data is done (including if and where data are processed across borders). Indicate if system prompts and outputs are logged and if any data pertaining to students are used for the purpose of training or fine-tuning.

Step 3: Purpose Limitation and Lawful Basis Establishment. In simple terms, delineate the educational purpose and the legal/administrative basis for the data to be processed. Show minimisation by establishing that each data point is linked to a need. If the data subject is a minor, outline some special measures that are to be taken, along with the need for obtaining consent or authorisation, as appropriate.

Step 4: Conduct a Scheduled Consultation. Record a brief consultation involving students, teachers, administrators, and appropriate supporting functions (e.g. disability services, privacy/security). Consensus is not the objective, but to have clear documentation of stated perceived advantages, uses that are not acceptable, and scenarios associated with significantly negative impacts.

Step 5: Assess and document the risk of harm. This risk assessment must address at least: (1) safety and welfare, (2) privacy, (3) equity/non-discrimination, (4) accountability/contested claims, (5) reliability, and (6) validity for the intended

purpose of the AI system. For each risk, document the potential impact (or harm) of the risk, the likelihood of occurrence, the risk's detectability, and the identity of stakeholders who may be disproportionately impacted by the risk.
Step 6: Construct supervisory and regulatory mitigations. Controls must be grounded in present realities and not be intended, for example, supervision, mandatory human intervention, human review, prescribed instructions (primarily system failure response and staff result intervention), training designed around the system's failure, and staff intervention.
Step 7: Assess and document residual risks as part of the record. Changes in risk after mitigation are documented. Determine ownership of the remaining risks. For any high residual risk, document that a responsible authority, presumably a senior executive, has approved the residual risk after conducting a privacy and security assessment.
Step 8: Upload and cite the system-usage statement. Upload a brief document in which you describe the purpose for which the data are used and the purpose for which the data are retained. This document should also provide information about limitations and the process for appealing an outcome or expressing concerns.
Step 9: Determine and document the set of circumstances that will activate a review and the frequency with which you will conduct the review.

2.5.2 Review Periods and Monitoring Triggers

Educational AI systems develop because of factors such as model updates, revisions of vendor contracts, changes to the curriculum, and variations in student demographics. Therefore, governance requires a combination of audits on a timeline and event-driven reviews.

Minimum requirements for reviews on a timeline include gate surveillance pre-deployment, post-launch review surveillance early within 30-60 days, quarterly reviews, and a yearly renewal audit that documentation and vendor commitments are reverified. Additional factors should also trigger the institution to perform an immediate review if there is a model rip and term changes, the vendor alters the contract, the system adds larger or novel assessment populations, serious incidents occur, or there are observational reports suggesting drift.

Audits need to confirm a) compliance with the approved scope and usage ledger, if real b) the generated outputs are trustworthy and appropriate for their designated use, c) equity outcomes, if positive, are changing, d) safety outcomes and their resolution, if positive, are changing, and e) the implemented privacy/security controls are changing. Every audit needs to contain a succinct record of observations of the audit, actions that need to be taken to correct the observations, the role that each action needs to be assigned to, and the timelines or deadlines by which the actions should be implemented.

2.5.3. Appeal and Recourse Workflow

If a constitutionally AI system can analyse and potentially affect the learning pathways (or modifications of learning activities aimed at the identification of the further development of certain psychophysical functions of a student), feedback on assessments, judgments (or the system of student assessments and evaluations), and support systems, student support, appeal, and recourse become governance imperatives. Institutions should consider implementing a rudimentary mechanism of appeal, setting, retention, and administrative governance (including, but not limited to, appropriate retention and distribution of records) of relevant evidence and providing a pathway for timely human review. These should include uncontested AI determination, reassessment of student work, unflagging, refining prompts and workflows, user retraining, and system suspension in the relevant context.

Service expectations must also be explicit. In the context of safety and privacy-sensitive issues, these should be prioritised, and in the context of recourse on disputable issues, there should be defined timelines to review to ensure that recourse can occur within the academic calendar.

2.5.4 Risk Thresholds and Go/No-Go Criteria

The deployment of AI in a system is governed by prescriptive decision rules for Responsible Deployment. Institutions should implement appropriate decision rules to determine the level of risk split across safety and well-being, privacy and data protection, equity and non-discrimination, reliability and validity, and accountability and contestability, assigning appropriate thresholds to each level to determine if a system can proceed, proceed with specific constraints, or be paused.

A deployment should be classified as \"no-go\" when there are residual risks surrounding safety that pose a risk without mechanisms to effectively mitigate them; when there are risks that are both highly consequential and cannot be prohibited; when determined privacy is not acceptable (e.g. without any required data minimisation and when there is no assurance that data retention or deletion will occur); when there is a lack of contestability when outcomes are determined without the existence of, or the ability to exercise, a backing appeals mechanism; or when there is a reasonable possibility of serious and widespread systemic disadvantage to protected or marginalised populations without a reasonable way to mitigate these risks.

The decision to continue under constraints, "go with constraints\" is warranted when the risk is still moderate but has been lowered, if risk scope restrictions are manageable, there is a requirement for a human review, adequate monitoring has been assigned and funded, and there is a pilot with predetermined measurable criteria to exit the pilot phase. A complete "go\" decision is only warranted with low residual risk (or moderate risk, acceptable within documented existing risk controls) as piloted, with evidence demonstrating that the system continues to function in an acceptable manner within the relevant context, and sufficient foundational governance documents are in existence and current (DPIA, use notice, logging plan, audit schedule, and appeal mechanism workflow). More systems should be paused or rolled back after approvals if there is an increase in incident rates beyond preset thresholds, data or algorithm drift without timely mitigation, vendor terms change in an undesirable way, or if there are new prohibited use cases that cannot be controlled.

2.6 Multi-Stakeholder Perspectives in Education

Participating in human-AI learning ecosystems requires an understanding of the diverse perspectives of the community and stakeholders. The pedagogy of teaching and student welfare is a concern for teachers, whereas students are more concerned with the usability and relevance of technology. Policymakers are targeting educational purposes, but developers are focusing on expansionary and usable aspects of AI. As Sanusi et al. (2024) found, it is necessary to bridge these perspectives through iterative dialogue and co-creation mechanisms, where each group recognises its contribution to shaping outcomes. Structured frameworks of participatory design aid the process, stakeholder-first AI literacy strategies (Dominguez Figaredo and Stoyanovich, 2023), and deliberation that involves the voices of various stakeholders.

2.7 Summary of Literature Gaps

Although there has been significant progress in the literature over the past few years, several gaps remain. First, it has been found that little longitudinal evidence exists regarding the sustainability of stakeholder engagement methods. Second, most AI literacy frameworks focus on teachers or students, whereas models that consider the community perspective are less common. Third, governance systems tend to focus on policies at higher levels without considering local issues. Finally, more empirical data on the long-term impact of generative AI on feedback, evaluation, and curriculum customisation are needed. These gaps are important to address to create resilient and inclusive human-AI learning ecosystems that are also ethically grounded.

3.1 Conceptual Framework

The theoretical framework presented in this chapter aims to integrate various approaches to the concept of participatory artificial intelligence (AI) within the educational context. It also combines participatory design, responsible AI, and digital literacy theoretical underpinnings, and includes the principles of inclusivity, transparency, and engagement. The framework can be considered a scaffold that will help us better understand how AI can change and become more than just a technological tool and a partner in the learning ecosystem. The framework aims to achieve two main objectives: first, to demonstrate how participatory approaches democratise AI design and adoption in education; and second, to underscore the importance of ethical considerations and literacy-building among stakeholders. This lays the groundwork for practical applications in classrooms, policies and governance structures.

Figure 5. Decision map of a human–AI learning ecosystem

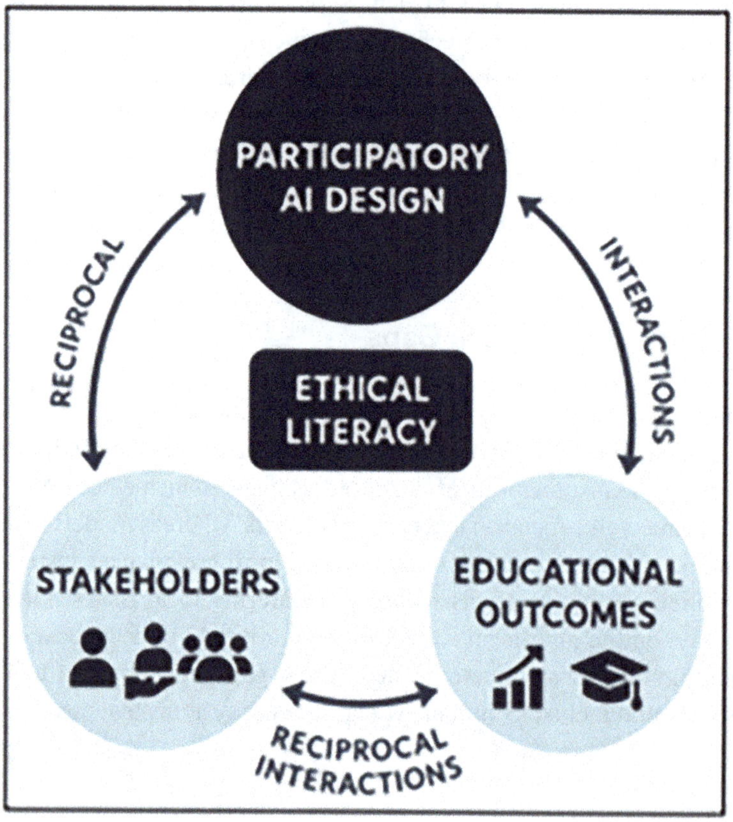

In Figure 5, we map the decision points where the deployment of AI may affect educational outcomes (instructional feedback, student support referral, integrity flagging, accommodation, and resource allocation). The figure elucidates what is most critical for leaders to exercise governance: where human decision-making is imperative, where AI is a non-consultative adviser, and where the line must be drawn on automation. It also identifies the most salient failure modes for each decision point (hallucination, bias, privacy leakage, and over-reliance) so that safeguards may be assigned to the appropriate stage in the workflow, rather than being abstracted to a principle.

3.2 Core Dimensions of Participatory AI in Education

The model is organised along three anchoring dimensions: (a) participatory co-design, (b) AI literacy and competency, and (c) responsible governance. These dimensions are interactively dynamic, a system that appreciates human agency with the utilisation of computational intelligence. Participatory co-design plays an important role because it eliminates the problem of technological determinism by involving students, educators, and communities in the AI development process (Delgado et al., 2023). AI literacy guarantees people's capacity to critically examine, interact with, and co-design AI systems (Chiu & Sanusi, 2024; Almatrafi et al., 2024). Finally, the principles associated with governance are fairness, transparency, and accountability, which coincide with the ethical imperatives (Memarian & Doleck, 2023; Kashyap et al., 2024).

Figure 6. Implementation levers and required governance artifacts

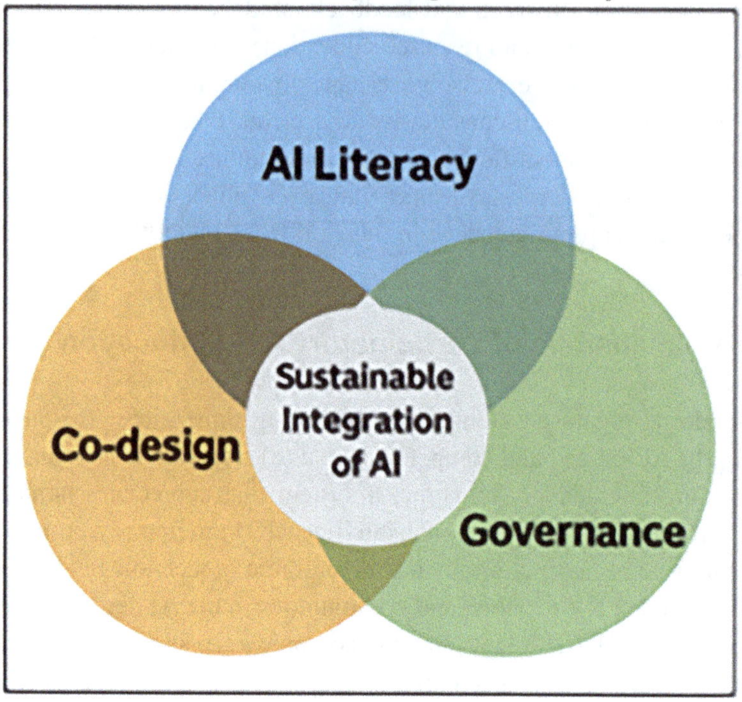

In Figure 6, we map the three dimensions of the chapter reframed as levers for implementation and assign to each of the levers a specific set of concrete artefacts needed to sustain responsible and scalable operation. Co-design produces role-specific requirements and guardrails (approved and prohibited uses and classroom workflow constraints). AI literacy produces user-role-specific training modules and competency evaluations (students, educators, and administrators). Governance produces auditable documents and decision gates (e.g. DPIA-style assessment, logging and retention plan, monitoring cadence, and appeal mechanism) that keep the system contestable and accountable after deployment.

3.3 Stakeholder Roles in Human–AI Ecosystems

Participatory AI ecosystems involve stakeholders in design, implementation, and appraisal activities, as opposed to (being passive recipients of) technology. Educators usually serve as mediators between AI and students to ensure that automated systems support educational goals (Van Leeuwen et al., 2023). AI-driven experiences are not only consumed by students; they can become co-authors of new learning experiences, which are shaped by adaptive dashboards, personalised learning feedback, and collaborative platforms (Pozdniakov et al., 2025). Policymakers and leaders of institutions create regulatory and ethical systems by incorporating guidelines that facilitate innovation and social responsibility (Ahrweiler et al., 2025). Technology developers are expected to produce systems that demonstrate cultural sensitivity, inclusivity, and fairness (Dominguez Figaredo and Stoyanovich, 2023). Collectively, these players have a way of making human-AI systems participatory, fair, and context-sensitive.

Figure 7. RACI for stakeholder responsibilities across the AI lifecycle

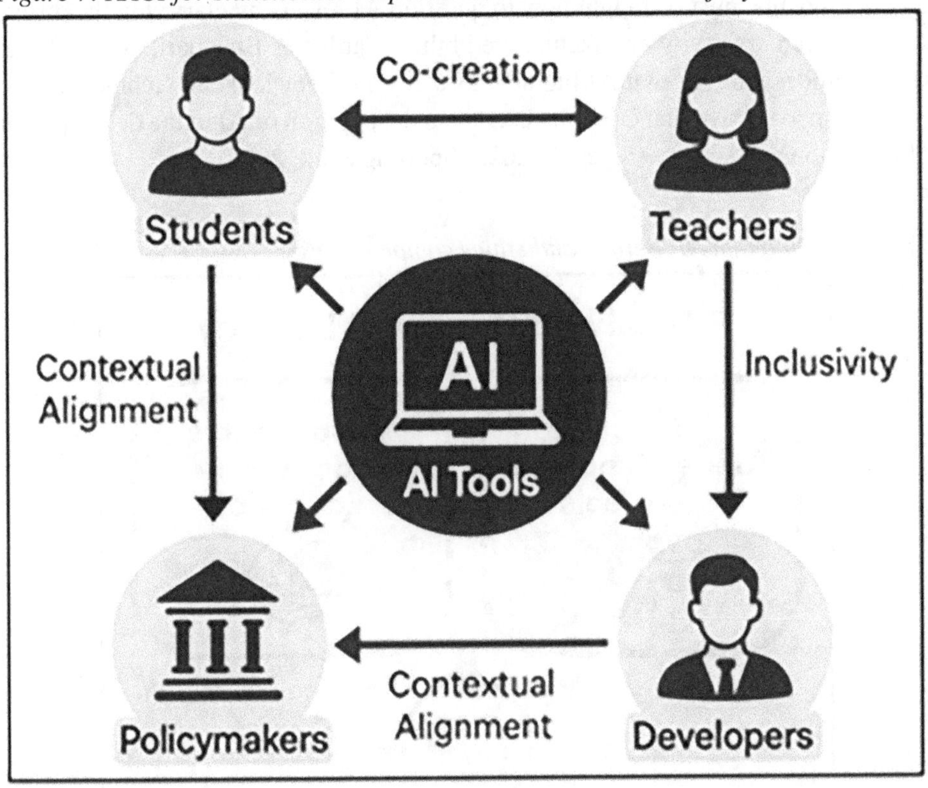

Figure 7 provides a RACI perspective on real-world risk across lifecycle stages, including procurement, configuration, classroom integration, monitoring, incident response, and appeals. provides a real-world perspective on a persistent question of leadership. This is done by allocating accountability for approvals, policy compliance, and issue resolution, as well as naming those who need to be consulted (disability services, privacy/security, etc.) prior to scope creep. This is a way to clarify decision rights and avoid governance gaps, which are often the result of dispersed responsibilities across IT, academia, and vendors.

3.4 Ethical and Critical AI Literacy

Ethical literacy is an important component of this model that allows stakeholders to question, challenge, and redesign AI-driven processes. Essential AI literacy involves informed knowledge of how algorithms are biased, the transparency of the data being used, and the sociopolitical realities that shape the workings of AI (Memarian & Doleck, 2023; Dominguez Figaredo & Stoyanovich, 2023). As another example, teachers should be trained to implement AI-generated analytics effectively without relying too much on the suggestions made by machines (Khosravi et al., 2025). Students must be taught how to question AI results by clarifying the difference between creativity and factual credibility (Pardos & Bhandari, 2024). Thus, ethical guides will see that AI literacy goes beyond knowledge to technical skills, but it is a perspective that critically considers the position of AI in the development of education and society (Su et al., 2023; Sperling et al., 2024).

Figure 8. Minimum AI literacy and ethics competencies

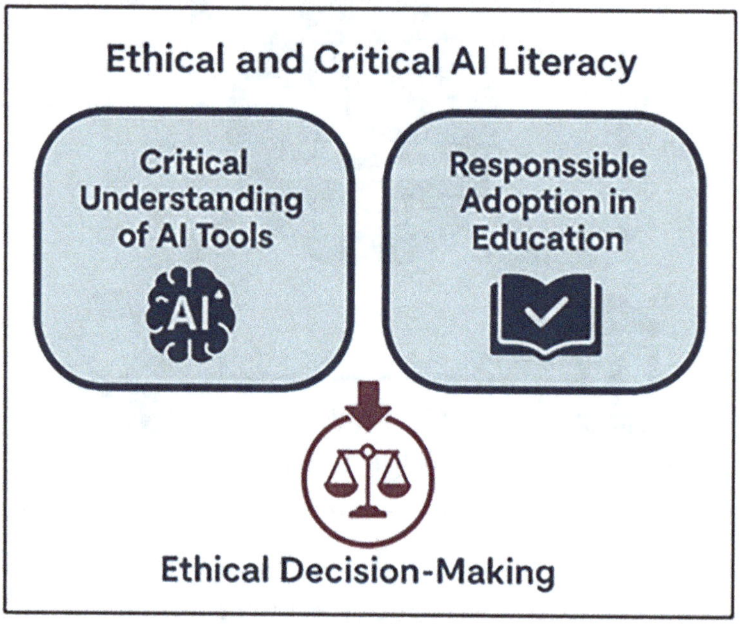

Figure 8 correlates literacy to governance by assigning minimal governance literacy to each of the identified roles (students, teachers, school administrators, and support staff) with governance training, validation (if any), and access controls required. These components are operationalised to connect the normative and aspirational proximity to ethics of "responsible use": mitigating model risk (i.e. be aware when uncertain), avoid and report when outputs are biased, do not document sensitive information about students when AI is employed, or use a transparency protocol to report AI use, and escalate within the AI use concerns governance framework. This operationalises "responsible use" by normatively describing and prescriptively articulating behavioural expectations, thereby facilitating the human layer to interlock with the technical controls to provide scalable oversight.

3.5 Application Scenarios of the Framework

The theoretical perspective is used in different fields of learning and research, including education. Participatory AI also supports the co-design of digital tests that improve literacy and critical thinking in higher education (Martin 2025). In the K-12 context, co-designed with teachers, AI dashboards allow the monitoring of the development of individual learners with diverse backgrounds in terms of discreetly increasing skills and catching up with others (Van Leeuwen et al., 2023). The policy level can also leverage the use of participatory AI by informing the design of the curriculum, as technological advances can be aligned with cultural and ethical priorities (Sanusi et al., 2024; Al-Zahrani & Alasmari, 2024). The framework will foster equity at a global level, ensuring that marginalised communities are not disregarded in terms of AI-based education developments (Hsu et al., 2022). Demonstrating flexibility to the contexts, the framework has been able to display flexibility in application in participatory processes, as well as being inclusive and accountable to the public.

Figure 9. Use-case portfolio by risk tier and required controls

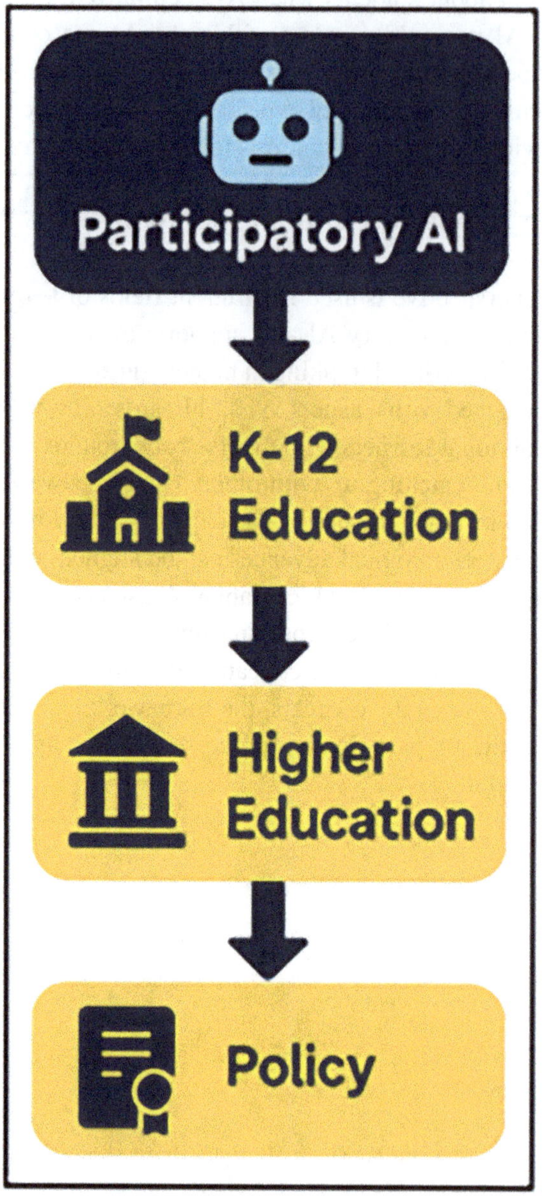

Figure 9 classifies different education AI use cases in the form of a portfolio by risk level (low, moderate, and high) and outlines the minimum required controls of education AI for each risk level. This is designed to address a specific governance concern: which use cases can be approved now? Which use cases require a constrained pilot? Which use cases are unacceptable? The figure indicates that high-risk use cases, such as those involving high-stakes grading, disciplinary action, admissions, or automated accusations of academic dishonesty, need to be either tightly controlled or prohibited altogether. In contrast, lower-risk use cases, such as drafting assistance, can be allowed under a minimum set of controls and ongoing risk supervision.

3.6 Synthesis of the Framework

The synthesis of this conceptual framework indicates that AI in education is a co-evolutionary process affected by the agency of stakeholders, participatory design, and ethical concerns. Rather than viewing AI as an imposition on the rest of the world, the framework places it within human-AI ecosystems, with feedback loops, allowing for continuous refinement (Karran et al., 2025). The combination of participatory design, AI literacy, and governance presents a roadmap for addressing the potential and challenges related to the implementation of AI. Finally, the framework makes it possible to note that the effectiveness of AI in education depends not only on its technological advancement but also on the shared capacity to align AI innovations with human values, equity, and critical thinking (Yang et al., 2024; Kashyap et al., 2024).

Figure 10. End-to-end operating model for responsible deployment

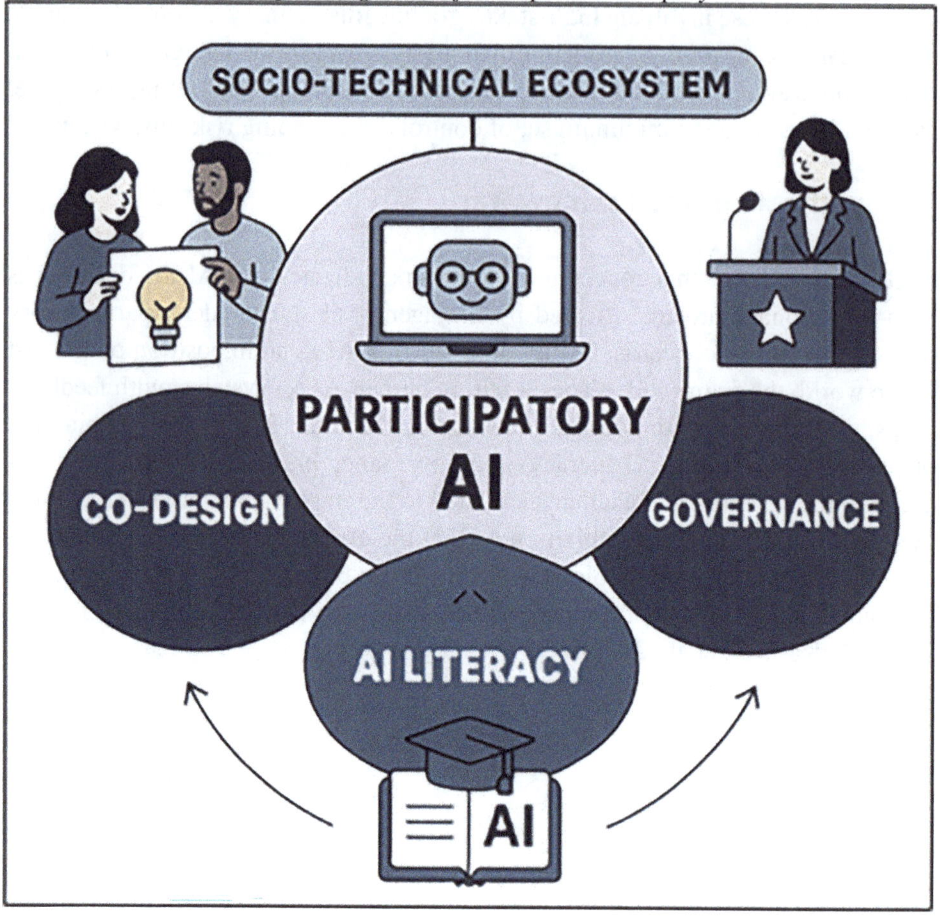

Figure 10 summarises the chapter into one operational model that can be used as a process for leadership. This operational model outlines the necessary governance gates and artefacts from the initial proposal to post-deployment monitoring: a DPIA-style assessment prior to the launch of the process, a temporary pilot phase governed by exit criteria, clearly defined go/no-go thresholds for each phase, a predetermined recurring audit schedule with specific events to trigger the audit, and an appeals/recourse pathway that operationalises feedback into a monitoring and control system. The purpose of the figure is to enable the manager to turn the concept of "ethical AI" from a purely theoretical idea into a cyclical process for governance that is repeatable and can demonstrate continuous improvement over time.

4. ETHICAL, SOCIAL, AND CULTURAL CHALLENGES

4.1 Ethical Challenges

Ethical issues related to artificial intelligence in education (AIED) bring forth the concepts of fairness, transparency, privacy, and accountability as part of the burning moral issues (Al-Zahrani & Doleck, 2023; Al-Zahrani & Alasmari, 2024). These problems have direct implications for the process of student evaluation, the decisions made by teachers, and the organisation of learning pathways. It is unfair to make predictive models treat all students differently, and adaptive systems are likely to inherit biases that were present in the training datasets when the system was trained on an unbalanced dataset (Dominguez Figaredo and Stoyanovich, 2023). It is important to make it transparent as well; if educators are unable to explain the reasoning behind an AI tool, the responsibility becomes ambiguous (Delgado et al., 2023). The use of such a large volume of data related to performance, demographics, and behaviour raises additional concerns related to privacy (Kashyap et al., 2024).

Figure 11. Ethical challenges in AI-enhanced education

Figure 11 highlights fairness, transparency, accountability, and privacy as the pillars of responsible AI, distinguishing the sources of risk from mitigation levers across the AI lifecycle.

4.2 Social Challenges

The applied AI technique has completely changed the nature of the classroom, particularly its equality and accessibility (Ahmed et al. 2024). One of the problems is the expanded digital segregation issue, in which high-achieving schools have access to AI tutors because of the resources available to them, whereas low-income schools do not; therefore, the achievement gap is further widened (Sanusi et al., 2024). Student–teacher relationships are also changing, with algorithmic feedback bypassing the judgments of the teacher; they may no longer be trusted, reducing the human and emotional aspects (Jin et al., 2025). Another challenge is the issue of inclusivity, as AI requires high levels of digital literacy, thus leaving out learners who are not trained in technologies (Sperling et al., 2024). In addition, AI labels such as struggling, gifted, etc., can label students in a durable manner that stigmatises them (Karran et al., 2025).

Figure 12. Social dynamics of AI integration

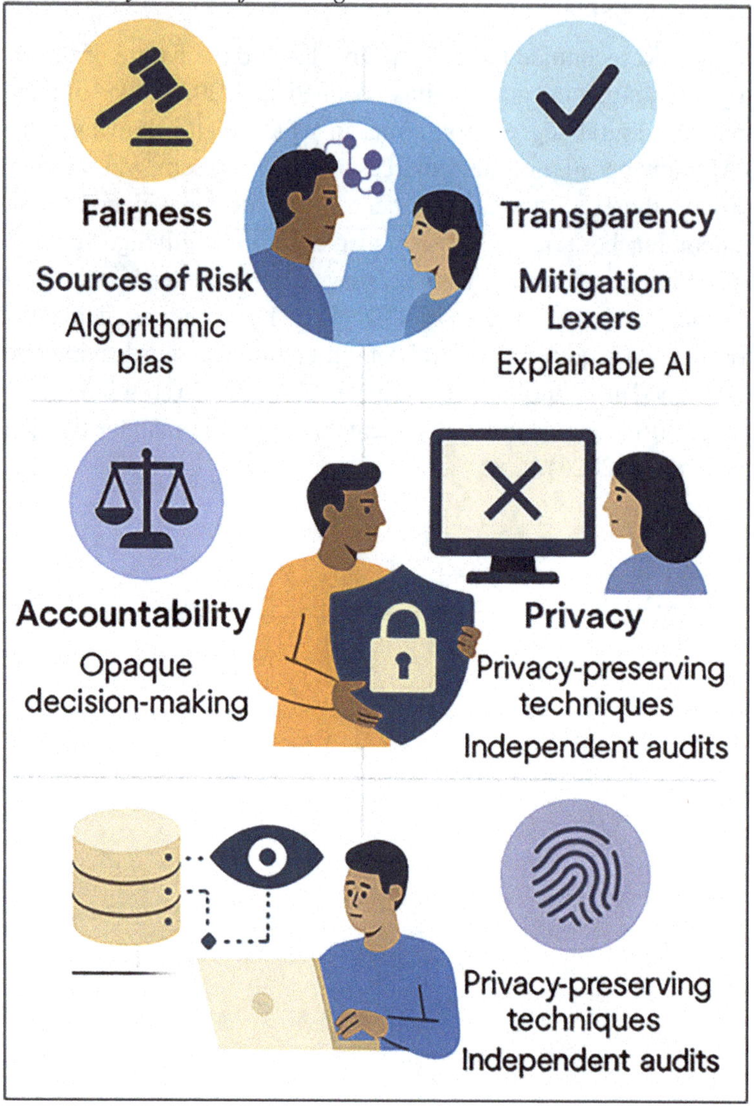

Figure 12 illustrates the digital divide, shifts in authority, and inclusivity risks, demonstrating how AI reshapes equity and classroom relationships.

4.3 Cultural Challenges

AI technologies often ignore local values, traditions, and languages because they are mostly trained on Western datasets (Su et al., 2023). Such divergence may lead to pedagogical disagreements when the intervention fails to resonate with the cultural landscapes of the learners (Yang et al., 2024). Language is an important factor; AI-generated content could be in other languages rather than local ones, or to bring out culture (Zhao 2024). In addition, cultural traditions regarding authority and cooperation determine how learners understand AI educators or grade checkers (Van Leeuwen et al., 2023). The nature of personalised learning, which is characteristic of AI, is dangerous to communal practices (Ahrweiler et al., 2025).

Figure 13. Cultural dimensions of AI in education

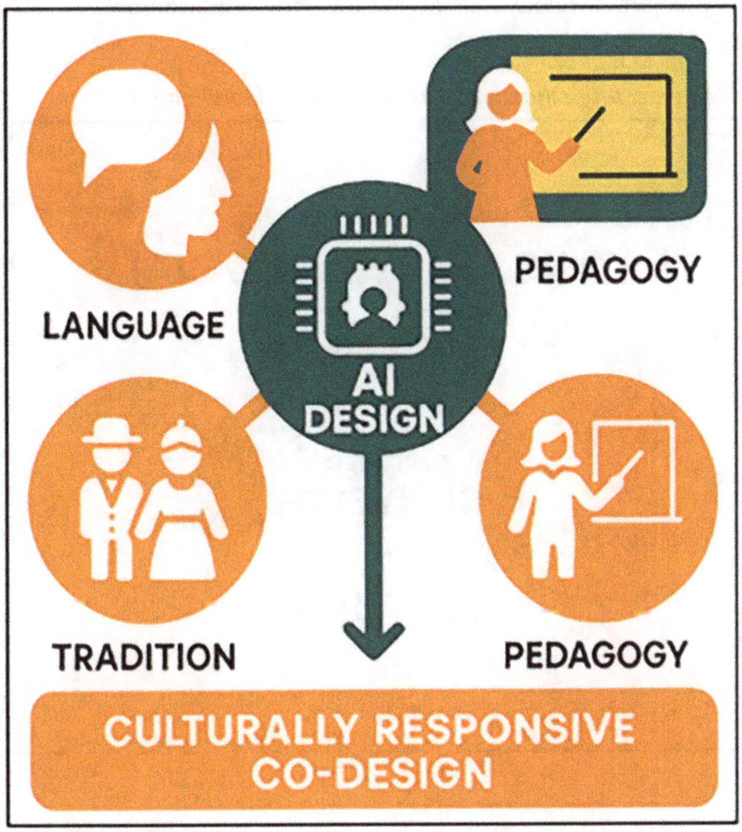

Figure 13 demonstrates the convergence of language, tradition, and pedagogy with AI design, emphasising the significance of culturally responsive co-design.

4.4 Intersection of Challenges

This poses an increased threat, along with ethical, social, and cultural issues. For example, biased algorithms (ethical) could unfairly disadvantage learners who are members of marginalised groups (social) and fail to acknowledge culturally relevant pedagogies (cultural) (Van den Broek et al., 2024; Martin 2025). Compounded harm more closely affects vulnerable groups, an aspect that was brought forth from an intersectional perspective, demanding a comprehensive intervention (Hsu et al., 2022). In the absence of this framework, the risks of interventions only deal with superficial problems without considering the underlying causes.

Figure 14. Intersecting ethical, social, and cultural challenges

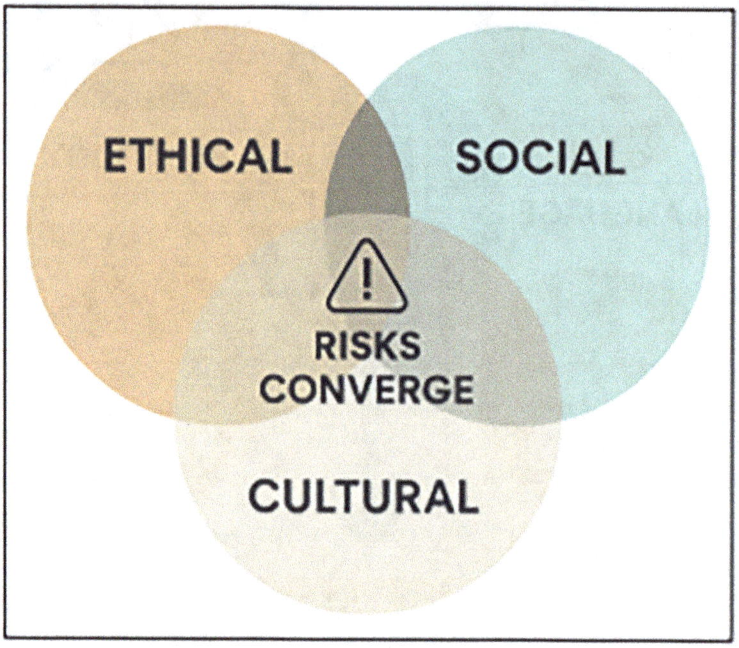

Figure 14 depicts overlaps in the fields, where risks converge, and why a comprehensive approach to solving the problems is necessary.

4.5 Towards Responsible AI in Education

There is an urgent need to incorporate diversity, cultural awareness, and responsiveness into AI design and implementation. Interactions between educators, students, and communities through participatory design can lead to solutions that provide AI with diverse values (Delgado et al., 2023; Ahrweiler et al., 2025). Robust governance policies must go hand in hand with co-design endeavours to create fairness and accountability (Karran et al., 2025). The possibility of using critical thinking in their attitude towards the results of AI is a concern that requires increasing AI literacy among teachers and learners (Almatrafi et al., 2024; Chiu & Sanusi, 2024). Public AIED must be defined as an action that includes constant assessment, the delivery of answers and responses, and the ability to accommodate appropriate contexts (Khosravi et al., 2025). Finally, the task is to achieve a balance between innovation and protection, thereby improving learning and maintaining ethical, social, and cultural integrity.

Figure 15. Framework for responsible AI in education

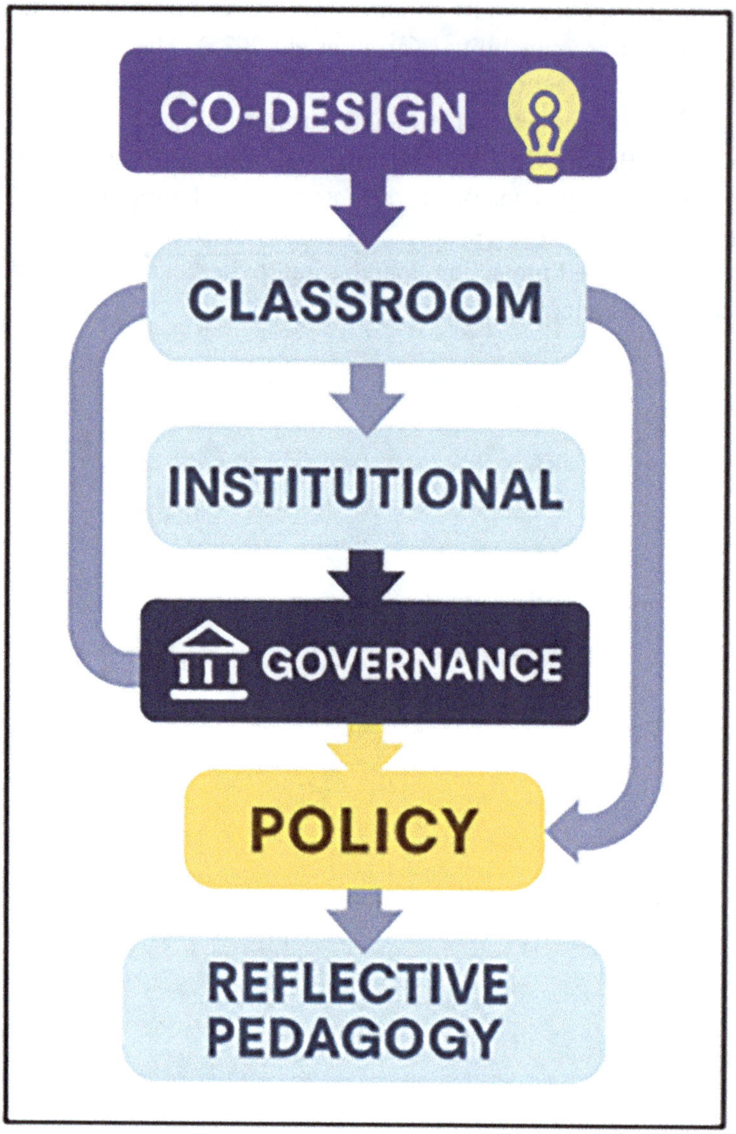

Figure 15 shows the framework for responsible AI in education. This value denotes a path of responsibility among co-design, governance, and reflective pedagogy, and the need to undergo sequential revision at all three levels: classroom, institutional, and policy.

5. ETHICAL, SOCIAL, AND EDUCATIONAL IMPLICATIONS OF PARTICIPATORY AI

Artificial Intelligence (AI) further triggers important ethical, social, and educational assumptions in existing societies, including learning environments. This is the case with participatory AI, where teachers, students, policymakers, and developers participate in the design and development of systems. The former provides an insightful lens on how to manage inclusivity, fairness, and human-centred design concerns in education. Compared to the top-down system of handling technology, the participatory system allows for the introduction of the principles of democracy into the process of manufacturing AI because it is aligned with the ethical principles of equity, transparency, and accountability (Delgado et al., 2023; Kashyap et al., 2024). In this section, the author considers the development of ethical CLs, social interactions, and educational activities that should be employed to integrate PAI into learning without any culpability.

5.1 Ethical Dimensions of Participatory AI

Ethics are sine qua non with respect to the adoption of responsible AI. This problem can be resolved by focusing on fairness, transparency, accountability, privacy, and inclusivity, which can mitigate the risks associated with implementing participatory AI (Dominguez Figaredo and Stoyanovich, 2023; Memarian and Doleck, 2023). Participatory models do not demand efficiency as one of the hallmarks of modern AI development; instead, the programs receive input into the design systems to ensure that the algorithms are not only fair but also sensitive to contexts (Su et al., 2023). Transparency is essential in education because, without explanations regarding algorithmic suggestions, teacher-student trust may be lost (Leeuwen et al., 2023). Privacy issues are also a massive concern since AI applications often deal with sensitive information about students, thus requiring regulatory platforms that will not affect rights but will encourage innovation in the field (Kashyap et al., 2024). By including it, participatory ethics would not only be used in designing pragmatics, but would also be part and parcel of maintaining fairness and communal responsibility among communities (Sperling et al., 2024).

Figure 16. Ethical principles in participatory AI

Figure 16 depicts the ethical principles of participatory AI. This character represents fairness, transparency, accountability, privacy, and inclusivity as ethical concepts that are interrelated. They formulated a balanced framework in combination with directing responsible AI innovations.

5.2 Social Implications and Stakeholder Involvement

Participatory AI has wider social importance than technical implementation and encompasses issues of trust, legitimacy, and access. In this way, students, educators, policymakers, and communities will trust AI systems as they will obtain their legitimacy and create joint educational values (Ahrweiler et al., 2025; Pozdniakov et al., 2025). Through participatory design, the fear of authoritative control can be mitigated as it moves educators and learners to the position of enacteurs rather than recipients of the outcomes of the algorithms (Van Leeuwen et al., 2023). However, involvement should be relevant, since tokenism efforts run the risk of becoming part of the problem of already established power imbalances (Hsu et al., 2022). With the expanded ecosystem of stakeholders, one can ensure that educational technology meets domestic priorities and cultural circumstances, aligning with the social context rather than being implemented solely because of external or corporate interests (Sanusi et al., 2024).

Figure 17. Stakeholder ecosystem in participatory AI

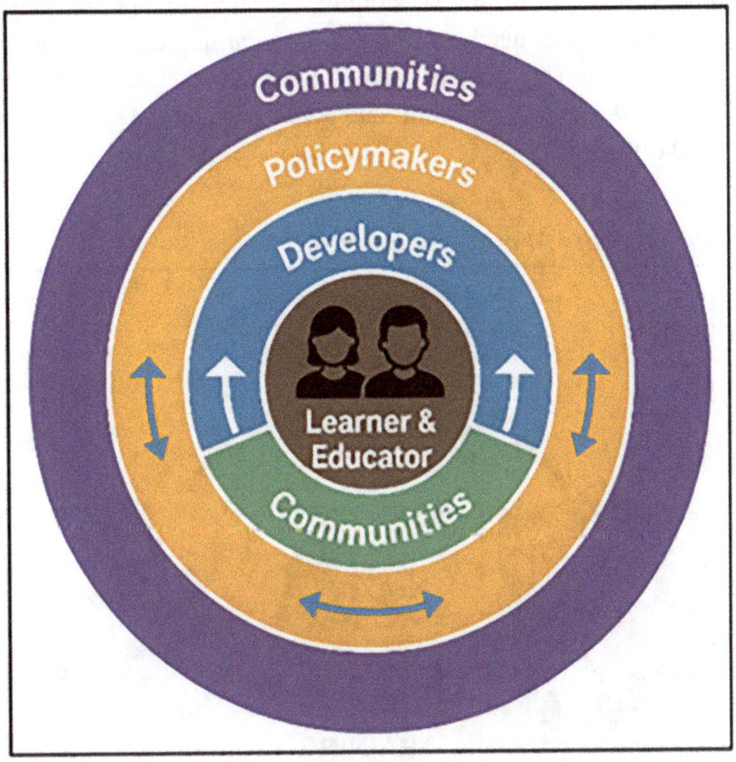

Figure 17 shows concentric circles of stakeholders, including educators, learners, policymakers, developers, and communities. The interdependence of their roles has significant implications for the outcome of participatory AI.

5.3 Educational Transformation through Participatory AI

Education has become a significant platform for engaging in participatory AI. In contrast to conventional paradigms, where students and teachers are treated as passive users receiving AI-powered insights, participatory approaches allow them to become participants in the design of systems and tools (Van den Broek et al., 2024; Martin, 2025). In addition to improving learning outcomes, this process of democratisation facilitates the AI literacy aspect of questioning and challenging the recommendations made by algorithms (Chiu and Sanusi, 2024). Participatory engagement also benefits teachers because they have the opportunity to customise AI tools for educational purposes instead of altering their teaching to suit unbending AI results (Khosravi et al., 2025). Moreover, the participatory framework helps curricula meet the various needs of learners and learning circumstances to make applications in education inclusive and fair (Almatrafi et al., 2024; Zhao, 2024). The introduction of co-design in classrooms and policies makes the sphere of education innovative and diverse.

Figure 18. Participatory AI in education

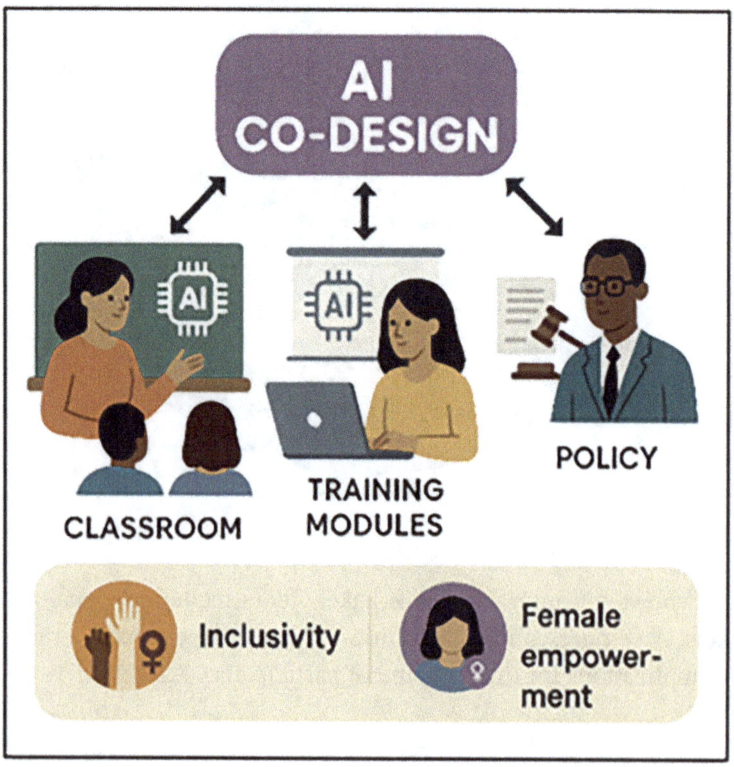

As shown in Figure 18, AI co-design can be effectively employed in classrooms, training modules, and the policy-making process, thereby making it more inclusive and empowering women in terms of participation.

5.4 Addressing Challenges and Risks

The potential outlook is not the only aspect that has flaws and limitations in participatory AI. Disparities in resources can restrict meaningful engagement possibilities, including Internet disparities and vertical building structures (Sperling et al., 2024). Stakeholder conflicts mainly manifest in situations where the terrain of commercial innovation and social responsibility harmonisation is the cause of ethical controversies (Karran et al., 2025). Involvement does not always guarantee the absence of bias, as it may develop in other circumstances due to a failure to protect against it (Dominguez Figaredo and Stoyanovich, 2023). The only way these risks can be addressed is by utilising interactive governance procedures that will reduce the risk of accountability, transparency, and eternal evaluation (Memarian & Doleck, 2023). It should also be noted that training campaigns, which aim to render teachers and students less illiterate on the subject of AI, should play a critical role in ensuring that AI system usage is controlled reflexively (Su et al., 2023; Al-Zahrani and Alasmari, 2024). Simultaneously, it can also serve as a means of educating about justice and reformation, thanks to the traditional approach followed by its foundation, which is based on inclusiveness and flexibility of the curriculum.

Figure 19. Risks and mitigation strategies in participatory AI

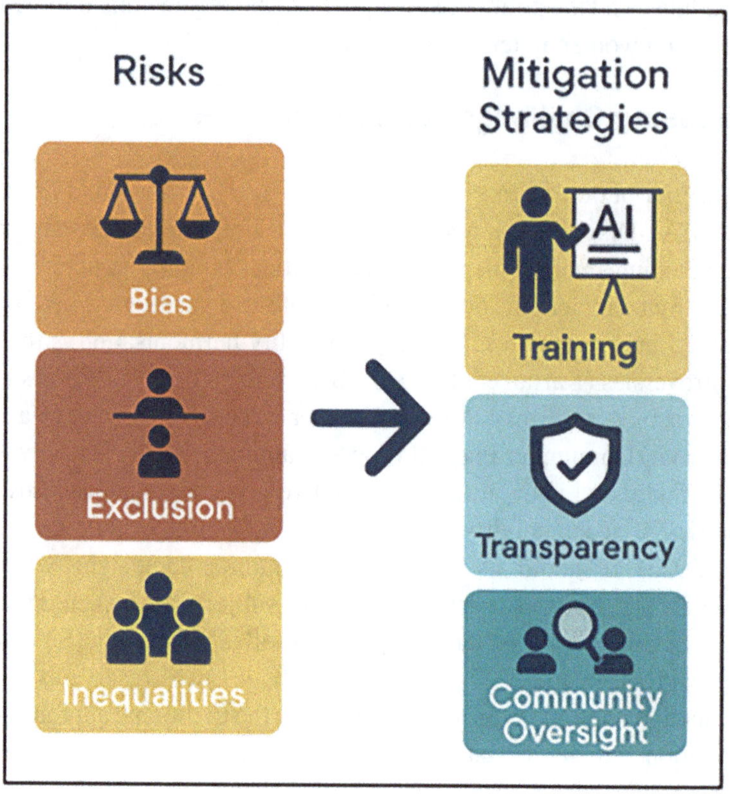

Figure 19 depicts the risks and mitigation strategies for participation in AI. This parameter also comprises risks that may be considered as bias, exclusion, and inequalities, as well as mitigation tactics, which include training, transparency, and community oversight.

6. POLICY AND GOVERNANCE OF PARTICIPATORY AI

The successful impact of Artificial Intelligence on educational activities presupposes that, along with the need to meet legal and legislative regulations, ethical considerations advocated to achieve equity, diversity, and responsibility should be taken into account. Participatory AI supports the steering of governance because multiple stakeholders, such as educators and students, participate in comparing policies and communities, thus making good decisions and transforming the top-down mechanism. When it comes to measuring the aspect of trust and communal accountability within society, AI systems would be capable of internalising the notion of quite similar values into government systems considering the element of participatory design (Delgado et al., 2023; Karran et al., 2025).

6.1 Regulatory Frameworks and Standards

The problem of artificial intelligence (AI) system fairness, accountability, and transparency has become one of the pressing issues upon which international organisations have begun to comment. The values of participatory AI mentioned above, applied to the education industry, can be explained by the fact that the decision-making process in the case includes teachers and learners. They include the need to share information and rules in different forms within the fairness and the option to gain knowledge about algorithmic practices with the assistance of transparency as an element of governance (Dominguez Figaredo and Stoyanovich, 2023; Memarian and Doleck, 2023). Participatory AI encourages greater participatory authority, as opposed to the strict authority inclined to adhere to international standards.

Figure 20. Alignment of participatory AI with global AI policies

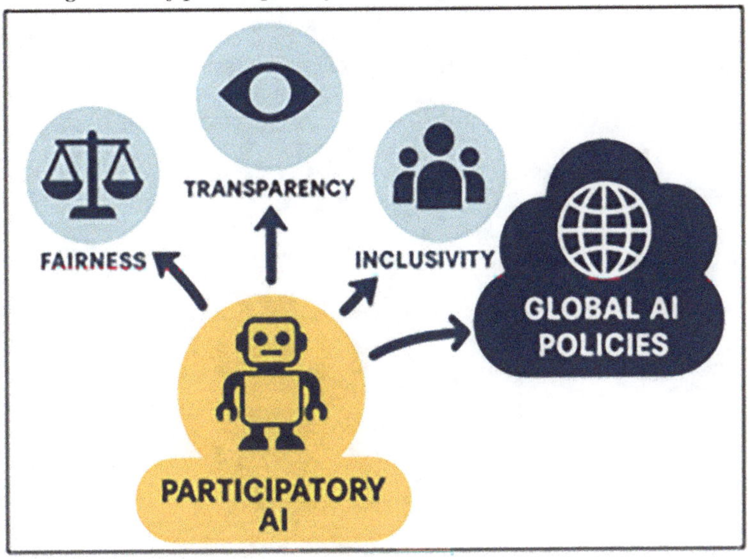

Figure 20 illustrates that participatory AI principles resonate with the framework of fairness, transparency, and inclusivity, thereby increasing consistency in global and educational policies.

6.2 National and Institutional Policies

AI strategies are gaining popularity among governments as methods to help them achieve a balance between innovation and fairness at the national level. The same applies to educational institutions that implement AI literacy courses, have participatory review boards, and other regional governance councils (Chiu & Sanusi, 2024; Almatrafi et al., 2024). The inclusion of the participatory form of AI in governance is changing governance models, where the decision-making process is becoming widespread rather than compliance alone, and the roles of teachers and students are being noted. Such institutional practices are accountable because they address the priorities of the country to realities in the classroom and direct the objectives of policies to local needs (Sperling et al., 2024; Sanusi et al., 2024).

Figure 21. National and institutional AI governance structures

Figure 21 displays governance processes, such as national AI councils, institutional ethics boards, and community forums, in which it is proposed that the incorporation of governance at several levels would make them coherent.

6.3 Governance Challenges

Since these developments have been made, governance systems have several shortcomings. The emergence of regulatory disparities between different regions of the world, inconsistent application, and uneven access to digital resources among various population groups threaten the efficiency of participatory AI (Ahmed et al., 2024; Sanusi et al., 2024). Moreover, the effects of institutional hierarchies are a barrier to effective participatory engagement, as they favour powerful voices and opinions over marginalised communities (Sperling et al., 2024). In the absence of responsive approaches, governance will become prone to uneven development behind technological advancement and contribute to injustice as systemic separation is reached (Broek et al., 2024).

Figure 22. Key challenges in AI governance

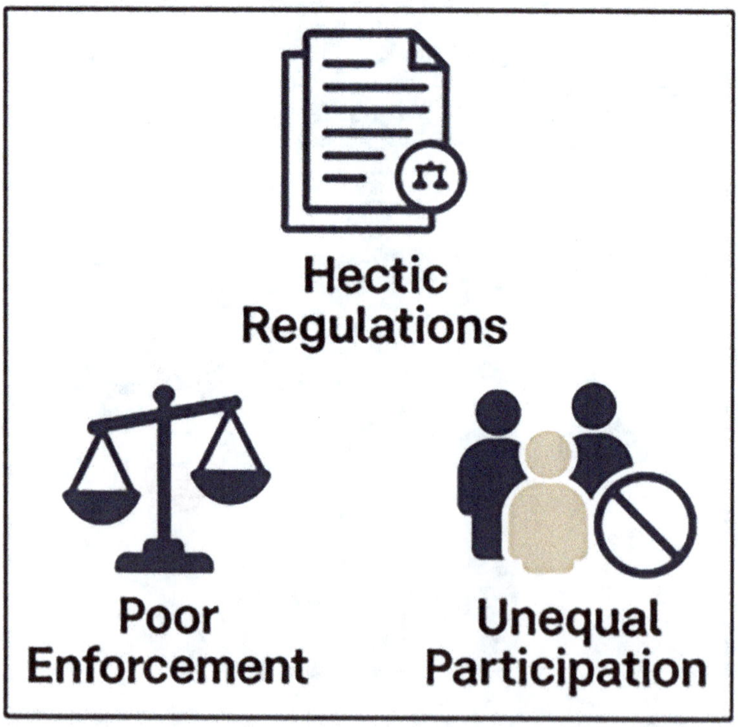

Figure 22 shows the key challenges of AI governance. These character lowlights are hectic regulations, poor enforcement, and unequal participation as key issues of governance.

6.4 Towards Inclusive and Adaptive Governance

Future governance must be dynamic and open-minded to contemplate the eventuality of co-design and communication with stakeholders at an early stage of any policymaking and implementation process. The main idea behind adaptive governance is the closed loop of consultations, drafting, reviewing, and amending to achieve resilience in high-velocity technological environments (Karran et al., 2025; Khosravi et al. 2025). Margin governance emphasises the importance of marginalised voices and promotes balance and equal relations, as it is considered a prerequisite for policies to be deemed context-relevant and socially fair (Ahrweiler et al., 2025; Van Leeuwen et al., 2023). The synthesis of the two styles positions governance as an interactive and multilateral practice that reflects the experiences of students and teachers.

Figure 23. Adaptive governance model for participatory AI

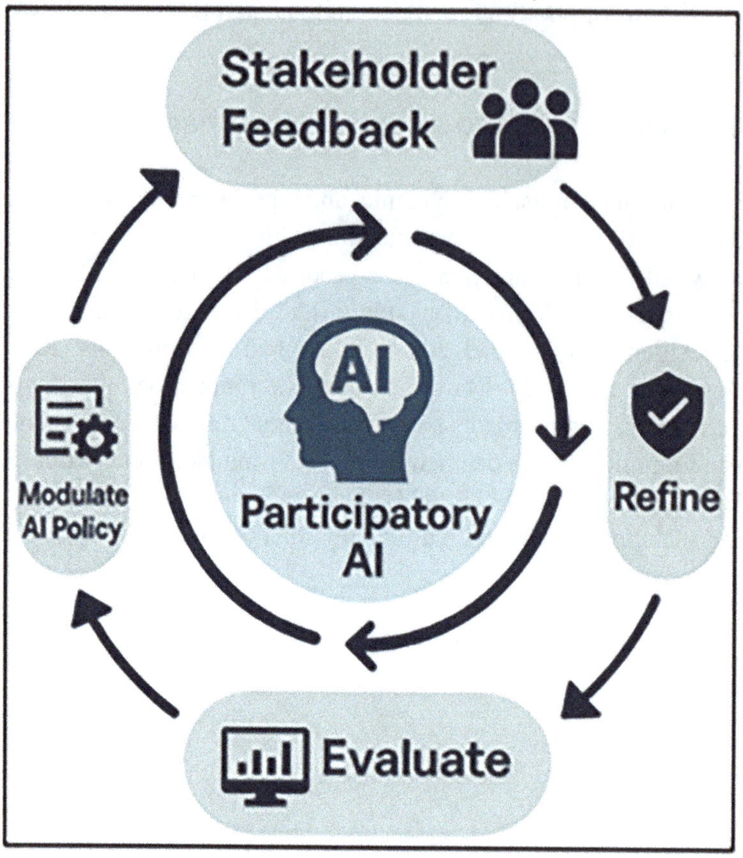

Figure 23 depicts the recursive process of governance, where stakeholder comments can grant warranties, facilitate calculations, and modulate AI policy reciprocals.

6.5 A 90-Day Pilot Blueprint (Milestones, KPIs, and Retrospective)

Unlike an open-ended rollout, the responsible implementation of participatory AI in education should begin with a 90-day pilot program. The 90-day pilot project implements adaptive governance through the incorporation of decision gates, defined measurements, and an established learning cycle. The aim is to determine, based on evidence instead of 'assuming' intent, whether the system should be sanctioned for wider use, sanctioned with conditions, or if use should be stopped or the system retired.

Milestone 1 (Day 30): Control Readiness and Check. By Day 30, the institution must validate that governance is actionable within the daily workflow. Minimum observable outputs should encompass a governed scope (what is approved and what should be prohibited), role-specific access and training completion, logging/recordkeeping adequate for review, and an initial incident/complaint assessment. The Day 30 decision should primarily focus on controllability. If the prohibited uses of the AI tool cannot be deterred or detected, the pilot should be paused until appropriate controls are put in place.

Milestone 2 (Day 60): Value, Safety, and Equity Review. By 60 days, the institution should develop a mid-pilot finding brief describing the first evidence of educational value, reliability, safety, response/reaction times, and inequities (if any) among student groups and/or learning contexts. The Day 60 value vs. risk decision should be a tradeoff. If there are risk signals and the value is marginal, the default should be to redesign or stop; expansion is a poor choice.

Milestone 3 (Day 90): Go/Go-with-Constraints/No-Go. By 90 days, the institution should finalise a decision memo and draft of the governance documentation (updating any governance artefacts, for example, DPIA-style assessment, or equivalent), and should be able to confirm that the documents properly articulate the ongoing (to be around and/or reset) monitoring plan (audit cadence and triggers) and recourse/response directions). Approval should be given, but governance should include strong requirements for monitoring and response frameworks, and funds should be allocated to monitoring and response frameworks.

Five KPIs (to be tracked for 90 days).

(1) **Scope compliance rate:** the percentage of documented/observed usage patterns of the system or program that comply with the approved use cases, the rate at which use-case prohibitions and use-case blanket restrictions are incorporated, and the rate at which such restrictions are enforced.

(2) **Learning value signal:** (an outcome proxy) a learning outcome from the program/system/learning artefact that has been preselected and is appropriate to the context, for example, scored rubrics, any revision improvement goals, quick feedback cycle times, or completion rates of practice tasks has been increased.

(3) **Safety/well-being incident rate:** overall count and severity of harmful/inappropriate outputs per-based-use frequency and resolution time, including escalation and resolution times.

(4) **The equity impact indicator** demonstrates that errors, negative experiences, or adverse outcomes do not cluster disproportionately (e.g. quantitative stratification when feasible, or, otherwise, a structured qualitative review).
(5) **Operational burden:** educator time cost and support load (helpdesk, investigations, training overhead) compared to the perceived overall outcome.

90-Day Pilot Retrospective (Template).

Context: tested use cases; cohort and context; model/vendor/version; and any alterations during the pilot.

KPI results: outcomes and trends per KPI; constraints and confidence caveats.

Incidents and appeals: overview, root causes, resolution time, and implemented correction actions.

What worked: practices/controls that managed to mitigate risk while sustaining value.

What failed: known insufficient positive outcomes (e.g. reliability, bias, privacy, and misuse) and their reasons.

Decision: Go/Go-with-constraints/No-go with clearly defined conditions, responsibilities, and timeframes.

Next 90 days: Top five actions with owners, due dates, and success measures to track results.

6.6 K–12 GenAI Writing Support Mini Case

A district conducted a 90-day trial with a generative writing assistant for 7–8 English Language Arts classes to improve the quality of revisions and reduce the amount of time teachers spend giving first-pass feedback. The district framed this tool as revision coaching rather than assessment. The participation of this generative writing assistant was limited to a defined cohort of classes in a 90-day trial.

Decisions (scope and constraints): The approved uses of the tool included brainstorming, outlining, clarifying prompts, and revision (structure, clarity, and grammar). Prohibited uses included grading, automated scoring, or the submission of AI-authored paragraphs as original work without attribution. Teachers were provided with the stipulation that any AI feedback was summative and that feedback should be revisited. Students had to disclose (with a checkbox and brief statement) when AI was used to draft or revise.

Operational artefacts (examples): The pilot had a weekly dashboard and a one-page model card as tools to maintain evidence of ongoing governance and support the review process.

Weekly Dashboard Preview: Week 6 Requests Scope Compliance Rate 92% (Target 95%): The primary cause was AI-generated text not being flagged. This was mitigated by UI reminders and established classroom routines. Learning Value Signal Gains (Previously Revised vs. Unrevised): 0.4 (Target 0.3) with the strongest improvement gains being in the overall structure and clarity of the text. The rate of Safety Incidents was 1.1 out of 1,000 (target: 2.0), mostly tone-related issues, which were resolved using prompt guardrails. Equity Indicator: Usefulness gap for English Language Learners was closed with the addition of bilingual exemplars and scaffolding in the prompts. Operational Burden Time Use 22 min avg. \ teacher\ wk (Target 30 min) with grade shifting from line edits to conferencing (85% in tier 2) Instructional Time Focus 80% tier 1 routines 100% required time. Volunteers required flex time

Intended Use of excerpt of the model card Scope and Purpose: Intended Use: AI-driven revision coaching and brainstorming. Scope: Not Grading, discipline, admissions, or integrity accusations. Main Scope Risks: Overreliance, inconsistent framing, norm bias, hallucinated claims, and prompt-driven privacy leakage. Controls: Prompt "no identifiers", retention limits for logs, teacher-only incident tagging, and mandatory human review in the tier where outputs may sway summative evaluation.

Results (after 90 days). The district noted small but steady gains in the quality of revisions and the speed of feedback cycles. An initially noted rise in the use of unreported AI-generated texts during the mid-pilot phase fell off as disclosure routines and "coach-not-writer" prompts were strengthened. The major design lesson was centred on equity. Feedback in the textile was generic and thus unhelpful to English language learners until the district implemented scaffolds and made provisions for bilingual texts.

Lessons learned. Integrity outcomes improved, first and foremost, when the workflow made the use of AI transparent and normalised, rather than punitive. Second, for "writing support", a tough policy, UI design, and classroom routines were needed to establish a firm boundary between coaching and content creation. Third, with equity, the risk of usefulness gaps, as detected through feedback from students, was visible, and the gaps were addressable through scaffolding.

7. TECHNOLOGICAL ADVANCEMENTS IN PARTICIPATORY AI

The high dynamic rate of participatory AI is attributed to technological advancements, as this rate enhances inclusivity, openness, and collaboration in the decision-making process. These trends do not emerge in efficiency-oriented frameworks because the adoption of human values would be integrated with the entire lifecycle of an AI, thus creating systems that are not only technically sound but also socially and ethically acceptable (Delgado et al., 2023; Karran et al., 2025).

7.1 Human-Centered AI Frameworks

A more significant participation of AI is the explainable AI (XAI) and reinforcement learning with human feedback (RLHF). XAI enhances transparency in the process by explaining how AI algorithms make suggestions and predictions, thereby providing a more trustworthy association between educators, students, and communities (Memarian and Doleck, 2023; Dominguez Figaredo and Stoyanovich, 2023). Simultaneously, RLHF tries to consider stakeholders because their needs and concerns will be included in the optimisation process, which leaves the results produced less contextual and morally accountable (Van Leeuwen et al., 2023).

Figure 24. Human-centered AI frameworks

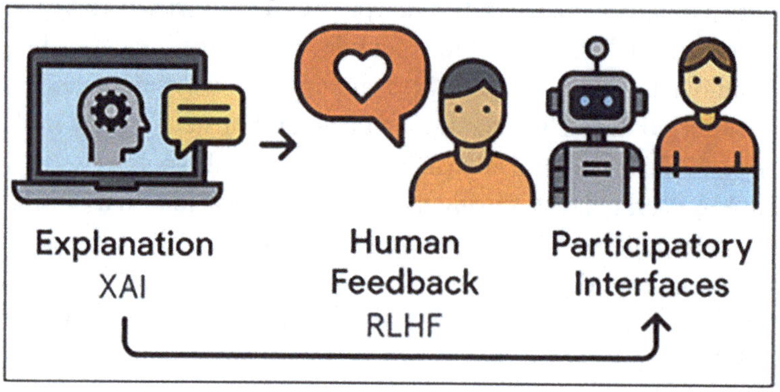

Figure 24 illustrates the integration of human judgment into AI system design using XAI, RLHF, and participation interfaces.

7.2 Interactive Design Platforms

More recent technologies in participatory AI have led to the emergence of systems that can facilitate real-time collaborative learning, providing educators, learners, and policymakers with opportunities to influence the development of these systems directly. Transforming access to and promoting access to participatory dashboards and open-source tools help level hierarchies within institutions by enabling various stakeholders to influence and control the development of AI tools (Chiu & Sanusi, 2024; Sperling et al., 2024).

Figure 25. Interactive design platforms in participatory AI

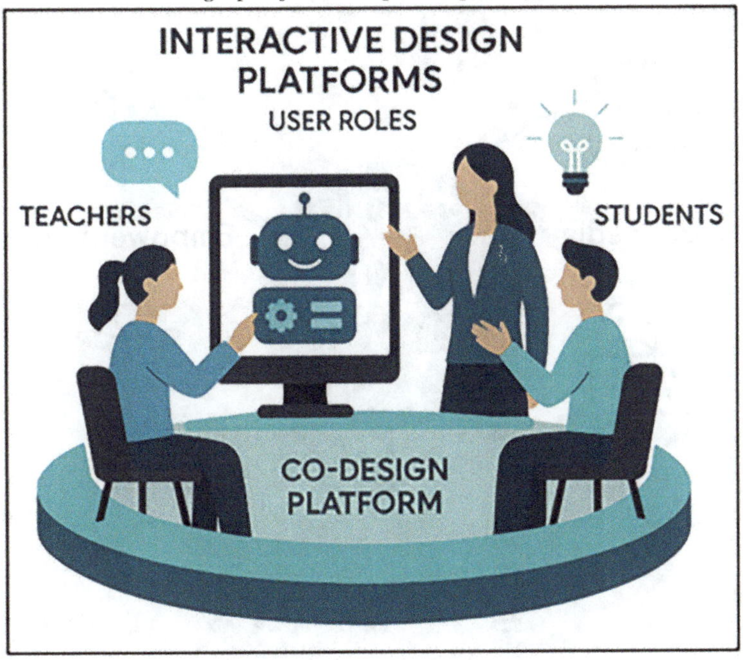

The former is also depicted in Figure 25, where the benefit of collaboration between various user roles in terms of creating AI occurs via co-design platforms.

7.3 Multimodal AI for Participation

The development of multimodal AI systems that can process text, images, language, and behavioural information has greatly enhanced the cohesiveness of participatory design. These technologies ensure access to AI with the involvement of stakeholders with different linguistic, cultural, or literacy backgrounds, and learners with disabilities (Zhao, 2024; Yang et al., 2024). Multimodal AI offers a broader client engagement base because engagement is diversified across various channels.

Figure 26. Multimodal AI for inclusive participation

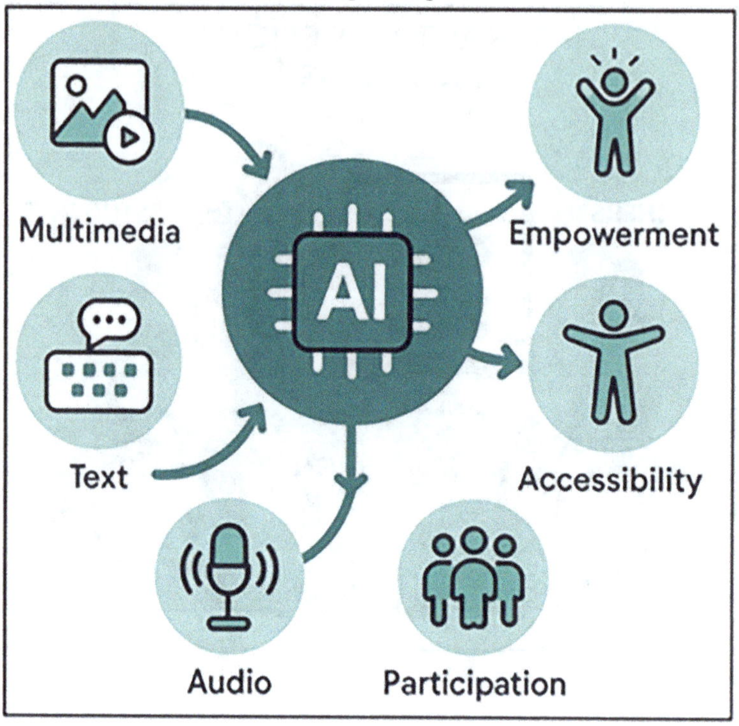

Figure 26 illustrates how accessibility is enhanced through multimodal inputs, including multimedia, text, and audio tools that foster inclusivity.

7.4 Automation with Ethical Oversight

Although the automation of participatory AI has resulted in a more productive process, the necessity of human control cannot be neglected. Through the process of using review checkpoints, educators and communities can maintain control over sensitive decisions arising in the field of grading, evaluation of students, and resource allocation (Van den Broek et al., 2024; Martin 2025). This equilibrium highlights the participatory principle that human beings should not be left out of the loop to ensure accountability and fairness.

Figure 27. Automation and oversight in participatory AI

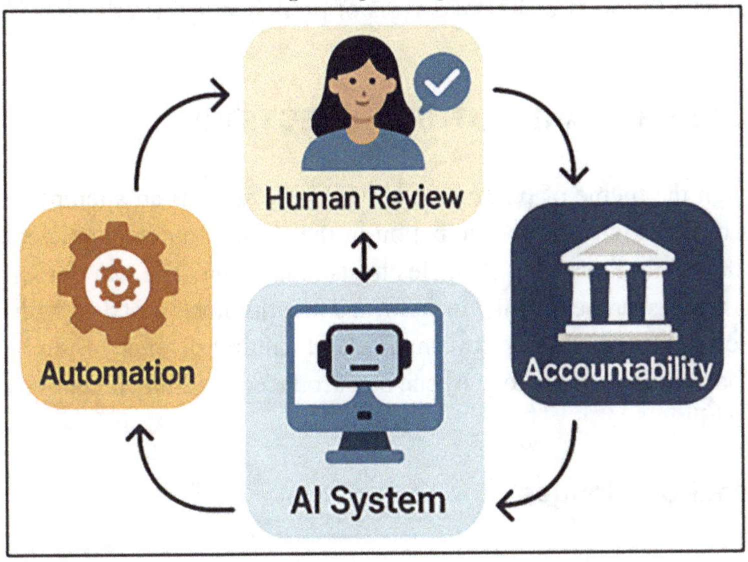

Figure 27 represents the automated procedures that are performed with strengthened human review mechanisms to ensure accountability.

7.5 Emerging Trends and Opportunities

More recent technological changes, including federated learning, blockchain-based governance, and recreational AI literacy programs, have altered the practice of participation in the field. FL enables privacy-safe information sharing because different distributed training may be held, and central information gathering is not required (Kashyap et al., 2024). Blockchain technology provides clear auditing procedures that resolve the problems of trust and accountability (Su et al., 2023). Moreover, AI literacy programs enable educators and learners to question, modify, and collaboratively design AI systems (Almatrafi et al., 2024; Khosravi et al., 2025). Taken together, these trends point to a future with inclusive, resilient, and globally scaled participatory AI.

Figure 28. Emerging trends in participatory AI

Figure 28 shows the interrelationship between federated learning, blockchain auditing, and AI literacy as linked drivers of participatory AI growth.

8. CHALLENGES AND FUTURE DIRECTIONS

Although the theme of participatory AI can be seen as an attempt to enhance the paths to inclusivity and participation in the form of a democratic experience, the system still faces various obstacles to its realisation. The way forward in this domain is that researchers, policymakers, and practitioners must deal with the complexities of ethics, scalability, governance, and cultural diversity. Simultaneously, the development of participatory AI can be introduced as a human-centred approach to sustainability.

8.1 Ethical Challenges

The interlacing of different human mindsets in the development of AI provokes several ethical concerns. Participatory frameworks are based on inclusivity; however, in real-life cases, there is an imbalance in the representation of stakeholders, as marginalised voices are usually outweighed by those that are more technologically literate and have institutional power (Holstein et al., 2019). This imbalance has the potential to institutionalise bias in participatory processes. To address this, deliberate expertise in achieving such recruitment, inclusive facilitation approaches, and tools that facilitate continuous audits of algorithmic results must be in place so that the preferential result is not only a dream realised but also a reality (Jobin et al., 2019).

8.2 Scalability and Practical Implementation

Although small-scale projects point to the promise of a participatory approach, scaling them to larger educational systems, nations, or even the use of AI worldwide adds considerable complexity. Various stakeholder groups tend to have competing interests, and the need for resources in the form of time, skills, and money tends to exceed what institutions or governments can provide (Selwyn, 2019; Holmes et al., 2021). This has seen participatory pipeline scaling as one of the research questions that have come to the fore, requiring new methodological approaches that are more inclusive yet efficient, enabling implementation on a broader scale.

8.3 Data Privacy and Security Concerns

AI using a participatory approach regularly involves the exchange of sensitive information relating to education, health, and the community with various stakeholders. Strong protective measures, such as the use of federated learning or the application of differential privacy algorithms, are essential to ensure that participants are not afraid to take part in the project, which also destroys the trust that is built (Zawacki-Richter et al., 2019; Su et al., 2023). It is necessary to balance confidentiality and free cooperation by implementing frameworks that combine technical protection, open communication, and a clear understanding of how data are used, stored, and safeguarded.

8.4 Governance and Accountability

The question of who takes control of the participatory AI decision-making process remains unanswered. The task is usually decentralised between developers, policymakers, educators, and communities; however, in turn, the division alleviates the task of holding a culprit liable or biased (Floridi & Cowls, 2019; Williamson & Piattoeva, 2022). Not all regulatory responses are the same across jurisdictions; hence, enforcement is fragmented. To overcome these issues, the trend in governance should shift to more adaptive models that strike the right balance between innovation and democratic governance, which involves setting open conflict resolution procedures and establishing ethical guidelines that are binding (Jobin, Ienca & Vayena, 2019).

8.5 Cultural and Contextual Diversity

Participatory AI is characterised by not applying universality but by considering cultural settings. Models originating in Western settings may not consider the values and practices of societies with other traditions of governance and education (Eubanks, 2018; Robertson, 2021). Such disconnection threatens to create digital colonialism, in which world systems are remodelled abroad according to external priorities. Culturally sensitive participatory practices should be emphasised in the future, as much of it is to be done at a local level, but it should not depart entirely from the global norms of equity and inclusivity (Knox 2020).

8.6 Future Opportunities

Nonetheless, it is necessary to note that participatory AI has substantial potential to change the interaction between intelligent systems and humans. Under the proposed conditions of AI literacy being developed both in schools and in the community, people will have the means to improve the process of actively engaging in design processes as well as becoming serious co-creators and no longer being mere users (Luckin, 2018; Selwyn, 2022). Participatory systems with a policy focus have the potential to integrate the voices of communities into regulatory frameworks; thus, innovation is more socially acceptable (Floridi & Cowls, 2019). It is more efficient and does not exclude the participation of people, as hybrid models combining automation and structured human control would not leave the most sensitive fields, such as education and healthcare untouched (Williamson & Piattoeva, 2022). Furthermore, an interdisciplinary effort by educators, engineers, ethicists, and social scientists would pave the way for holistic designs that are not only well-defined in terms of proficiency but also socially responsive (Holmes et al., 2019; Khosravi et al., 2025). Overall, these directions indicate where participatory AI could take a step beyond theoretical idealism into a realistic base of equitable, democratic, and people-centred information.

9. CONCLUSION

As noted in this chapter, participatory artificial intelligence (AI) is a promising technological and sociocultural paradigm shift. In contrast to conceiving AI as an agency left only to professionals, participatory AI aims to promote shared accountability, inclusion, and transparency, as it directly incorporates the human voice into intuitive system design, implementation, and governance. This perspective plays a significant role in education, governance, and social activities as AI technologies increasingly influence opportunities, access to knowledge, and decision-making. Various pieces of literature have provided frameworks on AI literacy, collaborative and co-design projects, and models where the communities first incorporated into the process of AI design began to show that, in such cases, the results are not only more ethical but also closer to what is needed in real life. Nonetheless, according to this chapter, there are hurdles on the way towards scalability, data privacy, cultural diversity, and the establishment of governance that defines the balance between innovation and accountability. Unless these obstacles are dealt with carefully, there is a high possibility that they will strengthen inequality or erode public trust in artificial intelligence. The future direction lies in enhancing three key pillars: augmenting AI literacy and education to empower stakeholders with the knowledge and confidence to become involved; building multi-disciplinary partnerships that encompass the examination of technical, ethical, and social dimensions; and creating sound policy frameworks that can institutionalise the values of participation on a broad scale. The final result of participatory AI would, therefore, be a vision of human-centred innovation, where systems cannot be imposed on communities but rather co-designed with them, safeguarding that AI development leads to the achievement of fairness, inclusivity, and sustainable development of societies.

REFERENCES

Ahmed, Z., Shanto, S. S., Rime, M. H. K., Morol, M. K., Fahad, N., Hossen, M. J., & Abdullah-Al-Jubair, M. (2024). The generative AI landscape in education: Mapping the terrain of opportunities, challenges and student perception. *IEEE Access : Practical Innovations, Open Solutions, 12*, 147023–147050. Advance online publication. DOI: 10.1109/ACCESS.2024.3461874

Ahrweiler, P., Späth, E., Siqueiros García, J. M., Luque Capellas, B., & Wurster, D. (2025). Inclusive technology co-design for participatory AI intelligence. In *Participatory Artificial Intelligence in Public Social Services* (pp. 25–42). Springer., DOI: 10.1007/978-3-031-71678-2_2

Al-Zahrani, A. M., & Alasmari, T. M. (2024). Exploring the impact of AI on higher education: The dynamics of ethical, social, and educational implications. *Humanities & Social Sciences Communications, 11*, 302. DOI: 10.1057/s41599-024-03432-4

Almatrafi, O., Johri, A., & Lee, H. (2024). A systematic review of AI literacy conceptualisation, constructs, implementation, and assessment efforts (2019–2023). *Computers and Education Open, 6*, 100173. DOI: 10.1016/j.caeo.2024.100173

Chiu, T. K. F., & Sanusi, I. T. (2024). Define, foster, and assess student and teacher AI literacy and competency for all. *Computers and Education Open, 6*, 100182. DOI: 10.1016/j.caeo.2024.100182

Delgado, F., Yang, S., Madaio, M., & Yang, Q. (2023). *The participatory turn in AI design: Theoretical foundations and the current state of practice. Equity and Access in Algorithms, Mechanisms, and Optimization (EAAMO '23)*. ACM., DOI: 10.1145/3617694.3623261

Domínguez Figaredo, D., & Stoyanovich, J. (2023). Responsible AI literacy: A stakeholder-first approach. *Big Data & Society, 10*(2), 20539517231219958. Advance online publication. DOI: 10.1177/20539517231219958

Domínguez Figaredo, D., & Stoyanovich, J. (2023). Responsible AI literacy: A stakeholder-first approach. *Big Data & Society, 10*(2), 20539517231219958. DOI: 10.1177/20539517231219958

Hsu, Y.-C., Huang, T.-H., Verma, H., Mauri, A., Nourbakhsh, I., & Bozzon, A. (2022). Empowering local communities using artificial intelligence. *Patterns (New York, N.Y.), 3*(7), 100449. DOI: 10.1016/j.patter.2022.100449 PMID: 35510187

Jin, F. J.-Y., Maheshi, B., Lai, W., Li, Y., Chen, G., Charwat, N., & Tsai, Y.-S. (2025). Students' perceptions of GenAI-powered learning analytics in the feedback process: A feedback-literacy perspective. *Journal of Learning Analytics, 12*(1). Advance online publication. DOI: 10.18608/jla.2025.8609

Karran, A. J., et al. (2025). Multi-stakeholder perspective on responsible AI in education. *npj Science of Learning, 10,* 13. DOI: 10.1038/s41539-025-00333-2

Kashyap, R., Samuel, Y., Friedman, L. W., & Samuel, J. (2024). Editorial: Artificial intelligence education & governance. *Frontiers in Artificial Intelligence, 7,* 1443386. DOI: 10.3389/frai.2024.1443386 PMID: 39011026

Khosravi, H., Shibani, A., Jovanović, J., Pardos, Z. A., & Yan, L. (2025). Generative AI and learning analytics: Pushing boundaries, preserving principles. *Journal of Learning Analytics, 12*(1), 1–11. DOI: 10.18608/jla.2025.8961

Martin, A. F. (2025). Participatory co-design and evaluation of a novel AI-integrated assessment aimed at improving critical AI literacy. *Behavioral Sciences (Basel, Switzerland), 15*(6), 808. DOI: 10.3390/bs15060808 PMID: 40564589

Memarian, B., & Doleck, T. (2023). Fairness, Accountability, Transparency, and Ethics (FATE) in AI and higher education: A systematic review. *Computers & Education: Artificial Intelligence, 5,* 100152. DOI: 10.1016/j.caeai.2023.100152

Pardos, Z. A., & Bhandari, S. (2024). ChatGPT-generated help produces learning gains equivalent to human tutor-authored help on mathematics skills. *PLoS One, 19*(5), e0304013. DOI: 10.1371/journal.pone.0304013 PMID: 38787823

Pozdniakov, S., Brazil, J., Mohammadi, M., Dollinger, M., Sadiq, S., & Khosravi, H. (2025). AI-assisted co-creation: Bridging skill gaps in student-generated content. *Journal of Learning Analytics, 12*(1), 129–151. DOI: 10.18608/jla.2025.8601

Sanusi, I. T., Agbo, F. J., Dada, O. A., Yunusa, A. A., Aruleba, K. D., Obaido, G., Olawumi, O., & Oyelere, S. S.Centre for Multidisciplinary Research and Innovation (CEMRI). (2024). Stakeholders' insights on artificial intelligence education: Perspectives of teachers, students, and policymakers. *Computers and Education Open, 7,* 100212. DOI: 10.1016/j.caeo.2024.100212

Sperling, K., Stenberg, C.-J., McGrath, C., Åkerfeldt, A., Heintz, F., & Stenliden, L. (2024). In search of artificial intelligence (AI) literacy in teacher education: A scoping review. *Computers and Education Open, 6,* 100169. DOI: 10.1016/j.caeo.2024.100169

Su, J., Ng, D. T. K., & Chu, S. K. W. (2023). Artificial intelligence (AI) literacy in early childhood education: The challenges and opportunities. *Computers & Education: Artificial Intelligence*, *4*, 100124. DOI: 10.1016/j.caeai.2023.100124

Van den Broek, S., Sankaran, S., & de Wit, J. (2024). Exploring the supportive role of artificial intelligence in participatory design: A systematic review. *Proceedings of the Participatory Design Conference (PDC '24)*. ACM. DOI: 10.1145/3661455.3669868

Van Leeuwen, A., Strauß, S., & Rummel, N. (2023). Participatory design of teacher dashboards: Navigating the tension between teacher input and theories on teacher professional vision. *Frontiers in Artificial Intelligence*, *6*, 1039739. DOI: 10.3389/frai.2023.1039739 PMID: 37304525

Yang, H., Zhang, D., Guo, W., & He, Y. (2024). Constructing a STEM projects design framework for middle school AI courses: Developing students' AI literacy as project goals. *IEEE Access : Practical Innovations, Open Solutions*, *12*, 1. Advance online publication. DOI: 10.1109/ACCESS.2024.3512499

Zhao, Y.-Y. (2024). The creative cosmos beyond humans: A symphony of participatory design and visual AI. *Frontiers in Communication*, *9*, 1440384. DOI: 10.3389/fcomm.2024.1440384

Chapter 11
Secure Coding and Generative AI:
Building Ethical Foundations for Student Coders

Hanh Le
http://orcid.org/0009-0007-8172-0809
University of the Cumberlands, USA

ABSTRACT

As generative AI tools, such as GitHub Copilot and ChatGPT, become embedded in programming education, they are reshaping how students learn and write code. While these tools increase access, speed, and engagement, they also raise concerns related to insecure code, plagiarism, and reduced understanding of core concepts. This chapter examines how educators can strike a balance between the benefits of AI-assisted coding and the technical and ethical responsibilities associated with secure software development. Drawing on classroom cases and student insights, it presents a framework that integrates AI literacy, secure-by-design principles, and ethical reflection. Key topics include common vulnerabilities in AI-generated code, strategies for pairing AI output with human review, and approaches for assessing human-AI collaboration. The chapter offers practical recommendations for curriculum redesign and educator training to help students develop safe, responsible, and ethical coding practices in an AI-rich learning environment.

INTRODUCTION

The rapid integration of generative artificial intelligence (AI) tools into computer science education has transformed how students engage in coding, problem-solving,

DOI: 10.4018/979-8-3373-6063-8.ch011

and software development. Platforms such as GitHub Copilot and ChatGPT are now familiar companions in both introductory and advanced programming courses, offering learners instant code suggestions, debugging assistance, and adaptive explanations that enhance their understanding of the material. These tools promise unprecedented access and efficiency, enabling students to overcome syntactic barriers, accelerate project development, and experiment more freely with complex programming patterns. As institutions seek equitable learning futures, generative AI has become a catalyst for expanding participation and reducing traditional entry barriers in computing education.

Yet the accelerating adoption of AI-assisted coding also introduces significant pedagogical, ethical, and security challenges. Early research shows that while AI can support learning, it can also generate insecure code, obscure fundamental reasoning, and encourage reliance on automated solutions without critical evaluation. Students may adopt vulnerable patterns—such as hardcoded credentials, unsafe input handling, or misconfigured APIs—without understanding their implications. Additionally, issues of plagiarism, authorship, and accountability complicate assessments of student work, raising questions about the boundaries of ethical tool use. These emerging risks underscore the need for frameworks that equip learners not only to utilize AI effectively but also to do so responsibly and securely.

This chapter examines how educators can navigate this evolving landscape. It argues that secure-by-design thinking and ethical reflection must become central components of AI-augmented programming instruction. Drawing on classroom case studies, student interviews, and analyses of real AI-generated vulnerabilities, the chapter proposes a pedagogical model that integrates AI literacy, foundational security principles, and human-AI collaborative practice. Rather than seeing AI as a replacement for human reasoning, the model positions AI as a partner whose outputs must be interrogated, validated, and contextualized within secure software development processes.

By exploring instructional strategies, assessment approaches, and recommendations for curriculum redesign, this chapter provides educators and institutions with actionable guidance for preparing the next generation of programmers to navigate both the opportunities and risks of AI-enhanced coding. It contributes to broader conversations on how human intelligence and generative AI can coexist in learning environments that are equitable, secure, and ethically grounded.

By blending theoretical insights, case studies, and practical strategies, the chapter encourages computer students to think beyond coding to consider the societal impact of their work. Whether in the classroom, lab, or industry, ethical competence is no longer optional; it is essential for building trustworthy systems with the assistance of AI and shaping a digital future.

The following Research Questions guide this study:

RQ1: How do students use generative AI tools in programming tasks, and what security vulnerabilities or ethical risks commonly emerge from AI-assisted code generation in educational settings?
RQ2: How can educators effectively integrate secure-by-design principles, AI literacy, and ethical reasoning into programming curricula that incorporate generative AI tools?
RQ3: What instructional strategies and assessment approaches best support responsible human-AI collaboration, enhance students' critical evaluation of AI-generated code, and strengthen their secure coding competencies?

This chapter is structured to guide the reader through a logical progression from theoretical foundations to empirical insights and their broader implications. Section 2 establishes the conceptual groundwork by introducing the theoretical frameworks that underpin the study, providing a lens through which the subsequent analysis of AI-assisted programming can be interpreted. Section 3 presents a comprehensive review of the literature, covering the emergence of generative AI tools in programming education, the ethical concerns associated with AI-generated code, such as plagiarism, hallucinations, and accountability gaps, as well as the security vulnerabilities that may be introduced by AI-assisted coding. This section further explores pedagogical strategies for teaching secure-by-design principles in AI-enriched learning environments, methods for integrating human-AI collaboration in the classroom, the development of AI literacy, including prompt engineering and explainability, and assessment frameworks for evaluating student engagement with AI tools. Section 4 details the qualitative research methodology employed, including the research design, data collection procedures, and analytical techniques used to ensure rigor and validity. Section 5 presents the principal findings, illustrated with case studies that exemplify key themes, and critically examines their theoretical, educational, and practical implications. Finally, Section 6 concludes the chapter by reflecting on its limitations, highlighting its contributions to the field of AI-assisted programming education, and suggesting directions for future research that can build on these insights.

BACKGROUND AND THEORETICAL FRAMEWORKS

The rapid integration of generative AI tools into programming education has created new opportunities for learning but also new challenges for security, ethics, and skill development. As students increasingly rely on AI-generated code to complete assignments, debug programs, and understand unfamiliar concepts, educators are grappling with how these tools are reshaping classroom practices and expectations.

To analyze these shifts, this chapter draws on three complementary theoretical perspectives: Deskilling of Jobs Theory (DJT), Job Characteristics Theory (JCT), and Technology Threat Avoidance Theory (TTAT). Together, these frameworks offer a sociotechnical foundation for understanding how AI alters skill acquisition, motivation, and security behaviors in computer science learning environments.

Deskilling of Jobs Theory

The Deskilling of Jobs Theory (DJT), grounded in Marxist labor critique and later developed by Harry Braverman (1974), posits that technological advancements can erode workers' autonomy, craftsmanship, and decision-making power by shifting control from humans to automated systems. Braverman's analysis documented how industrial automation fragmented skilled labor and reduced the cognitive complexity of work, leaving workers dependent on machine outputs rather than their own expertise. When applied to programming education, DJT offers a compelling lens for understanding how generative AI tools may unintentionally displace essential learning processes.

In traditional programming instruction, students develop competence through debugging, code tracing, iterative refinement, and problem decomposition. These activities not only build technical skills but also foster professional identity, confidence, and a sense of ownership over one's solutions. However, when generative AI provides completed functions or detailed fixes, students may bypass foundational cognitive steps. This AI assistance can lead to overreliance on system-generated code, superficial understanding of software architecture, and diminished familiarity with secure coding practices. The long-term implications include weaker retention of core concepts, reduced capacity for independent reasoning, and potentially lower confidence when AI tools are unavailable.

In this sense, AI-assisted learning may mirror the labor deskilling process by automating away the exact skills that education is intended to cultivate. Suppose students increasingly delegate judgment, problem-solving, and code construction to AI systems. In that case, they may graduate with narrower expertise, fewer creative problem-solving abilities, and a limited understanding of the security vulnerabilities embedded in the code they deploy. DJT therefore emphasizes the importance of designing learning environments that preserve student agency, ensure active engagement with AI outputs, and prevent the erosion of essential programming and security competencies.

Job Characteristics Theory

While DJT highlights the reduction of autonomy and skill, Job Characteristics Theory (JCT), introduced by Hackman and Oldham (1976), provides a psychological and motivational framework for understanding how work design—here, learning task design—shapes student engagement and performance. JCT identifies five core job dimensions: skill variety, task identity, task significance, autonomy, and feedback. These dimensions influence three critical psychological states that drive motivation: experienced meaningfulness, experienced responsibility, and knowledge of results.

In programming education, generative AI tools directly affect these dimensions. For example, AI systems can increase feedback immediacy by offering real-time explanations, code suggestions, and error corrections. This form of continuous, automated feedback can help students iterate more efficiently and reduce frustration. Yet the same tools can inadvertently reduce autonomy and task identity. When AI suggests solutions preemptively or provides nearly finished code fragments, students may engage in passive acceptance rather than deliberate construction, weakening their sense of ownership over learning tasks. Skill variety may also decrease if AI-generated templates limit exposure to diverse approaches, algorithms, or syntactic patterns.

Mapping JCT onto the use of AI in education provides a proper evaluation mechanism for instructors and curriculum designers. If AI tools make tasks too simple or overly guided, students may disengage, feeling that the work lacks meaningful challenge or fails to represent authentic problem-solving. On the other hand, when used purposefully, generative AI can expand task variety by enabling more ambitious projects, increase autonomy by reducing dependence on instructors for support, and strengthen task significance by helping students see real-world applications earlier in their learning. JCT thus encourages educators to structure AI-supported assignments in ways that preserve meaningfulness, sustain motivation, and reinforce students' identity as capable, responsible coders.

Technology Threat Avoidance Theory

While DJT and JCT focus on skill formation and motivational quality, the Technology Threat Avoidance Theory (TTAT), developed by Liang and Xue (2009), emphasizes how individuals perceive and respond to technological risks. TTAT posits that protective behaviors—such as secure coding practices, verification of AI outputs, or caution in tool adoption—emerge from four key perceptions: perceived severity, perceived vulnerability, safeguard effectiveness, and self-efficacy. This framework is crucial for understanding how students and instructors approach generative AI in contexts where security, ethics, and academic integrity are of paramount importance.

In programming courses, TTAT helps explain why some students misuse or avoid AI tools. Learners who perceive high risk—such as a fear of plagiarism accusations, a lack of clarity about policy guidelines, or anxiety about security vulnerabilities—may avoid using AI even when it could support their learning. Conversely, students who underestimate risks may adopt AI-generated solutions without critical evaluation, leading to insecure or ethically compromised code. Educators may also fall into one of these extremes: either restricting AI access entirely due to perceived threats or encouraging widespread use without sufficient guardrails.

TTAT emphasizes the importance of institutional safeguards, training, and clear guidelines that enable students to understand both the benefits and risks of generative AI. When learners develop AI literacy, can evaluate outputs critically, and feel confident in applying secure-by-design principles, the perceived threat diminishes, and constructive, responsible AI use becomes more likely. Without such structures, students may experience confusion, unintentionally misuse tools, or avoid technology altogether—limiting opportunities for learning and slowing the adoption of secure coding practices.

Background and Theoretical Frameworks Summary

The rapid expansion of generative artificial intelligence (AI) has reshaped contemporary approaches to software engineering education, prompting educators, researchers, and institutions to reevaluate how students learn technical skills in an era of automation. Tools such as ChatGPT, GitHub Copilot, and other intelligent tutoring systems have shifted the locus of activity from traditional problem-solving toward AI-assisted development, altering students' cognitive load, learning pathways, and sense of agency. This transformation raises essential questions regarding technological dependence, deskilling, and the evolving nature of professional expertise. Prior studies highlight benefits such as personalization, increased productivity, and improved accessibility, yet they also warn of unintended consequences—including reduced confidence, superficial understanding, and diminished opportunities for authentic practice. As AI becomes embedded in curricular and extracurricular learning contexts, a theoretical grounding is required to interpret these shifts and guide sustainable educational design.

To examine these dynamics, this chapter draws on several interrelated theoretical frameworks that illuminate how learners interact with intelligent systems, how skills evolve under conditions of automation, and how technological mediation reshapes human roles. The combination of these frameworks provides a multidimensional lens for analyzing students' lived experiences, educators' instructional strategies, and the broader sociotechnical implications of AI-enabled learning. Together, they offer a foundation for evaluating both the pedagogical value and the potential risks associated with generative AI in programming education.

The chapter is structured around four core theoretical perspectives: sociotechnical systems theory, which explains how technology and human activity co-evolve; activity theory, which elucidates how AI tools mediate learning, goals, and actions; cognitive load theory, which clarifies how automation reshapes cognitive effort and skill formation; and theories of deskilling and reskilling, which address how automation influences professional identity, confidence, and long-term expertise. Each framework contributes a distinct viewpoint on the changing landscape of AI-enhanced learning, and together they help articulate the implications for curriculum design, competency development, and the future role of the software engineer.

Table 1. Mapping interview questions to research questions and theoretical frameworks

Research Question (RQ)	Theoretical Framework	Interview Questions	Rationale / Link to Theory
RQ1: How do students use generative AI tools in programming tasks, and what security vulnerabilities or ethical risks commonly emerge from AI-assisted code generation in educational settings?	Deskilling of Jobs Theory (DJT)	1. Can you describe how you use AI tools when writing or debugging code? 2. Have you noticed situations where AI-generated code introduced errors or security risks? 3. How confident do you feel in completing coding tasks without AI assistance? 4. Are there coding tasks you avoid because you rely on AI? 5. How often do you review or modify AI-generated code before using it?	DJT highlights the potential erosion of skills and overreliance on technology. These questions probe students' dependence on AI, understanding of fundamental skills, exposure to vulnerabilities, and possible reduction in autonomous problem-solving.

continued on following page

Table 1. Continued

Research Question (RQ)	Theoretical Framework	Interview Questions	Rationale / Link to Theory
RQ2: How can educators effectively integrate secure-by-design principles, AI literacy, and ethical reasoning into programming curricula that incorporate generative AI tools?	Job Characteristics Theory (JCT)	1. How do assignments or projects involving AI tools help you understand secure coding practices? 2. Do AI-supported tasks provide opportunities for autonomy and problem-solving? 3. How does feedback from AI tools or instructors affect your learning? 4. How do you experience task variety when using AI tools? 5. Do AI-assisted tasks make you feel more responsible for the final code outcome?	JCT focuses on task design, motivation, and engagement. Questions examine how AI-mediated learning supports or undermines the variety of skills, task identity, autonomy, and feedback. They also explore students' perceptions of the meaningfulness and responsibility associated with coding tasks.
RQ3: What instructional strategies and assessment approaches best support responsible human-AI collaboration, enhance students' critical evaluation of AI-generated code, and strengthen their secure coding competencies?	Technology Threat Avoidance Theory (TTAT)	1. How do you decide whether to trust AI-generated code? 2. What strategies do you use to verify or secure AI-assisted code? 3. How do ethical or security concerns influence your use of AI tools? 4. Can you describe instances where you avoided using AI due to potential risks? 5. What types of guidance or instruction help you use AI responsibly?	

LITERATURE REVIEW

The Rise of Generative AI Tools in Programming Education

Generative AI tools such as GitHub Copilot and ChatGPT have rapidly reshaped programming education by offering instantaneous code suggestions, automated debugging support, and context-sensitive explanations that reduce cognitive load for learners. These systems enable students to experiment with complex coding patterns without fully mastering underlying algorithms or syntax, thereby lowering barriers to entry for novices and enhancing exploratory learning (Avila-Chauvet et al., 2023; Barke et al., 2023; Kuhail et al., 2023).

Recent empirical studies demonstrate strong student motivation to adopt AI-assisted workflows, particularly as these tools accelerate task completion, assist in project scaffolding, and provide personalized feedback loops (Avila-Chauvet et al., 2023). Avila-Chauvet et al. (2023), for example, found that students completing behavioral programming tasks in online courses used ChatGPT to clarify conceptual misunderstandings, seek alternative implementations, and validate logic structures.

At the professional level, the widespread uptake of AI tools within industry further reinforces their relevance in educational settings. Daigle (2024) reports that the majority of software teams now incorporate generative AI into daily workflows, and many organizations expect new graduates to be proficient with these tools.

However, literature also highlights concerns. Crowston and Bolici (2025) argue that the growing ubiquity of AI-generated code may weaken the development of foundational skills and reduce students' confidence in their ability to solve problems independently. Similarly, Barke et al. (2023) found that programmers often defer decision-making to AI-generated suggestions, which may inhibit reflective thinking during complex tasks.

Collectively, these findings reveal both the pedagogical potential and the emerging risks of integrating generative AI into programming education.

Ethical Concerns in AI-Generated Code: Plagiarism, Hallucinations, and Lack of Accountability

Generative AI introduces distinct ethical challenges in programming education. One major issue is plagiarism: students may submit AI-generated solutions without attribution, creating ambiguity around authorship and undermining the integrity of learning outcomes (Kuhail et al., 2023; Puccio et al., 2025). Kuhail et al. (2023)

additionally found that many learners perceive AI tools as authoritative sources, leading them to accept generated solutions uncritically.

Another primary concern is hallucination—AI systems producing code that is syntactically correct but functionally flawed, insecure, or entirely fabricated. Khurana et al. (2024) show that even carefully designed prompts can elicit incorrect explanations or misleading code, particularly when queries involve ambiguous or domain-specific requirements.

These issues also raise questions about accountability. When AI-produced code contains errors, who is responsible—the student, the instructor, or the model itself? Barke et al. (2023) emphasize that AI's persuasive presentation style can cause users to trust its outputs even when they diverge from established best practices.

To address these concerns, researchers emphasize the importance of transparent instructional models that teach students how to critically evaluate AI outputs, articulate ethical reasoning, and document the role of AI in their work.

Common Security Vulnerabilities Introduced by AI-Generated Code

Growing evidence suggests that AI-generated code often contains security vulnerabilities. Sridhara et al. (2023) identified common issues as hardcoded credentials, improper input validation, insecure API usage, missing sanitization steps, logic errors, and SQL injection risks. These vulnerabilities arise because generative models reproduce patterns from training data without considering context-specific security constraints.

In professional settings, developers often fail to recognize these flaws, and students with limited cybersecurity knowledge are even less equipped to detect or correct them (Crowston & Bolici, 2025). Rinta-Kahila et al. (2023) describe how reliance on automation can deepen "vicious cycles of skill erosion," where users increasingly trust automated outputs while gradually losing the ability to identify risks.

Given the prevalence of insecure code generated by AI, cybersecurity education must now include explicit attention to evaluating AI outputs for security weaknesses.

Teaching Secure-by-Design Principles in AI-Assisted Coding Environments

Given the challenges above, secure-by-design principles have become essential in programming curricula. Secure-by-design instruction emphasizes preventive practices—such as input validation, proper authentication, robust error handling, and systematic review procedures—especially as studies show that AI-generated code often introduces vulnerabilities that students may overlook (Crowston & Bolici, 2025; Rinta-Kahila et al., 2023; Sridhara et al., 2023).

In AI-assisted learning environments, these principles take on new urgency. Educators must train students to treat AI-generated code as preliminary scaffolding rather than authoritative solutions. Stefaniak and Moore (2024) argue that generative AI can support inclusive and reflective design deliberation by prompting learners to evaluate and justify design decisions. Applying such deliberation to code security encourages students to explicitly interrogate AI-generated logic and consider potential attack surfaces or vulnerabilities. Embedding secure-by-design frameworks within AI-assisted tasks not only improves students' technical competence but also reinforces ethical responsibility and professional readiness.

Classroom Strategies for AI Tool Integration: Pairing Code Generation with Human Review and Explanation

Effective instructional design requires striking a balance between automation and human judgment. Numerous studies recommend pairing AI-generated outputs with structured human review, debugging exercises, and explanation requirements (Crowston & Bolici, 2025; Sridhara et al., 2023).

For example, instructors may:

- Require students to annotate AI-generated code,
- Explain the reasoning behind corrections,
- Identify potential vulnerabilities, or
- Justify the selection of one AI-generated solution over alternatives.

Barke et al. (2023) found that programmers who critically reflect on AI suggestions develop deeper technical understanding and avoid blind reliance. These strategies help shift learning from passive acceptance to active engagement and metacognitive reasoning.

Case studies in online courses show similar benefits. Avila-Chauvet et al. (2023) demonstrate that when students combine ChatGPT explanations with instructor-led verification activities, their conceptual understanding and autonomy increase significantly.

AI Literacy: Prompt Engineering, Explainability, and Understanding Limitations

AI literacy encompasses understanding how generative AI works, how prompts influence outputs, and how to critically evaluate the limitations, biases, and potential risks associated with generated code. Holmes et al. (2022) emphasize that AI literacy is now a core digital competency comparable to algorithmic thinking and debugging.

Explainability exercises are efficient. When students unpack the reasoning behind AI-generated code—questioning assumptions, reviewing logic flow, and validating outputs—they strengthen analytical skills and reduce overreliance. Khurana et al. (2024) stress that prompt design must be taught explicitly, as poorly structured prompts often lead to hallucinations or misleading instructions.

Riazi et al. (2023) extend this discussion by highlighting the importance of trustworthiness and methodological rigor when working with AI tools, suggesting new validity criteria for evaluating AI-mediated writing or coding processes. These practices collectively support responsible, informed human-AI collaboration.

Rubrics and Assessment Methods for Evaluating Human-AI Coding Collaboration

Traditional assessment methods, focused on correctness and code completeness, are insufficient for evaluating learning in AI-assisted contexts. Scholars advocate for developing hybrid assessment frameworks that capture:

- The quality of human review and modification,
- The student's ability to identify AI errors,
- Reflective documentation of AI contributions, and
- Ethical reasoning associated with human-AI collaboration (Sridhara et al., 2023).

Crowston and Bolici (2025) argue that assessments must measure skill retention and independent problem-solving to ensure that AI does not mask gaps in conceptual understanding. Assessment strategies may include:

- Reflection logs documenting how AI was used,
- Secure code audits,
- Comparative analyses of multiple AI-generated solutions, or
- Oral examinations to verify student understanding.

Such rubrics promote accountability, transparency, and evaluative judgment.

Case Studies from University-Level and High School Computer Science Courses

Empirical studies across educational levels reveal diverse approaches to integrating AI tools. At the university level, instructors have implemented assignments that require students to refactor AI-generated code, while documenting security considerations, explaining logic flows, and validating AI-suggested algorithms (Crowston & Bolici, 2025). These strategies align with industry trends, where software teams often combine AI-generated scaffolding with manual review (Daigle, 2024).

In high school contexts, AI tools have been introduced as collaborative assistants in project-based learning. Students work in groups to analyze AI-generated options, compare alternative solutions, and conduct peer audits for plagiarism, security, and stylistic clarity (Stefaniak & Moore, 2024).

These case studies demonstrate that AI tools can enhance learning only when embedded within structured, reflective pedagogical frameworks.

Synthesis and Research Gaps

The current body of literature makes clear that generative AI has become a transformative force in programming education, offering benefits such as accelerated learning, enhanced engagement, and personalized instructional support (Barke et al., 2023; Stefaniak & Moore).. Students utilize AI tools to scaffold their understanding, explore alternative solutions, and receive immediate feedback (Avila-Chauvet et al., 2023).

At the same time, significant challenges persist. Ethical concerns—such as plagiarism, hallucination, and ambiguous accountability—are not systematically addressed in most curricula (Kuhail et al., 2023; Puccio et al., 2025). Additionally, the prevalence of security vulnerabilities in AI-generated code underscores the need for explicit secure coding instruction (Crowston & Bolici, 2025). Deskilling effects, as documented by Crowston and Bolici (2025) and Rinta-Kahila et al. (2023), further highlight the risks associated with overreliance on automation.

Despite the growing integration of generative AI tools in programming education, several critical gaps remain in the current research. First, few studies employ longitudinal designs to examine how sustained AI use impacts long-term skill retention, secure coding competence, and ethical reasoning. Without this perspective, it is challenging to determine whether the short-term benefits of AI assistance translate into lasting knowledge and practical proficiency.

Second, there is limited guidance on designing assessment frameworks that effectively evaluate collaboration between human learners and AI systems. Existing rubrics rarely account for students' abilities to critically assess AI outputs, apply cybersecurity reasoning, or engage in reflective practice, leaving instructors with insufficient tools to measure meaningful learning outcomes in AI-assisted coding contexts.

Third, the integration of AI literacy and security instruction remains underdeveloped in most programming curricula. Key skills such as prompt engineering, explainability, risk awareness, and secure-by-design principles are often introduced only superficially, if at all, limiting students' capacity to use AI tools responsibly and safely.

Fourth, minimal cross-level comparative research has been conducted to investigate how AI tools affect learners at different stages, from novices and high school students to advanced computer science majors. Understanding these differential effects is essential for tailoring instructional strategies and support mechanisms to diverse learner populations.

Finally, although theoretical frameworks such as Deskilling Theory, Job Characteristics Theory, and Technology Threat Avoidance Theory offer powerful lenses for interpreting the impact of AI on programming education, few empirical studies have applied these models directly to AI-supported learning environments. Leveraging these frameworks could provide deeper insights into both the opportunities and challenges posed by AI integration.

Addressing these gaps is essential for developing curricula that harness the benefits of generative AI while safeguarding students' long-term competencies, ethical awareness, and cybersecurity readiness. By filling these research and pedagogical voids, educators can ensure that AI-assisted programming education supports not only immediate performance gains but also sustainable skill development and responsible practice.

METHODOLOGY

This chapter outlines the methodological approach used to investigate how generative AI tools shape students' programming practices, secure coding competencies, and ethical reasoning in educational contexts. As AI systems such as ChatGPT and GitHub Copilot become increasingly integrated into learning environments, understanding students' lived experiences requires a method that captures personal meaning, internal reasoning, and emergent concerns. For this reason, the study employs a qualitative, hermeneutic phenomenological design, which focuses on interpreting how individuals make sense of their interactions with technology—particularly as automation reshapes skill expectations and learning processes.

Semi-structured interviews were selected to elicit rich, first-person accounts that illuminate not only what students do with AI-generated code but also *how they experience* issues such as reduced cognitive effort, exposure to vulnerabilities, and ethical uncertainty. Case studies embedded within the analysis provide additional contextual depth by illustrating how theoretical constructs manifest in real instructional settings. This methodological design aligns directly with the study's three research questions examining (1) AI use patterns and emerging risks, (2) curricular strategies for secure-by-design, ethical, and AI-literate instruction, and (3) pedagogical and assessment approaches that support responsible human–AI collaboration.

To enhance analytic rigor, interview transcripts were systematically coded using MaxQDA, allowing the researcher to blend inductive thematic discovery with deductive analysis grounded in the study's theoretical framework: Deskilling of Jobs Theory (DJT), Job Characteristics Theory (JCT), and Technology Threat Avoidance Theory (TTAT). Reflexive journaling throughout the research process helped mitigate bias by documenting interpretive decisions, reactions, and assumptions that emerged during the research process. Ethical standards, including confidentiality, informed consent, and secure data storage, were consistently upheld throughout the study. Together, these methodological components establish a rigorous foundation for analyzing how generative AI reshapes learning in programming education.

Research Design and Methodological Approach

This study adhered to establishing best practices in qualitative inquiry, employing a phenomenological research design to explore how individuals experience the integration of generative AI within programming education and software development. Phenomenology, as described by Peoples (2021), seeks to uncover the essence of lived experiences by examining how individuals perceive, interpret, and make meaning of phenomena. This perspective was especially relevant given the rapidly evolving nature of AI-assisted coding tools and the complex cognitive, ethical, and pedagogical questions they introduce.

A qualitative design enabled the collection of rich, contextualized accounts that would not have been accessible through quantitative methods. Rather than aiming for broad generalizability, the study focused on illuminating the nuanced ways students and practitioners engage with generative AI, how these tools shape their understanding of programming tasks, and how they navigate emerging concerns related to security, ethics, and skill development. Semi-structured interviews were chosen to strike a balance between consistency across participants and the flexibility needed for in-depth reflection.

Participant Selection

Participants were recruited using purposive sampling to ensure direct experience with programming tasks and generative AI tools. A total of twelve participants were included in the final sample, representing both university-level computer science students and high school learners enrolled in computer science courses. This composition was intentionally designed to capture perspectives from individuals at different stages of the educational pipeline, from secondary education to higher education. Including participants from both levels allowed the study to examine how exposure to programming, software development practices, and emerging AI-assisted tools may differ across learning environments. University-level participants typically had more advanced exposure to formal coursework in software engineering, algorithms, and system design, while high school participants provided insights into earlier stages of programming education and foundational skill development. Together, these perspectives offered a broader understanding of how learners at different academic levels experience and adapt to the integration of AI technologies in computer science education. All participants reported using at least one AI system, such as ChatGPT or GitHub Copilot, for coding, debugging, or conceptual understanding.

The sampling strategy intentionally sought diversity across:

- Educational levels (high school, undergraduate)
- Programming experience (introductory to advanced)
- Familiarity with AI tools
- Prior exposure to secure coding concepts

This variation enriched the dataset by capturing different interpretations and practices. Participants were invited through academic contacts, computing departments, and educator referrals. Each received an information sheet outlining the study's purpose, procedures, and voluntary nature. No compensation was provided.

Data Collection Procedures

Data was collected through semi-structured interviews conducted via Zoom. Interview sessions lasted between 45 and 75 minutes. This format enabled consistent coverage of core topics while providing participants with the flexibility to elaborate on issues they found meaningful. The interview guide included open-ended questions on:

- Experiences with AI-assisted coding
- Perceived impacts on skill development

- Awareness of security vulnerabilities in AI-generated code
- Ethical considerations such as plagiarism, attribution, and reliability
- Classroom activities, assignments, and instructional strategies
- Visions for future integration of AI in computing education

Interviews were recorded with participant consent and transcribed verbatim. The transcripts were anonymized by removing names, institutions, and other identifiable details. All data were stored on encrypted, password-protected devices.

Analytical Approach

Data analysis employed a thematic coding strategy combining inductive and deductive methods. The process involved several stages:

1. Initial holistic reading: transcripts were read in full to gain familiarity with tone, key experiences, and emotional markers.
2. Preliminary coding: codes were created to capture emerging ideas about AI usage, learning challenges, risk perceptions, and security concerns.
3. Deductive coding: additional codes were applied based on the conceptual constructs from DJT, JCT, and TTAT.
4. Theme development: related codes were grouped and refined into overarching themes aligned with the three research questions.
5. Cross-case comparison: differences and commonalities were examined across participants to strengthen the validity of interpretations.

MaxQDA was used to organize codes, construct coding hierarchies, visualize patterns, and facilitate systematic analysis. This tool supported transparency and consistency throughout the interpretive process.

Researcher Positionality

The researcher's background in software development, computing education, and AI-assisted coding shaped both the motivation for the study and the interpretive lens applied during analysis. Recognizing this potential influence, reflexive journaling was incorporated throughout the data collection and analysis process. Journals documented analytic decisions, reflections on unexpected participant perspectives, and examination of personal assumptions.

This practice enhanced reflexivity by:

- Acknowledging how professional experience with AI tools informs interpretation
- Identifying moments where assumptions might affect meaning-making
- Supporting transparency in how themes were constructed

Through ongoing reflection, the researcher aimed to minimize bias while remaining attentive to the complexity of participants' lived experiences.

Trustworthiness and Research Quality

Multiple strategies were implemented to enhance credibility, dependability, and confirmability. Triangulation was achieved by comparing participant accounts across diverse roles, including novices, advanced students, and industry practitioners. This cross-perspective analysis strengthened the robustness of emerging themes.

Member checking was performed with selected participants, who reviewed preliminary interpretations to ensure accuracy and resonance with their intended meaning. Their feedback provided valuable confirmation and refinement of analytical insights.

Additionally, the researcher maintained a reflexive journal throughout the study. This practice supported transparency by documenting analytical decisions, personal assumptions, and potential biases. Reflexivity helped ensure that interpretations were grounded in participants' narratives rather than the researcher's preconceptions.

Ethical Considerations

Ethical standards were consistently upheld throughout the research process. Approval was obtained from the Institutional Review Board (IRB), and all participants provided informed consent. Measures were taken to ensure anonymity, including the use of pseudonyms and the removal of identifiable information from transcripts. Data were stored securely on password-protected devices accessible only to the researcher.

Participants retained the right to withdraw at any point without penalty. The study prioritized respect for autonomy, confidentiality, and transparency—key principles in ethical qualitative research.

FINDINGS AND DISCUSSION

This study examined the impact of generative AI tools on students' programming practices, security awareness, and ethical decision-making in high school and university-level computer science courses. Through semi-structured interviews with 12 participants, the study uncovered patterns of use, areas of vulnerability, and instructional opportunities. The findings are organized by the three research questions and interpreted through the theoretical lenses of the Deskilling of Jobs Theory (DJT), Job Characteristics Theory (JCT), and Technology Threat Avoidance Theory (TTAT). These frameworks illuminate how AI tools influence skill development, motivational dynamics, and students' protective responses to technological risks.

> RQ1: How do students use generative AI tools in programming tasks, and what security vulnerabilities or ethical risks commonly emerge?

The integration of generative AI tools into programming education has transformed how students approach coding, problem-solving, and software development tasks. These tools provide immediate code suggestions, debugging assistance, and explanations, enabling learners to complete tasks more efficiently and explore complex programming concepts with guidance. However, alongside these benefits, AI-assisted coding introduces new challenges, including the potential for security vulnerabilities, ethical lapses, and a reliance on automated outputs that may reduce critical thinking and engagement. Investigating how students interact with AI in practice and identifying the common risks that arise is essential for understanding both the opportunities and limitations of these technologies in educational contexts. This research question, therefore, examines not only patterns of AI use but also the associated security and ethical considerations that must be addressed to ensure responsible and effective learning outcomes.

Theme 1: Reliance on AI and Reduced Cognitive Engagement

Participants frequently used AI tools to generate code, debug assignments, and explain concepts. While this increased efficiency and reduced frustration, several students reported minimal independent reasoning. One participant described their process as "copying what the AI gives and tweaking it just enough to run," indicating a shallow approach to learning. This new way of learning reflects the concerns raised in DJT: as automated systems assume more responsibility for complex tasks, users may lose opportunities to practice or internalize essential skills. The study found early indications of cognitive offloading, reduced problem-solving engagement, and an emerging belief that mastery is less necessary when AI can perform most coding tasks.

Theme 2: Exposure to Security Risks and Ethical Dilemmas

Many participants noted that AI-generated code introduced vulnerabilities, including missing input validation, hardcoded credentials, and insecure database queries. Students also reported concerns about plagiarism, overreliance on AI-generated explanations, and uncertainty about how to attribute AI-assisted work ethically.

TTAT helps explain these behaviors: students who perceived high levels of threat or vulnerability were more cautious, engaging in more thorough testing or validation. At the same time, those who underestimated risks tended to trust AI outputs without deeper inspection. This variability underscores the importance of raising awareness about AI risks in educational contexts.

Discussion of RQ1 Findings

These findings confirm that generative AI tools simultaneously enhance efficiency and pose ethical and security challenges. Students' overreliance may undermine long-term skill retention, consistent with DJT, while the perceived risks influence protective behaviors, as outlined by TTAT. Educators must therefore strike a balance between the use of AI and strategies that promote cognitive engagement and ethical responsibility.

> RQ2: How can educators integrate secure-by-design principles, AI literacy, and ethical reasoning into AI-augmented curricula?

As generative AI tools become increasingly embedded in programming education, the role of educators has expanded from delivering technical instruction to guiding students in the responsible and secure use of AI-assisted coding. Integrating secure-by-design principles ensures that learners develop the skills to anticipate and mitigate potential vulnerabilities in their code. At the same time, AI literacy equips them to understand, evaluate, and effectively interact with AI outputs. Additionally, fostering ethical reasoning encourages students to critically reflect on the implications of AI use, including accountability, intellectual property, and fairness. This research question focuses on the pedagogical strategies and curricular approaches that support the development of these competencies, aiming to prepare students to navigate AI-augmented programming environments with both technical proficiency and ethical awareness.

Theme 1: Embedding Secure Coding Practices

Students reported that structured activities—such as refactoring AI-generated code, identifying vulnerabilities, and documenting security decisions—helped strengthen their technical skills. When instructors embedded secure-by-design concepts (such as input validation, authentication, and error handling) into assignments, students developed a stronger ability to recognize and correct errors generated by AI. This discovery resonates with JCT: well-designed learning tasks increased students' sense of responsibility, autonomy, and skill variety, fostering deeper motivation and learning.

Theme 2: Developing AI Literacy and Critical Evaluation Skills

Participants emphasized the importance of learning how AI models work, understanding hallucinations, and practicing prompt engineering. Activities such as "explain your reasoning" exercises, model comparison tasks, and reflective journals helped students maintain autonomy and task identity even when using highly automated tools. By strengthening AI literacy, instructors reduce the risk of blind trust and help students remain competent, critical users.

Discussion of RQ2 Findings

The results indicate that integrating AI literacy and secure-by-design instruction supports responsible, engaged learning. JCT provides a helpful lens: when tasks are designed to require independent judgment and provide meaningful feedback, students remain motivated and retain control over their learning process. These findings suggest that pedagogical design can directly counteract the deskilling tendencies identified under RQ1.

> RQ3: What instructional strategies and assessment approaches support responsible human-AI collaboration?

The increasing prevalence of AI-assisted tools in programming education necessitates a rethinking of both instructional practices and assessment methods. Beyond mastering coding tasks, students must learn to collaborate effectively with AI systems, critically evaluate AI outputs, and maintain accountability for the decisions embedded in their code. This research question examines the pedagogical strategies that promote responsible human-AI collaboration, including structured guidance, reflective practice, and scaffolding of AI interactions. It also explores assessment approaches that capture not only the correctness of students' code but also their engagement with AI suggestions, ethical reasoning, and ability to identify and mitigate potential security or functional risks. Addressing these dimensions is essential for fostering competent, responsible, and critically aware programmers in AI-augmented learning environments.

Theme 1: Human-in-the-Loop Code Review

Participants noted that structured review processes, such as peer critique sessions, instructor-led code walks, and collaborative debugging, significantly enhanced their understanding. Students became more aware of AI limitations and more confident in identifying and correcting vulnerabilities. Consistent with TTAT, students who recognized potential threats were more likely to engage in protective behaviors such as validating output, testing edge cases, and documenting AI use.

Theme 2: Assessment and Rubrics for Human-AI Collaboration

Assignments that rewarded critique, verification, modification, and ethical reflection led to more thoughtful engagement with AI tools. Students appreciated rubrics that acknowledged the human-AI partnership rather than simply evaluating the correctness of the final code.

These structured evaluations also align with JCT by reinforcing task significance and providing clear feedback, which in turn supports deeper learning and understanding.

Discussion of RQ3 Findings

Human-in-the-loop approaches and explicit assessment structures are essential for developing responsible AI use. They encourage students to think critically, take ownership of their work, and recognize the role of human judgment in secure and ethical coding. These practices also reduce the risk of DJT-related skill erosion.

Figure 1. Understanding generative AI reshares programming education

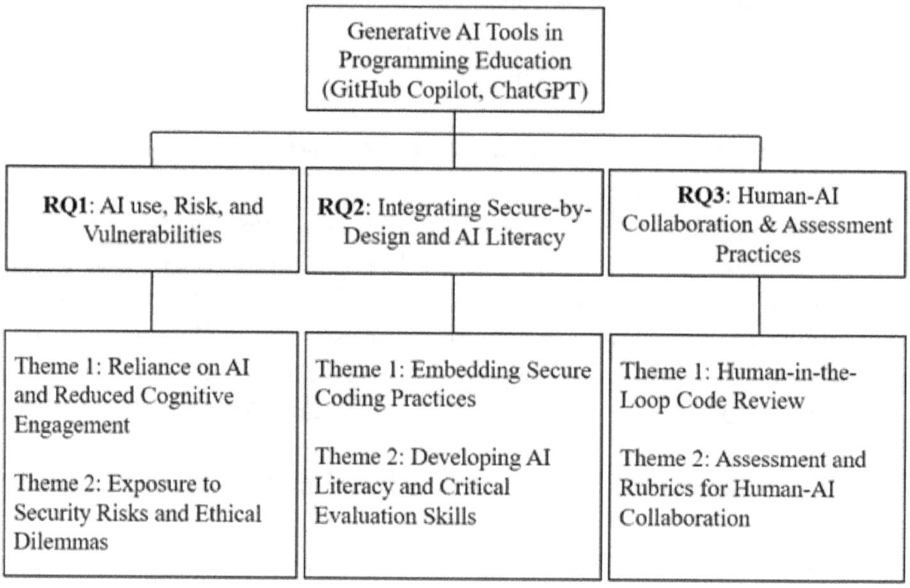

Figure 1 describes how Generative AI reshapes programming education through skill erosion (DJT), motivation and task design (JCT), and risk perception (TTAT).

Overall Discussion

Taken together, the findings reveal a complex interplay between student behaviors, instructional design, and the affordances of generative AI. The study shows that:

- AI increases efficiency but risks long-term skill erosion (DJT).
- Motivational and cognitive outcomes depend heavily on task design (JCT).
- Students' responses to AI-generated risks vary based on perceived threat and personal efficacy (TTAT).

The results suggest that effective AI integration requires striking a balance between automation and intentional pedagogical strategies that preserve core cognitive skills. Educators should design assignments that require verification, encourage ethical reasoning, and embed secure coding practices. AI literacy must become a foundational component of programming education, and assessments should reflect the realities of human-AI collaboration.

Ultimately, the findings indicate that generative AI can be a powerful educational asset—but only when accompanied by thoughtful design, critical evaluation, and structured oversight that ensure students continue to develop the skills, judgment, and security awareness necessary for professional practice in an AI-augmented world.

IMPLICATIONS AND LIMITATIONS

Implications

The findings of this study present several important implications for educators, curriculum designers, and academic institutions aiming to integrate generative AI tools into programming education in a secure, ethical, and pedagogically sound manner. First, the results underscore the need to embed secure-by-design principles throughout AI-assisted coding curricula. As generative models often produce code containing hardcoded secrets, unsafe defaults, or vulnerable logic structures, students must be trained to inspect and refine these outputs critically. Designing assignments that require verification, modification, threat modeling, and documentation of AI-generated code can foster deeper engagement with security concepts while reducing the risk of over-reliance and long-term deskilling.

Second, the study highlights the growing necessity of AI literacy initiatives. Students increasingly rely on generative systems without fully understanding their internal limitations, failure modes, or potential to produce plausible but incorrect output. Explicit instruction in prompt engineering, explainability, model constraints, and responsible use is essential for developing informed and cautious users. This reliance on AI aligns with Technology Threat Avoidance Theory, which emphasizes the importance of building protective behaviors and threat awareness. By equipping students with foundational AI literacy, educators can promote safer and more intentional use of generative tools.

Third, the findings reinforce the importance of human-in-the-loop pedagogical strategies and assessment frameworks. Students benefit most when AI is positioned as a collaborator rather than an infallible authority. Rubrics that reward critical thinking, debugging, ethical reflection, and secure coding behaviors encourage students to interrogate AI outputs actively rather than accept them passively. These approaches not only strengthen technical skills but also support motivational factors described in Job Characteristics Theory—such as task significance, autonomy, and skill variety—thereby enhancing learning outcomes and maintaining student agency in the development process.

Fourth, the study points to an urgent need for professional development among educators. Many instructors lack experience with generative AI tools, secure coding pedagogy, or assignment design tailored to AI-assisted learning environments. Without institutional investment in ongoing training, educators may struggle to anticipate risks, support students effectively, or design appropriate learning activities. Professional development should therefore focus on AI literacy, practical demonstrations of security vulnerabilities in AI-generated code, and strategies for balancing automation with independent problem-solving. Institutional support will be crucial in ensuring that generative AI enhances rather than undermines programming education.

Ultimately, the findings align with broader calls within the literature for comprehensive curriculum redesign. Scholars consistently emphasize that integrating generative AI into computing education requires a systemic approach that combines ethical instruction, security training, and reflective practice. Effective curricula may include scaffolded challenges that progressively increase the student's responsibility, structured reflection exercises on AI decision-making, and integrated assessments that evaluate human-AI collaboration rather than code correctness alone. Institutions should also consider establishing guidelines for the responsible use of AI, promoting collaborative learning environments, and ensuring that foundational programming skills remain central despite the rise of automation (Crowston & Bolici, 2025).

Together, these implications suggest that responsible integration of generative AI requires more than simply allowing students to use new tools. It demands intentional pedagogical design, institutional investment, and a commitment to fostering ethical, secure, and critically informed future software developers.

Limitations

Despite the contributions of this study, several limitations should be acknowledged to contextualize the findings. First, the qualitative research design relied on in-depth interviews with a relatively small sample of 12 participants. While this approach enabled rich, nuanced insights, it also limits the transferability of results across diverse educational settings, institutions, and student populations. Larger samples or mixed-methods designs would strengthen the generalizability of future work.

Second, the scope of the study focused primarily on university-level and high school computer science courses. Other instructional contexts—such as vocational training programs, coding bootcamps, workforce reskilling initiatives, or professional development environments—may experience AI integration differently. These settings often involve varied learner motivations, skill levels, and instructional constraints, suggesting that future research should explore a broader range of educational ecosystems.

Third, the findings relied heavily on self-reported perceptions, reflections, and experiences. Although interviews provide valuable access to students' internal reasoning, they are inherently vulnerable to biases such as social desirability, selective memory, and inaccurate self-assessment of AI reliance or skill proficiency.

Supplementing interview data with classroom observations, code artifact analysis, or performance-based assessments could offer a more holistic picture of how generative AI affects actual learning behavior and the development of secure coding practices.

A fourth limitation concerns the rapidly evolving nature of generative AI technologies. Tools such as ChatGPT and GitHub Copilot undergo continuous updates that alter capabilities, interface designs, and underlying models. As a result, findings tied to specific tool behaviors, error patterns, or security vulnerabilities may shift over time. Longitudinal studies and periodic reassessments will be essential to capture the dynamic trajectory of AI-assisted programming education.

Finally, this research did not explicitly examine the perspectives of educators, curriculum designers, or industry professionals who increasingly shape expectations for AI literacy and secure programming competencies. Including these stakeholders could provide additional insight into institutional readiness, policy development, and pedagogical alignment.

Despite these limitations, the study offers meaningful contributions to understanding how generative AI tools are reshaping programming education. The findings provide practical guidance for fostering ethical, secure, and pedagogically sound human-AI collaboration, while also highlighting critical areas for future empirical investigation.

CONCLUSION

Generative AI tools are reshaping the landscape of programming education, offering unprecedented opportunities for efficiency, engagement, and personalized learning. Tools such as GitHub Copilot and ChatGPT enable students to generate, debug, and experiment with code in previously inaccessible ways, fostering rapid exploration and iterative problem-solving. However, this transformation is not without challenges. Overreliance on AI can contribute to deskilling, reduce critical engagement with fundamental coding concepts, and introduce ethical and security risks, including plagiarism, hallucinated outputs, and insecure code patterns.

This chapter has demonstrated that a balanced, structured approach to AI-assisted programming instruction is essential. By integrating secure-by-design principles, AI literacy, and ethical reflection into curricula, educators can preserve students' autonomy, skill development, and sense of professional responsibility. Theoretical frameworks, such as the Deskilling of Jobs Theory, Job Characteristics Theory, and Technology Threat Avoidance Theory, provide valuable insights into how AI tools influence cognitive engagement, motivation, and risk perception in learning environments.

Practical strategies, including human-in-the-loop code review, reflective exercises, prompt engineering, and targeted assessment rubrics, support responsible human-AI collaboration and reinforce secure coding practices. Case studies from both university and high school settings illustrate that deliberate instructional design can mitigate deskilling effects while enhancing students' critical evaluation skills and ethical awareness.

Looking forward, ongoing research and curriculum innovation are necessary to ensure that AI tools serve as augmentative partners rather than substitutes for human reasoning. By fostering skill retention, security consciousness, and ethical literacy, educators can prepare the next generation of programmers to navigate AI-augmented software development responsibly, confidently, and creatively.

REFERENCES

Avila-Chauvet, L., Mejía, D., & Acosta Quiroz, C. (2023). CHATGPT as a support tool for online behavioral task programming. *SSRN*. Retrieved from https://ssrn .com/abstract=4329020

Barke, S., James, M., & Polikarpova, N. (2023). Grounded copilot: How programmers interact with code-generating models. *Proceedings of the ACM on Programming Languages, 7*(OOPSLA1), 85-111. DOI: 10.1145/3586030

Braverman, H. (1974). *Labor and monopoly capital.* Monthly Review Press. DOI: 10.14452/MR-026-03-1974-07_1

Crowston, K., & Bolici, F. (2025). Deskilling and upskilling with AI Systems. *nformation Research an International Electronic Journal, 30*(iConf), 1009-1023. DOI: 10.47989/ir30iConf47143

Daigle, K. (2024). *Survey: The AI wave continues to grow on software development teams.* Retrieved from https://github.blog/author/kdaigle/

Hackman, J. R., & Oldham, G. R. (1976). Motivation through the design of work: Test of a theory. *Organizational Behavior and Human Performance, 16*(2), 250–279. DOI: 10.1016/0030-5073(76)90016-7

Holmes, W., Bialik, M., & Fadel, C. (2022). Artificial intelligence in education: Promises and implications. In *Artificial Intelligence in Education.* Promise and Implications for Teaching and Learning.

Khurana, A., Subramonyam, H., & Chilana, P. K. (2024). Why and when llm-based assistants can go wrong: Investigating the effectiveness of prompt-based interactions for software help-seeking. *arXiv.org*. Retrieved from /arxiv.2402.08030DOI: 10.1145/3640543.3645200

Kuhail, M. A., Mathew, S. S., Khalil, A., Khalil, A., & Shah, S. J. (2023). "Will I be replaced?" Assessing ChatGPT's effect on software development and programmer perceptions of AI tools. *arXiv.org*. Retrieved from DOI: 10.2139/ssrn.4571482

Liang, H., & Xue, Y. (2009). Avoidance of information technology threats: A theoretical perspective. *Management Information Systems Quarterly, 33*(1), 71–90. DOI: 10.2307/20650279

Peoples, K. (2021). *How to write a phenomenological dissertation: A step-by-step guide* (Vol. 56). SAGE.

Puccio, B., Castagna, F., Tucker, A., & Veltri, P. (2025). Towards medical AI misalignment: a preliminary study. doi:/arXiv.2505.18212DOI: 10.48550

Riazi, M., Rezvani, R., & Ghanbar, H. (2023). Trustworthiness in L2 writing research: A review and analysis of qualitative articles in the Journal of Second Language Writing. *Research Methods in Applied Linguistics*, *2*(3), 100065. Advance online publication. DOI: 10.1016/j.rmal.2023.100065

Rinta-Kahila, T., Penttinen, E., Salovaara, A., Soliman, W., & Ruissalo, J. (2023). The vicious circles of skill erosion: A case study of cognitive automation. *Journal of the Association for Information Systems*, *24*(5), 1378–1412. DOI: 10.17705/1jais.00829

Sridhara, G. G, R. H., & Mazumdar, S. (2023). CHATGPT: A study on its utility for ubiquitous software engineering tasks. *arXiv.org*. doi:/arXiv.2305.16837DOI: 10.48550

Stefaniak, J., & Moore, S. (2024). The Use of Generative AI to Support Inclusivity and Design Deliberation for Online Instruction. *Online Learning : the Official Journal of the Online Learning Consortium*, *28*(3), 181–205. DOI: 10.24059/olj.v28i3.4458

KEY TERMS AND DEFINITIONS

AI-Enhanced Learning: Instructional processes supported by AI technologies that provide adaptive feedback, personalized pathways, and intelligent tutoring to improve learning outcomes.

Algorithmic Bias: Systematic unfairness is embedded in AI outputs due to biased training data or model design. In education and healthcare, algorithmic bias raises concerns regarding reliability, ethics, and equitable access to AI-generated information.

Automated Code Generation: The use of AI models to produce executable programming code based on natural-language prompts. This technology reshapes developer workflows, student learning processes, and instructional strategies.

Cognitive Offloading: The act of transferring mental tasks to external systems to save cognitive resources. AI tools may encourage excessive offloading, reducing students' ability to internalize conceptual knowledge.

Deskilling: The process by which human expertise diminishes due to automation or over-reliance on intelligent systems. In AI-supported programming education, deskilling may occur when learners outsource cognitive tasks to AI tools instead of developing foundational skills.

Generative Artificial Intelligence (GenAI): AI systems are capable of producing new content—such as text, code, or images—by learning patterns from large datasets. Tools like ChatGPT and GitHub Copilot exemplify GenAI in educational and programming contexts.

Human–AI Collaboration: Cooperative interaction in which humans and AI systems work together to complete tasks. In software engineering, this includes co-writing code, debugging, or generating documentation with AI assistance.

Skill Augmentation: The enhancement of human capabilities through AI assistance. Rather than replacing skills, AI amplifies the efficiency, accuracy, and productivity of developers and students.

Technological Dependence: A condition in which learners or developers become reliant on AI tools to perform tasks they previously completed independently, potentially reducing confidence and long-term competency.

Chapter 12

Exploring the Shift From Traditional Education Models to AI-Supported Human Collaboration

Muhammad Faraz Manzoor
http://orcid.org/0000-0001-6489-2157
University of Management and Technology, Lahore, Pakistan

Daksh Dave
http://orcid.org/0009-0005-4046-1703
Virginia Tech, USA

ABSTRACT

This chapter reviews how artificial intelligence is reshaping education by moving traditional teacher-centered systems toward more personalized, creative, and inquiry-driven learning. It outlines the historical shift from conventional instruction to AI-supported models that use adaptive pathways, competency-based structures, collaborative learning, and continuous assessment. The discussion explains how teacher responsibilities are expanding toward roles as learning designers, AI supervisors, and ethical stewards, while students gain greater autonomy, agency, and metacognitive skills. Key ethical and policy concerns, including privacy, bias, accessibility, and governance, are addressed to guide responsible adoption. Global cases show varied approaches and offer lessons for effective integration. The chapter closes with a view of emerging AI-native ecosystems featuring hybrid learning spaces, lifelong AI assistance, and analytics-driven credentialing aimed at building a more equitable and human-centered educational future.

DOI: 10.4018/979-8-3373-6063-8.ch012

1. INTRODUCTION

Education has entered a period of rapid transformation. Traditional approaches created for industrial and post-industrial societies are increasingly unable to meet the demands of a world shaped through digital technologies, intelligent systems, and continuous global change (Ayeni et al., 2024)(Hughes, 2023). Learners, educators, and institutions are navigating a landscape where knowledge creation, problem solving, and communication are influenced through artificial intelligence (Korres et al., 2025). This chapter explores the transition from conventional educational structures toward models where human expertise and AI systems work together. It highlights the need to rethink how learning is designed, delivered, and experienced in an era where intelligence is distributed across people and machines.

1.1. Background: Evolution of Education from Industrial-Era Models to Digital-Age Needs

The dominant template for modern schooling took shape during the industrial era. Factories required punctuality, discipline, predictability, and uniform skill sets. Schools mirrored these priorities. Students were grouped according to age, taught through standardized curricula, and assessed through system-wide examinations. The flow of information moved mainly in one direction from teacher to learner. Knowledge retention and procedural accuracy were valued above creativity and adaptability (Schrager, 2018).

As societies transitioned toward information economies, the limitations of these models became more visible. Digital technologies expanded access to content, altered workplace expectations, and accelerated innovation cycles (SARIDAŞ, 2025). Learners needed stronger competencies in critical thinking, collaboration, and interdisciplinary problem solving. Early digital tools such as multimedia resources, online repositories, and basic learning management systems brought change, yet they did not fundamentally reshape the structure of schooling. They operated as supplements rather than catalysts for new pedagogical logics. The emergence of artificial intelligence marks a far deeper shift because it introduces systems capable of analyzing data, personalizing learning pathways, and engaging in interactive knowledge construction (Chakraborty, 2024).

1.2. The Emergence of AI as a Transformative Force

Artificial intelligence introduces novel cognition in learning by analyzing large volumes of data, identifying patterns, and generating insights previously unavailable. Adaptive learning systems adjust difficulty based on student performance, while intelligent tutoring systems provide guidance and feedback akin to human instructors. Generative AI supports writing, coding, design, and reflection, expanding learners' capabilities (Gupta, 2024). Beyond automation, AI enables individualized interactions, offering targeted explanations for struggling students and advanced tasks for high performers. Educators gain analytics on misconceptions, progress gaps, and behavioral trends, positioning AI as a cognitive partner rather than a mere tool and prompting a re-evaluation of educational roles and relationships (Villegas-Ch et al., 2025).

1.3. Why Human–AI Collaboration Matters Now

The need of cooperation between humans and AI can be explained by the complexity of the contemporary learning environments. Human judgment, emotional intelligence, ethical reasoning, creativity and contextual awareness are also inimitable. The AI systems offer computing power, pattern matching, content creation, and real-time feedback at an extent that man cannot maintain. With such strengths combined, the learning environments will be more responsive, inclusive and dynamic (Li et al., 2025).

The need to develop a stronger collaboration is increased by current global challenges. Technological change is very fast and it requires constant learning. The use of AI-based processes in the workplace grows, and it demands people to have the ability to communicate effectively with intelligent machines. Students are forced to learn how to challenge artificial intelligence generated results, how to learn about AI system weaknesses, and how to condition the machine intelligence towards constructive purposes. Learning institutions need to equip learners however to utilize AI tools but to collaborate with them. The cooperation between humans and AI becomes the focus of the future-proof skills, facilitation of personalized learning processes, and alternative approaches to teaching (Atchley et al., 2024).

1.4. Purpose, Scope, and Significance of This Chapter

The purpose of this chapter is to explore the reformation of education in terms of human-AI collaboration. It explores the ways in which historical practices defined the existing systems and how AI-guided practices are producing new opportunities in learning and teaching. The discussion spans conceptual frameworks, pedagogical shifts, institutional implications, and ethical considerations. It also identifies the emerging competencies required for educators and learners to engage effectively with intelligent technologies (Chan & Tsi, 2023).

The significance of this exploration lies in its potential to guide educational stakeholders as they navigate ongoing transformation. Many institutions are experimenting with AI tools without a cohesive vision of how these technologies should integrate with human expertise. This chapter brings clarity to that relationship, highlighting practices that support collaboration, preserve human strengths, and maximize AI's contributions to meaningful learning (Qureshi, 2025).

1.5 Structure of the Chapter

The chapter begins with a historical analysis that traces the development of educational systems from industrial models to digital-age expectations. It then explores the evolution and capabilities of artificial intelligence within learning environments (Merino-Campos, 2025). Following this, the chapter discusses human–AI collaboration as a conceptual and practical framework for rethinking contemporary education. Subsequent sections examine pedagogical models, shifts in teacher roles, changes in student experiences, and ethical and policy implications. The chapter also presents examples that illustrate global approaches to AI-supported education (Atchley et al., 2024). It concludes with a discussion of emerging directions for designing learning ecosystems shaped through human–AI interaction.

2. HISTORICAL CONTEXT: TRADITIONAL MODELS OF EDUCATION

Conventional education systems developed in response to socio-economic demands for stability, uniformity, and centralized control. Industrial-era schooling emphasized standardized curricula, age-based grouping, and teacher-led instruction. These models enabled large-scale literacy and administrative efficiency but were structured around predictability rather than adaptability. As later analyses note, such systems were not designed for complex and rapidly changing knowledge environments(Education and Academy, 2024; Zinkina et al., 2016).

Teacher-centered instruction reflected industrial labor needs. Classrooms prioritized authority, linear content delivery, standardized textbooks, and examination-based assessment. Teachers functioned as primary knowledge sources, while students engaged in repetition and procedural practice. This structure supported scalability but reinforced memorization over conceptual depth (Schrager, 2018; Tieso, 2003).

Rote learning limited inquiry, creativity, and transfer of knowledge to unfamiliar contexts. Uniform pacing constrained individual readiness, leaving advanced learners unchallenged and struggling learners unsupported. Feedback was episodic rather than continuous, allowing misconceptions to persist. As formative assessment research demonstrates, limited feedback mechanisms weakened learning progression (Black & Wiliam, 1998; Debbarma & Deb, 2025).

The transition to digital and knowledge economies widened the gap between schooling and workplace demands. Industries increasingly required collaboration, data-informed reasoning, adaptability, and multi-step problem solving—competencies insufficiently cultivated through standardized instruction (Husain, 2023; Winthrop et al., 2016). Although curricula began referencing new skills, instructional structures remained constrained by rigid testing systems and overloaded syllabi, slowing institutional adaptation (Winthrop et al., 2016).

Before artificial intelligence, several technologies sought modernization. E-learning platforms digitized content but largely preserved linear pedagogy. Multimedia tools enhanced presentation but did not personalize instruction. Massive Open Online Courses expanded access yet struggled with completion rates and individualized feedback. While these innovations advanced digital delivery, they lacked adaptive analytics and cognitive responsiveness. The emergence of AI introduced systems capable of analyzing patterns, interpreting learner behavior, and enabling deeper personalization (Liu & Yu, 2022).

3. THE RISE OF AI IN EDUCATION

The field of artificial intelligence has developed to become no longer a niche of research but rather an essential part of modern-day learning (Figure 1). Its capacitance to process information, pattern recognition, and facilitate the making of decisions has promoted the educational systems to pursue new teaching models. These trends are examples of the advancements in computer science, data analysis, and cognitive technologies that allow the machines to perform tasks that were previously related to human logic. With the changing educational requirements where individuals have shifted towards individualization, flexibility and sophisticated skill acquisition, AI has been a critical component when redefining new pedagogical practices (Hasanain Mohammed Manji Al-Rzoky & Abdulredha, 2025).

3.1 Defining AI, machine learning, generative AI, and intelligent agents

Artificial intelligence refers to computational systems designed to perform tasks associated with human cognitive functions, including interpretation, prediction, and problem solving. It encompasses multiple subdomains with distinct capabilities.

Machine learning is a core area of AI in which algorithms learn patterns from data and improve performance through iterative exposure rather than explicit programming. In education, machine learning models are used to detect learning gaps, predict performance, and recommend targeted content (Mohammad Talha Siddiqui, 2025; Nuthakki, buddiga, et al., 2024).

Generative AI is a subfield focused on producing new content—such as text, images, or code—based on patterns learned from large datasets(Nuthakki, Uttiramerur, et al., 2024). In learning contexts, it supports writing assistance, conceptual clarification, and structured problem solving.

Intelligent agents are autonomous systems that respond to environmental inputs, make decisions, and interact with users. In education, they function as virtual tutors or feedback systems, offering real-time guidance and adaptive support(SARIDAŞ, 2025).

Figure 1. AI technology stack in education

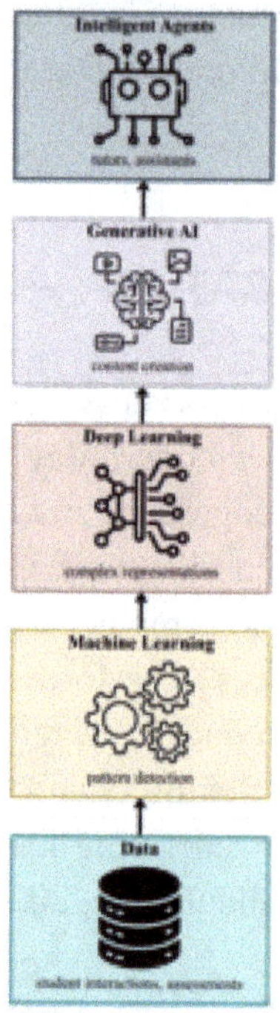

3.2 Key technological milestones in AI for education

The evolution of AI in education reflects a steady progression from rule-based expert systems, which automated structured reasoning in early computer-assisted instruction, to adaptive learning systems that personalized content based on student performance. Advances in natural language processing enabled more interactive tools such as automated grading and conversational tutoring, while deep learning improved real-time analytics, speech recognition, and predictive modeling. More recently, generative AI has expanded capabilities by producing explanations and instructional content, marking a shift from automation toward more interactive and collaborative educational systems (Alkhatlan & Kalita, 2018)(Rismanchian & Doroudi, 2025).

3.3 Current AI applications: personalization, tutoring systems, analytics, assessment

AI contributes to education primarily through personalization, tutoring, analytics, and assessment. Machine learning algorithms analyze learner behavior, performance trends, and engagement patterns to generate individualized learning pathways, recommending tasks and resources aligned with proficiency levels, thereby reducing cognitive load for beginners while extending enrichment to advanced learners (Figure 2). Intelligent tutoring systems provide interactive guidance by responding to student queries, diagnosing misconceptions, and offering stepwise support, with demonstrated improvements in mathematics, science, and language outcomes. Learning analytics draw on data from digital interactions—such as time on task, error patterns, and participation—to inform instructional decisions and identify at-risk learners through predictive modeling. AI-powered assessment tools further enhance evaluation by enabling automated scoring, performance tracking, and rapid feedback, with natural language processing supporting consistent grading of written responses and digital testing environments facilitating continuous formative assessment and timely learning adjustments (Villegas-Ch et al., 2025) (Saleem et al., 2025).

Figure 2. AI applications across the learning cycle

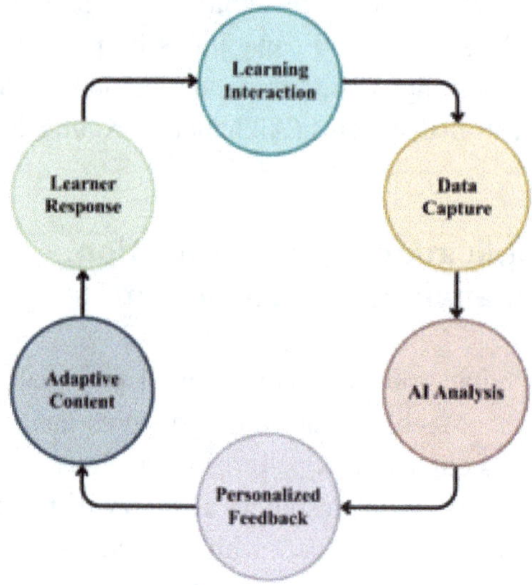

3.4 Emerging tools

Recent years have seen the rise of powerful AI tools that increasingly shape the learning and teaching experience. Generative AI models like ChatGPT support learners by providing explanations, study guides, examples, and feedback, while assisting teachers in content creation, assessment design, and lesson planning. Khanmigo, an AI-driven tutoring system integrated with Khan Academy, offers structured guidance that fosters critical thinking and inquiry within curriculum-aligned lessons. Tools like Copilot enhance computational thinking and coding skills by providing code suggestions, debugging support, and practice opportunities for both novices and experienced programmers. Adaptive platforms such as DreamBox, Coursera modules, and Century Tech personalize instruction by analyzing real-time learner data to adjust pacing, sequencing, and content presentation, improving engagement, retention, and conceptual mastery. Together, these AI tools illustrate a diverse, learner-centered ecosystem that spans tutoring, content generation, coding assistance, and data-informed personalized guidance (Langreo, 2024; OpenAI, 2025).

3.5 How AI changes the roles of teachers and learners

The integration of AI in education is transforming the roles of both teachers and students. Teachers are shifting from being sole content deliverers to facilitators, designers, and mentors, with AI handling repetitive tasks such as grading, lesson planning, and data tracking, allowing educators to focus on interpersonal communication, emotional support, and higher-order thinking. They guide students in interpreting AI-generated outputs, evaluating information quality, and applying ethical reasoning, while supporting AI literacy and technology integration. Students, in turn, become active participants who co-construct knowledge with AI, engage in experimentation, iteration, and collaborative exploration, and receive personalized feedback that enhances self-regulation and metacognition. Critical analysis skills are increasingly necessary to identify errors or biases in AI outputs, reinforcing digital literacy and responsible engagement. Human agency remains central, with AI expanding rather than replacing capabilities, fostering curiosity, creativity, and inquiry, and underscoring the need for professional development, ethical frameworks, and pedagogical redesign to support human-centered education (Qureshi, 2025).

4. HUMAN-AI COLLABORATION: A NEW EDUCATIONAL PARADIGM

The emergence of artificial intelligence in learning environments has encouraged a reorientation of educational practices. Instead of functioning as isolated tools, AI systems now participate in interactive processes that shape how knowledge is acquired, constructed, and applied (Figure 3). This paradigm introduces collaborative relationships where human judgment, creativity, and emotional intelligence merge with machine generated insights, analytics, and automation. The shift reflects a movement from technology enhanced instruction toward learning ecosystems in which human and artificial agents share responsibilities and influence pathways of understanding. This section explores the conceptual, pedagogical, and relational changes that define this paradigm (Creely et al., 2025).

Figure 3. Human–AI complementarity model

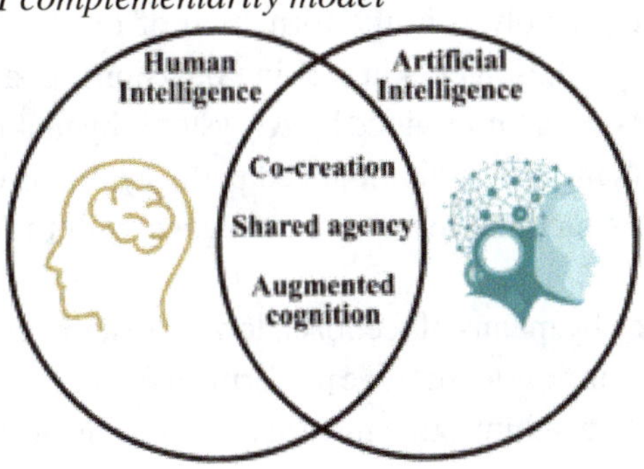

4.1 The conceptual shift: AI as collaborator, not replacement

A central theme in contemporary discourse on educational technology is the repositioning of AI as a collaborator rather than a substitute for human roles. Early narratives often focused on automation, suggesting that AI might displace teachers through advanced capabilities. Research now emphasizes the complementary nature of AI systems, which excel in data processing, pattern identification, and adaptive feedback while lacking emotional sensitivity and contextual judgment. This complementary relationship forms the foundation of collaborative learning ecosystems.

The idea of AI as a partner means that the capabilities of the technology are to be reimagined. It turns into a system aiding the execution of cognitive functions, exploration, and constant guidance. Teamwork also involves the recognition of human capabilities including empathy, moral thinking, improvisation, and the skill of working in a grey environment. These are some of the strengths that cannot be reproduced in algorithmic processes. Research in human centered artificial intelligence emphasizes that human and machine intelligence act in a synergistic manner meaning that none of the agents can present results that cannot be obtained by the other agent.

This change of conditions contributes to the institutional thinking, as well. Schools and universities are beginning to consider models that combine the knowledge of the teacher with AI obtained insights. Policies promote responsible incorporation as opposed to complete automation. The cooperative framing alleviates anxiety levels in teachers and encourages the use of AI supported teaching. It makes AI a friendly entity that will increase the capacity and decrease the amount of work instead of a threat (Qureshi, 2025)(Yan, 2025).

4.2 Human-AI Shared Agency in Learning

Shared agency is the approach to learning, in which both human beings and AI systems are actively involved in the formation of results. Human learners are traditionally characterized as agents in making decisions, goals and tracking their progress. These processes are now aided by AI systems by making real time suggestions, adaptive sequencing and individualized pathways. This common framework affects the manner in which the learners can engage with the content and control their learning.

AI improves agency by means of feedback loops. Systems compare performance trends and recommend on how to improve performance. The learners react by making changes in study habits, searching other materials or working on other representations. The communication is not linear but dynamic. Shared agency therefore increases the control of the learner since AI gives the learner more insights on which informed decision making can be done.

Shared agency is also experienced by teachers. AI applications compare the performance of classes in general, point out misconceptions, and students who require help. Teachers use this knowledge in instructional design. The synthesis of both the teacher intuition and the AI generated data makes the decision making a more enriched environment. The studies of collaborative agency show that the collaboration between agencies contributes to a better metacognition and engages more intensely.

Shared agency requires ethical responsibility. Students need to know how AI systems can actually make suggestions, and teachers need to make sure that suggestions do not limit exploration or promote biases. Clear-cut agreement on the working of the system promotes trust and autonomy. Such a balance would be needed to maintain healthy collaborative structures (Yan, 2025)(Aldino et al., 2025).

4.3 Co-creation of knowledge through AI tools

Co-creation entails the generation of knowledge using mutual interaction between learners, educators and AI systems. Classical teaching was aimed at passing information. Co-creation makes the students become active participants and interact with AI assisted prompts, simulations and creative processes. The learners sharpen ideas by interacting with generated models, hypothesize and forge other interpretations.

Artificial intelligence tools promote co-creation in several aspects. Generative systems come up with drafts, explanations, and visualizations, which the learners critique and refine. Such a loop resembles the real-world knowledge production processes in a professional setting. The intelligent tutoring systems facilitate the process of inquiry by giving step-by-step hints to guide the thought process as opposed to simply answering the questions. Adaptive platforms introduce the input of the learners into the changing sequences of contents.

Educators are also collaborators of AI. They use learning analytics information to plan specific activities, distinguish instruction and create meaningful learning experiences through designing richness. AI brings in information and teachers place these informations into contexts of curriculum and classroom realities. The co-creation process is known to be a partnership of human innovation and machine intelligence interacting with each other.

The co-creative tasks often provide students with a sense of improved motivation as AI tools are able to provide real-time feedback and tailored discovery options. Interaction with systems that recreate expert level reasoning is a stimulus to inquiry. The research on digital co-creation suggests that these interactions enhance understanding, broaden the conceptual framework, and become innovative (Eagle, 2025).

4.4 Teacher Augmentation vs. Teacher Automation

Augmentation and automation represent complementary approaches to integrating AI in education. Teacher automation involves transferring routine instructional or administrative tasks—such as grading, standardized feedback, and content delivery—to AI systems, reducing workload but potentially narrowing the educator's role. Teacher augmentation, by contrast, supports professional practice through AI-assisted lesson planning, data interpretation, and personalized intervention, while preserving human strengths such as empathy, cultural awareness, and ethical judgment. Research indicates that augmented teachers achieve better classroom outcomes by improving time management and feedback quality, whereas automation is most effective for scaling instruction in resource-limited settings. A balanced integration of both approaches requires principles that safeguard teacher agency and maintain pedagogical integrity (Qureshi, 2025).

4.5 Students as AI-Empowered Learners: From Consumers to Creators

Traditional systems usually put students in the role of information consumers. This orientation towards creation, exploration and active problem solving is shifted to AI supported learning environment. The interactions with the generative tools, simulations, code assistants, and adaptive inquiry platforms provide students with a chance to become a designer of knowledge.

AI empowers learners with the help of personalized scaffolding. The students are explained in a manner that best suits their cognitive profiles, and they will be able to tackle complex tasks with more confidence. They produce essays, projects, prototypes and the visualizations together with AI systems. This change creates a feeling of ownership since the learners get to feel that they are competent contributors.

The reorientation towards creation as opposed to consumption is also consistent with the current skill models that focus on creativity, innovation, and digital literacy. The experience with AI will teach students to be more critical of information and refine the output of the system as well as apply computational knowledge to the real context. It promotes reevaluation of thoughts and resilience since students repeat human-AI interaction cycles of work.

The studies on AI as assisted creativity indicate that there is a higher engagement and learning among the students who have been using the AI-based tools like generative AI in brainstorming, creating content, and experimenting. These tools make the creative opportunities democratic since learners who possess varied abilities will be able to engage meaningfully in design oriented tasks. AI thus, becomes an engine of increasing involvement and recognizing different talents (Gervacio, 2024)(Wang, 2025).

4.6 AI as a Cognitive Partner: Enhancing Problem Solving, Creativity, Critical Thinking

Artificial Intelligence Systems are cognitive companions when they take part in the cognitive processes which aid the comprehension of humans. Such collaboration will improve problem-solving since AI systems can break down problems, create possible solutions, and give step-by-step instructions. Learners are able to examine many solutions options, compare results and contemplate reasoning approaches. Cognitive partnership promotes a more thorough understanding since the students analyze their processing of thoughts as well as machine generated thoughts.

Artificial intelligence enhances creativity. Generative tools generate new combinations, drive ideation and eliminate obstacles to skill constraints. A visual representational scholar is able to make AI generated pictures to experiment with aesthetical ideas. Model outputs allow writers to explore the different tone and style. These processes increase the creativity possibilities and preserve the control of people.

The critical thinking is enhanced since learners will be required to question AI outputs, evaluate their credibility, and detect inaccuracies. AI at times generates misleading or partial information. Such restrictions given to learners promote source investigation and doubting. This interaction cultivates discernment, an essential skill in information rich environments.

The distributed cognition process is also supported by AI as a cognitive partner, in which human and machine agents are involved in thinking. Students transfer the repetitive processes to AI and dedicate the force of interpretation, synthesis, and higher order thinking. Analytics, also, provide teachers with the cognitive partnership concept that unveils hidden patterns that could not be observed manually. These understandings can be used in instructional planning and enhance pedagogical thinking.

The introduction of AI as a cognitive partner has become a marker of a change in the educational practice. It transforms learning as an individual undertaking to a collective thinking process where human beings and machines work together in their strengths. Such a collaboration helps to create flexible, reflexive and creative minds who are also prepared to face modern challenges (Riva, 2025).

5. PEDAGOGICAL MODELS FOR THE AI ERA

Artificial intelligence is changing educational practices greatly as it is being incorporated in the mechanism of teaching and learning (Figure 4). Classroom teaching methods that have traditionally been influenced by pedagogical methods are being transformed into learner-centered and more flexible and dynamic models. The features facilitating such developments by AI include adaptive feedback, smart content, continuous analytics and individualized learning. The subsequent parts of the paper consider key pedagogical paradigms that can meet the requirements of the AI age and discuss the way in which they are improved with the help of intelligent systems (Oyebola Olusola Ayeni et al., 2024).

Figure 4. AI-enhanced pedagogical models map

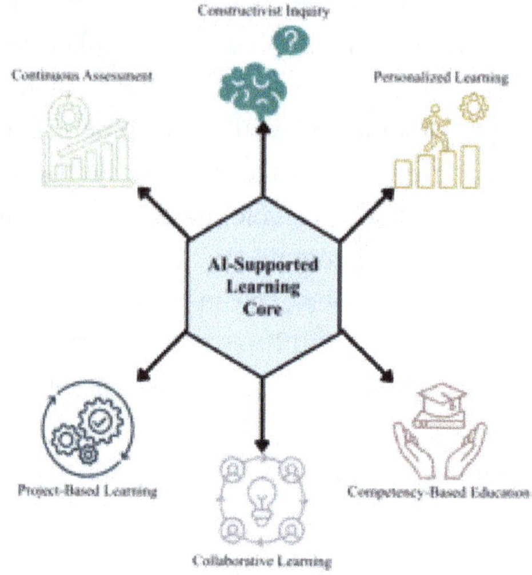

5.1 AI-Supported Constructivism and Inquiry-Based Learning

Constructivist sees learning as a dynamic process where people construct knowledge as a result of exploration, reflection, and interaction. Inquiry based learning builds on this philosophy by applying structured investigation, formulating problems, experimenting and reasoning. AI can greatly improve these methods since it provides tools that do not limit learner autonomy in exploration.

AI systems provide learners with curated resources, contextual hints, and real time feedback that guide inquiry processes while preserving agency. Intelligent search tools can reduce enormous information and help students find legitimate sources in the most shortest time possible. Generative AI models replicate the reasoning pattern of experts and assist learners to express hypotheses or narrow research questions. Students engage in dialogic learning, which allows them to explore concepts, test assumptions and get scaffolding to overcome conceptual blocks.

Quality of reflection is also enhanced with the help of AI supported inquiry. Intelligent systems read through the responses or partial solutions provided by learners and point out the misconceptions. This aids in metacognitive development since the students are able to understand how they think. Research on digital inquiry settings has shown that learners employing AI improved tools show greater engagement and their problem solving skills are better than their counterparts who use traditional tools. AI therefore strengthens constructivist learning without undermining its core principle of learner agency (El Fathi et al., 2025).

5.2 Personalized and Adaptive Learning Pathways

Personalized learning involves the customization of materials, speed and learning strategies based on the needs of the student. This personalization is optimized in adaptive pathways, which is the ongoing analysis of data, which guides real time changes. AI is effective in these processes due to its ability to identify the patterns of performance and customize learning processes.

Adaptive learning systems monitor interactions of the learners, assess their mastery, and modify task sequences. They provide more elaboration whenever a learner is struggling and speed up learning in cases where mastery is manifesting. Such a fluid route of instructional delivery moves the instructional paradigm off the one-size-fits-all models and recognizes that there are many different learning processes that exist in classrooms (Kang, 2023).

The success of individualized directions can be justified by the studies of the field of learning analytics, according to which a predictive system is used to identify those students who need intervention and provide a specific mechanism of assistance. AI systems enhance the insights of the teacher by providing early warning signals, which facilitate the provision of instructional response in a timely manner. Table 1 provides a summary of the differences between personalization using traditional and AI.

Table 1. Traditional vs AI-supported personalization

Feature	Traditional Personalization	AI Supported Personalization
Data use	Limited teacher observation	Continuous real time data streams
Pacing	Fixed	Dynamic and learner specific
Feedback	Periodic	Immediate and adaptive
Content selection	Instructor curated	Algorithmically optimized based on mastery
Intervention timing	Often delayed	Early prediction and timely support

Students in AI assisted personalized learning have a tendency to be more motivated since they can work at the level of their competence. These environments will not only minimize frustration among struggling learners, but will also increase the opportunities of enrichment among improved learners. These systems are adaptive, which is an indication of a transition to an inertiated curriculum development as opposed to a responsive curriculum design.

5.3 Competency-Based Education (CBE) Strengthened Through AI Insights

Competency-based education is focused on skills control and not the amount of time spent in the learning environments. The students move on when they show competence. The AI systems play a major role in the sustainability and accuracy of CBE frameworks.

Assessment analytics gauge performance in the various tasks and situations. Artificial intelligence systems make inferences on big data to find new strengths and gaps that would give a more holistic view of competence than individual event measures. The insights assist the educators to identify the readiness to progress and direct the learners to the specific exercises.

CBE demands a high frequency of practical skills. The simulations made possible by AI can assist real performance activities in which learners can use knowledge in practice. These simulations produce elaborate analytics represented in decision making processes, speed, accuracy, and strategy. Such information adds value to the evaluation of teachers and helps in sound decisions regarding mastery.

AI also works to promote individual channels within CBE. In cases where the learners cannot master specific competencies, AI recommends specific materials and practice tasks. It is hard to be this specific manually, as it requires computer intervention. Besides, AI can be used to provide scalable monitoring solutions, allowing institutions to address large groups of children and still provide them with personalized care.

The granularity of data, real performance possibilities and constant monitoring enhances rigour and accessibility of CBE models (Faucher et al., 2025).

5.4 Collaborative Learning Ecosystems and AI-Mediated Teamwork

Collaborative learning focuses on social interaction, collective problem solving and construction of knowledge. The concept of AI improves cooperation with the help of communication, coordination, and equal participation.

The AI mediated collaboration systems are used to analyze the patterns of interaction, detect the members of the group that are not engaged, and provide the prompts to facilitate participation. This comes to overcome the problem of the conventional group work whereby unequal contribution tends to influence results. The smart platforms also assist in pairing the learners with their complementary forces to create balanced teams.

Distributed teamwork is facilitated by virtual collaboration environments with the help of AI. Students can exchange documents, build projects and communicate using the integrated systems which offer real time suggestions and organizational support. AI will be able to summarize the conversations, emphasize the main points, and monitor development towards group objectives.

The studies on AI that promoted cooperation show better accomplishment of tasks and deeper conceptualization since learners have ongoing guidance that facilitates interactions. Communication skills are also developed in such environments since learners are able to express reasoning in an organised structure which has been refined using the machine knowledge.

AI mediated teaming is also helpful to teachers. Teachers track the group dynamics using dashboards, which are used to illustrate communication frequency, pattern of contribution, and shared decision making. This information assists teachers to only intervene when the need arises and at the same time maintain autonomy in students.

5.5 Project-Based and Design-Thinking Models Enriched Through AI Tools

Design thinking and project-based learning would nurture learners to be authentic and work on real world problems. Such models include brainstorming, planning, prototyping, testing and refinement. AI provides intelligent assistance to such stages by being creative, analytical, and efficient in processing information.

At the ideation stage, generative AI sources stimulus content, creates other viewpoints, and simulates brainstorming. This will enable the learners to diversify their thoughts and think outside the box. AI can be considered an advantage of design thinking frameworks since AI-powered systems can help frame the problem and help the person develop empathy by analyzing sentiments and modeling a scenario.

The AI tools facilitate workflow management in the planning and organization process. Smart assistants create schedules, approximate time required to complete tasks, and pinpoint possible risks. This assists teams to be focused and organized when undertaking complicated projects.

Prototyping will be easier because AI helps with the coding, visualization and simulation. Users that lack technical knowledge can create prototypes by being directed by AI powered applications. This democratizes the project-based learning and minimizes the reliance on technical skills of high level.

Test and trial also become better as AI compares performance information, user feedback and prototype behavior. These insights are used to revise and aid evidence-based decision making. In research on design education, the concept of AI-assisted iteration has been highlighted to result in improved quality solutions and improved reflection.

5.6 Assessment Transformation: Continuous, Formative, AI-Driven Evaluation

The application of AI in assessment practices is transforming them. The classical assessment paradigms were based on periodical testing which provided minimal information on the continuing learning. AI changes the evaluation toward continuous and formative practices that monitor the progress in various dimensions.

AI-based assessment systems assess the answers of the learners, identify the misperceptions and provide personalized feedback. This minimizes the delays and facilitates prompt instructional change. Essays, reflections, and explanations can be scored automatically with the help of natural language processing. These systems point out structural, conceptual and stylistic characteristics in student writing, which aids in development with minute commentaries.

Machine learning will forecast the future and determine learners who are likely to be left behind. Teachers get analytics which inform intervention strategies. These forecasts are based on the trends in interaction, correctness, time usage, and job performance.

Authentic assessment is also facilitated by AI. Simulations and interactive exercises generate large volumes of data data, which indicates decision making, strategy application and flexibility. This kind of information gives a subtle insight as opposed to conventional examination. Table 2 depicts the variations of conventional and AI supported evaluation.

Table 2. Traditional vs AI-driven assessment

Feature	Traditional Assessment	AI Driven Assessment
Frequency	Infrequent	Continuous
Feedback	Delayed	Immediate and adaptive
Data type	Limited responses	Multi dimensional behavioral data
Focus	Outcome	Process and progression
Intervention	Reactive	Proactive and predictive

6. REIMAGINING THE ROLE OF TEACHERS

The implementation of artificial intelligence in the learning setting does not only change the learning process of students, but it also changes the way of defining a professional identity among teachers (Figure 5). The teachers will also continue to play the core role, but their tasks are increasing to new areas with the assistance of AI. Teachers do not act purely as information conveyers, they are also planners of the learning setting, overseers of the AI software, ethical leaders, and human relationship facilitators. These innovations necessitate new skills, new instructional processes and new models of professional learning that can assist teaching in AI enriched classrooms.

Figure 5. Teacher role transformation model

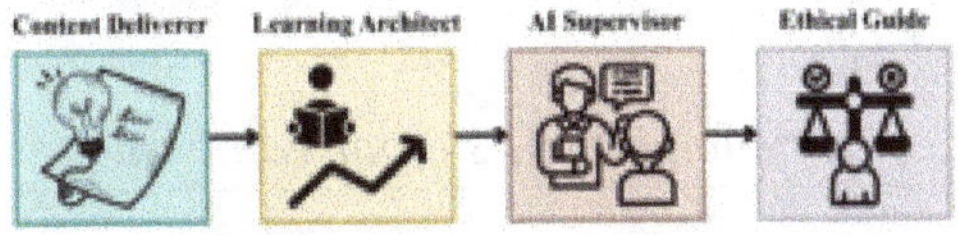

6.1 Teachers as Learning Architects and AI Supervisors

The teachers become more of learning designers who create instructional ecosystems in which AI tools become meaningful sequences. The role consists of choosing technologies that satisfy the curricular objectives, setting up AI-powered platforms, and setting up interactions between students and intelligent systems. The teachers define the cases of assistance of AI, the cases of necessity of human teaching, and the ways of the reinforcement and enrich the other one.

The other upcoming responsibility is the supervision of AI. Educators control the work of the systems, decipher the insights generated by AI, and make sure that the recommendations are consistent with pedagogical purposes. Supervision assists in keeping the classrooms transparent where AI plays an active role in making decisions concerning pacing, feedback and intervention. Studies on human-AI interaction emphasize the need to have human supervision to help avoid excessive dependence on algorithmic results. Educators are going to review the precision, ethical concerns, and situational correctness of AI recommendations and make sure that they facilitate learning instead of undermining it.

6.2 Essential new Teacher Skills: AI Literacy, Prompt Engineering, Data Ethics

Educators should have innovative skills to operate in AI assisted settings. When taught AI literacy, people are aware of how various systems of AI work, what data they utilize, and what restrictions they introduce. Such literacy will help teachers to use AI tools in a responsible way and understand the results of the systems correctly.

With the emergence of generative AI, prompt engineering is becoming an important skill. Those teachers capable of creating specific prompts facilitate students to get a better explanation, more profound insights, and more organized feedback. Timely strategies also affect the quality of instructional materials created with the help of AI in planning lessons.

Another important field of awareness is data ethics. AI systems gather and analyze the information about learners in an endless loop. Educators should be aware of privacy, ethical use of the data, and any possible prejudice. Table 3 shows teacher competencies that are needed in AI enriched classrooms.

Table 3. Key teacher competencies in AI supported instruction

Competency	Description
AI literacy	Understanding AI functions, benefits, and limits
Prompt engineering	Creating effective prompts for generative AI tools
Data ethics awareness	Ensuring safe and equitable data practices
Analytical interpretation	Understanding AI analytics to guide instruction
System supervision	Monitoring AI behavior and maintaining alignment with learning goals

6.3 Reducing Administrative Load Through Automation

AI can help to save much of the administrative load on the teacher who is likely to spend a lot of time. Objective responses are graded by automated grading systems and written assignments can be scored preliminarily by natural language processing tools. This will liberate teachers who would be engaged in repetitive evaluation and more time will be spent on instructional design.

Through AI supported platforms, the administrative processes of attendance tracking, lesson scheduling, and progress reporting, as well as communication with parents, can be automated. Such systems help to unify all the data to facilitate easy interpretation, and lower mistakes of manual input. Studies on teacher workload show that the automation process leads to increased job satisfaction as teachers will be able to spend more time on the pedagogical process.

Early learning issues are also identified with the help of automation. AI applications examine the patterns of participation, completion of assignments and performance to provide early warning signals. The teachers get the chance to intervene sooner and ensure that the complications do not escalate to the point where they need further intensive attention.

6.4 Enhancing Teacher Creativity, Productivity, and Emotional Presence

The support of lesson generation, with activity and resource development helps AI tools enhance teacher creativity. Generative AI is able to provide suggestions on instructional strategies, generate illustrative examples, and generate multimedia content, which can be customized by teachers and used in the classroom. This innovative augmentation stimulates innovation and decreases the number of time needed to come up with high quality materials.

There is an increase in productivity because routine tasks are automated and there is an improvement in the planning processes. Teachers undertake the role of refining assessment, differentiating resources, analyzing wide patterns of classroom performance using AI. With these improvements, teachers will have time to interact more with the students, guide them, and engage in reflections.

The emotional presence is enhanced in AI enhanced classes. With AI performing some of the administrative duties, educators get extra time to perform interpersonal work including conflict resolution, motivation creation, and emotional support. Social-emotional learning studies have concluded that human presence is still critical in fostering empathy, resilience and community in the learning spaces. The AI will not be able to substitute the human relational capacity, but it will provide the circumstances where teachers will be able to devote more of their attention to these aspects.

6.5 Professional Development Models for AI-Integrated Classrooms

The professional growth should be adjusted to help teachers implement AI in a responsible and successful way. Conventional training methods cannot be used as AI systems need to learn constantly, test, and practice their gains. Good models are made up of workshops, coaching, collaborative inquiry and practical explorations.

An avenue worth trying is the iterative learning cycle in which the educators start using AI tools in their classes, record the results, and distribute them among their colleagues. This is a process that fosters professional communities of practice. The mentioned studies on teacher learning indicate that peer supported experimentation results in greater adoption and stronger instructional innovation.

Micro-credential programs offer targeted learning pathways in areas such as AI literacy, ethical AI use, data interpretation, and generative AI teaching strategies. These credentials validate teacher expertise and encourage ongoing development. Institutions also provide mentorship programs where experienced technology integrators guide colleagues in implementing AI safely and meaningfully.

Continuous professional development ensures that teachers remain informed as AI technologies evolve. Training programs that adopt flexible, modular, and practice-centered structures prepare educators for long-term engagement with intelligent systems.

Reimagining the teacher's role in the AI era involves balancing technological efficiency with human-centered values. Teachers function as architects, supervisors, creators, and emotional anchors in learning environments shaped through AI. Their capacity to integrate AI responsibly and purposefully determines the quality of the educational transformation underway.

7. STUDENT EXPERIENCE IN AN AI-COLLABORATIVE LEARNING ENVIRONMENT

The introduction of the artificial intelligence into the learning settings changes not only the practice of instruction, but also the experience of studying. Students engage with systems that read their development, react to their necessities and help them explore knowledge in a more independent manner. The AI-enhanced environments transform students into the passive consumers of pre-existing information into the participants of the learning process, in which they engage with intelligent systems to form their learning experiences. Such spaces also lead to more profound thinking, creative learning, and acquisition of critical digital skills.

7.1 Personalized Learning Trajectories

AI systems create personalized learning paths that adapt to student performance, interests, and pace, unlike traditional classrooms with uniform progression. These platforms monitor accuracy, time on tasks, error patterns, and activity, offering additional explanations or advanced material as needed. Personalized pathways enhance motivation by matching assignments to ability levels, preventing frustration for struggling learners and boredom for advanced students. Studies in adaptive learning show measurable improvements in persistence and conceptual understanding due to timely, individualized support.

7.2 AI-Supported Creativity and Exploration

AI tools enhance creative expression and discovery learning. Generative models help students write, create images, run simulations, and code, overcoming initial obstacles in visualization or task organization. They support brainstorming, experimentation, and divergent thinking by suggesting alternatives that challenge assumptions—such as hypothetical scenarios in literature, alternative hypotheses in science, or stylistic variants in visual arts. Intelligent tutoring systems further promote exploration by guiding inquiry without giving direct answers, offering cues, resources, and prompts. Research shows that AI-supported exploration builds learner confidence and fosters more inclusive participation in creative activities.

7.3 Developing Metacognition With AI Feedback

Metacognition—the ability to monitor and control one's thinking—is enhanced in AI-enriched environments through detailed, immediate, and personalized feedback. AI systems highlight misconceptions, inefficient strategies, and progress trends, prompting students to evaluate and adjust their learning methods. Reflective prompts encourage learners to explain reasoning, justify choices, and assess AI outputs for trustworthiness and errors. Studies show that active engagement with AI-supported reflection improves self-regulation, persistence, and critical thinking, preparing students for collaborative human–AI learning environments.

7.4 Building Digital and AI Literacy as Core Competencies

Digital literacy remains essential, but AI-enriched environments require broader competencies. Learners must understand how AI gathers data, predicts outcomes, and generates content, supporting responsible and safe use (Figure 6). AI literacy includes knowing when to rely on AI, when to question its outputs, assessing credibility, and adjusting strategies. Such skills prepare students for academic and professional contexts dominated by AI. Curricular frameworks increasingly embed AI literacy, teaching algorithmic behavior, bias detection, and ethical considerations, summarized in Table 4.

Table 4. Core components of AI literacy for students

Component	Description
Understanding AI functions	Basic awareness of how algorithms operate
Data awareness	Knowing how data is collected and used
Critical evaluation	Assessing the quality of AI generated outputs
Ethical considerations	Recognizing fairness, privacy, and bias implications
Collaborative use	Working effectively with AI to accomplish tasks

Figure 6. Student growth dimensions pyramid

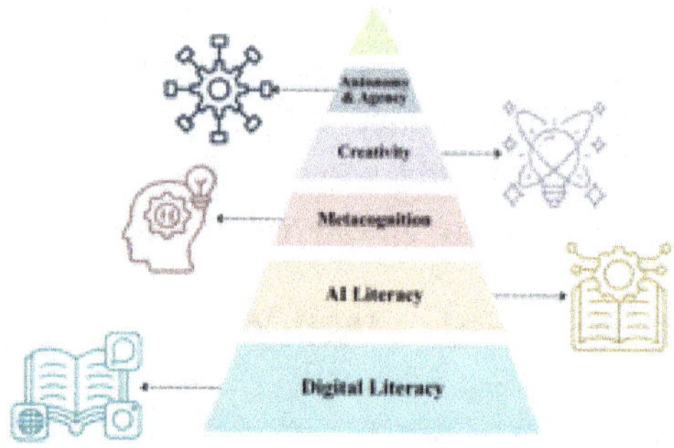

7.5 Empowering Student Autonomy and Agency

AI-based learning environments foster student responsibility and self-directed learning. Adaptive systems support self-pacing, letting learners decide when to review, advance, or explore additional material, aligning with their goals and readiness. AI guides independent problem solving by providing context rather than prescriptive instructions, enabling students to navigate resources, interpret feedback, and make informed decisions. Through co-creation with AI tools, learners gain confidence, critically analyze outputs, and refine their work, promoting agency and resilience. Research shows that AI-supported autonomy strengthens intrinsic motivation and academic outcomes. Overall, AI reshapes student experience by enhancing personalization, creativity, metacognition, digital literacy, and agency, preparing learners for contemporary, technology-driven societies.

8. ETHICAL, SOCIAL, AND POLICY CONSIDERATIONS

The integration of artificial intelligence into education introduces new ethical, social, and policy concerns that influence how learning environments are designed and governed. AI systems process vast amounts of learner data, generate recommendations, shape learning trajectories, and participate in evaluative processes. Such functions are to be taken into serious consideration to avoid the likelihood that the system of education is not equitable, transparent, safe, and puts the human well-being at the centre of its activities. The debate on AI and its role in education goes beyond the technical needs and addresses more framework questions of equity, human rights, psychological growth, and institutional accountability.

8.1 Data Privacy, Security, and Transparency

AI-based learning platforms rely on extensive data collection to provide personalized experiences, including information on performance, behavior, communication, and even emotions, raising privacy concerns. Schools must clearly communicate what data is collected, how it is used, and who has access to maintain trust and protect student rights. Security is also critical, as robust measures are needed to prevent unauthorized access, breaches, and misuse of sensitive information, which could compromise learning systems. Transparency in AI operations is essential; students and teachers should understand how recommendations are generated, ensuring ethical and responsible use while avoiding misunderstandings or false confidence.

8.2 Bias, Fairness, and Consequences of Algorithmic Decision-Making

AI models reflect the data they are trained on, and if that data contains past inequalities or stereotypes, the systems can replicate or amplify biases, affecting student evaluation, placement, and recommendations. Ensuring equity requires continuous monitoring of outputs across demographic groups, with educators analyzing trends in feedback, learning pathways, and performance forecasts to detect potential bias. Overreliance on AI can also distort teacher perceptions, highlighting the need for human critical intervention. Addressing bias in AI not only promotes academic fairness but also supports students' emotional well-being, motivation, and self-esteem.

8.3 Digital Divides: Ensuring Equitable AI Access

AI-assisted learning requires robust infrastructure, including high-speed internet, compatible devices, and reliable technology. Students from disadvantaged backgrounds may face barriers due to poor connectivity or lack of devices, exacerbating existing inequalities. Promoting equity involves strategies such as device-sharing programs, low-bandwidth AI tools, community access centers, and targeted funding for under-resourced areas. Additionally, digital literacy training is essential to ensure that all learners can effectively engage with AI platforms and participate without discrimination.

8.4 Psychological Impacts of AI Reliance

AI in learning can affect both cognition and emotion. While instant support and guidance from AI can accelerate learning, overreliance may reduce perseverance, creativity, and independent problem-solving. Frequent detailed feedback may enhance learning but can also raise anxiety or lower confidence, requiring careful design to support growth rather than judgment. Human interaction remains essential for empathy, encouragement, and social development, as AI cannot fully replicate these relational aspects. Educators should also guide students to critically understand AI's capabilities to prevent overdependence or anthropomorphizing the technology.

8.5 Regulatory Frameworks and Governance Models for Safe AI in Education

The rapid expansion of AI in education requires governance frameworks emphasizing safety, equity, accountability, and ethical practice. Policies should cover data protection, transparency, accessibility, and responsible use, guiding institutions in selecting technologies and establishing vendor ethics. National AI strategies increasingly include education, focusing on risk assessment, compliance, and clear responsibility for data governance and AI implementation. Regulatory measures may limit automated decisions in high-stakes areas, ensuring human oversight, inclusivity, and accommodation for learners with diverse needs. Continuous evaluation is essential, as guidelines must evolve alongside technological advances and stakeholder feedback.

8.6 Responsible AI Guidelines for Educators, Students, and Institutions

Responsible AI use in education requires coordinated commitments from teachers, learners, and institutions, guided by ethical practices and clear goals. Teachers should view AI as an ally, understand its strengths and limitations, verify outputs, and adapt interactions to the classroom context, while educating students on ethical use, data privacy, and critical evaluation. Students must engage with AI consciously, challenge outputs, respect academic integrity, and avoid over-reliance. Institutions play a central role by implementing open data policies, providing training, testing AI tools, and establishing reporting mechanisms for harmful or biased behaviors. Effective and ethical integration depends on ongoing governance, ensuring that AI enhances learning without compromising fairness, safety, or human dignity.

9. CASE STUDIES AND GLOBAL PERSPECTIVES

The application of AI in education is in many regions, and each of them has specific priorities, influences of cultures, and policy frameworks. The experimentation with AI in countries includes the need to solve personalization, shortage of teachers, equity gaps, and data-driven decision making. Such international projects can give an invaluable account of what AI can do to enhance the learning process as long as they are based on the local requirements and standards of learning. The analysis of regional applications, institutional achievements, experiences of early adopters, and cross-cultural interpretations can assist in identifying the variety of approaches to human-AI collaboration and the reasons that determine its success.

9.1 Regional Approaches to AI in Education

In the United States, AI adoption is largely innovation-driven. For example, the EdTech firm *Carnegie Learning* implements AI-powered adaptive mathematics platforms across over 1,000 schools, improving student problem-solving accuracy by 15–20%. National guidelines emphasize responsible AI use, teacher oversight, equity, and transparency.

China has implemented AI at a national level to support large-scale personalization. *Squirrel AI* employs advanced learner profiling and adaptive algorithms to provide customized instruction to tens of thousands of students, showing improvements of 10–25% in mathematics and language scores in published studies. Government initiatives integrate AI competency training from early schooling to develop a digitally skilled workforce.

The European Union prioritizes ethical and regulated AI use. Pilot programs, such as adaptive engineering courses at *TU Delft*, provide individualized problem sets while maintaining faculty oversight and compliance with GDPR standards. Studies indicate improved learner engagement without compromising academic integrity. Other regions show diverse objectives: Singapore focuses on AI for lifelong learning; the UAE integrates AI into smart school systems; and African countries explore AI to address teacher shortages and expand access to quality education under resource constraints.

9.2 Exemplary Models of Human–AI Collaboration

Several institutions demonstrate effective integration of AI while preserving human agency. *Arizona State University* incorporates generative AI writing assistants in first-year composition courses, enabling students to receive formative feedback and brainstorm ideas, monitored by instructors; studies report increased student confidence and engagement. In China, middle schools using *Squirrel AI*-based tutoring platforms complement classroom instruction with teacher-monitored analytics dashboards, enhancing student practice and concept reinforcement, with measurable gains in mathematics and language performance. At *TU Delft*, adaptive problem sets in engineering courses allow instructors to track anonymized analytics, providing tailored support without increasing the risk of academic dishonesty. Table 5 summarizes these institutions' key characteristics and outcomes.

Table 5. Characteristics of effective human-AI collaborative institutions

Feature	Description
Teacher oversight	Educators supervise AI interactions and contextualize system outputs
Ethical alignment	AI tools comply with ethical and privacy standards
Student empowerment	Learners use AI to create, explore, and self-regulate
Integrated professional development	Teachers receive training in AI literacy and system navigation
Balanced automation	Routine tasks are automated while complex tasks remain human-led

These case studies show that successful institutions treat AI as an enhancement rather than a replacement, emphasizing collaboration, transparency, and human judgment.

9.3 Lessons Learned From Early Adopters

Early experiences with AI in education highlight several key lessons for effective integration. Teacher involvement is critical; schools that provided insufficient training saw resistance or ineffective use, whereas knowledgeable educators could interpret data and make informed pedagogical decisions. Transparency in AI systems fosters trust, as students respond better when the reasoning behind recommendations is clear. Scalability must be planned carefully, since adaptive solutions that succeed in small settings may fail at larger scales without proper infrastructure and monitoring. Data governance is essential to balance privacy with meaningful insights, and institutions without frameworks faced ethical and operational challenges. Overall, successful adoption requires iterative refinement, stakeholder feedback, and alignment with educational values rather than a plug-and-play approach.

9.4 Cross-Cultural Interpretations of AI in Learning

The role and adoption of AI in education are strongly influenced by cultural norms. In societies emphasizing technological progress and standardized achievement, AI is often integrated into exams, tutoring, and centralized learning systems as a productivity and learning tool. In contrast, cultures that prioritize humanistic values—such as creativity, emotional engagement, and interpersonal relationships—approach AI more cautiously, emphasizing responsible use and ethical safeguards, as seen in many European contexts. Student perceptions of AI also vary: in cultures that value teacher authority, AI is viewed as a complementary tool, whereas in more experimental or collaborative learning cultures, it is seen as an accessible partner that democratizes knowledge. Linguistic diversity and local context further shape AI interaction, with multilingual and culturally relevant systems promoting inclusivity. Comparative studies indicate that AI adoption is most effective when aligned with local expectations, teaching norms, and cultural values, highlighting the importance of situational flexibility, ethical accountability, and thoughtful human–AI collaboration.

10. FUTURE DIRECTIONS: DESIGNING AI-NATIVE LEARNING ECOSYSTEMS

The principles of AI are transforming the nature of education and an emphasis is placed on the creation of learning environments where AI serves as a core, not an adjunct, component. AI-native learning ecosystems are a form of future where real-world locations, online environments, pedagogies, and assessment are in agreement with smart technologies. These ecosystems facilitate fluid learning processes that transform to the needs of the learners and expectations of the society. The future of education will be dependent on the creation of flexible, adaptable, and collaborative spaces that will consider AI to be a crucial companion in human growth.

10.1 The Future Classroom: Hybrid, Fluid, AI-Augmented Spaces

The future of the classroom will be defined by the hybrid form of classrooms which are eclipsed with the physical and digital classrooms. Rather than rigid rows of desks, the classrooms will have flexible setups, which promote group work, individual investigation, and activities facilitated by artificial intelligence. Interactive surfaces, mixed-reality tools, and VR enabled simulations will be provided in everyday teaching, and students will be able to shift between practical tasks and AI-assisted investigation without issues.

Classroom management systems based on AI will constantly be tracking the progress of learners, patterns, and altering the flows of instructions. The suggested systems can be the grouping of strategies, emerging challenges highlighted, or suggestions of enrichment opportunities. The dashboards will see teachers visualizing real-time learning analytics and therefore act strategically instead of uniformly. These conditions facilitate a dynamic model of instruction in which learning is modeled based on the needs of students but not strict schedules.

The hybrid classrooms will also not be confined to the school building. Students will be exposed to AI-mediated learning experiences at home or community centers or distance locations. A permeable barrier between in-school and out-of-school learning arises in a digital companionship where the mode aids in maintaining constant interaction. Studies conducted in blended learning settings have demonstrated that learners perform well in an environment where they have flexibility and a flexible pacing and this means that the future learning environment will be mobility-focused, interactive, and engage feedback provided by AI regularly.

Inclusive spaces are also a priority of AI-augmented spaces. The intelligent systems have the capability of modifying interfaces to students with disabilities, multimodal content, language translation, and customized assistance. This makes diversity in the classroom a enriching experience as opposed to being a hindrance. The future classroom thus acts as a dynamic ecosystem in which there are physical and digital layers, which are in constant contact with each other to facilitate deeper learning.

10.2 AI as a Lifelong Learning Companion

AI will no longer be limited to formal education and be used as a lifelong learning companion in future learning ecosystems. Students will leave school with their own AI systems that are aware of their learning history, cognitive styles, interests and the long-term aspirations. Professional growth, career shifts, and personalized reskilling or upskilling recommendations may be developed with the help of these AI companions.

Technological change is fast and every individual needs to keep changing with the times. AI will be able to track the tendencies in the labor market, evaluate skills and competencies demanded, and propose learning paths according to the needs. In the case of adults who have work and personal life, AI companions will provide flexible micro-learning experiences that become part of the everyday routine.

Reflective practices may also be enabled by these systems. By being prodded, rated, and overviewing of progress, AI companions assist users to become aware of metacognition and planning skills during the long term. Research in lifelong learning has shown that the personalized and systematic guidance can be of great value to a person, particularly when they are required to work in a complex or shifting work environment.

AI companions will also facilitate well-being, and will remind users of balanced workloads, recommend stress-management strategies or pair them with human mentors or support networks. Emotional and cognitive support integration is useful in making lifelong learning sustainable, as opposed to an overwhelming experience.

Moreover, AI systems of a lifetime can develop civic participation with the support of customized news feeds, philosophical reflections, and ethical deliberations. Such aspects make AI companions more than learning assistants, but also informative companions of citizens. Learners will also change their AI systems with the progression of their lifespan, adjusting to new ambitions, opportunities, and challenges.

10.3 New Credentialing Systems Supported by AI Analytics

Conventional mechanisms of credentialing are based on grading, transcripts, and standardized testing. The systems tend to give little information on the skills of the learners and they are unable to represent competences in areas of complexity. AI provides novel possibilities to change the credentialing process to a more transparent, descriptive, and meaningful one.

To identify trends in problem solving, collaboration, creativity, and persistence, AI analytics may be used to record the micro-level performance data of a variety of tasks. Multi-dimensional profile of strengths in cognitive, social, and behavioral domains is possible with AI, as opposed to just one score in order to summarize learning. These profiles provide more detailed descriptions of what learners can do in a higher education and employment situation.

Online degrees will become more popular. Students may earn badges or micro-certifications for demonstrating mastery of specific skills, such as data interpretation, teamwork, or ethical reasoning. AI is used as the core of the performance evidence checking process based on automated analysis of assignments, simulations, and collaborative work. Accrediting bodies are able to have standard requirements but have individualized access to certification.

The AI support will also enhance the portfolio based credentialing. Students can be assisted by systems to catalogue artifacts, comment on progress, and self-reflect on progress. Evaluations based on AI can recognize correspondence to the standards of the students in terms of their professional life and provide feedback on how it can be improved. The employers can view dynamic credential profiles which show actual abilities as opposed to fixed grades.

Credentialing with AI analytics is also more fair. The conventional examinations might be biased in terms of learning styles or socio-economic status. Models that operate on AI consider performance data at a large scale, instead of relying on individual high-pressure assessments. As an illustration, rather than a single test, AI is able to integrate evidence gathered on hundreds of learning interactions, which is a more balanced perspective of competence.

REFERENCES

Aldino, A. A., Tsai, Y. S., Gupte, S., Henderson, M., Nath, D., Gašević, D., & Chen, G. (2025). Analytics of Learner-Centered Feedback: A Large-Scale Case Study in Higher Education. *Computers & Education, 237*, 105360. DOI: 10.1016/j.compedu.2025.105360

Alkhatlan, A., & Kalita, J. (2018). Intelligent Tutoring Systems: A Comprehensive Historical Survey with Recent Developments. *International Journal of Computer Applications, 181*(43), 1–20. DOI: 10.5120/ijca2019918451

Atchley, P., Pannell, H., Wofford, K., Hopkins, M., & Atchley, R. A. (2024). Human and AI collaboration in the higher education environment: opportunities and concerns. *Cognitive Research: Principles and Implications 2024 9:1, 9*(1), 20-. DOI: 10.1186/s41235-024-00547-9

Ayeni, O. O., Al Hamad, N. M., Chisom, O. N., Osawaru, B., & Adewusi, O. E. (2024). AI in education: A review of personalized learning and educational technology. *GSC Advanced Research and Reviews, 18*(2), 261–271. DOI: 10.30574/gscarr.2024.18.2.0062

Ayeni, O. O., Mohd, N., Hamad, A., Chisom, O. N., Osawaru, B., & Adewusi, O. E. (2024). AI in education : A review of personalized learning and educational technology. *GSC Advanced Research and Reviews, 18*(2), 261–271. DOI: 10.30574/gscarr.2024.18.2.0062

Black, P., & Wiliam, D. (1998). Assessment and Classroom Learning. *Assessment in Education: Principles, Policy\& Practice, 5*(1), 7–74. DOI: 10.1080/0969595980050102

Chakraborty, S. (2024). *Generative AI in Modern Education Society.*

Chan, C. K. Y., & Tsi, L. H. Y. (2023). *The AI Revolution in Education: Will AI Replace or Assist Teachers in Higher Education?* Creely, E., Carabott, · Kelly, Carabott, K., Creely, E., & Carabott, K. (2025). Teaching and learning with AI: an Integrated AI-Oriented Pedagogical Model. *The Australian Educational Researcher 2025 52:6, 52*(6), 4633–4654. DOI: 10.1007/s13384-025-00913-6

Debbarma, S., & Deb, M. (2025). *Play-Based Learning vs . Traditional Learning : A Comprehensive Comparative Analysis. 13*(3).

Eagle, B. A. (2025). *Co-Creating with AI in Higher Education : A Human-AI Collaborative Storybook Project Xindi Lyu.* 2–7.

Education and Academy. (2024). *How Industrialization Shaped Modern Education Systems.*

El Fathi, T., Saad, A., Larhzil, H., Lamri, D., & Al Ibrahmi, E. M. (2025). Integrating generative AI into STEM education: enhancing conceptual understanding, addressing misconceptions, and assessing student acceptance. *Disciplinary and Interdisciplinary Science Education Research 2025 7:1, 7*(1), 6-. DOI: 10.1186/s43031-025-00125-z

Faucher, M. A., Sing, E., Harris, S., Hutson, E., & Hoelscher, S. H. (2025). Artificial Intelligence and Competency-Based Education: A Rapid Scoping Review. *Journal of Midwifery & Women's Health, 70*(6), 865–881. Advance online publication. DOI: 10.1111/jmwh.70009 PMID: 40810696

Gervacio, A. P. (2024). Exploring how generative AI contributes to the motivated engagement and learning production of science-oriented students. *Environment and Social Psychology, 9*(11), 11. DOI: 10.59429/esp.v9i11.3194

Gupta, T. (2024). Adaptive Learning Systems: Harnessing AI to Personalize Educational Outcomes. *International Journal for Research in Applied Science and Engineering Technology, 12*(11), 458–464. DOI: 10.22214/ijraset.2024.65088

Hughes, S. (2023). *Here's why AI makes traditional education models obsolete.*

Husain, F. N. (2023). Impact of Multiple Intelligences and 21st Century Skills on Future Work Force. *International Education Studies, 16*(3), 16. DOI: 10.5539/ies.v16n3p16

Kang, P. K. (2023). AI in Education: Personalized Learning Through Adaptive Systems. *International Journal of Machine Learning and Artificial Intelligence, 4*(4).

Khan, F. A.Hasanain Mohammed Manji Al-Rzoky. (2025). The Transformative Role of Artificial Intelligence in Healthcare. *Journal of Postgraduate Medical Institute, 39*(2), 92–94. DOI: 10.54079/jpmi.39.2.3779

Korres, O., Paños-Castro, J., Alkhawaja, L., & Idris, M. (2025). Exploring the impact of Artificial Intelligence on students' skills for sustainable development in education. *Frontiers in Education, 10*, 1691148. DOI: 10.3389/feduc.2025.1691148

Langreo, L. (2024). ChatGPT, Bard, Copilot, Khanmigo: What AI Tools Do Teachers Use?

Li, T., Krajcik, J. S., & Spiro, R. (2025). The Transformative Collaboration of Human Intelligence and Artificial Intelligence in Designing Knowledge-in-Use Science Assessment for Learning. *Journal of Science Education and Technology, 2025*, 1–27. DOI: 10.1007/s10956-025-10275-4

Liu, M., & Yu, D. (2022). Towards intelligent E-learning systems. *Education and Information Technologies, 28*(7), 1. DOI: 10.1007/s10639-022-11479-6 PMID: 36532790

Merino-Campos, C. (2025). The Impact of Artificial Intelligence on Personalized Learning in Higher Education: A Systematic Review. *Trends in Higher Education 2025, Vol. 4, Page 17, 4*(2), 17. DOI: 10.3390/higheredu4020017

Nuthakki, S., buddiga, S. K. pranitha, & Koganti, S. (2024). Exploring Deep Learning Models for Image Recognition: A Comparative Review. *Signal & Image Processing : An International Journal, 15*(3), 01–10. DOI: 10.5121/sipij.2024.15301

Nuthakki, S., Uttiramerur, A. D., Nuthakki, Y., & Munjala, M. B. (2024). Navigating the Medical Landscape: A Review of Chatbots for Biomarker Extraction from Diverse Medical Reports. *International Journal For Multidisciplinary Research, 6*(1), 13154. Advance online publication. DOI: 10.36948/ijfmr.2024.v06i01.13154

OpenAI. (2025). *Khan Academy explores GPT-4 to power Khanmigo — limited pilot program.*

Qureshi, I. (2025). The Impact of AI on Teacher Roles: Towards a Collaborative Human-AI Pedagogy. *AI EDIFY Journal*, 2(1), 1–11.

Rismanchian, S., & Doroudi, S. (2025). The Evolution of Research on AI and Education Across Four Decades: Insights from the AIxEd Framework. *International Journal of Artificial Intelligence in Education, 2025*(5), 1–24. DOI: 10.1007/s40593-025-00483-9

Riva, G. (2025). *The Architecture of Cognitive Amplification: Enhanced Cognitive Scaffolding as a Resolution to the Comfort-Growth Paradox in Human-AI Cognitive Integration.*

Saleem, D. S., Aziz, M. U., Iqbal, D. M. J., & Abbas, S. (2025). AI in Education: Personalized Learning Systems and Their Impact on Student Performance and Engagement. *The Critical Review of Social Sciences Studies, 3*(1), 2445–2459. DOI: 10.59075/c35qa453

Sarıdaş, G. (2025). The Use of Artificial Intelligence Agents in Education. *International Society That Learns Journal*, 2(1), 61–72. DOI: 10.64782/istlj22286172

Schrager, A. (2018). *The modern education system was designed to teach future factory workers to be "punctual, docile, and sober."*

Siddiqui, M. T. (2025). AI-Enabled Pedagogy: Advancing Education Through Innovative Teaching Tools and the AI-TEACH Model. *Journal of Informatics Education and Research*, *5*(1), 2526–2539. DOI: 10.52783/jier.v5i1.2261

Tieso, C. L. (2003). Ability grouping is not just tracking anymore. In *Roeper Review* (Vol. 26, Issue 1, pp. 29–36). DOI: 10.1080/02783190309554236

Villegas-Ch, W., Buenano-Fernandez, D., Navarro, A. M., & Mera-Navarrete, A. (2025). Adaptive intelligent tutoring systems for STEM education: analysis of the learning impact and effectiveness of personalized feedback. *Smart Learning Environments 2025 12:1, 12*(1), 41-. DOI: 10.1186/s40561-025-00389-y

Wang, N. C. (2025). Scaffolding Creativity: Integrating Generative AI Tools and Real-world Experiences in Business Education. *Conference on Human Factors in Computing Systems - Proceedings, 1*. DOI: 10.1145/3706599.3720283

Winthrop, R., Williams, T. P., & McGivney, E. (2016). *Skills in the digital age — How should education systems evolve?* Yan, L. (2025). *From Passive Tool to Socio-cognitive Teammate: A Conceptual Framework for Agentic AI in Human-AI Collaborative Learning*.

Zinkina, J., Korotayev, A., & Andreev, A. (2016). Mass Primary Education in the Nineteenth Century. *Globalistics and Globalization Studies*, *26*(15), 63–70.

Chapter 13

Rethinking Education Through the Lens of Human-AI Collaboration:

Exploring the Shift From Traditional Education Models to AI-Supported Human Collaboration

Dwiki Dzaki Yudi Putra
http://orcid.org/0009-0000-9843-340X
Universitas Esa Unggul, Indonesia

Binastya Anggara Sekti
http://orcid.org/0000-0001-5489-4888
Universitas Esa Unggul, Indonesia

ABSTRACT

This chapter explores the paradigm shift in education from rigid traditional models to dynamic human-AI collaborative learning systems. Based on criticism of standard curricula and unfair assessment practices, this chapter advocates for the integration of artificial intelligence not as a replacement for educators, but as a cognitive partner that enriches human learning. Drawing on AI theories centred on social construction and human-centred approaches, this chapter proposes an inclusive and adaptive framework designed to support diverse learners through personalised feedback, real-time analysis, and collaborative problem-solving. Using case studies and practical models, this chapter highlights how human-AI collaboration can address existing systemic inequalities and foster a more equitable, learner-centred learning

DOI: 10.4018/979-8-3373-6063-8.ch013

environment. It offers conceptual and empirical insights for reimagining education as a partnership between human intelligence and machine learning—with the goal of creating an ethical, inclusive, and sustainable future of learning.

INTRODUCTION

The global education landscape is entering an era of profound and multidimensional disruption—technological, epistemological, and institutional—driven by rapid advances in artificial intelligence (AI). The term "profound disruption" here refers not merely to technological innovation but to fundamental shifts in how knowledge is produced, mediated, and validated in educational systems. Empirical data from UNESCO and OECD show that AI has begun transforming instructional design, assessment, and teacher–student interaction at scale. A comprehensive approach to AI education is needed to equip both students and teachers with the skills and knowledge necessary to navigate and thrive in an increasingly intelligent era (Wu & Sun, 2024).

Traditional education models, often characterised by rigidity and standardisation, are now under scrutiny. Historically designed for the industrial era, these models emphasised efficiency and uniformity but frequently neglected diversity and contextual learning. Foundational thinkers such as John Dewey and Lev Vygotsky have long advocated learner-centred and socially constructed knowledge, a principle that is now gaining renewed relevance through AI-supported collaboration. Interactive learning experiences that go beyond traditional education, commonly associated with classroom-based, teacher-led, and exam-oriented learning (Dass, Tanwar, & Datta, 2026).

At the intersection of educational reform and technological innovation, human–AI convergence presents new opportunities for transformation. These opportunities vary across stakeholders. For teachers, AI can function as an intelligent assistant that supports instructional design, assessment, and feedback. For students, AI enables personalised and adaptive learning pathways. For educational institutions, it offers data-driven insights to support strategic reform and the development of inclusive learning analytics. An enhancement in developing pedagogical approaches offering a new experiential and interactive learning way through art to enrich learning experiences (El-Mahdy, 2026).

Inclusivity refers to accessibility across diverse socio-cultural contexts, while equity denotes fairness in AI-mediated learning outcomes. Collaboration is understood as encompassing both human–AI interaction and peer-to-peer co-construction of knowledge. Rather than positioning AI solely as a replacement or enhancement tool, AI is framed along a spectrum ranging from augmentation to co-agency, in which it complements and amplifies human capabilities.

Ethical considerations are central to this discussion. Algorithmic bias, data sovereignty, and human agency must be critically addressed to ensure that AI integration aligns with humanistic educational goals. Tools such as ChatGPT, Khanmigo, and adaptive learning tutors illustrate both the potential and the challenges of AI in education: while enabling real-time feedback and multimodal engagement, they also raise concerns related to contextual sensitivity, bias, and interpretability. ChatGPT, a language model developed by OpenAI, has gained significant attention in education across Asia (Irwanto, 2025)

Human–AI collaboration is further examined as a means of redefining learning as a dynamic and relational process. Emphasis is placed on learning processes and outcomes, while reflections on the broader purpose of education are deferred to the concluding section. By engaging both classical and contemporary educational theories, an integrative framework for AI-supported, human-centred learning ecosystems is developed—one that balances technological innovation with ethical, social, and pedagogical integrity. As emphasized by UNESCO, the rapid emergence of artificial intelligence has introduced not only technological advancement but also profound epistemological and institutional transformations across global education systems, necessitating new ethical and pedagogical frameworks to ensure equitable learning.

These developments have the potential to revolutionise traditional educational models, which have long been criticised for their rigid structures, standardised curricula, and uniform assessment systems. At the intersection of educational reform and technological innovation, the convergence of human intelligence and artificial intelligence offers unexpected opportunities to redesign learning environments that are not only more inclusive and equitable but also adaptive, personalised, and collaborative.

This chapter explores the paradigm shift from a teacher-centred education model to a system that adopts AI-supported human collaboration. Rather than viewing AI as a replacement for educators, this new paradigm positions AI as an intelligent partner that enhances human capabilities. This shift requires not only technological integration but also a reconfiguration of pedagogical philosophy, instructional design, and assessment methods. Importantly, it also demands attention to ethical considerations, including algorithmic bias, data privacy, and the preservation of human agency.

With the emergence of tools such as ChatGPT, Khanmigo, and AI tutors integrated into learning management systems, educational institutions are now beginning to experiment with human-AI hybrid learning ecosystems. These ecosystems leverage real-time data, natural language processing, and generative capabilities to support personalised feedback, adaptive content delivery, and collaborative problem-solving.

However, while these innovations are promising, they also raise critical questions about the future role of educators, learners, and institutions in shaping a meaningful and equitable future for education.

In this chapter, we propose that the effective integration of AI into education requires a fundamental rethinking of learning itself: its purpose, process, and outcomes. Drawing on AI theories grounded in social constructionism, connectivism, and human-centred approaches, we aim to develop a collaborative human-AI learning framework that supports lifelong, learner-centred, and socially responsive education. This framework is situated within a broader context of equity and access, emphasising the importance of designing technology and pedagogy that serve diverse populations of learners across geographical regions and socio-economic contexts.

This exploration is not merely theoretical. Through empirical examples and case studies, we will demonstrate how human-AI collaboration can be realised in practice, providing insights for educators, policymakers, and technology developers who wish to create more dynamic and inclusive learning environments. This chapter serves as a conceptual foundation and practical guide for reflecting on education through the lens of AI-supported human collaboration. Table 1 shows the Key Shifts from Traditional to Human-AI Collaborative Education.

Table 1. Key shifts from traditional to human-AI collaborative education

Element	Traditional Model	Human-AI Collaborative Model
Role of Educator	Knowledge dispenser	Co-designer, facilitator
Role of Learner	Passive recipient	Active collaborator
Technology Use	Supplementary tool	Integral collaborator
Curriculum Design	Static, standardized	Dynamic, personalized
Feedback Mechanism	Delayed, summative	Real-time, formative

Case Study: AI-Supported Leaarning Analytics in a Singaporean Secondary School

In 2022, a visionary secondary school in Singapore implemented an artificial intelligence (AI)-based learning analytics platform to personalise mathematics teaching. The platform analyses students' problem-solving patterns, identifies common misconceptions, and recommends individually tailored learning resources. Teachers use dashboards to monitor overall class trends and provide timely interventions. The rapid development and widespread availability of affordable AI-powered tools have necessitated a rethinking of what it means to be critically literate in the digital world (Weninger & Xu, 2026).

As a result, students reported increased motivation thanks to instant feedback and progress visualisation. The school also noted significant improvements in learning outcomes, particularly among students who previously struggled with conventional teaching methods. Educators appreciated AI's ability to identify hidden learning gaps and valued their new role as strategic facilitators rather than content deliverers.

This case illustrates the paradigm shift introduced by human-AI collaboration—where students are empowered, teachers are repositioned as coaches, and AI acts as an adaptive partner in educational success.

LIMITATIONS OF TRADITIONAL EDUCATIONS MODELS

Despite centuries of development and refinement, traditional education models still operate predominantly within a framework shaped by the needs of the industrial era—emphasising uniformity, efficiency, and top-down transmission of knowledge. While this model once played a critical role in mass literacy and workforce development, it now faces increasingly sharp criticism amid rapid social transformation, digital disruption, and growing awareness of student diversity. Traditional education emphasizes esthetic skills, the digital age requires comprehensive technical and interdisciplinary skills (Wang & Wang, 2025).

One fundamental limitation is the lack of personalisation and contextual relevance. Standardised curricula are often designed with a one-size-fits-all approach, disregarding students' socio-cultural backgrounds, cognitive profiles, and emotional needs. This marginalises students who do not conform to dominant norms, including those with neurological differences, those from diverse linguistic backgrounds, and students from underrepresented communities. It also reinforces a deficit model of education—where learners are seen as empty vessels to be filled rather than as co-creators of knowledge. The increasing incidence of psychological health challenges among college students highlights the limitations of traditional education and intervention methods (Zhang & Shi, 2025).

Furthermore, traditional pedagogy often emphasises rote learning and passive information absorption, which hinders creativity, critical thinking, and collaborative inquiry. Students are positioned as passive recipients of pre-determined content, with little opportunity to shape their own learning experiences. This rigid structure not only undermines student motivation but also fails to develop essential 21st-century skills such as adaptability, problem-solving, and independent learning.

Assessment practices in traditional systems are also inherently limiting and unfair. The dominance of high-stakes summative assessments—such as national standardised tests—prioritises memorisation over mastery and disproportionately penalises students who excel in non-traditional ways, including through oral, visual, or collaborative modes. This assessment provides little room for formative feedback or iterative learning, and offers only a snapshot of student performance rather than a holistic picture of their growth and potential.

Another critical issue is the epistemological bias embedded in traditional curricula. Often rooted in Western-centric and canonical knowledge systems, these curricula can marginalise indigenous, local, or non-dominant worldviews, further distancing students from marginalised regions or cultures. This contributes to what experts refer to as epistemological injustice—systemic assessment that devalues certain forms of knowledge and experience.

Beyond issues of curriculum and pedagogy, structural inequalities continue to shape access to quality education. Schools in rural, underfunded, or conflict-affected areas often lack qualified teachers, adequate infrastructure, and digital resources. Traditional models, with their reliance on static classroom environments and rigid instruction schedules, are unable to address these inequalities—especially in an increasingly mobile, digital, and connected world. The iterative adoption of Agile practices can enhance both product quality and professional readiness (Sa'adah, Yuhana, Rochimah, & Afridian Rasyid, 2026).

Furthermore, the mismatch between school learning and real-world application remains a persistent challenge. Subject compartmentalisation, minimal interdisciplinary integration, and limited opportunities for authentic problem-solving result in a curriculum that feels abstract and irrelevant to students' life experiences. This leads to disengagement, increased dropout rates, and a widespread perception that formal education is out of step with the demands of contemporary life and work.

Finally, the teacher–student relationship in traditional models is often hierarchical and one-sided, positioning educators as the sole authority and reducing opportunities for student voice and autonomy. Unlike models that encourage guidance and collaborative learning, this dynamic can hinder the development of mutual trust, dialogue, and social-emotional growth, elements that are increasingly recognised as essential for meaningful learning. Table 2 shows the Key Limitations of Traditional Educations.

Table 2. Key limitations of traditional educations

Limitation	Description	Impact
Rigidity	Standardized curriculum and fixed pedagogy	Excludes diverse and neurodivergent learners
Summative Assessment	Focus on final exams and memory-based evaluation	Undermines deep learning, creativity, and learner confidence
Epistemic Bias	Dominace of Western-centric knowledge system	Marginalises local and indigenous worldviews
Structural Inequity	Geographic and socio-economic disparities in resource access	Widening achievement and opportunity gaps
Lack of Relevance	Disconnect from real-world challenges and interdisciplinary problems	Low engagement, reduced retention
Top-down Authority	Teacher-centred, unidirectional learning	Suppresses learner autonomy and collaboration

Case Study: High-Stakes Testing and Equity Gaps

A national review of high school graduation rates in Indonesia shows that students from rural areas score significantly lower on national graduation exams than their urban peers, even though their level of engagement in class is similar. Interviews revealed that exam-focused assessments fail to capture local knowledge and learning styles, thereby disproportionately disadvantaging students who do not follow the mainstream curriculum. The rapid advancement of Artificial Intelligence (AI) has opened up new frontiers of technological possibilities, yet the traditional education system in Indonesia has largely remained entrenched in conventional practices (Wong-A-Foe, 2023).

Case Study: Irrelevance of Curriculum and Risk of Dropping Out

A qualitative study in secondary schools in West Nusa Tenggara, Indonesia, found that many students drop out not because of academic failure, but because they feel that the subject matter taught in school is irrelevant to their daily lives. Students from agricultural communities, for example, expressed frustration that school subjects were not connected to agriculture, climate resilience, or local livelihoods. Teachers, bound by the national curriculum mandate, felt unable to adapt the curriculum to the needs of the community—highlighting the urgent need for a more responsive and context-sensitive model of education. Teaching and learning are not merely about process of conveying knowledge, but more as a model to form ideal educational subjects i.e., learning participants with characters (Saidi, Puspitasari, & Wijaya, 2016).

TOWARD HUMAN-AI COLLABORATIVE LEARNING

Unlike the limitations of traditional education models, the emergence of artificial intelligence (AI) technology has opened up opportunities for new forms of learning that emphasise collaboration, flexibility, and personalisation. Human-AI collaborative learning is based on the concept that AI systems function not only as tools or tutors, but also as learning partners and co-creators in the educational process. This reconceptualisation transforms the learning experience into a dynamic partnership, where learners interact with intelligent agents that support exploration, inquiry, and reflective practice. Artificial intelligence (AI) is among the key technologies reshaping modern industries by establishing mass customization and personalization (Nain & Samal, 2026).

One of the key features of human-AI collaboration is its ability to personalise learning experiences at scale. AI-supported platforms can analyse learners' behavioural data, preferences, strengths, and weaknesses to provide tailored learning pathways that evolve over time. These systems facilitate formative assessment, instant feedback, and responsive content adjustment in line with learners' ongoing development. For example, AI-supported recommendation systems can compile reading materials or question sets that align with learners' current understanding and future goals.

Another important dimension is the promotion of metacognitive skills through reflection and goal-setting facilitated by AI. Intelligent learning companions can encourage students to articulate their reasoning, evaluate their progress, and plan their next steps, thereby fostering a deeper awareness of their own learning processes. Thus, AI contributes to the development of students' autonomy and self-regulation, competencies that are essential for lifelong learning.

Additionally, AI can facilitate collaborative problem-solving by enabling distributed cognition between humans and machines. For example, AI systems can support group work by managing workflows, suggesting resources, or facilitating communication between peers with diverse expertise. In this scenario, AI functions not only as a facilitator but also as an active participant in meaning-making, providing insights generated from large-scale data processing.

Human-AI collaboration also offers significant benefits for educators. Rather than replacing teachers, AI can enhance their capabilities by automating administrative tasks, monitoring classroom engagement, and identifying students who need additional support. Teachers can then focus on high-level instructional design and provide social-emotional guidance that remains uniquely human. The synergy between human empathy and AI efficiency enables a more holistic educational environment.

However, realising the full potential of human-AI collaboration requires deliberate design, grounded in ethical and pedagogical principles. Systems must be transparent, interpretable, and aligned with educational values to ensure trust and effectiveness.

Importantly, human-AI interactions must be designed to preserve student autonomy, respect diversity, and promote inclusive participation.

As the shortcomings of traditional education become increasingly apparent, the emergence of artificial intelligence (AI) offers not only opportunities for technological improvement, but also pedagogical transformation. Going beyond the conventional understanding of AI as a tool or tutor, the human-AI collaborative learning paradigm views AI as a partner that participates in knowledge formation, supports the role of humans, and facilitates collective intelligence.

Redefining Roles in the Learning Ecosystem

The core of this paradigm is a shift from hierarchical and linear instruction to connected and collaborative learning experiences. In a human-AI collaborative learning environment, AI is not a substitute for teachers, but rather a partner in pedagogical settings. AI helps analyse learning progress, adjusts material delivery, encourages reflective thinking, and facilitates interaction between learners. Teachers transition from information disseminators to learning experience designers, while learners become active knowledge creators who effectively interact with both humans and intelligent systems in meaningful dialogue. AI Technology Management focuses on strategically integrating AI into organizations to enhance innovation and value creation (Sekti, 2025a).

Unlike previous waves of educational technology, AI facilitates dynamic two-way feedback. This feedback enables systems to continuously update, personalise, and organise learning based on real-time data—including emotional states, collaborative behaviour, and metacognitive signals. This facilitates timely interventions, promoting responsive and relational learning processes.

Beyond Personalisation: Toward Collective Intelligence

Although personalisation remains one of the key strengths of AI, true human-AI collaboration must go further to support collective intelligence, where groups of learners and intelligent agents work together to solve complex problems. AI systems can identify patterns of expertise among learners, recommend optimal group divisions, and facilitate distributed cognition through shared artefacts and dialogue facilitation. These collaborative AI functions reflect and extend Vygotsky's principles of social learning, adapted for hybrid digital spaces.

For example, in AI-enhanced project-based learning environments, students can co-design digital artefacts with generative AI (e.g., co-writing short stories with GPT-4, generating simulations for scientific inquiry, or designing inclusive interfaces using multimodal prompts). This not only develops domain knowledge but also creative thinking, ethical reasoning, and mutual dependence—skills that are critical for a future society shaped by rapid technological change.

Enabling Human Flourishing through AI-Augmented Metacognition

One of the greatest transformative potentials of AI lies in its ability to strengthen metacognitive capacities. Intelligent learning companions can encourage students to plan, monitor, and evaluate their learning strategies—thereby fostering independence and resilience. Through natural language interaction, generative AI can facilitate reflective dialogue, encouraging students to articulate their thoughts, overcome misunderstandings, and develop higher-order thinking skills.

Additionally, AI systems can be designed to monitor student well-being, detect inactivity, or recommend social-emotional interventions—contributing to a holistic, human-centred educational experience. This positions AI not only as a learning accelerator but also as an ethical partner supporting student development.

Supporting Teachers through Augmented Pedagogy

Teachers remain irreplaceable in this collaborative paradigm—not because of AI, but thanks to AI. By automating administrative tasks, managing personalised learning, and visualising student progress, AI frees teachers to focus on emotional support, contextual assessment, and cultural responsiveness. Teachers can also collaborate with AI to co-design learning pathways, receive pedagogical advice, and engage in reflective practice through data-driven feedback.

To support this vision, professional development must go beyond digital literacy to AI pedagogical literacy—equipping educators to critically engage with AI systems, co-design ethical implementation strategies, and lead human-AI co-design processes in their own contexts.

Pedagogical Frameworks for Human–AI Integration

To effectively embed AI into educational ecosystems, pedagogical models must provide a theoretical foundation that guides instructional design and practice. Three frameworks—TPACK, SAMR, and Universal Design for Learning (UDL)—offer useful lenses for integrating AI in classrooms.

1. TPACK (Technological Pedagogical Content Knowledge) emphasises the balance between content mastery, pedagogical strategy, and technological fluency. AI enhances TPACK by enabling adaptive scaffolding and data-informed pedagogy.

2. SAMR (Substitution, Augmentation, Modification, Redefinition) maps how technology transforms learning tasks. AI supports the redefinition phase, allowing the creation of new tasks such as generative content co-design and intelligent tutoring systems.
3. Universal Design for Learning (UDL) ensures accessibility by accommodating diverse learner profiles. AI systems aligned with UDL can personalise learning materials for neurodiverse and multilingual learners.

Together, these frameworks inform a systemic approach to AI integration, supporting inclusivity, adaptability, and teacher autonomy.

Teacher Professional Development and AI Literacy

Educators play a central role in shaping ethical and pedagogical AI integration. However, most training remains technocentric, focusing on tool operation rather than critical and contextual application. Building AI literacy requires:

1. AI Pedagogical Literacy Training – workshops and micro-credentials focusing on ethics, inclusivity, and learner agency;
2. Communities of Practice – peer-led networks sharing best practices and co-designing AI learning materials;
3. Institutional Support Systems – policies that allocate time, resources, and mentoring for experimentation with AI tools.

Global initiatives such as Finland's "Elements of AI" curriculum and Singapore's national AI teacher training programmes demonstrate that systemic support significantly enhances educators' confidence and competence in AI-mediated instruction. Pre-service teachers can play a crucial role in integrating AI-based tools into the new educational landscape (Reyes-Rojas, Díaz, Ruz-Reveco, Castro, & Reyes-González, 2026).

In summary, human-AI collaborative learning represents a transformative shift from conventional education. By combining human strengths and artificial intelligence, it enables a more responsive, inclusive, and engaging learning environment. The following chapters will explore how this collaboration can be implemented through theoretical frameworks, empirical evidence, and implementation strategies across various educational settings. Table 3 shows the Comparison Between Traditional and Human-AI Collaborative Learning Models.

Table 3. Comparison between traditional and human-AI collaborative learning models

Dimension	Traditional Education	Human-AI Collaborative Learning
Pedagogical Approach	Teacher-centered, didactic	Learner-centered, co-constructed
Content Delivery	Linear and uniform	Adaptive, generative and contextual
Role of Assessment	High-stakes, summative	Formative, dynamic, and continuous
Role of Educator	Knowledge transmitter	Learning architect and empathic facilitator
Learner Agency	Low, passive recipient	High, reflective co-designer
Nature of Collaboration	Human-human only	Human-AI-human interaction and synergy
Cultural Adaptability	Standardised, top-down	Localised, participatory, responsive

Case Study: AI-Enchanced Peer Learning at an Indonesian University

In 2023, a large public university in Indonesia launched a pilot project integrating artificial intelligence (AI) into a flipped classroom approach for undergraduate computer science students. The AI system, based on natural language processing and adaptive learning algorithms, was integrated into the university's learning management system (LMS) and designed to act as a peer learning assistant. Traditional learning management systems often fail to sustain student motivation in computer science education, where consistent practice is crucial for skill development (Duong, Huang, Nguyen, & Chen, 2026).

Students received personalised learning paths based on their performance on formative quizzes. The AI assistant analysed contributions to discussion forums and suggested collaboration partners based on complementary skill profiles. The system also identifies potential misunderstandings in real-time and encourages reflective journal writing.

Instructors reported increased engagement, reduced grading time, and enhanced collaboration among students. Students noted that the AI's non-judgmental feedback encouraged experimentation and curiosity. Specifically, students from underrepresented groups reported stronger feelings of inclusion and participation.

This case illustrates how AI, when integrated wisely, can transform classroom dynamics from passive reception to active knowledge construction and collaboration. It highlights the potential of human-AI partnerships in creating inclusive, fair, and participatory learning environments aligned with the goals of Education 4.0.

Case Study: Generative Collaborative Design in Multilingual Classrooms

In a pilot project in East Kalimantan, Indonesia, secondary school students worked with a generative artificial intelligence (AI) platform that enabled them to create short films in Indonesian and the indigenous Dayak language. The AI system helped translate, visualise, and co-write the script. Teachers facilitated this process by guiding students to reflect on cultural values and storytelling ethics. Students reported increased pride in their local identity, while teachers noted improvements in collaboration, language proficiency, and engagement. This case study demonstrates how AI can serve as a cultural bridge and creative partner, facilitating inclusive learning through human-AI synergy.

ETHICAL AND EQUITY CONSIDERATIONS IN HUMAN-AI COLLABORATION

The rapid adoption of artificial intelligence (AI) technology in education requires critical evaluation of its ethical and equity implications. While AI has the potential to democratise access to quality learning, its implementation without deliberate safeguards can reinforce existing inequalities.

One major issue is algorithmic bias. AI systems trained using non-representative data can inadvertently disadvantage marginalised students. For example, natural language processing tools may perform poorly on non-native English speakers or those from diverse cultural backgrounds, leading to biased assessments and misinterpretations.

Another issue is data privacy. AI in education often relies on large datasets that include personal metrics, behaviour, and performance. Without a robust data governance framework, student privacy and autonomy may be at risk. Transparent data usage policies, informed consent procedures, and AI ethics audits are essential to mitigate these risks. Information Security Awareness (ISA) is a crucial component in strengthening cybersecurity resilience at both individual and organizational levels (Sekti, 2025b).

Equitable access is also vital. The digital divide—marked by inequalities in infrastructure, device availability, and digital literacy—can lead to uneven benefits from AI tools. Human-AI collaboration must be contextualised within local educational realities, ensuring that disadvantaged schools and regions are not left behind.

Ethical design is key to ensuring that AI complements rather than replaces the human element in teaching and learning. AI systems must be built with values such as inclusivity, transparency, and fairness at their core. Additionally, teachers, students, and communities must be involved in co-designing AI tools to align with pedagogical and cultural needs.

As artificial intelligence (AI) becomes increasingly integrated into the education ecosystem, issues of ethics and fairness are no longer peripheral concerns but central to the design, implementation, and governance of human-AI collaboration. Without deliberate efforts to address the ethical implications of AI systems and their impact on social-political aspects, technology that promises to democratise learning could instead exacerbate existing inequalities and marginalise vulnerable learners.

Algorithmic Bias and Epistemic Injustice

One of the most widespread ethical challenges in artificial intelligence (AI) is algorithmic bias—the root causes of which lie in historical data imbalances, exclusive training data sets, and embedded socio-cultural norms. In the context of education, this bias can manifest through language processing tools that misinterpret non-standard dialects, recommendation systems that reinforce stereotypes, or predictive analytics that disadvantage students from underrepresented backgrounds.

Beyond bias, educational AI systems can reinforce epistemic injustice by prioritising dominant cultural knowledge over local and indigenous epistemologies. AI models trained primarily on Western-centric content risk overlooking non-Western worldviews, reinforcing a homogeneous vision of what is considered "valid knowledge". This is a serious issue in multilingual and multiethnic societies such as Indonesia, India, and many parts of Africa and Latin America, where cultural relevance is essential for student engagement and identity affirmation.

Data Privacy, Surveillance, and Consent

Artificial intelligence (AI)-based learning systems often require extensive data collection—including behavioural analysis, keyboard typing patterns, emotional expressions, and social interaction networks. While such data facilitates personalisation and responsiveness, it also poses significant risks to students' privacy, autonomy, and psychological safety. As digital health solutions proliferate, the protection of personal health information has become paramount, necessitating a comprehensive framework that addresses privacy concerns while fostering innovation (Awotunde, 2026).

In many cases, students and educators are unaware of how their data is collected, analysed, or monetised. This creates an imbalance of power where invisible surveillance becomes commonplace in learning environments. Additionally, minors may be subject to profiling and tracking without adequate protection, particularly in countries where data protection laws are still underdeveloped.

Ethical collaboration between humans and AI requires transparent data policies, consent processes tailored to adolescents, and mechanisms that allow students to control their data. Equally important is the development of trustworthy AI—systems that are explainable, accountable, and aligned with the values of the educational community.

Equity of Access and the Digital Divide

Technological innovations often outpace infrastructure readiness. In many regions—particularly rural and remote areas in the Global South—schools still lack reliable internet access, functional hardware, and trained educators. Implementing artificial intelligence (AI) without addressing these gaps can widen educational disparities, resulting in uneven distribution of benefits.

Furthermore, access to AI tools is not only about devices and bandwidth, but also digital literacy, language inclusivity, and content relevance. Students with disabilities, non-native language speakers, and students from minority groups may find AI systems inaccessible or frustrating if they are not designed with Universal Design for Learning (UDL) principles in mind.

Ethical Co-Design and Participatory Development

To ensure that artificial intelligence (AI) supports a future of equitable learning, AI must be designed with, not just for, communities. This involves engaging students, teachers, parents, and local stakeholders as partners in the development of AI systems—prioritising cultural appropriateness, pedagogical relevance, and ethical sensitivity.

Community-driven design promotes trust and contextual ownership, especially in historically marginalised environments. It also creates opportunities for intergenerational knowledge exchange, language preservation, and local innovation. A participatory approach not only increases social acceptance but also serves as an ethical safeguard by incorporating real-world experiences into the AI lifecycle.

Moral Responsibility and Educational Autonomy

The integration of artificial intelligence (AI) into education should not replace the role of human moral reasoning. Systems that provide recommendations—related to student abilities, behaviour, or educational paths—should not be given unquestioned authority. Teachers and students should be empowered to challenge, ignore, and criticise AI decisions, maintaining the central role of human judgement in the educational process.

Furthermore, AI systems must align with human values such as dignity, justice, empathy, and freedom. This requires the development of an AI ethics framework tailored to education—distinct from commercial or industrial applications—with a focus on relational, developmental, and citizenship dimensions in learning.

In conclusion, the ethical and fair implementation of AI in education requires interdisciplinary collaboration between educators, technologists, policymakers, and ethicists. By prioritising these issues, we can shape a future where AI supports human prosperity rather than threatens it. Table 4 shows the Ethical Risks and Mitigation Strategies in Human-AI Education.

Table 4. Ethical risks and mitigation strategies in human-AI education

Ethical Concern	Potential Risk	Mitigation Strategy
Algorithmic Bias	Discrimination against minorities and marginalised learners	Diverse training data, community review, bias audits
Data Privacy	Surveillance, misuse of personal data	Transparent data governance, informed consent, opt-out mechanisms
Epistemic Exclusion	Cultural alienation, loss of local knowledge	Pluralistic content, multilingual systems, indigenous inclusion
Access Inequality	Digital divide leading to exclusion	Investment in infrastructure; inclusive design
Loss of Human Agency	Overdependence on AI recommendations	Promote critical thinking; teacher-AI balance
Trust and Transparency	"Black box" systems reduce accountability	Explainable AI, pedagogical transparency, learner-facing dashboards

Case Study: Community-Driven AI Curriculum Desing in Rural Schools

A rural education initiative in Central Java, Indonesia, collaborated with local educators and parents to design an artificial intelligence (AI)-supported curriculum tailored to local values and infrastructure. Instead of importing existing tools, they jointly developed a chatbot using Indonesian and local dialects to guide students through agricultural science modules relevant to their environment.

The AI system operates offline and uses solar-powered devices. Teachers report that students become more engaged when content is tailored to the local context. Community leaders are also invited to review AI outputs to ensure cultural appropriateness, facilitating intergenerational collaboration. Artificial Intelligence is a transformative technology reshaping industries (Sekti, 2025c). This community-based approach demonstrates how ethical issues can be addressed through participatory design and localisation, aligning AI capabilities with principles of fairness and inclusivity.

In a participatory project in the mountains of West Papua, a coalition of educators, traditional leaders, and university researchers collaborated to develop an AI-supported biodiversity education curriculum. The AI system, implemented via solar-powered tablets, includes modules for identifying local plants and animals, supported by multimodal classification trained using images and narratives provided by community elders.

Rather than replacing teachers, the AI tool functions as a cultural mediator and research assistant. Students interview elders, upload local observations, and collaboratively create knowledge maps with the system. Teachers curate AI outputs to ensure alignment with traditional ecological wisdom. This initiative not only preserves indigenous knowledge systems but also creates an inclusive model of collaborative knowledge production between humans and AI.

FUTURE DIRECTIONS AND POLICY IMPLICATIONS

As AI continues to evolve, the intersection of AI and education calls for a proactive policy framework that ensures innovation is utilised in an ethical, inclusive, and sustainable manner. The future of human-AI collaboration in education depends not only on technological advances, but also on institutional willingness to support systemic change.

One emerging direction is the development of explainable and transparent AI systems tailored to the educational context. These systems should be designed to support pedagogical goals and enable students and educators to understand how recommendations or feedback are generated. This aligns with the growing call for "pedagogical explainability" in AI.

Another important area is professional development for educators. Teachers need structured training to critically engage with AI tools, understand their limitations, and help design their use. Countries such as Finland and Singapore have launched national strategies to improve teachers' skills in digital pedagogy, offering models for other countries to follow.

Policies must also address infrastructure gaps, particularly in Global South countries. Investments in internet connectivity, energy access, and low-cost devices are prerequisites for equitable AI adoption. Initiatives such as Indonesia's "Merdeka Belajar" reform can be expanded to integrate AI in an inclusive and meaningful way (Wiyono, Komariah, Hidayat, & Kusumaningrum, 2025). Ethical governance mechanisms, such as AI ethics boards, participatory design protocols, and impact assessments, should be institutionalised within education systems. These mechanisms should be dynamic and involve representatives from underserved communities, ensuring responsiveness to evolving needs.

The future of human-AI collaboration in education will not be determined solely by technological advances, but rather by policy choices, institutional vision, and societal values. The question is no longer whether AI will enter the classroom, but how AI will be regulated, for whom AI will be designed, and with what consequences. In this context, a visionary policy framework must go beyond the rhetoric of digital transformation and adopt systemic, inclusive, and participatory strategies that redefine the goals and processes of education itself (Li et al., 2025).

Toward Policy for Collaborative Intelligence

Developing education policies must recognise that the convergence of human and machine intelligence is not merely a technological shift—it is a redefinition of epistemology, agency, and community in the learning process. Such policies should:

1. Foster a collaborative intelligence ecosystem in which students, educators, AI agents, and communities collectively create knowledge;
2. Promote human-AI partnerships in project-based and interdisciplinary learning models;
3. Recognise and protect human dignity, autonomy, and decision-making in all AI-mediated learning environments.

This requires adjustments to assessment systems, accreditation models, and curriculum design to align with the dynamic and co-evolutionary nature of learning in the AI era.

Educator Preparedness and AI Pedagogical Literacy

Teachers are critical to the success of any AI-driven transformation. Yet, current professional development programs remain largely technocentric, focusing on how to use digital tools rather than on why, when, and for whom these tools should be used. Future directions must include:

1. Nationwide AI pedagogy training programs that centre ethics, inclusion, and learner agency;
2. Peer-led learning communities of practice focused on AI-enhanced instructional design;

3. Pre-service teacher curricula that incorporate critical AI literacy, including algorithmic bias, human–AI interaction, and digital equity.

Teachers should be empowered not only as end users but as co-designers of AI ecosystems, capable of making pedagogically sound and context-sensitive decisions.

Infrastructure and Inclusion: Closing the Digital Equity Gap

Policies must prioritise infrastructure equity as a foundation for AI integration. This means investing in:

1. High-speed internet access for remote and rural areas;
2. Low-cost, durable devices that support AI applications;
3. Offline AI solutions that function without full connectivity (e.g., edge AI, locally trained models);
4. Multilingual and culturally adaptive AI interfaces to ensure content relevance and accessibility.

Ethical Governance and Participatory Regulation

The rapid adoption of AI in education demands robust ethical governance grounded in participatory values. Future-oriented policy frameworks should include:

1. AI ethics boards in education ministries, composed of educators, technologists, ethicists, parents, and students;
2. Mandatory algorithmic audits to detect and address bias in educational platforms;
3. National frameworks for explainability and data sovereignty, ensuring that AI systems are transparent, understandable, and accountable;
4. Guidelines for learner-informed consent and age-appropriate data privacy protection.

Cross-Sectoral Collaboration and Public-Private Partnerships

AI in education is inherently transdisciplinary. Governments must foster collaborative ecosystems involving academia, civil society, edtech industries, and international organisations. Effective partnerships can:

1. Support sandbox experiments for testing new AI-powered pedagogical models;
2. Establish interoperability standards for AI integration across platforms and institutions;

3. Provide funding incentives for ethical and inclusive AI research in education;
4. Encourage co-design with indigenous and local communities, especially in postcolonial contexts where cultural autonomy must be preserved.

Public–private partnerships must move beyond commercialization and focus on social innovation and community empowerment.

Global Solidarity and Knowledge Sharing

In an interconnected world, no single country or community can address the challenges and opportunities of AI in isolation. Future policy must be situated within a framework of global solidarity, recognising education as a shared human right and collective responsibility. This includes:

1. Participating in UNESCO-led AI-in-Education global frameworks;
2. Contributing to open-source AI educational tools and multilingual datasets;
3. Supporting South–South cooperation in AI capacity building and localisation;
4. Establishing global ethics charters that reflect diverse epistemologies and values.

Finally, global collaboration will be essential. Multilateral organisations (e.g., UNESCO, World Bank) can facilitate cooperation, knowledge exchange, and funding mechanisms to bridge the gap between high-performing and low-performing education systems. Cross-national research on culturally responsive AI design should be prioritised to avoid one-size-fits-all solutions.

Overall, realising the full potential of human-AI collaboration in education depends on policies that prioritise human values, fairness, and flexibility. As we envision the future of learning, it is important to ensure that AI reinforces—rather than replaces—the relational and ethical dimensions of education. Table 5 shows the Strategic Policy Domains for Future Human–AI Collaboration in Education.

Table 5. Strategic policy domains for future human–AI collaboration in education

Policy Domain	Strategic Focus	Example Action Steps
Collaborative Intelligence	Redesign learning goals to integrate human–AI co-creation	Reform curriculum and assessment to support co-agency
Teacher Capacity	Prepare educators as critical, ethical users and co-designers of AI	AI pedagogy certification; community of practice
Infrastructure Equity	Ensure foundational access to AI-powered learning tools	Rural broadband, affordable devices, offline AI

continued on following page

Table 5. Continued

Policy Domain	Strategic Focus	Example Action Steps
Ethical Governance	Institutionalise transparency, fairness, and accountability	Ethics boards, algorithm audits, student privacy laws
Public-Private Innovation	Align AI development with public good values	Funding ethical edtech innovation, open AI APIs for education
Global Cooperation	Share knowledge, tools, and ethical commitments across borders	Open repositories, joint South-South AI education labs

Case Study: National AI-in-Education Strategy in Singapore

The Singapore Ministry of Education has launched a national initiative to integrate artificial intelligence (AI) into primary and secondary education. The policy includes mandatory AI training modules for all teachers, AI-supported assessment systems to reduce the burden of assessment, and a national student data trust to protect personal information. Singapore University of Technology and Design (SUTD) is embarking on an educational innovation program called SUTD campusX to support its future of education (Sockalingam et al., 2025).

The initiative is supported by partnerships with local universities and EdTech companies to develop culturally relevant AI tools. A key feature is the establishment of an 'AI Ethics Committee for Education,' comprising educators, technology experts, and student representatives. The committee oversees ethical audits and ensures inclusivity in design and implementation.

This multi-stakeholder strategic approach demonstrates how national policies can support sustainable and equitable human-AI collaboration in learning systems.

Case Study: Cross-Country AI Literacy Initiative – "Teaching with AI Across Borders"

In 2024, an Asia-Africa-Latin America consortium launched a cross-country AI in Education programme that developed an open, multilingual teacher training course titled "Teaching with AI for Equity and Inclusion." The course was co-developed by educators and researchers from Indonesia, Kenya, Peru, and Finland, combining global ethical standards with locally relevant case studies. It includes modules on co-designing AI, mitigating bias, and culturally responsive teaching with generative tools.

Thousands of educators in 27 countries completed the programme in its first year, demonstrating the power of global collaboration for a fair human-AI learning future.

DESIGNING THE FUTURE OF COLLABORATIVE AND INCLUSIVE LEARNING

As the education system faces unprecedented technological change, social fragmentation, and ecological uncertainty, the urgent need to design a collaborative, inclusive, and contextually adaptive future of learning becomes increasingly pressing. Collaboration between humans and artificial intelligence (AI) offers powerful opportunities—but also profound responsibilities—to shape new models of education that reflect ethical intelligence, pluralistic values, and shared agency.

This future cannot be built through technological innovation alone. It must emerge through the deliberate design of ecosystems—where curriculum frameworks, community engagement, policy decisions, and research agendas align with shared goals for fair and sustainable learning systems.

To conclude the discussion on human-AI collaboration in education, this chapter outlines the future direction of collaborative and inclusive learning approaches. Key focuses include direct implications for curriculum design, community engagement, and public policy formation, as well as recommendations for further research directions that can strengthen AI's role in creating fair and adaptive education systems.

Implications for Curriculum Design

Curriculum must evolve from rigid, prescriptive structures toward flexible, modular, and co-created frameworks. In a collaborative AI ecosystem, the curriculum is no longer a fixed path, but a living architecture that can be adapted in real-time based on learners' interests, cultural contexts, and emerging societal challenges. AI enables personalised learning based on real-time data, so curricula need to be designed to accommodate individual student learning trajectories. In addition, interdisciplinary approaches, project-based learning, and 21st-century skills such as critical thinking, collaboration, and digital literacy need to be core components of future curriculum design.

Curriculum design that supports human–AI collaboration must also emphasise the development of metacognition and technological literacy. Students need to master not only content but also how to learn and interact ethically with AI systems. Therefore, the curriculum needs to include modules that teach an understanding of how AI works, its potential biases, and the responsibilities involved in its use (UNESCO, 2021). In this way, students do not become passive users but active partners in smart learning systems.

Additionally, the success of collaborative curriculum design requires structural flexibility in its implementation. Educational institutions need to provide space for teachers to adapt to local contexts, student abilities, and classroom social dynamics. A curriculum that is too rigid will hinder meaningful AI integration. Therefore, curriculum development must be modular and open to data-driven updates and regular evaluations.

Key features of future curricula include:

1. Competency-based progression, where learners advance based on mastery and application rather than seat time;
2. Integration of transdisciplinary inquiry, enabling students to solve complex real-world problems using tools from science, arts, humanities, and technology;
3. Embedded AI literacy and digital ethics, preparing learners to critically understand, evaluate, and design AI systems;
4. Opportunities for co-design, where students and teachers shape learning pathways together, supported by generative AI as a partner in ideation, planning, and assessment.

AI systems can assist by mapping prior knowledge, recommending personalised resources, and visualising learning growth—but the epistemological authority remains shared between humans and machines in service of deeper understanding and critical thinking. Table 6 shows the Comparison of Conventional and AI-Based Curriculum Designs.

Table 6. Comparison of conventional and AI-based curriculum designs

Curriculum Aspects	Conventional	AI-Based Collaborative
Structure	Fixed and linear	Flexible and adaptive
Learning Focus	Memorisation and exams	Skills and problem solving
Assessment	Summative	Formative and real-time
Student Role	Passive	Active and participatory

Case Study: Implementation of AI Curriculum in Finland

Implementing the 'Elements of AI' curriculum module designed for all levels of higher education and the general community. This module enhances public understanding of AI and provides critical skills on how it works and its ethical use, resulting in broad public participation in educational technology.

In addition, the success of collaborative curriculum design requires structural flexibility in its implementation. Educational institutions need to provide space for teachers to make adjustments to the local context, student abilities, and classroom social dynamics. A curriculum that is too rigid will hinder the meaningful integration of AI. Therefore, curriculum development must be modular and open to data-driven updates and regular evaluation results.

The Role of Community and Public Policy

Educational transformation does not only depend on technology, but also on the support and involvement of social actors such as local communities, schools, parents, and policymakers. Communities play a role as guardians of cultural and local contexts that must be integrated into the design of AI systems. Meanwhile, public policy must ensure equitable access to technology, regulate the ethical use of student data, and provide ongoing training for educators. A collaborative approach between the public, private, and civil society sectors is essential to creating a fair and sustainable education ecosystem.

Public policy also needs to encourage collaboration between educational institutions and the technology industry in the development and testing of AI tools that are relevant and responsive to field needs. The government can facilitate pilot projects, provide collaborative research funding, and set interoperability standards so that the technology used in schools can be integrated. This will accelerate adoption and reduce the digital divide between regions.

From the community perspective, community empowerment in the education process is becoming increasingly important. Community digital literacy programmes, parental involvement in AI-based learning, and communication forums between teachers and residents can strengthen social acceptance of change. In addition, community participation can serve as a social control mechanism for transparency and accountability in the use of AI in educational spaces. Table 7 shows the The Role of Actors in the Implementation of AI-Based Collaborative Education.

Table 7. The role of actors in the implementation of AI-based collaborative education

Actors	Strategic Role	Example of Implementation
Government	Regulations, funding, infrastructure	Incentives for educational AI Platforms
Community	Guardians of local values, social oversight	Community AI learning forums
Schools	Direct implementation, teacher training	Integration of AI into daily learning
Parents	Emotional and moral support	Family digital literacy

Case Study: The "Smart Villages" Programme in India

The Indian government is collaborating with research institutions and local communities to implement AI-based learning systems in remote villages. The programme involves AI training for local teachers, the use of educational platforms in various regional languages, and data-driven monitoring by the community. The results show an increase in student participation and active community involvement in the educational process.

Direction of Further Research

Future research needs to explore various aspects of human–AI collaboration in the context of education. Some priority areas include: (1) long-term evaluation of the effectiveness of AI in improving learning outcomes; (2) interdisciplinary studies on ethics, privacy, and fair algorithms; (3) development of AI models that are adaptive to local contexts and cultures; and (4) experiments in AI-based collaborative pedagogical design at various levels of education. Participatory action research involving teachers, students, and policymakers is highly recommended to generate findings that are relevant and directly impact practice.

In addition to focusing on effectiveness, research must also address questions regarding the subjective experiences of students and teachers in AI-supported learning environments. How they perceive agency, fairness, and engagement in the learning process are key indicators of success. Qualitative methods such as classroom ethnography and narrative studies are essential for capturing these nuances.

Furthermore, research is needed in the field of educational AI system design that prioritises principles of inclusivity and diversity. For example, how AI can be developed to recognise and value local dialects, unique learning styles, and cultural values of students across different regions. Interdisciplinary collaboration between computer science, pedagogy, anthropology, and psychology will enrich perspectives and strengthen the impact of technological solutions on educational equity. Table 8 shows the Priority Research Agenda in Human–AI Collaboration-Based Education.

Table 8. Priority research agenda in human–AI collaboration-based education

Research Focus	Objectives	Recommended Methods
Effectiveness of AI on learning outcomes	Measuring long-term result	Longitudinal experiments, controlled trials
Ethics and data privacy	Ensuring fair and safe use of AI	Interdisciplinary studies, policy reviews
User experience	Capturing student and teacher perceptions	Ethnography, in-depth interviews
Local adaptation of AI	Testing cultural and contextual relevance	Community case studies, participatory research

Case Study: Participatory Research in Ugandan Secondary Schools

A collaboration between a local university, the Ministry of Education, and secondary schools in Uganda developed a predictive AI system to identify the risk of school dropouts. Data was collected and analysed together with students, teachers, and the community to test the system in a local context. This research resulted in a 12% increase in student retention and increased trust in technology.

This chapter emphasises that AI-based collaborative learning must be designed as part of a systemic transformation involving curriculum design, inclusive policies, and community support. With a strategic and evidence-based approach, human–AI collaboration can be the key to realising a more equitable, resilient, and sustainable future for education.

CONCLUSIONS AND RECOMMENDATIONS

Human–AI collaboration in education should be understood not merely as the integration of advanced technologies, but as a systemic transformation toward more adaptive, equitable, and sustainable educational ecosystems. Such collaboration enables personalised, reflective, and data-driven learning while simultaneously requiring fundamental shifts in curriculum design, educational policy, and research practices. AI must be positioned as a cognitive partner rather than a replacement for teachers, with system designs that strengthen learners' autonomy, empathy, and critical thinking. Meaningful integration therefore depends on alignment with local contexts, human values, and clearly articulated pedagogical goals.

To realise this potential, the capacity of key educational actors, including teachers, school leaders, and policymakers, must be strengthened through continuous professional development, cross-sector knowledge exchange, and collaborative research partnerships. Ethical governance should be reinforced through regulatory frameworks that address algorithmic auditing, data protection, and inclusivity, alongside participatory design processes involving students and local communities. At the same time, governments and funding bodies must prioritise infrastructure equity by investing in connectivity, devices, and reliable electricity, particularly in frontier, outermost, and disadvantaged regions. Future research should focus on culturally and contextually adaptive AI systems and on diverse user experiences, adopting participatory and interdisciplinary approaches to ensure that human–AI collaboration contributes to a transformative, inclusive, and meaningful educational future for all.

REFERENCES

Awotunde, J. B. (2026). Data Privacy in Virtual Healthcare Environments and Ethical Guidelines for Metaverse Health Applications. In *Studies in Computational Intelligence* (Vol. 1224, pp. 543–576). DOI: 10.1007/978-3-031-99946-8_23

Dass, C., Tanwar, S., & Datta, P. (2026). Designing and Development of AR Based Application for Science Education. *GMSARN International Journal, 20*(1), 91–99. Retrieved from https://www.scopus.com/inward/record.uri?eid=2-s2.0-105011666784&partnerID=40&md5=2771cf9da160e9aaf3a82363f2a52a9d

Duong, H.-T., Huang, C.-L., Nguyen, B.-A., & Chen, H.-M. (2026). Analyzing student perceptions and behaviors in the use of an engaging visualization dashboard for peer code review activities. *Science of Computer Programming*, *249*, 103394. Advance online publication. DOI: 10.1016/j.scico.2025.103394

El-Mahdy, D. (2026). Intangible Re-imagined historical spaces between walls: Art installation as an interactive teaching tool in theory-based architecture curricula. *Thinking Skills and Creativity*, *60*, 102052. Advance online publication. DOI: 10.1016/j.tsc.2025.102052

Irwanto, I. (2025). Research on ChatGPT in education in Asia: A bibliometric analysis (2022–2025). *Discover Artificial Intelligence*, *5*(1), 244. Advance online publication. DOI: 10.1007/s44163-025-00505-4

Li, T., Krajcik, J. S., & Spiro, R. (2025). The Transformative Collaboration of Human Intelligence and Artificial Intelligence in Designing Knowledge-in-Use Science Assessment for Learning. *Journal of Science Education and Technology*. Advance online publication. DOI: 10.1007/s10956-025-10275-4

Nain, G., & Samal, U. (2026). Intelligence behind individualization: A survey on role of AI in mass customized and personalized production. *Technology in Society*, *85*, 103195. Advance online publication. DOI: 10.1016/j.techsoc.2025.103195

Reyes-Rojas, J., Díaz, B., Ruz-Reveco, C., Castro, A., & Reyes-González, D. (2026). Conceptualizing pre-service teachers' readiness for AI integration into teaching practices: An intelligent-TPACK approach. *Computers and Education Open*, *10*, 100320. Advance online publication. DOI: 10.1016/j.caeo.2025.100320

Sa'adah, U., Yuhana, U. L., Rochimah, S., & Afridian Rasyid, M. B. (2026). Bridging the skills gap through Agile methodologies in Vocational Software Development Education. *Array (New York, N.Y.)*, *29*, 100614. Advance online publication. DOI: 10.1016/j.array.2025.100614

Saidi, A. I., Puspitasari, D. G., & Wijaya, H. (2016). Interpreting the cultural values of learning space design based on traditional education system in Indonesia. *Advanced Science Letters*, *22*(12), 4367–4369. DOI: 10.1166/asl.2016.8157

Sekti, B. A. (2025a). AI Technology Management Concepts and Strategies. In *AI Technology Management and Value Creation* (pp. 1–32). DOI: 10.4018/979-8-3373-2497-5.ch001

Sekti, B. A. (2025b). Information Security Awareness. In *User-Centric Cybersecurity Implications for Sustainable Digital Transformation* (pp. 111–145). DOI: 10.4018/979-8-3373-3171-3.ch004

Sekti, B. A. (2025c). Machine Learning vs. AI: Key Concepts. In *Implementing Enterprise Cybersecurity With AI* (pp. 1–27). DOI: 10.4018/979-8-3373-2252-0.ch001

Sockalingam, N., Lo, K., Teo, J., Wei, C. C., Jiet, D. C. J., Herremans, D., Jun, M. L. M., Kurniawan, O., Wang, Y., & Leong, P. K. (2025). Towards the future of education: Cyber-physical learning. *Discover Education*, *4*(1), 82. Advance online publication. DOI: 10.1007/s44217-025-00474-x

Wang, J., & Wang, H. (2025). Cultivation of innovative thinking and career development in design education. *Humanities & Social Sciences Communications*, *12*(1), 1390. Advance online publication. DOI: 10.1057/s41599-025-05754-3

Weninger, C., & Xu, H. (2026). AI, representation, and critical digital literacy: Navigating visual bias in the digital age. *System*, *136*, 103896. Advance online publication. DOI: 10.1016/j.system.2025.103896

Wiyono, B. B., Komariah, A., Hidayat, H., & Kusumaningrum, D. E. (2025). The structural effects of evaluation types in the implementation process of the independent learning program in higher education. *Discover Sustainability*, *6*(1), 321. Advance online publication. DOI: 10.1007/s43621-025-01171-3

Wong-A-Foe, D. (2023). Navigating the Implications of AI in Indonesian Education: Tutors, Governance, and Ethical Perspectives. In *Communications in Computer and Information Science* (Vol. 1942 CCIS, pp. 349–360). DOI: 10.1007/978-981-99-7969-1_26

Wu, D., & Sun, X. (2024). Exploring Human-centered AI Literacy Education: Interpretation and Insights from UNESCO's AI Competency Framework for Teachers and Students. *Journal of Library and Information Science in Agriculture*, *36*(8), 4–19. DOI: 10.13998/j.cnki.issn1002-1248.24-0644

Zhang, X., & Shi, W. (2025). An AI-driven framework integrating predictive modeling and intervention strategies to enhance psychological health education among college students. *Discover Applied Sciences*, *7*(10), 1095. Advance online publication. DOI: 10.1007/s42452-025-07674-y

Chapter 14
Lifelong Learning and Skill Development in the Age of AI

Nithin Subba Rao
http://orcid.org/0009-0006-3542-9597
Michigan Technological University, USA

T. C. Manjunath
http://orcid.org/0000-0003-2545-9160
Rajarajeswari College of Engineering, Bengaluru, India

P. Selvakumar
http://orcid.org/0000-0002-3650-4548
Department of Science and Humanities, Nehru Institute of Technology, Coimbatore, India

S. Guru Basava Aradhya
http://orcid.org/0000-0002-3335-2681
Atria Institute of Technology, India

Revanayya Kantayya
http://orcid.org/0009-0009-2552-8550
Dayananda Sagar Business Academy, India

T. Toni
http://orcid.org/0009-0000-7775-1142
Salesian College, India

ABSTRACT

In an era increasingly defined by artificial intelligence (AI), automation, and rapid technological advancement, AI on work, education, and everyday life. The traditional model of acquiring a fixed set of skills early in life and relying on them throughout one's career is no longer viable. AI systems are evolving at an unprecedented pace, leading to the automation of routine and even some complex tasks, while simultaneously creating new roles and industries that demand new competencies. As such, individuals must constantly reskill and upskill to remain relevant in the job market, adapt to shifting career landscapes, and leverage the benefits of AI tools effectively and ethically.The necessity for lifelong learning is underscored by the disruptive impact of AI on the workforce.Automation technologies are projected to displace

DOI: 10.4018/979-8-3373-6063-8.ch014

millions of jobs globally, especially those involving repetitive manual labor or routine cognitive tasks. However, while AI renders some jobs obsolete, it also generates new opportunities in fields like data science, machine learning, cybersecurity.

INTRODUCTION: THE IMPORTANCE OF LIFELONG LEARNING IN THE AGE OF AI

In an era increasingly defined by artificial intelligence (AI), automation, and rapid technological advancement, AI on work, education, and everyday life. The traditional model of acquiring a fixed set of skills early in life and relying on them throughout one's career is no longer viable. AI systems are evolving at an unprecedented pace, leading to the automation of routine and even some complex tasks, while simultaneously creating new roles and industries that demand new competencies. As such, individuals must constantly reskill and upskill to remain relevant in the job market, adapt to shifting career landscapes, and leverage the benefits of AI tools effectively and ethically.The necessity for lifelong learning is underscored by the disruptive impact of AI on the workforce.(Abdeldayem et al., 2021) Automation technologies are projected to displace millions of jobs globally, especially those involving repetitive manual labor or routine cognitive tasks. However, while AI renders some jobs obsolete, it also generates new opportunities in fields like data science, machine learning, cybersecurity, AI ethics, robotics, and human-AI interaction. The catch is that these new jobs require specialized knowledge and adaptability, which means that static education is insufficient.(Avalekar et al., 2025) This dynamic necessitates a paradigm shift toward a learning model that is continuous and responsive to change. Governments, academic institutions, and employers are increasingly recognizing this need by promoting flexible learning pathways, online education platforms, micro-credentialing, and training programs tailored to emerging industry demands. For individuals, this shift implies not just a professional obligation but a mindset of intellectual curiosity and resilience.Moreover, lifelong learning in the age of AI is not confined to professional skill development. It encompasses the cultivation of digital literacy, critical thinking, ethical reasoning, and interdisciplinary awareness—attributes that are indispensable in navigating an AI-driven world. As AI systems are integrated into healthcare, education competencies empower individuals to engage meaningfully in shaping the development and governance of AI technologies.In addition, lifelong learning fosters human capabilities that AI cannot replicate—such as creativity, empathy, emotional intelligence, and moral judgment.

As machines take over increasingly complex tasks, the human touch becomes more valuable in fields such as mental health, education, arts, social work, and leadership.

These human-centric skills are not static; they too can beenhanced world, human flourishing is not about competing with machines but about complementing them in ways that emphasize what makes sniquely human.The institutional and societal dimensions of lifelong learning also demand attention. As AI transforms economic and social structures, it is imperative for public policy to support equitable access to lifelong learning opportunities.(Banala et al., 2025) Disparities in digital infrastructure, educational quality, and financial resources can exacerbate inequalities if not addressed proactively. Lifelong learning must be inclusive, reaching marginalized populations, rural communities, aging workers, and those whose roles are most vulnerable to automation. Programs that provide affordable retraining, digital skills boot camps, workplace learning initiatives, and support for adult learners are crucial in creating a resilient and into the fabric of daily life.Technological advancements themselves are enabling the evolution of lifelong learning. AI-driven personalized learning platforms can adapt content and pace to individual needs, optimizing retention and engagement. Virtual reality and simulation technologies are making hands-on training more immersive and effective. Massive open online courses (MOOCs), online degrees, and credentialing systems are democratizing access to world-class education. At the same time, data analytics allows for the continuous assessment and improvement of learning programs. These innovations, if designed ethically and inclusively, can help overcome traditional barriers to education such as time constraints, geographic limitations, and cost.(Bates & Davis, 2004) However, leveraging AI in learning also requires individuals to cultivate self-direction, digital fluency, and the ability to navigate an overwhelming amount of information critically and responsibly.Another essential aspect of lifelong learning is adaptability. The half-life of skills—the amount of time before a learned skill becomes half as valuable—has shortened dramatically. This means that workers need to periodically reinvent themselves, not just by learning new technical skills but by building the cognitive flexibility to pivot into new domains. Lifelong learners view change not as a threat but as an opportunity for growth. They develop metacognitive skills such as learning how to learn, managing learning goals, and evaluating their own progress. These skills are foundational in a world where AI can alter industries and job roles in just a few years. Importantly, adaptability also supports mental health and psychological resilience in times of uncertainty, empowering individuals to face the future with confidence and purpose.

THE ROLE OF AI IN SUPPORTING ADULT EDUCATION AND SKILL DEVELOPMENT

This is especially beneficial for adult learners who often juggle education with work, family, or other responsibilities. AI enables them to learn at their own convenience, maximizing both time efficiency and comprehension. Furthermore, personalized feedback, intelligent recommendations, and continuous assessments help maintain motivation and ensure mastery, improving retention and application of knowledge.AI also plays a crucial role in making adult education more accessible and inclusive. Language processing technologies such as real-time translation and speech-to-text tools support learners from diverse linguistic backgrounds, breaking down language barriers tat have historically hindered adult participation in education. Additionally, AI-driven accessibility tools such as screen readers, voice-activated commands, and predictive text input make learning more inclusive for people with disabilities. In rural or underserved regions, where access to traditional educational institutions may be limited, urgical procedures, or navigating customer service scenarios.(Calonge et al., 2023) These technologies provide experiential learning opportunities that traditional classrooms cannot offer, improving both skill acquisition and confidence. In fields such as manufacturing, healthcare, logistics, and emergency response, such hands-on training is invaluable. AI also supports soft skills development—such as communication, teamwork, leadership, and problem-solving—through virtual agents, role-playing simulations, and interactive learning experiences that mirror real-life interactions.Another important function of AI in adult education is career guidance and workforce alignment. Intelligent systems can analyze labor market trends, job descriptions, and skill demand data to recommend relevant courses, certifications, or learning paths to individual learners. AI-based career advising tools help adults identify their strengths, explore emerging career options, and make informed decisions about reskilling or upskilling. For example, a mid-career professional looking to transition into a new industry can use an AI-powered platform to assess transferable skills, identify gaps, and receive customized learning suggestions that align with future job prospects. (Chowdhary et al., 2025) These systems can also match learners with internship opportunities, mentors, and potential employers, bridging the gap between education and employment and accelerating career advancement.In addition to supporting learners, AI empowers educators, training providers, and institutions by providing deep use these insights to adapt teaching strategies, offer personalized assistance, and improve the effectiveness of their programs. For institutions, predictive analytics can inform curriculum design, resource allocation, and strategic planning, ensuring that offerings remain relevant to evolving changing industries. With the rise of microlearning and modular content, AI can deliver bite-sized learning materials to adults at the moment of need—whether on the job, during a commute, or in preparation for a task.

Chatbots, voice assistants, and AI-powered knowledge bases provide on-demand answers and guidance, transforming workplaces into dynamic learning environments. This approach supports lifelong learning by embedding education into the fabric of daily life, allowing adults to stay current with new tools, regulations, processes, and technologies without the need for extended classroom sessions.To fully realize the potential of AI in adult education, a collaborative approach is needed across sectors. Policymakers must create enabling frameworks that promote innovation while safeguarding rights. Employers should integrate AI-based learning tools into their training ecosystems and support a culture of lifelong learning. Educational institutions must redesign curricula and pedagogies to incorporate AI effectively, ensuring that both educators and learners are equipped to engage with these tools. Technology developers need to prioritize ethical design, user-centric interfaces, and interoperability to ensure that AI systems serve diverse learning needs. collaboration and cross-cultural learning. Platforms that use machine translation, automatic content generation, and collaborative tools allow adult learners from different parts of the world to share knowledge, exchange ideas, and learn from one another. This global interconnectedness fosters intercultural competence, broadens perspectives, and prepares adults to work in increasingly diverse and internationalized environments. Furthermore, AI can help preserve and revitalize indigenous knowledge and languages by digitizing and curating culturally relevant educational content, ensuring that adult learning is not only technologically advanced but also culturally grounded.In conclusion, AI is poised to play a transformative role in adult education and skill development. Its capacity to personalize learning, enhance access, simulate real-world experiences, provide data-driven guidance, and support lifelong learning makes it a powerful tool in the quest for an adaptable and inclusive workforce. As the demands of the digital economy continue to evolve, adults must continuously reskill and upskill to thrive—and AI offers innovative solutions to meet these demands effectively. However, realizing this potential requires intentional design, equitable access, and ethical implementation. By embracing AI thoughtfully, societies can ensure that adult education not only responds to today's challenges but also anticipates tomorrow's opportunities, fostering a culture of continuous growth, empowerment, and inclusion in the age of intelligent technology.

AI-POWERED ADAPTIVE LEARNING SYSTEMS FOR ADULTS

As artificial intelligence (AI) continues to reshape the landscape of modern education, one of its most transformative applications is in the development and deployment of adaptive learning systems. (Coates et al., 2025)These systems use AI algorithms and real-time data analytics to tailor the learning experience according to an individual learner's performance, preferences, and progress. For adult learners—who often bring varied educational backgrounds, professional experiences, and learning needs—AI-powered adaptive learning systems offer a highly effective, flexible, and personalized approach to education and skill development. These systems not only support lifelong learning and reskilling but also democratize access to high-quality education by overcoming traditional barriers such as time, location, and cost. In an era characterized by rapid technological change and shifting job markets, adaptive learning systems are emerging as indispensable tools for preparing adults to thrive in the digital economy.At their core, AI-powered adaptive learning systems are designed to respond to the learner in real time. Unlike static e-learning modules or classroom lectures, which treat all learners the same, adaptive systems use AI to constantly assess how a learner is interacting with content. (Dakhli & De Clercq, 2004)This includes analyzing response times, quiz scores, engagement patterns, and even keystroke dynamics. Based on this data, the system dynamically adjusts the difficulty level of questions, revisits misunderstood concepts, introduces new materials when appropriate, and suggests remedial or supplementary resources tailored to the learner's needs. (Daleure, 2017)For adult learners, many of whom return to education after a long hiatus or in pursuit of career advancement, this responsiveness ensures that the learning experience is both supportive and efficientAnother powerful feature of AI-adaptive learning systems is continuous formative assessment.

Rather than relying solely on end-of-course exams or static tests, these systems embed assessment into every interaction. As adults engage with content, answer questions, complete assignments, or participate in discussions, the AI collects data and evaluates understanding in real time. It then adapts instruction accordingly, providing immediate feedback, re-teaching misunderstood concepts, or advancing to more complex material when mastery is demonstrated. (Edarabia, 2017). This constant loop of feedback and adjustment enables learners to address gaps promptly and reinforces learning before misconceptions become entrenched. For adult learners, especially those learning independently or remotely, such real-time support mimics the benefits of one-on-one tutoring and significantly enhances self-directed learning.AI-powered adaptive systems also help adult learners make more informed decisions about their learning pathways and career trajectories. Many systems are integrated with labor market data, enabling them to suggest courses and skill sets aligned with current job trends and future opportunities. For example, a healthcare worker looking to transition into a technology role may be guided toward personalized pathways in health informatics, data analysis, or cybersecurity, with content curated based on individual goals and job market demands. Furthermore, AI systems can recommend micro-credentials, certifications, or supplementary training that align with the learner's aspirations, empowering them to build career-relevant skills efficiently and strategically.Incorporating elements of gamification and motivation strategies, adaptive systems can increase persistence and reduce dropout rates among adult learners. Many platforms reward progress with badges, leaderboards, milestones, and certificates—features that are particularly effective in maintaining motivation and a sense of achievement. The ability to visualize progress, receive encouraging messages, and set personal learning goals creates a positive learning experience and fosters a growth mindset. Moreover, by adapting the difficulty and complexity of tasks, these systems ensure that learners are constantly challenged but not overwhelmed—striking a balance that maintains engagement and encourages continuous effort.Accessibility is another crucial area where adaptive learning systems are making a significant impact. AI-enhanced features such as text-to-speech, speech recognition, real-time translation, and predictive text input help remove barriers for learners with disabilities or those from non-native language backgrounds.

AI-DRIVEN LEARNING ANALYTICS FOR ADULT EDUCATION

When powered by AI, this approach moves beyond basic data tracking to offer predictive insights, real-time feedback, and dynamic support tailored to individual learners. As adult education continues to evolve in response to technological change, workforce demands, and lifelong learning imperatives, AI-driven learning analytics stands out as a transformative tool with immense potential to enhance learner success and institutional effectiveness.At the heart of AI-driven learning analytics is the ability to collect and process vast amounts of data from a wide array of learning interactions. These may include time spent on tasks, quiz scores, forum participation, mouse clicks, keystrokes, video-watching behavior, device usage, course navigation paths, and more. (Fadlelmula & Qadhi, 2024)AI systems analyze this behavioral data using machine learning algorithms to identify patterns, detect anomalies, and infer learner engagement, comprehension, and progression. In adult education, this granular insighOne of the most impactful applications of AI-driven learning analytics is predictive modeling. These models use historical and real-time data to forecast future learner behaviors and outcomes. For example, they can predict whether a learner is likely to pass a course, disengage from content, or drop out altogether. Such predictions allow for early interventions—personalized messages, additional resources, check-ins from instructors—that can re-engage at-risk learners before issues escalate. For adult learners balancing education with other life commitments, these timely nudges can be critical in maintaining momentum and completing their educational goals(Fares et al., 2023). Institutions can also use predictive analytics to monitor cohort performance, allocate resources efficiently, and design support services that target the needs of specific populations, such as first-generation college students, older adults, or career switchers.metacognitive skills—such as planning, goal-setting, and self-assessment—that are essential for effective lifelong learning. For instance, an adult learner enrolled in a project management certification course might use a dashboard to track their quiz performance across modules, identify weak spots in risk management concepts, and revise their study schedule accordingly.

This level of insight and control enhances learner confidence, encourages persistence, and builds a stronger feedback loop allows instructors to refine their content, improve clarity, and adjust pacing to better support adult learners. It also helps identify successful teaching strategies and replicate best practices across courses and programs.(Gambhir & Bhattacharjee, 2021) For example, if analytics show that learners perform better in courses that incorporate peer discussion forums, educators might integrate collaborative elements into traditionally solo learning environments. Such data-informed pedagogy fosters a culture of continuous improvement in adult education.There is also a need to ensure that learning analytics enhance rather than replace the human element in education. While AI can provide powerful insights, it is educators, advisors, and mentors who interpret those insights in context and provide the empathy, encouragement, and social interaction that adult learners often need. A balanced approach that combines the analytical power of AI with the emotional intelligence of human educators is essential for maximizing the benefits of learning analytics.n conclusion, AI-driven learning analytics represent a transformative force in adult education. By turning raw data into meaningful insights, these systems personalize learning, support at-risk learners, guide career-aligned skill development, and enhance instructional quality. They offer a roadmap for optimizing learning experiences in an increasingly complex and dynamic educational landscape. However, realizing their full potential requires thoughtful implementation, attention to ethical concerns, and a commitment to using data not just to monitor learners, but to empower them. In doing so, AI-driven learning analytics can serve as a cornerstone of inclusive, effective, and lifelong education in the digital age.

UPSKILLING AND RESKILLING IN THE AGE OF AI: WHY IT MATTERS

The age of AI is characterized by relentless change, with entire industries transforming, job roles becoming obsolete, and new occupations emerging at a breathtaking pace. Against this backdrop, continuous learning is not merely a strategic advantage but a necessity for survival. Upskilling and reskilling serve as the bridge between technological advancement and human adaptability, ensuring that individuals and societies can navigate disruption, harness innovation, and thrive in a future shaped by intelligent machines.The driving force behind the rising demand for upskilling and reskilling is the disruptive not only routine manual tasks but also cognitive functions such as data analysis, decision-making, and customer service. Roles in manufacturing, transportation, finance, retail, and administrative support are particularly susceptible to automation, placing millions of workers at risk of displacement(Hassock & Hill, 2022). However, while AI eliminates certain job functions, it also creates new opportunities in fields such as data science, machine learning, robotics, cybersecurity, digital marketing, and AI ethics. These emerging roles require a different skill set—often more technical, analytical, and adaptable—than those required in the past. Upskilling and reskilling are critical to preparing workers for this transition, enabling them to seize new opportunities rather than be left behind by technological progress.For individuals, the need to upskill or reskill is tied directly to employability and career longevity. The traditional career model—where one learns a profession in youth and practices it until retirement—is becoming obsolete. In today's job market, skills have a shorter shelf life, and adaptability is the most valuable attribute.

Professionals must now update their skillsets every few years to remain relevant and competitive. This is especially important in sectors experiencing rapid digitization, such as healthcare, education, logistics, and financial services. A nurse, for example, may need to learn how to operate AI-driven diagnostic tools or use telemedicine platforms, while a logistics worker may need to understand data analytics or drone management. Reskilling also provides a lifeline to those whose roles are disappearing entirely—offering pathways to enter new industries and redefine their careers(Hui et al., 2023).From an economic perspective, large-scale upskilling and reskilling are essential to maintaining a productive and inclusive workforce. As the World Economic Forum and other institutions have highlighted, failing to invest in human capital as technology advances can lead to structural unemployment, widening income inequality, and social instability. Conversely, a workforce that is continuously learning and evolving is better positioned to support innovation, drive economic growth, and respond to the challenges of a knowledge-based economy. Governments and policy-makers are increasingly recognizing this imperative by launching sector investment in employee learning. AI-driven tools can analyze a worker's existing competencies, career history, and job goals to create a customized curriculum tailored to market demand. Chatbots, virtual tutors, and gamified learning environments enhance engagement and retention, while microlearning modules allow busy adults to build skills in short, manageable segments. This approach is especially effective for adult learners, who may need flexible, on-demand learning options to accommodate work and family responsibilities. AI can also assist in tracking progress, issuing digital credentials, and connecting learners with job opportunities— AI rather than be displaced by it.industrial jobs into green roles supports both environmental goals and economic resilience. Moreover, the convergence of AI with sustainability—such as AI applications for climate modeling or resource optimization—requires interdisciplinary skills that combine environmental literacy with digital expertise. Preparing the workforce for this intersection is essential for achieving inclusive and sustainable development in the AI age.Inequity in access to upskilling and reskilling opportunities remains a significant challenge that must be addressed to ensure inclusive growth. Many vulnerable populations—such as low-income workers, rural residents, migrants, women returning to the workforce, and older adults—face barriers to participation in learning programs due to lack of time, financial resources, internet connectivity, or prior educational attainment. Without targeted support, these groups risk being disproportionately affected by job displacement and digital exclusion.

AI-BASED TRAINING PROGRAMS FOR UPSKILLING AND RESKILLING

The transformative power of artificial intelligence (AI) is fundamentally reshaping education and workforce development, particularly in the realm of upskilling and reskilling. (Iyer et al., 2023)AI-based training programs offer dynamic, personalized, and scalable solutions to equip workers with the evolving skill sets required in today's rapidly changing labor markets. As technological innovation accelerates, the traditional model of education—frontloaded early in life—has become insufficient. Continuous learning is now essential to maintain employability, adapt to new industries, and thrive amid digital disruption. In this context, AI-based training programs emerge as critical tools that enable individuals, companies, and governments to respond effectively to shifting workforce demands. These programs leverage the capabilities of AI to deliver customized learning paths, automate skill assessments, offer real-time feedback, and facilitate immersive and interactive learning experiences. adaptive approach ensures that learners focus on areas where improvement is needed and are not burdened with redundant material. For instance, a mid-career professional transitioning into a data science role may already possess statistical knowledge but need focused training in programming languages like motivation, reduce dropout rates, and improve learning outcomes—key factors in the success of adult upskilling and reskilling.Moreover, AI-based training programs excel in providing real-time performance analytics and feedback, enabling learners to monitor their progress and adjust their strategies accordingly. Through sophisticated data analysis, AI can track learning behavior, quiz results, time spent on tasks, and engagement levels to offer actionable insights.(Iyer, 2022) These insights help learners identify strengths and weaknesses, while instructors and coaches can intervene with timely support when needed. Some platforms incorporate gamification elements powered by AI—such as achievement badges, adaptive quizzes, and leaderboards—which sustain learner engagement and motivation. Others employ virtual assistants or chatbots that answer questions, clarify concepts, or guide learners through modules, creating a seamless and supportive learning environment.

Figure 1. Lifelong learning in a digital age

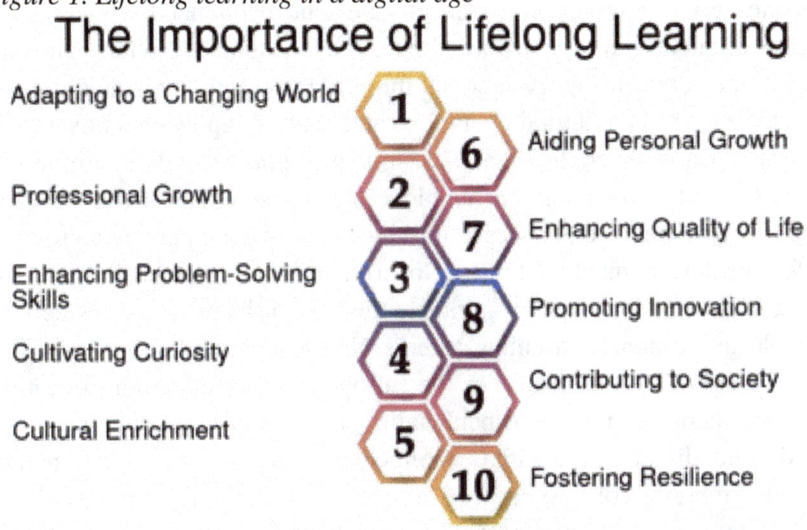

AI also enhances the accessibility and inclusivity of training programs. Many individuals in need of upskilling or reskilling face barriers such as time constraints, financial limitations, or geographical isolation. AI-based platforms, accessible via smartphones or laptops, enable self-paced and remote learning, breaking down traditional barriers to education.(Jetha et al., 2023) For instance, a warehouse worker in a rural area can access high-quality technical training in logistics automation, while a stay-at-home parent can pursue courses in digital marketing at night. In multilingual settings, AI can offer real-time translation and transcription, enabling learners to study in their preferred language. This democratization of access ensures that a broader and more diverse population can benefit from skill development, supporting social equity and inclusion.example, AI-driven simulations can train technicians to operate complex machinery, healthcare workers to conduct procedures, or pilots to respond to emergencies. By creating realistic scenarios that adapt based on learner responses, these systems reinforce practical skills and decision-making abilities. Such experiential learning is particularly valuable for high-risk industries or those requiring physical tasks that cannot be taught effectively through text or video alone.

AI ensures that these experiences are customized, repeatable, and continuously evolving based on user feedback and performance.Corporations and organizations are increasingly adopting AI-based training programs to future-proof their workforce and maintain competitiveness. In industries facing digital transformation—such as finance, retail, manufacturing, and healthcare—internal training platforms powered by AI are being used to close skills gaps, onboard employees to new roles, and support leadership development. These platforms can forecast future skill requirements based on business goals, assess existing competencies, and recommend individualized learning paths aligned with organizational needs. For example, a retail company introducing AI-powered inventory systems might deploy a training module that upskills frontline workers in digital operations and reskills supply chain managers in data analytics.(Kamalov et al., 2023) This strategic approach not only improves workforce agility but also strengthens employee retention, engagement, and performance.At the national level, AI-based training programs are playing a growing role in workforce development strategies. Governments and public institutions are collaborating with edtech companies, universities, and private-sector partners to design scalable and responsive training systems. National platforms such as India's SWAYAM, Singapore's SkillsFuture, or the European Union's Digital Education Action Plan are incorporating AI to personalize learning at scale, identify labor market trends, and align training with economic needs. AI can analyze job market data to identify emerging roles, suggest in-demand skills, and map pathways from declining occupations to growth areas. Such intelligence is crucial for directing public investment in training programs and guiding individuals toward sustainable and rewarding careers.The role of AI in supporting credentialing and recognition of skills is also transforming.

AI-DRIVEN CAREER GUIDANCE AND COUNSELING

In the contemporary world, where technological advancement, labor market fluidity, and the evolution of job roles are more rapid than ever before, traditional career counseling and large datasets to offer data-informed insights, skill assessments, and predictive analytics tailored to an individual's unique aspirations, aptitudes, personality traits, and real-time market demands.(Khan, 2023) The result is a reimagined approach to career guidance that is proactive rather than reactive, continuous rather than episodic, and highly accessible rather than limited by geographic or institutional constraints. AI is not merely augmenting human advisors; it is revolutionizing the entire paradigm of career development by making it more data-driven, equitable, and future-oriented.diverse data sets to generate highly personalized career recommendations. Traditional guidance methods often rely on subjective human judgment, general assessments, and outdated labor market information. In contrast, AI systems can synthesize data from a wide array of sources, including online resumes, job market analytics, skill repositories, educational records, psychometric evaluations, and even behavioral insights from user interactions on learning platforms. By doing so, these systems construct a comprehensive learner profile and map it against real-time labor market trends. For example, a platform might identify that a user with strong logical reasoning, experience in customer service, and coursework in statistics is a good fit for transitioning into business analytics. It can then suggest relevant certifications, internships, or skill development programs, creating a seamless bridge between current abilities and future goals.Moreover, AI tools are capable of delivering dynamic and adaptive career planning, which evolves as users grow and as industries change. Instead of offering a one-time career assessment—common in traditional models—AI-driven systems continuously learn from the user's interactions, completed training, updated interests, and external labor market shifts. As a result, career guidance becomes a living, breathing service that adjusts to new opportunities, personal development, and life changes. For instance, someone who begins as a web developer but later develops an interest in AI could be guided toward machine learning engineering pathways, complete with updated skill maps, emerging job roles, and recommended learning resources. This adaptive capability is essential in aAI-driven systems are also revolutionizing how individuals understand their own strengths and potential. Through psychometric testing powered by AI, personality analysis via NLP, and advanced skills diagnostics, these platforms offer deep self-insight that was previously only accessible through professional counselors(Koroteev & Tekic, 2021) AI can detect hidden talents, identify latent interests, and reveal how these align with current and future job roles. For example, by analyzing writing samples, coding tasks, or social media activity, an AI counselor can identify creativity, problem-solving ability, or leadership potential.

Additionally, AI can support continuous career coaching through intelligent virtual assistants or chatbots that are available 24/7. (Li, 2022)These AI companions can engage in natural conversations to answer questions, suggest career moves, explain industry requirements, and even help with soft skills like communication or networking. Advanced chatbots can simulate mock interviews, provide feedback on presentation skills, or guide users through decision trees to explore pros and cons of career options. The ability to receive immediate, empathetic, and intelligent support any time of day makes career guidance more responsive and user-centered. These virtual advisors can also nudge users to stay on track with learning goals, remind them of upcoming deadlines, and reinforce motivation—functions that are especially valuable for self-directed learners.Employers and HR professionals also benefit from AI-driven career counseling tools, particularly in internal talent mobility and succession planning. By analyzing employee data, performance metrics, and organizational goals, AI systems can recommend personalized career pathways within a company. This helps in identifying high-potential employees, aligning training resources with business needs, and reducing turnover by providing meaningful career progression opportunities.(Limbore et al., 2025) For example, a logistics coordinator with an aptitude for data analysis might be guided toward an operations research analyst role, supported by targeted upskilling. Developers must implement fairness-aware machine learning techniques and ensure diversity in training data. Moreover, users must be informed about how their data is used, and privacy must be safeguarded rigorously. Trust is foundational in career counseling, and ethical governance frameworks are essential to ensure that AI systems uphold this trust.Another challenge is the human element of empathy, moral judgment, and emotional intelligence—areas where AI, despite advances, remains limited. While AI can simulate supportive dialogue, it cannot fully replace the nuanced guidance of experienced human counselors who can read emotional cues, address complex personal issues, or provide moral support during crises. The most effective model, therefore, is a hybrid one—where AI serves as a powerful assistant to human advisors, freeing them from routine tasks and data analysis so they can focus on high-value, human-centric counseling.

AI IN THE WORKPLACE: OPPORTUNITIES AND CHALLENGES

AI has become a strategic tool for enhancing productivity, driving innovation, and enabling data-driven operations. As companies increasingly adopt AI technologies such as machine learning, natural language processing, robotic process automation (RPA), and intelligent chatbots, the workplace is evolving into a hybrid ecosystem of human-machine collaboration. However, alongside the promising opportunities that AI brings, there are also significant challenges—including ethical concerns, job AI systems often work alongside them, enhancing decision-making, providing insights, and enabling data-driven strategies. Decision support systems powered by AI can synthesize large volumes of unstructured data to help managers and executives make informed choices.(Lokhande et al., 2025) For example, AI-driven business intelligence tools analyze market trends, customer feedback, and operational data to offer actionable insights. In marketing, AI helps personalize customer experiences through behavioral analytics and targeted content. In HR, AI supports recruitment by screening resumes, analyzing candidate fit, and even conducting preliminary interviews using conversational AI. This augmentation of roles contributes to greater innovation and strategic agility within organizations.engineers, AI trainers, and automation specialists have emerged as high-growth careers. Moreover, interdisciplinary roles—such as those combining domain expertise with AI literacy (e.g., AI-driven legal analysts or AI-informed educators)—are gaining prominence. This shift underscores the growing importance of digital literacy and continuous learning in adapting to the AI-powered workplace. Companies that invest in upskilling and reskilling their workforce are better positioned to harness AI's potential while maintaining employee engagement and competitiveness.in lower-skilled, low-wage jobs are not supported with training and transition pathways.(Martin et al., 2020) Without proactive labor market policies, the digital divide could widen, exacerbating unemployment and social disparities. Employers must therefore strike a balance between technological adoption and human capital investment.accountability, and transparency.

Organizations must implement practices such as bias audits, explainable AI, inclusive data sourcing, and stakeholder engagement to build trust and mitigate harm. Additionally, interdisciplinary ethics committees and compliance officers should be involved in AI deployment decisions.employee buy-in and minimize resistance, organizations must prioritize change management, open communication, and inclusive participation in the AI adoption process.laws such as the GDPR is critical. Furthermore, workers need to be educated about their digital rights and the ways in which their data is being collected and used by AI systems within the organization. Transparent data practices not only protect legal compliance but also foster a culture of trust and ethical responsibility.and foresight. Leadership training programs should include modules on AI literacy, responsible innovation, and inclusive technology management. Moreover, cross-functional collaboration between IT, HR, legal, and business strategy teams is essential to align AI initiatives with organizational goals and values.placing human values, well-being, and dignity at the core of AI development and deployment. This paradigm shift emphasizes the complementarity between human intuition and machine intelligence. For example, AI can process millions of data points to detect fraud patterns, but it takes human judgment to interpret anomalies in a broader ethical context. Similarly, while AI can streamline workflows, human empathy remains irreplaceable in client relations, conflict resolution, and leadership. By framing AI as a partner rather than a competitor, organizations can foster a more harmonious and productive work environment.Looking ahead, the workplace of the future will be characterized by agility, intelligence, and personalization, all powered by AI.

AI-BASED PERFORMANCE SUPPORT SYSTEMS FOR EMPLOYEES

The emergence of Artificial Intelligence (AI)-based Performance Support Systems (PSS) marks a significant evolution in how organizations enhance employee productivity, learning, and job efficiency. These systems offer on-demand, contextual, and intelligent assistance to employees during their workflow, enabling them to perform tasks more accurately and confidently without interrupting their work for extensive training. Unlike traditional support systems that are static and often generic, AI-based PSS are dynamic, data-driven, and personalized—adapting in real-time to the unique needs, preferences, and performance gaps of individual workers. As workplaces become more complex and rapidly changing due to technological advancements, globalization, and hybrid work environments, AI-based performance support is gaining strategic importance.(McElroy et al., 2006) These tools are particularly valuable in task—such as the application being used, the user's historical behavior, and the task's complexity—and provide immediate guidance tailored to that situation. For instance, in customer service roles, AI-powered assistants can suggest appropriate responses to client queries, flag policy-related issues, or even offer product recommendations in real-time. In software development, intelligent code assistants like GitHub Copilot use natural language processing (NLP) to suggest code snippets, correct errors, and explain logic. This real-time support not only boosts accuracy and speed but also reduces cognitive overload, minimizes error rates, and fosters continuous learning in the flow of work.A key feature of AI-based PSS is personalization. These systems use machine learning algorithms to analyze vast amounts of employee data—including performance metrics, learning history, interaction patterns, and task success rates—to tailor interventions. Over time, the system becomes more attuned to individual learning curves, preferred formats (videos, checklists, simulations), and motivational triggers. For example, a medical technician using AI-assisted imaging software might receive customized feedback on diagnosis accuracy and interactive visual prompts to improve interpretation of scans.

In retail, frontline employees can use AI-based mobile apps that guide them through inventory management or customer engagement scenarios based on their past experiences and knowledge levels. (Negi, 2023)By aligning support with individual needs, AI-based systems enhance retention, engagement, and overall job satisfaction. FAQs, these AI systems can understand nuanced queries, interpret intent, and provide contextually relevant answers. For instance, in a financial services setting, an employee might ask, "What's the current interest rate for our small business loans?" and receive not just the rate, but accompanying documentation, relevant regulations, and customer eligibility criteria—all within seconds.(Pabalkar & Chanda, 2022) Collaboration is also enhanced by AI performance support. Smart systems can suggest colleagues or mentors to consult, automatically generate collaboration spaces based on shared challenges, and even summarize meeting notes or highlight key decisions for ongoing projects. In team-based environments, such as agile software development or healthcare delivery, these tools facilitate knowledge sharing and collective intelligence. AI can match employees working on similar problems, suggest experts within the organization, and promote peer-to-peer learning. As knowledge flows more freely and is curated by intelligent systems, organizational agility and innovation are strengthened.Another benefit of AI-based PSS lies in reducing on-boarding time and enhancing the productivity of new hires. New employees often face a steep learning curve and may require extensive training before reaching full productivity. AI-enabled support systems can accelerate this process by offering interactive walkthroughs, contextual guidance, and immediate access to experts or resources. For example, in a complex enterprise software environment, a new hire can rely on an AI assistant to navigate the platform, understand business rules, and avoid critical errors. This not only shortens time-to-productivity but also increases confidence and engagement among new recruits.The scalability of AI-based PSS is especially valuable for large and distributed organizations. Traditional support models—such as in-person mentoring or scheduled training—are often limited by geography, time, and resource constraints. AI systems, by contrast, are available 24/7, can support thousands of employees simultaneously, and can adapt to diverse roles, languages, and cultural contexts. Whether an employee is working remotely, in the field, or across time zones, AI ensures equitable access to performance support. (Paderanga et al., 2023).

Moreover, centralized analytics provide leadership with visibility into organizational capability, training effectiveness, and emerging skill gaps across departments or regions.which can erode trust. Organizations must establish transparent policies on data usage, anonymize sensitive data, and emphasize the developmental—not punitive—purpose of these tools. Additionally, the accuracy and fairness of AI recommendations depend on the quality and diversity of the training data. Systems must be regularly audited to avoid reinforcing biases or making inappropriate assumptions about employee capabilities or needs.Another concern is the risk of overdependence on AI. While performance support tools can enhance productivity, they should not replace critical thinking, problem-solving, or interpersonal judgment. Employees must retain the ability to question AI recommendations, make ethical decisions, and innovate beyond algorithmic boundaries. To achieve this balance, organizations should design AI systems that encourage reflection, offer explanations, and allow human override. Integrating AI with a culture of psychological safety and learning agility ensures that technology empowers rather than dictates performance.Leadership and organizational readiness are crucial for successful adoption of AI-based PSS. Managers and supervisors must be trained not only in using these systems but also in interpreting analytics, mentoring employees based on AI feedback, and fostering a supportive environment.

THE FUTURE OF WORK: IMPLICATIONS FOR LIFELONG LEARNING

Artificial Intelligence (AI), automation, robotics, cloud computing, remote work infrastructure, and other innovations are reshaping industries, redefining job roles, and altering how, when, and where work takes place. In this new paradigm, the traditional model of education followed market demands agility, continuous adaptation, and a proactive approach to skill development—making lifelong learning not just a personal asset but a societal necessity. As the boundaries between learning is essential for individuals to remain employable and for societies to ensure economic resilience and social equityOne of the most profound implications of the future of work is the accelerated obsolescence of skills. Technological innovation is shortening the shelf-life of technical knowledge, with some digital competencies becoming outdated within just a few years.(Radakovich & Nazha, 2021) Automation and AI are projected to eliminate or transform millions of jobs globally, particularly in sectors like manufacturing, logistics, customer service, and administrative support. At the same time, entirely new roles are emerging in areas such as data science, cybersecurity, AI ethics, digital marketing, and sustainability consulting. This duality—job displacement alongside job creation—means that workers must constantly acquire new skills to remain relevant and competitive. Lifelong learning becomes the bridge between displacement and opportunity, ensuring that individuals are not left behind by technological progress.Moreover, the demand for hybrid skill sets—combinations of technical proficiency and human-centric capabilities—is reshaping educational priorities. Future jobs will increasingly require individuals to blend digital literacy with creativity, emotional intelligence, critical thinking, adaptability, and cross-cultural communication. These “soft” or “durable” skills are less likely to be automated and are critical for roles involving complex decision-making, leadership, innovation, and customer engagement. Lifelong learning frameworks must therefore go beyond narrow technical training and support holistic development, enabling workers to thrive in multidisciplinary, team-based, and purpose-driven work environments. For example, a data analyst of the future may also need to understand ethical frameworks, collaborate effectively with marketing teams, and communicate insights clearly to non-technical stakeholders.

The rise of the gig economy and non-traditional employment models further amplifies the importance of lifelong learning. Increasing numbers of workers are engaging in freelance, contract, or platform-based work, which offers flexibility but often lacks formal career development support. In such decentralized labor markets, individuals must take greater ownership of their professional growth. Lifelong learning provides the tools for self-directed development, allowing gig workers to build a portable skillset, explore multiple career paths, and remain agile in a fluid job market. (Sadok et al., 2023)Digital learning platforms, micro-credentials, and peer-to-peer knowledge sharing communities play a pivotal role in supporting continuous learning for independent workers. AI-powered personalization, adaptive learning platforms, gamification, augmented and virtual reality, and mobile-first content are enabling learners to receive customized, real-time, and immersive educational experiences(Tubadji et al., 2021). These technologies support diverse learning styles and allow adults to learn at their own pace, on their own terms, and in the flow of work. For instance, a factory worker could use AR-based training to upskill on new machinery, while a sales executive might engage in microlearning modules between client meetings. As these innovations become mainstream, the focus of lifelong learning will shift from formal degrees to continuous, bite-sized, and experiential learning that aligns closely with evolving job demands.The implications of the future of work extend beyond individuals to organizations and policymakers. For businesses, fostering a culture of lifelong learning is no longer optional—it is a strategic imperative. Companies that fail to invest in employee development risk falling behind in innovation, productivity, and talent retention. Forward-thinking organizations are embedding learning into the fabric of their operations, integrating it with performance management, career progression, and organizational design. Some are even creating internal talent marketplaces and learning ecosystems that empower employees to explore new roles, projects, and skills within the organization. This internal mobility not only addresses talent shortages but also cultivates a more engaged and agile workforce.development and social inclusion. (Verma et al., 2023)This includes investing in adult education, vocational training, and digital infrastructure, as well as creating financial incentives and learning subsidies for underserved populations.

PREPARING FOR EMERGING JOBS AND SKILLS WITH AI

Forum predicts that while automation and AI may displace millions of jobs, they will also generate millions of new ones—.(Verma & Sehgal, 2023) The rise of AI is not simply a technological shift; it is a socio-economic transformation that calls for a fundamental reimagining of education, training, and workforce development strategies. Preparing individuals to meet the demands of these new roles requires a proactive approach that emphasizes lifelong learning, agility, and the integration of AI itself into the learning process.Emerging jobs are increasingly characterized by their hybrid nature, requiring a blend of domain expertise, digital literacy, and human-centric skills. Roles such as AI ethicist, machine learning operations (MLOps) engineer, virtual reality experience designer, automation specialist, data privacy consultant, and human-AI interaction designer exemplify this convergence.

These positions demand not only technical acumen—such as coding, data analysis, and algorithm development—but also competencies in ethics, design thinking, user experience, communication, and cultural awareness. Additionally, jobs in climate tech, sustainability analysis, and digital wellness are gaining prominence, driven by global imperatives like climate action, mental health, and digital equity. The rapid evolution of the job market means that many of the careers of the next decade are still being defined, making adaptability a critical attribute for workers.AI plays a vital role in preparing the workforce for these emerging roles through intelligent skills mapping, predictive analytics, personalized learning, and career path optimization.(Wang et al., 2021) AI-driven platforms can analyze labor market trends in real time, identifying in-demand skills and projecting future job opportunities based on industry trajectories. Moreover, by leveraging AI to support inclusive hiring and training practices, organizations can ensure that opportunities in emerging fields are accessible to a diverse talent pool.In the context of education, AI is transforming curriculum design and pedagogy to better reflect the realities of emerging jobs. Higher education institutions and vocational training providers are increasingly integrating AI-driven tools to co-create syllabi aligned with industry requirements. These curricula incorporate interdisciplinary learning, project-based assignments, and collaborative problem-solving, mirroring the team-oriented nature of modern workplaces.

Furthermore, AI-powered simulators and virtual labs offer learners the opportunity to engage in experiential learning, where they can apply theoretical knowledge in simulated environments that mimic real-world scenarios. For example, students in healthcare technology might use VR simulations to practice diagnostics, while aspiring robotics technicians could experiment with machine programming in a digital twin of a factory floor.AI is also revolutionizing career guidance and mentorship, providing intelligent support systems that help individuals explore new job roles, understand required skills, and plan learning trajectories. AI chatbots and virtual career advisors can analyze user preferences, past experiences, and labor market data to recommend tailored career paths. These tools democratize access to high-quality career counseling, which is especially valuable for underrepresented groups and individuals in remote or underserved regions. Additionally, AI can match learners with mentors and peer networks based on shared interests and goals, fostering social learning and peer support—critical components for motivation and long-term success in new career journeys.Another critical aspect of preparing for emerging jobs is the recognition of prior learning and skills acquired outside traditional settings. AI can facilitate this through the development of intelligent credentialing systems that assess and validate skills gained through work experience, online courses, volunteer work, or informal learning. For example, an AI system might evaluate a gig worker's roles without starting from scratch, reducing time and cost barriers and promoting equity in workforce development.

LIFELONG LEARNING STRATEGIES FOR A CHANGING JOB MARKET

In the era of accelerating technological advancements, globalization, and economic disruption, the concept of a stable, linear career trajectory has become outdated. Traditional education systems—once designed to prepare individuals for a single career over a lifetime—are no longer sufficient. The 21st-century labor market is fluid, dynamic, and increasingly shaped by artificial intelligence (AI), automation, and the platform economy. Jobs are being created, transformed, or rendered obsolete at an unprecedented pace, compelling individuals, institutions, and governments to adopt lifelong learning as a central strategy for career resilience and workforce competitiveness. Lifelong learning is no longer a luxury or a supplementary endeavor—it is a necessity for survival and success in a world where adaptability, agility, and continuous upskilling are paramount.encompasses a wide range of learning experiences—formal, informal, and non-formal—occurring through work, online platforms, peer networks, mentorship, and everyday life. As the job market undergoes rapid shifts due to emerging technologies and socio-economic changes, lifelong learning enables individuals to remain employable, transition between careers, and respond proactively to disruptions in their industries.aspirations. For example, a manufacturing worker displaced by automation may receive targeted suggestions to upskill in robotics programming, quality assurance, or supply chain analytics. These pathways often incorporate micro-credentials, digital badges, or stackable certificates, allowing learners to accumulate qualifications gradually and flexibly.

AI-driven platforms can analyze data from job postings, industry reports, economic indicators, and demographic trends to generate predictive insights. These insights can then inform curriculum development, public policy, and individual learning choices. For example, if a region anticipates a boom in green energy jobs, training providers can design programs in solar panel installation, environmental compliance, and energy efficiency management.adaptability, and collaboration—are becoming increasingly valuable. These attributes are harder to automate and are essential for navigating change, leading teams, and solving complex problems. Lifelong learning strategies should incorporate opportunities to build these capabilities through team-based projects, leadership training, reflective practice, and interdisciplinary coursework. Role-play scenarios, group discussions, and real-time feedback mechanisms can enhance engagement and skill acquisition in these areas.retirees seeking second careers or continued engagement. For example, midlife learners might benefit from executive education, industry certifications, or peer mentoring, while older adults may pursue digital literacy, entrepreneurship, or civic engagement programs. Policies such as learning accounts, portable education benefits, or government-sponsored reskilling grants can incentivize and support learning at any age.curriculum with universities, offer real-time project opportunities, or sponsor workforce development programs. Governments can create national learning strategies, invest in infrastructure, and monitor outcomes. NGOs and community organizations can support outreach, digital inclusion, and equitable access for marginalized populations. A collective approach enhances impact and sustainability, creating ecosystems that support learners throughout their lives.education—through job experience, volunteering, or self-study—that may not be documented in traditional qualifications. RPL frameworks allow these competencies to be assessed and translated into recognized credentials, helping individuals fast-track into new careers or education programs. Digital credentialing systems, powered by AI, can streamline RPL assessments and increase transparency, portability, and trust in alternative pathways.institutionalized learning as a core business strategy, offering internal academies, learning management systems, and innovation labs. At the societal level, national campaigns, media literacy initiatives, and community learning hubs can raise awareness and motivate lifelong learners of all backgrounds.sensitive programs, second-chance education for dropouts, and prison education initiatives are examples of inclusive lifelong learning models. AI can also support inclusivity by offering multilingual content, voice-based interfaces, and assistive technologies.pathways, and skills-matching tools.

CONCLUSION

AI is not simply a disruptive force—it is a powerful enabler that, when leveraged ethically and inclusively, can democratize education, personalize learning, and support human development across the lifespan. Embracing lifelong learning with AI is central to building resilient individuals, adaptive workforces, and more equitable and innovative societies.skills, transition into emerging careers, and continuously adapt to technological changes. Whether through AI-driven micro-learning platforms that deliver content in bite-sized modules, or intelligent career guidance tools that map competencies to labor market demands, AI helps bridge the gap between where individuals are and where they nsystems can identify learners at risk of disengagement and provide tailored interventions to support retention and completion. Through these capabilities, AI contributes to closing equity gaps and ensuring that lifelong learning opportunities are available to all, regardless of socioeconomic status, geographic location, or previous educational attainment. healthcare and manufacturing to information technology and green energy, AI-based training programs are already helping workers acquire competencies for the jobs of tomorrow. Meanwhile, AI-driven mentorship platforms and performance support systems offer real-time guidance and coaching, enhancing learning transfer and workplaprotect learners' rights. Educational institutions, employers, governments, and technology providers must collaborate to ensure that AI tools are designed with equity, pedagogical integrity, and accountability at their core. Clear ethical frameworks, inclusive design processes, and robust policy support are essential to safeguard against unintended harms and ensure that AI serves as a tool for empowerment rather than exploitation. holistic learning. Lifelong learning is not merely about acquiring technical skills—it is also about developing the capacity for reflection, adaptability, empathy, and civic engagement. AI must therefore be seen as a partner in the learning journey, enhancing rather than replacing the rich relational and experiential dimensions of education.The path forward must be inclusive, participatory, and responsive. Policymakers should invest in digital infrastructure, AI literacy, and capacity building to ensure that all individuals can benefit from AI-enhanced lifelong learning. Educational systems must embrace flexible and modular learning models that recognize diverse forms of knowledge, including informal and non-traditional learning. Employers must create cultures of continuous learning and provide workers with access to upskilling opportunities powered by AI. Learners themselves must be empowered with the digital and critical thinking skills needed to navigate AI tools effectively and ethically.As we look to the future, the synergy between AI and lifelong learning offers a compelling vision for human flourishing in a complex and uncertain world. It is a vision in which individuals are no longer constrained by geography, age, or background, but are empowered to learn, grow, and thrive at every stage of life. It is a future where education becomes a continuous, personalized, and inclusive journey, supported by intelligent systems that respond to human needs, aspirations, and potential. It is a future in which knowledge becomes more accessible, skills more adaptable, and societies more resilient in the face of change.Ultimately, embracing lifelong learning with AI is not merely a strategic imperative—it is a moral and social commitment. It is a recognition that in the age of intelligent machines, our most important investment remains in human intelligence, creativity, and capacity. By aligning AI with the goals of lifelong learning, we can build a more just, dynamic, and enlightened future—one in which all individuals have the opportunity to participate fully, contribute meaningfully, and live with dignity in a world transformed by technology. This is the promise of lifelong learning in the age of AI: not just to survive disruption, but to shape a better, more inclusive, and more empowered future for all.

REFERENCES

Abdeldayem, M. M., Aldulaimi, S. H., & Kharabsheh, R. (2021). Development of human capital resources to increase economic growth and innovation in the GCC Countries. *International Journal of Green Management and Business Studies*, *1*(1), 62–79.

Avalekar, U. A., Mehta, V., Mishra, B. R., Prasanna, L., Rajlakshmi, P. V., & Manjunath, T. C. (2025). The Current Advances in AI-Driven Education. In Babulak, E. (Ed.), *Educational AI Humanoid Computing Devices for Cyber Nomads* (pp. 173–196). IGI Global Scientific Publishing., DOI: 10.4018/979-8-3693-8985-0.ch008

Banala, S., Panyaram, S., & Selvakumar, P. (2025). Artificial Intelligence in Software Testing. In Chelliah, P., Venkatesh, R., Natraj, N., & Jeyaraj, R. (Eds.), *Artificial Intelligence for Cloud-Native Software Engineering* (pp. 237–262). IGI Global Scientific Publishing., DOI: 10.4018/979-8-3693-9356-7.ch009

Bates, P., & Davis, F. A. (2004). Social capital, social inclusion, and services for people with learning disabilities. *Disability & Society*, *19*(3), 195–207. DOI: 10.1080/0968759042000204202

Calonge, D. S., Shah, M. A., Aguerrebere, P. M., Abdulla, N., Connor, M., Badr, M., & Blakemore, E. (2023). Should I stay or should I go? International students' challenges and opportunities to secure employment in their host country after graduation. A scoping review using PRISMA. *Journal of Applied Learning and Teaching*, *6*(2), 1. https://journals.sfu.ca/jalt/index.php/jalt/index

Chowdhary, S., Selvakumar, P., Sangeetha, B., Sarvaani, V. V., Anute, N., & Sharma, M. (2025). The Role of Social Capital in Entrepreneurial Development. In Martínez-Falcó, J., Sánchez-García, E., & Marco-Lajara, B. (Eds.), *Support Networks for Entrepreneurs: Social Capital and Strategic Collaborations* (pp. 311–338). IGI Global Scientific Publishing., DOI: 10.4018/979-8-3693-9836-4.ch013

Coates, J. M., Santhanalakshmi, K., Dinesh, N., Gandhimathi, S., & Chandel, P. S. Mohit, (2025). Assessment and Evaluation in Transnational Staff Development. In G. Morris & J. Ye (Eds.), Training and Development in Transnational Higher Education (pp. 387–406). IGI Global Scientific Publishing. DOI: 10.4018/979-8-3373-1897-4.ch019

Dakhli, M., & De Clercq, D. (2004). Human capital, social capital, and innovation: A multi-country study. *Entrepreneurship and Regional Development*, *16*(2), 107–128. DOI: 10.1080/08985620410001677835

Daleure, G. (2017). UAE goes global. In Emiratization in the UAE labor market: Opportunities and challenges (pp. 7–26). DOI: 10.1007/978-981-10-2765-9_2

Edarabia. (2017). UAE Minister of Higher Education targets skills gap. Retrieved January 9, 2024, from. https://www.edarabia.com/uaeminister-higher-education-targets-skills-gap/

Fadlelmula, F. K., & Qadhi, S. M. (2024). A systematic review of research on artificial intelligence in higher education: Practice, gaps, and future directions in the GCC. *Journal of University Teaching & Learning Practice*, *21*(06), 2. DOI: 10.53761/pswgbw82

Fares, O. H., Butt, I., & Lee, S. H. M. (2023). Utilization of artificial intelligence in the banking sector: A systematic literature review. *Journal of Financial Services Marketing*, *28*(4), 835–852. DOI: 10.1057/s41264-022-00176-7

Gambhir, B., & Bhattacharjee, A. (2021). Embracing the role of artificial intelligence in accounting and finance: Contemplating the changing skillset expectations. *Development and Learning in Organizations*, *36*(1), 17–20. DOI: 10.1108/DLO-01-2021-0016

Hassock, L., & Hill, C. (2022). Employability and employment: The role of higher education in a rapidly changing world. In *Higher education and job employability* (pp. 155–178). Springer International Publishing., DOI: 10.1007/978-3-031-05716-8_8

Hui, X., Reshef, O., & Zhou, L. (2023). The short-term effects of generative artificial intelligence on employment: Evidence from an online labor market. DOI: 10.2139/ssrn.4527336

Iyer, S., Gernal, L., Subramanian, R., & Mehrotra, A. (2023). Impact of digital disruption influencing business continuity in UAE higher education. *Educational Technology Quarterly*, *2023*(1), 18–57. DOI: 10.55056/etq.29

Iyer, S. S. (2022). Applicaiton of digital technologies: Integrated Blockchain with emerging technologies. In Ramakrishna, Y. (Ed.), *Handbook of research on supply chain resiliency, efficiency, and visbility in the post-pandemic era* (pp. 267–272). IGI Global., DOI: 10.4018/978-1-7998-9506-0.ch014

Jetha, A., Bonaccio, S., Shamaee, A., Banks, C. G., Bültmann, U., Smith, P. M., Tompa, E., Tucker, L. B., Norman, C., & Gignac, M. A. (2023). Divided in a digital economy: Understanding disability employment inequities stemming from the application of advanced workplace technologies. *SSM. Qualitative Research in Health*, *3*(1), 100293. DOI: 10.1016/j.ssmqr.2023.100293

Kamalov, F., Santandreu Calonge, D., & Gurrib, I. (2023). New era of Artificial Intelligence in Education: Towards a sustainable multifaceted revolution. *Sustainability (Basel), 15*(16), 12451. DOI: 10.3390/su151612451

Khan, S. (2023). UAE economic performance surpasses expectations amid investment in new sectors. National NOW Times. Retrieved December 14, 2023, from. https://www.thenationalnews.com/business/economy/2023/11/27/uae-economic-performance-surpasses-expectations-amid-investment-in-new-sectors/

Koroteev, D., & Tekic, Z. (2021). Artificial Intelligence in oil and gas upstream: Trends, challenges, and scenarios for the future. *Energy and AI, 3*(1), 100041. DOI: 10.1016/j.egyai.2020.100041

Li, L. (2022). Reskilling and upskilling the future-ready workforce for industry 4.0 and beyond. *Information Systems Frontiers, 1*(1), 1–16. DOI: 10.1007/s10796-022-10308-y PMID: 35855776

Limbore, N. V., Anute, N., Ahluwalia, G. K., Chordiya, P. B., & Kalshetti, P. (2025). Ethical Leadership and Corporate Responsibility. In Harriott, S. (Ed.), *Innovative Approaches to Managing Conflict and Change in Diverse Work Environments* (pp. 193–218). IGI Global Scientific Publishing., DOI: 10.4018/979-8-3693-9556-1.ch009

Lokhande, M., John Deva Prasanna, D. S., Selvakumar, P., Ragupathi, T., Vaissnave, V., & Manjunath, T. C. (2025). Novel ML Algorithms for Healthcare. In A. Ajibesin, N. G., & S. Thangavel (Eds.), Synergizing Data Envelopment Analysis and Machine Learning for Performance Optimization in Healthcare (pp. 113–134). IGI Global Scientific Publishing. DOI: 10.4018/979-8-3373-0081-8.ch005

Martin, J. P., Stefl, S. K., Cain, L. W., & Pfirman, A. L. (2020). Understanding first-generation undergraduate engineering students' entry and persistence through social capital theory. *International Journal of STEM Education, 7*(2), 37–42. DOI: 10.1186/s40594-020-00237-0

McElroy, M. W., Jorna, R. J., & van Engelen, J. (2006). Rethinking social capital theory: A knowledge management perspective. *Journal of Knowledge Management, 10*(5), 124–136. DOI: 10.1108/13673270610691233

Negi, V. (2023). Artificial intelligence: Next-level customer service. *Advances in Logistics, Operations, and Management Science, 2*(5), 226–240. DOI: 10.4018/979-8-3693-0418-1.ch015

Pabalkar, V., & Chanda, R. (2022). Role of artificial intelligence in healthcare. In International conference on information and management engineering (pp. 353–360). Springer Nature Singapore. DOI: 10.1007/978-981-99-2746-3_37

Paderanga, C., Soni, A., & Nisa, N. (2023). Artificial intelligence adoption among accountants in the UAE: An integrated AI acceptance-avoidance model. Global Scientific and Academic Research Journal of Economics. *Business and Management, 2*(11), 61–86.

Radakovich, N., & Nazha, A. (2021). The future of artificial intelligence in healthcare. In *Machine learning in Cardiovascular medicine* (pp. 371–394). Academic Press., DOI: 10.1016/B978-0-12-820273-9.00016-6

Sadok, H., Mahboub, H., Chaibi, H., Saadane, R., & Wahbi, M. (2023). *Applications of Artificial Intelligence in finance: Prospects, Limits and risks. In 2023 international conference on digital age & technological advances for sustainable development (ICDATA).* IEEE., DOI: 10.1109/ICDATA58816.2023.00034

Tubadji, A., Denney, T., & Webber, D. J. (2021). Cultural relativity in consumers' rates of adoption of artificial intelligence. *Economic Inquiry, 59*(3), 1234–1251. DOI: 10.1111/ecin.12978

Verma, D., Kansra, P., & Kaur, S. (2023). A theoretical perspective of artificial intelligence in hostility of cyber threats in the banking sector. In *Advanced machine learning algorithms for complex financial applications* (pp. 43–54). IGI Global., DOI: 10.4018/978-1-6684-4483-2.ch004

Verma, P., & Sehgal, S. (2023). Leveraging artificial intelligence for enhancing customer experience and efficiency in the banking industry. In *AI and emotional intelligence for modern business management* (pp. 282–310). IGI Global., DOI: 10.4018/979-8-3693-0418-1.ch019

Wang, Q., Zhao, L., Chang-Richards, A., Zhang, Y., & Li, H. (2021). Understanding the impact of social capital on the innovation performance of construction enterprises: Based on the mediating effect of knowledge transfer. *Sustainability (Basel), 13*(9), 5099. DOI: 10.3390/su13095099

Compilation of References

AACSB / AACSB International. (2025, February). Framework for human-centric AI-first teaching. *AACSB Insights.* https://www.aacsb.edu/insights/articles/2025/02/a-framework-for-human-centric-ai-first-teaching

Aayog, N. I. T. I. (2021). *National strategy for artificial intelligence: Education sector*. Government of India.

Abdalla, H., & Moussa, A. (2024). Culturally responsive teaching: Navigating models and implementing effective strategies. *Acta Pedagogia Asiana*, *3*(2), 91–100. DOI: 10.53623/apga.v3i2.432

Abdeldayem, M. M., Aldulaimi, S. H., & Kharabsheh, R. (2021). Development of human capital resources to increase economic growth and innovation in the GCC Countries. *International Journal of Green Management and Business Studies*, *1*(1), 62–79.

Abraham, M. M., & Dev, S. (2026). AI-driven surveillance in India: Reconciling privacy, national security and legal oversight. *Journal of Data Protection and Privacy*, *8*(2), 183–207. DOI: 10.69554/BZBZ5748

Accenture. (2021). Artificial intelligence services. https://www.accenture.com/us-en/services/data-ai

Aceves, T. C., & Orosco, M. J. (2014). *Culturally responsive teaching* (Document No. IC-2). University of Florida, Collaboration for Effective Educator, Development, Accountability, and Reform Centre. http://ceedar.education.ufl.edu/tools/innovation-configurations/

Agbese, M., Alanen, H.-K., Antikainen, J., Erika, H., Isomaki, H., Jantunen, M., Kemell, K.-K., Rousi, R., Vainio-Pekka, H., & Vakkur, V. (2023). Governance in Ethical, Trustworthy AI Systems: Extension of the ECCOLA Method for AI Ethics Governance Using GARP. *E-Informatica Software Engineering Journal*, *17*(1), 230101. DOI: 10.37190/e-Inf230101

Agesilaou, A., & Kyza, E. A. (2022). Whose data are they? Elementary school students' conceptualization of data ownership and privacy of personal digital data. *International Journal of Child-Computer Interaction, 33*, 100462. DOI: 10.1016/j.ijcci.2022.100462

Ahamed, H. R., & Hanirex, D. K. (2024, August). A deep learning-enabled approach for real-time monitoring of learner activities in adaptive e-learning environments. In *2024 7th International Conference on Circuit Power and Computing Technologies (ICCPCT)* (Vol. 1, pp. 846-851). IEEE. DOI: 10.1109/ICCPCT61902.2024.10673041

Ahmed, F. (2024). The digital divide and AI in education: Addressing equity and accessibility. *AI Edify Journal, 1*(2), 12–22.

Ahmed, Z., Shanto, S. S., Rime, M. H. K., Morol, M. K., Fahad, N., Hossen, M. J., & Abdullah-Al-Jubair, M. (2024). The generative AI landscape in education: Mapping the terrain of opportunities, challenges and student perception. *IEEE Access : Practical Innovations, Open Solutions, 12*, 147023–147050. Advance online publication. DOI: 10.1109/ACCESS.2024.3461874

Ahrweiler, P., Späth, E., Siqueiros García, J. M., Capellas, B. L., & Wurster, D. (2025). Inclusive technology co-design for participatory AI. *Participatory Artificial Intelligence in Public Social Services: From Bias to Fairness in Assessing Beneficiaries*, 35-62.

Ahrweiler, P., Späth, E., Siqueiros García, J. M., Capellas, B. L., & Wurster, D. (2025). *Inclusive Technology Co-design for Participatory AI.*, DOI: 10.1007/978-3-031-71678-2_2

Ahuja, K., & Bala, I. (2021). Role of Artificial Intelligence and IoT in Next Generation Education System. In *Intelligence of Things: AI-IoT Based Critical-Applications and Innovations* (pp. 189–208). Springer International Publishing. DOI: 10.1007/978-3-030-82800-4_8

AI-ALOE. (2024). *The return of Jill Watson*. National AI Institute for Adult Learning and Online Education. https://aialoe.org/the-return-of-jill-watson/

Airaj, M. (2024). Ethical artificial intelligence for teaching-learning in higher education. *Education and Information Technologies, 29*(13), 17145–17167. DOI: 10.1007/s10639-024-12545-x

Ajmani, L., Foriest, J., Taylor, J., Pittman, K., Gilbert, S., & Devito, M. (2024). Whose Knowledge is Valued? Epistemic Injustice in CSCW Applications. *Proceedings of the ACM on Human-Computer Interaction, 8*(CSCW2), 1–28. DOI: 10.1145/3687062

Akbari, R. N., & Fithry, A. (2024). MENGANALISIS PENGARUH HAK CIPTA DALAM GANGGUAN AI PADA SEKTOR MEDIA. *Prosiding SNAPP : Sosial Humaniora, Pertanian. Kesehatan Dan Teknologi*, *2*(1), 377–383. DOI: 10.24929/snapp.v2i1.3159

Akdemir, A. S., & Ulaş, A. H. (2024). Culturally responsive teaching in the age of artificial intelligence. In Akdemir, A. S. (Ed.), *Emerging Trends, Multilingualism, and AI Integration in Language Studies* (pp. 42–53). Shanlax Publications.

Akgün, S., & Greenhow, C. (2021). Artificial intelligence in education: Addressing ethical challenges in K–12 settings. *AI and Ethics*, *2*(3), 431–440. DOI: 10.1007/s43681-021-00096-7 PMID: 34790956

Al-Azawei, A., Parslow, R., & Lundqvist, K. (2016). Building an effective learning environment with intelligent tutoring systems. *Computers in Human Behavior*, *63*, 685–696. DOI: 10.1016/j.chb.2016.05.069

Albosaif, W. K., Aljughaiman, A. M., & Alsayed, A. K. (2025). The role of diversity in enrichment programs in shaping the career paths of gifted individuals: An analysis of influential factors and emerging trends. *International Journal of Advanced and Applied Sciences*, *12*(11), 82–92. DOI: 10.21833/ijaas.2025.11.009

Aldino, A. A., Tsai, Y. S., Gupte, S., Henderson, M., Nath, D., Gašević, D., & Chen, G. (2025). Analytics of Learner-Centered Feedback: A Large-Scale Case Study in Higher Education. *Computers & Education*, *237*, 105360. DOI: 10.1016/j.compedu.2025.105360

Alexander Sotiriou, S., & Bogner, X. F. (2023). Discovery Space: A Technology-Enhanced Classroom for Deeper Learning in STEM. In *Reimagining Education - The Role of E-Learning, Creativity, and Technology in the Post-Pandemic Era*. IntechOpen. DOI: 10.5772/intechopen.1002649

Alfredo, R., Echeverria, V., Jin, Y., Yan, L., Swiecki, Z., Gašević, D., & Martinez-Maldonado, R. (2024). Human-centred learning analytics and AI in education: A systematic literature review. *Computers and Education: Artificial Intelligence*, *6*, 100215. DOI: 10.1016/j.caeai.2024.100215

Ali, F. (2021). Teachers in AI-augmented classrooms. *Computers and Education: Artificial Intelligence.*

Ali, M. (2024). AI and Intelligent Tutoring Systems: A New Paradigm for Student-Centered Learning. *Journal of AI Integration in Education*, *1*(2), 1–11.

Alkhatlan, A., & Kalita, J. (2018). Intelligent Tutoring Systems: A Comprehensive Historical Survey with Recent Developments. *International Journal of Computer Applications, 181*(43), 1–20. DOI: 10.5120/ijca2019918451

Almatrafi, O., Johri, A., & Lee, H. (2024). A systematic review of AI literacy conceptualisation, constructs, implementation, and assessment efforts (2019–2023). *Computers and Education Open, 6*, 100173. DOI: 10.1016/j.caeo.2024.100173

Alvén, F. (2024). Controversial issues in history teaching. *Journal of Curriculum Studies, 56*(5), 537–553. DOI: 10.1080/00220272.2024.2322502

Al-Zahrani, A. M., & Alasmari, T. M. (2024). Exploring the impact of AI on higher education: The dynamics of ethical, social, and educational implications. *Humanities & Social Sciences Communications, 11*, 302. DOI: 10.1057/s41599-024-03432-4

Amershi, S., Weld, D., Vorvoreanu, M., Fourney, A., Nushi, B., Collisson, P., & Horvitz, E. (2019, May). Guidelines for human-AI interaction. In *Proceedings of the 2019 chi conference on human factors in computing systems* (pp. 1-13).

Aminullah, M., Susanto, H., Nadilla, D. F., & Mardiani, F. (2025). Challenges And Strategies Of History Teachers In Utilizing Digital Learning Media: A Case Study At SMKN 1 Banjarmasin. *Jurnal Pendidikan Ips, 15*(3), 751–758. DOI: 10.37630/jpi.v15i3.3257

Amoakwa, A., Asante, G., & Gyimah, E. (2025). Implementing History Curriculum in Basic Schools: Techniques and Challenges. *East African Journal of Education Studies., 8*(3), 306–317. DOI: 10.37284/eajes.8.3.3524

Analytics, Q. T. (2025). Validation of Teachers AI-TPACK Scale. *International Journal of Education and Research Review.* https://qtanalytics.in/journals/index.php/IJERR/article/view/3919

Anggiani, A., Dewi, O., Simanjuntak, C., Barus, A., & Sari, I. (2025). Challenges and Opportunities for High School History Teachers in Using TikTok and Other Social Media for Learning. *Riwayat: Educational Journal of History and Humanities., 8*(3), 2623–2631. DOI: 10.24815/jr.v8i3.47375

Artificial Intelligence Act, E. U. (2024). Available on https://artificialintelligenceact.eu/article/50/

ASER Centre. (2025). *Annual status of education report: AI integration update*. Pratham Foundation.

Atari, M., Xue, M. J., Park, P. S., Blasi, D. E., & Henrich, J. (2023, September 22). Which humans? DOI: 10.31234/osf.io/5b26t

Atchley, P., Pannell, H., Wofford, K., Hopkins, M., & Atchley, R. A. (2024). Human and AI collaboration in the higher education environment: Opportunities and concerns. *Cognitive Research: Principles and Implications*, *9*(1), 20. DOI: 10.1186/s41235-024-00547-9

Atenas, J., Havemann, L., & Nerantzi, C. (2025). Critical and creative pedagogies for artificial intelligence and data literacy: An epistemic data justice approach for academic practice. *Research in Learning Technology*, *32*, 3296. DOI: 10.25304/rlt.v32.3296

Avalekar, U. A., Mehta, V., Mishra, B. R., Prasanna, L., Rajlakshmi, P. V., & Manjunath, T. C. (2025). The Current Advances in AI-Driven Education. In Babulak, E. (Ed.), *Educational AI Humanoid Computing Devices for Cyber Nomads* (pp. 173–196). IGI Global Scientific Publishing., DOI: 10.4018/979-8-3693-8985-0.ch008

Avila-Chauvet, L., Mejía, D., & Acosta Quiroz, C. (2023). CHATGPT as a support tool for online behavioral task programming. *SSRN*. Retrieved from https://ssrn.com/abstract=4329020

Awotunde, J. B. (2026). Data Privacy in Virtual Healthcare Environments and Ethical Guidelines for Metaverse Health Applications. In *Studies in Computational Intelligence* (Vol. 1224, pp. 543–576). DOI: 10.1007/978-3-031-99946-8_23

Ayeni, O. O., Al Hamad, N. M., Chisom, O. N., Osawaru, B., & Adewusi, O. E. (2024a). AI in education: A review of personalized learning and educational technology. *GSC Advanced Research and Reviews*, *18*(2), 261–271. DOI: 10.30574/gscarr.2024.18.2.0062

Baeza-Yates, R. (2023). An introduction to responsible AI. *European Review (Chichester, England)*, *31*(4), 406–421. DOI: 10.1017/S1062798723000145

Bai, Y., Kadavath, S., Kundu, S., Askell, A., Kernion, J., Jones, A., . . . Kaplan, J. (2022). Constitutional AI: Harmlessness from AI Feedback. *arXiv preprint arXiv:2212.08073.*

Baidoo-Anu, D., & Owusu Ansah, L. (2023). Education in the era of generative Artificial Intelligence (AI): Understanding the potential benefits of ChatGPT in promoting teaching and learning. *Journal of AI.*, *7*(1), 52–62. DOI: 10.61969/jai.1337500

Baker-Bell, A. (2020). *Linguistic justice: Black language, literacy, identity, and pedagogy*. Routledge. DOI: 10.4324/9781315147383

Baker, R. S., & Hawn, A. (2022). Algorithmic bias in education. *International Journal of Artificial Intelligence in Education, 32*(4), 1052–1092. DOI: 10.1007/s40593-021-00285-9

Bakhanova, E., Garcia, J. A., Raffe, W. L., & Voinov, A. (2020). Targeting social learning and engagement: What serious games and gamification can offer to participatory modeling. *Environmental Modelling & Software, 134*, 104846. DOI: 10.1016/j.envsoft.2020.104846

Bakhanova, E., Garcia, J. A., Raffe, W. L., & Voinov, A. (2023). Gamification framework for participatory modeling: A proposal. *Group Decision and Negotiation, 32*(5), 1167–1182. DOI: 10.1007/s10726-023-09838-w

Bakhtin, M. M. (1981). *The dialogic imagination: Four essays*. University of Texas Press.

Balasubramanian, S., Devarajan, H. R., Raparthi, M., Dodda, S. B., Maruthi, S., & Adnyana, I. M. D. M. (2023). Ethical considerations in ai-assisted decision-making for end-of-life care in healthcare. *Power System Technology, 47*(4), 167–182. DOI: 10.52783/pst.168

Balfour, S. P. (2013). Assessing writing in MOOCs: Automated essay scoring and calibrated peer review. *Research & Practice in Assessment, 8*, 40–48.

Banala, S., Panyaram, S., & Selvakumar, P. (2025). Artificial Intelligence in Software Testing. In Chelliah, P., Venkatesh, R., Natraj, N., & Jeyaraj, R. (Eds.), *Artificial Intelligence for Cloud-Native Software Engineering* (pp. 237–262). IGI Global Scientific Publishing., DOI: 10.4018/979-8-3693-9356-7.ch009

Bandi, A., Adapa, P. V. S. R., & Kuchi, Y. E. V. P. K. (2023). The Power of Generative AI: A Review of Requirements, Models, Input–Output Formats, Evaluation Metrics, and Challenges. *Future Internet, 15*(8), 260. Advance online publication. DOI: 10.3390/fi15080260

Banerjee, A., & Dey, D. (2022). Speech-to-text and text-to-speech systems for inclusive education in India. *IEEE Access : Practical Innovations, Open Solutions, 10*, 121456–121468. DOI: 10.1109/ACCESS.2022.3222563

Banerjee, D. (2024). The Impact of Digital Tools on the Teaching of History: A Comparative Study of Traditional and Technology-Integrated Teaching Methods. *International Journal For Multidisciplinary Research, 3*(3), 22919. DOI: 10.36948/ijfmr.2024.v06i03.22919

Bañuelos Capistrán, J., Zavala Scherer, D., & Lugo Rodríguez, N. (2025). Art, community and AI: Images for an affective memory. *Frontiers in Communication, 10*, 1567694. DOI: 10.3389/fcomm.2025.1567694

Bardia, A., & Agrawal, A. (2025). MindCraft: Revolutionizing education through AI-powered personalized learning and mentorship in rural India. *arXiv preprint arXiv:2502.05826*. https://doi.org//arXiv.2502.05826DOI: 10.48550

Barke, S., James, M., & Polikarpova, N. (2023). Grounded copilot: How programmers interact with code-generating models. *Proceedings of the ACM on Programming Languages, 7*(OOPSLA1), 85-111. DOI: 10.1145/3586030

Barnes, E., & Hutson, J. (2024). Navigating the ethical terrain of AI in higher education: Strategies for mitigating bias and promoting fairness. *Forum for Education Studies, 2*(2), 1229. DOI: 10.59400/fes.v2i2.1229

Barreiro, A., & Pérez-Manjarrez, E. (2025). Collective memory, moral judgements, and history education. *Current Opinion in Psychology, 66*, 102113. DOI: 10.1016/j.copsyc.2025.102113

Bartelds, H., Savenije, G., & Van Boxtel, C. (2020). Students' and teachers' beliefs about historical empathy in secondary history education. *Theory and Research in Social Education, 48*(4), 529–551. DOI: 10.1080/00933104.2020.1808131

Basham, J. D.. (2024). *Universal design for learning and artificial intelligence*. International Journal of Pedagogy, Development and Lifelong Learning., DOI: 10.30935/ijpdll/14694

Bataineh, A. Q., Abu-AlSondos, I. A., Almazaydeh, L., El Mokdad, S. S., & Allahham, M. (2023, December). Enhancing natural language processing with machine learning for conversational AI. In *IET Conference Proceedings CP870* (Vol. 2023, No. 39, pp. 229-237). Stevenage, UK: The Institution of Engineering and Technology.

Bates, P., & Davis, F. A. (2004). Social capital, social inclusion, and services for people with learning disabilities. *Disability & Society, 19*(3), 195–207. DOI: 10.1080/0968759042000204202

Bayne, S. (2015). What's the matter with technology? *International Journal of Educational Technology in Higher Education, 12*(1), 1–12. DOI: 10.1186/s41239-015-0004-y

Bearman, M., & Ajjawi, R. (2023). Learning to work with the black box: Pedagogy for a world with artificial intelligence. *British Journal of Educational Technology, 54*(5), 1160–1173. DOI: 10.1111/bjet.13337

Bekturganov, K., & Nurpeissova, E. (2025). Digital History: Students' Opportunities to Eradicate National Nihilism Using Smart Products. *3i intellect idea innovation - интеллект идея инновация. 1*(1), 308-314. DOI: 10.52269/22266070_2025_1_308

Bender, E. M., & Friedman, B. (2018). Data statements for NLP: Toward mitigating system bias and enabling better science. *Transactions of the Association for Computational Linguistics, 6*, 587–604. DOI: 10.1162/tacl_a_00041

Bender, E. M., Gebru, T., McMillan-Major, A., & Shmitchell, S. (2021, March). On the dangers of stochastic parrots: Can language models be too big? In *Proceedings of the 2021 ACM conference on fairness, accountability, and transparency* (pp. 610-623). DOI: 10.1145/3442188.3445922

Benjamin, R. (2019). *Race after technology: Abolitionist tools for the new Jim Code*. Polity Press.

Bergmann, J., & Sams, A. (2012). *Flip your classroom: Reach every student in every class every day*. International Society for Technology in Education.

Bhagat, S., Meenakshi, Bakshi, P., & Aman. (. (2025). Integrating technology in history education: Digital pathways and transformative practices aligned with nep 2020. *International Journal on Science and Technology., 16*(2), 1–12. DOI: 10.71097/IJSAT.v16.i2.4531

Bharat, N. L. C. (2025). AI in education: Transforming teachers' roles and the quest for value-based learning. https://nlcbharat.org/ai-in-education-transforming-teachers-roles-and-the-quest-for-value-based-learning/

Biesta, G. (2010). *Good education in an age of measurement: Ethics, politics, democracy*. Paradigm Publishers.

bin Antin, A. & Dzulkifli, D.N. (2025). A concept paper on readiness in artificial intelligence (AI) mastery and its impact on 21st century pedagogy among pre-service history teachers. *International Journal of Research and Innovation in Social Science (IJRISS), 9*(7), 1630–1636. DOI: 10.47772/IJRISS.2025.907000135

Birhane, A., Isaac, W., Prabhakaran, V., Diaz, M., Elish, M. C., Gabriel, I., & Mohamed, S. (2022, October). Power to the people? Opportunities and challenges for participatory AI. In *Proceedings of the 2nd ACM Conference on Equity and Access in Algorithms, Mechanisms, and Optimization* (pp. 1-8). DOI: 10.1145/3551624.3555290

Birkstedt, T., Minkkinen, M., Tandon, A., & Mäntymäki, M. (2023a). AI governance: Themes, knowledge gaps and future agendas. *Internet Research, 33*(7), 133–167. DOI: 10.1108/INTR-01-2022-0042

Bishop, J. L., & Verleger, M. A. (2013). The flipped classroom model: A complete evidence-based review. *ASEE Annual Conference & Exposition.* DOI: 10.18260/1-2--22585

Black, P., & Wiliam, D. (1998). Assessment and Classroom Learning. *Assessment in Education: Principles, Policy\& Practice, 5*(1), 7–74. DOI: 10.1080/0969595980050102

Błoch, A., Oms, G., & Santana, C. (2025). Decolonizing Archival Narratives: Exploring Digital Bias in the Catalogs of Portuguese-Colonized African Territories. *Journal of African History, 66*, e19. DOI: 10.1017/S0021853725100601

Bobby, L. Asirit, L., & H. Hua, J. (. (2023a). Converging perspectives: Assessing AI readiness and utilization in Philippine higher education. *Polaris Global Journal of Scholarly Research and Trends, 2*(3), 1–50. DOI: 10.58429/pgjsrt.v2n3a152

Bozkir, E., Özdel, S., Lau, K. H. C., Wang, M., Gao, H., & Kasneci, E. (2024). Embedding Large Language Models into Extended Reality: Opportunities and Challenges for Inclusion, Engagement, and Privacy. In *Proceedings of the 6th Conference on ACM Conversational User Interfaces, CUI 2024*. DOI: 10.1145/3640794.3665563

Braverman, H. (1974). *Labor and monopoly capital.* Monthly Review Press. DOI: 10.14452/MR-026-03-1974-07_1

Bronfenbrenner, M. (1973). Equality and equity. *The ANNALS of the American Academy of Political and Social Science, 409*(1), 9-23. (Original work published 1973)DOI: 10.1177/000271627340900103

Brown, M., & Klein, C. (2020). Whose Data? Which Rights? Whose Power? A Policy Discourse Analysis of Student Privacy Policy Documents. *The Journal of Higher Education, 91*(7), 1149–1178. DOI: 10.1080/00221546.2020.1770045

Brown, T. B., Mann, B., Ryder, N., Subbiah, M., Kaplan, J., Dhariwal, P., & Amodei, D. (2020). Language models are few-shot learning models. *Advances in Neural Information Processing Systems, 33*, 1877–1901. DOI: 10.48550/arXiv.2005.14165

Brown, T., Mann, B., Ryder, N., Subbiah, M., Kaplan, J. D., Dhariwal, P., & Amodei, D. (2020). Language models are few-shot learners. *Advances in Neural Information Processing Systems, 33*, 1877–1901.

Bryk, A. S., & Schneider, B. (2002). *Trust in schools: A core resource for improvement.* Russell Sage Foundation.

Bulathwela, S., Pérez-Ortiz, M., Holloway, C., Cukurova, M., & Shawe-Taylor, J. (2024a). Artificial Intelligence Alone Will Not Democratise Education: On Educational Inequality, Techno-Solutionism and Inclusive Tools. *Sustainability (Basel), 16*(2), 781. DOI: 10.3390/su16020781

Bulger, M. (2016). *Personalized learning: The conversations we are not having.* Data & Society Research Institute. DOI: 10.69985/OBUE9001

Buolamwini, J., & Gebru, T. (2018). Gender shades: Intersectional accuracy disparities in commercial gender classification. In *Proceedings of the 1st Conference on Fairness, Accountability and Transparency* (pp. 77–91). PMLR.

Burgos-Videla, C., Parada-Ulloa, M., & Martínez-Díaz, J. (2025). Critical thinking in the classroom: The historical method and historical discourse as tools for teaching social studies. *Frontiers in Sociology, 10*, 1526437. DOI: 10.3389/fsoc.2025.1526437

Butalov, D. (2025, February 26). *Navigating the AI-Driven Transformation in Education.* EdTech Digest. Retrieved from https://www.edtechdigest.com/2025/02/26/navigating-the-ai-driven-transformation-in-education/

Cain, W. (2023). Prompting Change: Exploring Prompt Engineering in Large Language Model AI and Its Potential to Transform Education. *TechTrends, 68*(1), 47–57. DOI: 10.1007/s11528-023-00896-0

Calonge, D. S., Shah, M. A., Aguerrebere, P. M., Abdulla, N., Connor, M., Badr, M., & Blakemore, E. (2023). Should I stay or should I go? International students' challenges and opportunities to secure employment in their host country after graduation. A scoping review using PRISMA. *Journal of Applied Learning and Teaching, 6*(2), 1. https://journals.sfu.ca/jalt/index.php/jalt/index

Capraro, V., Lentsch, A., Acemoglu, D., Akgun, S., Akhmedova, A., Bilancini, E., Bonnefon, J.-F., Brañas-Garza, P., Butera, L., Douglas, K. M., Everett, J. A. C., Gigerenzer, G., Greenhow, C., Hashimoto, D. A., Holt-Lunstad, J., Jetten, J., Johnson, S., Kunz, W. H., Longoni, C., & Viale, R. (2024). The impact of generative artificial intelligence on socioeconomic inequalities and policy making. *PNAS Nexus, 3*(6), 1–18. DOI: 10.1093/pnasnexus/pgae191 PMID: 38864006

Carnegie Learning. (2025). *The state of AI in education 2025* [White paper]. https://discover.carnegielearning.com/hubfs/PDFs/Whitepaper%20and%20Guide%20PDFs/2025-AI-in-Ed-Report.pdf

Casal-Otero, L., Catala, A., Fernández-Morante, C., Taboada, M., Cebreiro, B., & Barro, S. (2023a). AI literacy in K-12: A systematic literature review. *International Journal of STEM Education, 10*(1), 29. DOI: 10.1186/s40594-023-00418-7

CAST. (2018). *Universal Design for Learning guidelines* (v2.2). http://udlguidelines.cast.org

CAST. (2025). Artificial intelligence & UDL. https://www.cast.org/what-we-do/artificial-intelligence/

CBSE. (2024). *AI in Indian classrooms: NEP implementation report*. Central Board of Secondary Education.

Celik, I. (2022). Towards Intelligent-TPACK: An empirical study on teachers' professional knowledge to ethically integrate artificial intelligence (AI)-based tools into education. *Computers in Human Behavior, 138*, 107468. DOI: 10.1016/j.chb.2022.107468

Celik, I.. (2023). Towards Intelligent-TPACK: An empirical study. *Computers in Human Behavior, 139*, 107547. Advance online publication. DOI: 10.1016/j.chb.2022.107547

Cengage Group. (2025). AI's impact on education in 2025. https://www.cengagegroup.com/news/perspectives/2025/ais-impact-on-education-in-2025/

Cenoz, J., & Gorter, D. (2015). *Multilingual education: Between language learning and translanguaging*. Cambridge University Press. DOI: 10.1017/9781009024655

Chakraborty, S. (2024). *Generative AI in Modern Education Society.*

Chamo, N., Biberman-Shalev, L., Bar-Tal, S., & Broza, O. (2025). Heutagogy Meets Generative AI in Teacher Education: Examining an Evolving Synergy. *Journal of Posthumanism., 5*(7), 1189–1208. DOI: 10.63332/joph.v5i7.2906

Chan, C. K. Y., & Tsi, L. H. Y. (2023). *The AI Revolution in Education: Will AI Replace or Assist Teachers in Higher Education?* Creely, E., Carabott, · Kelly, Carabott, K., Creely, E., & Carabott, K. (2025). Teaching and learning with AI: an Integrated AI-Oriented Pedagogical Model. *The Australian Educational Researcher 2025 52:6, 52*(6), 4633–4654. DOI: 10.1007/s13384-025-00913-6

Chan, C. K. Y. (2023). A comprehensive AI policy education framework for university teaching and learning. *International Journal of Educational Technology in Higher Education, 20*(1), 38. DOI: 10.1186/s41239-023-00408-3

Chan, C. K. Y., & Hu, W. (2023). Students' voices on generative AI: Perceptions, benefits, and challenges in higher education. *International Journal of Educational Technology in Higher Education, 20*(1), 43. Advance online publication. DOI: 10.1186/s41239-023-00411-8

Chatzichristofis, S. (2025). Reframing AI in Education: A Pedagogical Opportunity, Not a Technocratic Threat. *Journal of Research in Science Teaching*, *63*(1), 97–103. DOI: 10.1002/tea.70024

Chaudhari, S., Aggarwal, P., Murahari, V., Rajpurohit, T., Kalyan, A., Narasimhan, K., Deshpande, A., & Castro da Silva, B. (2025). RLHF deciphered: A critical analysis of reinforcement learning from human feedback for LLMs. *ACM Computing Surveys*, *58*(2), 1–37. DOI: 10.1145/3743127

Chaudhry, M. A. (2021). Artificial intelligence in education: A high-level academic and industry note. *SSRN*. https://doi.org/DOI: 10.2139/ssrn.3953227

Chen, R., Koedinger, K., & VanLehn, K. (2019). Learning about learning: What MOOCs reveal about pedagogical design. In *Artificial Intelligence in Education* (pp. 234–238). Springer., DOI: 10.1007/978-3-030-23204-7_64

Chine, D. R., Brentley, C., Thomas-Browne, C., Richey, J. E., Gul, A., Carvalho, P. F., Branstetter, L., & Koedinger, K. R. (2022). *Educational Equity Through Combined Human-AI Personalization: A Propensity Matching Evaluation.*, DOI: 10.1007/978-3-031-11644-5_30

Chiu, T. K. F. (2025). Developing Intelligent-TPACK (I-TPACK): A new framework for human–AI collaboration. *Interactive Learning Environments*. Advance online publication. DOI: 10.1080/10494820.2025.2545053

Chiu, T. K. F., & Sanusi, I. T. (2024). Define, foster, and assess student and teacher AI literacy and competency for all. *Computers and Education Open*, *6*, 100182. DOI: 10.1016/j.caeo.2024.100182

Chiu, T. K., Ahmad, Z., Ismailov, M., & Sanusi, I. T. (2024). What are artificial intelligence literacy and competency? A comprehensive framework to support them. *Computers and Education Open*, *6*, 100171. DOI: 10.1016/j.caeo.2024.100171

Choi, B. (2025). Identifying Issues and Seeking Improvements in History Education Through the Use of Generative AI. *Education Research International*, *45*(1), 283–300. DOI: 10.34245/jed.45.1.283

Choudhury, M., & Deshmukh, A. (2022). Designing linguistic diversity in AI systems. *Proceedings of CHI 2022 Workshops*. DOI: 10.48550/arXiv.2203.12632

Chowdhary, S., Selvakumar, P., Sangeetha, B., Sarvaani, V. V., Anute, N., & Sharma, M. (2025). The Role of Social Capital in Entrepreneurial Development. In Martínez-Falcó, J., Sánchez-García, E., & Marco-Lajara, B. (Eds.), *Support Networks for Entrepreneurs: Social Capital and Strategic Collaborations* (pp. 311–338). IGI Global Scientific Publishing., DOI: 10.4018/979-8-3693-9836-4.ch013

Christiano, P. F., Leike, J., Brown, T., Martic, M., Legg, S., & Amodei, D. (2017). Deep reinforcement learning from human preferences. *Advances in Neural Information Processing Systems*, •••, 30.

Chukhlomin, V. (2024). Socratic Prompts: Engineered Dialogue as a Tool for AI-Enhanced Educational Inquiry. *Latin American Business and Sustainability Review*, *1*(1), 1–13. DOI: 10.70469/labsreview.v1i1.10

Coates, J. M., Santhanalakshmi, K., Dinesh, N., Gandhimathi, S., & Chandel, P. S. Mohit, (2025). Assessment and Evaluation in Transnational Staff Development. In G. Morris & J. Ye (Eds.), Training and Development in Transnational Higher Education (pp. 387–406). IGI Global Scientific Publishing. DOI: 10.4018/979-8-3373-1897-4.ch019

Cohn, C., Snyder, C., & Fonteles, J., T. s., A., Montenegro, J., & Biswas, G. (. (2024). A multimodal approach to support teacher, researcher and AI collaboration in STEM+C learning environments. *British Journal of Educational Technology*, *56*, 595–620. DOI: 10.1111/bjet.13518

Conn, Z. (2024). A HOUSE WITH EXPOSED BEAMS: INQUIRY-BASED LEARNING AND HISTORIANS' ETHICAL RESPONSIBILITIES AS SCHOLAR-TEACHERS. *History and Theory*, *63*(4), 106–127. DOI: 10.1111/hith.12366

Cooper, G. (2023). Examining Science Education in ChatGPT: An Exploratory Study of Generative Artificial Intelligence. *Journal of Science Education and Technology*, *32*(3), 444–452. DOI: 10.1007/s10956-023-10039-y

Cordeiro, C. M., Adomaitis, L., & Huang, L. (2026). The AI-policy-governance nexus: How regulation and AI shift corporate governance toward stakeholders. *Technology in Society*, *84*, 103117. Advance online publication. DOI: 10.1016/j.techsoc.2025.103117

Corrales, M., Rodríguez, F., Merchán, M., Merchán, P., & Pérez, E. (2024). Comparative Analysis between Virtual Visits and Pedagogical Outings to Heritage Sites: An Application in the Teaching of History. *Heritage.*, *7*(1), 366–379. DOI: 10.3390/heritage7010018

Costa, C. J., Aparicio, M., & Aparicio, J. T. (2025, May). Gamifying Human-AI Interaction: Using Large Language Models for Enhanced Engagement and Learning. In *2025 IEEE 5th International Conference on Human-Machine Systems (ICHMS)* (pp. 325-331). IEEE.

Costa, C. J. (2025). Integrating LLM usage in gamified systems. *WSEAS Transactions on Mathematics*, *24*, 258–267. DOI: 10.37394/23206.2025.24.25

Crawford, K. (2021). *Atlas of AI: Power, politics, and the planetary costs of artificial intelligence.* Yale University Press.

Crompton, H. (2025). The evolution of education through artificial intelligence. *International Journal of Research in Education and Science, 13*(2), 1–15.

Crompton, H., & Burke, D. (2024). Artificial intelligence in higher education: The state of the field. *International Journal of Educational Technology in Higher Education, 21*(1), 22. Advance online publication. DOI: 10.1186/s41239-023-00392-8

Crowston, K., & Bolici, F. (2025). Deskilling and upskilling with AI Systems. *nformation Research an International Electronic Journal, 30*(iConf), 1009-1023. DOI: 10.47989/ir30iConf47143

CRPE. (2025). New research finds schools of education fail to prepare teachers to use AI. https://crpe.org/new-research-finds-schools-of-education-fail-to-prepare-teachers-to-use-ai/

Cuban, L. (2001). *Oversold and underused: Computers in the classroom.* Harvard University Press. DOI: 10.4159/9780674030107

Dai, D., Suzuki, S., & Chen, G. (2025). Generative AI for professional communication training in intercultural contexts: Where are we now and where are we heading? *Applied Linguistics Review, 16*(2), 763–774. DOI: 10.1515/applirev-2024-0184

Daigle, K. (2024). *Survey: The AI wave continues to grow on software development teams*. Retrieved from https://github.blog/author/kdaigle/

Dakhli, M., & De Clercq, D. (2004). Human capital, social capital, and innovation: A multi-country study. *Entrepreneurship and Regional Development, 16*(2), 107–128. DOI: 10.1080/0898562041000l677835

Daleure, G. (2017). UAE goes global. In Emiratization in the UAE labor market: Opportunities and challenges (pp. 7–26). DOI: 10.1007/978-981-10-2765-9_2

Dass, C., Tanwar, S., & Datta, P. (2026). Designing and Development of AR Based Application for Science Education. *GMSARN International Journal, 20*(1), 91–99. Retrieved from https://www.scopus.com/inward/record.uri?eid=2-s2.0-105011666784&partnerID=40&md5=2771cf9da160e9aaf3a82363f2a52a9d

De Andrade, T., & Gobbi, M. (2025). O algoritmo como arquivista: Curadoria algorítmica, apagamentos estruturais e a luta pela memória coletiva no século XXI. *Revista Memorare., 12*(1), e27026–e27026. DOI: 10.59306/memorare.v12e12025e27026

Debbarma, S., & Deb, M. (2025). *Play-Based Learning vs . Traditional Learning : A Comprehensive Comparative Analysis. 13*(3).

Delaben, R., Bual, J., & Madrigal, D. (2025). Student's Achievement of Learning Competencies and Challenges in Learning World History in Public High Schools. *Technium Social Sciences Journal.*, *72*, 312–331. DOI: 10.47577/tssj.v72i1.12903

Delgado, F., Yang, S., Madaio, M., & Yang, Q. (2023). *The participatory turn in AI design: Theoretical foundations and the current state of practice. Equity and Access in Algorithms, Mechanisms, and Optimization (EAAMO '23)*. ACM., DOI: 10.1145/3617694.3623261

Deterding, S., Dixon, D., Khaled, R., & Nacke, L. (2011, September). From game design elements to gamefulness: defining" gamification". In *Proceedings of the 15th international academic MindTrek conference: Envisioning future media environments* (pp. 9-15). DOI: 10.1145/2181037.2181040

Devlin, J., Chang, M.-W., Lee, K., & Toutanova, K. (2019). BERT: Pre-training of deep bidirectional transformers for language understanding. In *Proceedings of NAACL-HLT 2019* (pp. 4171–4186). Association for Computational Linguistics. DOI: 10.48550/arXiv.1810.04805

Dewey, J. (1938). *Experience and education*. Kappa Delta Pi.

Dieterle, E. (2022). The cyclical ethical effects of using artificial intelligence in education. *AI & Society*. Advance online publication. DOI: 10.1007/s00146-022-01467-8 PMID: 36185064

Dignum, V. (2021). The role and challenges of education for responsible AI. *London Review of Education, 19* (1), 1, 1–11. DOI: 10.14324/LRE.19.1.01

Dignum, V. (2019). *Responsible artificial intelligence: How to develop and use AI in a responsible way*. Springer. DOI: 10.1007/978-3-030-30371-6

DiMaggio, P., & Hargittai, E. (2001). From the 'digital divide' to 'digital inequality': Studying Internet use as penetration increases. Working Papers 47, Princeton University, School of Public and International Affairs, Center for Arts and Cultural Policy Studies. Accessed on https://ideas.repec.org/p/pri/cpanda/15.html

Dodge, J., Sap, M., Marasović, A., Agnew, W., Ilharco, G., Groeneveld, D., & Gardner, M. (2021). Documenting Large Webtext Corpora: A Case Study on the Colossal Clean Crawled Corpus. In *Proceedings of the 2021 Conference on Empirical Methods in Natural Language Processing*. Association for Computational Linguistics. DOI: 10.18653/v1/2021.emnlp-main.98

Domínguez Figaredo, D., & Stoyanovich, J. (2023). Responsible AI literacy: A stakeholder-first approach. *Big Data & Society*, *10*(2), 20539517231219958. Advance online publication. DOI: 10.1177/20539517231219958

Downes, S. (2012). *Connectivism and connective knowledge: Essays on meaning and learning networks*. National Research Council Canada.

Druga, S., Vu, S. T., Likhith, E., & Qiu, T. (2019). Inclusive AI literacy for kids around the world. [Association for Computing Machinery.]. *Proceedings of FabLearn, 2019*, 104–111. DOI: 10.1145/3311890.3311904

Duckworth, A. (2016). *Grit: The power of passion and perseverance*. Scribner.

Duong, H.-T., Huang, C.-L., Nguyen, B.-A., & Chen, H.-M. (2026). Analyzing student perceptions and behaviors in the use of an engaging visualization dashboard for peer code review activities. *Science of Computer Programming, 249*, 103394. Advance online publication. DOI: 10.1016/j.scico.2025.103394

Dwivedi, Y. K., Kshetri, N., Hughes, L., Slade, E. L., Jeyaraj, A., Kar, A. K., Baabdullah, A. M., Koohang, A., Raghavan, V., Ahuja, M., Albanna, H., Albashrawi, M. A., Al-Busaidi, A. S., Balakrishnan, J., Barlette, Y., Basu, S., Bose, I., Brooks, L., Buhalis, D., & Wright, R. (2023). Opinion Paper: "So what if ChatGPT wrote it?" Multidisciplinary perspectives on opportunities, challenges and implications of generative conversational AI for research, practice and policy. *International Journal of Information Management, 71*, 102642. 10.1016/j.ijinfomgt.2023.102642. DOI: 10.1016/j.ijinfomgt.2023.102642

Dynamic Pixel. (2025). Human–AI collaboration in teaching and learning. https://www.dynamicpixel.co.in/blog/human-ai-collaboration-in-teaching-and-learning-a-transformative-shift-in-education/

Eagle, B. A. (2025). *Co-Creating with AI in Higher Education : A Human-AI Collaborative Storybook Project Xindi Lyu*. 2–7.

Edarabia. (2017). UAE Minister of Higher Education targets skills gap. Retrieved January 9, 2024, from. https://www.edarabia.com/uaeminister-higher-education-targets-skills-gap/

EDDS Education. (2025, June 5). *Ensuring Fairness in AI for Education: A Framework for Trustworthy Systems*. Retrieved from https://www.edds-education.org/post/ensuring-fairness-in-ai-for-education-a-framework-for-trustworthy-systems

Edling, S., Sharp, H., Löfström, J., & Ammert, N. (2020a). The good citizen: Revisiting moral motivations for introducing historical consciousness in history education drawing on the writings of Gadamer. *Citizenship. Social and Economics Education, 19*(2), 133–150. DOI: 10.1177/2047173420936622

Edling, S., Sharp, H., Löfström, J., & Ammert, N. (2020b). Why is ethics important in history education? A dialogue between the various ways of understanding the relationship between ethics and historical consciousness. *Ethics and Education, 15*(3), 336–354. DOI: 10.1080/17449642.2020.1780899

EdTech Digest. (2025). Carnegie Learning Report: The state of AI in education 2025. https://www.edtechdigest.com/2025/05/05/carnegie-learning-report-the-state-of-ai-in-education-2025/

Education and Academy. (2024). *How Industrialization Shaped Modern Education Systems*.

Edutopia. (2024). Using AI to enhance Universal Design for Learning. https://www.edutopia.org/article/using-ai-in-universal-design-for-learning/

Eguchi, A., Okada, H., & Muto, Y. (2021). Contextualizing AI Education for K-12 Students to Enhance Their Learning of AI Literacy Through Culturally Responsive Approaches. *KI - Künstliche Intelligenz, 35*(2), 153–161. DOI: 10.1007/s13218-021-00737-3

El Fathi, T., Saad, A., Larhzil, H., Lamri, D., & Al Ibrahmi, E. M. (2025). Integrating generative AI into STEM education: enhancing conceptual understanding, addressing misconceptions, and assessing student acceptance. *Disciplinary and Interdisciplinary Science Education Research 2025 7:1, 7*(1), 6-. DOI: 10.1186/s43031-025-00125-z

Elements of AI. (2025). *Free online introduction to AI.* https://www.elementsofai.com/

El-Mahdy, D. (2026). Intangible Re-imagined historical spaces between walls: Art installation as an interactive teaching tool in theory-based architecture curricula. *Thinking Skills and Creativity, 60*, 102052. Advance online publication. DOI: 10.1016/j.tsc.2025.102052

eSchool News. (2024, November 13). *Equitable access to AI in classrooms is a problem–the solution is.* Retrieved from https://www.eschoolnews.com/digital-learning/2024/11/13/equitable-access-ai-professional-development/

European Commission. (2024). *DigCompEdu implementation report.*

European Commission. (2024). *Regulation of the European Parliament and of the Council laying down harmonized rules on Artificial Intelligence (AI Act).* European Union.

Evurulobi, C., Dagunduro, A., & Ajuwon, O.Chinasa Iroabughichi EvurulobiAdebukola Olufunke DagunduroOlanike Abiola Ajuwon. (2024). Digital narratives and historical representation: A review - analyzing how digital mediums are revolutionizing the way history is taught and perceived. *World Journal of Advanced Research and Reviews.*, *24*(1), 2083–2096. DOI: 10.30574/wjarr.2024.24.1.2852

Ewart, K. (2025). Leveraging Generative AI for Culturally Responsive Teaching: A Shift in Educator Planning and Practice. In R. Jake Cohen (Ed.), *Proceedings of Society for Information Technology & Teacher Education International Conference* (pp. 2030-2035). Orlando, FL, USA: Association for the Advancement of Computing in Education (AACE). Available on https://www.learntechlib.org/p/225764

Fadlelmula, F. K., & Qadhi, S. M. (2024). A systematic review of research on artificial intelligence in higher education: Practice, gaps, and future directions in the GCC. *Journal of University Teaching & Learning Practice*, *21*(06), 2. DOI: 10.53761/pswgbw82

Falavarjani, M., & Mousavi, A. (2024). Rethinking fairness in classroom assessment: The influence of cultural dimensions. *American Journal of STEM Education*, *2*, 22–49.

Fareed, M., Nassif, A., & Nofal, E. (2024). Exploring the Potentials of Artificial Intelligence Image Generators for Educating the History of Architecture. *Heritage.*, *7*(3), 1727–1753. DOI: 10.3390/heritage7030081

Fares, O. H., Butt, I., & Lee, S. H. M. (2023). Utilization of artificial intelligence in the banking sector: A systematic literature review. *Journal of Financial Services Marketing*, *28*(4), 835–852. DOI: 10.1057/s41264-022-00176-7

FAS (Federation of American Scientists). (2024). Establish a teacher AI literacy development program.

Faucher, M. A., Sing, E., Harris, S., Hutson, E., & Hoelscher, S. H. (2025). Artificial Intelligence and Competency-Based Education: A Rapid Scoping Review. *Journal of Midwifery & Women's Health*, *70*(6), 865–881. Advance online publication. DOI: 10.1111/jmwh.70009 PMID: 40810696

Federiakin, D., Molerov, D., Zlatkin-Troitschanskaia, O., & Maur, A. (2024, November). Prompt engineering as a new 21st century skill. [). Frontiers Media SA.]. *Frontiers in Education*, *9*, 1366434. DOI: 10.3389/feduc.2024.1366434

Felix, C. V. (2020). The role of the teacher and AI in education. In *Innovations in higher education teaching and learning* (Vol. 15, pp. 133–146). Emerald Publishing., DOI: 10.1108/S2055-3641202015

Fesenko, A., Gurevych, R., Yarova, A., Gotsuliak, V., Dovhalets, O., & Perekhodko, N. (2025). Neuroethics and the Politics of Historical Memory: Rethinking Polish-Ukrainian Relations Through Education. *BRAIN. Broad Research in Artificial Intelligence and Neuroscience, 16*(2), 169–177. DOI: 10.70594/brain/16.2/13

Firmansyah, H., & Atmaja, T. (2025). Transformation of history learning methods in the digital era: Challenges and opportunities in schools. [IJED]. *Indonesian Journal of Educational Development, 6*(1), 264–277. DOI: 10.59672/ijed.v6i1.4791

Florian, L., & Black-Hawkins, K. (2011). Exploring inclusive pedagogy. *British Journal of Sociology of Education, 32*(2), 175–194. DOI: 10.1080/01425692.2011.559310

Floridi, L., & Cowls, J. (2022). A unified framework of five principles for AI in society. *Machine learning and the city: Applications in architecture and urban design*, 535-545.

Foka, A., & Griffin, G. (2024). AI, Cultural Heritage, and Bias: Some Key Queries That Arise from the Use of GenAI. *Heritage., 7*(11), 6125–6136. DOI: 10.3390/heritage7110287

Forbes (Walther, C.). (2025). AI is changing how we learn: The new role of human teachers. https://www.forbes.com/sites/corneliawalther/2025/03/01/ai-is-changing-how-we-learn-the-new-role-of-human-teachers/

Fortuna, A., Prasetya, F., Samala, A. D., Rawas, S., Criollo-C, S., Kaya, D., Raihan, M., Andriani, W., Safitri, D., & Nabawi, R. A. (2025). Artificial intelligence in personalized learning: A global systematic review of current advancements and shaping future opportunities. *Social Sciences & Humanities Open, 12*, 102114. DOI: 10.1016/j.ssaho.2025.102114

Fowlin, J., Coleman, D., Ryan, S., Gallo, C., Soares, E., & Hazelton, N. (2025). Empowering Educators: Operationalizing Age-Old Learning Principles Using AI. *Education Sciences, 15*(3), 393. DOI: 10.3390/educsci15030393

Freire, P. (1970). Pedagogy of the Oppressed. *Continuum : an Interdisciplinary Journal on Continuity of Care.*

Fridrich, A. (2025). Georgia Tech's Jill Watson outperforms ChatGPT in real classrooms. *LinkedIn.* (LinkedIn post)

Friedman, B., Hendry, D. G., & Borning, A. *A survey of value sensitive design methods, foundations and trends® in human–computer interaction 11 (2)(2011) 63–125.*

Frontiers in Education. (2025). AI teachers (AI-based robots as teachers): History, potential, concerns, and recommendations. *Frontiers in Education, 10*, Article 1541543. DOI: 10.3389/feduc.2025.1541543

Frontiers in Education. (2025). Generative AI use in K–12 education: A systematic review. *Frontiers in Education, 10*, Article 1647573. DOI: 10.3389/feduc.2025.1647573

Gallotta, R., Todd, G., Zammit, M., Earle, S., Liapis, A., Togelius, J., & Yannakakis, G. N. (2024). Large language models and games: A survey and roadmap. *IEEE Transactions on Games*, 1–18. DOI: 10.1109/TG.2024.3461510

Gambhir, B., & Bhattacharjee, A. (2021). Embracing the role of artificial intelligence in accounting and finance: Contemplating the changing skillset expectations. *Development and Learning in Organizations, 36*(1), 17–20. DOI: 10.1108/DLO-01-2021-0016

García-Méndez, S., de Arriba-Pérez, F., & Somoza-López, M. D. C. (2025). A review on the use of large language models as virtual tutors. *Science & Education, 34*(2), 877–892. DOI: 10.1007/s11191-024-00530-2

García, O., & Kano, N. (2014). Translanguaging as process and pedagogy: Developing the English writing of Japanese students in the US. In Conteh, J., & Meier, G. (Eds.), *The multilingual turn in languages education: Opportunities and challenges* (pp. 258–277). Multilingual Matters. DOI: 10.21832/9781783092246-018

García, O., & Wei, L. (2014). Translanguaging, bilingualism, and bilingual education. In Wright, W., Boun, S., & García, O. (Eds.), *The handbook of bilingual and multilingual education* (pp. 223–240). Wiley-Blackwell.

Gay, G. (2000). *Culturally responsive teaching: Theory, research, and practice.* Teachers College Press.

Gay, G. (2015). The what, why, and how of culturally responsive teaching: International mandates, challenges, and opportunities. *Multicultural Education Review, 7*(3), 123–139. DOI: 10.1080/2005615X.2015.1072079

Ge, W., Sun, Y., Wang, Z., Zheng, H., He, W., Wang, P., . . . Wang, B. (2025). SRLAgent: Enhancing Self-Regulated Learning Skills through Gamification and LLM Assistance. *arXiv preprint arXiv:2506.09968.*

Gee, J. P. (2007). *What video games have to teach us about learning and literacy* (2nd ed.). Palgrave Macmillan.

Gerdes, A. (2022). A participatory data-centric approach to AI Ethics by Design. *Applied Artificial Intelligence*, *36*(1), 2009222. Advance online publication. DOI: 10.1080/08839514.2021.2009222

Gervacio, A. P. (2024). Exploring how generative AI contributes to the motivated engagement and learning production of science-oriented students. *Environment and Social Psychology*, *9*(11), 11. DOI: 10.59429/esp.v9i11.3194

Gholiagha, S., Neyer, J., Sienknecht, M., Wolska, M. A., Kiesel, D., Riehmann, P., Voigt, J., Wiegmann, M., López García, I., Girgensohn, K., Stein, B., & Fröhlich, B. (2025). From annotation to reflection: How participatory AI training enhances critical thinking. *AI & Society*, •••, 1–14. DOI: 10.1007/s00146-025-02539-9

Gianni, A. M., Nikolakis, N., & Antoniadis, N. (2025). An LLM based learning framework for adaptive feedback mechanisms in gamified XR. *Computers & Education: X Reality, 7*, 100116.

Gilman, M. E. (2023). *Democratizing AI: Principles for meaningful public participation*. Data & Society.

Gilster, P. (1997). *Digital literacy*. Wiley.

Glickman, M., & Sharot, T. (2025). How human–AI feedback loops alter human perceptual, emotional and social judgements. *Nature Human Behaviour*, *9*(2), 345–359. DOI: 10.1038/s41562-024-02077-2 PMID: 39695250

Goel, A. K., & Polepeddi, L. (2016). Jill Watson: A virtual teaching assistant for online education. *Georgia Tech Working Paper.*

Goel, A. K.. (2024). Jill Watson: A virtual teaching assistant powered by ChatGPT. *arXiv.* https://arxiv.org/abs/2405.11070

Goleman, D. (1995). *Emotional intelligence*. Bantam Books.

Goslen, A., Kim, Y. J., Rowe, J., & Lester, J. (2025). LLM-based student plan generation for adaptive scaffolding in game-based learning environments. *International Journal of Artificial Intelligence in Education, 35*(2), 533–558. DOI: 10.1007/s40593-024-00421-1

Grab, M. O. (2025). Teaching for equity: An exploration of AI's role in culturally responsive teaching in higher education settings. *Innovative Higher Education*. Advance online publication. DOI: 10.1007/s10755-025-09801-4

Grata, A., & Llaneta, R. (2024). *Understanding Philippine History Education in the Age of Disinformation: A Phenomenological Exploration*. International Journal of Education and Humanities., DOI: 10.58557/(ijeh).v4i4.262

Grever, M., & Vlies, T. (2017). Why national narratives are perpetuated: A literature review on new insights from history textbook research. *London Review of Education, 15*(2), 286–301. DOI: 10.18546/LRE.15.2.11

Grubaugh, S. (2023). Harnessing AI to power constructivist learning: An evolution of educational paradigms. *Journal of Education Technology in Mathematics, 2*(1), 43. Advance online publication. DOI: 10.3390/jetm20200043

Gruber, A., & Köse, N. (2025). Language education amid digital disruption: In-service and pre-service teacher perspectives on AI language bias and curriculum integration. *Language Awareness*, 1–19. Advance online publication. DOI: 10.1080/09658416.2025.2590680

Guesmi, M., Chatti, M. A., Tayyar, A., Ain, Q. U., & Joarder, S. (2022). Interactive Visualizations of Transparent User Models for Self-Actualization: A Human-Centered Design Approach. *Multimodal Technologies and Interaction, 6*(6), 42. DOI: 10.3390/mti6060042

Guillen-Aguinaga, M., Aguinaga-Ontoso, E., Guillen-Aguinaga, L., Guillen-Grima, F., & Aguinaga-Ontoso, I. (2025). Data quality in the age of AI: A review of governance, ethics, and the FAIR principles. *Data, 10*(12), 201. DOI: 10.3390/data10120201

Gunter, D. (2025). Integrating Marginalized Voices into History Education. *Journal of Educational Impact.*, *2*(1), 56–64. DOI: 10.70617/eduimpact.2025.12

Gupta, M., & Kaul, S. (2024). AI in inclusive education: A systematic review of opportunities and challenges in the Indian context. *MIER Journal of Educational Studies Trends & Practices, 14*(2), 429–461. DOI: 10.52634/mier/2024/v14/i2/2702

Gupta, T. (2024). Adaptive Learning Systems: Harnessing AI to Personalize Educational Outcomes. *International Journal for Research in Applied Science and Engineering Technology, 12*(11), 458–464. DOI: 10.22214/ijraset.2024.65088

Güven, İ. (2025). Yapay zekâya (YZ) ilişkin teorik çerçeve ve eğitimsel temeller. [Theoretical framework and educational foundations of artificial intelligence (AI)] In Güven, İ., & Ayantaş, T. (Eds.), *Sosyal bilgiler eğitiminde yapay zekâ (YZ)* [*Artificial intelligence (AI) in social studies education*]. Pegem Akademi.

Hackman, J. R., & Oldham, G. R. (1976). Motivation through the design of work: Test of a theory. *Organizational Behavior and Human Performance, 16*(2), 250–279. DOI: 10.1016/0030-5073(76)90016-7

Hammedi, W., Leclercq, T., Poncin, I., & Alkire, L. (2021). Uncovering the dark side of gamification at work: Impacts on engagement and well-being. *Journal of Business Research, 122*, 256–269. DOI: 10.1016/j.jbusres.2020.08.032

Han, I. (2021). Immersive virtual field trips and elementary students' perceptions. *British Journal of Educational Technology*, *52*(1), 179–195. DOI: 10.1111/bjet.12946

Hansen, T. F. (2006). The evolution of genetic architecture. *Annual Review of Ecology, Evolution, and Systematics*, *37*(1), 123–157. DOI: 10.1146/annurev.ecolsys.37.091305.110224 PMID: 17017054

Harnes, H. (2025). What can empirical research tell us about how to develop students' historical empathy? A scoping review. *History Education Research Journal.*, *22*(1), 1–18. DOI: 10.14324/HERJ.22.1.18

Hassan, Y. M., & Aboulhassan, A. (2024, November). A framework for adaptive game play and adversary creation based on gamer behavioral analysis and large language (llm) models. In *2024 International Mobile, Intelligent, and Ubiquitous Computing Conference (MIUCC)* (pp. 413-417). IEEE.

Hassan, S., & De Filippi, P. (2021). Decentralized autonomous organization. *Internet Policy Review*, *10*(2). Advance online publication. DOI: 10.14763/2021.2.1556

Hassock, L., & Hill, C. (2022). Employability and employment: The role of higher education in a rapidly changing world. In *Higher education and job employability* (pp. 155–178). Springer International Publishing., DOI: 10.1007/978-3-031-05716-8_8

He, K., Liu, X., Xu, Y., Bustamante, A. S., & Warschauer, M. (2025). "Carlitos the Curious Caterpillar": Exploring teacher–AI co-creation of culturally responsive educational materials. In *Interaction Design and Children (IDC '25)* (pp. 1–19). ACM. DOI: 10.1145/3713043.3727056

Hemmer, P., Schemmer, M., Kühl, N., Vössing, M., & Satzger, G. (2025). Complementarity in human–AI collaboration. *European Journal of Information Systems*, *34*(6), 979–1002. Advance online publication. DOI: 10.1080/0960085X.2025.2475962

Heras, S. C., Gargalo, C. L., Weitze, C. L., Mansouri, S. S., Gernaey, K. V., & Krühne, U. (2021). A framework for the development of Pedagogical Process Simulators (P2Si) using explanatory models and gamification. *Computers & Chemical Engineering*, *151*, 107350. DOI: 10.1016/j.compchemeng.2021.107350

Hernández, A. D., Mosquera, D., & Gallegos, F. (2025). Lessons from the margins: Contextualizing, reimagining, and hacking generative AI in the Global South. *Harvard Data Science Review*.

Hetharion, B., Yafie, E., Bakri, T., Ilyas, S., Nirmala, B., & Setyaningsih, D. (2025). Using Emerging Digital Technologies Adoption for History Teaching: A Teacher-Centric Unified Theory of Acceptance and Use of Technology Analysis of Motivational and Environmental Influences. *European Journal of Educational Research., 14*(3), 999–1014. DOI: 10.12973/eu-jer.14.3.999

He, Z., Su, J., Chen, L., Wang, T., & Lc, R. (2024). 'I Recall the Past': Exploring How People Collaborate with Generative AI to Create Cultural Heritage Narratives. *Proceedings of the ACM on Human-Computer Interaction, 9*(2), 1–30. DOI: 10.1145/3711006

Hinterreiter, S., Spinde, T., Oberdörfer, S., Echizen, I., & Latoschik, M. E. (2024). News Ninja: Gamified annotation of linguistic bias in online news. *Proceedings of the ACM on Human-Computer Interaction, 8*(CHI PLAY), 1-29. DOI: 10.1145/3677092

Hirpara, N., Weber, M., Szakonyi, A., Cardona, T., & Singh, D. (2024, November). Exploring the Role of GenAI in Shaping Education. In *International Conference on Intelligent Human Computer Interaction* (pp. 121-134). Cham: Springer Nature Switzerland.

Holmes, W., Bialik, M., & Fadel, C. (2019). *Artificial intelligence in education: Promises and implications for teaching and learning*. Center for Curriculum Redesign.

Holmes, W., Persson, J., Choi, J., & Maeda, Y. (2022). *Artificial intelligence and the future of teaching and learning: Insights and recommendations*. US Department of Education.

Holmes, W., Porayska-Pomsta, K., Holstein, K., Sutherland, E., Baker, T., Shum, S. B., Santos, O. C., Rodrigo, M. T., Cukurova, M., Bittencourt, I. I., & Koedinger, K. R. (2022). Ethics of AI in Education: Towards a Community-Wide Framework. *International Journal of Artificial Intelligence in Education, 32*(3), 504–526. DOI: 10.1007/s40593-021-00239-1

Holstein, K., McLaren, B. M., & Aleven, V. (2021). Designing for human–AI complementarity in K–12 education. *arXiv*. https://arxiv.org/abs/2104.01266

Horban, O., Stadnyk, M., Vintoniv-Bakharieva, S., Panasiuk, L., & Yatyshchuk, O. (2025). Artificial Intelligence as an Integral Component of the Digital Culture within Contemporary Higher Education. *Journal of Educational Technology and Learning Creativity, 3*(2), 451–467. DOI: 10.37251/jetlc.v3i2.2333

Horvatić, D., & Lipic, T. (2021). Human-Centric AI: The Symbiosis of Human and Artificial Intelligence. *Entropy (Basel, Switzerland), 23*(3), 332. DOI: 10.3390/e23030332 PMID: 33799841

Hsu, Y.-C., Huang, T.-H., Verma, H., Mauri, A., Nourbakhsh, I., & Bozzon, A. (2022). Empowering local communities using artificial intelligence. *Patterns (New York, N.Y.), 3*(7), 100449. DOI: 10.1016/j.patter.2022.100449 PMID: 35510187

Huang, L. (2023). Ethics of Artificial Intelligence in Education: Student Privacy and Data Protection. *Science Insights Education Frontiers, 16*(2), 2577–2587. DOI: 10.15354/sief.23.re202

Huang, L., Yu, W., Ma, W., Zhong, W., Feng, Z., Wang, H., Chen, Q., Peng, W., Feng, X., Qin, B., & Liu, T. (2025). A survey on hallucination in large language models: Principles, taxonomy, challenges, and open questions. *ACM Transactions on Information Systems, 43*(2), 1–55. DOI: 10.1145/3703155

Huber, S. E., Kiili, K., Nebel, S., Ryan, R. M., Sailer, M., & Ninaus, M. (2024). Leveraging the potential of large language models in education through playful and game-based learning. *Educational Psychology Review, 36*(1), 25. DOI: 10.1007/s10648-024-09868-z

Hu, E. J., Shen, Y., Wallis, P., Allen-Zhu, Z., Li, Y., Wang, L., & Chen, W. (2022). LoRA: Low-rank adaptation of large language models. *International Conference on Learning Representations (ICLR).*

Hughes, S. (2023). *Here's why AI makes traditional education models obsolete.*

Hughes, C.. (2023). AI and intellectual property in education. *Journal of Academic Ethics.*

Hui, X., Reshef, O., & Zhou, L. (2023). The short-term effects of generative artificial intelligence on employment: Evidence from an online labor market. DOI: 10.2139/ssrn.4527336

Husain, F. N. (2023). Impact of Multiple Intelligences and 21st Century Skills on Future Work Force. *International Education Studies, 16*(3), 16. DOI: 10.5539/ies.v16n3p16

Hu, W., & Shao, Z. (2025). Design and Evaluation of a GenAI-Based personalized Educational Content System Tailored to Personality Traits and Emotional Responses for Adaptive Learning. *Computers in Human Behavior Reports, 19*, 100735. DOI: 10.1016/j.chbr.2025.100735

Huynh, L., & McNamara, D. S. (2025). GenAI-Powered Text Personalization: Natural Language Processing Validation of Adaptation Capabilities. *Applied Sciences (Basel, Switzerland), 15*(12), 6791. DOI: 10.3390/app15126791

Hydari, M. Z., Adjerid, I., & Striegel, A. D. (2023). Health wearables, gamification, and healthful activity. *Management Science, 69*(7), 3920–3938. DOI: 10.1287/mnsc.2022.4581 PMID: 37547027

Ifenthaler, D., & Schumacher, C. (2023). Reciprocal issues of artificial and human intelligence in education. *Journal of Research on Technology in Education, 55*(1), 1–6. DOI: 10.1080/15391523.2022.2154511

IJERT. (2025). Human–AI collaboration in education. https://www.ijert.org/human-ai-collaboration-in-education-enhancing-learning-environments

IJOPR. (2025). Transforming learning or creating dependency? *International Journal of Online Pedagogical Research.*

Iniesto, F.. (2021). Ethical implications of artificial intelligence in education. *Educational Research Review.*

Integranxt. (2025). AI in education: Reimagining the role of teachers. https://integranxt.com/blog/ai-in-education-reimagining-the-role-of-teachers/

Irwanto, I. (2025). Research on ChatGPT in education in Asia: A bibliometric analysis (2022–2025). *Discover Artificial Intelligence, 5*(1), 244. Advance online publication. DOI: 10.1007/s44163-025-00505-4

Ishak, N., & Ahmad, A. (2025). History Education and Students' Historical Consciousness in Malaysian Primary Schools. *International Journal of Academic Research in Progressive Education and Development., 14*(2). Advance online publication. DOI: 10.6007/IJARPED/v14-i2/25307

Ismaniati, C. (2025). Mediating TPACK and AI intentions among teachers. *ERIC.* https://files.eric.ed.gov/fulltext/EJ1472857.pdf

ITU. (2022). *Measuring digital development: Facts and figures.*

Iyer, S. S. (2022). Applicaiton of digital technologies: Integrated Blockchain with emerging technologies. In Ramakrishna, Y. (Ed.), *Handbook of research on supply chain resiliency, efficiency, and visbility in the post-pandemic era* (pp. 267–272). IGI Global., DOI: 10.4018/978-1-7998-9506-0.ch014

Iyer, S., Gernal, L., Subramanian, R., & Mehrotra, A. (2023). Impact of digital disruption influencing business continuity in UAE higher education. *Educational Technology Quarterly, 2023*(1), 18–57. DOI: 10.55056/etq.29

Jackson, J., Starr, J., and Weaver, D. (2024, August). *A Framework for Digital Equity. Digital Promise.* DOI: 10.51388/20.500.12265/223

Jaillant, L., & Rees, A. (2022). Applying AI to digital archives: Trust, collaboration and shared professional ethics. *Digit. Scholarsh. Humanit.*, *38*(2), 571–585. DOI: 10.1093/llc/fqac073

Jeon, J., Wei, L., Tai, K. W. H., & Lee, S. (2025). ç Generative AI and its dilemmas: Exploring AI from a translanguaging perspective. *Applied Linguistics*, *46*(4), 709–717. DOI: 10.1093/applin/amaf049

Jetha, A., Bonaccio, S., Shamaee, A., Banks, C. G., Bültmann, U., Smith, P. M., Tompa, E., Tucker, L. B., Norman, C., & Gignac, M. A. (2023). Divided in a digital economy: Understanding disability employment inequities stemming from the application of advanced workplace technologies. *SSM. Qualitative Research in Health*, *3*(1), 100293. DOI: 10.1016/j.ssmqr.2023.100293

Jiang, T., Sun, Z., Fu, S., & Lv, Y. (2024). Human-AI interaction research agenda: A user-centered perspective. *Data and Information Management*, *8*(4), 100078. DOI: 10.1016/j.dim.2024.100078

Jin, F. J.-Y., Maheshi, B., Lai, W., Li, Y., Chen, G., Charwat, N., & Tsai, Y.-S. (2025). Students' perceptions of GenAI-powered learning analytics in the feedback process: A feedback-literacy perspective. *Journal of Learning Analytics*, *12*(1). Advance online publication. DOI: 10.18608/jla.2025.8609

Johnson, M. (2021). Scalable approach to reducing gender bias in Google translate. Accesed on https://ai.googleblog.com/2020/04/a-scalable-approach-to-reducing-gender.html

Johnson, D., Deterding, S., Kuhn, K. A., Staneva, A., Stoyanov, S., & Hides, L. (2016). Gamification for health and wellbeing: A systematic review of the literature. *Internet Interventions : the Application of Information Technology in Mental and Behavioural Health*, *6*, 89–106. DOI: 10.1016/j.invent.2016.10.002 PMID: 30135818

Jones, R. (2025). Culture machines. *Applied Linguistics Review*, *16*(2), 753–762. DOI: 10.1515/applirev-2024-0188

Kamalov, F., Santandreu Calonge, D., & Gurrib, I. (2023). New era of Artificial Intelligence in Education: Towards a sustainable multifaceted revolution. *Sustainability (Basel)*, *15*(16), 12451. DOI: 10.3390/su151612451

Kamar, E. (2016, July). Directions in Hybrid Intelligence: Complementing AI Systems with Human Intelligence. In *IJCAI* (pp. 4070-4073).

Kang, P. K. (2023). AI in Education: Personalized Learning Through Adaptive Systems. *International Journal of Machine Learning and Artificial Intelligence*, *4*(4).

Kansteiner, W. (2022). Digital Doping for Historians: Can History, Memory, And Historical Theory Be Rendered Artificially Intelligent? *History and Theory*, *61*(4), 119–133. DOI: 10.1111/hith.12282

Karaoulas, A. (2025). Supervision and Teaching in Education: Historical Development and Contemporary Transformation in The Digital Age. *International Journal of Research in Education Humanities and Commerce.*, *6*(3), 73–91. DOI: 10.37602/IJREHC.2025.6306

Karran, A. J., et al. (2025). Multi-stakeholder perspective on responsible AI in education. *npj Science of Learning, 10,* 13. DOI: 10.1038/s41539-025-00333-2

Kashyap, R., Samuel, Y., Friedman, L. W., & Samuel, J. (2024). Editorial: Artificial intelligence education & governance. *Frontiers in Artificial Intelligence*, *7*, 1443386. DOI: 10.3389/frai.2024.1443386 PMID: 39011026

Kasinathan, G.. (2023). Inclusive AI: Bridging language, disability, and digital divides in Indian classrooms. *International Journal of Inclusive Education*. Advance online publication. DOI: 10.1080/13603116.2023.2184212

Kaushik, V., Narayana, A., Satha, D. S., Grace, J., Elankavi, R., & Chavan, G. (2025). Generative Ai For Multicultural Music Education. *ShodhKosh: Journal of Visual and Performing Arts*, *6*(5s), 547–557. DOI: 10.29121/shodhkosh.v6.i5s.2025.6910

Khakpour, A., & Colomo-Palacios, R. (2021). Convergence of gamification and machine learning: A systematic literature review. *Technology. Knowledge and Learning*, *26*(3), 597–636. DOI: 10.1007/s10758-020-09456-4

Khan Academy. (2025). *Khanmigo: AI-powered tutoring.*

Khan, S. (2023). UAE economic performance surpasses expectations amid investment in new sectors. National NOW Times. Retrieved December 14, 2023, from. https://www.thenationalnews.com/business/economy/2023/11/27/uae-economic-performance-surpasses-expectations-amid-investment-in-new-sectors/

Khan, F. A.Hasanain Mohammed Manji Al-Rzoky. (2025). The Transformative Role of Artificial Intelligence in Healthcare. *Journal of Postgraduate Medical Institute*, *39*(2), 92–94. DOI: 10.54079/jpmi.39.2.3779

Khan, L. M. (2017). Amazon's antitrust paradox. *The Yale Law Journal, 126*(3), 710–805.

Khosravi, H., Shibani, A., Jovanović, J., Pardos, Z. A., & Yan, L. (2025). Generative AI and learning analytics: Pushing boundaries, preserving principles. *Journal of Learning Analytics*, *12*(1), 1–11. DOI: 10.18608/jla.2025.8961

Khurana, A., Subramonyam, H., & Chilana, P. K. (2024). Why and when llm-based assistants can go wrong: Investigating the effectiveness of prompt-based interactions for software help-seeking. *arXiv.org*. Retrieved from /arxiv.2402.08030DOI: 10.1145/3640543.3645200

Khurana, S. (2025). Decolonizing Artificial Intelligence: Indigenous Knowledge Systems, Epistemic Pluralism, and the Ethics of Technology. *Journal of Computer Allied Intelligence.*, *3*(3), 1–10. DOI: 10.69996/jcai.2025013

Kim, J. (2023). Leading teachers' perspective on teacher-AI collaboration in education. *Education and Information Technologies*, *29*(7), 8693–8724. DOI: 10.1007/s10639-023-12109-5

Kindenberg, B. (2024). ChatGPT-Generated and Student-Written Historical Narratives: A Comparative Analysis. *Education Sciences*, *14*(5), 330. DOI: 10.3390/educsci14050530

Kindenberg, B. (2025). The Role of AI in Historical Simulation Design: A TPACK Perspective on a French Revolution Simulation Design Experience. *Education Sciences*, *15*(2), 192. DOI: 10.3390/educsci15020192

King, A. (1993). From sage on the stage to guide on the side. *College Teaching*, *41*(1), 30–35. DOI: 10.1080/87567555.1993.9926781

Kirs, E. (2023). Historical reflection as a source of inspiration for youth resistance in illiberal regimes – a qualitative study of the FreeSZFE movement in Hungary. *Journal of Youth Studies*, *28*(1), 213–235. DOI: 10.1080/13676261.2023.2261861

Kittur, A., Chi, E. H., & Suh, B. (2008, April). Crowdsourcing user studies with Mechanical Turk. In *Proceedings of the SIGCHI conference on human factors in computing systems* (pp. 453-456). DOI: 10.1145/1357054.1357127

Kittur, A., Nickerson, J. V., Bernstein, M., Gerber, E., Shaw, A., Zimmerman, J., & Horton, J. (2013, February). The future of crowd work. In *Proceedings of the 2013 conference on Computer supported cooperative work* (pp. 1301-1318). DOI: 10.1145/2441776.2441923

Kocielnik, R., Amershi, S., & Bennett, P. N. (2019, May). Will you accept an imperfect ai? Exploring designs for adjusting end-user expectations of ai systems. In *Proceedings of the 2019 CHI conference on human factors in computing systems* (pp. 1-14).

Koedinger, K. R., Corbett, A. T., & Perfetti, C. A. (2012). The knowledge–learning–instruction framework: Bridging the science–practice chasm to enhance robust student learning. *Cognitive Science, 36*(5), 757–798. DOI: 10.1111/j.1551-6709.2012.01245.x PMID: 22486653

Koehn, P. (2020). *Neural machine translation.* Cambridge University Press. DOI: 10.1017/9781108608480

Kong, S. C., Cheung, W. M. Y., & Zhang, G. (2021). Evaluation of an artificial intelligence literacy course for university students with diverse study backgrounds. *Computers and Education: Artificial Intelligence, 2,* 100026. DOI: 10.1016/j.caeai.2021.100026

Kong, S., & Yang, Y. (2024). A Human-Centered Learning and Teaching Framework Using Generative Artificial Intelligence for Self-Regulated Learning Development Through Domain Knowledge Learning in K–12 Settings. *IEEE Transactions on Learning Technologies, 17,* 1588–1599. DOI: 10.1109/TLT.2024.3392830

Korir, M., Slade, S., Holmes, W., Héliot, Y., & Rienties, B. (2023). Investigating the dimensions of students' privacy concern in the collection, use and sharing of data for learning analytics. *Computers in Human Behavior Reports, 9,* 100262. DOI: 10.1016/j.chbr.2022.100262

Koroteev, D., & Tekic, Z. (2021). Artificial Intelligence in oil and gas upstream: Trends, challenges, and scenarios for the future. *Energy and AI, 3*(1), 100041. DOI: 10.1016/j.egyai.2020.100041

Korres, O., Paños-Castro, J., Alkhawaja, L., & Idris, M. (2025). Exploring the impact of Artificial Intelligence on students' skills for sustainable development in education. *Frontiers in Education, 10,* 1691148. DOI: 10.3389/feduc.2025.1691148

Kosta, D. (2025, January 13). *State AI guidance for K-12 schools (updated July 2025).* AI for Education Initiative. Retrieved from https://aiforeducation.org/state-guidance-2025

Kouzelis, L., & Spantidi, O. (2024). Enhancing Historical Extended Reality Experiences: Prompt Engineering Strategies for AI-Generated Dialogue. *Applied Sciences (Basel, Switzerland), 14*(15), 6405. DOI: 10.3390/app14156405

Koyama, S. (2023). The potential of transnational history education: Attempts at university teaching practice in East Asia. *Memory Studies, 16*(6), 1663–1670. DOI: 10.1177/17506980231204203

KPMG. (2022). *Future of education in India: AI opportunities and challenges.* KPMG India.

Krohmann, S., Rank, S., Schmidt-Kraepelin, M., Thiebes, S., & Sunyaev, A. (2025). Quest for quality: A review of design knowledge on gamified AI training data annotation systems. *Behaviour & Information Technology*, **•••**, 1–26. DOI: 10.1080/0144929X.2025.2568932

Kuhail, M. A., Mathew, S. S., Khalil, A., Khalil, A., & Shah, S. J. (2023). "Will I be replaced?" Assessing ChatGPT's effect on software development and programmer perceptions of AI tools. *arXiv.org*. Retrieved from DOI: 10.2139/ssrn.4571482

Kulynych, B., Madras, D., Milli, S., Raji, I. D., Zhou, A., & Zemel, R. (2020, July). Participatory approaches to machine learning. In *International Conference on Machine Learning Workshop* (Vol. 7).

Kumar, V., Singh, V., Pandey, A., & Tiwari, P. (2021). AI-powered personalized learning systems: A review. *International Journal of Educational Technology in Higher Education, 18*(1), 1–23. DOI: 10.1186/s41239-021-00292-2 PMID: 34926790

Ladson-Billings, G. (1995). Toward a theory of culturally relevant pedagogy. *American Educational Research Journal, 32*(3), 465–491. DOI: 10.3102/00028312032003465

Lameras, P., Arnab, S., Hill, V., Lee, J., & Brown, K. (2021). Power to the teachers: An exploratory review on artificial intelligence in education. *Information (Basel), 12*(11), 459. Advance online publication. DOI: 10.3390/info13010014

Lampou R. (2023). *The Integration of Artificial Intelligence in Education: Opportunities and Challenges.*

Landrum, T. J., & McDuffie, K. A. (2010). Learning styles in the age of differentiated instruction. *Exceptionality, 18*(1), 6–17. DOI: 10.1080/09362830903462441

Langreo, L. (2024). ChatGPT, Bard, Copilot, Khanmigo: What AI Tools Do Teachers Use?

Lazovsky, G., Raz, T., & Kenett, Y. (2024). The Art of Creative Inquiry—From Question Asking to Prompt Engineering. *The Journal of Creative Behavior, 59*(1), e671. DOI: 10.1002/jocb.671

Le Dinh, T., Le, T. D., Uwizeyemungu, S., & Pelletier, C. (2025). Human-Centered Artificial Intelligence in Higher Education: A Framework for Systematic Literature Reviews. *Information (Basel), 16*(3), 240. DOI: 10.3390/info16030240

Learn-Work Ecosystem Library. (2025, July 8). *AI Literacy Framework for Primary & Secondary Education—OECD-EC.* Retrieved from https://learnworkecosystemlibrary.com/initiatives/ai-literacy-framework-for-primary-secondary-education-oecd-ec/

LeBoeuf, R. (2025, February 12). *From regulation to innovation: What the EU AI Act means for EdTech*. FeedbackFruits Blog. Retrieved from https://feedbackfruits.com/blog/2025-eu-ai-act-edtech

Lee, B. (2023). Digital Tools & Inquiry-Based Learning in History Education. *Muallim Journal of Social Science and Humanities.*, *7*(4), 78–88. DOI: 10.33306/mjssh/255

Lee, J., Hicke, Y., Yu, R., Brooks, C., & Kizilcec, R. F. (2024). The life cycle of large language models in education: A framework for understanding sources of bias. *British Journal of Educational Technology*, *55*(5), 1982–2002. DOI: 10.1111/bjet.13505

Lee, S., Jeon, J., & Choe, H. (2025). Enhancing pre-service teachers' global Englishes awareness with technology: A focus on AI chatbots in 3D metaverse environments. *TESOL Quarterly*, *59*(1), 49–74. DOI: 10.1002/tesq.3300

Leslie, L. G., Jali, N., Yahia, S. B., Shiang, C. W., & Junaini, S. N. (2025, August). Exploring Large Language Models in Gamified Environments: A Systematic Literature Review. In *2025 14th International Conference on Information Technology in Asia (CITA)* (pp. 119-124). IEEE. DOI: 10.1109/CITA66455.2025.11198821

Liang, H., & Xue, Y. (2009). Avoidance of information technology threats: A theoretical perspective. *Management Information Systems Quarterly*, *33*(1), 71–90. DOI: 10.2307/20650279

Liao, S. J., Han, P., & Xu, Y. (2025). Capability and Potential of Generative Artificial Intelligence (AI) Tools in Science Education: An Exploratory Study of ChatGPT-Powered Tools (DALL-E and Globe Explore), Midjourney and Gatekeep in Multimodal Science Education. *Journal of College Science Teaching*, *54*(6), 477–493. DOI: 10.1080/0047231X.2025.2480575

Li, L. (2022). Reskilling and upskilling the future-ready workforce for industry 4.0 and beyond. *Information Systems Frontiers*, *1*(1), 1–16. DOI: 10.1007/s10796-022-10308-y PMID: 35855776

Limbore, N. V., Anute, N., Ahluwalia, G. K., Chordiya, P. B., & Kalshetti, P. (2025). Ethical Leadership and Corporate Responsibility. In Harriott, S. (Ed.), *Innovative Approaches to Managing Conflict and Change in Diverse Work Environments* (pp. 193–218). IGI Global Scientific Publishing., DOI: 10.4018/979-8-3693-9556-1.ch009

Lim, W. M., Gunasekara, A., Pallant, J. L., Pallant, J. I., & Pechenkina, E. (2023). Generative AI and the future of education: Ragnarök or reformation? A paradoxical perspective from management educators. *International Journal of Management Education*, *21*(2), 100790. Advance online publication. DOI: 10.1016/j.ijme.2023.100790

Lin, P., & Van Brummelen, J. (2021, May). Engaging teachers to co-design integrated AI curriculum for K-12 classrooms. In *Proceedings of the 2021 CHI conference on human factors in computing systems* (pp. 1-12). DOI: 10.1145/3411764.3445377

Li, T., Krajcik, J. S., & Spiro, R. (2025). The Transformative Collaboration of Human Intelligence and Artificial Intelligence in Designing Knowledge-in-Use Science Assessment for Learning. *Journal of Science Education and Technology, 2025*, 1–27. DOI: 10.1007/s10956-025-10275-4

Literacy Framework, A. I. (2025). *Empowering learners for the age of AI*. https://ailiteracyframework.org

Liu, M., & Yu, D. (2022). Towards intelligent E-learning systems. *Education and Information Technologies, 28*(7), 1. DOI: 10.1007/s10639-022-11479-6 PMID: 36532790

Liu, P., Yuan, W., Fu, J., Jiang, Z., Hayashi, H., & Neubig, G. (2023). Pre-train, prompt, and predict: A systematic survey of prompting methods in natural language processing. *ACM Computing Surveys, 55*(9), 1–35. DOI: 10.1145/3560815

Liu, W., Jamaludin, K. A., & Hamzah, M. I. (2025). Systematic review of culturally responsive teaching and implications for technical communication education. *Multidisciplinary Reviews, 8*(4), 2025117. DOI: 10.31893/multirev.2025117

Li, X., & Yu, S. (2025). Culturally responsive AI module in early childhood teacher education: An action research. *Journal of Early Childhood Teacher Education*, 1–17. Advance online publication. DOI: 10.1080/10901027.2025.2552973

Loewen, S., Crowther, D., Isbell, D. R., Kim, K. M., Maloney, J., Miller, Z. F., & Rawal, H. (2019). Mobile-assisted language learning: A Duolingo case study. *ReCALL, 31*(3), 293–311. DOI: 10.1017/S0958344019000065

Lokhande, M., John Deva Prasanna, D. S., Selvakumar, P., Ragupathi, T., Vaissnave, V., & Manjunath, T. C. (2025). Novel ML Algorithms for Healthcare. In A. Ajibesin, N. G., & S. Thangavel (Eds.), Synergizing Data Envelopment Analysis and Machine Learning for Performance Optimization in Healthcare (pp. 113–134). IGI Global Scientific Publishing. DOI: 10.4018/979-8-3373-0081-8.ch005

Long, D., & Magerko, B. (2020, April). What is AI literacy? Competencies and design considerations. In *Proceedings of the 2020 CHI conference on human factors in computing systems* (pp. 1-16). DOI: 10.1145/3313831.3376727

Lorè, N., & Heydari, B. (2024). Strategic behavior of large language models and the role of game structure versus contextual framing. *Scientific Reports, 14*(1), 18490. DOI: 10.1038/s41598-024-69032-z PMID: 39122801

Louie, B., Björling, E. A., Kuo, A. C., & Alves-Oliveira, P. (2022). Designing for culturally responsive social robots: An application of a participatory framework. *Frontiers in Robotics and AI*, *9*, 983408. Advance online publication. DOI: 10.3389/frobt.2022.983408 PMID: 36340576

Luckin, R., Holmes, W., Griffiths, M., & Forcier, L. B. (2016). *Intelligence unleashed: An argument for AI in education*. Pearson Education.

Luprichová, J. (2025). Enhancing Historical Understanding, Gender Perspectives, and Critical Thinking. *Resource*, *12*, 188–197. DOI: 10.53349/re-source.2025.is1.a1391

Ly, C., Peng, E., Liu, K., Qin, A., Howe, G., Cheng, A., & Cuadra, A. (2025). Museum in the Classroom: Engaging Students with Augmented Reality Museum Artifacts and Generative AI. *Proceedings of the Extended Abstracts of the CHI Conference on Human Factors in Computing Systems*. 1-8. DOI: 10.1145/3706599.3719787

Macgilchrist, F. (2019). Digital inequalities and the ethics of EdTech. *Learning, Media and Technology*.

Maimela, C., & Mbonde, P. (2025). Artificial intelligence in South African universities: Curriculum transformation and decolonisation—aid or obstacle? *Frontiers in Sociology*, *10*, 1543471. DOI: 10.3389/fsoc.2025.1543471

Malysheva, O., Tokareva, E., Orchakova, L., & Smirnova, Y. (2022). The effect of online learning in modern history education. *Heliyon*, *8*(7), e09965. Advance online publication. DOI: 10.1016/j.heliyon.2022.e09965

Mandeville, C. P., Nilsen, E. B., Herfindal, I., & Finstad, A. G. (2023). Participatory monitoring drives biodiversity knowledge in global protected areas. *Communications Earth & Environment*, *4*(1), 240. DOI: 10.1038/s43247-023-00906-2

Martin, K. (2023). The evolving role of educators in the age of AI. https://katielmartin.com/2023/06/20/the-evolving-role-of-educators-in-the-age-of-ai/

Martin, A. F. (2025). Participatory co-design and evaluation of a novel AI-integrated assessment aimed at improving critical AI literacy. *Behavioral Sciences (Basel, Switzerland)*, *15*(6), 808. DOI: 10.3390/bs15060808 PMID: 40564589

Martinez-Maldonado, R. (2023). Human-centred learning analytics: Four challenges in realising the potential. *Journal of Learning Letters*. DOI: 10.59453/FIZJ7007

Martin, J. P., Stefl, S. K., Cain, L. W., & Pfirman, A. L. (2020). Understanding first-generation undergraduate engineering students' entry and persistence through social capital theory. *International Journal of STEM Education*, *7*(2), 37–42. DOI: 10.1186/s40594-020-00237-0

Masten, A. S. (2014). *Ordinary magic: Resilience in development.* Guilford Press.

Matthew, U. O., Bakare, K. M., Ebong, G. N., Ndukwu, C. C., & Nwanakwaugwu, A. C. (2023). Generative Artificial Intelligence (AI) Educational Pedagogy Development: Conversational AI with User-Centric ChatGPT4. *Journal of Trends in Computer Science and Smart Technology*, *5*(4), 401–418. DOI: 10.36548/jtcsst.2023.4.003

Mayasari, R. (2022). Leveraging AI for Universal Design for Learning. In *AI in Education* (EdTech Books). https://edtechbooks.org/ai_in_education/leveraging_ai_for_universal_design_for_learning

Maynez, J., Narayan, S., & McDonald, R. (2020). On faithfulness and factuality in abstractive summarization. *Proceedings of ACL.* DOI: 10.18653/v1/2020.acl-main.173

McCallum, L. (2024). New takes on developing intercultural communicative competence: Using AI tools in telecollaboration task design and task completion. *Journal for Multicultural Education*, *18*(1/2), 153–172. DOI: 10.1108/JME-06-2023-0043

McElroy, M. W., Jorna, R. J., & van Engelen, J. (2006). Rethinking social capital theory: A knowledge management perspective. *Journal of Knowledge Management*, *10*(5), 124–136. DOI: 10.1108/13673270610691233

McNulty, N. (2025, March 21). *Comparative analysis of generative AI policies in education: Australia, Japan, New Zealand, Korea, United Kingdom.* Retrieved from https://niallmcnulty.com/ai-policies-international-overview

Memarian, B., & Doleck, T. (2023). Fairness, Accountability, Transparency, and Ethics (FATE) in AI and higher education: A systematic review. *Computers & Education: Artificial Intelligence*, *5*, 100152. DOI: 10.1016/j.caeai.2023.100152

Mengesha, Z., Heldreth, C., Lahav, M., Sublewski, J., & Tuennerman, E. (2021). "I don't think these devices are very culturally sensitive."—Impact of automated speech recognition errors on African Americans. *Frontiers in Artificial Intelligence*, *4*(725911), 725911. Advance online publication. DOI: 10.3389/frai.2021.725911 PMID: 34901836

Mercer, N. (2000). *Words and minds: How we use language to think together.* Routledge.

Merino-Campos, C. (2025). The Impact of Artificial Intelligence on Personalized Learning in Higher Education: A Systematic Review. *Trends in Higher Education 2025, Vol. 4, Page 17*, *4*(2), 17. DOI: 10.3390/higheredu4020017

Mestre, A. (2024, May). Towards a Hybrid Intelligence Paradigm: Systematic Integration of Human and Artificial Capabilities. In *International Conference on Research Challenges in Information Science* (pp. 149-156). Cham: Springer Nature Switzerland. DOI: 10.1007/978-3-031-59468-7_17

Miao, F., & Shiohira, K. (2024). *AI competency framework for students*. UNESCO Publishing.

Michalon, B. & Camacho- Zúñiga, C. (2023). ChatGPT, a brand-new tool to strengthen timeless competencies. *Frontiers in Education, 8 (*1251163), DOI: 10.3389/feduc.2023.1251163

Michel-Villarreal, R., Vilalta-Perdomo, E., Salinas-Navarro, D. E., Thierry-Aguilera, R., & Gerardou, F. S. (2023). Challenges and Opportunities of Generative AI for Higher Education as Explained by ChatGPT. *Education Sciences*, *13*(9), 856. Advance online publication. DOI: 10.3390/educsci13090856

Mierwald, M. (2024). Chatting about the Past with Artificial Intelligence. *Journal of Educational Media. Memoria y Sociedad : Revista del Departamento de Historia y Geografia*, *16*(2), 143–173. DOI: 10.3167/jemms.2024.160206

Mikalef, P., Conboy, K., Lundström, J. E., & Popovič, A. (2022). Thinking responsibly about responsible AI and 'the dark side' of AI. *European Journal of Information Systems*, *31*(3), 257–268. DOI: 10.1080/0960085X.2022.2026621

Miles, J. (2018). Teaching history for truth and reconciliation: The challenges and opportunities of narrativity, temporality, and identity. *McGill Journal of Education*, *53*(2). Advance online publication. DOI: 10.7202/1058399ar

Miller, B., & Spohnholz, J. (2023). Collaboratively Reforming General Education History Teaching and Learning: A Roadmap for the Twenty-First Century. *Proceedings of the H-Net Teaching Conference.* Vol 1. 77-87. DOI: 10.33823/phtc.v1i1.203

Miragoli, M. (2024). Conformism, Ignorance & Injustice: AI as a Tool of Epistemic Oppression. *Episteme (Edinburgh)*, *22*(2), 522–540. DOI: 10.1017/epi.2024.11

Mishra, P., & Koehler, M. J. (2006). Technological pedagogical content knowledge: A framework for teacher knowledge. *Teachers College Record*, *108*(6), 1017–1054. DOI: 10.1111/j.1467-9620.2006.00684.x

Mishra, P., Warr, M., & Islam, R. (2023). TPACK in the age of generative AI. *Journal of Digital Learning in Teacher Education*, *39*(4), 273–278. DOI: 10.1080/21532974.2023.2247480

MIT CAIL. (2025). *Collaborative AI for learning (CAIL)*. https://education.mit.edu/project/collaborative-ai-for-learning-cail/

Mittal, U., Sai, S., Chamola, V., & Sangwan, D. (2024). A Comprehensive Review on Generative AI for Education. *IEEE Access : Practical Innovations, Open Solutions, 12*, 142733–142759. DOI: 10.1109/ACCESS.2024.3468368

Mohamed, S., Png, M., & Isaac, W. (2020). Decolonial AI: Decolonial Theory as Sociotechnical Foresight in Artificial Intelligence. *Philosophy & Technology, 33*(4), 659–684. DOI: 10.1007/s13347-020-00405-8

Moldovan, S., Moldovan, I., & Rice, T. (2025). Speculative Memory and Machine Augmentation: A Polyvocal Rendering of Brutalist Architecture Through AI and Photogrammetry. *Heritage., 8*(10), 401. DOI: 10.3390/heritage8100401

Mollema, W. J. T. (2024). Decolonial AI as Disenclosure. *Open Journal of Social Sciences, 12*(2), 574–603. DOI: 10.4236/jss.2024.122032

Mollès, D., & Parada-Ulloa, M. (2025). The classroom as a space of resistance. Cooperation, gratitude and collective memory between neuroscience and social science. *Frontiers in Sociology, 10*, 1567675. Advance online publication. DOI: 10.3389/fsoc.2025.1567675

Morschheuser, B., Hamari, J., Koivisto, J., & Maedche, A. (2017). Gamified crowdsourcing: Conceptualization, literature review, and future agenda. *International Journal of Human-Computer Studies, 106*, 26–43. DOI: 10.1016/j.ijhcs.2017.04.005

Moskalyuk, M., & Len, A. (2025). Digital Technologies and Their Role in Studying History. *Open Educational E-Environment of Modern University*, (18), 92–102. DOI: 10.28925/2414-0325.2025.188

Moustaghfir, S., & Brigui, H. (2024). Navigating Critical Thinking in the Digital Era: An Informative Exploration. *International Journal of Linguistics. Literature and Translation, 7*(1), 137–143. DOI: 10.32996/ijllt.2024.7.1.11x

Muis, A., Lukin, S., Sharif, S., Rashid, N., & Hamid, Z. (2024). Nation-Building through History Education: Mutual Goals in Shaping Student Character. *International Journal of Academic Research in Progressive Education and Development., 13*(3), 2391–2397. DOI: 10.6007/IJARPED/v13-i3/22157

Muldoon, J., & Wu, B. (2023). Artificial Intelligence in the Colonial Matrix of Power. *Philosophy & Technology, 36*(4), 1–24. DOI: 10.1007/s13347-023-00687-8

Muzanenhamo, P., & Power, S. (2024). ChatGPT and accounting in African contexts: Amplifying epistemic injustice. *Critical Perspectives on Accounting*, *99*, 102735. DOI: 10.1016/j.cpa.2024.102735

Naidoo, V., & Chadhaa, K. K. (2025). Culturally responsive AI chatbots: From framework to field evidence. *Computers in Human Behavior: Artificial Humans*, *6*, 100224. Advance online publication. DOI: 10.1016/j.chbah.2025.100224

Nain, G., & Samal, U. (2026). Intelligence behind individualization: A survey on role of AI in mass customized and personalized production. *Technology in Society*, *85*, 103195. Advance online publication. DOI: 10.1016/j.techsoc.2025.103195

Narayanan, K. S., & Kumaravel, A. (2024). Hybrid gamification and AI tutoring framework using machine learning and adaptive Neuro-fuzzy inference system. *Journal of Advanced Research in Applied Sciences and Engineering Technology*, *42*(2), 221–233. DOI: 10.37934/araset.42.2.221233

National Digital Inclusion Alliance. (2019). Definitions. Retrieved from https://www.digitalinclusion.org/definitions/

NCERT. (2025). *AI Series Phase II*. https://ciet.ncert.gov.in/activity/aiseriesteacher-II

Negi, V. (2023). Artificial intelligence: Next-level customer service. *Advances in Logistics, Operations, and Management Science*, *2*(5), 226–240. DOI: 10.4018/979-8-3693-0418-1.ch015

Ng, D. T. K., Leung, J. K. L., Chu, S. K. W., & Qiao, M. S. (2021). Conceptualizing AI literacy: An exploratory review. *Computers and Education: Artificial Intelligence*, *2*, 100041.

Ng, D. T. K., Leung, J. K. L., Su, J., Ng, R. C. W., & Chu, S. K. W. (2021). Teachers' AI digital competencies and twenty-first-century skills in the post-pandemic world. *Educational Technology Research and Development*, *70*(1), 137–161. DOI: 10.1007/s11423-023-10203-6 PMID: 36844361

Nguyen, A., Hong, Y., Dang, B., & Huang, X. (2024). Human-AI collaboration patterns in AI-assisted academic writing. *Studies in Higher Education*, *49*(5), 847–864. DOI: 10.1080/03075079.2024.2323593

Ni, L., & Shin, C. (2025). Humanism Enhancing Student Motivation in History Learning Through AI-Driven e-Cooperative and e-Collaborative Methods in Rural Education. *Randwick International of Education and Linguistics Science Journal.*, *6*(1), 99–108. DOI: 10.47175/rielsj.v6i1.1132

Nkolika, C. (2025). Pedagogical Challenges Encountered by Teachers in Some Content Areas of the Reintroduced History Curriculum in Junior Secondary Schools in Awka Education Zone. *Indonesian Journal of Innovative Teaching and Learning.*, *2*(1), 72–80. DOI: 10.64420/ijitl.v2i1.176

Noble, S. U. (2018). *Algorithms of oppression: How search engines reinforce racism*. New York University Press. DOI: 10.18574/nyu/9781479833641.001.0001

Nuranti, E. Q., Yulianti, E., & Husin, H. S. (2022). Predicting the Category and the Length of Punishment in Indonesian Courts Based on Previous Court Decision Documents. *Computers*, *11*(6), 88. DOI: 10.3390/computers11060088

Nussbaum, M. C. (1997). *Cultivating humanity*. Harvard University Press.

Nuthakki, S., buddiga, S. K. pranitha, & Koganti, S. (2024). Exploring Deep Learning Models for Image Recognition: A Comparative Review. *Signal & Image Processing : An International Journal, 15*(3), 01–10. DOI: 10.5121/sipij.2024.15301

Nuthakki, S., Uttiramerur, A. D., Nuthakki, Y., & Munjala, M. B. (2024). Navigating the Medical Landscape: A Review of Chatbots for Biomarker Extraction from Diverse Medical Reports. *International Journal For Multidisciplinary Research*, *6*(1), 13154. Advance online publication. DOI: 10.36948/ijfmr.2024.v06i01.13154

Nyaaba, M., & Zhai, X. (2025). Developing a theory-grounded AI tool for generating culturally responsive lesson plans. *Computers and Education: Artificial Intelligence*. DOI: 10.1016/j.caeai.2025.100474

Nyaaba, M., Wright, A., & Choi, G. L. (2024). Generative AI and digital neocolonialism in global education: Towards an equitable framework. *arXiv preprint arXiv:2406.02966*.

O'neil, C. (2017). *Weapons of math destruction: How big data increases inequality and threatens democracy*. Crown.

O'Reilly, C. (2025). History of AI in education: From origins to future. *TSH Anywhere.* https://www.tshanywhere.org/post/history-ai-education-origins-future

Ocrospoma, G., Fuster-Guillén, D., Ocaña-Fernández, Y., & Villalba-Condori, K. O. (2023). Enseñanza recíproca influenciado por los niveles de alfabetización informacional en estudiantes de Ciencias de la Comunicación. *PUBLICACIONES*, *53*(2), 125–155. DOI: 10.30827/publicaciones.v53i2.26819

OECD & Education International. (2023). Opportunities, guidelines and guardrails for effective and equitable use of AI in education. In *OECD Digital Education Outlook 2023*. OECD Publishing.

OECD. (2019). *OECD AI principles.* https://oecd.ai

OECD. (2021). *AI and education: Challenges and opportunities.* OECD Publishing.

OECD. (2025, January 23). *Trends Shaping Education 2025.* Retrieved from https://www.oecd.org/en/publications/trends-shaping-education-2025_ee6587fd-en/full-report/global-trends-and-the-future-of-education-in-2025_7358e77a.html

Ofosu-Asare, Y. (2024). Cognitive imperialism in artificial intelligence: Counteracting bias with indigenous epistemologies. *AI & Society*, *40*(4), 3045–3061. DOI: 10.1007/s00146-024-02065-0

Oger, A., Gorisse, G., Fleury, S., & Christmann, O. (2025). MemorIA, an Architecture for Creating Interactive AI Historical Agents in Educational Contexts. *Computer Animation and Virtual Worlds*, *36*(3), e70032. DOI: 10.1002/cav.70032

Oksuzoglu, G. (2024). Construction of collective memory through official history education in North Cyprus (1971-2003). *Turkish History Education Journal.*, *13*(1), 142–169. DOI: 10.17497/tuhed.1423137

Oliveira, G., Grenha Teixeira, J., Torres, A., & Morais, C. (2021). An exploratory study on the emergency remote education experience of higher education students and teachers during the COVID-19 pandemic. *British Journal of Educational Technology*, *52*(4), 1357–1376. DOI: 10.1111/bjet.13112 PMID: 34219758

Ooi, K.-B., Tan, G. W.-H., Al-Emran, M., Al-Sharafi, M. A., Capatina, A., Chakraborty, A., Dwivedi, Y. K., Huang, T.-L., Kar, A. K., Lee, V.-H., Loh, X.-M., Micu, A., Mikalef, P., Mogaji, E., Pandey, N., Raman, R., Rana, N. P., Sarker, P., Sharma, A., & Wong, L.-W. (2025). The Potential of Generative Artificial Intelligence Across Disciplines: Perspectives and Future Directions. *Journal of Computer Information Systems*, *65*(1), 76–107. DOI: 10.1080/08874417.2023.2261010

OpenAI. (2025). *Khan Academy explores GPT-4 to power Khanmigo — limited pilot program.*

OPH. (2025). AI in education: Legislation and recommendations. https://www.oph.fi/en/artificial-intelligence-education-legislation-and-recommendations

Ożegalska-Łukasik, N. & Łukasik, S. (2023). Culturally responsive artificial intelligence – problems, challenges and solutions. *Intercultural Relations, 7*(2(14), 106-119. DOI: 10.12797/RM.02.2023.14.07

Pabalkar, V., & Chanda, R. (2022). Role of artificial intelligence in healthcare. In International conference on information and management engineering (pp. 353–360). Springer Nature Singapore. DOI: 10.1007/978-981-99-2746-3_37

Paderanga, C., Soni, A., & Nisa, N. (2023). Artificial intelligence adoption among accountants in the UAE: An integrated AI acceptance-avoidance model. Global Scientific and Academic Research Journal of Economics. *Business and Management*, *2*(11), 61–86.

Pahune, S., & Akhtar, Z. (2025). Transitioning from MLOps to LLMOps: Navigating the unique challenges of large language models. *Information (Basel)*, *16*(2), 87. DOI: 10.3390/info16020087

Paiz, J. M., Toncelli, R., & Kostka, I. (2025). *Artificial intelligence, real teaching: A guide to AI in ELT*. University of Michigan Press. DOI: 10.3998/mpub.14329762

Pane, J. F., Steiner, E. D., Baird, M. D., & Hamilton, L. S. (2015). *Continued progress: Promising evidence on personalized learning*. RAND Corporation. DOI: 10.7249/RR1365

Pan, S., Luo, L., Wang, Y., Chen, C., Wang, J., & Wu, X. (2024). Unifying large language models and knowledge graphs: A roadmap. *IEEE Transactions on Knowledge and Data Engineering*, *36*(7), 3580–3599. DOI: 10.1109/TKDE.2024.3352100

Pansoni, S., Tiribelli, S., Paolanti, M., Frontoni, E., & Giovanola, B. (2023). Design of an Ethical Framework for Artificial Intelligence in Cultural Heritage. *2023 IEEE International Symposium on Ethics in Engineering, Science, and Technology (ETHICS)*, 1-5. DOI: 10.1109/ETHICS57328.2023.10155020

Papagiannidis, E., Enholm, I. M., Dremel, C., Mikalef, P., & Krogstie, J. (2023a). Toward AI Governance: Identifying Best Practices and Potential Barriers and Outcomes. *Information Systems Frontiers*, *25*(1), 123–141. DOI: 10.1007/s10796-022-10251-y PMID: 35464171

Papert, S. (1996). *The Connected Family: Bridging the digital generation gap*. Longstreet Press.

Paradiso Solutions. (2025). 7 best adaptive learning platforms in 2025. https://www.paradisosolutions.com/blog/best-adaptive-learning-platforms/

Pardos, Z. A., & Bhandari, S. (2024). ChatGPT-generated help produces learning gains equivalent to human tutor-authored help on mathematics skills. *PLoS One*, *19*(5), e0304013. DOI: 10.1371/journal.pone.0304013 PMID: 38787823

Paris, D. (2012). Culturally sustaining pedagogy: A needed change in stance, terminology, and practice. *Educational Researcher*, *41*(3), 93–97. DOI: 10.3102/0013189X12441244

Paris, D., & Alim, H. S. (2017). *Culturally sustaining pedagogies*. Teachers College Press.

Park, S. (2024). AI chatbots and linguistic injustice. *Journal of Universal Language, 25*(1), 99–119. DOI: 10.22425/jul.2024.25.1.99

Pataranutaporn, P., Danry, V., Leong, J., Punpongsanon, P., Novy, D., Maes, P., & Sra, M. (2021). AI-generated characters for supporting personalized learning and well-being. *Nature Machine Intelligence, 3*(12), 1013–1022. DOI: 10.1038/s42256-021-00417-9

Pawan, F., Li, S., Nijiati, S., Dopwell, M., Harris, A., & Iruoje, T. (2023). Culturally- and Linguistically-Responsive Online Teacher Learning Professional Development. *Online Learning : the Official Journal of the Online Learning Consortium, 27*(4). Advance online publication. DOI: 10.24059/olj.v27i4.4003

Pearson, A. (2024). Creativity: Firing on all generative AI cylinders. *Journal of Digital and Social Media Marketing, 12*(1), 52–64. DOI: 10.69554/VSKL5622

Peoples, K. (2021). *How to write a phenomenological dissertation: A step-by-step guide* (Vol. 56). SAGE.

Petter, S., Barber, C. S., & Barber, D. (2020). Gaming the system: The effects of social capital as a resource for virtual team members. *Information & Management, 57*(6), 103239. DOI: 10.1016/j.im.2019.103239

Pham, N., Ngoc, H. P., & Nguyen-Duc, A. (2025). Fairness for machine learning software in education: A systematic mapping study. *Journal of Systems and Software, 219*, 112244. DOI: 10.1016/j.jss.2024.112244

Piaget, J. (1970). *Science of education and the psychology of the child*. Orion Press.

Piller, I. (2016). *Linguistic diversity and social justice*. Oxford University Press. DOI: 10.1093/acprof:oso/9780199937240.001.0001

Poce, A., De Medio, C., Valente, M., Contardi, L., Torre, E., Pirchi, S., & Tolaini, M. (2025). Digital OBL, AI and Robotics for inclusive heritage education experiences. *Ubiquity Proceedings., 6*(1), 28. Advance online publication. DOI: 10.5334/uproc.196

Polit, D. F., & Beck, C. T. (2006). The content validity index: A critical review. *Research in Nursing & Health, 29*, 489–497. DOI: 10.1002/nur.20147 PMID: 16977646

Polson, M. C., & Richardson, J. J. (2013). *Foundations of intelligent tutoring systems*. Psychology Press. DOI: 10.4324/9780203761557

Pope, A., &, R. (2024). Exploring Historians' Critical Use of Generative AI Technologies for History Education. *Proceedings of the Association for Information Science and Technology*, 61. DOI: 10.1002/pra2.1188

Popescu, A. I., & Burlacu, M. (2025). Knowledge Governance and AI Awareness in Higher Education. *MDPI, 15*(6), 144. Retrieved from https://www.mdpi.com/2075-4698/15/6/144

Pozdniakov, S., Brazil, J., Mohammadi, M., Dollinger, M., Sadiq, S., & Khosravi, H. (2025). AI-assisted co-creation: Bridging skill gaps in student-generated content. *Journal of Learning Analytics, 12*(1), 129–151. DOI: 10.18608/jla.2025.8601

Qureshi, I. (2025). The Impact of AI on Teacher Roles: Towards a Collaborative Human-AI Pedagogy. *AI EDIFY Journal, 2*(1), 1–11.

Radakovich, N., & Nazha, A. (2021). The future of artificial intelligence in healthcare. In *Machine learning in Cardiovascular medicine* (pp. 371–394). Academic Press., DOI: 10.1016/B978-0-12-820273-9.00016-6

Radeta, M., Freitas, R., Rodrigues, C., Zuniga, A., Nguyen, N. T., Flores, H., & Nurmi, P. (2024). Man and the machine: Effects of AI-assisted human labeling on interactive annotation of real-time video streams. *ACM Transactions on Interactive Intelligent Systems, 14*(2), 1–22. DOI: 10.1145/3649457

Raffel, C., Shazeer, N., Roberts, A., Lee, K., Narang, S., Matena, M., & Liu, P. J. (2020). Exploring the limits of transfer learning with a unified text-to-text transformer. *Journal of Machine Learning Research, 21*(140), 1–67. DOI: 10.5555/3455716.3455856

Raji, I. D., Smart, A., White, R. N., Mitchell, M., Gebru, T., Hutchinson, B., & Barnes, P. (2020, January). Closing the AI accountability gap: Defining an end-to-end framework for internal algorithmic auditing. In *Proceedings of the 2020 conference on fairness, accountability, and transparency* (pp. 33-44). DOI: 10.1145/3351095.3372873

RAND Corporation. (2025). *AI training in U.S. school districts: 2025 update.*

Rane, N. L., Choudhary, S. P., & Rane, J. (2024). Education 4.0 and 5.0: Integrating Artificial Intelligence (AI) for personalized and adaptive learning. *Journal of Artificial Intelligence and Robotics, 1*(1), 29–43. DOI: 10.61577/jaiar.2024.100006

Redecker, C. (2017). *European framework for the digital competence of educators (DigCompEdu)*. Publications Office of the European Union.

Ren, X., & Wang, R. (2025). Integrating human–AI collaboration into translation education: A comprehensive protocol for assessment, diagnosis, and strategy development. *PLOS ONE, 20*(12 December). DOI: 10.1371/journal.pone.0338089

Ren, X. (2025). Policy, Pedagogy, and Technological Disruption: Teacher Agency in AI-Integrated Educational Ecosystems. *Business and Social Sciences Proceedings, 2*, 31–37. DOI: 10.71222/azryt912

Resta, P., & Laferrière, T. (2015). Digital equity and intercultural education. *Education and Information Technologies, 20*(4), 743–756. DOI: 10.1007/s10639-015-9419-z

Reyes-Galindo, V., Jaramillo-Correa, J. P., Carrasco Nava, K., De-la-Rosa-González, A. E., Flores Flores, D., Martínez, M., Monroy-De-la-Rosa, L. A., Morelos Zamora, M. Á., Ramírez Morales, B. E., Ramírez Morales, O. T., Rodríguez, M., Salazar Zamora, M., Zamora Callejas, C., Zamora Callejas, R., Zamora, C., Zamora, T., González-Camacho, V. A., Rebollo, E., Torres-Jardón, R., & Mastretta-Yanes, A. (2023). Evaluating pollution-related damage and restoration success in urban forests with participatory monitoring and digital tools. *Conservation Biology, 37*(5), e14112. Advance online publication. DOI: 10.1111/cobi.14112 PMID: 37204008

Reyes-Rojas, J., Díaz, B., Ruz-Reveco, C., Castro, A., & Reyes-González, D. (2026). Conceptualizing pre-service teachers' readiness for AI integration into teaching practices: An intelligent-TPACK approach. *Computers and Education Open, 10*, 100320. Advance online publication. DOI: 10.1016/j.caeo.2025.100320

Riazi, M., Rezvani, R., & Ghanbar, H. (2023). Trustworthiness in L2 writing research: A review and analysis of qualitative articles in the Journal of Second Language Writing. *Research Methods in Applied Linguistics, 2*(3), 100065. Advance online publication. DOI: 10.1016/j.rmal.2023.100065

Ribble, M. (2015). *Digital citizenship in schools*. ISTE.

Ribeiro, M. T., Wu, T., Guestrin, C., & Singh, S. (2020). Beyond accuracy: Behavioral testing of NLP models with CheckList. *arXiv preprint arXiv:2005.04118*. DOI: 10.18653/v1/2020.acl-main.442

Richter, S., Slowinski, P., & Richter, A. (2024). A constructivist approach to integrating AI in marketing education. *Marketing Education Review*. Advance online publication. DOI: 10.1177/02734753241288876

Rinta-Kahila, T., Penttinen, E., Salovaara, A., Soliman, W., & Ruissalo, J. (2023). The vicious circles of skill erosion: A case study of cognitive automation. *Journal of the Association for Information Systems, 24*(5), 1378–1412. DOI: 10.17705/1jais.00829

Rismanchian, S., & Doroudi, S. (2025). The Evolution of Research on AI and Education Across Four Decades: Insights from the AIxEd Framework. *International Journal of Artificial Intelligence in Education, 2025*(5), 1–24. DOI: 10.1007/s40593-025-00483-9

Riva, G. (2025). *The Architecture of Cognitive Amplification: Enhanced Cognitive Scaffolding as a Resolution to the Comfort-Growth Paradox in Human-AI Cognitive Integration*.

Rivas, P., & Zhao, L. (2023). Marketing with ChatGPT: Navigating the Ethical Terrain of GPT-Based Chatbot Technology. *AI, 4*(2), 375–384. DOI: 10.3390/ai4020019

Riyat, S., Gandhi, J., Kumar, A., Das, K., Panigra, A., Jennifer, D., & Manav, O. M. (2025). Reinventing Digital Illustration With Generative Ai Tools. *ShodhKosh: Journal of Visual and Performing Arts, 6*(5s), 1–11. DOI: 10.29121/shodhkosh.v6.i5s.2025.6876

Rollins, M. (2023). *AI-assisted constructivism*. LinkedIn.

Rose, D. H., & Dalton, B. (2009). Learning to read in the digital age. *Mind, Brain and Education : the Official Journal of the International Mind, Brain, and Education Society, 3*(2), 74–83. DOI: 10.1111/j.1751-228X.2009.01057.x

Roshanaei, M. (2024). Towards best practices for mitigating artificial intelligence implicit bias in shaping diversity, inclusion and equity in higher education. *Education and Information Technologies, 29*(14), 18959–18984. DOI: 10.1007/s10639-024-12605-2

Rospigliosi, P. (2023). Artificial intelligence in teaching and learning: What questions should we ask of Chat GPT? *Interactive Learning Environments, 31*(1), 1–3. DOI: 10.1080/10494820.2023.2180191

Ruiz-Rojas, L., Salvador-Ullauri, L., & Acosta-Vargas, P. (2024). Collaborative Working and Critical Thinking: Adoption of Generative Artificial Intelligence Tools in Higher Education. *Sustainability (Basel), 16*(13), 5367. DOI: 10.3390/su16135367

Sa'adah, U., Yuhana, U. L., Rochimah, S., & Afridian Rasyid, M. B. (2026). Bridging the skills gap through Agile methodologies in Vocational Software Development Education. *Array (New York, N.Y.), 29*, 100614. Advance online publication. DOI: 10.1016/j.array.2025.100614

Sadok, H., Mahboub, H., Chaibi, H., Saadane, R., & Wahbi, M. (2023). *Applications of Artificial Intelligence in finance: Prospects, Limits and risks. In 2023 international conference on digital age & technological advances for sustainable development (ICDATA)*. IEEE., DOI: 10.1109/ICDATA58816.2023.00034

Sahu, P. (2025). AI and digital tools supporting multilingual primary education in India. *International Journal of Multidisciplinary Educational Research, 14*(5[2]). Advance online publication. DOI: 10.5281/zenodo.10982345

Saidi, A. I., Puspitasari, D. G., & Wijaya, H. (2016). Interpreting the cultural values of learning space design based on traditional education system in Indonesia. *Advanced Science Letters*, *22*(12), 4367–4369. DOI: 10.1166/asl.2016.8157

Sakki, I. (2025). Collective memory and history textbooks. *Current Opinion in Psychology*, *65*, 102073. DOI: 10.1016/j.copsyc.2025.102073

Saleem, D. S., Aziz, M. U., Iqbal, D. M. J., & Abbas, S. (2025). AI in Education: Personalized Learning Systems and Their Impact on Student Performance and Engagement. *The Critical Review of Social Sciences Studies*, *3*(1), 2445–2459. DOI: 10.59075/c35qa453

Samala, A. D., Zhai, X., Aoki, K., Bojic, L., & Zikic, S. (2024). An In-Depth Review of ChatGPT's Pros and Cons for Learning and Teaching in Education. [IJIM]. *International Journal of Interactive Mobile Technologies*, *18*(02), 96–117. DOI: 10.3991/ijim.v18i02.46509

Samuel, Y., Brennan-Tonetta, M., Samuel, J., Kashyap, R., Kumar, V., Krishna Kaashyap, S., Chidipothu, N., Anand, I., & Jain, P. (2023a). Cultivation of human centered artificial intelligence: Culturally adaptive thinking in education (CATE) for AI. *Frontiers in Artificial Intelligence*, *6*, 1198180. Advance online publication. DOI: 10.3389/frai.2023.1198180 PMID: 38106981

Samuli Laato. (2022). *How to explain AI systems to end users: a systematic literature review and research agenda.*

Sánchez-Martín, J., Guillén-Peñafiel, R., & Hernández-Carretero, A. (2025). Artificial Intelligence in Heritage Tourism: Innovation, Accessibility, and Sustainability in the Digital Age. *Heritage.*, *8*(10), 428. DOI: 10.3390/heritage8100428

Sandhu, S., Harris, R., & Copsey-Blake, M. (2023). School history, identity and ethnicity: An examination of the experiences of young adults in England. *Journal of Curriculum Studies*, *55*(2), 153–170. DOI: 10.1080/00220272.2023.2184212

Sanusi, I. T., Agbo, F. J., Dada, O. A., Yunusa, A. A., Aruleba, K. D., Obaido, G., Olawumi, O., & Oyelere, S. S.Centre for Multidisciplinary Research and Innovation (CEMRI). (2024). Stakeholders' insights on artificial intelligence education: Perspectives of teachers, students, and policymakers. *Computers and Education Open*, *7*, 100212. DOI: 10.1016/j.caeo.2024.100212

Sarıdaş, G. (2025). The Use of Artificial Intelligence Agents in Education. *International Society That Learns Journal, 2*(1), 61–72. DOI: 10.64782/istlj22286172

Sato, E., Shyyan, V., Chauhan, S., & Christensen, L. (2024). Putting ai in fair: A framework for equity in ai-driven learner models and inclusive assessments. *Egitimde ve Psikolojide Ölçme ve Degerlendirme Dergisi, 15*(Special Issue), 263–281. DOI: 10.21031/epod.1526527

Savenije, G., & De Bruijn, P. (2017). Historical empathy in a museum: Uniting contextualisation and emotional engagement. *International Journal of Heritage Studies, 23*(9), 832–845. DOI: 10.1080/13527258.2017.1339108

Schiff, D. (2022). Education for AI, not AI for Education: The Role of Education and Ethics in National AI Policy Strategies. *International Journal of Artificial Intelligence in Education, 32*(3), 527–563. DOI: 10.1007/s40593-021-00270-2

Schrager, A. (2018). *The modern education system was designed to teach future factory workers to be "punctual, docile, and sober."*

Scitepress. (2024). The role of generative AI in personalised learning within constructivist frameworks. In *Proceedings of the 16th International Conference on Computer Supported Education* (pp. 1–10). https://doi.org/DOI: 10.5220/126887240001

Seaborn, K., & Fels, D. I. (2015). Gamification in theory and action: A survey. *International Journal of Human-Computer Studies, 74*, 14–31. DOI: 10.1016/j.ijhcs.2014.09.006

Sekti, B. A. (2025a). Adversarial Machine Learning in Industrial Cybersecurity: Challenges and Solutions. In *AI-Enhanced Cybersecurity for Industrial Automation* (pp. 363–386). IGI Global Scientific Publishing. DOI: 10.4018/979-8-3373-3241-3.ch018

Sekti, B. A. (2025a). AI Technology Management Concepts and Strategies. In *AI Technology Management and Value Creation* (pp. 1–32). DOI: 10.4018/979-8-3373-2497-5.ch001

Sekti, B. A. (2025b). Foundations of Artificial Intelligence Ethics. In *Navigating Social Trust in the AI Era* (pp. 23–47). DOI: 10.4018/979-8-3373-7011-8.ch002

Sekti, B. A. (2025b). Information Security Awareness. In *User-Centric Cybersecurity Implications for Sustainable Digital Transformation* (pp. 111–145). DOI: 10.4018/979-8-3373-3171-3.ch004

Sekti, B. A. (2025c). Machine Learning vs. AI: Key Concepts. In *Implementing Enterprise Cybersecurity With AI* (pp. 1–27). DOI: 10.4018/979-8-3373-2252-0.ch001

Sellar, S., & Gulson, K. N. (2021). Becoming information centric: The emergence of new cognitive infrastructures in education policy. *Journal of Education Policy, 36*(3), 309–326. DOI: 10.1080/02680939.2019.1678766

Selwyn, N. (2019). *Should robots replace teachers? AI and the future of education.* Polity Press.

Sharma, G., & Kalra, A. (2020). Designing accessible voice user interfaces for low-literacy users. In *Proceedings of IDC 2020* (pp. 77–88). ACM. DOI: 10.1145/3392063.3394431

Sharma, S., Mittal, P., Kumar, M., & Bhardwaj, V. (2025). The role of large language models in personalized learning: A systematic review of educational impact. *Discover Sustainability, 6*(1), 1–24. DOI: 10.1007/s43621-025-01094-z

Shneiderman, B. (2020). *Human-centered AI.* Oxford University Press.

Shute, V. J. (2008). Focus on formative feedback. *Review of Educational Research, 78*(1), 153–189. DOI: 10.3102/0034654307313795

Siddiqui, M., Mansoori, M., Siddiqui, M., & Yadav, A.Mohammad Talha Siddiqui. (2025). AI-Enabled Pedagogy: Advancing Education Through Innovative Teaching Tools and the AI-TEACH Model. *Journal of Informatics Education and Research., 5*(1), 2526–2539. DOI: 10.52783/jier.v5i1.2261

Siemens, G. (2005). Connectivism: A learning theory for the digital age. *International Journal of Instructional Technology and Distance Learning, 2*(1), 3–10.

Silfver, M., & Myyry, L. (2022). Integrating historical and moral consciousness in history teaching. *Historical Encounters: A journal of historical consciousness, historical cultures, and history education. 9*(2), 18-29. DOI: 10.52289/hej9.203

Singh, R., & Singh, A. (2025). *Integrating AI in Education: Navigating UNESCO Global Guidelines, Emerging Trends, and Its Intersection with Sustainable Development Goals.* ResearchGate. Retrieved from https://www.researchgate.net/publication/389936132_Integrating_AI_in_Education_Navigating_UNESCO_Global_Guidelines_Emerging_Trends_and_Its_Intersection_with_Sustainable_Development_Goals

Singh, A., & Gupta, P. (2025). Perspective of generative AI for UNESCO inclusive education. *SSRN.* DOI: 10.2139/ssrn.5181859

Sleeter, N., Schrum, K., Swan, A., & Broubalow, J. (2020). "Reflective of my best work": Promoting inquiry-based learning in a hybrid graduate history course. *Arts and Humanities in Higher Education, 19*(3), 285–303. DOI: 10.1177/1474022219833662

Snow, R., O'connor, B., Jurafsky, D., & Ng, A. Y. (2008, October). Cheap and fast–but is it good? Evaluating non-expert annotations for natural language tasks. In *Proceedings of the 2008 conference on empirical methods in natural language processing* (pp. 254-263).

Sockalingam, N., Lo, K., Teo, J., Wei, C. C., Jiet, D. C. J., Herremans, D., Jun, M. L. M., Kurniawan, O., Wang, Y., & Leong, P. K. (2025). Towards the future of education: Cyber-physical learning. *Discover Education*, *4*(1), 82. Advance online publication. DOI: 10.1007/s44217-025-00474-x

Song, D., Lee, W., & Oh, H. (2021, August). Context-aware and data-driven feedback generation for programming assignments. In *Proceedings of the 29th ACM Joint Meeting on European Software Engineering Conference and Symposium on the Foundations of Software Engineering* (pp. 328-340). DOI: 10.1145/3468264.3468598

Southworth, J., Migliaccio, K., Glover, J., Glover, J. N., Reed, D., McCarty, C., Brendemuhl, J., & Thomas, A. (2023). Developing a model for AI Across the curriculum: Transforming the higher education landscape via innovation in AI literacy. *Computers and Education: Artificial Intelligence*, *4*, 100127. DOI: 10.1016/j.caeai.2023.100127

Spanellis, A., & Harviainen, J. T. (2021). *Transforming society and organizations through gamification*. Springer International Publishing. DOI: 10.1007/978-3-030-68207-1

Sperling, K., Stenberg, C.-J., McGrath, C., Åkerfeldt, A., Heintz, F., & Stenliden, L. (2024). In search of artificial intelligence (AI) literacy in teacher education: A scoping review. *Computers and Education Open*, *6*, 100169. DOI: 10.1016/j.caeo.2024.100169

Srnicek, N. (2017). *Platform Capitalism*. Polity Press.

Stanford University. (2025a, January 9). *Report outlines Stanford principles for use of AI*. Retrieved from https://news.stanford.edu/stories/2025/01/report-outlines-stanford-principles-for-use-of-ai

Stanford University. (2025b, January 9). *Report of the AI at Stanford Advisory Committee*. Retrieved from https://provost.stanford.edu/2025/01/09/report-of-the-ai-at-stanford-advisory-committee/

Stanovsky, E.. (2019). Evaluating gender bias in machine translation. In *Proceedings of the 57th Annual Meeting of the ACL* (pp. 1679–1684). DOI: 10.18653/v1/P19-1163

Stefaniak, J., & Moore, S. (2024). The Use of Generative AI to Support Inclusivity and Design Deliberation for Online Instruction. *Online Learning : the Official Journal of the Online Learning Consortium, 28*(3), 181–205. DOI: 10.24059/olj.v28i3.4458

Stoddard, J. (2021). Difficult knowledge and history education. *Pedagogy, Culture & Society, 30*(3), 383–400. DOI: 10.1080/14681366.2021.1977982

Su, J., Ng, D. T. K., & Chu, S. K. W. (2023). Artificial intelligence (AI) literacy in early childhood education: The challenges and opportunities. *Computers & Education: Artificial Intelligence, 4*, 100124. DOI: 10.1016/j.caeai.2023.100124

Sukhera, J. (2022). Narrative reviews: Flexible, rigorous, and practical. *Journal of Graduate Medical Education, 14*(4), 414–417. DOI: 10.4300/JGME-D-22-00480.1 PMID: 35991099

Suppes, P. (1978). The future of the PLATO project. *Educational Technology, 18*(6), 7–12.

Suresh, H., & Guttag, J. V. (2019). A framework for understanding the unintended consequences of machine learning. *Communications of the ACM, 63*(11), 62–71. DOI: 10.1145/3376897

Swiss Cyber Institute. (2025, July 4). *The EU AI Act: Implications for Ethical AI in Education.* Retrieved from https://swisscyberinstitute.com/blog/eu-ai-act-implications-ethical-ai-education/

Szabó, F., & Szoke, J. (2024). How does generative AI promote autonomy and inclusivity in language teaching? *ELT Journal, 78*(4), 478–488. DOI: 10.1093/elt/ccae052

Tadimalla, S. Y., & Kunkeler, T. (2024, October). Exploring Capital and Privilege in Computing and Engineering Education Through Gamification. In *2024 IEEE Frontiers in Education Conference (FIE)* (pp. 1-9). IEEE. DOI: 10.1109/FIE61694.2024.10893030

Tan, C., & Koh, K. (2022). AI in Singapore education.

Tang, K., Cooper, G., Rappa, N., Cooper, M., Sims, C., & Nonis, K. (2024). A dialogic approach to transform teaching, learning & assessment with generative AI in secondary education: A proof of concept. *Pedagogies, 19*(3), 493–503. DOI: 10.1080/1554480X.2024.2379774

Tan, X., Li, Y., & Liu, J. (2024). Artificial intelligence in teaching and teacher professional development: A systematic review. *Computers and Education: Artificial Intelligence, 7*, 100269. Advance online publication. DOI: 10.1016/j.caeai.2024.100269

Tan, Z., Zeng, Q., Tian, Y., Liu, Z., Yin, B., & Jiang, M. (2024, November). Democratizing Large Language Models via Personalized Parameter-Efficient Fine-tuning. In *Proceedings of the 2024 Conference on Empirical Methods in Natural Language Processing* (pp. 6476-6491). DOI: 10.18653/v1/2024.emnlp-main.372

Tao, Y., Viberg, O., Baker, R. S., & Kizilcec, R. F. (2024). Cultural bias and cultural alignment of large language models. *PNAS Nexus*, *3*(9), pgae346. DOI: 10.1093/pnasnexus/pgae346 PMID: 39290441

Taulli, T., & Deshmukh, G. (2025). *Building Generative AI Agents: Using LangGraph, AutoGen, and CrewAI. Building Generative AI Agents: Using LangGraph.* AutoGen, and CrewAI., DOI: 10.1007/979-8-8688-1134-0

TeachAI. (2024). AI literacy training for educators.

TeachBetter. (2025). The future of education with AI. https://teachbetter.ai/the-future-of-education-with-ai-2025/

The Organization for Economic Co-operation and Development (OECD). (2001). *Understanding the digital divide.* OECD Publications.

Tieso, C. L. (2003). Ability grouping is not just tracking anymore. In *Roeper Review* (Vol. 26, Issue 1, pp. 29–36). DOI: 10.1080/02783190309554236

Tıkız-Ertürk, G., & Taşpınar, H. K. (2023). Applications of artificial intelligence (AI) in EFL classrooms. In S. Uçar (Ed.), *Digital pedagogy in the 21st century: Emerging technologies in foreign language classrooms* (ss. 27–44). Efe Akademi Publishing.

Tirado-Olivares, S., Navío-Inglés, M., O'Connor-Jiménez, P., & Cózar-Gutiérrez, R. (2023). From Human to Machine: Investigating the Effectiveness of the Conversational AI ChatGPT in Historical Thinking. *Education Sciences*, *13*(8), 803. DOI: 10.3390/educsci13080803

Toktamysov, S., Alwaely, S., & Gallyamova, Z. (2022). Digital technologies in history training: The impact on students' academic performance. *Education and Information Technologies*, *28*(2), 2173–2186. DOI: 10.1007/s10639-022-11210-5

Torkamaan, H., Steinert, S., Pera, M. S., Kudina, O., Freire, S. K., Verma, H., Kelly, S., Sekwenz, M.-T., Yang, J., van Nunen, K., Warnier, M., Brazier, F., & Oviedo-Trespalacios, O. (2024). Challenges and future directions for integration of large language models into socio-technical systems. *Behaviour & Information Technology*, •••, 1–20. DOI: 10.1080/0144929X.2024.2431068

Tubadji, A., Denney, T., & Webber, D. J. (2021). Cultural relativity in consumers' rates of adoption of artificial intelligence. *Economic Inquiry, 59*(3), 1234–1251. DOI: 10.1111/ecin.12978

Tucci, V., & Hursh, D. (1991). Competent Learner Model: Instructional programming for teachers and learners. *Education & Treatment of Children*, •••, 349–360.

U.S. Department of Education, Office of Educational Technology. (2023). *Artificial intelligence and the future of teaching and learning: Insights and recommendations*. Washington, DC: USDOE. https://tech.ed.gov/files/2023/05/AI-Teaching-Learning-Report-2023.pdf

U.S. Department of Education. (2023). *Artificial intelligence and the future of teaching and learning.* https://www.ed.gov/sites/ed/files/documents/ai-report/ai-report.pdf

Ukwandu, E., Omisade, O., Jones, K., Thorne, S., & Castle, M. (2025). The future of teaching and learning in the context of emerging artificial intelligence technologies. *Futures, 171*, 103616. DOI: 10.1016/j.futures.2025.103616

Umar, F. (2024). Engaging with History in the Digital Age: A Study of Technology-Based Distance Learning in History. *Journal of Policy Research, 10*(2), 873–878. DOI: 10.61506/02.00308

UNC (University of North Carolina). (2025). Embedding human values into AI tools that help students. https://ed.unc.edu/2025/03/24/embedding-human-values-into-ai-tools-that-help-students/

UNESCO. (2013). *Media and information literacy.*

UNESCO. (2019). *Beijing consensus on artificial intelligence and education*. Paris: UNESCO. https://unesdoc.unesco.org/ark:/48223/pf0000370307

UNESCO. (2021). *Artificial intelligence and education: Guidance for policy-makers.*

UNESCO. (2021). *Reimagining our futures together: A new social contract for education*. UNESCO Publishing.

UNESCO. (2021a). *AI and education: Guidance for policy-makers* (Miao, F., Holmes, W., Huang, R., & Zhang, H.). Paris: UNESCO. https://unesdoc.unesco.org/ark:/48223/pf0000376709

UNESCO. (2023). *Ethics of artificial intelligence in education.*

UNESCO. (2025). *AI competency framework for teachers.* https://www.unesco.org/en/articles/ai-competency-framework-teachers

United Nations Educational, Scientific and Cultural Organization (UNESCO). (2022). *Recommendation on the ethics of artificial intelligence*. https://unesdoc.unesco.org/ark:/48223/pf0000381137

University of San Diego. (2025). *39 examples of artificial intelligence in education.* https://onlinedegrees.sandiego.edu/artificial-intelligence-education/

University of Toronto. (2025, March 31). *Guidance on the Use of Generative Artificial Intelligence*. Retrieved from https://www.sgs.utoronto.ca/about/guidance-on-the-use-of-generative-artificial-intelligence/

Vakulik, V., Sheviakov, O., Slavska, Y., & Vakulik, S. (2024). Teaching History in High School as A Way to Build a Complex of Self-Identifications of High School Students. *Pedagogy and Education Management Review.*, *2*(16), 56–67. DOI: 10.36690/2733-2039-2024-2-56-67

Vallée, E., & Hsu, Y.-C. (2023). Protecting Students: Data Privacy in the African Union. *TechTrends*, *67*(2), 203–206. DOI: 10.1007/s11528-023-00834-0

Van den Broek, S., Sankaran, S., & de Wit, J. (2024). Exploring the supportive role of artificial intelligence in participatory design: A systematic review. *Proceedings of the Participatory Design Conference (PDC '24)*. ACM. DOI: 10.1145/3661455.3669868

Van Deursen, A. J., & Van Dijk, J. A. (2019). The first-level digital divide shifts from inequalities in physical access to inequalities in material access. *New Media & Society*, *21*(2), 354–375. DOI: 10.1177/1461444818797082 PMID: 30886536

Van Leeuwen, A., Strauß, S., & Rummel, N. (2023). Participatory design of teacher dashboards: Navigating the tension between teacher input and theories on teacher professional vision. *Frontiers in Artificial Intelligence*, *6*, 1039739. DOI: 10.3389/frai.2023.1039739 PMID: 37304525

VanGorder, M. (2025). Imagining the Past. *Teaching History: A Journal of Methods. 49*(1), 56-65. DOI: 10.33043/7753574bb

Vaswani, A., Shazeer, N., Parmar, N., Uszkoreit, J., Jones, L., Gomez, A. N., & Polosukhin, I. (2017). Attention is all you need. *Advances in Neural Information Processing Systems*, *30*. Advance online publication. DOI: 10.48550/arXiv.1706.03762

Vaughan, J. W. (2018). Making better use of the crowd: How crowdsourcing can advance machine learning research. *Journal of Machine Learning Research*, *18*(193), 1–46.

Vavrus, M. (2008). Culturally responsive teaching. In T. L. Good (Ed.), *21st century education: A reference handbook* (Vol. 2, pp. 49–57). SAGE. https://www.scribd.com/document/636505197/VavrusCulturallyResponsiveTeaching

Verma, D., Kansra, P., & Kaur, S. (2023). A theoretical perspective of artificial intelligence in hostility of cyber threats in the banking sector. In *Advanced machine learning algorithms for complex financial applications* (pp. 43–54). IGI Global., DOI: 10.4018/978-1-6684-4483-2.ch004

Verma, P., & Sehgal, S. (2023). Leveraging artificial intelligence for enhancing customer experience and efficiency in the banking industry. In *AI and emotional intelligence for modern business management* (pp. 282–310). IGI Global., DOI: 10.4018/979-8-3693-0418-1.ch019

Vesselinov, R., & Grego, J. (2012). *Duolingo effectiveness study*. City University of New York.

Vidal, J., Estoquia, C., & Concepcion, M. (2025). Quasi-Development: Access alone to Artificial Intelligence like ChatGPT Is Not Enough.

Villegas-Ch, W., Buenano-Fernandez, D., Navarro, A. M., & Mera-Navarrete, A. (2025). Adaptive intelligent tutoring systems for STEM education: analysis of the learning impact and effectiveness of personalized feedback. *Smart Learning Environments 2025 12:1, 12*(1), 41-. DOI: 10.1186/s40561-025-00389-y

Villena-Taranilla, R., & Diago, P. (2025). Challenges and Implications of Virtual Reality in History Education: A Systematic Review. *Applied Sciences (Basel, Switzerland), 15*(10), 5589. DOI: 10.3390/app15105589

Vinella, F. L., Koppelaar, S., & Masthoff, J. (2022). Forming Teams of Learners Online in a User as Wizard Study with Openness, Conscientiousness, and cognitive Ability. *Adjunct Proceedings of the 30th ACM Conference on User Modeling, Adaptation and Personalization*, 283–292. DOI: 10.1145/3511047.3537660

Vuorikari, R., et al. (2022). AI literacy in Europe.

Vuorikari, R. (2022, June). DigComp helping shape the education ecosystem in Europe. In *Annual Conference of European Distance and E-Learning Network* (pp. 137-143). Cham: Springer International Publishing. DOI: 10.1007/978-3-031-20518-7_11

Vygotsky, L. S. (1978). *Mind in society: The development of higher psychological processes*. Harvard University Press.

Waghid, Y., & Waghid, Z. (2021). *Artificial intelligence and education: Philosophical perspectives on innovation and equity*. Springer.

Walker, E., Johnson, T., & Lomas, J. E. (2022). Prediction and intervention in educational environments. *International Journal of Artificial Intelligence in Education, 32*(2), 456–489. DOI: 10.1007/s40593-021-00256-7

Walter, Y. (2024). Embracing the future of Artificial Intelligence in the classroom: The relevance of AI literacy, prompt engineering, and critical thinking in modern education. *International Journal of Educational Technology in Higher Education, 21*(1), 1–29. DOI: 10.1186/s41239-024-00448-3

Walther, C. (2025). AI is changing how we learn. *Forbes*. https://www.forbes.com/sites/corneliawalther/2025/03/01/ai-is-changing-how-we-learn-the-new-role-of-human-teachers/

Wang, R., & Demszky, D. (2023). Is ChatGPT a Good Teacher Coach? Measuring Zero-Shot Performance For Scoring and Providing Actionable Insights on Classroom Instruction. In *Proceedings of the Annual Meeting of the Association for Computational Linguistics* (pp. 626–667). Retrieved from https://www.scopus.com/inward/record.uri?eid=2-s2.0-85172178508&partnerID=40&md5=c3131386676854c615e0acae66264a4b

Wang, H., Fu, T., Du, Y., Gao, W., Huang, K., Liu, Z., Chandak, P., Liu, S., Van Katwyk, P., Deac, A., Anandkumar, A., Bergen, K., Gomes, C. P., Ho, S., Kohli, P., Lasenby, J., Leskovec, J., Liu, T.-Y., Manrai, A., & Zitnik, M. (2023). Scientific discovery in the age of artificial intelligence. *Nature, 620*(7972), 47–60. DOI: 10.1038/s41586-023-06221-2 PMID: 37532811

Wang, J., & Wang, H. (2025). Cultivation of innovative thinking and career development in design education. *Humanities & Social Sciences Communications, 12*(1), 1390. Advance online publication. DOI: 10.1057/s41599-025-05754-3

Wang, M., & Guo, W. (2023). The Potential Impact of ChatGPT on Education: Using History as a Rearview Mirror. *ECNU Review of Education, 8*, 41–48. DOI: 10.1177/20965311231189826

Wang, N. C. (2025). Scaffolding Creativity: Integrating Generative AI Tools and Real-world Experiences in Business Education. *Conference on Human Factors in Computing Systems - Proceedings, 1*. DOI: 10.1145/3706599.3720283

Wang, Q., Zhao, L., Chang-Richards, A., Zhang, Y., & Li, H. (2021). Understanding the impact of social capital on the innovation performance of construction enterprises: Based on the mediating effect of knowledge transfer. *Sustainability (Basel), 13*(9), 5099. DOI: 10.3390/su13095099

Warschauer, M., & Matuchniak, T. (2010). New technology and digital learning: Addressing educational inequity. *Harvard Educational Review, 80*(4), 698–730.

Warsinsky, S., Schmidt-Kraepelin, M., Thiebes, S., Wagner, M., & Sunyaev, A. (2022, May). Gamified expert annotation systems: meta-requirements and tentative design. In *International Conference on Design Science Research in Information Systems and Technology* (pp. 154-166). Cham: Springer International Publishing. DOI: 10.1007/978-3-031-06516-3_12

Washington, P. (2024). A perspective on crowdsourcing and human-in-the-loop workflows in precision health. *Journal of Medical Internet Research, 26*, e51138. DOI: 10.2196/51138 PMID: 38602750

Webb, P., Sellar, S., & Gulson, K. (2019). Anticipating education: Governing habits, memories and policy-futures. *Learning, Media and Technology, 45*(3), 284–297. DOI: 10.1080/17439884.2020.1686015

Weidinger, L., et al. (2022). Taxonomy of risks in language models. *NeurIPS Datasets and Benchmarks.*

Wei, J., Wang, X., Schuurmans, D., Bosma, M., Xia, F., Chi, E., & Zhou, D. (2022). Chain-of-thought prompting elicits reasoning in large language models. *Advances in Neural Information Processing Systems, 35*, 24824–24837.

Weng, K., Jia, M., Nguyen, T. T., Hu, X., Zhang, G., & Zeng, Q. (2026). Coupled data-driven and experience-informed neural networks for prediction of pile base resistance with consideration of data limitation. *Engineering Applications of Artificial Intelligence, 165*, 113384. Advance online publication. DOI: 10.1016/j.engappai.2025.113384

Weninger, C., & Xu, H. (2026). AI, representation, and critical digital literacy: Navigating visual bias in the digital age. *System, 136*, 103896. Advance online publication. DOI: 10.1016/j.system.2025.103896

Williams, R., Ali, S., Devasia, N., DiPaola, D., Hong, J., Kaputsos, S., Jordan, B., & Breazeal, C. (2022). AI+Ethics Curricula for Middle School Youth: Lessons Learned from Three Project-Based Curricula. *International Journal of Artificial Intelligence in Education*, 1 - 59. DOI: 10.1007/s40593-022-00298-y

Williamson, B., & Eynon, R. (2020). Historical perspectives on AI and education. *Learning, Media and Technology.*

Williamson, B., & Hogan, M. (2020). Commercialisation of education in the AI era. *Learning, Media and Technology, 45*(3), 245–259. DOI: 10.1080/17439884.2020.1772849

Williamson, B., & Piattoeva, S. (2023). EdTech policy agendas. *Learning, Media and Technology.*

Winthrop, R., Williams, T. P., & McGivney, E. (2016). *Skills in the digital age — How should education systems evolve?* Yan, L. (2025). *From Passive Tool to Socio-cognitive Teammate: A Conceptual Framework for Agentic AI in Human-AI Collaborative Learning.*

Wiyono, B. B., Komariah, A., Hidayat, H., & Kusumaningrum, D. E. (2025). The structural effects of evaluation types in the implementation process of the independent learning program in higher education. *Discover Sustainability, 6*(1), 321. Advance online publication. DOI: 10.1007/s43621-025-01171-3

Wong-A-Foe, D. (2023). Navigating the Implications of AI in Indonesian Education: Tutors, Governance, and Ethical Perspectives. In *Communications in Computer and Information Science* (Vol. 1942 CCIS, pp. 349–360). DOI: 10.1007/978-981-99-7969-1_26

Wood, E. A., Ange, B. L., & Miller, D. D. (2021). Are We Ready to Integrate Artificial Intelligence Literacy into Medical School Curriculum: Students and Faculty Survey. *Journal of Medical Education and Curricular Development, 8*, 23821205211024078. Advance online publication. DOI: 10.1177/23821205211024078 PMID: 34250242

World Economic Forum. (2025). How AI and human teachers can collaborate to transform education. https://www.weforum.org/stories/2025/01/how-ai-and-human-teachers-can-collaborate-to-transform-education/

Wu, D., & Sun, X. (2024). Exploring Human-centered AI Literacy Education: Interpretation and Insights from UNESCO's AI Competency Framework for Teachers and Students. *Journal of Library and Information Science in Agriculture, 36*(8), 4–19. DOI: 10.13998/j.cnki.issn1002-1248.24-0644

Xenos, M., & Velli, V. (2018, September). A serious game for introducing software engineering ethics to university students. In *International Conference on Interactive Collaborative Learning* (pp. 579-588). Cham: Springer International Publishing.

Xing, X., Wang, W., Ma, L., Yang, W., & Zheng, J. (2025). Lifecycle-Aware code generation: Leveraging Software Engineering Phases in LLMs. *arXiv preprint arXiv:2510.24019.*

Xue, L., Constant, N., Roberts, A., Kale, M., Al-Rfou, R., Siddhant, A., & Raffel, C. (2021). mT5: A massively multilingual pre-trained text-to-text transformer. In *Proceedings of NAACL 2021*. DOI: 10.18653/v1/2021.naacl-main.41

Yang, F., Liu, J., & Li, K. (2025). LLM-Guided Reinforcement Learning for Interactive Environments. *Mathematics*, *13*(12), 1932. DOI: 10.3390/math13121932

Yang, H., Zhang, D., Guo, W., & He, Y. (2024). Constructing a STEM projects design framework for middle school AI courses: Developing students' AI literacy as project goals. *IEEE Access : Practical Innovations, Open Solutions*, *12*, 1. Advance online publication. DOI: 10.1109/ACCESS.2024.3512499

Yang, W. (2022a). Artificial Intelligence education for young children: Why, what, and how in curriculum design and implementation. *Computers and Education: Artificial Intelligence*, *3*, 100061. DOI: 10.1016/j.caeai.2022.100061

Yankouskaya, A., Babiker, A., Rizvi, S., Alshakhsi, S., Liebherr, M., & Ali, R. (2025). LLM-D12: A Dual-Dimensional Scale of Instrumental and Relational Dependencies on Large Language Models. *ACM Transactions on the Web*.

Yan, L., Pammer-Schindler, V., Mills, C., Nguyen, A., & Gašević, D. (2025). Beyond efficiency: Empirical insights on generative AI's impact on cognition, metacognition and epistemic agency in learning. *British Journal of Educational Technology*, *56*(5), 1675–1685. DOI: 10.1111/bjet.70000

Yusuf, A., Pervin, N., Román-González, M., & Noor, N. (2024). Generative AI in education and research: A systematic mapping review. *Review of Education*, *12*(2), e3489. DOI: 10.1002/rev3.3489

Yu, Y., & Hu, W. (2025). Three-Dimensional Modeling and AI-Assisted Contextual Narratives in Digital Heritage Education: Course for Enhancing Design Skill, Cultural Awareness, and User Experience. *Heritage.*, *8*(7), 280. DOI: 10.3390/heritage8070280

Zamfirescu-Pereira, J. D., Wong, R. Y., Hartmann, B., & Yang, Q. (2023, April). Why Johnny can't prompt: how non-AI experts try (and fail) to design LLM prompts. In *Proceedings of the 2023 CHI conference on human factors in computing systems* (pp. 1-21). DOI: 10.1145/3544548.3581388

Zehr, H. (2015). *Changing lenses: A new focus for crime and justice*. Herald Press.

Zembylas, M. (2021). A decolonial approach to AI in higher education teaching and learning: Strategies for undoing the ethics of digital neocolonialism. *Learning, Media and Technology*, *48*(1), 25–37. DOI: 10.1080/17439884.2021.2010094

Zerilli, J., Bhatt, U., & Weller, A. (2022). How transparency modulates trust in artificial intelligence. *Patterns (New York, N.Y.)*, *3*(4), 100455. DOI: 10.1016/j.patter.2022.100455 PMID: 35465233

Zhang, K. (2021). AI technologies for education: Recent research and future directions. *Computers and Education: Artificial Intelligence.*

Zhang, X., & Shi, W. (2025). An AI-driven framework integrating predictive modeling and intervention strategies to enhance psychological health education among college students. *Discover Applied Sciences*, *7*(10), 1095. Advance online publication. DOI: 10.1007/s42452-025-07674-y

Zhang, Y., & Dong, C. (2024). Exploring the digital transformation of generative ai-assisted foreign language education: A socio-technical systems perspective based on mixed-methods. *Systems*, *12*(11), 462. DOI: 10.3390/systems12110462

Zhao, Y., et al. (2022). Humanistic aspects of AI in educational contexts. *Journal of Educational Technology.*

Zhao, Y.-Y. (2024). The creative cosmos beyond humans: A symphony of participatory design and visual AI. *Frontiers in Communication*, *9*, 1440384. DOI: 10.3389/fcomm.2024.1440384

Zhong, H. (2024). Optimal Integration: Human, Machine, and Generative AI. *Machine, and Generative AI (July 18, 2024).*

Zimmerman, B. J. (2013). Theories of self-regulated learning and academic achievement: An overview and analysis. *Self-regulated learning and academic achievement*, 1-36.

Zinkina, J., Korotayev, A., & Andreev, A. (2016). Mass Primary Education in the Nineteenth Century. *Globalistics and Globalization Studies*, *26*(15), 63–70.

Zou, J. Y., & Schiebinger, L. (2018). AI can be sexist and racist; it is time to make it fair. *Nature*, *559*(7714), 324–326. DOI: 10.1038/d41586-018-05707-8 PMID: 30018439

Zytko, D. J., Wisniewski, P., Guha, S. P. S., Baumer, E., & Lee, M. K. (2022). Participatory Design of AI Systems: Opportunities and Challenges Across Diverse Users, Relationships, and Application Domains. *CHI Conference on Human Factors in Computing Systems Extended Abstracts*, 1–4. DOI: 10.1145/3491101.3516506

About the Contributors

Faizan Ahmad is a Lecturer in Computer Science at Cardiff School of Technologies, Cardiff Metropolitan University. Prior to joining Cardiff Met, Dr. Faizan worked as a Tenure-Track Assistant Professor/Founding Director of the Research Centre for Human-Computer Interaction (2018-2022) and Research Associate (2010-2011) in a well-reputed university of Pakistan where they were responsible for curriculum design, teaching, research, supervisory, moderation, and consultancy in human-computer interaction domain. Dr. Faizan received their Ph.D. in Computer Science and Technology from the Institute of Computing Technology, Chinese Academy of Sciences in 2017, and their M.Eng. (Distinction) in Computer Applied Technology from the School of Computer Science and Engineering, Beihang University in 2013. With a broad teaching background in computer science to diverse audiences (e.g., face-to-face, online, and apprenticeship), Dr. Faizan Ahmad have successfully planned, developed, and led modules in the domains of Human-Computer Interaction (HCI), Artificial Intelligence (AI), Games, Web, and Mobile Application Development. Dr. Faizan's technical expertise spans from foundational subjects such as Programming Fundamentals to advanced topics like Usability and Interaction Design. Dr. Faizan Ahmad's research focuses on advancing Human-Centered Artificial Intelligence and AI-driven personalised learning within the context of Smart Learning Environments, Immersive Education Technologies, and Industry 5.0. Dr. Faizan is particularly interested in designing emotionally adaptive, cognitively engaging systems that integrate Human-Computer Interaction (HCI), Gamification, and Multimodal Learning Analytics. A core strand of their work explores the use of emerging technologies such as Digital Twins and the Metaverse to create scalable, inclusive, and personalised educational experiences. Through this interdisciplinary lens, they aim to develop intelligent learning systems that respond to learners' behavioural, emotional, and performance data in real time, enhancing both learner engagement and pedagogical impact.

Jay Kumar Pandey is currently working as an Assistant Professor in the Department of Electrical & Electronics Engineering at Shri Ramswaroop Memorial University, Barabanki (U.P.) India. Dr. Pandey has completed his Ph.D. and has done his M.Tech. with specialization in Power Control (Instrumentation) and also done his MBA from Finance and Marketing. His subjects of interest are related to Artificial Intelligence, Biomedical & Healthcare, Image Processing, Machine Learning and Renewable energy. He has 15 years of teaching and research experience has published more than 30 research papers in National and International journals / conferences & Book Chapters in CRC, NOVA, Taylor & Francis, Springer and IGI Publisher. Dr. Pandey is an editor of books (edited) published by reputed publishers Apple Academy Press, IGI, Elsevier, Wiley-IEEE, NOVA, Bentham Science, IAP, Emerald Publication, Taylor & Francis & Cambridge Scholar .Dr. Pandey is also Editor of Journal of Technology Innovations and Energy United States. Dr. Pandey having reviewer in different conference/Journal/Book Chapters like (The Journal of Supercomputing in Springer Nature, IGI publishing, Journal of Security and Communication Networks Hindawi, Journal of Biomimetics, Biomaterials and Biomedical Engineering (JBBBE) Scientific Net, Switzerland, Advanced Engineering Forum (AEF) Scientific Net, Switzerland)

Momina Shaheen, Fellow, Higher Education Academy (UK), is Lecturer in Computing, in University of Roehampton, London, United Kingdom. She has 364 citations, an h-index of 9, and an i10-index of 8. Her most recent publications cover topics like disaster identification using federated learning algorithms, and AI applications in healthcare and smart cities.. She earned her master's in software engineering from Bahria University Islamabad Campus in 2016. She has more than 6 years of experience in research and academia. She has supervised and initiated a number of projects in her career. She has lead different project in the area of Machine Learning, Data Science, Artificial Intelligence, Internet of things, Cognitive Sciences and Distributed Systems.

***

Tolgahan Ayantaş In 2018, they were appointed as a research assistant in the Department of Social Studies Education at Ankara University's Faculty of Educational Sciences. They completed their master's degree in Social Studies Education at Ankara University's Institute of Educational Sciences in 2019 and their PhD in the same field at Gazi University's Institute of Educational Sciences in 2024. They have served as a researcher in two separate EU Erasmus+ projects focusing on computational thinking and continue to advise on TÜBİTAK 2209-A student projects. Moreover, they have published numerous book chapters and articles in their field. Their areas of focus include Social Studies education, the training of Social Studies teachers, professional development models for teachers, the teaching of historical topics in Social Studies, history education, digitalisation in education, computational thinking, and textbook writing.

Nandita Chakrabarty is an Assistant Professor in Special Education at the Faculty of Disability Management and Special Education (FDMSE), Ramakrishna Mission Vivekananda Educational and Research Institute (RKMVERI), a Deemed-to-be University accredited by NAAC with an A++ grade, located in Coimbatore, Tamil Nadu, India. Her academic work focuses on inclusive education, disability studies, and pedagogical innovations that support diverse learners. Dr Chakrabarty has contributed to research and teacher education programs aimed at strengthening evidence-based practices in special education. She is committed to advancing accessible and equitable learning environments through interdisciplinary approaches and community engagement. She may be contacted at nanditachakrabarty21@gmail.com, ORCID: 0009-0006-6237-0172.

Parag Chatterjee received the B.E. degree in Computer Science & Engineering from the Karnatak University, Dharwad, India, in 1998 and received M.Tech. degree from IIEST Shibpur, Kolkata, India, in 2007. He has an academic experience of 20 years. Currently he is working as an Assistant Professor in the Department of CSE at Global Institute of Management and Technology, Krishnanagar, West Bengal, India. His current research interests include Data ware Housing, Data mining and Wireless sensor. He has 15 publication in national and international journals and 3 Patents.

Daksh Rajesh Dave is a Master's candidate in Computer Engineering at Virginia Tech, advised by Dr. Eric Burger. His research sits at the intersection of AI systems, cybersecurity, and networks, with a focus on graph-based recommender systems, large language model (LLM)–driven analytics, and Zero-Trust intrusion detection for 5G and cloud-native infrastructures. He has worked on industry-facing projects, including SAPPPKG for large-scale recommendations, Tenko/Zero-Trust anomaly detection for network defense, and O-RAN security and fuzzing

Nayla Fadiya is an information technology professional with research interests in the Internet of Things (IoT) and Early Warning Systems. Her work focuses on the design and implementation of sensor-based systems, real-time data acquisition, and intelligent monitoring solutions to support risk mitigation and decision-making processes. She has been involved in projects that integrate hardware, software, and network technologies to improve system reliability and responsiveness. With a strong commitment to applied research and technological innovation, Nayla continues to contribute to the development of smart systems for environmental monitoring and safety applications.

Revanayya Kantayya is a distinguished academician and researcher in the field of Commerce and Management, currently associated with the Department of Commerce and Management at Dayananda Sagar Business Academy, Bangalore, Karnataka. Known for his strong academic credentials and commitment to scholarly excellence, he has made significant contributions to teaching, research, and academic development in higher education. His academic journey reflects dedication, perseverance, and a consistent pursuit of excellence in commerce and management studies. Dr. Revanayya completed his Ph.D. in Commerce from the Central University of Karnataka, where his research contributed to advancing knowledge in contemporary commerce and business-related disciplines. His academic competence is further validated by successfully clearing both the UGC National Eligibility Test (NET) and the Karnataka State Eligibility Test (KSET), demonstrating his strong conceptual foundation and eligibility for university-level teaching and research. An outstanding performer throughout his academic career, Dr. Revanayya secured First Rank in his Master of Commerce (M.Com) program and was honored with a Gold Medal in recognition of his exceptional academic achievement. His scholarly potential was further acknowledged through the prestigious Doctoral Fellowship Award for the academic year 2017–18, which supported his research pursuits during his doctoral studies. At Dayananda Sagar Business Academy, Bengaluru (560082), Dr. Revanayya actively engages in teaching undergraduate and postgraduate students, fostering analytical thinking and practical understanding of commerce and management concepts. His areas of academic interest include commerce education, business management practices, financial studies, and research methodology. He is committed to creating an engaging learning environment that encourages critical inquiry, ethical business practices, and professional development among students.

Hanh Le is a passionate researcher and accomplished Full Stack Software Developer with deep expertise in software development, data analytics, data science, and cloud computing. She holds a Ph.D. in Information Technology and a Master's in Computer Science, bringing both academic rigor and a solution-driven mindset to her work. With extensive experience in front-end and back-end development, she specializes in scalable, database-driven applications that support evidence-based decision-making. Dr. Le has led transformative tech initiatives across healthcare, law enforcement, and retail, translating complex needs into high-performing systems. She values interdisciplinary collaboration, believing that impactful innovation often arises at the intersection of fields. Her blend of technical skill, research excellence, and collaborative spirit continues to drive progress in academia and industry alike.

T.C. Manjunath was born on 6th February 1967. He did his B.E. from RV College of Engg. in 1989 (B'lore Univ), M.E. in Robotics & Automation from Govt.'s LD College of Engg., (Gujarat Univ., Ahmedabad) in 1992 with FCD-First Rank & PhD in Systems & Control Engg. from IIT Bombay in the year 2007, got best research scholar award for the entire IITB. He is currently working as the Dean Research (R & D) and as Professor in Dept. of Computer Science & Engg. with specialization in IoT, Cyber Security, Blockchain Technology in Rajarajeswari College of Engineering, Bengaluru, Karnataka. He has got a teaching (academic), research & administrative experience of more than 35+ years (10 years as Principal & 8 years as HoD, 1 year as Dean Research & rest as faculty) and has published more than 1500+ research papers in various national & international journals & conferences, with 175+ patents, 100+ book-chapters, 25 awards, 100s of Keynote talks and also published 25 text books in various field of science, engineering & technology, completed projects worth Rs. 9 Crores till date & guided 10 PhD scholars in VTU. He is a member of 30 Professional Society Chapters and is a fellow of IE, IETE, AMIEE, Sr. Member of IEEE and a chartered engineer.

Kübra Okumuş Dağdeler is an associate professor in the Department of Foreign Language Education at Sivas Cumhuriyet University, Türkiye. She holds a bachelor's degree in English Language Teaching from Gazi University, and master's and doctorate degrees in the same field from Atatürk University. Her research mainly focuses on educational technology in English Language Teaching, specifically Mobile-Assisted Language Learning (MALL), digital peer feedback, personalized learning, and the integration of artificial intelligence tools into EFL/ESL instruction. She has published in a range of national and international outlets, including SSCI, Scopus, and ESCI-indexed journals. She also engages with international collaborative networks, notably COST Actions.

P. Selvakumar is currently an Associate Professor in the Department of Science and Humanities at Nehru Institute of Technology, Coimbatore, Tamil Nadu, India. Prior to joining Nehru Institute of Technology, he held positions as an Assistant Professor in the Department of Science and Humanities various engineering colleges in Coimbatore, Tamil Nadu, India, spanning from 2011 to 2023. Dr.P. Selvakumar's academic and research interests lie primarily in the field of phytochemistry. He has made significant contributions to his field, with an impressive record that includes 30 journal publications, 12 patents, and 20 conference papers. Additionally, he has organized 5 seminars and conferences, further demonstrating his commitment to academic and scientific exchange. Throughout his career, Dr. P.Selvakumar has been recognized for his dedication and excellence in teaching, having been honored with several awards, including the Best Teacher Awards. He holds a prominent position in the academic community, contributing actively to research.

P. S. Rajakumar received M. Tech degree in Computer Science and Engineering (CSE) from Dr M.G.R. Educational and Research Institute, India and a PhD degree in CSE from Jawaharlal Nehru Technological University, Hyderabad, India. His distinguished career spanning 32 years of academic experience. He has published more than 60 articles which include Scopus & Web of Science (WoS). He has also published 5 books with ISBN. He holds multifarious memberships from the prominent professional bodies specifically from LMCSI, LMISTE, SMIEEE, FIEI, MACM and LMTSI. His research interest and areas are Data mining, SVM classifier, IoT, cloud computing, DL and ML. Presently he is Supervising 04 Scholars under Ph.D Programe, 04 Scholars were Completed Their Public Viva Voce. He has won many awards and accolades during his career and presently serving as a Dean – Activities and Professor in the Department of CSE at Dr M.G.R. Educational and Research Institute, Chennai, Tamil Nadu, India.

Nithin Subba Rao A distinguished manufacturing excellence leader with over 15 years of experience in the automotive industry, Nithin Subba Rao has established himself as a transformational force in operational optimization and cost reduction. He holds a Master's degree in Mechanical Engineering from Michigan Technological University and an MBA in Operations Management, combining technical expertise with strategic business acumen. As a Six Sigma Black Belt with 10+ approved patents in manufacturing process improvement, Nithin Subba Rao has demonstrated exceptional capability in driving operational transformation and delivering measurable results. His track record includes delivering over $80 million in combined cost savings and restructuring benefits while implementing Industry 4.0 technologies across multiple manufacturing facilities. Nithin Subba Rao's expertise spans digital transformation, lean manufacturing, ERP integration, and the development of sustainable continuous improvement cultures that drive long-term competitive advantage. His personal philosophy of continuous improvement – symbolized by naming his daughter "Aarohi," meaning continuous improvement / ascending – reflects his deep commitment to daily progress and systematic excellence. He firmly believes that consistency beats intensity, working toward his goals one step at a time with a target of 1% daily improvement, a principle that has delivered miraculous results in both his personal and professional life.

Guru Basava Aradhya S. is a distinguished academic leader and Professor with 19 years of experience. Holding a PhD in Management and several international patents, his expertise encompasses HR analytics, AI-driven management, and strategic growth. He has published extensively in Scopus and ABDC journals and authored influential books on HR metrics and strategy. Currently, he serves as Professor and Head in School of Business Management, Noida International University, Uttar Pradesh.

S. Magesh is a distinguished academician and entrepreneur with multifaceted credentials in Engineering, Science, Arts, Administration, Technology, Linguistics, and Management. He began his academic career in 1999, advancing to Professor and Head of the Computer Science Department with 17 years in academia and 10 years in corporate roles. He has published 24 indexed journals, 2 patents, and 2 books. Magesh is currently performing research in Deep Learning at Dr. M.G.R. Educational and Research Institute, Chennai, India. His academic contributions have been recognized through publications in Web of Science, ESCI, SCOPUS, Springer, and Compendex.

Srijanani S is a student who is pursuing B.E Computer Science and Engineering in Velammal Engineering College .Srijanani is an accomplished web developer with a strong passion for creating dynamic and user-friendly websites. Her academic background provided a solid foundation in programming, web development, and software engineering. Her journey is marked by valuable experiences, diverse internships, and notable participation in hackathons. Srijanani' s idea of blood warmer system for blood transfusion using Hardware and IOT secured best place in Hackathon organised in Velammal Engineering College. Her significant contribution in designing of Health Monitoring System for detecting sudden abnormalities using IOT has been shortlisted for the Smart India Hackathon. Srijanani has enriched her professional portfolio with internships at four different companies, each offering unique challenges and learning opportunities. Srijanani' technical skill set includes proficiency in HTML, CSS, JavaScript, various JavaScript frameworks such as React and Angular. She is also well-versed in back-end technologies like Node.js and Express, as well as database management systems like MongoDB and SQL.

Ratan Sarkar is an Assistant Professor in the Department of Education, Tezpur University (A Central University), Assam, India. Previously, he served nearly seven years as Assistant Professor in the Department of Teachers' Training (B.Ed.), Prabhat Kumar College, Contai (Vidyasagar University), and as Guest Faculty at National Institute for Empowerment of Persons with Intellectual Disabilities, Regional Centre, Kolkata. He holds a Ph.D. in Education from Pondicherry University, an M.Ed. and M.Phil. in Special Education from Ramakrishna Mission Vivekananda Educational and Research Institute, Belur Math, and an M.A. in Education and Technology from Tata Institute of Social Sciences, Mumbai. He began his academic journey with a

B.Ed. in Special Education (Jadavpur University) and a B.A. in English (Hons) from Siliguri College (University of North Bengal), Darjeeling. Dr. Sarkar has published extensively in leading journals (SAGE, Springer, Routledge, Wiley), authored books, chapters, and reviews, and led projects under the Ministry of Education, Govt. of India. His works on inclusive education, EdTech, disability studies, policy advocacy to advance equitable learning ecosystems.

Binastya Anggara Sekti has been a lecturer at the Faculty of Computer Science, Esa Unggul University, Jakarta, since 2016. He is actively involved in the Artificial Intelligence and Information Security Study Group. He holds a Bachelor's degree in Informatics Engineering from the Bandung Institute of Technology and a Master's degree in Information Systems Management from Trisakti University, Jakarta. Prior to entering academia, he accumulated over 25 years of professional experience as an IT practitioner in various companies across Jakarta. His work focused on developing data centers for internet service providers and delivering IT solutions for the manufacturing and oil & gas sectors. His research interests include artificial intelligence, cybersecurity, and the development of IT infrastructure.

Rafael Luberto Sinaga is an artificial intelligence researcher at Esa Unggul University, Jakarta, Indonesia. His research interests include artificial intelligence, machine learning, data analytics, and intelligent information systems. He has been actively involved in academic research and applied projects focusing on the development and implementation of AI-based solutions to address real-world challenges across various domains. His work demonstrates strong analytical skills, critical thinking, and a commitment to technological innovation. Rafael actively contributes to scientific publications and collaborative research initiatives aimed at advancing the application of artificial intelligence in education, industry, and digital transformation.

Tess Toni is an Assistant Professor in the Department of English at Salesian College, Siliguri, where she has been serving since 2024. Her academic interests primarily include Gender Studies, Diaspora, and the use of social media by the current generation. She has actively participated in numerous national and international seminars, contributing to scholarly discussions in her areas of expertise. She completed both her B.A. and M.A. in English from Mahatma Gandhi University, Kottayam, Kerala. At present, she teaches courses on Indian Literature in English, Postcolonial Literature, History of English Literature, and Women's Writing, and also helps students to enhance their communication skills.

Azizaturridha Fitria Wibowo is a motivated individual with interests in information technology, digital systems, and applied computing. She has been involved in academic and practical activities related to system development, data processing, and web-based applications, with a focus on efficiency and usability. Her work reflects strong analytical thinking and a problem-solving mindset in addressing real-world challenges. Azizaturridha is known for her adaptability and collaborative approach, and she continues to develop her skills in emerging technologies to support innovative and sustainable digital solutions in academic and professional environments.

Dwiki Dzaki Yudi Putra is an information technology professional with an interest in information systems and the development of innovative digital solutions. His areas of interest include the application of emerging technologies to improve system efficiency, support digital transformation, and address practical challenges in organizational and societal contexts. He is engaged in exploring user-oriented and sustainable technology solutions, with a focus on bridging technical development and conceptual understanding in information systems research and practice.

Index

A

B

C

D

E

G

H

I

L

M

N

P

R

S

T

W

www.ingramcontent.com/pod-product-compliance
Lightning Source LLC
LaVergne TN
LVHW081318300926
849161LV00008B/1798
9798337360638